PARLIAMENT BUILDING, OTTAWA.

PLAN OF MOSAIC FLOOR.

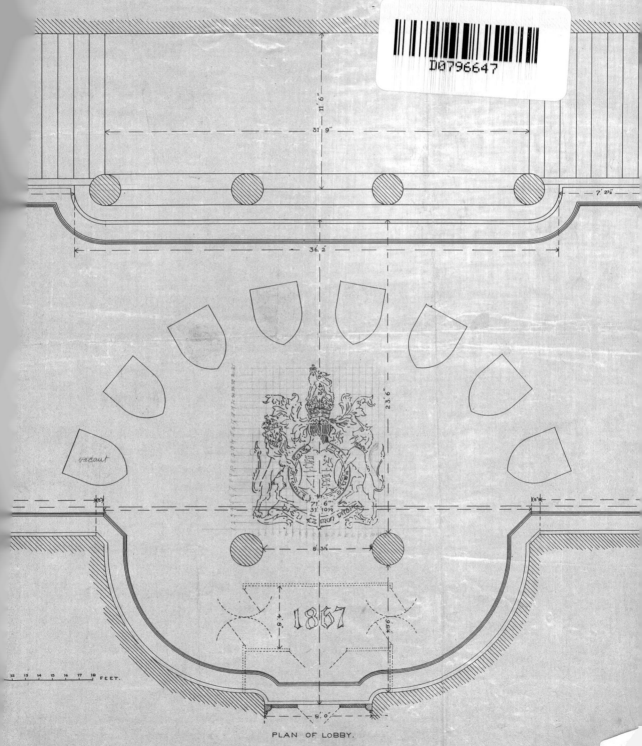

vacant

1867

12 13 14 15 16 17 18 FEET.

PLAN OF LOBBY.

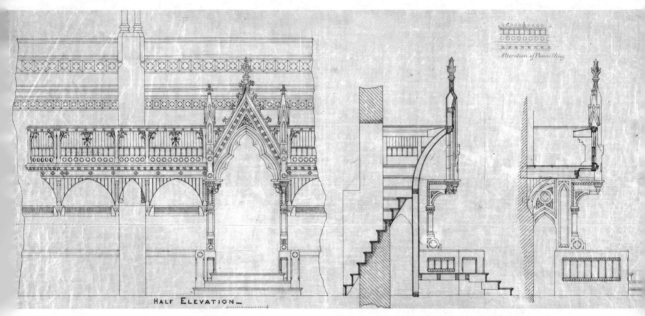

HALF ELEVATION

ESSENTIAL READINGS

IN CANADIAN GOVERNMENT AND POLITICS

SECOND EDITION

EDITED BY

PETER H. RUSSELL
FRANÇOIS ROCHER
DEBRA THOMPSON
AMANDA BITTNER

 emond 2016 / TORONTO, CANADA

Emond Montgomery Publications Limited
60 Shaftesbury Avenue
Toronto ON M4T 1A3
http://www.emond.ca/highered

Printed in Canada on FSC® certified paper.
Reprinted November 2019.

We acknowledge the financial support of the Government of Canada.
Nous reconnaissons l'appui financier du gouvernement du Canada.   Canadä

Vice-president, publishing: Anthony Rezek
Acquisitions editor: Mike Thompson
Managing editor, development: Kelly Dickson
Developmental and permissions editor: Francine Geraci
Director, editorial and production: Jim Lyons
Editorial assistant: Samantha Preddie
Production editor and coordinator: Laura Bast
Copy editor: Paula Pike
Proofreaders: Cindy Fujimoto and Laura Bast
Text designer and typesetter: Tara Wells
Cover designers: Stephen Cribbin and Simon Evers
Cover image: Architectural drawings for the main tower of the original Parliament Buildings, Ottawa. *Hand Book to the Parliamentary and Departmental Buildings, Canada*, by Joseph Bureau (1867). Courtesy Library and Archives Canada.
Back cover photo: Mike Thompson

Library and Archives Canada Cataloguing in Publication

Essential readings in Canadian government and politics / edited by Peter H. Russell, François Rocher, Debra Thompson, Amanda Bittner. — Second edition.

Includes bibliographical references and index.
ISBN 978-1-55239-662-9 (paperback)

1. Canada—Politics and government—Textbooks.   I. Rocher, François, editor   II. Russell, Peter H., editor   III. Bittner, Amanda, editor   IV. Thompson, Debra, 1980-, editor

JL75.E85 2016   320.971   C2015-905101-0

Contents

Part 1: Understanding Canada

Part 2: Canada's Institutions and Representation

Part 3: Governing Canada

Part 4: Canadian Society: Identities and Diversities

Preface

This project originated with a brief conversation that took place, appropriately enough, on Parliament Hill, during which Emond Publishing editor Mike Thompson suggested to Peter Russell the idea for this book. While articulating the guiding principle was relatively easy—that is, a book that would pull together a broad selection of primary and secondary readings that students of Canadian politics should have some familiarity with—making the final selections was considerably more difficult, if still very enjoyable.

In preparing this second edition, that task was somewhat easier, given the extensive feedback we received from instructors, although we readily concede that another group of four scholars would have undoubtedly come up with a different list. Despite that, we believe these selections represent a very solid introduction to the key issues, people, and perspectives at the heart of Canadian politics and political science, enhanced by a strong historical element that we think students will also greatly benefit from. We hope that these pieces will spark lively discussions and debate, and also help build an appreciation for the breadth of thought and writing in this field.

There are several key changes to this edition, most obviously that almost half of the selections are new, and, while there are slightly fewer readings than in the first edition, many excerpts are now a little longer, providing readers with more depth. Perhaps the most significant change is the new four-part thematic structure, intended to more closely match the themes covered in a typical Canadian politics course. This includes a new part (Part 2) focusing on Canadian political institutions, voting, and related areas. In addition, Part 3 now includes a section exploring Canada's foreign policy and international relations.

As with the first edition, we welcome suggestions and feedback on the selections in this volume. In the meantime, we hope readers will agree that this editorial team—a group with quite varied backgrounds and academic interests—has produced an appropriately diverse and engaging set of readings that do justice to the richness, nuance, and complexity of Canadian political life.

The publisher wishes to thank the following people for providing their feedback on the first edition, and suggestions for this second edition: Matt James (University of Victoria), Paul Kopas (University of British Columbia), Larry LeDuc (University of Toronto), Christian Leuprecht (Queen's University/Royal Military College), Antonia Maioni (McGill University), Jonathan Malloy (Carleton University), Luc Turgeon (University of Ottawa), and Nelson Wiseman (University of Toronto).

The publisher and the authors also wish to thank Linda White for her contribution to the first edition of this book.

About the Authors

Peter H. Russell is a professor of political science (emeritus) at the University of Toronto.

François Rocher is a professor of political science at the University of Ottawa.

Debra Thompson is an assistant professor of African American Studies at Northwestern University.

Amanda Bittner is an associate professor of political science at Memorial University.

Prime Ministers of Canada, 1867–Present

Election year	Prime minister(s) following the election
1867	John A. Macdonald (Conservative)
1872	John A. Macdonald (Conservative)
1874	Alexander Mackenzie (Liberal)
1878	John A. Macdonald (Conservative)
1882	John A. Macdonald (Conservative)
1887	John A. Macdonald (Conservative)
1891	Macdonald/Abbott/Thompson/Bowell/Tupper (Conservative)
1896	Wilfrid Laurier (Liberal)
1900	Wilfrid Laurier (Liberal)
1904	Wilfrid Laurier (Liberal)
1908	Wilfrid Laurier (Liberal)
1911	Robert Borden (Conservative)
1917	Robert Borden/Arthur Meighen (Unionist)
1921	William Lyon Mackenzie King (Liberal)
1925	William Lyon Mackenzie King (Liberal)/Arthur Meighen (Conservative)
1926	William Lyon Mackenzie King (Liberal)
1930	R.B. Bennett (Conservative)
1935	William Lyon Mackenzie King (Liberal)
1940	William Lyon Mackenzie King (Liberal)
1945	William Lyon Mackenzie King/Louis St. Laurent (Liberal)
1949	Louis St. Laurent (Liberal)
1953	Louis St. Laurent (Liberal)
1957	John Diefenbaker (Conservative)
1958	John Diefenbaker (Conservative)
1962	John Diefenbaker (Conservative)
1963	Lester Pearson (Liberal)
1965	Lester Pearson/Pierre Trudeau (Liberal)
1968	Pierre Trudeau (Liberal)
1972	Pierre Trudeau (Liberal)
1974	Pierre Trudeau (Liberal)
1979	Joe Clark (Conservative)
1980	Pierre Trudeau/John Turner (Liberal)
1984	Brian Mulroney (Conservative)
1988	Brian Mulroney/Kim Campbell (Conservative)
1993	Jean Chrétien (Liberal)
1997	Jean Chrétien (Liberal)
2000	Jean Chrétien/Paul Martin (Liberal)
2004	Paul Martin (Liberal)
2006	Stephen Harper (Conservative)
2008	Stephen Harper (Conservative)
2011	Stephen Harper (Conservative)
2015	Justin Trudeau (Liberal)

PART 1
Understanding Canada

Introduction

Canada has never been an easy country to understand. This is as true for its own people as for those who view it from the outside. It has never been a state based on a people with one language and one culture. From its founding in 1867 to the present day, the Canadian federation has been based on compromise and the accommodation of cultural and linguistic diversity. The writings included in this part mark critical milestones in the evolving nature of the different aspirations that have animated Canada's experience as a nation-state and the efforts to maintain its unity.

Part 1 begins with an 1840 speech delivered by Louis-Hippolyte LaFontaine during the first election in the United Province of Canada, an amalgamation of Lower and Upper Canada that Britain imposed upon the *Canadiens* after the rebellions of 1837–1838. Although LaFontaine had been a supporter of the *patriotes* in the rebellion, he now urges his people to cooperate with English Canadians to achieve responsible democratic government. This landmark speech—LaFontaine went on to win the election campaign, becoming the first prime minister of the United Province of Canada—is followed by a letter from three Canadian politicians sent to the British colonial secretary in 1858, seeking his support for a federation of Britain's North American colonies. Speeches by two of Canada's founding fathers, John A. Macdonald and George-Étienne Cartier, come next. It was the partnership of these two leaders—one English Canadian and the other French Canadian—that made Confederation possible in 1867. In their speeches we can see the colonial nature of Canada's beginnings. Macdonald and Cartier share a strong allegiance to the British monarchical system and an equally strong distaste for what they view as the excesses of American democracy. But they differ in their aspirations for the federation they are founding. While Macdonald views federalism not as an ideal but as a pragmatic compromise and believes that the new federal

parliament has been given "all the powers that are incident to sovereignty," Cartier emphasizes the deep cultural diversity that will give the new federation its distinctive identity.

The two items that follow their speeches show the emergence of differing perspectives on
the English–French relationship in Canada. The early 20th-century pamphlet written by
Henri Bourassa, a staunch Canadian patriot in the Cartier mould, argues that Canada will
best maintain its unity and its distinctiveness from the United States by fostering English–
French dualism throughout Canada. The centralizing trends that followed in the Second
World War and post-war reconstruction prompted the government of Quebec to appoint the
Tremblay Royal Commission to examine the constitutional issues raised by these centraliz-
ing developments. The Tremblay report calls for a return to the Quebecois understanding
of Confederation being founded on a partnership between English and French Canadians.
But, unlike Henri Bourassa earlier in the century, the Quebec commissioners believe the
survival of the French-Canadian culture now depends entirely on Quebec.

The "Quiet Revolution" that capped Quebec's emergence as a secular and industrialized
society dramatically radicalized the constitutional aspirations of much of francophone Quebec. Instead of calling for a return to the spirit of Confederation, Quebec political leaders in
the 1960s mobilized support for a restructuring of the Canadian federation to properly reflect
Quebec's place as one of Canada's founding peoples. Excerpts from a 1965 book by Daniel
Johnson, leader of the Union Nationale party who would become premier of Quebec in 1966,
indicate the challenge that will plunge Canada into a quarter century of mega constitutional
politics. The title of Johnson's book, *Égalité ou Indépendence*, indicates the ultimatum that
Quebec now poses to Canada. The Canadian who would lead Canada in responding to Quebec's challenge was another Quebecker, Pierre Elliott Trudeau. His essay on "Federalism,
Nationalism, and Reason," published on the eve of his becoming prime minister of Canada,
warns of the coming clash between Quebec nationalism and Canadian nationalism.

Preston Manning's 1987 speech to the Western Assembly on Canada's economic and political future reflects the growing strength of western Canada in the Canadian federation, and
a desire to have its reform tradition of populist democracy play a major role in Canadian
politics. Charles Taylor's essay on "Shared and Divergent Values" looks back on the intense
constitutional politics of the 1970s and '80s that resulted in the patriation of Canada's Constitution with a charter of rights and freedoms and recognition of Aboriginal rights, but left
old and new cleavages in the Canadian body politic. Taylor contends that embracing Canada's deep diversity should be seen as the country's greatest source of strength and unity.

Aboriginal peoples did not participate in Confederation. Although they continued to
engage in a treaty-making process with Canada from Confederation to the early years of the
20th century, they were not acknowledged as partners in Confederation. References to them
in Taylor's essay indicate that Canada's heavy season of constitutional politics afforded Aboriginal peoples an opportunity to place their aspirations on the country's constitutional
agenda. The Royal Commission on Aboriginal Peoples (RCAP), appointed in 1991, was the
first time a representative group of Aboriginal and non-Aboriginal Canadians had come
together to consider the place of Aboriginal peoples in Canada. *People to People, Nation to
Nation* is an overview of the commission's 1996 final report. It calls for rebuilding the relationship of Aboriginal peoples with Canada on the basis of mutual respect, partnership, and
fair sharing.

The final two writings included in this part reflect on how Canada may cope with unresolved constitutional issues and a population harbouring divergent senses of national identity. Both point to understanding Canada as a multinational democracy. Peter Russell's essay "Canada—A Pioneer in the Management of Constitutional Politics in a Multi-national Society," written in 2000 after the rejection of the Charlottetown Accord in the 1992 referendum and the narrow win for the federalist side in Quebec's 1995 referendum, considers the lessons to be learned from these mega constitutional failures about managing the process of constitutional change in deeply divided societies. James Tully's discussion of Canada as a multinational democracy places the Canadian experience in a larger international context. Tully draws on modern democratic theory to elucidate a set of principles for operating a multinational democracy such as Canada.

Further Suggested Reading

Janet Ajzenstat, Paul Romney, Ian Gentles, and William D. Gairdner, eds. *Canada's Founding Debates*. Toronto: University of Toronto Press, 1999.

Michael Asch. *On Being Here to Stay: Treaties and Aboriginal Rights in Canada*. Toronto: University of Toronto Press, 2014.

Eugene Forsey. "The Crown and the Constitution." In *Freedom and Order*. Toronto: McClelland & Stewart, 1974.

Alain-G. Gagnon, ed. *Contemporary Canadian Federalism: Foundations, Traditions, Institutions*. Toronto: University of Toronto Press, 2009.

Alain-G. Gagnon and Raffaele Iacovino. *Federalism, Citizenship and Quebec: Debating Multinationalism*. Toronto: University of Toronto Press, 2007.

Roger Gibbins and Guy Laforest, eds. *Beyond the Impasse: Toward Reconciliation*. Montreal: Institute for Research on Public Policy, 1998.

John George Lambton (Earl of Durham). *The Durham Report*, 1839. New edition abridged by Gerald M. Craig. Montreal and Kingston: McGill-Queen's University Press, 2006.

Kenneth McRoberts. *Misconceiving Canada: The Struggle for National Unity*. Toronto: Oxford University Press, 1997.

Kenneth McRoberts and Dale Postgate. *Quebec: Social Change and Political Crisis*, revised edition. Toronto: McClelland & Stewart, 1988.

John Meisel, Guy Rocher, Arthur Silver, and Institute for Research on Public Policy (IRPP), eds. *As I Recall/Si je me souviens bien: Historical Perspectives*. Montreal: IRPP, 1999.

Peter H. Russell. *Constitutional Odyssey: Can Canadians Become a Sovereign People?* 3rd edition. Toronto: University of Toronto Press, 2004.

John Ralston Saul. *Louis-Hippolyte LaFontaine and Robert Baldwin*. Toronto: Penguin Canada, 2010.

André Siegfried. *The Race Question in Canada*, 1907. Montreal and Kingston: McGill-Queen's University Press/Carleton Library Series, 1966.

Triadafilos Triadafilopoulos. *Becoming Multicultural: Immigration and the Politics of Membership in Canada and Germany*. Vancouver: University of British Columbia Press, 2012.

Jeremy Webber. *Reimagining Canada: Language, Culture, Community and the Canadian Constitution*. Montreal and Kingston: McGill-Queen's University Press, 1994.

1 Address to the Electors of Terrebonne

Louis-Hippolyte LaFontaine (1840)

EDITORS' INTRODUCTION

Britain responded to the rebellions of 1837–1838 in Lower and Upper Canada by passing the 1840 Act of Union, *uniting Lower and Upper Canada together in the Province of Canada. Louis-Hippolyte LaFontaine, who had been a strong supporter of the reformist Patriotes, emerged as the strongest French-Canadian leader in the united province. In the United Province of Canada's first election, he ran in the constituency of Terrebonne, and urged its electors to take the path of political cooperation with reform-minded English-speaking citizens, rather than violence, to achieve responsible, democratic government. It is this emphasis on responsible government—that is, the constitutional requirement for the prime minister and the government to maintain the confidence of a majority of members of Parliament in the House of Commons—that became the central principle of Canadian democracy. LaFontaine, among others, championed responsible government in his speeches, and went on to win the election, becoming the first prime minister of the United Province of Canada.*

LaFontaine's speech also laid the foundation for an alliance with Robert Baldwin, the leader of liberal reformers in the western part of the province (Canada West, formerly Upper Canada). In 1848, LaFontaine and Baldwin formed the first Canadian government under elected English and French leaders with full control of domestic affairs.

Three weeks after LaFontaine gave this speech on August 25, 1840, an English translation appeared in the Toronto Examiner *newspaper, and was very influential among reformers in English Canada. Political historian John Ralston Saul has called LaFontaine's address "the key founding statement of what we understand Canada to be."*

To the Electors of the County of Terrebonne

Gentlemen,

The Union has at last been decreed! In the opinion of the English Parliament, Canada must henceforth be but one Province. Whether this great political measure is in accordance with the true interests of the population, who will now have to submit to a single Legislature, is a problem which time alone may solve. History will say that it was thrust by force upon the inhabitants of Lower and Upper Canada. To render this measure legitimate, their consent must be obtained. Their voice can only make itself heard in the House of Assembly, where, nevertheless, the Act of the Imperial Parliament, with its numerous injustices, will permit no more than a portion of their legitimate Representatives to take their places in the first session of the new Legislature.

The exercise of arbitrary power granted to the Governor in Chief may postpone a general election for a length of time, just as it may also suddenly and unexpectedly call you to the campaign hustings. Whether that event be near or distant, I shall not lose sight of my old commitments. Having been elected to represent you in the Assembly of Lower Canada during two Parliaments, if you have approved of my conduct and my principles, as I have reason to believe, I again offer my services in the United Legislature. I offer them to you in the conviction that the time has come when one who sincerely loves his country must not shrink from those sacrifices that are the consequences of a political life. Despite the unanimity which has usually reigned in the sentiments of the electors of your county, I hope to meet you in great numbers at the campaign hustings. I am counting upon the well-known patriotism of a population of twenty-five thousand souls, who are called upon to name but a single Representative, even while a little town of only a few dozen electors will enjoy the same privilege.

The events that the future has in store for our country are of the highest importance. Canada is the land of our ancestors; it is our homeland, as it should be the adopted homeland of the various populations that come from diverse parts of the globe to make their way into its vast forests, the future resting place of their families and their hopes. Like us, their paramount desire must be the happiness and prosperity of Canada. It is the heritage which they should strive to transmit to their descendants in this young and hospitable country. Above all, their children should be, like ourselves, CANADIANS.

On the continent of America, the greatest benefit that the population enjoys is social equality; it reigns to the highest degree. If, in some of the old countries of another hemisphere, that equality should seem to suffice for the satisfaction of the wishes and wants of the inhabitants, it is insufficient alone to satisfy the vigorous populations of the new world. In addition to social equality, we must have political liberty. Without it, we will have no future; without it, our needs will remain unsatisfied, and we would strive in vain to attain that state of well-being which the abundant resources of nature in America would seem to warrant. With constant and directed efforts, with steadfastness and prudence towards this essential goal of our prosperity, we will secure for ourselves political liberty. To prevent us from enjoying it, one would need to destroy the social equality that forms the distinctive character of the population of Upper Canada as well as that of Lower Canada. For this social equality must necessarily lead to political liberty. It is an irresistible need in the British colonies of North America. The habits of a people are stronger than laws imposed upon it, and we know of nothing that will weaken them. There can exist in Canada no privileged caste above and beyond the mass of its inhabitants. Titles may be created and flourish for a day, but the next day, the children of the favoured few will be seen trailing the sullied parchment of nobility through the mud of the streets.

But what is the method of obtaining this political liberty, so essential to the peace and happiness of the colonies, and to the development of its vast resources? The method is the popular endorsement of the adoption of laws; it is the consent of the people to vote for taxes and to regulate their use; it is also the efficient participation of the people in the action of government; it is their legitimate influence over the machinery of the administration, and their effective constitutional control over those individuals to whom that administration is entrusted; it is, in a word, that which is the great question of the day: Responsible Government, such as it was recognized and promised in the Assembly of Upper Canada for the purpose of obtaining the consent of its members to the principle of the union, and not such as it may now be being defined in certain places.

This principle forms the basis of no new theory. It is the primary engine of the British Constitution. Lord Durham, in recognizing the necessity of its application to the colonies in their local affairs, has touched upon the root of the problem and has recommended the only workable remedy. In these times, the importance of this question is such that no candidate who has political principles, and attaches any value to them, should hesitate to express his opinion on this subject. I am not one of those with a blind confidence in the promises of the Governor General. Far from it; I believe that in practice he will not readily carry out this principle, and my opinion is that the extent to which he may do so will depend on the composition of the new House of Assembly. For my part, I do not hesitate to say that I am in favour of this British principle of Responsible Government. I see, in its operation, the only guarantee we can have of a good and effective government. The colonists must have control over their own affairs. All their efforts must be directed towards this end, and to bring it about, it will be necessary that the Colonial administration be formed and directed *by and with* the majority of the Representatives of the people, as the only means of "administering the Government of these provinces in accordance with the wishes and interests of the people, and to pay to their sentiments, as expressed through their Representatives, the deference that is justly due to them."

Another question, no less important, is that which arises out of the Union of the two provinces. The Union is an act of injustice and despotism; it is imposed upon us without our consent, and in that it deprives Lower Canada of the legitimate number of its Representatives. It wrests from us the use of our language in the proceedings of the Legislature, contrary to the faith of treaties and *the word* of the Governor General. It compels us to pay, without our consent, a debt which we never contracted, and it empowers the Executive to take illegal possession of an enormous portion of the revenues of the country, under the name of a Civil List, without the consent of the people's Representatives.

Does it follow, therefore, that the Representatives of Lower Canada should pledge themselves beforehand, and, unconditionally, demand the repeal of the Union? No, they should not do so. They should wait before adopting a determination, the immediate result of which might be to place us, for an indefinite time, under the draconian legislation of a Special Council, and leave us without any representation at all. It is an error, too prevalent among political parties in the Colonies, to believe that they may hope for sympathy from this or that Imperial Minister. Whether a Minister in London is Tory, Whig, or Radical will make no difference to the political situation of the Colonies. The past is there to convince us of this.

The Reformers in both provinces form an immense majority. Those of Upper Canada, or at least their Representatives, have assumed the responsibility of the Act of Union, and of all its unjust and tyrannical conditions, by confiding, for all its details, in the discretion of the Governor General. They will not, they cannot, approve of the manner in which the inhabitants of Lower Canada are treated by this Act. If they have been deceived in their expectations, they must protest against these conditions which subject their political interests and ours to the whims of the Executive. If they do not, they will place the Reformers of Lower Canada in a false position in reference to them, and would thus incur the risk of retarding the progress of reform for long years to come. They, as well as ourselves, will have to suffer the internal divisions which such a state of things would invariably give birth to. It is in the interest of the Reformers in both Provinces to meet on the field of legislation, in a spirit of peace, of union, of friendship and of fraternity. Unity of purpose is more necessary now than ever. I have no doubt that the Reformers of Upper Canada feel this necessity as deeply as ourselves, and that in the first session of the Legislature they will give us unequivocal proof of that feeling, as a pledge of mutual and enduring confidence.

When the work of the regular and constitutional legislation is taken up again, another important question, which is of more immediate interest to the inhabitants of Lower Canada, will, in all probability, demand the attention of your deputies. I allude to the question of seigniorial rights. I agree most sincerely with the opinion expressed by you on this subject, in the sixth resolution of a meeting in your county, held on the 11th of June, 1837, in which you declared that:

> With a view to ensure sooner or later a triumph of these democratic principles, which can alone form the basis of a free and enduring Government on this continent, we must employ all the means in our power to equalize the ranks of society, to wrest from Government all hope of establishing in this country a new aristocracy, however weak it may be, and that this assembly considers that one of the most effective measures to attain this end is to abolish seigniorial rights, by granting to those who enjoy them a just and reasonable compensation, and to establish a tenure entirely free, where our values and needs can be urgently asserted.

Education is the primary blessing which Government can confer upon a people. In the past, we had schools that were shut up by the Legislative Council. The public monies will be better spent on their reopening than on paying a police force which is repulsive to and abhorred by all. The establishment of our colleges makes lies every day of those false and injurious assertions, propagated by passion and prejudice, that are intended to brand Canadians with a reputation of ignorance and indifference to the advantages of education.

The development of our vast internal resources urgently requires the opening of an easy line of navigation from the sea to the great lakes. The St. Lawrence is the natural canal for the conveyance of a great portion of the products of the west. If, to attract towards us that source of public and private wealth, it requires the hand of man to come in aid of the means afforded to us by nature, we must not hesitate to give it judicious and prudent cooperation.

Such are my views of the leading features of our political position. If they are yours, you will prove it on the day when, in common with your brother Reformers, you will be called upon to choose a member to represent you in the United Legislature.

I have the honour to be,

Your devoted Servant,

L.H. LaFontaine

Montreal, 25 August 1840.

2 "Not Derived from the People": Letter from the Fathers of Confederation to the British Colonial Secretary

Alexander Galt (1858)

EDITORS' INTRODUCTION

This letter, signed by three Fathers of Confederation but drafted primarily by Alexander Galt, contains what Peter Russell, in his book Constitutional Odyssey, *describes as "perhaps the most haunting lines in Canada's history." In their proposal to the Colonial Office in London, written just as the United States was moving inexorably toward a bloody civil war, Galt, George-Étienne Cartier, and John Ross took pains to point out that "the basis of Confederation now proposed differs from that of the United States in several important particulars. It does not profess to be derived from the people but would be the constitution provided by the imperial parliament, thus affording the means of remedying any defect."*

While the letter is prescient of the federal union of the British North American colonies that lies ahead, it resonates with apprehension about applying the American doctrine of the sovereignty of the people to Canada. Neither at the time of this letter nor at the time of Confederation, a decade later, had the Canadians constituted themselves a single people to be governed by the will of the majority. Under these circumstances, they preferred that custody of their Constitution remain in the hands of the Imperial Parliament in London.

To British Colonial Secretary Edward Bulwer-Lytton

London, 25th October, 1858.

Dear Sir Edward:

In the official communication which we have this day the honour to address to you, on the Confederation of the British North American provinces, we have felt it improper to offer any opinion upon the details which will form the subject of the proposed discussion by Delegates. It is also our duty not to cause embarrassment by advancing views which may yet have to be greatly modified. We venture, however, in compliance with your desire for a confidential communication on these points to suggest:

That the Federal Government should be composed of a Governor-General, or Viceroy, to be appointed by the Queen, of an Upper House or Senate elected upon a territorial basis of representation, and of a House of Assembly, elected on the basis of population, the Executive to be composed of ministers responsible to the legislature.

That the powers of the Federal legislators and Government should comprehend the Customs, Excise and all trade questions, Postal Service, Militia, Banking, Currency, Weights and Measures and Bankruptcy, Public Works of a National Character, Harbours and Light-houses, Fisheries and their protection, Criminal justice, Public Lands, Public Debt and Government of unincorporated and Indian Territories. It will form a subject for mature deliberation whether the powers of the Federal Government should be confined to the points named, or should be extended to all matters and not specially entrusted to the local legislatures.

The Confederation might involve the constitution of a Federal Court of Appeal.

The general revenue, having first been charged with the expense of collection and civil government, to be subject to the payment of interest on the public debts of the Confederation to be constituted from the existing obligations of each—the surplus to be divided each year according to population. The net revenue from the Public Lands in each province to be its exclusive property, except in the case of the territories.

It may be expedient for a limited time to provide from the general revenue a certain fixed contribution for educational and judicial purposes until provision is made for the same by each member of the Confederation.

It will be observed that the basis of Confederation now proposed differs from that of the United States in several important particulars. It does not profess to be derived from the people but would be the constitution provided by the imperial parliament, thus affording the means of remedying any defect, which is now practically impossible under the American constitution. The local legislature would not be in a position to claim the exercise of the same sovereign powers which have frequently been the cause of difference between the American states and their general government. To this may be added that by the proposed distribution of the revenue each province would have a direct pecuniary interest in the preservation of the authority of the Federal Government. In these respects it is conceived that the proposed Confederation would possess greater inherent strength than that of the United States, and would combine the advantage of the unity for general purposes of a legislative union with so much of the Federation principle as would join all the benefits of local government and legislation upon questions of provincial interest. …

G.E. Cartier.
JNO. Ross.
A.T. Galt.

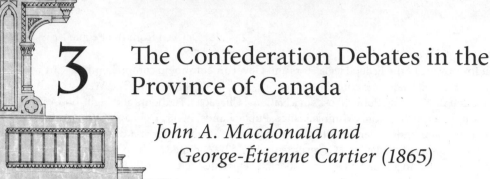

3 The Confederation Debates in the Province of Canada

John A. Macdonald and George-Étienne Cartier (1865)

EDITORS' INTRODUCTION

Of the three colonies that came together in 1867 to form Canada—the Province of Canada (which combined what are now the provinces of Ontario and Quebec), New Brunswick, and Nova Scotia—Canada was the only one whose legislature conducted a full, detailed debate on the terms of the proposed federal union. This debate took place in Quebec City from early February to mid-March 1865. The debate was based on the 72 Resolutions agreed to by delegates from the British North American colonies at a conference held in Quebec City in October 1864. John A. Macdonald and George-Étienne Cartier were leading members of the "Grand Coalition" of Conservatives and Liberals that was formed in 1864 to govern the Province of Canada with the primary objective of settling its constitutional future. At the end of the debate a motion supporting the 72 Resolutions was adopted by a majority of 91 to 33. The majority in favour among members of the Legislative Assembly from Canada West (today's Ontario) was 54 to 8. Among members from Canada East (today's Quebec) it was 37 to 25. The 72 Resolutions, with a few changes agreed to at a conference in London that same year, became the basis of Canada's founding constitution, the British North America Act, *enacted by the Parliament of the United Kingdom in 1867.*

(Note to the reader: At the time, Hansard often recorded proceedings in the third person.)

Legislative Assembly

Monday, February 6, 1865.

Attorney General Macdonald moved, "That an humble Address be presented to Her Majesty, praying that She may be graciously pleased to cause a measure to be submitted to the Imperial Parliament, for the purpose of uniting the Colonies of Canada, Nova Scotia, New Brunswick, Newfoundland, and Prince Edward Island, in one Government, with provisions based on certain Resolutions, which were adopted at a Conference of Delegates from the said Colonies, held at the city of Quebec, on the 10th October, 1864." He said: Mr. Speaker, in fulfillment of the promise made by the Government to Parliament at its last session, I have moved this resolution. I have had the honour of being charged, on behalf of the Government, to submit a scheme for the Confederation of all the British North American Provinces—a scheme which has been received, I am glad to say, with general, if not universal, approbation in Canada. The scheme, as propounded through the press, has received almost no opposition. While there may be occasionally, here and there, expressions of dissent from some of the details, yet the scheme as a whole has met with almost universal approval, and the Government has the greatest satisfaction in presenting it to this House. ...

The subject, however, though looked upon with favour by the country, and though there were no distinct expressions of opposition to it from any party, did not begin to assume its present proportions until last session. Then, men of all parties and shades of politics became alarmed at the aspect of affairs. They found that such was the opposition between the two sections of the province, such was the danger of impending anarchy, in consequence of the irreconcilable differences of opinion, with respect to representation by population, between Upper and Lower Canada, that unless some solution of the difficulty was arrived at, we would suffer under a succession of weak governments—weak in numerical support, weak in force, and weak in power of doing good. All were alarmed at this state of affairs. We had election after election, we had ministry after ministry, with the same result. Parties were so equally balanced, that the vote of one member might decide the fate of the Administration, and of course of legislation for a year or a series of years. This condition of things was well calculated to arouse the earnest consideration of every lover of his country, and I am happy to say it had that effect. None were more impressed by this momentous state of affairs, and the grave apprehensions that existed of a state of anarchy destroying our credit, destroying our prosperity, destroying our progress, than were the members of this present House; and the leading statesmen on both sides seemed to have come to the common conclusion, that some step must be taken to relieve the country from the dead-lock and impending anarchy that hung over us. With that view, my colleague, the President of the Council, made a motion founded on the dispatch addressed to the Colonial Minister, to which I have referred, and a committee was struck, composed of gentlemen of both sides of the House, of all shades of political opinion, without any reference to whether they were supporters of the Administration of the day or belonged to the Opposition, for the purpose of taking into calm and full deliberation the evils which threatened the future of Canada. ...

The report of that committee was laid before the House, and then came the political action of the leading men of the two parties in this House, which ended in the formation of the present Government. The principle upon which that Government was formed has been announced, and is known to all. It was formed for the very purpose of carrying out the object which has now received to a certain degree its completion, by the resolutions I have had the honour to place in your hands. As has been stated, it was not without a great deal of difficulty and reluctance that the Government was formed. The gentlemen who compose this Government had for many years been engaged in political hostilities to such an extent that it affected even their social relations. But the crisis was great, the danger was imminent, and the gentlemen who now form the present Administration found it to be their duty to lay aside all personal feelings, to sacrifice in some degree their position, and even to run the risk of having their motives impugned, for the sake of arriving at some conclusion that would be satisfactory to the country in general. The present resolutions were the result. And, as I said before, I am proud to believe that the country has sanctioned, as I trust that the representatives of the people in this House will sanction, the scheme which is now submitted for the future government of British North America. (Cheers.) ...

[W]e returned to Quebec, and then the Government of Canada invited the several governments of the sister colonies to send a deputation here from each of them for the purpose of considering the question, with something like authority from their respective governments. The result was, that when we met here on the 10th of October, on the first day on which we assembled, after the full and free discussions which had taken place at Charlottetown, the first resolution now before this House was passed unanimously, being received with acclamation as, in the opinion of every one who heard it, a proposition which ought to receive, and would receive, the sanction of each government and each people. The resolution is, "That the best interests and present and future prosperity of British North America will be promoted by a Federal Union under the Crown of Great Britain, provided such union can be effected on principles just to the several provinces." It seemed to all the statesmen assembled—and there are great statesmen in the Lower Provinces, men who would do honour to any government and to any legislature of any free country enjoying representative institutions—it was clear to them all that the best interests and present and future prosperity of British North America would be promoted by a Federal Union under the Crown of Great Britain. And it seems to me, as to them, and I think it will so appear to the people of this country, that, if we wish to be a great people; if we wish to form—using the expression which was sneered at the other evening—a great nationality, commanding the respect of the world, able to hold our own against all opponents, and to defend those institutions we prize; if we wish to have one system of government, and to establish a commercial union, with unrestricted free trade, between people of the five provinces, belonging, as they do, to the same nation, obeying the same Sovereign, owning the same allegiance, and being, for the most part, of the same blood and lineage; if we wish to be able to afford to each other the means of mutual defence and support against aggression and attack—this can only be obtained by a union of some kind between the scattered and weak boundaries composing the British North American Provinces. (Cheers.) …

I trust the scheme will be assented to as a whole. I am sure this House will not seek to alter it in its unimportant details; and, if altered in any important provisions, the result must be that the whole will be set aside, and we must begin *de novo*. If any important changes are made, every one of the colonies will feel itself absolved from the implied obligation to deal with it as a Treaty, each province will feel itself at liberty to amend it *ad libitum* so as to suit its own views and interests; in fact, the whole of our labours will have been for nought, and we will have to renew our negotiations with all the colonies for the purpose of establishing some new scheme. I hope the House will not adopt any such a course as will postpone, perhaps for ever, or at all events for a long period, all chances of union. All the statesmen and public men who have written or spoken on the subject admit the advantages of a union, if it were practicable: and now when it is proved to be practicable, if we do not embrace this opportunity the present favourable time will pass away, and we may never have it again. …

The Conference having come to the conclusion that a legislative union, pure and simple, was impracticable, our next attempt was to form a government upon federal principles, which would give to the General Government the strength of a legislative and administrative union, while at the same time it preserved that liberty of action for the different sections which is allowed by a Federal Union. And I am strong in the belief that we have hit upon the happy medium in those resolutions, and that we have formed a scheme of government which unites the advantages of both, giving us the strength of a legislative union and the sectional freedom of a federal union, with protection to local interests. In doing so we had the advantage of the experience of the United States. It is the fashion now to enlarge on the defects of the Constitution of the United States, but I am not one of those who look upon it as a failure. (Hear, hear.) I think and believe that it is one of the most skillful works which human intelligence ever created; is one of the most perfect organizations that ever governed a free people. To say that it has some defects is but to say that it is not the work of Omniscience, but of human intellects. We are happily situated in having had the opportunity of watching its operation, seeing its working from its infancy till now. It was in the main formed on the model of the Constitution of Great Britain, adapted to the circumstances of a new country, and was perhaps the only practicable system that could have been adopted under the circumstances existing at the time of its formation. We can now take advantage of the experience of the last seventy-eight years, during which that Constitution has existed, and I am strongly of the belief that we have, in a great measure, avoided in this system which we propose for the adoption of the people of Canada, the defects which time and events have shown to exist in the American Constitution. In the first place, by a resolution which meets with the universal approval of the people of this country, we have provided that for all time to come, so far as we can legislate for the future, we shall have as the head of the executive power, the Sovereign of Great Britain. (Hear, hear.) …

In the Constitution we propose to continue the system of Responsible Government, which has existed in this province since 1841, and which has long obtained in the Mother Country. This is a feature of our Constitution as we have it now, and as we shall have it in the Federation, in which, I think, we avoid one of the great defects in the Constitution of the United States. There the President, during his term of office, is in a great measure a despot, a one-man power, with the command of the naval and military forces—with an immense amount of patronage as Head of the Executive, and with the veto power as a branch of the legislature, perfectly uncontrolled by responsible advisers, his cabinet being departmental officers merely, whom he is not obliged by the Constitution to consult with, unless he chooses to do so. With us the Sovereign, or in this country the representative of the Sovereign, can act only on the advice of his ministers, those ministers being responsible to the people through Parliament. …

Ever since the union was formed the difficulty of what is called "State Rights" has existed, and this had much to do in bringing on the present unhappy war in the United States. They commenced, in fact, at the wrong end. They declared by their Constitution that each state was a sovereignty in itself, and that all the powers incident to a sovereignty belonged to each state, except those powers which, by the Constitution, were conferred upon the General Government and Congress. Here we have adopted a different system. We have strengthened the General Government. We have given the General Legislature all the great subjects of legislation. We have conferred on them, not only specifically and in detail, all the powers which are incident to sovereignty, but we have expressly declared that all subjects of general interest not distinctly and exclusively conferred upon the local governments and local legislatures, shall be conferred upon the General Government and Legislature. We have thus avoided that great source of weakness which has been the cause of disruption of the United States. We have avoided all conflict of jurisdiction and authority, and if this Constitution is carried out, as it will be in full detail in the Imperial Act to be passed if the colonies adopt the scheme, we will have in fact, as I said before, all the advantages of a legislative union under one administration, with, at the same time the guarantees for local institutions and for local laws, which are insisted upon by so many in the provinces now, I hope, to be united. ...

As may be well conceived, great difference of opinion at first existed as to the constitution of the Legislative Council. In Canada, the elective principle prevailed; in the Lower Provinces, with the exception of Prince Edward Island, the nominative principle was the rule. We found a general disinclination on the part of the Lower Provinces to adopt the elective principle; indeed, I do not think there was a dissenting voice in the Conference against the adoption of the nominative principle, except from Prince Edward Island. The delegates from New Brunswick, Nova Scotia and Newfoundland, as one man, were in favour of nomination by the Crown. And nomination by the Crown is of course the system which is most in accordance with the British Constitution. We resolved then, that the constitution of the Upper House should be in accordance with the British system as nearly as circumstances would allow. An hereditary Upper House is impracticable in this young country. Here we have none of the elements for the formation of a landlord aristocracy—no men of large territorial positions—no class separated from the mass of people. An hereditary body is altogether unsuited to our state of society, and would soon dwindle into nothing. ...

I shall not go over the other powers that are conferred on the General Parliament. Most of them refer to matters of financial and commercial interest, and I leave those subjects in other and better hands. Besides all the powers that are specifically given in the 37th and last item of this portion of the Constitution, confers on the General Legislature the general mass of sovereign legislation, the power to legislate on "all matters of general character, not specifically and exclusively reserved for the local governments and legislatures." This is precisely the provision which is wanting in the Constitution of the United States. It is here that we find the weakness of the American system—the point where the American Constitution breaks down. (Hear, hear.) It is in itself a wise and necessary provision. We thereby strengthen the Central Parliament, and make the Confederation one people and one government, instead of five peoples and five governments, with merely a point of authority connecting us to a limited and insufficient extent. ...

There are numerous subjects which belong, of right, both to the Local and the General Parliaments. In all these cases it is provided, in order to prevent a conflict of authority, that where there is concurrent jurisdiction in the General and Local Parliaments, the same rule should apply as now applies in cases where there is concurrent jurisdiction in the Imperial and in the Provincial Parliaments, and that when the legislation of the one is adverse to or contradictory of the legislation of the other, in all such cases the action of the General Parliament must overrule, ex-necessitate, the action of the Local Legislature. (Hear, hear.) ...

In conclusion, I would again implore the House not to let this opportunity to pass. It is an opportunity that may never recur. At the risk of repeating myself, I would say, it was only by a happy concurrence of circumstances, that we were enabled to bring this great question to its present position. If we do not take advantage of the time, if we show ourselves unequal to the occasion, it may never return, and we shall hereafter bitterly and unavailingly regret having failed to embrace the happy opportunity now offered of founding a great nation under the fostering care of Great Britain, and our Sovereign Lady, Queen Victoria. (Loud cheers, amidst which the honourable gentleman resumed his seat.)

The House, at eleven p.m., adjourned.

Legislative Assembly

Tuesday, February 7, 1865.
Attorney General Cartier rose to continue the debate on Confederation. ...

Everyone who knew anything of his past public course was aware that he was opposed to the principle of representation by population while Upper and Lower Canada were under one Government. He did not regret his opposition. If such a measure had been passed, what would have been the consequence? There would have been constant political warfare between Upper and Lower Canada. True it was that the members from Upper Canada, being in the majority, it might have been imagined they would have carried everything before them; but as far as justice to Lower Canada was concerned, such might not have been the case. The consequence of representation by population would have been that one territory would have governed another, and this fact would have presented itself session after session in the House, and day after day in the public prints. (Hear, hear.) The moment this principle had been conceded as the governing element, it would have initiated between the two provinces a warfare which would have been unremitting. (Hear, hear.) ...

In 1858 he first saw that representation by population, though unsuited for application as a governing principle as between the two provinces, would not involve the same objection if other partners were drawn in by a federation. In a struggle between two—one weak, and the other a strong party—the weaker could not but be overcome; but if three parties were concerned, the stronger would not have the same advantage; as when it was seen by the third that there was too much strength on one side, the third would club with the weaker combatant to resist the big fighter. (Cheers and laughter.) He did not oppose the principle of representation by population from an unwillingness to do justice to Upper Canada. He took this ground, however, that when justice was done to Upper Canada, it was his duty to see that no injustice was done to Lower Canada. He did not entertain the slightest apprehension that Lower Canada's rights were in the least jeopardized by the provision that in the General Legislature the French Canadians of Lower Canada would have a smaller number of representatives than all the other origins combined. ...

Confederation was, as it were, at this moment almost forced upon us. We could not shut our eyes to what was going on beyond the lines, where a great struggle was going on between two Confederacies, at one time forming but one Confederacy. We saw that a government, established not more than 80 years ago, had not been able to keep together the family of states which had broke up four or five years since. We could not deny that the struggle now in progress must necessarily influence our political existence. We did not know what would be the result of that great war—whether it would end in the establishment of two Confederacies or in one as before. However, we had to do with five colonies, inhabited by men of the same sympathies and interests, and in order to become a great nation they required only to be brought together under one General Government. The matter resolved itself into this, either we must obtain British North American Confederation or be absorbed into an American Confederation. (Hear, hear, and dissent.) ...

In our Federation the monarchical principle would form the leading feature, while on the other side of the lines, judging by the past history and present condition of the country, the ruling power was the will of the mob, the rule of the populace. Every person who had conversed with the most intelligent American statesmen and writers must have learned that they all admitted that the governmental powers had become too extended, owing to the introduction of universal suffrage, and mob rule had consequently supplanted legitimate authority; and we now saw the sad spectacle of a country torn by civil war, and brethren fighting against brethren. The question for us to ask ourselves was this: Shall we be content to remain separate—shall we be content to maintain a mere provincial existence, when, by combining together, we could become a great nation? It had never yet been the good fortune of any group of communities to secure national greatness with such facility. In past ages, warriors had struggled for years for the addition to their country of a single province. ...

Here, in British North America, we had five different communities inhabiting five separate colonies. We had the same sympathies, and we all desired to live under the British Crown. We had our commercial interests besides. It was of no use whatever that New Brunswick, Nova Scotia and Newfoundland should have their several custom houses against our trade, or that we should have custom houses against the trade of those provinces. In ancient times, the manner in which a nation grew up was different from that of the present day. Then the first weak settlement increased into a village, which, by turns, became a town and a city, and the nucleus of a nation. It was not so in modern times. Nations were now formed by the agglomeration of communities having kindred interests and sympathies. Such was our case at the present moment. Objection had been taken to the scheme now under consideration, because of the words "new nationality." Now, when we were united together, if union were attained, we would form a political nationality with which neither the national origin, nor the religion of any individual, would interfere. It was lamented by some that we had this diversity of races, and hopes were expressed that this distinctive feature would cease. The idea of unity of races was utopian—it was impossible. Distinctions of this kind would always exist. Dissimilarity, in fact, appeared to be the order of the physical world and the moral world, as well as in the political world. But with regard to the objection based on this fact, to the effect that a great nation could not be formed because Lower Canada was in great part French and Catholic, and Upper Canada was British and Protestant, and the Lower Provinces were mixed, it was futile and worthless in the extreme. Look, for instance, at the United Kingdom, inhabited as it was by three great races. (Hear, hear.) Had the diversity of race impeded the glory, the progress, the wealth of England? Had they not rather each contributed their share to the greatness of the Empire? Of the glories of the senate, the field, and the ocean, of the successes of trade and commerce, how much was contributed by the combined talents, energy, and courage of the three races together? (Cheers.) In our own Federation we should have Catholic and Protestant, English, French, Irish and Scotch, and each by his efforts and his success would increase the prosperity and glory of the new Confederacy. (Hear, hear.) He viewed the diversity of races in British North America in this way: we were of different races, not for the purpose of warring against each other, but in order to compete and emulate for the general welfare. (Cheers.) We could not do away with the distinctions of race. We could not legislate for the disappearance of the French Canadians from American soil, but British and French Canadians alike could appreciate and understand their position relative to each other. They were placed like great families beside each other, and their contact produced a healthy spirit of emulation. It was a benefit rather than otherwise that we had a diversity of races. ...

This scheme, he repeated, met with the approval of all moderate men. The extreme men, the socialists, democrats and annexationists were opposed to it. The French Canadian opponents of the project were, it appeared, afraid that their religious rights would suffer under the new arrangement. Fancy the celebrated *Institut Canadien*, of Montreal, under the lead of citizen Blanchet, taking religion under their protection! (Laughter.)

Mr. Dougall loudly proclaimed that the British Protestant minority would be entirely placed at the mercy of the French Canadians. He (Hon. Mr. Cartier) thought the arguments of the young French gentlemen belonging to the national democratic party who cried out that their religion and nationality would be destroyed, ought in all reason to be sufficient to satisfy the scruples and calm the fears of Mr. Dougall. The *True Witness*, which was also one of the enemies of the scheme, said that if it were adopted the French Canadians were doomed; while his brother in violence, the *Witness*, said that the Protestants were doomed. (Hear, hear, and laughter.) At a meeting recently held in Montreal on the subject, he (Hon. Mr. Cartier) observed that Mr. Cherrier had enrolled himself among the enemies of the project. Well, this fine quiet old gentleman announced that he had come out of his political retirement for the purpose of opposing Federation. All he (Hon. Mr. Cartier) could say was that he never knew Mr. Cherrier was a strong politician. However, it appeared that he had come out once more on the political stage for the purpose of opposing this villainous scheme, which was intended to destroy the nationality and religion of the French Canadians—all brought about by that confounded Cartier! (Laughter and cheers.)

Allusion has been made to the opinion of the clergy. Well he would say that the opinion of the clergy was for Confederation (Hear, hear.) Those who were high in authority, as well as those who occupied more humble positions, were in favour of Federation, not only because they saw in it so much security for all they held dear, but because it was just to their Protestant fellow-subjects as well, because they were opposed to political bickering and strife. This opposition to a state of political dissension and trouble was the general feeling of the clergy, and because they saw in Confederation a solution of those difficulties which had existed for some time, due regard being had to just rights, they were favourable to the project. The fact, however, was that when we saw such extreme opponents as Mr. Clerk, of the *True Witness*, Mr. Dougall, of the *Witness*, and the young gentlemen of the *Institut Canadien* combined to resist Confederation, because each party argued it would produce the most widely different results—we might look upon this fact, he repeated, as one of the strongest arguments in favour of Confederation. (Hear.) We had, on the other hand, all the moderate men, all that was respectable and intelligent, including the clergy, favourable to Federation. (Hear, hear, and oh, oh.) He did not, of course, mean to say that there were not respectable opponents to the project—what he did mean, however, was that it met general approval from the classes referred to. He was opposed, he might as well state most distinctly, to the democratic system which obtained in the United States. In this country of British North America we should have a distinct form of government, the characteristic of which would be to possess the monarchical element. When we had Confederation secured, there was not the least doubt but that our Government would be more respectable—that it would have more prestige, and command more respect from our neighbours. (Hear, hear.)

4 The French Language and the Future of Our Race

Henri Bourassa (1912)

EDITORS' INTRODUCTION

Henri Bourassa was a prominent Quebec politician and journalist. From the 1890s through the first half of the 20th century, he was the leading exponent of Canada as an independent Anglo-French nation. In 1910 he founded Le Devoir, *which has remained to this day one of Canada's most influential French-language newspapers. On June 28, 1912, he addressed the first Congrès de la langue française au Canada. The speech was published as a pamphlet in 1913, entitled "La langue française et l'avenir de notre race," and appears below in translation.*

At the very time Henri Bourassa was putting forward his vision of an English–French Canada, English-Canadian opinion was moving in the opposite direction. In 1913, Ontario's Department of Education circulated a directive aimed at eliminating French language teaching in both public and separate schools.

Mr. President, Honourable Members, Ladies and Gentlemen,

It is difficult for me to believe that the organization of this magnificent congress did not have a discreet ulterior motive in giving me a topic that deals with the realm of the future. However, since I lay no claim to the gift of prophecy, I trust you will allow me to proceed with the forecasting of the future, relying on the teachings of the past and the lessons of the present day.

I have been asked to speak to you about the French language and its influence on the future of the race. If you will bear with me, we shall study the question from two points of view.

First of all we shall consider what the influence of the language may be on the future of the race itself; then we shall study the role of the language in the relations that must exist between the French race and the races that live with it on the American continent. …

The 1867 Constitution and the Language

What are the exact terms of the Act of 1867? We do no need to discuss this tonight. All that is helpful to recall to those who have forgotten and to impress more strongly on their minds is that as far as federal laws and administration are concerned, the principle of absolute equality between the two languages is recognized to the letter; and that is enough. In fact if the law recognizes the principle, common sense as well as justice says that this principle must receive the sanction of all the means that are necessary to assure its application. In other words to suggest that under the authority of the 1867 constitution the rights of the French language exist only for Quebec is to say that the pact of 1867 was a trap, that Cartier, Macdonald, Brown, Howe and all the authors of this magnificent constitution were in league to deceive the people of Lower Canada!

As for me, I do not believe it; I think the true interpretation of the constitutional law that governs us is the one given it twenty-four years later by its chief author, Sir John A. Macdonald, in the memorable words the President of the Senate quoted the other day. I shall simply recall their content. It was that since 1867 in Canada there has no longer been a conquered race or a triumphant race, a ruling race or a subject race, but that on the contrary there is complete equality under the authority of the law itself for all that concerns the political, social, and moral rights of the two races, particularly for the public and private use of the two languages.

If French and English make up the double vocabulary of the Canadian people as a whole, how is it that there are narrow provincialists who affirm that any one of the legislatures of the Dominion of Canada can deprive the French-speaking citizens of any province of the means of giving their children knowledge and complete possession of this language in all the schools where their money is accepted just the same as the money of English-speaking people?

If the two languages are official, according to the very terms of the constitution, these languages have the right to coexist everywhere that the Canadian people lead a public life: at church, at school, in Parliament, in court, and in all public services. …

Means of Preserving the Language—The Schools

I wish to speak to you this evening of only two means of assuring the permanence, life, and fruitfulness of the French language in Canada.

The first and most important of all is teaching, that is, the schools. In 1875, eight years after the inauguration of the constitution, Edward Blake—another great statesman who was not afraid of the truth, even when it was dangerous for him—proclaimed on the floor of the Commons that the principle of separate schools should be adopted all across Western Canada, so that the two races and two religious beliefs could teach as they chose, but with state aid; because, he said, this is the very principle on which the federal pact was arranged between Upper and Lower Canada. Between the French Canadians and the English Canadians, and between the Canadian Protestants and the Canadian Catholics; and if this principle is good for the Canada of old, it should be equally good for the Canada of the future.

Those in the English provinces who are opposed to the teaching of French in public and separate schools are really the violators of the fundamental spirit of the Canadian constitution; and those of our fellow countrymen who preach to us a doctrine of subservience and who say that it is monstrous to claim for the French language equal rights with the English language are violating the sprit of the constitution just as much. No, the pact drawn up by those two great statesmen Sir John A. Macdonald and Sir George-Étienne Cartier was not a pact of subservience; quite the opposite, it was a straightforward and honourable treaty, signed by the sons of two great nations that wished to join forces in order to end past divisions and hatreds for ever, so that from this fruitful union a great people might be born, conceived in justice.

Those in the English provinces who preach the exclusion of French and those in our French province who teach a lesson of subservience are both betraying the constitution and the faith sworn in it. …

Towards French Sources

The second element necessary for the preservation of the language is to nourish it continually at the source from which it springs, at the only source that can assure its vitality and purity, that is, France. ...

But you will say that there is danger to our national unity. This nourishing at the sources of French thought can give rise to mental reservations and feelings of regret among the French Canadians; can isolate them from the British Empire and even from the Canadian Confederation. Those who talk like this show that they do not know the first thing about American history and are also ignorant of the human heart.

To think that by drawing intellectual light from the source that is France, or by seeking the nourishment the language needs, the French Canadian is going to become more French or less British or less Canadian is almost as sensible as believing that the cultured American wonders if he should not return to the Crown of England simply because he continues to read Shakespeare or Thackeray instead of nourishing his mind with the literature of the dime novels that fill the railway trains of the United States. The educated American is intellectually more English today than he was twenty-five years ago. He has learned that if he is to make gigantic material accomplishments by himself, to develop his territory, industry, and commerce in a really astonishing way, and to amaze the world with his political, industrial, and commercial vitality, he cannot ignore fifteen centuries of British civilization, from which he has drawn the best part of his blood and thought. But is he therefore less American, less devoted to his splendid homeland?

In the same way the French Canadian knows that if his language is not to become a dead language or a patois, as they call it in the "Parisian French" shops in Toronto, it must continue to find its nourishment in the homeland where it was formed.

A Canadian Literature

But if our language must become more and more French in form, it must become even more Canadian in content.

It must give birth to a Canadian literature, it must help us to write and read Canadian history, it must teach us to write well and to plead in favour of Canadian laws, and it must make us understand the spirit and the letter of the Canadian laws and constitution. And *Canadian* is not meant here in the narrow sense of our province or of our race, but in the complete and national meaning of this name that belongs to all the races that inhabit Canada. With the aid of this French language in an improved and living form we must seek out the origins of the English and American civilization; we must study the history of England and the United States; we must come to know the English and the Celts better and make ourselves better known to them.

Neither Isolation Nor Amalgamation

And this brings me to the second part of this study. I said that for the preservation and growth of the language we must bring ourselves closer to the intellectual life of France and at the same time *nationalize* our language along with all the other elements of our national life. Likewise when we define the scope of our claims we must keep in mind our situation with regard to the other races that share this land with us. We must be as wary of isolation as of assimilation. We cannot allow ourselves to be absorbed by any other race in Canada; but also we should not live like the Hebrews in Egypt, accepting the offer of seductive flesh-pots as compensation for their slavery. In Canada we must play the role of allies, brothers, associates. Therefore our duty forces us to investigate the ideas of those who fear and fight against the preservation and growth of the French language. Some see in this a danger to the unity of our faith and moral discipline; others an obstacle to national unity. …

The French Language and the Upholding of Confederation

Not only does the maintaining of the French language offer no danger to the religious and national unity of the country, but I am sure that the preservation and expansion of the French language in each of the English provinces of Canada is the only positive moral guarantee of both the unity of the Canadian Confederation and the maintaining of the British institutions in Canada.

Human institutions are preserved only by the survival of the vital principles that fostered these institutions. I have proved that the Canadian Confederation is the result of a contract between the two races in Canada, French and English, based on equality and recognizing equal rights and reciprocal duties. Canadian Confederation will last only as long as this equality of rights is recognized as the basis of the public right in Canada, from Halifax to Vancouver.

At first glance it is difficult to explain the blindness of those who—and they are numerous—honestly want to bring about the gradual destruction of the French language, or the blindness of those more moderate people who agree to allow it to live on in the Province of Quebec, but strive to prevent its penetration elsewhere. However, this mentality is easily explained.

First of all their ignorance of history and the absence of any philosophy deprive the English-Canadian statesmen and journalists of really knowing the depths of the human soul and the concept of distant repercussions of events in the history of nations. They do not know the past, or they forget about it; and consequently their vision of the future is short-sighted and limited.

In the second place the habit of colonial servitude hampers them from seeing beyond the borders of the country they live in. Most Anglo-Canadians know only two countries, England and Canada; and many of them are hesitant to decide which of these is their real homeland.

Finally, the absence of an intellectual culture and the intense pursuit for wealth that permeates Canadian society as well as American society very often make us disregard the immense superiority of the latent moral forces that brood under the conspicuous brutal force. This is particularly true of politicians who seek driving powers of immediate interest.

There are some Anglo-Canadians who honestly believe that since the English language is the language of the mother country, it should also be the colony's. They seem to forget this very important fact: that the English language is the language not only of England, but also of the United States.

Our Relations with the United States

Please allow me a digression. The remarks I wish to make on this subject are not dictated by a feeling of animosity toward the great Republic. No, these racial hatreds, this habit of criticizing foreign peoples, are among the most obvious proofs of the limits of our public mentality and of our "colonialism." I admire the American people. They came at the appointed time in the design of Providence to offer their contribution to the harmony of nations. But I sincerely believe that in the true interests of America and the human race the United States and Canada must remain two separate nations. I am sure that the honest American opinion that does not fall prey to the temptations of greed in continually enlarging national territory is identical in this matter to the feelings of the Canadian people.

Now if Canada is to remain separate from the United States it is high time our fellow English Canadians opened their eyes and ears and broadened their outlook to realize that a real danger threatens the unity of the Canadian people and the preservation of its political existence. This danger is the slow but sure infiltration of Americanism that creeps into all the phases of our national, political, and social life.

Perhaps this will surprise you, but in reality Quebec, Champlain's old city, so French in its character, is more Canadian and more British than Montreal. Montreal is more Canadian and more British than Toronto. Toronto is more Canadian and more British than Winnipeg. Why? Because thanks to the predominance of the French language in Quebec City you have protected yourselves better from the American invasion than Montreal. Not only to the traveller passing through but also to the careful observer, that particularly "loyalist" city Toronto seems half won over to American ideas, to the American mentality, to American customs, to American speech, and to the American way of life; and this dangerous situation is to be feared far more than any commercial treaty or attack on the constitution, since it is the moral and personal winning over of the individuals who make up the nation. …

French Groups and Canadian Unity

However, the biggest obstacle that could be thrown up against the slow but sure conquest of the English provinces by American thinking—especially in the western provinces—would be the implanting in each of these provinces of French-Canadian groups that were as strong as possible. They could be given their own schools and French-speaking priests so that they could set up their own parishes and they would be like so many small Provinces of Quebec. In this way there would be men everywhere for whom the American ideal, the cult of the gold calf, the profits of commerce and industry, would not be the principal objective. There would also be the people in all parts of Canada who were behind the times, *dumb* enough—forgive me this word, gentlemen—to hold on to an ideal above that of wealth and success; people who would continue to do outside the Province of Quebec what they have done in the Province of Quebec for the last one hundred and fifty years: that is, keep the British institutions intact while at the same time claiming the right everywhere to express freely their thoughts on all political matters that concern Canada and the Empire.

The Tremblay Report

David Kwavnick (1954)

5

EDITORS' INTRODUCTION

The Tremblay Commission was established by the Duplessis government in Quebec in 1953 to conduct an inquiry into problems arising from what were seen as centralizing encroach-ments on the powers and resources granted to the provinces at the time of Confederation. Despite being given only a year in which to complete its work, the commission produced a massive five-volume report on the traditional culture of Quebec and the powers needed to secure it. The commission's report was prepared in French. Sections of its recommendations reproduced below are from an English translation edited by David Kwavnick in 1973.

The report puts forward a dualistic vision of Canada, with Quebec the homeland of a distinct communal French-Canadian culture, and Canada outside of Quebec as the home of an Anglo Canada with a more individualistic and economically driven culture. As for Quebec's constitutional aspiration, on the eve of the Quiet Revolution, as expressed in this report, they remain conservative—protecting Quebec's provincial jurisdiction from a centralizing Canadian state.

General Outline and Summary of Recommendations

The constitutional imbroglio which has played a dominant part in Canada's recent history has appeared to be mainly fiscal and its most outstanding episodes have been in regard to taxes. But it has its origin in a fundamental divergence of opinion on the interpretation of Canadian federalism.

The situation which has gradually developed in this country, especially since the last war, is one whose control and remedy requires a re-examination of our attitudes towards the foundations of our constitutional and political system. There is not and there cannot be any question (despite suggestions from certain quarters) of a mere redistribution, through one method or another, of the funds required for the public administration. The real need is for a re-appraisal of the socio-political reality's lasting requirements, with a re-adjustment of the fiscal system made consequent thereto.

Therefore, we ourselves have sought to grasp the problem in its entirety. We are firmly of the belief that the entire constitutional system is bound up with the questions of taxes and

Source: Excerpted from *The Tremblay Report: Report of the Royal Commission of Inquiry on Constitutional Problems*, edited by David Kwavnick. Montreal and Kingston: McGill-Queen's University Press. Originally published by McClelland & Stewart, 1973. Reprinted by permission.

of the allocation of taxes which, in turn, also involves the fundamental liberties and political lot both of the individual as a citizen, and of the two great cultural communities which make up our population.

To encompass the present situation in its true dimensions and in its profound causes, we have considered it our duty to study it first of all in the perspectives of history and according to the basic principles of political philosophy. For every human society is, in fact, a constantly evolving living complex whose state, at any given point of time, can only be understood by reference to the past and to a certain concept of order.

History

… The constitutional policy of the Province of Quebec has never, since 1867, departed from the strict federalist interpretation of the Constitution, nor from the proper juridical status and mutual relations of the parties constituting the Canadian state. It is its own best witness that it has taken seriously the agreement reached in 1867 and, in every circumstance, has done what was necessary to promote the sprit of that agreement in Canadian political life.

This fidelity to the federative principle it asserted resoundingly, and at the cost of heavy sacrifice, with regard to taxation and, notably, on the question of subsidies which is the central issue in the present federal–provincial controversy. …

In a word—and this is the salient point to be gleaned from these pages of history—the attitude of the Province of Quebec in fiscal matters, as in all other matters of a constitutional nature, has never changed. It holds to an interpretation, according to the spirit of federalism, of the agreement reached in 1867.

THE PROBLEM OF CULTURE AND FEDERALISM

The Basic Question

Federalism and the problem of cultures are, to some degree, correlative. Here we touch the very root of the debate which has agitated Canadian opinion for years. The duality of cultures is the central premise of the Canadian political problem, no matter from what angle it may be approached. If the population were homogeneous, with the same religion, the same language, the same traditions and the same concept of order and of life, Canada might, especially in these days of swift and easy communications, satisfy the geographic and economic diversity of its vast territory with a modified federalism and even, in certain fields, with a fairly wide measure of administrative decentralization.

But such is not the case. Two great communities of differing origin and culture constitute its human components and each of them intends to live according to its own concepts and to preserve its own identity from one generation to another. The phenomenon is all the more ineradicable inasmuch as the difference in cultures almost exactly corresponds to the difference in religion. This fact has dominated the country's history for almost two centuries and it has conditioned all main stages of its constitutional evolution.

The Idea of Culture

Since this duality of cultures is the principle premise of the Canadian political problem, we have endeavoured to deal with it in its primary elements. We have therefore taken up and analyzed the basic ideas of culture, nation, society and state both *per se* and in their reciprocal relationships. We have attempted to isolate the predominating features of the two great Canadian cultures: what it is that distinguishes them and even what places them in opposition to each other. We have recalled the social consequences resulting from the opposition of cultures ever since the conquest in the province of Quebec; and finally, we have sought to define Quebec's special role within the Canadian Confederation, insofar as it constitutes the national focus of French-Canadian culture.

Federalism

Only federalism as a political system permits two cultures to live and develop side by side within a single state: that was the real reason for the Canadian state's federative form. Therefore we have studied federalism, first as a system of social organization resting on the four sociological and philosophical bases: the Christian concept of Man and society, the variety and complexity in social life, the idea of the common good, and the principle of every society's complementary functions. In the second place, we have studied federalism as a political and juridical system.

Competing Theses

According to the ideas held regarding the two major matters just mentioned, one either reaches the centralizing position habitually taken by the federal government or else one reaches the autonomist position which is traditionally that of the Province of Quebec.

As regards taxes, political economy, social policy and educational subsidies, these are the two theses which stand opposed. The federal government looks at Canada as a whole; it talks about "Canadian unity" without specifying whether it will be the product of group fusions or of their voluntary co-operation; of "Canadian culture" as if culture, which has Man himself as its object and has reference to a certain general concept of life, will allow no differentiation of inspiration or ways of life as between one group and another, of the "Canadian nation," as if the nation were not primarily and essentially a community of culture. Starting from there it considers it normal that, throughout the country, Canadians of every group should, for example, be subjected to the same system of social security and that the Constitution should be interpreted in the most centralizing way. Our chapters on the federal government's theories and practices on constitutional matters, with respect to education as well as in regard to economic, social and fiscal subjects clearly illustrate what we have just written. These bring to light the eminently practical effects of a whole series of concepts which, at first glance, might be considered essentially theoretical and speculative. As a matter of fact, the interpretation given, at the state level, to concepts such as culture, nation, society and citizenship expresses itself in laws, institutions and ways of life and thus tends either towards the conservation of a particular culture and the stimulation of its development or else it tends to undermine its capacity to perpetuate itself and, eventually, impoverishes its sources.

Federalism, as a political system, may vary according to the purposes for which it is intended. When its sole objective is to adapt the political system to the geographical and economic diversity of any given country, it can be more or less flexible and relaxed. On the contrary, if, within the framework of a single state, it aims at ensuring the parallel development of distinctive cultures, it is extensive and rigid.

Culture and the Sociological Milieu

Every particular culture needs a focus wherein to maintain and renew itself from generation to generation. That is to say, it requires a centre where each of its particulars, including language, traditions and ways of life must be currently necessary and a requisite for success to every person making up the collectivity. Thus, the required centre is one wherein the people who embody it may live according to their concepts, where they may express themselves freely according to their spirit and where they themselves … may erect, according to their idea, the institutions necessary for the full expansion of individual and collective life. To fulfill its purpose and allow the cultural groups present within a single state to develop themselves according to their respective particularisms and thereby contribute to the prosperity of the whole, federalism must be broad enough to assure to each of them the political initiative in such functions of collective life as lie closest to the ideological, intellectual and social exigencies of the culture itself. By these we mean education, public charities, mutual assistance, labour and family organization, etc.

Despite the ambiguity of some of its sections, that is precisely what the Constitution of 1867 sought to bring about in Canada. Through its method of distributing powers, it assigned to the two orders of government those prerogatives which correspond to the objectives of cultural federalism. Since 1867, the Canadian reality has grown. It has become articulated and integrated but it has not changed insofar as its cultural components and its political requirements are concerned. And it is to these we must revert, no matter from what angle the state's structure and functioning may be studied. Without such a reference to the heart of the matter, technically efficient solutions may be found for this or that problem, but none will be found which will be politically just.

The Province of Quebec and French-Canadian Culture

If Anglo-Canadian culture is today spread throughout nine of the ten Canadian provinces and if it can count upon their organized life for its diffusion and renewal, French-Canadian culture on the other hand has only one real focus, and that is the Province of Quebec. This, then, is how the case of French Canada and of the Province of Quebec rests with regard to English Canada and the Canadian state. If, as is its legitimate ambition, Canada should eventually give birth to an authentic "nation" in whose midst the two groups will live in friendship, finding their full flowering in a co-operation made all the more fruitful because it is based on mutual trust, the role of the Province of Quebec, as national focus and primary political centre of one of the two groups, will be a truly great one, and one of which it must itself become aware, while the rest of the country has every interest not to underestimate the importance of its role. …

Recommendations

FEDERAL–PROVINCIAL RELATIONS

The Problem

In order to give a better idea of the direction and scope of our recommendations, we think it may be useful to re-state our problem's main elements. On the one hand:

1. The primary purpose of Canadian federalism is to allow the two great cultural communities which made up our population a) to live and develop themselves according to their respective particularisms and b) to co-operate in the building and progress of a common fatherland;
2. With regard to French-Canadian culture, the Province of Quebec assumes alone the responsibilities which the other provinces jointly assume with regard to Anglo-Canadian culture;
3. The Canadian reality, both economic and sociological, has undergone a profound transformation since 1867, but its cultural elements have not changed, so that the basic problem still remains the same.

Furthermore:

4. a) Transportation and integration of the economic and social complex have made economic stability one of the major political goals; b) ideas regarding the state's economic and social role have also evolved, with intervention by the state in the economy's functioning being today admissible, both in theory and in practice, while a new school of economists claims it can give it a scientific basis and standards;
5. Industrial concentration has created fiscal inequalities as between the provinces, and these should be remedied, as far as possible.

In the third place:

6. Control of the economy and equalization of fiscal conditions as between the provinces are the main reasons today invoked by the federal government as justifying its social as well as its fiscal policy. It considers both of these, over and above their special purposes, as being indispensable instruments of economic control. The federal government, moreover, relies on an interpretation of the Constitution according to which it is vested with the main economic powers, and possesses "unlimited" power to tax and "absolute" power to spend. Thus, it concludes that it alone can exercise all initiatives needed to control the economy, to maintain employment, and to equalize fiscal resources between the provinces. As a consequence, it seems to think that pursuit of economic and social goals has, in some way, priority over cultural objectives, and also that the federal government itself has similar priority over the provinces.

Such is the basic conflict of which the fiscal problem is the most visible manifestation. In short, it arises from a unitary non-federative interpretation of the Constitution and of the very notion of a state, and it arises also from a technically administrative but non-political concept of the state's role in economic and social affairs.

For our part, we hold that there is no opposition between the state's economic and social goals and its cultural objectives, and we believe that both of them can be effectively realized in a federative system, provided there is an awareness of the political nature of the problem and of the steps that must be taken in order to ensure a harmonious solution in a country as differentiated as Canada.

1. Politics, in the best sense of the word, has for its objective not merely welfare but good living, that is, the hierarchic totality of conditions needed for full assertion of

human individuality. If it is true that the citizen serves the state, it is equally true that the state is in Man's service.

2. In a federative system, the state is composed of two orders, and not merely one single order of government, each of them acting by its own authority within its special domain but in coordination within the framework of constitutional law. Autonomy for the component parts and co-ordination of policies are the conditions required to make this type of state efficacious, particularly in these days when the various functions of collective life are so fully integrated.

3. The institutions of communal life are the sociological expression of the culture, and one of its modes of renewal. Cultural policy and social policy are, therefore, only extensions of each other; they must have the same inspiration and they must be entrusted to the government which, being itself a participant in the culture, can best grasp its spirit and express it through laws.

4. The various kinds of taxes are in a qualitative relationship to the functions of collective life. In a federative state of the cultural type, they should be distributed between the orders of government according to the functions with which the latter are vested. Thus, since taxes on incomes have a direct incidence on persons and institutions, they should belong to the government on which cultural and social responsibility is incumbent. Since taxes on business operations and on the circulation of goods have a direct economic incidence and, if employed on the regional and local level, would tend to raise barriers within the same country, they should logically belong to that government which is vested with the larger economic responsibility and whose jurisdiction extends over the whole territory.

5. If equality of services between the several parts of a federative state is desirable, it cannot, however, be considered an absolute. Consequently, it cannot be established as a permanent system for the redistribution of funds nor, more especially, can it be sought to the detriment of the higher interests of one or more groups.

General Solution

RETURN TO THE CONSTITUTION

In our opinion, only a frank return to the Constitution can conciliate the principles enumerated above with the practical exigencies of Canadian politics today. We, therefore, recommend to the government of the Province of Quebec that it should invite the federal government and the governments of the other provinces, as constituent parts of the state, to undertake jointly a re-adaptation of the public administration according to the spirit of federalism. This re-shaping, carried out within the framework of the Constitution, would aim at re-interpreting its master-ideas in the four major provisions which a fiscal policy for our times, conforming both to federalism and to the state's general needs, ought to provide.

Two of these provisions, in their choice and arrangement of fiscal structures, imply options as to the principles from which Canadian policy should proceed.

Equality or Independence

Daniel Johnson (1965)

6

EDITORS' INTRODUCTION

Daniel Johnson was first elected as a Union Nationale member to the Quebec legislature in 1946. He served as a minister in the Duplessis government before becoming leader of the Union Nationale party in 1961. In 1965 he published Égalité ou indépendance *and had his party adopt it as its platform for constitutional reform. In 1966 he defeated Jean Lesage's Liberals and became premier of Quebec. Johnson's threat to lead Quebec to independence if Quebec could not achieve equality with the rest of Canada through constitutional reform led to the 1967 Confederation of Tomorrow Conference in Toronto. In February 1968, at the first of a long series of federal–provincial constitutional conferences, Johnson squared off over these same issues with a newly appointed federal minister of justice, Pierre Elliott Trudeau.*

The Independence of Quebec

With assimilation definitively set aside, a status quo unable to satisfy anyone, us refusing to continue a policy of mending and interminable begging, there remain only two solutions: equality or independence, a new constitution or separation.

I think that we must not, *a priori*, reject the separatist solution. Because complete independence for Quebec, for reasons not dependent on itself, may become the only issue compatible with the survival and progress of the French Canadian nation. If others appear to be ready to sacrifice our culture, if need be, to save the Confederation, my attitude is completely different. Without animosity, however without bending, I must clearly state that Confederation is not an end in itself; and that if, after making every effort to make it equally habitable for our two cultural communities, we note that our efforts are in vain, the Confederation will seem to us unsalvageable. There are some who want to save Canada even at the expense of Quebec's autonomy. I, myself, am ready to save Quebec's autonomy even at the price of Confederation.

In saying this, I am only adapting to today's context a doctrine that was always part of my party. On at least two occasions, Mr. Duplessis repeated in the House what he had already

Source: Excerpted and translated from *Égalité ou indépendance. 25 ans plus tard à l'heure du lac Meech* by Daniel Johnson. Montréal: VLB Éditeur, 1990. © VLB Éditeur. Reprinted by permission.

proclaimed at the federal–provincial conference of 1950: "If they don't want to respect the pact of 1867, if they don't want us in the Confederation, the province of Quebec itself will take measures to survive." On December 1, 1959, one month before his death, Mr. Paul Sauvé also said this, speaking of a more equitable sharing of revenues: "I say with as much sincerity as I can muster, that if, in 1962, all the country's authorities do not realize that it is a question of life or death, I do not see how the Canadian Confederation will be able to continue to function."

I am thus not one of those who take separatists lightly. It really is too easy to go to Toronto or elsewhere and receive praise for saying, for instance, "Don't worry about Quebec separatists; they are nothing more than a handful of dreamers who want to build another Great Wall of China or another Berlin Wall outside their province."

Undoubtedly, there are extremists everywhere, but the separatists I know, and there are some in my very own party, have never had the thought that in our era, Quebec could be self-sufficient while ignoring the rest of the continent. Independence is not autarky, and those who confuse the two do so expressly to confuse things.

Every country, no matter the degree of liberation it may have achieved, must necessarily harmonize its economy with those of its surrounding neighbours. If it is independent, this will be done through treaties, agreements, and trade accords. Most importantly, this harmonizing must not always be done through others or according to the interests of others. It is to be the result of genuine cooperation.

The separatists, if I understand them, believe that, in the current state of things, this cooperation is no longer possible between the two communities that share Canada. They believe that political separation is a prerequisite for all future cooperation.

Those Who Fear Separatism

Certain politicians, in one language or the other, made speeches, some of which added further insult, in order to defeat separatism. I do not believe this is the correct method. Verbal violence appears to be as unjustifiable and inefficient as other forms of violence.

In my opinion, we will not prevent the dislocation of Canada by crusades and indictments. The weapon that must be used is that of comprehension and justice.

Why do some advocate total independence for Quebec? It is because they have had enough of begging and lame compromises. It is because they have lost their hope of feeling at home throughout Canada. It is because they want to leave their minority status, their situation of dependence.

Youth is impatient. It has a thirst for the absolute. Never will we be able to satisfy it with half-measures, crumbs or percentages of rights. It wants just solutions that are clear-cut and radical.

However, today as in the past, separatism to me does not necessarily appear as the only solution for now. In his recent work, *L'Option politique du Canada français* (*The Political Option of French Canada*), Philippe Garigue states that separatism would cause a split not only between English Canada and French Canada, but also within French Canada, because more than a million of us live outside Quebec. It is necessary to envision this event. Furthermore, as in 1791, separatism will not remove the problem of co-existence of two nations on one territory, since an important Anglophone minority, which has indisputable historical rights, also lives in our province.

Serious separatists are the first to recognize that Quebec could not live isolated anyway and that independence would not at all make the need for harmonious collaboration with the rest of the country and continent disappear. They say this: Let's become independent first and it will become much easier to establish in equality the conditions of such cooperation. This argument has weight. However, in the viewpoint created by the constitutional parliamentary committee, I prefer, for my part, before resorting to the ultimate recourse of separatism, to attempt all that can be attempted, so that the French Canadian nation can feel at home, as in a real homeland, in all of Canada.

It seems to me that we can attain equality through negotiation, without necessarily going as far as independence, which includes, needless to say, a certain number of risks that are quite difficult to evaluate.

With this in mind, I asked the constitutional committee, on May 13, 1964, to prepare a study on the consequences of independence.

Also, I continue to believe in the possibility of a dialogue and establishing in Canada a new constitution which would set up from the top, for the entire country, a truly bi-national body, where the agents of both cultural communities could work together, on equal footing, to manage their common interests.

I do not believe this exalting task to be beneath the moral and intellectual forces of Canadians of both cultures.

And in any case, it's this or separation.

The French Canadian nation, in development for the past three centuries, needs a climate of freedom to fully flourish. There cannot be cultural equality without cultural autonomy. And there cannot be cultural autonomy without political autonomy. The French Canadian nation must have a homeland. If it fails to happen politically from one ocean to the other, in a new, bi-national federalism, it will have no choice but to create an independent Quebec.

I know well that this is an extreme solution, a solution of last resort. It is a little bit like a strike. But for a union undertaking negotiation, it would not be wise at the start to exclude a strike option, even if it hopes to avoid it.

If secession became the only way for French Canadians to be themselves, to stay French, then it would not only be their right, it would be their duty to become separatists.

For my part, I have no doubt that, in this case, the Union Nationale will be the only party capable of achieving independence with order, with respect to individual freedoms and vested interests.

Canada or Quebec

This equality, will we attain it? The answer does not depend on us alone. This is why it appears premature to me to concern ourselves excessively now with the form of a new constitutional regime.

Before deciding on the container, let us decide on the content.

Some talk of a special status for Quebec, while remaining careful to not define what they mean by this. Here is a very convenient term that can mean almost anything. As I explained earlier, there are many examples of federations where some member states benefit from a special status. But I know of none that can apply exactly to the Canadian situation. Because this situation is unique.

Others speak of associated states. Interesting formula, but again, one should specify what one means by this, because all sorts of associations can exist. The minority shareholder is also an associate in a company.

What is important above all is to determine what the essential powers are for the affirmation of the French Canadian nation.

There are, for nations as much as for individuals, fundamental freedoms that are not to be begged for and which cannot be reason for compromises or underhanded dealings.

The right of self-determination, for the French Canadian nation, is of this order. It is a collective heritage that I consider fully acquired and I would never agree to renegotiate.

What we want is more than the powers that were accorded to us by the 1867 constitution.

What we want, in fact, is the right to decide for ourselves, or to have an equal part in decisions on all areas that concern our life as a nation.

After all, are we masters of our house when Ottawa alone governs everything concerning radio and television, media which are perhaps in our time the most efficient cultural instruments?

Are we masters of our house when Ottawa refuses to protect, with appropriate tariffs, the products of certain vital French Canadian industries?

Are we masters of our house when Ottawa can use immigration in a way to modify ethnic equilibrium, to the point of rendering us minorities in the State of Quebec?

Are we masters of our house when a decision of the Bank of Canada can affect the credit of our businesses, of our financial institutions and even of the State of Quebec?

Are we masters of our house when the federal tax department can skim the profits from the exploitation of natural resources which belong to the Quebec community and, through taxes on our companies, prevent us from planning our economy, according to our own needs?

Are we masters of our house when, through estate taxes, the federal government can encroach upon our civil code?

Are we masters of our house when nationalization is the only way to repatriate the taxes from our business into Quebec?

Are we masters of our house when the Supreme Court, of which the judges are all appointed by Ottawa, is the ultimate interpreter of our French code and the only tribunal to which we can submit our grievances against the federal government?

Here are the methods that Ottawa has to interfere directly into our national life. Here are the situations we must remedy if we want self-determination as a nation.

It is this I was thinking of when, in 1962, I adopted for the Union Nationale agenda an article that went like this:

> Draw up, in all areas, the master plans that will let the Quebec community flourish completely, following its own dreams and taking initiative for its own solutions, even if it requires demanding and obtaining participation from Ottawa as necessary for the realisation of these plans.

I admit it is not easy to obtain Ottawa's participation in initiatives favouring the growth of the Quebec community. But in which imbroglio would we throw ourselves into, if we were to, as required by the so-called repatriation formula, solicit participation from the other nine provinces?

Can you see the head of the state of Quebec undertaking a pilgrimage to each provincial capital to humbly beg each of the other Premiers to agree to have his legislature adopt a law allowing us, for example, to govern French radio and television?

Will we have to ask permission from another province, which population is barely half the size of Quebec City, to give priority to the French language in our national state?

Will we multiply by ten the difficulties the central government has already created? To what haggling will we have to bend to defeat the ten vetoes?

This is why I spoke of a straitjacket regarding the amendment formula that we disguise under the name of "repatriation formula." At a time when we feel the absolute necessity of expanding the powers of Quebec, it is not the time, it seems to me, to multiply the obstacles and to close the door on fruitful negotiations.

Federation, associated states, confederation, special status, republic, whatever it is, the new constitutional regime will have to give the French Canadian nation all the powers that are necessary to control its own destiny.

After three centuries of labour, our nation has earned the right to live freely. So much the better if it can feel at home from ocean to ocean. This implies that we are recognized as having complete equality. If not, we will have to have Quebec independence.

Canada or Quebec, wherever the French Canadian nation finds freedom, that is where home will be.

Quebec, March 1965.

7 Federalism, Nationalism, and Reason

Pierre Elliott Trudeau (1968)

EDITORS' INTRODUCTION

Pierre Trudeau was a leading Quebec intellectual who, along with Jean Marchand and Gerard Pelletier, was invited to join the federal Liberal Party and run for Parliament in 1965 to strengthen the Pearson Liberal government in facing the challenges arising from Quebec's "Quiet Revolution." His essay on federalism, nationalism, and reason is based on a paper he presented in 1964 to a joint meeting of the Canadian Political Science Association and the Canadian Law Teachers Association. It was included in Federalism and the French Canadians, *a collection of his writings edited by John Saywell and published in 1968, on the eve of his becoming leader of the Liberal Party and prime minister of Canada.*

Trudeau's essay contains the intellectual underpinning of the counterattack against Quebec nationalism that he will lead as Canada's prime minister. While it criticizes the emotional appeal of nationalism as incompatible with the rationalism necessary for the accommodations that must be made in a federation like Canada's, in calling on Quebeckers to grow out of the social and economic backwardness of their province and enjoy the benefits of modern Canada, Trudeau offers a competing Canadian nationalism to Quebec nationalism.

State and Nation

The concept of federalism with which I will deal in this paper is that of a particular system of government applicable within a sovereign state; it flows from my understanding of state and nation. Hence I find it necessary to discuss these two notions in part I of this paper, but I need only do so from the point of view of territory and population. Essentially, the question to which I would seek an answer is: what section of the world's population occupying what segment of the world's surface should fall under the authority of a given state?

Until the middle of the eighteenth century, the answer was largely arrived at without regard to the people themselves. Of course in much earlier times, population pressures guided by accidents of geography and climate had determined the course of the migrations which were to spill across the earth's surface. But by the end of the Middle Ages, such migrations had run

Source: Excerpted from *Federalism and the French Canadians*. Macmillan of Canada, 1968. Notes omitted. Reprinted by permission of the Estate of Pierre Elliott Trudeau. See http://www.trudeaufoundation.ca.

their course in most of Europe. The existence of certain peoples inhabiting certain land areas, speaking certain languages or dialects, and practising certain customs, was generally taken as data—*choses données*—by the European states which arose to establish their authority over them.

It was not the population who decided by what states they would be governed; it was the states which, by wars (but not "people's wars"), by alliances, by dynastic arrangements, by marriages, by inheritance, and by chance, determined the area of territory over which they would govern. And for that reason they could be called territorial states. Except in the particular case of newly discovered lands, the population came with the territory; and except in the unusual case of deportations, very little was to be done about it.

Political philosophers, asking questions about the authority of the state, did not inquire why a certain population fell within the territorial jurisdiction of a certain state rather than of another; for the philosophers, too, territory and population were just data; their philosophies were mainly concerned with discovering the foundations of authority over a *given* territory and the sources of obedience of a *given* population.

In other words, the purpose of Locke and Rousseau, not unlike that of the medieval philosophers and of the ancient Stoics, was to explain the origins and justify the existence of political authority *per se*; the theories of contract which they derived from natural law or reason were meant to ensure that within a given state bad governments could readily be replaced by good ones, but not that one territorial state could be superseded by another.

Such then was the significance of social contract and popular sovereignty in the minds of the men who made the Glorious Revolution, and such it was in the minds of those who prepared the events of 1776 in America and 1789 in France. As things went, however, the two latter "events" turned out to be momentous revolutions, and the ideas which had been put into them emerged with an immensely enhanced significance.

In America, it became necessary for the people not merely to replace a poor government by a better one, but to switch their allegiance from one territorial state to another, and in their own words, to

> declare, that these United Colonies, are, and of right ought to be, free and independent states; that they are absolved from all allegiance to the British crown, and that all political connection, between them and the state of Great Britain, is and ought to be totally dissolved; and that, as free and independent states, they have full power to levy war, conclude peace, contract alliances, establish commerce, and to do all other acts and things which independent states may of right do.

Here then was a theory of government by consent which took on a radically new meaning. Since sovereignty belonged to the people, if appeared to follow that any given body of people could at will transfer their allegiance from one existing state to another, or indeed to a completely new state of their own creation. In other words, the consent of the population was required not merely for a social contract, which was to be the foundation of civil society, or for a choice of responsible rulers, which was the essence of self-government; consent was also required for adherence to one territorial state rather than to another, which was the beginning of national self-determination.

Why the theory of consent underwent such a transformation at this particular time is no doubt a matter for historical and philosophical conjecture. …

Consequently, it might be said that in the past the (territorial) state had defined its territorial limits which had defined the people or nation living within. But henceforth it was to be the people who first defined themselves as a nation, who then declared which territory belonged to them as of right, and who finally proceeded to give their allegiance to a state of their own choosing or invention which would exercise authority over that nation and that territory. Hence the expression "nation-state." As I see it, the important transition was from the *territorial state* to the *nation-state*. But once the latter was born, the idea of the *national state* was bound to follow, it being little more than a nation-state with an ethnic flavour added. With it the idea of self-determination became the principle of nationalities.

Self-determination did not necessarily proceed from or lead to self-government. Whereas self-government was based on reason and proposed to introduce liberal forms of government into existing states, self-determination was based on will and proposed to challenge the legitimacy and the very existence of the territorial states.

Self-determination, or the principle of nationalities (I am talking of the doctrine, for the expressions became current only later), was bound to dissolve whatever order and balance existed in the society of states prevailing towards the end of the eighteenth century. But no matter; for it was surmised that a new order would arise, free from wars and inequities. As each of the peoples of the world became conscious of its identity as a collectivity bound together by natural affinities, it would define itself as a nation and govern itself as a state. An international order of nation-states, since it would be founded on the free will of free people, would necessarily be more lasting and just than one which rested on a hodge-podge of despotic empires, dynastic kingdoms, and aristocratic republics. In May 1790, the Constituent Assembly had proclaimed: "La nation française renonce à entreprendre aucune guerre dans un but de conquête et n'emploiera jamais de forces contre la liberty d'aucun peuple."

Unfortunately, things did not work out quite that way. The French Revolution, which had begun as an attempt to replace a bad government by a good one, soon overreached itself by replacing a territorial state by a nation-state, whose territory incidentally was considerably enlarged. In 1789, the *Déclaration des droits de l'homme et du citoyen* had stated: "Le principe de toute souveraineté réside essentiellement dans la Nation. Nul corps, nul individu ne peut exercer d'autorité qui n'en émane expressément." But who was to be included in the nation? Danton, having pointed out in 1793 that the frontiers of France were designated by Nature, the French nation willed possession of that part of Europe which spread between the Rhine, the Pyrenees, the Atlantic Ocean, and the Alps. …

The political history of Europe and of the Americas in the nineteenth century and that of Asia and Africa in the twentieth are histories of nations labouring, conspiring, blackmailing, warring, revolutionizing, and generally willing their way towards statehood. It is, of course, impossible to know whether there has ensued therefrom for humanity more peace and justice than would have been the case if some other principle than self-determination had held sway. In theory, the arrangement of boundaries in such a way that no important national group be included by force in the territorial limits of a state which was mainly the expression of the will of another group, was to be conducive to peaceful international order. In practice, state boundaries continued to be established and maintained largely by the threat of or the use of force. The concept of right in international relations became, if anything, even more a function of might. And the question whether a national minority was "important" enough to be entitled to independence remained unanswerable except in terms of the political and physical power that could be wielded in its favour. Why did Libya become a country in 1951 and not the Saar in 1935, with a population almost as great? Why should Norway be independent and not Brittany? Why Ireland and not Scotland? Why Nicaragua and not Quebec?

As we ask ourselves these questions, it becomes apparent that more than language and culture, more than history and geography, even more than force and power, the foundation of the nation is will. For there is no power without will. The Rocky Mountains are higher than the Pyrenees but they are not a watershed between countries. The Irish Sea and the Straits of Florida are much narrower than the Pacific Ocean between Hawaii and California, yet they are more important factors in determining nationhood. Language or race do not provide, in Switzerland or Brazil, the divisive force they are at present providing in Belgium or the United States.

Looking at the foregoing examples, and at many others, we are bound to conclude that the frontiers of nation-states are in reality nearly as arbitrary as those of the former territorial states. For all their anthropologists, linguists, geographers, and historians, the nations of today cannot justify their frontiers with noticeably more rationality than the kings of two centuries ago; a greater reliance on general staffs than on princesses' dowries does not necessarily spell a triumph of reason. Consequently, a present-day definition of the word "nation" in its juristic sense would fit quite readily upon the population of the territorial states which existed before the French and American revolutions. A nation (as in the expressions: the French nation, the Swiss nation, the United Nations, the President's speech to the nation) is no more and no less than the entire population of a sovereign state. (Except when otherwise obvious, I shall try to adhere to that juristic sense in the rest of this paper.) Because no country has an absolutely homogeneous population, all the so-called nation-states of today are also territorial states. And the converse is probably also true. The distinction between a nation-state, a multi-national state, and a territorial state may well be valid in reference to historical origins; but it has very little foundation in law or fact today and is mainly indicative of political value judgments.

Of course, the word "nation" can also be used in a sociological sense, as when we speak of the Scottish nation, or the Jewish nation. As Humpty Dumpty once told Alice, a word means just what one chooses it to mean. It would indeed be helpful if we could make up our minds. Either the juristic sense would be rejected, and the word "people" used instead (the people of the Soviet Union, the people of the United States; but what word would replace "national"? People's? Popular?); in that case "nation" would be restricted to its sociological meaning, which is also closer to its etymological and historical ones. Or the latter sense would be rejected, and words like "linguistic," "ethnic," or "cultural group" be used instead. But lawyers and political scientists cannot remake the language to suit their convenience; they will just have to hope that "the context makes it tolerably clear which of the two [senses] we mean."

However, for some people one meaning is meant to flow into the other. The ambiguity is intentional and the user is conveying something which is at the back of his mind—and sometimes not very far back. In such cases the use of the word "nation" is not only confusing, it is disruptive of political stability. Thus, when a tightly knit minority within a state begins to define itself forcefully and consistently as a nation, it is triggering a mechanism which will tend to propel it towards full statehood.

That, of course, is not merely due to the magic of words, but to a much more dynamic process which I will now attempt to explain. When the erstwhile territorial state, held together by divine right, tradition, and force, gave way to the nation-state, based on the will of the people, a new glue had to be invented which would bind the nation together on a durable basis. For very few nations—if any—could rely on a cohesiveness based entirely on "natural" identity, and so most of them were faced with a terrible paradox: the principle of national self-determination which had justified their birth could just as easily justify their death. Nationhood being little more than a state of mind, and every sociologically distinct group within the nation having a contingent right of secession, the will of the people was in constant danger of dividing up—unless it were transformed into a lasting consensus. …

Nationalism and Federalism

Many of the nations which were formed into states over the past century or two included peoples who were set apart geographically (like East and West Pakistan, or Great Britain and Northern Ireland), historically (like the United States or Czechoslovakia), linguistically (like Switzerland or Belgium), racially (like the Soviet Union or Algeria). Half of the aforesaid countries undertook to form the national consensus within the framework of a unitary state; the other half found it expedient to develop a system of government called federalism. The process of consensus-formation is not the same in both cases. It is obviously impossible, as well as undesirable, to reach unanimity on all things. Even unitary states find it wise to respect elements of diversity, for instance by administrative decentralization as in Great Britain, or by language guarantees as in Belgium; but such limited securities having been given, a consensus is obtained which recognizes the state as the sole source of coercive authority within the national boundaries. The federal state proceeds differently; it deliberately reduces the national consensus to the greatest common denominator between the various groups composing the nation. Coercive authority over the entire territory remains a monopoly of the (central) state, but this authority is limited to certain subjects of jurisdiction; on other subjects, and within well-defined territorial regions, other coercive authorities exist. In other words, the exercise of sovereignty is divided between a central government and regional ones.

Federalism is by its very essence a compromise and a pact. It is a compromise in the sense that when national consensus on *all* things is not desirable or cannot readily obtain, the area of consensus is reduced in order that consensus on *some* things be reached. It is a pact or quasi-treaty in the sense that the terms of that compromise cannot be changed unilaterally. That is not to say that the terms are fixed forever; but only that in changing them, every effort must be made not to destroy the consensus on which the federated nation rests. For what Ernest Renan said about the nation is even truer about the federated nation: "L'existence d'une nation est … un plébiscite de tous les jours." This obviously did not mean that such a plebiscite could or should be held every day, the result of which could only be total anarchy; the real implication is clear: the nation is based on a social contract, the terms of which each new generation of citizens is free to accept tacitly, or to reject openly.

Federalism was an inescapable product of an age which recognized the principle of self-determination. For on the one hand, a sense of national identity and singularity was bound to be generated in a great many groups of people, who would insist on their right to distinct statehood. But on the other hand, the insuperable difficulties of living alone and the practical necessity of sharing the state with neighbouring groups were in many cases such as to make distinct statehood unattractive or unattainable. For those who recognized that the first law of politics is to start from the facts rather than from historical "might-have-been's," the federal compromise thus became imperative.

But by a paradox I have already noted in regard to the nation-state, the principle of self-determination which makes federalism necessary makes it also rather unstable. If the heavy paste of nationalism is relied upon to keep a unitary nation-state together, much more nationalism would appear to be required in the case of a federal nation-state. Yet if nationalism is encouraged as a rightful doctrine and noble passion, what is to prevent it from being used by some group, region, or province within the nation? If "nation algérienne" was a valid battle cry against France, how can the Algerian Arabs object to the cry of "nation kabyle" now being used against them?

The answer of course, is that no amount of logic can prevent such escalation. The only way out of the dilemma is to render what is logically defensible actually undesirable. The advantages *to the minority group* of staying integrated in the whole must on balance be greater than the gain to be reaped from separating. This can easily be the case when there is no real alternative for the separatists, either because they are met with force (as in the case of the U.S. Civil War), or because they are met with laughter (as in the case of the *Bretons bretonnisants*). But when there is a real alternative, it is not so easy. And the greater the advantages and possibilities of separatism, the more difficult it is to maintain an unwavering consensus within the whole state.

One way of offsetting the appeal of separatism is by investing tremendous amounts of time, energy, and money in nationalism, *at the federal level*. A national image must be created that will have such an appeal as to make any image of a separatist group unattractive. Resources must be diverted into such things as national flags, anthems, education, arts councils, broadcasting corporations, film boards; the territory must be bound together by a network of railways, highways, airlines; the national culture and the national economy must be protected by taxes and tariffs; ownership of resources and industry by nationals must be made a matter of policy. In short, the whole of the citizenry must be made to feel that it is only within the framework of the federal state that their language, culture, institutions, sacred traditions, and standard of living can be protected from external attack and internal strife.

It is, of course, obvious that a national consensus will be developed in this way only if the nationalism is emotionally acceptable to all important groups within the nation. Only blind men could expect a consensus to be lasting if the national flag or the national image is merely the reflection of one part of the nation, if the sum of values to be protected is not defined so as to include the language or the cultural heritage of some very large and tightly knit minority, if the identity to be arrived at is shattered by a colour-bar. The advantage as well as the peril of federalism is that it permits the development of a regional consensus based on regional values; so federalism is ultimately bound to fail if the nationalism it cultivates is unable to generate a national image which has immensely more appeal than the regional ones.

Moreover, this national consensus—to be lasting—must be a living thing. There is no greater pitfall for federal nations than to take the consensus for granted, as though it were reached once and for all. The compromise of federalism is generally reached under a very particular set of circumstances. As time goes by these circumstances change; the external menace recedes, the economy flourishes, mobility increases, industrialization and urbanization proceed; and also the federated groups grow, sometimes at uneven paces, their cultures mature, sometimes in divergent directions. To meet these changes, the terms of the federative pact must be altered, and this is done as smoothly as possible by administrative practice, by judicial decision, and by constitutional amendment, giving a little more regional autonomy here, a bit more centralization there, but at all times taking great care to preserve the delicate balance upon which the national consensus rests.

Such care must increase in direct proportion to the strength of the alternatives which present themselves to the federated groups. Thus, when a large cohesive minority believes it can transfer its allegiance to a neighbouring state, or make a go of total independence, it will be inclined to dissociate itself from a consensus the terms of which have been altered in its disfavour. On the other hand, such a minority may be tempted to use its bargaining strength to obtain advantages which are so costly to the majority as to reduce to naught the advantages to the latter of remaining federated. Thus, a critical point can be reached in either direction beyond which separatism takes place, or a civil war is fought.

When such a critical point has been reached or is in sight, no amount, however great, of nationalism can save the federation. Any expenditure of emotional appeal (flags, professions of faith, calls to dignity, expressions of brotherly love) at the national level will only serve to justify similar appeals at the regional level, where they are just as likely to be effective. Thus the great moment of truth arrives when it is realized that *in the last resort* the mainspring of federalism cannot be emotion but must be reason.

To be sure, federalism found its greatest development in the time of the nation-states, founded on the principle of self-determination, and cemented together by the emotion of nationalism. Federal states have themselves made use of this nationalism over periods long enough to make its inner contradictions go unnoticed. Thus, in a neighbouring country, Manifest Destiny, the Monroe Doctrine, the Hun, the Red Scourge, the Yellow Peril, and Senator McCarthy have all provided glue for the American Way of Life; but it is apparent that the Cuban "menace" has not been able to prevent the American Negro from obtaining a renegotiation of the terms of the American national consensus. The Black Muslims were the answer to the argument of the Cuban menace; the only answer to both is the voice of reason.

It is now becoming obvious that federalism has all along been a product of reason in politics. It was born of a decision by pragmatic politicians to face facts as they are, particularly the fact of the heterogeneity of the world's population. It is an attempt to find a rational compromise between the divergent interest-groups which history has thrown together; but it is a compromise based on the will of the people.

Looking at events in retrospect, it would seem that the French Revolution attempted to delineate national territories according to the will of the people, without reference to rationality; the Congress of Vienna claimed to draw state boundaries according to reason, without reference to the will of the people; and federalism arose as an empirical effort to base a country's frontiers on both reason and the will of the people.

I am not heralding the impending advent of reason as the prime mover in politics, for nationalism is too cheap and too powerful a tool to be soon discarded by politicians of all countries; the rising *bourgeoisies* in particular have too large a vested interest in nationalism to let it die out unattended. Nor am I arguing that as important an area of human conduct as politics could or should be governed without any reference to human emotions. But I would like to see emotionalism channelled into a less sterile direction than nationalism. And I am saying that within sufficiently advanced federal countries, the auto-destructiveness of nationalism is bound to become more and more apparent, and reason may yet reveal itself even to ambitious politicians as the more assured road to success. This may also be the trend in unitary states, since they all have to deal with some kind of regionalism or other. Simultaneously in the world of international relations, it is becoming more obvious that the Austinian concept of sovereignty could only be thoroughly applied in a world crippled by the ideology of the nation-state and sustained by the heady stimulant of nationalism. In the world of today, when whole groups of so-called sovereign states are experimenting with rational forms of integration, the exercise of sovereignty will not only be divided within federal states; it will have to be further divided between the states and the communities of states. If this tendency is accentuated the very idea of national sovereignty will recede and, with it the need for an emotional justification such as nationalism. International law will no longer be explained away as so much "positive international morality," it will be recognized as true law, a "coercive order … for the promotion of peace."

Thus there is some hope that in advanced societies, the glue of nationalism will become as obsolete as the divine right of kings; the title of the state to govern and the extent of its authority will be conditional upon rational justification; a people's consensus based on reason will supply the cohesive force that societies require; and politics both within and without the state will follow a much more functional approach to the problems of government. If politicians must bring emotions into the act, let them get emotional about functionalism!

The rise of reason in politics is an advance of law; for is not law an attempt to regulate the conduct of men in society rationally rather than emotionally? It appears then that a political order based on federalism is an order based on law. And there will flow more good than evil from the present tribulations of federalism if they serve to equip lawyers, social scientists, and politicians with the tools required to build societies of men ordered by reason.

Who knows? Humanity may yet be spared the ignominy of seeing its destinies guided by some new and broader emotion based, for example, on continentalism.

Canadian Federalism: The Past and the Present

Earlier in this paper, when discussing the concept of national consensus, I pointed out that it was not something to be forever taken for granted. In present-day Canada, an observation such as that need not proceed from very great insight. Still, I will start from there to examine some aspects of Canadian federalism.

Though, technically speaking, national self-determination only became a reality in Canada in 1931, it is no distortion of political reality to say that the Canadian nation dates from 1867, give or take a few years. The consensus of what is known today as the Canadian nation took shape in those years; and it is the will of that nation which is the foundation of the state which today exercises its jurisdiction over the whole of the Canadian territory.

Of course, the will of the Canadian nation was subjected to certain constraints, not least of which was the reality of the British Empire. But, except once again in a technical sense, this did not mean very much more than that Canada, like every other nation, was not born in a vacuum, but had to recognize the historical as well as all other data which surrounded its birth.

I suppose we can safely assume that the men who drew up the terms of the Canadian federal compromise had heard something of the ideology of nationalism which had been spreading revolutions for seventy-five years. It is likely too that they knew about the Civil War in the United States, the rebellions of 1837–8 in Canada, the Annexation Manifesto, and the unsatisfactory results of double majorities. Certainly they assessed the centrifugal forces that the constitution would have to overcome if the Canadian state was to be a durable one: first, the linguistic and other cultural differences between the two major founding groups, and secondly the attraction of regionalisms which were not likely to decrease in a country the size of Canada.

Given these data, I am inclined to believe that the authors of the Canadian federation arrived at as wise a compromise and drew up as sensible a constitution as any group of men anywhere could have done. Reading that document today, one is struck by its absence of principles, ideals, or other frills; even the regional safeguards and minority guarantees are pragmatically presented, here and there, rather than proclaimed as a thrilling bill of rights. It has been said that the binding force of the United States of America was the idea of liberty, and certainly none of the relevant constitutional documents let us forget it. By comparison, the Canadian nation seems founded on the common sense of empirical politicians who had wanted to establish some law and order over a disjointed half-continent. If reason be the governing virtue of federalism, it would seem that Canada got off to a good start.

Like everything else, the Canadian nation had to move with the times. Many of the necessary adjustments were guided by rational deliberation: such was the case, for instance, with most of our constitutional amendments, and with the general direction imparted to Canadian law by the Privy Council decisions. It has long been a custom in English Canada to denounce the Privy Council for its provincial bias; but it should perhaps be considered that if the law lords had not leaned in that direction, Quebec separatism might not be a threat today: it might be an accomplished fact. From the point of view of the damage done to Quebec's understanding of the original federal compromise there were certainly some disappointing—even if legally sound—judgments (like the New Brunswick, Manitoba, and Ontario separate school cases) and some unwise amendments (like the B.N.A. No. 2 Act, 1949); but on balance, it would seem that constitutional amendment and judicial interpretation would not by themselves have permanently damaged the fabric of the Canadian consensus if they had not been compounded with a certain type of adjustment through administrative centralization.

Faced with provinces at very different stages of economic and political development, it was natural for the central government to assume as much power as it could to make the country as a whole a going concern. Whether this centralization was always necessary, or whether it was not sometimes the product of bureaucratic and political empire-builders acting beyond the call of duty, are no doubt debatable questions, but they are irrelevant to the present inquiry. The point is that over the years the central administrative functions tended to develop rather more rapidly than the provincial ones; and if the national consensus was to be preserved some new factor would have to be thrown into the balance. This was done in three ways.

First, a countervailing regionalism was allowed and even fostered in matters which were indifferent to Canada's economic growth. For instance, there was no federal action when Manitoba flouted the constitution and abolished the use of the French language in the legislature. …

Second, a representative bureaucracy at the central level was developed in such a way as to make the regions feel that their interests were well represented in Ottawa. ...

Third, tremendous reserves of nationalism were expended, in order to make everyone good, clean, unhyphenated Canadians. Riel was neatly hanged to all who would exploit petty regional differences. The Boer War was fought, as proof that Canadians could overlook their narrow provincialisms when the fate of the Empire was at stake. Conscription was imposed in two world wars, to show that in the face of death all Canadians were on an equal footing. And lest nationalism be in danger of waning, during the intervals between the above events Union Jacks were waved, Royalty was shown around, and immigration laws were loaded in favour of the British Isles. ...

In short, during several generations, the stability of the Canadian consensus was due to Quebec's inability to do anything about it. Ottawa took advantage of Quebec's backwardness to centralize; and because of its backwardness that province was unable to participate adequately in the benefits of centralization. The vicious circle could only be broken if Quebec managed to become a modern society. But how could this be done? The very ideology which was marshalled to preserve Quebec's integrity, French-Canadian nationalism, was setting up defence mechanisms the effect of which was to turn Quebec resolutely inward and backwards. It befell the generation of French Canadians who came of age during the Second World War to break out of the dilemma; instead of bucking the rising tides of industrialization and modernization in a vain effort to preserve traditional values, they threw the flood-gates open to forces of change. And if ever proof be required that nationalism is a sterile force, let it be considered that fifteen years of systematic non-nationalism and sometimes ruthless anti-nationalism at a few key points of the society were enough to help Quebec to pass from a feudal into a modern era.

Technological factors could, practically alone, explain the sudden transformation of Quebec. But many agents from within were at work, eschewing nationalism and preparing their society to adapt itself to modern times. Typical amongst such agents were the three following: Laval's *Faculté des sciences sociales* began turning out graduates who were sufficiently well equipped to be respected members of the central representative bureaucracy. The *Confédération des travailleurs catholiques du Canada* came squarely to grips with economic reality and helped transform Quebec's working classes into active participants in the process of industrialization. The little magazine *Cité Libre* became a rallying point for progressive action and writing; moreover it understood that a modern Quebec would very soon call into question the imbalance towards which the original federal compromise had drifted, and it warned that English-Canadian nationalism was headed for a rude awakening; upholding provincial autonomy and proposing certain constitutional guarantees, it sought to re-establish the Canadian consensus on a rational basis.

The warnings went unheeded; Ottawa did not change. But Quebec did: bossism collapsed, blind traditionalism crumbled, the Church was challenged, new forces were unleashed. When in Europe the dynasties and traditions had been toppled, the new societies quickly found a new cohesive agent in nationalism; and no sooner had privilege within the nation given way to internal equality than privilege *between* nations fell under attack; external equality was pursued by way of national self-determination. In Quebec today the same forces are at work: a new and modern society is being glued together by nationalism, it is discovering its potentialities as a nation, and is demanding equality with all other nations. This in turn is causing a backlash in other provinces, and Canada suddenly finds herself wondering wheth-er she has a future. What is to be done?

If my premises are correct, nationalism cannot provide the answer. Even if massive invest-ments in flags, dignity, protectionism, and Canadian content of television managed to hold the country together a few more years, separatism would remain a recurrent phenomenon, and very soon again new generations of Canadians and Quebeckers would be expected to pour their intellectual energies down the drain of emotionalism. If, for instance, it is going to remain *morally wrong* for Wall Street to assume control of Canada's economy, how will it be-come *morally right* for Bay Street to dominate Quebec's—or for that matter, Nova Scotia's?

It is possible that nationalism may still have a role to play in backward societies where the *status quo* is upheld by irrational and brutal forces; in such circumstances, *because there is no other way*, perhaps the nationalist passions will still be found useful to unleash the revolutions, upset colonialism, and lay the foundations of welfare states; in such cases, the undesirable consequences will have to be accepted along with the good.

But in the advanced societies, where the interplay of social forces can be regulated by law, where the centres of political power can be made responsible to the people, where the eco-nomic victories are a function of education and automation, where cultural differentiation is submitted to ruthless competition, and where the road to progress lies in the direction of international integration, nationalism will have to be discarded as a rustic and clumsy tool.

No doubt, at the level of individual action, emotions and dreams will still play a part; even in modern man, superstition remains a powerful motivation. But magic, no less than totems and taboos, has long since ceased to play an important role in the normal governing of states. And likewise, nationalism will eventually have to be rejected as a principle of sound govern-ment. In the world of tomorrow, the expression "banana republic" will not refer to independ-ent fruit-growing nations but to countries where formal independence has been given priority over the cybernetic revolution. In such a world, the state—if it is not to be outdis-tanced by its rivals—will need political instruments which are sharper, stronger, and more finely controlled than anything based on mere emotionalism: such tools will be made up of advanced technology and scientific investigation, as applied to the fields of law, economics, social psychology, international affairs, and other areas of human relations; in short, if not a pure product of reason, the political tools of the future will be designed and appraised by more rational standards than anything we are currently using in Canada today.

Let me hasten to add that I am not predicting which way Canada will turn. But because it seems obvious to me that nationalism—and of course I mean the Canadian as well as the Quebec variety—has put her on a collision course, I am suggesting that cold, unemotional rationality can still save the ship. Acton's prophecy, one hundred years ago, is now in danger of being fulfilled in Canada. "Its course," he stated of nationality, "will be marked with ma-terial as well as moral ruin, in order that a new invention may prevail over the works of God and the interests of mankind." This new invention may well be functionalism in politics; and perhaps it will prove to be inseparable from any workable concept of federalism.

"The West Wants In"

Preston Manning (1987)

Introduction

As Delegates are aware, this Assembly was called to accomplish two purposes: 1. To develop an "Agenda for Change"—a list of basic reforms required by Western Canadians to improve our economic and social condition, and our position within Canadian Confederation. 2. To recommend an appropriate political vehicle for advancing the West's Agenda for Change over the next few years, including the next federal election.

Over the past few hours, we have been presented with various proposals for constitutional, economic, and social change. Tomorrow, Delegates will decide which of those should be included in the West's Agenda for Change.

Source: Preston Manning, "Choosing a Political Vehicle to Represent the West: A Presentation to the Western Assembly on Canada's Economic and Political Future." Vancouver, May 29–31, 1987. Reprinted by permission.

Over the past few hours we have also heard an analysis of the existing federal political parties as potential vehicles for advancing the West's Agenda for Change.

My task is now to explore with you the advisability of creating a new, broadly-based federal political party with its roots in the West, as an appropriate vehicle for carrying forward the West's Agenda for Change.

In doing so, I am assuming that while the West will continue to whole-heartedly support the promotional efforts of groups like the Triple-E Senate Committee and Canada West Foundation, it is important to consider the necessity of a political vehicle which will carry the West's Agenda for Change directly into the political arena.

In discussing such a political vehicle, I am also assuming that the vast majority of Western Canadians want into, not out of, Confederation, and therefore reject a separatist party as an appropriate vehicle for political action.

A New Party in the Reform Tradition

Let me make clear from the outset that when we refer to the possibility of creating a new political party to represent the West, we are not talking about another splinter party or single-issue party, or yet another party of the strange and extreme. The West has produced too many of these in the past years, and there is no need for another.

Rather, if we think at all about the creation of a new federal political party to carry our concerns and contribution into the national political arena, we should be thinking about the creation of a new vehicle to represent the great political "reform tradition" which runs like a broad and undulating stream throughout the length and breadth of Canadian politics but which currently finds no suitable means of expression in any of the traditional federal parties.

The "reform tradition" to which I refer began in the mid-19th century when a group of reformers in the Canadian colonies—Joseph Howe in Nova Scotia, Robert Baldwin and Egerton Ryerson in Upper Canada, and Louis Lafontaine in Quebec—decided to fight against the vested political interests and inflexible colonial structures of their day to achieve responsible and responsive government.

In the 1860s, it was the Fathers of Confederation who embodied the reform tradition when Liberals like George Brown and Conservatives like Sir John A. Macdonald and Georges Cartier set aside old party structures and allegiances to create the great Liberal–Conservative coalition which brought into being the nation of Canada.

It would appear that the trauma of Confederation exhausted the spirit of radical political reform in Atlantic Canada and Ontario, for from that day to this those two regions of the country have been content to express themselves politically within the traditional framework of a two-party system dominated by the Liberal and Conservative parties.

There are, however, two great regions of this country where the spirit of political reform continues to manifest itself—usually in times of constitutional or economic stress—in the form of new political movements that seek to implement change by challenging and, on occasion, displacing, the traditional party structures.

One of those regions, of course, is the Province of Quebec; the other is the great Canadian Northwest.

If we could have afforded it, I would like to have lined the walls of this Assembly room with the portraits of the Western Reformers—the men and women who, since 1870, have sought to change Canada and advance Western Canadian interests through the creation of new political structures and programs.

Such a gallery of Western Reformers would include the following:

- Louis Riel, the first Western reformer, whose efforts resulted in the creation of the Province of Manitoba, and his Indian allies of later times, like Poundmaker, who fought the imposition of the federal welfare state on his proud people.
- F.W.G. Haultain and the Independent members of the old Territorial Legislature. Haultain was the man who resisted efforts to carve the Canadian Northwest into multiple provinces—who called himself a Big Westerner in favour of one big Western Province—and who negotiated the terms of the "Autonomy Bills" by which Alberta and Saskatchewan became Provinces.
- From 1905 into the 1920s it was the so-called "Farmers' Movement" which embodied the Western spirit of reform and which brought into being the Progressive Party—the first Western reform movement to break across the Canadian Shield and win substantial support in other parts of Canada. Its heroes included John Bracken, J.S. Woodsworth, and Thomas Crerar of Manitoba; Henry Wise Wood of Alberta; and Agnes Campbell McPhail, the first female Member of Parliament in Canada.
- In the 1921 federal election, the Progressives captured the second-largest number of seats in the Canadian House of Commons, and used their influence to secure the Crow's Nest freight rate reform and the Natural Resources Transfer Agreement.
- The Depression parties, the Canadian Commonwealth Federation or CCF in Saskatchewan under Tommy Douglas and M.J. Coldwell; the Social Credit movement in Alberta under William Aberhart and Ernest C. Manning, later expanded into British Columbia by W.A.C. Bennett; and the Reconstruction Party of H.H. Stevens with its base in the Province of British Columbia.

These are just some of the reformers of Western Canada—men and women who, when faced with unfair treatment by vested interests, or insensitive government controlled by Central Canadian parties, created new vehicles as instruments of change.

And if you are prepared to think of yourselves as Reformers—as people who want change in the conduct of our public affairs and who are prepared to create new structures to secure those changes—then the critics and the commentators who dismiss this Assembly as some isolated gathering of Western malcontents will be proven wrong.

If we talk about creating a new federal political party in this context, we are talking about reviving a tradition which is older than Confederation itself and as Western as Riel and the Farmers' Movement.

I would like to think that those reformers of by-gone days are looking down from some great Assembly in the sky and asking of our generation, "Do you have the courage and ability to lead on from where we left off?"

And tomorrow we will provide an answer to that question when we vote on whether to work within the existing party structures or to create a new structure to advance the West's Agenda.

Having, therefore, set our discussion of political vehicles in context, let me turn to the central question, "Is a new federal political party needed to advance the West's interests and concerns?"

Is a New Federal Party Needed? Four Reasons

Over the past three months, members of your Steering Committee and other Assembly committees have talked to a large number of Western Canadians, from Vancouver Island to the Manitoba–Ontario border. Not all of these are agreed that a new federal political party is required. But those who have been considering this option advance four main reasons for doing so. These reasons are:

1. Because the West is in deep trouble economically and structurally, yet no federal political party makes Western concerns and interests its top priority.
2. Because the Federal PCs are in decline all across the West, and this situation is creating a dangerous political vacuum.
3. Because the Federal Liberals and NDP as presently constituted are inappropriate vehicles for representing Western Canada.
4. Because the Federal Parliament, as dominated by the Central Canadian parties, is lacking in leaders and vision, and requires an influx of fresh blood and new ideas through a strong new competitor at the polls.

For the next few minutes, let us examine each of these reasons more carefully.

1. *The West is in deep trouble economically and structurally, yet no federal political party makes Western concerns and interests its top priority.*

In the words of my friend Ted Byfield, "People of every political stripe know that something is grievously wrong in Western Canada. Farmers can't afford to seed their crops, mines are closed, oil rigs lie derelict, shipyards are idle, food banks are besieged, the savings of many lifetimes have vanished, homes have lost their value, and a host of unemployed burst the welfare roils of every town and city."

Such economic conditions call for new directions, new proposals—for fundamental changes in national economic and social policy. Yet there is nothing really new for the West coming out of Ottawa from any of the traditional parties. Their top political priorities continue to be to hold or increase their support in Quebec and Ontario.

When something isn't working, you try to fix it. And if the old tools for fixing things don't work, you search for new tools.

2. *The federal Progressive Conservatives are in decline all across the West, thereby creating a dangerous political vacuum.*

If a federal election were to be held tomorrow, it is probably safe to say that about 50% of Western Canadians would not vote. This is exactly what happened in the recent Pembina by-election in Alberta. If this same voting pattern were to occur in a general election, some

80 Western seats would be up for grabs to whoever could organize 15–20% of the voters, an extremely unhealthy situation in a democratic state.

What are some of the reasons people advance for their lack of confidence in the federal Conservatives as a vehicle for advancing the West's interests? Let me cite just a few.

Some people mention their high expectations that the Mulroney government would introduce major changes in the scale and structure of the federal government during its first 18 months in office, and their profound disappointment when these changes didn't occur.

Others mention the government's slowness to remove the iniquitous Petroleum Gas Revenue Tax, its mishandling of the CF-18 contract, its slowness to enunciate a Western diversification policy, the continuation of patronage politics and appointments, and the failure to implement proposed reforms in the Unemployment Insurance program after spending years and millions of dollars on developing reform proposals.

As the popularity of the Mulroney Government declines across the country, there are many who have sadly concluded that the Progressive Conservative Party at the federal level has a congenital inability to govern. Certainly, its track record for most of the 20th century has been one of continuous disappointment: the periodic election of Conservative governments with enormous promise—Bennett in 1930, Diefenbaker in 1958, and Brian Mulroney in 1984—only to see those mandates melt away in confusion and failure within five short years or less.

Whatever the reasons for the decline of the Federal PCs, if that Party is in fact headed for another 20 years in the political wilderness, they cannot be considered an appropriate vehicle for the implementation of the reform program required to raise the fortunes and influence of Western Canada within Confederation.

3. *The federal Liberals and NDP, as presently constituted, are also inappropriate vehicles for representing the interests of Western Canada.*

With respect to the Liberal Party of Canada, this is the party which said that it would reform itself after its defeat in the last general election. But this great reformation has not occurred, perhaps because the Liberals mistakenly believe that they can be returned to power as a result of the demise of the Conservatives, without undergoing any fundamental transformation.

On the Prairies, particularly in the rural areas, the professional Liberal politician is still defined as "a politician who puts party and patronage ahead of principles and province."

In Alberta, and throughout the petroleum sector, the federal Liberals are still referred to as "the gang of thieves that stole the 60 billion." The "60 billion" refers, of course, to the transfer of wealth from Western Canada to Central Canada which occurred under the infamous National Energy Program and federal petroleum pricing policies.

The National Energy Program provides perhaps the greatest reason why the resource-producing regions of this country should not entrust the conduct of the national government to the Liberal Party until at least another generation passes. The NEP constituted a deliberately planned and executed raid on the resource wealth of Western Canada for the short-term benefit of the federal Treasury and Eastern consumers. It was an unmitigated disaster for the producing provinces and the producing sector, the effects of which are felt to this day. Yet there has never been any apology from the Liberal Party of Canada; no formal inquiry as to how a national party with long government experience could ever have been induced to adopt such a policy; and no ironclad assurances announced to ensure that such a policy would not be instituted again if the price of petroleum were to rise once more. ...

Three Options

And so to summarize, the West is in deep trouble, but no existing federal political party makes our needs its number one priority. The West is in need of new instruments to advance new solutions, but the traditional political instruments at its disposal are flawed and unsympathetic. The present leaders of the federal parties offer no fresh vision for Canada and the West, and if a federal election were held today 50% of our people would not vote because they do not like any of the options.

The question arises, "What to do?" Only three options present themselves:

1. To continue to attempt to work within the existing structures, notwithstanding their past failures and bleak possibilities for the future. This is the position of those that support the status quo.
2. To pursue some extreme option—such as to threaten secession, and to actually take steps to bring that secession about. This is an option which is urged upon us by parties like the W.C.C.
3. Thirdly, there is the reform option—to seek constructively to change the structures and conditions which lie at the root of the West's difficulties and discontent through direct political action. ...

Directions to the Architects

If this Assembly were to support the concept of bringing into being a new federal political party to advance the West's Agenda, it is obvious that we should not be so foolish as to give the architects of that new party a "blank cheque" or a vague mandate. ...

As one who has studied all the previous Western reform movements in considerable detail, I would like to suggest that the following general specifications should be followed by those responsible for putting together any new federal political party to represent the West in the closing decade of the 20th century:

1. *A new federal political party representing the West should have a positive orientation and vision.*

A new federal party, born out of Western concerns and aspirations, should not be simply a negative reaction to the status quo. It should not simply be a party of protest with a litany of complaints and concerns, but rather a party of reform, with some positive alternatives to offer.

One of the problems of splinter parties and some interest groups in the West at the present time is that they are essentially reactionary and negative, rather than positive and pro-active. People want to hear what the West is FOR; they have heard enough about what the West is against. To quote the historian Thomas Lowery, "In every generation Canadians have had to rework the miracle of their political existence. ... Canada is a supreme act of faith." A federal political party which is incapable of inspiring that act of faith is unfit to govern Canada!

2. *A new federal party representing the West should have standards of performance, policy, and people that exceed those of the existing federal political parties.*

If you were to take a survey in most Western communities today and ask people what organizations render the greatest service to their communities, the name of a federal political party would not occur on a list of the top fifty. One of the reasons for this is that the standards of performance in federal politics have sunk to low levels.

The federal parties do virtually no screening of candidates or workers—as witnessed by the number of mediocre candidates and outright influence peddlers who managed to get themselves elected as Progressive Conservatives in the last federal election.

The federal parties do virtually no original or creative policy work any more—all this is left up to others. Federal political parties provide virtually no training or orientation for their own candidates or workers, other than media and public relations training. When these people get to Ottawa, many of them know little or nothing about the art of representation, or legislating, or public finance, or how to deal with the federal bureaucracy. They must "learn on the job," under a crushing workload, and the results are less than satisfactory.

Any business organization or social agency or union which invested as little money and effort in establishing standards and developing people as do our federal political parties, would be out of business in a year.

A new federal political party has a chance to establish higher standards and appropriate support services for people entering public life through that vehicle, and these standards and support levels should be established at the very outset.

3. *A new federal political party representing the West should be ideologically balanced.*

In order to ensure that we could draw support from the disaffected members of the Liberals and the NDP as well as the Conservatives, it is important that a new Western political party have a strong social conscience and program as well as a strong commitment to market principles and freedom of enterprise.

A new federal party which embodies the principal political values of the West will transcend some of the old categories of left and right. It will provide a home for the socially-responsible businessman and the economy-conscious social activist. It should be a party whose members and leaders are characterized as people with "hard heads and soft hearts," i.e., people who attach high importance to wealth creation and freedom of economic activity on the one hand, but who are also genuinely concerned and motivated to action on behalf of the victims of the many injustices and imperfections in our economic and social systems.

We need a political party in which Canadian youth—who are presently alienated for the most part from the federal political party system—will feel at home. Canadian youth have special interest in jobs, in the economy of the future, in environmental protection and conservation, and in conflict resolution on a world scale—concerns which once again are not easily classified on the old "left–right" spectrum and which again call for ideological innovation and balance. ...

4. *A new federal political party representing the West should be committed to preserving and strengthening Canada through the institution of needed reforms.*

As has been emphasized by other speakers to this Assembly, most of us wish to believe that the West's future lies within, not without, Confederation. "The West Wants In" should be our motto, and any new federal political party created in the West should be designed to achieve that objective, and not the separation of the West from Confederation.

In this connection, let us attempt to channel the separatist sentiment in the West (sentiments which are perfectly understandable under the present circumstances) into separation of Western Canadians from the obsolete federal political party structures which no longer serve us well. If Western Canadians want to separate from something, let them separate by the hundreds of thousands from the Federal PCs, the Federal Liberals, and the Federal NDP—rather than attempting to separate Western Canada itself from the rest of our country.

The West wants in, and when the West gets "in" in a true and meaningful sense, we will be in a position not simply to advance our own interests but to provide support and stimulus to all the resource-producing regions of the country, and the nation as a whole.

5. *A new federal political party representing the West should*
   have "room to grow" into a truly national party.

This brings me to the fifth specification which should be given to the architects of any new federal political party originating from the West.

They should build on a foundation broad enough and strong enough to support geographic expansion, so that the party built on that foundation has the potential to become a truly national party with the passage of time.

The federal Liberal Party is a national party with its roots in Quebec. The federal Conservative Party is a national party with its origin and roots in Upper Canada.

There is no reason under heaven why this country could not support a truly national party with its roots in the resource-producing regions—a party which, unlike the NDP, will remain loyal to its region of origin.

A new federal party, created initially to represent the West, should aspire to become that new national party, and nothing should be done in the early stages of its conception and birth to preclude it from eventually gaining support all across the country, particularly in those regions of Ontario, Quebec, Atlantic Canada and Northern Canada which share many of our concerns and aspirations.

Conclusions and Recommendations

Tomorrow, Delegates to this Assembly will be presented with a ballot/resolution calling for them to recommend to Western Canadians a political vehicle for securing action on the West's Agenda for Change over the next few years, including the next federal election.

The options presented on that ballot/resolution will include:

- Supporting and attempting to reform the Progressive Conservative Party of Canada.
- Supporting and attempting to reform the Liberal Party of Canada.
- Supporting and attempting to reform the New Democratic Party of Canada.
- Supporting and attempting to broaden the Confederation of Regions Party.
- Supporting and encouraging Western separatism as advocated by the Western Canada Concept.

- Creating and supporting a new broadly-based federal political party with its roots in the West, and,
- Pursuing and supporting some other alternative to be suggested by the Delegates.

If, after due consideration to the arguments contained in this presentation, as well as the viewpoints expressed on the other alternatives, the Delegates to this Assembly should decide in favour of creating and supporting a new broadly-based federal political party with its roots in the West, then I would invite your support for the following recommendations which will also be put in the form of a Resolution to be included with tomorrow's ballot.

RECOMMENDATION 1: That this Assembly direct its Steering Committee to begin preparations for the Founding Convention of a new federal political party to be held prior to November 15th, 1987.

RECOMMENDATION 2: That this Assembly direct its Steering Committee and the organizers of any Founding Convention for a new Western-based federal political party as follows:

(a) That the Agenda for the Founding Convention include provisions for:
  - Defining the ideological position and platform of the new party.
  - Selecting the name and establishing a constitution of the new party.
  - Selecting a leader.

(b) That the following guidelines be adhered to in organizing the creation of a new federal political party:
  - A positive orientation and vision—not merely negative or reactionary.
  - Establishment of high standards.
  - Achievement of ideological balance.
  - Committed to preserving and strengthening Canada—"The West Wants In."
  - Provision of room to grow from a regionally based party to a truly national party capable of forming a national government.

(c) That the immediate objective of the new political party to be created at the Foundation Convention in the fall of 1987 would be to field at least 80 candidates in federal constituencies across the West in the next federal election.

RECOMMENDATION 3: That this Assembly direct its Steering Committee to communicate with all Western Members of Parliament to invite them to provide leadership in Parliament for a Western-based reform movement, by separating themselves from their existing federal parties, sitting as a united bloc together in Parliament, and, if feasible, seeking to enter into a coalition arrangement with the Mulroney Government to better advance the interests and concerns of the West.

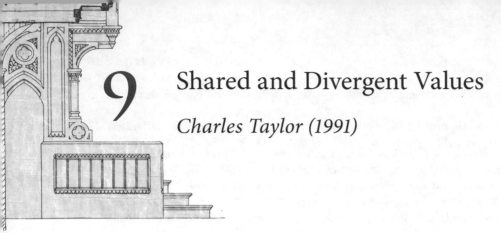

9 Shared and Divergent Values

Charles Taylor (1991)

EDITORS' INTRODUCTION

Charles Taylor is one of Canada's most eminent philosophers. He was for many years a professor at McGill University, where he taught in both the philosophy and political science departments. Although Taylor is recognized internationally for his philosophical work, he has been engaged throughout his career in the political life of his country, most recently as a member of the Consultation Commission on Accommodation Practices Related to Cultural Differences (see reading 69 in this volume).

In this essay, Taylor discusses how the recognition of diverse cultures within the country has been a source of strength and unity for Canada. He suggests that Canada's success in managing diversity may provide the world with a more relevant version of liberal democracy than the more unitary American paradigm.

Are there divergences of value between the different regions of Canada? In a sense, these are minimal. There appears to be a remarkable similarity throughout the country, and across the French/English difference, when it comes to the things in life which are important. Even when it comes to the values that specifically relate to political culture, there seems to be broad agreement. About equality, nondiscrimination, the rule of law, the mores of representative democracy, about social provision, about violence and firearms, and a host of issues.

This was not always the case. Half a century ago, it seemed that there were serious differences between the two major groups as far as political culture was concerned. Pierre Trudeau wrote about this.[1] The ravages of Maurice Duplessis on the rule of law, which he seemed to be able to get away with—his treatment of Jehovah's witnesses and Communists—seemed to indicate that Quebec and French Canada had different views about the toleration of dissent. Some people were ready to believe that the two societies gave quite different values to the maintenance of unity around certain cherished truths and standards when these conflicted with the goods of tolerance, freedom, or permitted diversity. Not that the rest-of-Canada was all that liberal in those days. Various minorities and dissidents had a rough time. But the particular grounds for illiberalism were rather strikingly different in Quebec, seemingly

Source: Excerpted from *Options for a New Canada*, edited by Ronald L. Watts and Douglas M. Brown. Toronto: University of Toronto Press, 1991. Some notes omitted. Reprinted by permission.

organized around the values of a traditional, ultramontane Catholicism. They made the province stand out as exotic and disturbing in the eyes of other Canadians.

This difference has disappeared today. Partly one might say that French Canada has rejoined "English Canada"; more accurately one might say that the forces within Quebec that were always striving for a liberal society have won out. Perhaps it would be more insightful to say that both parts of Canada have been swept up into the liberal consensus that has become established in the whole western world in the wake of the World War II. As we shall see below, some English-speaking Canadians seem still to doubt this, to harbour a suspicion of Quebec's liberal credentials, but this is quite unfounded in the 1990s. Or rather, suspicions are in order, but just as they are about any other Atlantic society, for none of these is exempt from racism, chauvinism, and similar ills.

Ironically, at the very moment when we agree upon so much, we are close to breakup. We have never been closer to breakup in our history, although our values have never been so uniform. The road to uniformity goes beyond the ironing out of differences between the two major cultures. There has also been a steady erosion of urban–rural differences in outlook over the last half century. And the prodigious effect of modern communications has probably lessened all the various regional differences as well.

Why Canada?

So what is the problem? It emerges when you ask another kind of question, also in the realm of values in some broad sense. Not what do people cherish as good, but what is a country for? That is, what ought to be the basis of unity around which a sovereign political entity can be built? This is a strange question in a way; it is not one that would likely be asked in many countries. But it arises here because there are alternatives, and therefore a felt need for justification. These alternatives exist for us—in our understanding of our situation—even when they are not very likely, when they enjoy minimal support and are hardly in the cards politically. They can still exist as a challenge to self-justification because they existed historically, and we retain the sense that our existing arrangements emerge out of a choice that excluded them.

In Canada-outside-Quebec (COQ)[2] the alternatives are two: the country or bits of it could join, or could have joined the United States; and the bits could also have failed to join together—and indeed, could one day deconfederate again. So there are two existential questions for COQ which we can call the unity and distinctness questions respectively. For Quebec there is one big question, which is too familiar and too much on the agenda today to need much description. It is the issue of whether to be part of Canada or not; and if so, how. I stress that neither of the existential alternatives may be strong options in COQ today, but that does not stop them functioning as reference points for self-definition; as ways of defining the question: what do we exist for?

In a sense the existential questions of the two societies are interwoven. Perhaps COQ would not feel the need for self-definition, for an answer to the question, "What is Canada for?" to anything like the same degree if Quebec were not contemplating answering its existential question in a radical form. But once the country's existence is threatened in this way all the suppressed alternatives rise to the surface in the rest-of-Canada as well.

So what are the answers? It will be easier to set out the problem by taking "English Canada" first. The answer here used to be simple. Way back when it really fitted into our official name of "British North America," the distinctness question answered itself; and unity seemed to be the corollary of the drive for distinctness in face of the American colossus. But as the Britishness, even "Englishness" of non-Quebec Canada declines, this becomes less and less viable as an answer. We are all the Queen's subjects, but this seems to mean less to less people; and more awkwardly, it means quite a bit to some still, but nothing at all to others, and thus cannot be the basis of unity.

What binds Canada together outside Quebec is thus no longer a common provenance, and less and less a common history. But people find the bonding elements in political institutions and ways of being. This is not a total break from the old identity, because Britishness also defined itself largely in terms of political institutions: parliamentary government, a certain juridical tradition, and the like. The slide has been continuous and without a sharp break from the old to the new. There are even certain continuing elements, but the package is different.

Canadians feel that they are different from the Americans, because (a) they live in a less violent and conflict-ridden society. This is partly just a matter of luck. We do not have a history that has generated an undeclared, low-level race war continuously feeding itself in our cities. But it is also a matter of political culture. From the very beginning Americans have put a value on energetic, direct defense of rights, and therefore are ready to mitigate their condemnation of violence. There is more understanding of it south of the border, more willingness to make allowances for it. And this has something to do with the actual level of violence being higher there, as well as with a number of strange penchants of American society, such as that expressed in the powerful lobby for personal firearms. Canadians tend to put more value on "peace, order and good government." At least, this is how we see ourselves, which is perhaps what is important for our purposes; but there seems to be some truth in the perception.

As a consequence, there is more tolerance here of rules and restrictions that are justified by the need for order. With it there is more of a favourable prejudice (at least in English Canada), and a free gift of the benefit of the doubt to the police forces. Hence the relative absence of protest when the *War Measures Act* was invoked in 1970; hence also the strange reluctance of the Canadian public to condemn the RCMP, even after all the revelations of its dubious behaviour.

We might add that Americans' tolerance of conflict extends into the domain of law as well. They are more litigious than we are. They think that is a good thing, that it reflects well on them. No one should take any guff from anyone. We tend to deplore it. From an American point of view, we seem to have an endless appetite for guff. But perhaps the long-term effect of the 1982 Charter will be to diminish this difference.

Related to this first point, Canadians (b) see their political society as more committed to collective provision, over against an American society that gives greater weight to individual initiative. Appeals for reduced government can be heard from the right of the political spectrum in both countries, but the idea of what reduced government actually means seems to be very different. There are regional differences in Canada, but generally Canadians are proud of and happy with their social programs, especially health insurance, and find the relative absence of these in the U.S. disturbing. The fact that poverty and destitution have been left to proliferate in American cities as they have during the Reagan years is generally seen here as a black mark against that society. Canadian practice may not be as much better as many of us believe; but the important point is that this is seen as a difference worth preserving.

Thus these two answers, (a) *law and order* and (b) *collective provision*, help to address the distinctness question. They explain why we are and want to remain a distinct political unit. But what answers the unity question? Why be a single country, and what common goals ought to animate this country? In one sense, (a) and (b) can serve here as well, if one thinks (as many Canadians instinctively do) that we need to hang together in order to maintain this alternative political culture as a viable option in North America. And then (b) can be logically extended into one of the principal declared common objectives of the Canadian federation in recent decades: (c) the equalization of life conditions and life chances between the regions. The solidarity of collective provision, which within each regional society generates such programs as Medicare, can be seen as finding its logical expression in a solidarity of mutual help between regions.

And so Canadian federalism has generated the practices of large-scale redistribution of fiscal resources through equalization payments, and attempts have been made at regional development. This too contrasts with recent American practice and provides a further answer to the distinctness question. We perhaps owe the drive to equality to the fact that we have been confronted with existential questions in a way that our neighbours have not since 1865. The Canadian federal union has been induced to justify itself, and greater interregional solidarity may be one of the fruits of this underlying angst.

But this bonding principle has also been a worrying source of division, because it is widely seen as a locus of failed aspirations and disappointed expectations. The principles of *regional equality and mutual help* run against a perceived reality of central Canadian domination in the outlying regions, a grievous mismatch of promise and performance. ...

It is clear that this issue of regional equality is a very troubled one in Canada. That is because it is on one hand an indispensable part of the answer to the unity question; while on the other it seems to many so largely unrealized, and on top of it all, we agree less and less on what it actually means.

But even if things were going swimmingly in this domain, we still would not have a full answer to the unity question. English Canada has been becoming more and more diverse, less and less "English," over the decades. The fact that it has always been an immigrant society, i.e., one which functions through admitting a steady stream of new arrivals, on top of the fact that it could not aspire to make immigrants over to its original mould, has meant that it has *de facto* become more and more multicultural over the years. It could not aspire to assimilate the newcomers to an existing mould, because this was originally British, hence ethnic. In the United States, which has always operated on a strong sense that it incarnates unrivalled political institutions, the drive to make everyone American could proceed apace. It was never as clear what the Canadian identity amounted to in political terms, and insofar as it was conceived as British it could not be considered normative for new arrivals. First, it was only the identity of one part of the country, and second, it could not but come to be seen as one ethnic background among others.

Canadians have seen their society as less of a melting pot than the United. States; and there has been some truth in this. In contrast to the neighbour society, people have spoken of a Canadian "mosaic." So this has even become for some a new facet of their answer to the distinctiveness question, under the rubric (d) *multiculturalism*. This is also far from trouble-free. Questions are being posed in both the major cultures about the pace and even goals of integration, or assimilation of immigrants into the larger anglophone or francophone society. This is particularly troubling in Quebec, which has much less historic experience of assimilating immigrants and a much higher proportion of whose francophone population is *pure laine*.

This makes even more acute the need for a further point of unity, a common reference point of identity, which can rally people from many diverse backgrounds and regions. In a quite astonishing way, (e) the *Charter of Rights* has come to fill this role in English Canada in recent years. It is astonishing, because nine years ago it did not exist. Nor was there that much of a groundswell of support demanding its introduction before it became a bone of contention between federal and provincial governments in the run-up to the patriation of 1981–82. But the Meech Lake debate showed how important it has become in COQ not just as an additional bulwark of rights, but as part of the indispensable common ground on which all Canadians ought to stand. For many people, it has come in the space of a few years to define in part the Canadian political identity. And since in COQ the national identity has to be defined in terms of political institutions for reasons rehearsed above, this has been a fateful development.

Why Quebec?

How about Quebec? How can it go about answering its existential question? The terms are very different. In Quebec, there is not a distinctness issue. The language and culture by themselves mark us off from Americans, and also from other Canadians. Much of (a) to (e) is seen as a "Good Thing" in Quebec. Regarding (a)—law and order—people do not compare themselves a lot with the U.S., but there is no doubt that Quebecers are spontaneously on the side of law and order, and are even more horrified by internecine conflict than other Canadians. ...

Regarding (b)—collective provision—it goes without saying that people are proud of their social programs in the province, and want to keep them. Point (d)—multiculturalism—is more problematic. As a federal policy, multiculturalism is sometimes seen as a device to deny French-speaking minorities their full recognition, or even to reduce the importance of the French fact in Canada to that of an outsize ethnic minority. And within Quebec itself, the growing diversity of francophone society is causing much heartburn and anxiety. Point (c)—regional equality and mutual self-help—is generally supported in Quebec, and even (e)—the Charter was favourably seen until it came to be perceived as an instrument for the advancement of the uniformity of language regimes across the country. Even now its other provisions are widely popular.

But these do not go very far to answer the question, what is a country for? There is one obvious answer to this question, which has continued down through the decades for over two centuries: (f) you need a country to defend or promote the nation. The nation here was originally "la nation canadienne-française." Now without entirely abandoning the first formulation, it tends to be put as *la nation québécoise*. This does not betoken any change in ethnic identity, of course. It reflects rather a sense, which presents itself as realistic, but may be too pessimistic, that the really survivable elements of la nation canadienne-française are only to be found in Quebec.

But the real point here is that (f) makes the survival and/or flourishing of this nation/language one of the prime goals of political society. No political entity is worth allegiance that does not contribute to this. The issue: independent Quebec versus remaining in Canada turns simply on different judgments about what does contribute to this. ...

Equality of What?

[A] great area of conflict is between the demands of a special status for Quebec, and those of regional equality, once this is interpreted as requiring equality between the provinces. But whereas over the two models of liberalism there is really a genuine philosophic difference underlying all the misunderstanding, here there is still much mutual misperception and cross-purposes.

For in fact, the two demands come out of quite different agendas, as has often been remarked. The demand for special status is usually one for assuming a wider range of responsibilities and hence for greater autonomy. The call for regional equality comes generally from those who feel that their interests have been given insufficient weight in federal policy-making, and hence aims for more clout in this process. One side wants to take a greater distance from the central government and legislature; the other wants a weightier place within these. That is why it has taken the form in recent years of a call for reform in federal institutions, notably the Senate.

So understood, these demands are not logically opposed. Of course, they can at many points get in each other's way. There has been a fear among provinces that look to a more active federal government to equalize conditions across the regions, that excessive powers to Quebec might end up weakening the power of the centre to act. This may indeed be, but it is not fated to do so. It is not the reflection of a logical conflict, such as that between equality of all provinces on one hand, and special powers for one of them on the other. The demands for special status and strong central government can possibly be made compatible. What has made this difficult in practice has been precisely the refusal to depart from uniformity. This has meant that any "concession" to Quebec has had to be offered to all the provinces. Fortunately, these have not always been taken up, and so we have evolved quite a considerable *de facto* special status for Quebec, as I remarked above. But it has never been possible to proceed in that direction openly and explicitly, because of the pressure for uniformity. In the Meech Lake Accord itself, designed to address the difficulties of Quebec, most of what was accorded to Quebec had to be distributed to all the others.

The language of "equality" between provinces has in fact been a source of confusion, screening the reality of what is at stake and making solutions more difficult. Equality is a notoriously difficult concept to apply, and depends on the respect one makes salient. It could be argued that Quebec needs powers that other provinces do not, to cope with problems and a vocation that other provinces do not have. Accordingly, this point could be seen as a move towards equality (to each province according to its tasks), not away from it. Moreover, the special status has nothing to do with having more clout at the centre. It involves something quite different.

All of this should encourage us to think that it may not be beyond human wit to fever a way to satisfy these different demands together. There are (a) provinces that want more say in the decisions of the federal government. There are others who, while not disinterested in this first goal are mainly concerned with (b) maintaining an active federal government as a force for economic and social equalization between regions. Then there is Quebec, which (c) wants the powers it thinks essential to the preservation and promotion of its distinct society.

To this we now have to add the aboriginal dimension. That means that our arrangements have to accommodate the need for forms of self-government and self-management appropriate to the different first nations. This may mean in practice allowing for a new form of jurisdiction in Canada, perhaps weaker than the provinces, but, unlike municipalities, not simply the creatures of another level of government.

Putting all this together will be very difficult. It will take much ingenuity and good will. Perhaps more of either than we possess. But the task will be utterly impossible if we persist in describing the problem in the misleading and often demagogic language of equality versus inequality of provinces. Put in these terms the problem is a false one, and the present importance of this formulation is a sign of our lack of lucidity and the decline of good will. It reflects the deep mutual suspicions that have come to cloud our political scene.

The game of multidimensional constitutional tug-of-war that we have been playing in Canada these past years has made our situation worse, partly by creating or strengthening unhealthy linkages, whereby aspirations that are, as such, perfectly compatible come to be seen as deadly rivals. Examples are the linkages made between linguistic duality and multiculturalism, or those between aboriginals and Québécois, or those between regional equality and the distinct society. It may already be too late to climb out of the skein of resentments and mutual suspicion, and it will take far-sighted and courageous leadership to do so. But it will also require that we see each others' aspirations for what they are, as free as possible from the rhetoric of resentment.

Levels of Diversity

Various solutions can be glimpsed beyond the present stalemate. One set would be based on a dualism in which Quebec would no longer be a federal unit just like the others. The other possible range would have as its basis a four- or five-region federalism decentralized enough to accommodate Quebec as a member on all fours with the rest. Either type of solution would have to accommodate difference in a way we have not yet succeeded in doing—at least openly and admittedly.

Can we do it? It looks bad, but I would like to close by saying a few words about what this might mean.

In a way, accommodating difference is what Canada is all about. Many Canadians would concur in this. That is why the recent bout of mutual suspicion and ill-will in the constitutional debate has been so painful to many of our compatriots. It is not just that the two sources of difference I have been describing are becoming more salient. Old questions may be reopened. To some extent Trudeau's remarkable achievement in extending bilingualism was made possible by a growing sympathy towards the French fact among political and social elites in COQ. The elites pushed the bilingual process at a pace faster than many of their fellow citizens wanted. For many people lower down in the hierarchy, French was being "stuffed down their throats," but granted the elite-run nature of the political accommodation process in this country, they seemed to have no option but to take it.

During the Meech debate the procedures of elite negotiation came under sharp criticism and challenge. Moreover, the COQ elites were themselves split on how to respond to the new package, in a way they had not been on bilingualism. It was therefore not surprising that we began to see a rebellion against the accommodation of French. This might be the harbinger of greater resistance to come. Already one hears westerners saying that Canadian duality is an irrelevancy to them, that their experience of Canada is of a multicultural mosaic. The very bases of a two-language federation are being questioned again. This important axis of difference is under threat.

More fundamentally, we face a challenge to our very conception of diversity. Many of the people who rallied around the Charter and multiculturalism to reject the distinct society are proud of their acceptance of diversity. And in some respects rightly so. What is enshrined here is what one might call first-level diversity. There are great differences in culture and outlook and background in a population that nevertheless shares the same idea of what it is to belong to Canada. Their patriotism or manner of belonging is uniform, whatever their other differences, and this is felt to be a necessity if the country is to hold together.

This is far from accommodating all Canadians. For Quebecers, and for most French Canadians, the way of being a Canadian (for those who still want to be) is by their belonging to a constituent element of Canada, *la nation québécoise*, or *canadienne-française*. Something analogous holds for aboriginal communities in this country. Their way of being Canadian is not accommodated by first-level diversity. And yet many people in COQ are puzzled by the resulting sense of exclusion, because first-level diversity is the only kind to which they are sensitive, and which they feel they fully acknowledge.

To build a country for everyone, Canada would have to allow for second-level or "deep" diversity, where a plurality of ways of belonging would also be acknowledged and accepted. Someone of, say, Italian extraction in Toronto, or Ukrainian extraction in Edmonton, might indeed feel Canadian as a bearer of individual rights in a multicultural mosaic. His or her belonging would not "pass through" some other community, although the ethnic identity might be important to him or her in various ways. But this person might nevertheless accept that a Québécois, or a Cree, or a Déné, might belong in a very different way, that they were Canadian through being members of their national communities. And reciprocally, the Québécois, Cree, or Déné would accept the perfect legitimacy of the "mosaic" identity.

Is this utopian? Could people ever come to see their country this way? Could they even find it exciting and an object of pride that they belong to a country that allows deep diversity? Pessimists say no, because they do not see how such a country could have a sense of unity. The model of citizenship has to be uniform, or people would have no sense of belonging to the same polity. Those who say this tend to take the United States as their paradigm, which has indeed been hostile to deep diversity, and has sometimes tried to stamp it out as "un-American."

But these pessimists should bear in mind three things. First, deep diversity is the only formula on which a united federal Canada can be rebuilt, once we recall the reasons why we all need Canada—such as those above, i.e., law and order, collective provision, and regional equality and mutual self-help.

Second, in many parts of the world today, the degree and nature of the differences resemble Canada's rather than the United States. If a uniform model of citizenship fits better the classical image of the western liberal state, it is also true that this is a straightjacket for many political societies. The world needs other models to be legitimated, in order to allow for more humane and less constraining modes of political cohabitation. Instead of pushing ourselves to the point of breakup in the name of the uniform model, we would do our own and some other peoples a favour by exploring the space of deep diversity. To those who believe in according people the freedom to be themselves, this would be counted a gain in civilization.

In this exploration we would not be alone. Europe-watchers have noticed how the development of the Community has gone along with an increased breathing space for regional societies—Breton, Basque, Catalan—which were formerly threatened with the steamroller of the national state.

Finally, after dividing to form two polities with uniform citizenship, both successor-states would find that they had failed after all to banish the challenge of deep diversity; because the only way that they can do justice to their aboriginal populations is by adopting a pluralist mould. Neither Quebec nor COQ could succeed in imitating the United States, or the European national states in their chauvinist prime. Why not recognize this now, and take the road of deep diversity together?

Notes

1. "La Province de Québec au moment de la grève" in Pierre Trudeau (ed.), *La Grève de l'Amiante* (Montréal: les Éditions Cité Libre, 1956).

2. In Quebec we speak blithely of "English Canada," but the people who live there do not identify with this label. We need a handy way of referring to the rest of the country as an entity, even if it lacks for the moment political expression. In order to avoid the clumsy three-word hyphenated expression, I plan to use "COQ" henceforth in this paper. I hope the reader will not take this as a sign of encroaching barbarism, or Québécois self-absorption (although it might partake in small measure of both).

People to People, Nation to Nation

Royal Commission on Aboriginal Peoples (1996)

10

EDITORS' INTRODUCTION

In the wake of the confrontation of Mohawk warriors with the Canadian Armed Forces at Oka and Kahnawake in the summer of 1990, the Mulroney government established the Royal Commission on Aboriginal Peoples. The commission was co-chaired by George Erasmus, Grand Chief of the Assembly of First Nations, and René Dussault, a Quebec judge. Its membership included leading members of the Inuit, Métis, and non-status Indian communities; Bertha Wilson, a retired Supreme Court of Canada justice; and Allan Blakeney, a former premier of Saskatchewan. The commission had a broad mandate to study and make recommendations on all aspects of the relationship between Aboriginal peoples and Canada. It began its work in 1991 and submitted its five-volume final report in 1996. "Looking Forward, Looking Back" is the opening section of a widely distributed summary of the commission's findings and recommendations entitled People to People, Nation to Nation.

While few of the commission's hundreds of recommendations were immediately enacted, its report set a standard, agreed on by Aboriginal and non-Aboriginal leaders, for measuring progress in reforming relations with Aboriginal peoples in Canada. The key elements of that standard are eliminating the wide gap in the living conditions of Aboriginal and non-Aboriginal Canadians, but doing so through nation-to-nation treaty relationships.

Looking Forward, Looking Back

After some 500 years of a relationship that has swung from partnership to domination, from mutual respect and co-operation to paternalism and attempted assimilation, Canada must now work out fair and lasting terms of coexistence with Aboriginal people.

The Starting Point

The Commission has identified four compelling reasons to do so:

- Canada's claim to be a fair and enlightened society depends on it.
- The life chances of Aboriginal people, which are still shamefully low, must be improved.

Source: Excerpted from *People to People, Nation to Nation*. Ottawa: Government of Canada, 1996.
See http://www.aadnc-aandc.gc.ca/eng/1100100014597/1100100014637.

- Negotiation, as conducted under the current rules, has proved unequal to the task of settling grievances.
- Continued failure may well lead to violence.

CANADA AS A FAIR AND ENLIGHTENED SOCIETY

Canada enjoys a reputation as a special place—a place where human rights and dignity are guaranteed, where the rules of liberal democracy are respected, where diversity among peoples is celebrated. But this reputation represents, at best, a half-truth.

A careful reading of history shows that Canada was founded on a series of bargains with Aboriginal peoples—bargains this country has never fully honoured. Treaties between Aboriginal and non-Aboriginal governments were agreements to share the land. They were replaced by policies intended to

... remove Aboriginal people from their homelands.
... suppress Aboriginal nations and their governments.
... undermine Aboriginal cultures.
... stifle Aboriginal identity. ...

THE LIFE CHANCES OF ABORIGINAL PEOPLE

The third volume of our report, *Gathering Strength*, probes social conditions among Aboriginal people. The picture it presents is unacceptable in a country that the United Nations rates as the best place in the world to live.

Aboriginal people's living standards have improved in the past 50 years—but they do not come close to those of non-Aboriginal people:

- Life expectancy is lower.
- Illness is more common.
- Human problems, from family violence to alcohol abuse, are more common too.
- Fewer children graduate from high school.
- Far fewer go on to colleges and universities.
- The homes of Aboriginal people are more often flimsy, leaky and overcrowded.
- Water and sanitation systems in Aboriginal communities are more often inadequate.
- Fewer Aboriginal people have jobs.
- More spend time in jails and prisons.

Aboriginal people do not want pity or handouts. They want recognition that these problems are largely the result of loss of their lands and resources, destruction of their economies and social institutions, and denial of their nationhood.

They seek a range of remedies for these injustices, but most of all, they seek control of their lives.

FAILED NEGOTIATIONS

A relationship as complex as the one between Aboriginal and non-Aboriginal people is necessarily a matter of negotiation. But the current climate of negotiation is too often rife with conflict and confrontation, accusation and anger.

Negotiators start from opposing premises. Aboriginal negotiators fight for authority and resources sufficient to rebuild their societies and exercise self-government—as a matter of right, not privilege. Non-Aboriginal negotiators strive to protect the authority and resources of Canadian governments and look on transfers to Aboriginal communities as privileges they have bestowed.

Frequent failure to come to a meeting of minds has led to bitterness and mistrust among Aboriginal people, resentment and apathy among non-Aboriginal people.

In our report, we recommend four principles for a renewed relationship—to restore a positive climate at the negotiating table—and a new political framework for negotiations. ...

RISK OF VIOLENCE

Aboriginal people have made it clear, in words and deeds, that they will no longer sit quietly by, waiting for their grievances to be heard and their rights restored. Despite their long history of peacefulness, some leaders fear that violence is in the wind.

What Aboriginal people need is straightforward, if not simple:

- Control over their lives in place of the well-meaning but ruinous paternalism of past Canadian governments.
- Lands, resources and self-chosen governments with which to reconstruct social, economic and political order.
- Time, space and respect from Canada to heal their spirits and revitalize their cultures.

> *We are getting sick and tired of the promises of the federal government. We are getting sick and tired of Commissions. We are getting sick and tired of being analyzed ... We want to see action.*
>
> Norman Evans
> Pacific Métis Federation

The Ghosts of History

Every Canadian will gain if we escape the impasse that breeds confrontation between Aboriginal and non-Aboriginal people across barricades, real or symbolic. But the barricades will not fall until we understand how they were built.

Studying the past tells us who we are and where we came from. It often reveals a cache of secrets that some people are striving to keep hidden and others are striving to tell. In this case, it helps explain how the tensions between Aboriginal and non-Aboriginal people came to be, and why they are so hard to resolve.

Canadians know little about the peaceful and co-operative relationship that grew up between First Peoples and the first European visitors in the early years of contact. They know even less about how it changed, over the centuries, into something less honourable. In our report, we examine that history in some detail, for its ghosts haunt us still.

The ghosts take the form of dishonoured treaties, theft of Aboriginal lands, suppression of Aboriginal cultures, abduction of Aboriginal children, impoverishment and disempowerment of Aboriginal peoples. Yet at the beginning, no one could have predicted these results, for the theme of early relations was, for the most part, co-operation.

The relationship between Aboriginal and non-Aboriginal people evolved through four stages:

- There was a time when Aboriginal and non-Aboriginal people lived on separate continents and knew nothing of one another.
- Following the years of first contact, fragile relations of peace, friendship and rough equality were given the force of law in treaties.
- Then power tilted toward non-Aboriginal people and governments. They moved Aboriginal people off much of their land and took steps to "civilize" and teach them European ways.
- Finally, we reached the present stage—a time of recovery for Aboriginal people and cultures, a time for critical review of our relationship, and a time for its renegotiation and renewal.

Many of today's malfunctioning laws and institutions—the *Indian Act* and the break-up of nations into bands, to name just two—are remnants of the third stage of our history. But there was honour in history, too; indeed, the foundations of a fair and equitable relationship were laid in our early interaction. …

TREATY MAKING

Treaty making among Aboriginal peoples dates back to a time long before Europeans arrived. Aboriginal nations treated among themselves to establish peace, regulate trade, share use of lands and resources, and arrange mutual defence. Through pipe smoking and other ceremonies, they gave these agreements the stature of sacred oaths.

European traditions of treaty making date to Roman times, but in the seventeenth century, they took on new importance. They became the means for the newborn states of Europe to control their bickering and warfare—indeed, to end it for long periods. Treaties were a way of recognizing each other's independence and sovereignty and a mark of mutual respect.

In the colonies that became Canada, the need for treaties was soon apparent. The land was vast, and the colonists were few in number. They feared the might of the Aboriginal nations surrounding them. Colonial powers were fighting wars for trade and dominance all over the continent. They needed alliances with Indian nations.

The British colonial government's approach to the treaties was schizophrenic. By signing, British authorities appeared to recognize the nationhood of Aboriginal peoples and their equality as nations. But they also expected First Nations to acknowledge the authority of the monarch and, increasingly, to cede large tracts of land to British control—for settlement and to protect it from seizure by other European powers or by the United States.

The Aboriginal view of the treaties was very different. They believed what the king's men told them, that the marks scratched on parchment captured the essence of their talks. They were angered and dismayed to discover later that what had been pledged in words, leader to leader, was not recorded accurately. They accepted the monarch, but only as a kind of kin figure, a distant "protector" who could be called on to safeguard their interests and enforce treaty agreements. They had no notion of giving up their land, a concept foreign to Aboriginal cultures.

*In my language, there is no word for "surrender." There is no word. I cannot
describe "surrender" to you in my language, so how do you expect my
people to [have] put their X on "surrender"?*

> Chief Francois Paulette
> Treaty 8 Tribal Council, Yellowknife, Northwest Territories

... The purpose of the treaties, in Aboriginal eyes, was to work out ways of sharing lands
and resources with settlers, without any loss of their own independence. But the representatives of the Crown had come to see the treaties merely as a tool for clearing Aboriginal
people off desirable land.

To induce First Nations to sign, colonial negotiators continued to assure them that treaty
provisions were not simply agreed, but *guaranteed* to them—for as long as the sun shone
and the rivers flowed.

Stage 4: Renewal and Renegotiation

Policies of domination and assimilation battered Aboriginal institutions, sometimes to the
point of collapse. Poverty, ill health and social disorganization grew worse. Aboriginal
people struggled for survival as individuals, their nationhood erased from the public mind
and almost forgotten by themselves.

Resistance to assimilation grew weak, but it never died away. In the fourth stage of the
relationship, it caught fire and began to grow into a political movement. One stimulus was
the federal government's White Paper on Indian Policy, issued in 1969.

*The fact is that when the settlers came, the Indians were there, organized
in societies and occupying the land as their forefathers had done for
centuries. This is what Indian title means ...*

> Supreme Court of Canada
> Calder v. Attorney General of British Columbia (1973)

The White Paper proposed to abolish the *Indian Act* and all that remained of the special
relationship between Aboriginal people and Canada—offering instead what it termed *equality*. First Nations were nearly unanimous in their rejection. They saw this imposed form of
"equality" as a coffin for their collective identities—the end of their existence as distinct
peoples. Together with Inuit and Métis, they began to realize the full significance of their
survival in the face of sustained efforts to assimilate them. They began to see their struggle
as part of a worldwide human rights movement of Indigenous peoples. They began to piece
together the legal case for their continuity as peoples—nations within Canada—and to speak
out about it.

They studied their history and found evidence confirming that they have rights arising
from the spirit and intent of their treaties and the *Royal Proclamation of 1763*. They took
heart from decisions of Canadian courts, most since 1971, affirming their special relationship
with the Crown and their unique interest in their traditional lands. They set about beginning
to rebuild their communities and their nations with new-found purpose.

> *The relationship between the government and Aboriginals is trust-like*
> *rather than adversarial, and ... contemporary recognition and affirmation*
> *of Aboriginal rights must be defined in light of this historic relationship.*
>
> Supreme Court of Canada
> R. v. Sparrow (1990)

The strong opposition of Aboriginal people to the White Paper's invitation to join mainstream society took non-Aboriginal people by surprise. The question of who Aboriginal people are and what their place is in Canada became central to national debate.

A dozen years of intense political struggle by Aboriginal people, including appeals to the Queen and the British Parliament, produced an historic breakthrough. "Existing Aboriginal and treaty rights" were recognized in the *Constitution Act, 1982*.

This set the stage for profound change in the relationship among the peoples of Canada, a change that most governments have nevertheless found difficult to embrace.

The Way Forward

The policies of the past have failed to bring peace and harmony to the relationship between Aboriginal peoples and other Canadians. Equally, they have failed to bring contentment or prosperity to Aboriginal people.

In poll after poll, Canadians have said that they want to see justice done for Aboriginal people, but they have not known how. In the following chapters, we outline a powerful set of interlinked ideas for moving forward.

In the years since the White Paper, Canadian governments have been prodded into giving Aboriginal communities more local control. They have included more Aboriginal people in decision making and handed over bits and pieces of the administrative apparatus that continues to shape Aboriginal lives.

But governments have so far refused to recognize the continuity of Aboriginal nations and the need to permit their decolonization at last. By their actions, if not their words, governments continue to block Aboriginal nations from assuming the broad powers of governance that would permit them to fashion their own institutions and work out their own solutions to social, economic and political problems. It is this refusal that effectively blocks the way forward.

The new partnership we envision is much more than a political or institutional one. It must be a heartfelt commitment among peoples to live together in peace, harmony and mutual support.

For this kind of commitment to emerge from the current climate of tension and distrust, it must be founded in visionary principles. It must also have practical mechanisms to resolve accumulated disputes and regulate the daily workings of the relationship.

We propose four principles as the basis of a renewed relationship.

1. **Recognition**
   The principle of mutual recognition calls on non-Aboriginal Canadians to recognize that Aboriginal people are the original inhabitants and caretakers of this land and have

distinctive rights and responsibilities flowing from that status. It calls on Aboriginal people to accept that non-Aboriginal people are also of this land now, by birth and by adoption, with strong ties of love and loyalty. It requires both sides to acknowledge and relate to one another as partners, respecting each other's laws and institutions and co-operating for mutual benefit.

2. **Respect**
The principle of respect calls on all Canadians to create a climate of positive mutual regard between and among peoples. Respect provides a bulwark against attempts by one partner to dominate or rule over another. Respect for the unique rights and status of First Peoples, and for each Aboriginal person as an individual with a valuable culture and heritage, needs to become part of Canada's national character.

3. **Sharing**
The principle of sharing calls for the giving and receiving of benefits in fair measure. It is the basis on which Canada was founded, for if Aboriginal peoples had been unwilling to share what they had and what they knew about the land, many of the newcomers would not have lived to prosper. The principle of sharing is central to the treaties and central to the possibility of real equality among the peoples of Canada in the future.

4. **Responsibility**
Responsibility is the hallmark of a mature relationship. Partners in such a relationship must be accountable for the promises they have made, accountable for behaving honourably, and accountable for the impact of their actions on the well-being of the other. Because we do and always will share the land, the best interests of Aboriginal and non-Aboriginal people will be served if we act with the highest standards of responsibility, honesty and good faith toward one another.

> *The Six Nations of the Iroquois Confederacy have described the spirit of the relationship as they see it in the image of a silver covenant chain. "Silver is sturdy and does not easily break," they say. "It does not rust and deteriorate with time. However, it does become tarnished. So when we come together, we must polish the chain, time and again, to restore our friendship to its original brightness."*
>
> *Chief Jacob E. Thomas*
> *Cayuga First Nation, Haudenosaunee (Iroquois) Confederacy*

We propose that treaties be the mechanism for turning principles into practice. Over several hundred years, treaty making has been used to keep the peace and share the wealth of Canada. Existing treaties between Aboriginal and non-Aboriginal people, however dusty from disuse, contain specific terms that even now help define the rights and responsibilities of the signatories toward one another.

We maintain that new and renewed treaties can be used to give substance to the four principles of a just relationship.

11 Canada—A Pioneer in the Management of Constitutional Politics in a Multi-national Society

Peter H. Russell (2000)

EDITORS' INTRODUCTION

Peter Russell is a widely published scholar on constitutional, judicial, and Aboriginal politics. He taught political science at the University of Toronto from 1958 to 1996 and has served as president of the Canadian Political Science Association, the Canadian Law and Society Association, and the Churchill Society for the Advancement of Parliamentary Democracy.

The following essay was originally presented at an international conference on constitutional reform in North America at the University of Augsberg in Germany. It advances the argument that Canada stumbled into the challenge of working out constitutional arrangements for a country that harbours "nations within" by virtue of the fact that its dominant English-speaking majority did not completely conquer the French nation, nor the Indigenous nations within its boundaries.

It is Canada's fate to have become a pioneer in managing a very challenging type of constitutional politics. This is the constitutional politics of a democratic political community among whose people there are very different senses of national allegiance and identity. In such a society the big background issue of constitutional politics always is: can these people or peoples constitute a political community?

Canada's engagement in this kind of constitutional politics has come about not through rational choice or abstract philosophy. We have stumbled into this situation without fully realizing what we were doing. Even now many Canadians, perhaps even a majority—especially in "English Canada" and among new immigrants—would not accept my characterization of Canada as a multi-national society. They yearn for a Canada with a single sense of national identity. In effect, they yearn for a different Canada than the one in which they find themselves. Indeed, their very sense of unease about our disunity is an important element in Canada's constitutional restlessness.

In large measure we Canadians stumbled into the situation we find ourselves in through incomplete conquests. In the eighteenth century, the British did not complete their conquest of New France by expelling the Canadiens as they had earlier done with the Acadians. Nor

Source: *The Politics of Constitutional Reform in North America: Coping with New Challenges*, edited by Rainer-Olaf Schlutze and Roland Sturm. Opladen, Germany: Leske + Budrich Publishers, 2000. Reprinted by permission.

did they carry through with a program of forced assimilation of French Catholics into their English/Protestant culture. Within 15 years of the conquest they recognized the conquered people's religion and civil law. The British did not do this out of any profound philosophical commitment to political or cultural pluralism. They did it mainly as a strategy for securing the loyalty of the Canadiens at a time when the Empire was threatened with rebellion in the American colonies to the south. Nonetheless it was a decisive move towards a deeply pluralist Canada and Empire.

The absence of any commitment to cultural pluralism was evident again in the nineteenth century when British constitutionalists responded to rebellions in their two Canadian provinces. Lord Durham's plan was to assimilate the French Canadians into the English culture which he believed would soon dominate a reunited Canada. But the Québécois defeated this effort by surviving with their own sense of identity and forcing a federal constitutional solution with a province in which they as a majority would have enough political power to secure the essential elements of their distinct society.

The other incomplete conquest concerns the Indigenous peoples. In the seventeenth and eighteenth centuries the British (like the French) for military and commercial reasons entered into treaty-like agreements with Aboriginal nations. The Royal Proclamation of 1763 which set out British policy for governing the lands ceded by France at the end of the Seven Years War recognized the Indian nations' possession of territory outside the settled British colonies and laid down that settlement in this territory could take place only on lands that were sold or ceded by the Indians to the Crown. The Royal Proclamation, though often ignored in the nineteenth and twentieth centuries, survives as part of Canada's constitutional law. In 1982 its primacy was acknowledged in section 25 of the new *Canadian Charter of Rights and Freedoms.*

In Canada as in the United States once the settlers clearly had the upper hand militarily and demographically, treaty-like relations with Indigenous peoples gave way to colonial domination. Still there is an important difference between the two countries. In Canada right up into the twentieth century, treaties were the principal means for acquiring new lands from the Indians for settlement and economic development in much of Ontario, the western prairies, north-eastern British Columbia and part of the Northwest Territories. While the practical impact of these treaties was massive dispossession, nonetheless they did entail recognition by the incoming settler state of the Aboriginal signatories' nationhood and their collective ownership of traditional lands. The United States also made hundreds of treaties with Indian nations and through Chief Justice John Marshall's jurisprudence accorded Indian peoples the status of "domestic, dependent nations." However, soon after the Civil War, Congress abolished all future treaty-making. The American west was won from the Indians through brutal warfare rather than duplicitous treaties.

The continuity of treaty relationships with Aboriginal peoples in Canada has had important consequences for the present day. In the 1960s and 70s, a resurgence of Aboriginal nationalism induced the federal government to abandon its program of assimilation and resume the process of making agreements with native peoples who continue to occupy their traditional lands. Taking advantage of the constitutional restructuring brought on by Québec nationalism, Aboriginal peoples were able to have their rights, including treaty rights, recognized in the *Constitution Act* of 1982. Federal and provincial governments in Canada now recognize Aboriginal peoples as "First Nations" and are engaged, all across the country, in a process of negotiating self-government agreements with them, as well as with the Métis nation and Inuit peoples.

It is the persistence over centuries of the Québécois and the Indigenous peoples of Canada in insisting on their recognition as distinct peoples or nations that obliges Canada, if it is to survive with its present borders and population, to manage the constitutional affairs of a multi-national community. Let us be clear that what is at issue here is not simply a multi-cultural state but a multi-national state. Virtually every state in the world is in fact multi-cultural and acknowledges this, in varying degrees, in its laws and policies. Canada goes much further with multi-culturalism than most, extending financial support and encouragement to many ethnic minorities besides French-speaking Canadians and Aboriginal peoples. Functioning as a multi-national political community means something much more difficult and problematic than multi-culturalism. It means, in the Canadian case, acknowledging that two groups, French Canadians and Indigenous peoples, are not just cultural minorities but political societies with the special rights of homeland peoples to maintain political jurisdictions in which they can ensure their survival as distinct peoples.

Most of the Canadian citizens who belong to these "nations within" have a dual sense of national identity. In varying degrees most Aboriginal Canadians and French-speaking Québecers identify with Canada as well as with their own historic nations—though they may be reluctant to recognize Canada as "their nation." Alongside them, the majority of Canadians acknowledge Canada as their nation—their only nation—and in varying degrees despair of accommodating the "nations within." Managing the constitutional affairs of a population with such conflicting and incoherent notions of national identity is not just Canada's challenge but the challenge of many areas in the world today where some kind of national autonomy within a larger political community is the main alternative to the splintering of states or international conflict. That is why Canada's fortunes in dealing with this challenge bear watching.

Throughout its first century the Canadian federation had very few constitutional affairs to manage. The Confederation Constitution was based on an agreement between English and French Canadian politicians laden with ambiguity and conflicting expectations about the future of the federation. Indigenous peoples were included only as mute subjects of the new central government. Constitutional sovereignty—the power to amend the constitutional text—remained in the hands of the British Parliament. The federation grew and its structure evolved without any grand attempts to settle or accommodate constitutional differences. The main developments were the strengthening of provincial rights, a very strong commitment to a federal ethic, the confining of French Canada primarily to Québec, and concerted efforts by the federal government, despite the treaty process, to assimilate native peoples into what was fervently believed to be the superior culture of the Europeans.

Canadians did not become embroiled in constitutional politics until after World War II when federal politicians—French as well as English—moved by a sense of Canadian nationalism became determined to terminate Canada's constitutional colonialism and "patriate" the country's Constitution. They then confronted the unresolved ambiguities and differences about the nature of Canada as a political community. For transferring the power to amend the Constitution from Britain to Canada meant deciding who or what in Canada—which government or governments, which people or peoples—would be constitutionally sovereign. By the mid-1960s it was becoming clear that this grand issue—a mega issue in constitutional politics if ever there was one—would not be easy to resolve. A secular nationalism was also now moving many French Québecers to insist that patriation, the fulfillment of Canadian nation-hood, should take place only if the position of Québec as the homeland of a nation within Canada was more strongly and explicitly secured in the Canadian Constitution. The result, of course, of this collision of nationalisms and constitutional visions was an entire generation of very heavy constitutional politics—what I have called "mega constitutional politics."

Fear not—I am not about to take you through the many chapters of this seemingly endless constitutional struggle—the Victoria Charter, Trudeau's initiatives, the 1980 Québec refer-endum, Patriation, the conferences with Aboriginal peoples, Meech Lake, the Charlottetown Accord, the 1995 Québec referendum and all of that. If you want details, there are many books written about all of these events, including one of my own (Russell 1993). (Indeed, I am in no position to complain about the struggle as I have truly dined out on it—in Canada and around the world). But I do wish to reflect on its outcome, and what we can learn from the experi-ence about constitutionalism in societies that are deeply divided in a multi-national sense.

The first thing to observe is that after a generation of constitutional wrangling Canadians are no closer to resolving explicitly in formal constitutional terms the big issues that divide them. Important constitutional changes were made in 1982—patriation, a constitutional bill of rights and constitutional recognition of Aboriginal rights. But Prime Minister Trudeau's government forced these changes through over the opposition of Québec's provincial gov-ernment and most of Canada's Aboriginal leaders. This led to the subsequent constitutional efforts—the inconclusive First Ministers' Conferences with Aboriginal leaders, the defeat of the Meech Lake Accord designed to accommodate Québec and the referendum defeat of the Charlottetown Accord designed to accommodate everyone. The miracle is not that this latter effort failed but that it came so close to succeeding!

At the end of all this, many observers of our constitutional scene would conclude that the Canadian political community is more deeply divided than it was at the beginning of this constitutional struggle. In the light of the nearly 50–50 split in the 1995 Québec referendum, the same might be said of Québec as a political community. And, as the Nisga'a Treaty with its provision for an Aboriginal nation to exercise a real share of law-making sovereignty in Canada runs into stiff opposition among non-Aboriginal Canadians, there is no sign of a clear consensus on the future of Aboriginal peoples in Canada. The one point on which Canadians are now constitutionally united is their exhaustion with contesting constitutional issues. It is this feeling of constitutional exhaustion that may in the end persuade Québec sovereignists not to proceed with yet another referendum. These failed efforts at reaching a constitutional consensus in Canada did succeed in changing one important feature of Can-ada's constitutional culture: they democratized it. Making the written Constitution the most important political issue in the country for a generation, talking about the Constitution as ideally a vision of our society, a mirror in which all Canadians can see themselves, a document inscribing what we are all about—all of this convinced the Canadian public that they must have a crucial say in making any important changes in the Constitution. Political elites may still play the lead role in negotiating and drafting constitutional proposals—that much of consti-tutional democracy remains intact. But for proposals for fundamental constitutional change to be legitimate in Canada they must now be ratified by the people voting in referendums.

This democratization of Canada's constitutional process has not been written into the country's Constitution—though it has been incorporated into the constitutional systems of Québec, the three western-most provinces and several Aboriginal nations. Nonetheless, I believe that for major constitutional changes in the structure of our federal institutions or the structure of the federation, in the status of Indigenous peoples, or in the *Charter of Rights and Freedoms*, a Canadian wide referendum would be a political imperative for all. For this reason Bruce Ryder and I in a paper on "Ratifying a Post-referendum Agreement on Québec Sovereignty" (Ryder/Russell 1997) argued that, if after a sovereignist win in a Québec referendum, federal, provincial and Aboriginal leaders negotiated an agreement on a fundamental change in Québec's constitutional status, their agreement would have to be submitted to a Canada-wide referendum.

At a very abstract philosophical level, a compelling case can be made for this democratization of the constitutional process: in a constitutional democracy, after all, shouldn't the people be sovereign and have the final say on their highest law, the Constitution? The trouble with applying this simple principle of popular sovereignty to a multi-national society like Canada is the absence of an agreement on who the sovereign people are or on how that will can be identified. Québec sovereignists would say the people of Québec are sovereign and a majority of them express the people's will. This view is repudiated by federalists within and outside Québec, many of whom would argue that some majority of Canadians—simple or extraordinary—is sovereign in Canada. Most Aboriginal people do not believe their nations ever surrendered their sovereignty—though they might have difficulty agreeing on how that sovereignty is expressed in the present context.

Thus in the Canadian case—and I would submit in other multi-national communities—that first step in the Lockean social contract whereby all consent to form a single sovereign people to be governed by an agreed upon political authority has not and may never be taken. In a setting such as this attempts at grand constitutional settlements are much more likely to exacerbate than to resolve societal conflict.

The recipe for managing constitutional affairs that this analysis yields is not one of constitutional *immobilisme*. One of the worst myths haunting Canada's constitutional affairs is that the only alternative to a grand resolution of constitutional issues is a constitutional deep-freeze. Through the 1990s since the demise of the Charlottetown Accord important changes have been taking place in the operation of our constitution. Changes in the roles and responsibilities of government in our federal system have occurred without formal constitutional amendment. Some of this was consolidated in a political agreement on the Social Union. The parties to this agreement were the federal government and all of the Canadian provinces except Québec. In this agreement, the provinces for the first time acknowledge the legitimacy of the federal government using its spending power to support initiatives in areas of exclusive provincial jurisdiction, and in exchange the federal government agrees to launch such shared-cost or block-funded programs only with the agreement of a majority of provincial governments.

Québec's non-participation in the Social Union agreement demonstrates the strength and limitation of this kind of change. In effect it underlines Québec's special status in the Canadian federation without requiring that Canadians agree on explicit recognition of this special status in the constitutional text—an agreement that would probably be impossible to secure.

Progress has also been made in reforming Aboriginal relations. The Royal Commission on Aboriginal Peoples—the first collaborative inquiry in world history of indigenous and non-indigenous people into the past, present and future of their mutual relationship—has mapped out the path to a post-colonial relationship through treaty-like agreements on land

and governance. Through such an agreement, Nunavut, the homeland of the Eastern Arctic Inuit, is now up and running as a new self-governing territory of Canada. Treaty negotiations on land and governance issues are currently under way at approximately 80 different "tables" in every part of Canada. The Supreme Court of Canada's 1997 decision in *Delgamuukw* confirming Aboriginal peoples' ownership and control of their traditional, unsurrendered lands gave strong legal backing to this modern treaty process.

Popular support for this process of recognizing Aboriginal nations as self-governing nations within Canada is, however, shaky. Many non-Aboriginal commentators in the popular media are shocked to learn that under the Nisga'a Agreement the Nisga'a people besides being citizens of Canada will be recognized as citizens of the Nisga'a nation and that the Nisga'a government will have supreme law-making authority on matters such as their own constitution, language and culture, the education of their children and the management of the 10% of their traditional lands and resources recognized in the Agreement as belonging to them. Similar provisions are contained in other agreements now being negotiated across the country. The Nisga'a people have ratified the agreement and a very unpopular British Columbian government has pushed it through the British Columbia legislature. It is now before the federal parliament which must also approve it before it becomes law. The Chrétien government having been a party to the treaty and with a majority in the House of Commons will ensure its safe passage, but not without an acrimonious political debate. If, as the opposition urged, the Nisga'a Agreement had been put to a referendum in B.C., it would very likely have been rejected. The Nisga'a agreement, the product of over twenty years of negotiations, is inevitably a compromise. It is bitterly attacked by native critics as giving up too much land and self-government, just as many non-Aboriginal Canadians question it for going too far the other way. In constitutional referendum campaigns fought through the mass media, nay-sayers have an easier time standing on the high ground of pure principle and scare-mongering about change than do the defenders of grubby compromise.

Thus we Canadians limp along adjusting constitutional relationships in our multi-national political community without definitively settling the question of who or what we are, and without any clear popular consensus on the nature of the country expressed in the text of our constitution. The lesson we may have taught ourselves, and perhaps other deeply divided political communities, is that it is best not to try reaching a grand and explicit popular agreement on fundamental constitutional principles. As a number of our constitutional commentators have observed, abeyance and avoidance of intractable abstract questions such as the locus of sovereignty and the identity of the nation are conditions of constitutional peace in Canada. Of course, there are some who do not want peace. The most militant of these are the Québec sovereignists. They, by definition, do not accept that sovereignty should be shared. And despite constitutional exhaustion, they may yet force the issue. If they do have another referendum, and if they win it (whatever "winning" means), I am not sure what the final outcome will be—a totally independent Québec, a Québec in some new partnership relation with Canada or the status quo. However, I am fairly certain of one thing which is that in a newly configured Canada or an independent Québec with its present borders, as in Canada as it now is, sovereignty will in fact be shared among peoples, and there will once again be a need to practice the quiet and delicate constitutional arts of sharing sovereignty in a multi-national society.

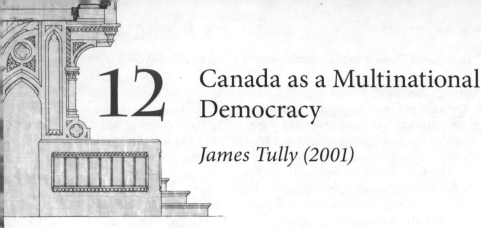

12 Canada as a Multinational Democracy

James Tully (2001)

EDITORS' INTRODUCTION

James Tully is a distinguished research professor at the University of Victoria. He has also taught at McGill University and the University of Toronto. Tully has gained worldwide recognition for his work in re-examining liberal political philosophy. He is also a leading scholar on democratic governance in an age of diversity, including the emergence of multinational states. In 2001, Tully and Professor Alain-G. Gagnon of McGill University co-edited the first full study of multinational democracies.

This excerpt, from James Tully's introduction to that volume, sets out the ingredients of a democratic constitution that are necessary to accommodate the reality of a multinational society.

The "Problematization" of the Constitutional Identity of a Multinational Society by Struggles over Recognition

A Multinational Society

Canada is described as a "free and democratic society" in section 1 of the *Canadian Charter of Rights and Freedoms*. For the purposes of this Introduction, a "multinational society" or "multinational democracy" is a type of "free and democratic society" which includes more than one "nation," or, more accurately, more than one "member" of the society demands recognition as a nation or nations. In the case of Canada, the present government of Quebec and many of the citizens demand recognition as a nation and the present leaders of the indigenous or "aboriginal" peoples and the majority of aboriginal people demand recognition as "first nations" or "indigenous peoples." For the sake of brevity, I will sometimes write simply that "Quebec" and the "aboriginal peoples of Canada" demand recognition as a nation and as first nations respectively. I mean by this shorthand that a majority of Quebecers and aboriginal people support these demands. A member of a multinational society that demands recognition as a nation may itself be a multinational society. Quebec, with eleven

Source: Excerpted from *Multinational Democracies*, edited by Alain-G. Gagnon and James Tully. Cambridge: Cambridge University Press, 2001. Notes omitted. Reprinted with the permission of Cambridge University Press.

aboriginal peoples in and across its borders demanding recognition as first nations, is a multinational democracy.

To investigate the features of a free, multinational democracy let us start (not uncritically) from the classic liberal account of a reasonably plural, free and democratic society presented by John Rawls, in *Political Liberalism* (1996), and its careful and innovative extension by Anthony Laden, in *Reasonably Radical: Deliberative Liberalism and the Politics of Identity* (2001), to free and democratic, multicultural and multinational societies. Rawls and Laden describe a free and democratic society as one that has a high degree of self-sufficiency and a place for all the main purposes of human life (Rawls 1996, pp. 40–3). A multinational society, like all free and democratic societies, meets these conditions. Moreover, a multinational society, like all free and democratic societies, is a fair system of social, political and economic cooperation in the broad and thick sense given to this phrase by Rawls. It is the congeries of democratic practices in which we acquire, exercise, question and modify our identities as national and multinational citizens (Rawls 1996, pp. 15–22, 41, 222, 269; Laden 2001, chs. 5–8).

"Cooperation" is more than socially coordinated action. "Cooperation is guided by publicly recognized rules and procedures that those cooperating accept and regard as properly regulating their conduct." Cooperation also involves the idea of "fair terms of cooperation"—"these are terms that every participant may reasonably accept, provided that everyone else likewise accepts them" (Rawls 1996, p. 16). The fair terms of cooperation apply to the basic structure of the society, to its political, economic and social institutions, and they are expressed in the constitutional principles of the society (Rawls 1996, pp. 257–8, 269–71; cp. SC 1998, paras. 50, 54). Accordingly, a demand for recognition as a nation or nations and its mode of institutional accommodation within a multinational society must be compatible with conditions of a fair system of social cooperation, or what the Supreme Court of Canada calls "unity," to be acceptable. Conversely, a demand for recognition is often supported by the claim that the prevailing terms of cooperation or unity are unacceptable in some respect, for example in the case of both Quebec and indigenous peoples.

A free and democratic society, whether multinational or uninational, is "free" in two relevant senses. The members of the society are free and the society as a whole is free. That is, the members of the society not only act democratically within the rules and procedures of cooperation; they also impose the rules on themselves and alter the rules and procedures democratically *en passant*. Such a society is "self-governing" or "self-determining," not in the radical sense that its members will into being the conditions of association. Rather, the members are free to either accept the conditions of association or enter into democratic negotiations to change the conditions that can be shown to be unjust; or, if the second of these options is blocked, to initiate the option to negotiate exit (SC 1998, paras. 83–105, 111–39). This is one of the most widely accepted principles of legitimacy in the modern world: for example, (1) of a liberal society as a fair system of social, political and economic cooperation, i.e. the rules are freely accepted and regarded as appropriate by the participants themselves (Rawls 1996, p. 16); (2) of "self-determination" as it is predicated of free societies or "peoples" in international law (SC 1998, paras. 111–39); and (3) of a free and democratic society in which the sovereign people or peoples impose the rules of the association on themselves as they obey those rules (Habermas 1998, pp. 49–74, 129–54, 253–64; Rawls 1996, pp. 396–409). The rules and procedures are neither imposed from the outside nor from an undemocratic element within. A member "nation" seeking recognition within the larger society itself will be free and democratic in these two senses as well, on pain of a performative contradiction (Tully 2000b).

A "nation" is a "people" with the right of self-determination. A multinational society is a "people" composed of peoples, a multi-peoples society or a multination. The multinational democracies studied in this volume have been recognized as self-determining, single nations or peoples by international law for centuries. The nations that demand recognition within multinational societies also and *eo ipso* demand recognition as "peoples." The terms "nations" and "peoples" have been used in overlapping ways over the last two hundred years and they are used interchangeably in discussions over, say, the Quebec "people" or "nation" and the "first nations" or "indigenous peoples." Since I wish to focus on the conditions of freedom and recognition in multinational societies, the concept of a people with the right of self-determination is appropriate, rather than the concept of a nation, which is appropriate for issues of nationalism.

A multinational society is usually but not always a federation. Israel and New Zealand, for example, are binational but not federal. I will concentrate on multinational federal societies because I wish to draw on Canada and because they are more complex than non-federal multinational societies. If we can clarify the main features of freedom and recognition in multinational federations, the non-federal cases should not be difficult. A federation is a society in which democratic self-government is distributed in such a way that citizens "participate concurrently in different collectivities" (SC 1998, para. 66)—in the democratic institutions of the society as a whole and of the federated members, such as provinces, states, nations or first nations. A "confederation," in contrast, is an association, not a society, in which citizens participate only in their "nation," not in the multinational confederation as a whole. The problem of multinational recognition in a confederation is correspondingly less complex and can be set aside for now.

Four Dimensions of Constitutional Identity

When a demand for the recognition of one or more nations or peoples arises in a multinational democracy, it "problematizes" the constitutional identity of the society. That is, the demand renders problematic the current (single-nation) constitutional identity of the society and proposes a change. Various solutions are then proposed to the problem in theory and practice. Looking back over fifty years of experience, three conflicting types of solution are standardly proposed around which citizens and governments mobilize: (1) defence of the status quo, with or without a degree of sub-constitutional change, (2) various forms of recognition of the nation or nations by changing the current constitutional identity, and (3) secession of the nation or nations and recognition as a new independent nation or nations, with or without some relation to the former society. As we see from the studies in this collection, each of the three types of strategic solution is defined by an evolving structure of argument which presents reasons for the justice and stability of its solution and the injustice and instability of the other two. Call the whole—including the reasons and causes of the demand, the proposals and solutions, the public discussions and negotiations, or refusals to negotiate, the amendments of the constitution and institutional changes, and the demands for recognition that this amendment in turn provokes—the "problematization" of the constitutional identity of a multinational democracy (Foucault 1984, p. 389 and Tully 1999b for the concept of problematization).

The "constitutional identity" of a multinational society, as of any free and democratic society, is its "basic constitutional structure," what I called above the publicly recognized and accepted rules and procedures by which the members of the society recognize each other and coordinate their cooperation. In the words of the Supreme Court of Canada, the constitution "embraces unwritten, as well as written rules," and includes "the global system of rules and principles which govern the exercise of constitutional authority" (Supreme Court 1998, para. 32). The constitution is the present system of rules of mutual recognition that gives a society its constitutional identity.

There are four major dimensions of the constitutional identity of a democratic society. First, a constitution recognizes the *members* of a society under their respective identities and enumerates their rights, duties and powers. For example, the Canadian constitution recognizes "citizens" with their rights, freedoms and duties, various types of "minorities" (linguistic, cultural, and individuals or groups disadvantaged because of race, ethnic origin, colour, religion, sex, age and mental or physical disability), "territories," "aboriginal peoples" and their rights, "provinces" with their legislative powers, the federation and its federal legislature, and the Canadian society as a whole. Second dimension, a constitution stipulates the *relations of governance* among the members, the rules and procedures that guide their conduct as members of a fair system of social cooperation (the totality of laws and regulations). Third, the constitution lays out a set of procedures and institutions of *discussion and alteration* of prevailing relations of governance over time. In Canada, these include the rights of public discussion, debate, assembly, voting, strike and dissent, courts, legislatures, procedures of federal–provincial renegotiation, the notwithstanding clause, treaty negotiations among first nations and federal and provincial governments, and procedures for amending the constitution. Fourth, the constitution includes the *principles, values and goods* that are brought to bear on the identification of members, the relations among them, and the discussion and alteration of their identities and relations over time. These principles, values and goods do not form a determinate and ordered set of principles of justice to which all the members agree. Rather, they are many, none is trump, different ones are brought to bear in different cases, and there is reasonable disagreement and contestation about which ones are relevant and how they should be applied in any case (SC 1998, paras. 49–54). Indeed, part of what makes the society free and democratic is reasonable disagreement among the members and their political traditions of liberalism, conservatism, socialism, republicanism, feminism, nationalism, multiculturalism, environmentalism and so on (Rawls 1999, pp. 140–3). These principles, values and goods comprise the public, normative warrants members appeal to in exchanging reasons over the justice and stability of their conflicting demands for and against recognition in any case (Rawls 1999, pp. 129–80; Laden 2001, chs. 5–7).

In cases of the recognition of nations in multinational societies, there are seven relevant principles. Following the Supreme Court, four principles are necessary (but not sufficient) to the "reconciliation of diversity with unity" in cases of multinationalism: the principles of federalism, democracy, the rule of law and constitutionalism, and the protection of minorities (SC 1998, paras. 32, 49, 55–82). In thin liberal democratic theories, two principles—democracy and rule of law—are said to be coequal and jointly sufficient for legitimacy (Habermas 1998, pp. 253–64). However, this is sufficient only for a subset of modern societies, those that are non-federal and do not acknowledge the protection of minorities as an independent principle.

In addition, three basic principles are indispensable to any free and democratic society: freedom, equality and distinctness. Free and equal are widely endorsed principles. By "freedom" I mean not only the freedoms associated with private autonomy (the freedom of the moderns), but also, and of primary concern in this case, the freedom associated with public autonomy, the democratic freedoms of members to participate in their society in the twofold sense explained in the section above. "Equality" includes not only the relatively uncontentious formal equality associated with thin liberal democracy, but also the substantive equality associated with thicker liberal societies (such as Rawls' "difference principle") and with social democracy (for example, social and economic rights for citizens and groups, and equalization transfers for provinces) (SC 1998, para. 64). Finally, it includes the equality of peoples. Members standardly disagree over the ranking, interpretation and application of these three aspects of equality.

Finally, members not only recognize each other as free and equal but also as the bearers of "distinct" or, as the Supreme Court puts it, "diverse identities" (SC 1998, paras. 43, 58, 59, 60, 74, 79–82). The freedom of expression of individual citizens, the principle of non-discrimination, equity policies, proportional representation, the protection of individual and group identities, languages and cultures, aboriginal rights, self-government and some federal arrangements (such as the special provisions for Quebec) are often justified in part by the principle of diversity or distinctness. Again, support varies and is contested, but public recognition of some forms of diversity and of "identity-related differences" is both unavoidable (language and culture being the most obvious examples) and good, either in itself or as a means to other goods, such as mutual respect.

PART 2
Canada's Institutions and Representation

Introduction

Canadian political life occurs largely within a set of formal institutions, some of them as old as Canada itself—such as Parliament and many of the rules and conventions that govern it—coupled with constraints, influences, and features that have evolved much more recently, such as the political media in a digital age. Closely entwined with the processes and mechanics of politics are concepts at the very core of our democracy: the *representation* of Canadians by members of Parliament in our House of Commons, and the expression of the popular will through voting and the electoral system. Some aspects of these institutions and processes might be understood through objective measurement and a study of data, or an examination of our Constitution, or voting laws; others may benefit from an approach that considers social trends and other shifting influences, or how power is exercised. But all of these institutions and processes, like the Canadian populace itself, continue to evolve—sometimes imperceptibly slowly, sometimes rapidly—and taken together, they have shaped Canada's politics as we know it.

Assessing Canadian politics today, it is clear that a number of factors exert an influence on Canada's political institutions and the nature of our representation. The French versus English cleavage remains, as ever, a dominant consideration in both society and electoral politics. Over the last century, the conception of a dualistic Canada has gradually come into conflict with an "equality-of-the-provinces" conception of the Canadian federation. This is due in part to the arrival of other provinces into the federation, and the strengthening of those provincial governments and identities, most notably the increasing political and economic influence of Western Canada in recent decades. Writing in 1967, Mildred Schwartz (Reading 25) considers the importance of regionalism in determining both public opinion and party organization. Writing soon after, Alan Cairns (Reading 19) notes the significant role that provinces have played in increasing their strength and power, leading to the development of this additional cleavage in Canadian society: one based on regionalism. His analysis points to the fact that institutions do indeed play an important role in creating, maintaining, and perpetuating societal cleavages.

Although multiple sources of conflict and controversy abound in Canadian politics, ultimately, today's political struggles and compromises are largely rooted in two (often conflicting) cleavages: French versus English, and region versus region, with Western Canada a notable actor in both cleavages.

In recent decades, we have seen the election to Parliament of several new parties, some of them expressions of regional interests and ambitions. In 2004, for example, the Liberal Party formed a minority government, facing an opposition that consisted of the Conservative Party (not the old Conservative Party, but a new amalgamation of the once-powerful Progressive Conservative Party and the more recent Reform/Alliance), the Bloc Québécois, and the NDP. In 2011, we saw the election of a Conservative Party majority, with the NDP sitting as the official opposition (the first time in Canadian history that it has served in that role), while the Liberals dropped to third-party status, and the Bloc Québécois all but disappeared. The 2011 vote also resulted in the election of the first-ever member of Parliament from the Green Party.

And so it appears that Canada has moved from a stable, two-party system seen at the turn of the 20th century (see essays by Carty, Johnston, and Smith in Carty, 1992),* and a 20th century dominated by the Liberals and Conservatives, to a multi-party system today that has in many ways been quite unstable. Not only have we seen older parties rise to new prominence in recent years—such as the NDP, which traces its roots to the organizing of western farmers as the CCF in the 1930s, and the reconstituted Conservative Party of Canada, which rose from the ashes after winning a mere two seats in the 1993 election to win its majority in 2011—but we have also seen the addition of new, regionally based parties into the system. The Bloc Québécois, a sovereigntist party based entirely in Quebec, has over the past 20 years competed for opposition status with the Reform Party, originally a "protest party" based in the West. The relative success of these parties illustrates the weight of regional cleavages in Canadian politics, as well as their conflictual nature, given that a certain amount of Reform's platform rested on anti-Quebec sentiment (see Reading 78 in Part 4, on the rise of the Reform Party). As with regionalism, the French/English cleavage remains important, although it is no longer reflected or expressed in traditional parties in the manner it once was.

One dynamic of interest to many political scholars is the relationship of local party organizations to the larger party they represent. As Carty notes in "The Politics of Tecumseh Corners" (Reading 22), the local context matters, and it affects how parties organize. Indeed, the very nature of political parties continues to shape Canadian politics. As André Siegfried, one of the fathers of Canadian electoral politics, noted over a century ago:

> In Canada the party is almost a sacred institution, to be forsaken only at the cost of one's reputation and career. It is held in esteem almost like one's religion, and its praises are sung in dithyrambs that are often a trifle absurd. Its members owe it absolute loyalty even in the smallest

---

* Works noted in this Introduction that are not among the excerpted readings in Part 2 can be found in the Further Suggested Reading section that follows this Introduction.

matters, and individual vagaries of opinion are sternly condemned. Oppose your party in defence of some doctrine which it formerly maintained itself but which the necessities of the moment have led it to abandon, and you will lose your reputation by your independence.

… In the eyes of politicians … "Party first, Principles afterwards!" might almost have been their cry. (André Siegfried, *The Race Question in Canada*, 142–144)

Along with examining the dynamics surrounding language and culture, Siegfried observed that religion was also an important consideration in Canadian politics at the turn of the last century, and his observation still holds today, although it must be moderated somewhat. Many scholars have noted the importance of religion over the years. Irvine and Gold (1980) illustrate the effect of family and socialization in passing down the importance of religion on partisanship, while Johnston (1985) takes their analysis one step further and points to the role of socialization outside of the family, as society helps to maintain the relationship between religion and partisanship. The Catholic/Protestant cleavage is another point of interest (see Blais, Reading 28; Mendelsohn and Nadeau, 1997, who point to the role of the media in tempering religion's role). Meanwhile, Bittner's work (Reading 30) demonstrates that political knowledge reduces the effect of religious cleavages. It is also important to note that, while the "old" religions retain a certain importance, a newer moral traditionalism and social conservatism have combined with organized religion to become a significant factor in the support enjoyed by, in particular, the Reform/Alliance/Conservative parties over the past 30 years. Clearly, further exploration of the role of one's religion—or lack thereof—in influencing voting decisions is necessary if we are to better understand this particular cleavage in Canadian politics.

In addition to the long-standing religious and regional cleavages in Canadian politics, several other social issues have become important since Siegfried's era. The importance of gender over the last century has grown significantly, with women coming to hold political office (including prime minister), party leadership, positions within the civil service, and so on. Women's issues, although certainly not *the* defining cleavage of Canadian politics, have taken on increased importance over the years, and some of the readings included in this section point to the importance of gender as a cleavage and as a representational issue (for example, Bashevkin, Reading 20; Gidengil et al., Reading 27; Gidengil and Everitt, Reading 32; Bittner, Reading 30).

In today's Canada, increased immigration has led to a diverse population, and multiculturalism has remained a significant issue in our politics (see also Readings 65–70 in Part 4). Meanwhile, issues relating to Canada's First Nations and Aboriginal Peoples, including claims to land rights, environmental matters such as pipelines, traditional practices, and self-government, continue to surface on the national political agenda (see Part 4, section II). Other scholars debate the importance of class-based cleavages (Brodie and Jenson, Reading 21; Johnston, 1992). The claims made by these different groups—women, various cultural and ethnic groups, First Nations Peoples, workers—have been election issues and the subject of parliamentary debates in recent years, and our political institutions' ability to address these matters is an important indicator of the health of our democracy.

The media, too, is an important institution, and plays a vital role in shaping Canadian democracy. In the early 21st century, technological advances have led to a globalized and connected citizenry, in which online discussion, debate, and information sharing have changed not only the media, but the nature of parliamentary activity, electoral campaigns, and political engagement. The role of the media in Canadian politics is examined in the final group of readings in this part, beginning with a selection from Harold Innis's landmark book *Empire and Communications* (Reading 31), which predates the digital age, but which considers the connection between communication forms and political power through a very broad, historical lens. The other, more recent selections by Gidengil and Everitt, Barney, and Small (Readings 32–34) examine not only the unprecedented technological changes of recent decades, and the impact of new tools such as Twitter, but also the ways in which gender norms, for example, are played out through traditional broadcast media.

Readings in other sections of Part 2, and in Further Suggested Reading below, also point to the influence of the media: Bittner (Reading 30) addresses the relationship between political knowledge and religion, noting that well-informed Catholics are less "different" from other Canadians. Mendelsohn and Nadeau (1997) point to the importance of the media in tempering differences between Catholics and Protestants, and in reinforcing the importance of regional cleavages in the minds of voters. And Johnston (1992) and Cutler (2002) both point to the important role the media plays in "priming" its audience on certain issues, and thus affecting the outcomes of elections and voting behaviour.

It is important to note that the nature of political science itself has evolved over the decades since the time of Siegfried and other pioneers. Reflections and observations of the type made by Siegfried (1907) and George Grant (1965), both of whom are representative of a more contemplative approach to political science scholarship, are few and far between at the turn of the 21st century, because the methodologies they tended to use to support their claims have been replaced by more rigorous approaches. In contemporary research, political scientists tend to use much more systematic observation, comparison, quantitative research, and sophisticated methodological tools in order to develop theories and (where possible) conclusions about Canadian politics.

Scholars now strive to provide an understanding of *why* people vote the way they do. As we noted above, Schwartz (in 1967) and Cairns (in 1968) made important observations about Canadian regionalism, but it is also worth noting that both scholars were early path-breakers in their use of statistical analysis to advance their arguments about the role of region in Canadian politics. Cairns, for example, through a sophisticated analysis of the impact of the electoral system and the party system, sought to explain why region has become so important in Canadian politics, as well as how and why the electoral system has exacerbated French/English differences in Parliament.

To what extent do the sorts of cleavages in Canadian politics and society that we have noted above reflect those cleavages found in countries with similar institutional frameworks? How do Canada's political institutions operate in comparison to other countries? Comparison with other countries' institutions is both valuable and necessary in the study of politics, and a great deal of Canadian scholarship draws from global and comparative literature. Several of the excerpts included in this section use comparison as they examine aspects of Canada's Parliament or its parties against what we know about the workings of the Westminster parliamentary system elsewhere, or the "first-past-the-post" election format (see the readings in this part by Carty and Cross; Pilon; Blais; Savoie; and Aucoin, Jarvis, and Turnbull).

Much of the contemporary work on Canada's Parliament and other institutions seeks to understand whether (or why) the Canadian system is broken, and what can be done to fix it. These issues are often articulated as questions in several readings in this part, such as: Why is power concentrated in the hands of the prime minister (Franks; Savoie; Aucoin, Jarvis, and Turnbull)? What ought to happen when the prime minister seeks to prorogue Parliament (Forsey)? And do our core political institutions (the Senate, the House of Commons, the electoral system) need changing? This important question is at the core of the readings by, respectively, Segal et al. (Reading 17); Aucoin et al. (Reading 18), and Pilon (Reading 23).

The readings in this section represent several key contributions to our understanding of Canada's political institutions and processes. (Note that Canada's courts, another key institutional pillar, are examined in Part 3, section 3.3.) But we must concede that this list of "essential" excerpts is certainly not exhaustive, and so the list of suggested recommended readings below will offer useful starting points for further study.

Further Suggested Reading
Parliament

Eugene Forsey. *How Canadians Govern Themselves.* Ottawa: Government of Canada, 1980; updated 2005.

George Grant. *Lament for a Nation.* Montreal and Kingston: McGill-Queen's University Press, 1965.

Christopher Kam. "Parliamentary 'Cowboys and Indians': Ministerial Responsibility and Bureaucratic Drift." *Governance* 13, 2000, 365–392.

Alison Loat and Michael MacMillan. *Tragedy in the Commons: Former Members of Parliament Speak Out on Canada's Failing Democracy.* Toronto: Random House, 2014.

Peter H. Russell. *Two Cheers for Minority Government: The Evolution of Canadian Parliamentary Democracy.* Toronto: Emond Montgomery, 2008.

Donald Savoie. *Breaking the Bargain: Public Servants, Ministers, and Parliament.* Toronto: University of Toronto Press, 2003.

The Electoral System and the Party System

Amanda Bittner and Royce Koop, eds. *Parties, Elections and the Future of Canadian Politics.* Vancouver: University of British Columbia Press, 2013.

R.K. Carty. *Canadian Political Party Systems: A Reader.* Peterborough, ON: Broadview Press, 1992.

R.K. Carty, William Cross, and Lisa Young. *Rebuilding Canadian Party Politics.* Vancouver: University of British Columbia Press, 2000.

David M. Farrell. *Electoral Systems: A Comparative Introduction.* London: Palgrave Macmillan, 2011.

Royce Koop. *Grassroots Liberals: Organizing for Local and National Politics.* Vancouver: University of British Columbia Press, 2011.

André Siegfried. *The Race Question in Canada.* London: Eveleigh Nash, 1907.

David Stewart and Ken Carty. "Does Changing the Party Leader Provide an Electoral Boost? A Study of Canadian Provincial Parties, 1960–1992." *Canadian Journal of Political Science* 26(2), 1993, 313–330.

Campaigns and Voters

Amanda Bittner. *Platform or Personality? The Role of Party Leaders in Elections.* Oxford: Oxford University Press, 2011.

Harold Clarke, Allan Kornberg, and Peter Wearing. *A Polity on the Edge: Canada and the Politics of Fragmentation.* Toronto: University of Toronto Press, 2000.

Fred Cutler. "Local Economies, Local Policy Impacts, and Federal Electoral Behaviour in Canada." *Canadian Journal of Political Science* 35(2), 2002.

W.P. Irvine and H. Gold. "Do Frozen Cleavages Ever Go Stale? The Bases of the Canadian and Australian Party Systems." *British Journal of Political Science* 10, 1980, 187–218.

Richard Johnston. "The Reproduction of the Religious Cleavage in Canadian Elections." *Canadian Journal of Political Science* 18, 1985.

Richard Johnston, André Blais, Henry E. Brady, and Jean Crête. *Letting the People Decide: Dynamics of a Canadian Election.* Montreal and Kingston: McGill-Queen's University Press, 1992.

Richard Johnston, André Blais, Elisabeth Gidengil, and Neil Nevitte. *The Challenge of Direct Democracy: The 1992 Canadian Referendum.* Montreal and Kingston: McGill-Queen's University Press, 1996.

Matthew Mendelsohn. "Rational Choice and Socio-Psychological Explanation for Opinion on Quebec Sovereignty." *Canadian Journal of Political Science* 36(3), 2003, 511–537.

Richard Nadeau and André Blais. "Explaining Election Outcomes in Canada: Economy and Politics." *Canadian Journal of Political Science* 26(4), 1993, 775–790.

Stuart Soroka and Christopher Wlezein. "Opinion Representation and Policy Feedback: Canada in Comparative Perspective." *Canadian Journal of Political Science* 37(3), 2005, 1–29.

Marianne Stewart and Harold Clarke. "The Dynamics of Party Identification in Federal Systems: The Canadian Case." *American Journal of Political Science* 42(1), 1998, 97–116.

The Media and Communications

Elizabeth Goodyear-Grant. *Gendered News: Media Coverage and Electoral Politics in Canada.* Vancouver: University of British Columbia Press, 2013.

Royce Koop and Harold J. Jansen. "Partisan Blogs and Blogrolls in Canada: Forums for Democratic Deliberation?" *Social Science Computer Review* 27(2), 2009, 155–173.

Matthew Mendelsohn and Richard Nadeau. "The Religious Cleavage and the Media in Canada." *Canadian Journal of Political Science* 30, 1997, 129–146.

Tamara A. Small, Harold Jansen, Frédérick Bastien, Thierry Giasson, and Royce Koop. "Online Political Activity in Canada: The Hype and the Facts." *Canadian Parliamentary Review* 37(4), 2014, 9–16.

Additional References

Donald V. Smiley. *The Federal Condition in Canada.* Toronto: McGraw-Hill Ryerson, 1987.

Linda White, Richard Simeon, Robert Vipond, and Jennifer Wallner. *The Comparative Turn in Canadian Political Science.* Vancouver: University of British Columbia Press, 2009.

Prorogation Revisited: Eugene Forsey on Parliament and the Governor General

13

Eugene Forsey and Helen Forsey (1984, 2009)

EDITORS' INTRODUCTION

Eugene Forsey was both a public official and an experienced commentator on Canadian political life. He taught at McGill, Carleton, and Waterloo universities. His political engagement began with the CCF, then with the Liberal Party of Canada, which led to his being nominated a senator in 1970. He was considered to be an expert on constitutional issues, especially the reserve powers of the Crown, and his observations still have bearing on contemporary parliamentary issues. His daughter, Helen Forsey, is a writer and activist based in rural eastern Ontario and Newfoundland and Labrador's Avalon Peninsula.

Prorogation (the dissolution of a session of Parliament) has recently become an increasingly salient issue in Canadian politics, in part because we have seen a series of minority parliaments over the past 20 years. The King–Byng affair of 1926—in which the governor general famously refused the prime minister's request to dissolve Parliament—may have occurred a long time ago, but the role of the governor general and the power of the prime minister continue to be debated and explored among scholars. Forsey, who passed away before the most recent prorogation of Parliament in December 2009, suggests that the solution is simple: the governor general ought to reject a prime minister's request to prorogue Parliament.

Below is the text of a document, typed and signed by my father, Eugene Forsey, the late Senator and constitutional expert. Dated August 15, 1984, it was among the papers I retrieved from his office and apartment after his death in 1991. It sets out very clearly the role of the Governor General "if no party gets a clear majority in the election."

The principles Eugene Forsey outlines in this paper apply directly to Mr. Harper's outrageous action last month in asking the Governor General to prorogue Parliament, and to the Governor General's action in granting his request. He has his hypothetical Governor General tell the Prime Minister:

"Prime Minister, responsible cabinet government means government by a cabinet with a majority in the House of Commons. I don't know whether you have such a majority. No one knows. The only way to find out is by summoning Parliament and letting it vote … It is not for me to

Source: rabble.ca, January 19, 2009. Reprinted by permission of Helen Forsey.

decide who shall form the Government. But it is for the House of Commons. I cannot allow you to prevent the House of Commons from performing its most essential function. To permit you to do that would be to subvert the Constitution. I cannot allow you to usurp the rights of the House of Commons."

The specific scenario outlined in my father's document differs slightly from the present case in that the 40th Parliament did meet—however briefly—after the October election, and did—however unwisely—pass the Speech from the Throne. But the principle remains the same. The Prime Minister and the Governor General prevented the House of Commons from performing its "most essential function": deciding who should govern.

It's all very well to say they only "delayed" that decision. If so, they had no business doing anything of the sort. As my father argued so compellingly in his many writings on the subject, any action taken to prevent the House of Commons from voting and possibly bringing the government down is a travesty of democracy. The classic example was the "King–Byng affair" of 1926, when Prime Minister Mackenzie King asked Lord Byng, the Governor General, to dissolve Parliament while a vote of non-confidence was pending.

In 1926, Mackenzie King wanted the critical vote "delayed" in order to hold a fresh election and use the campaign to hoodwink the electorate into putting him back into office. In 2008, Stephen Harper wanted the vote in the House "delayed" in order to keep hold of the reins of power, mount a massive propaganda war against the opposition at taxpayers' expense, and hope for political amnesia to set in over the holidays. Whether in the form of dissolution or prorogation, such "delay" constitutes a subversion of the Constitution, a usurpation of the rights of the House of Commons.

My father actually anticipated a rather similar use of prorogation to prevent Parliament from carrying out its responsibilities. And he stated what should happen in such a case:

"The only protection against such conduct is the reserve power of the Crown, the Governor General, to refuse such prorogation or dissolution, and, if necessary, to dismiss the Government which advised such prorogation or dissolution."

It doesn't get much clearer than that.

• • •

Note: *I have copied the document here as he typed it himself, with his formatting and underlining. The only change I have made is to flag with asterisks three segments that are less directly relevant to our current situation, and place them at the end. Those three segments, while not essential to the basic argument in the current context, give a taste of the rigorousness and thoroughness with which my father pursued, analyzed and documented all such matters.*

—Helen Forsey

Position of the Governor General If No Party Gets a Clear Majority in the Election

I have been asked what the Governor General does if no party gets a clear majority (more than half the seats in the House of Commons) in the general election.

I. The answer is, "Nothing."

The incumbent Prime Minister has a choice between two courses:

•

a) He can resign. The Governor General then sends for the Leader of the Opposition, and asks him to form a government.

b) He (the incumbent Prime Minister) can meet the new House of Commons. If it supports him, he remains in office. If it defeats him, he resigns, and the Governor General sends for the Leader of the Opposition.

This is what happened in Britain in 1886, 1892 and 1924.* In Canada, in 1926, Mackenzie King (who had been defeated in his own constituency, as had eight of his Ministers) had come out of the election of 1925 with 101 seats to the Conservatives' 116 (in a House of 245). He met the new House, and, till late in June, was sustained by it.

The Government in office, even if it has fewer seats than the official Opposition, is entitled to meet the new House, and let it decide whether to keep that Government in or throw it out.

There is no reason at all for any intervention by the Governor General. Indeed, any such intervention would be grossly improper.

It is not the business of the Governor General to decide who should form the Government. It is the business of the newly elected House of Commons.**

II. If no party gets a clear majority in the election, and the incumbent Government decides not to resign (as it has a perfect right to do) but attempts to carry on for an extended period without meeting the new House (financing the country's business by means of Governor General's special warrants, as provided for in the *Financial Administration Act*, Section 23), then, at some point, Her Excellency would have the right, indeed the duty, to insist that Parliament should be summoned; the right, the duty, to refuse to sign any more special warrants till it was summoned. She would have to say:

> "Prime Minister, responsible cabinet government means government by a cabinet with a majority in the House of Commons. I don't know whether you have such a majority. No one knows. The only way to find out is by summoning Parliament and letting it vote. If you will not advise me to summon Parliament forthwith, then I shall have to dismiss you and call on the Leader of the Opposition. It is not for me to decide who shall form the Government. But it is for the House of Commons. I cannot allow you to prevent the House of Commons from performing its most essential function. To permit you to do that would be to subvert the Constitution. I cannot allow you to usurp the rights of the House of Commons."

I have said, "for an extended period," and "at some point." What period? What point?

There can be no precise answer. How many grains make a heap? But if, let us say, for three months, or four, or five, or six, the newly elected Parliament had not been summoned, at some point there would most certainly be a public outcry:

> "Here! What's going on? Responsible government means government by a cabinet with a majority in the House of Commons. Has this Government, which is spending millions of public money, a majority in the House of Commons? The only way to find out is to summon Parliament and let the House vote. If this Government won't advise that action, then we'd better get a Government that will, and get it quick, and it's the duty of the Governor General to see that

we do get it. Her action is our only protection against a gross violation of the very essence of our Constitution."

I must emphasize that the courts could do absolutely nothing.

I must emphasize also that, in law, the Government could stay in office, and finance the ordinary business of government by Governor General's special warrants, for a very long time. True, it would have to summon Parliament within twelve months of the last sitting of the previous Parliament. But, having done so, it could then prorogue it, after a session of a few hours, and repeat the performance a year later. (Indeed, it could dissolve Parliament after a session of only a few hours, as Mr. King did on January 25, 1940.)

The only protection against such conduct is the reserve power of the Crown, the Governor General, to refuse such prorogation or dissolution, and, if necessary, to dismiss the Government which advised such prorogation or dissolution.***

(signed) Eugene Forsey
August 15, 1984

* In each case (Salisbury in 1886 and 1892, Baldwin in 1924. Salisbury was defeated in the newly elected House in 1886 and 1892, and Baldwin Salisbury was defeated in the newly elected House in 1924.)

** Immediately after the election of 1972, when for a few days, it looked as if the Conservatives would have 109 seats to the Liberals' 107, there was a considerable chorus of voices claiming that the Governor General should call on the Conservative leader, Mr. Stanfield, to form a Government. This would have necessitated his dismissing Mr. Trudeau. Every constitutional authority would agree that there could be circumstances which would warrant the Governor General's exercising his "reserve power" to dismiss a Government. But no constitutional authority would say this was one of such circumstances.

If, in 1972, Mr. Stanfield had in fact won 109 seats to Mr. Trudeau's 107, the Governor General would have had no warrant whatever, no right whatever, to usurp the authority of the House of Commons to decide which of the two should be Prime Minister.

If the Governor General, after the election of 1925, had dismissed Mr. King and called on Mr. Meighen to form a Government, then, when the new House met, it might have defeated Mr. Meighen, and the Governor General would have been compelled to call on Mr. King. Meanwhile, the welkin would have rung, and properly so, with denunciations of the unconstitutionality of His Excellency's intervention, his usurpation of the rights of the House of Commons.

If, after the election of 1972, the Governor General had dismissed Mr. Trudeau and called on Mr. Stanfield, exactly the same results could have followed.

*** If anyone questions the word "millions" above, in relation to Governor General's special warrants, he or she need only look up the official records for the occasions when such warrants have been used (during an election) to finance the ordinary business of government to the tune of hundreds of millions of dollars. I myself heard Mr. Michener, a few years back, tell a Senate Committee that he had once signed a single special warrant for hundreds of millions (it was either $200,000,000 or $400,000,000; I can easily, if need be, find the precise figure in the Proceedings of the Committee).

I must also emphasize that we have, in Canada, nothing like the United Kingdom's Army and Air Force Annual Act, and that, since 1896, it has never been the custom to make the voting of interim Supply by Parliament a condition precedent to a dissolution of Parliament.

The Parliament of Canada

C.E.S. Franks (1987)

14

EDITORS' INTRODUCTION

C.E.S. ("Ned") Franks is one of Canada's foremost scholars of Parliament, having taught at Queen's University for 35 years. A Fellow of the Royal Society of Canada, among other honours, he has penned hundreds of pieces both academic and non-academic, on a variety of subjects, including legislatures, public administration, aboriginal self-government, and sport.

This excerpt, which is the introduction to his 1987 book The Parliament of Canada, *explores the key functions of Parliament. It also sets out the arguments and themes of the book, in which Franks seeks to explain growing dissatisfaction with the Canadian system. His observations are still relevant decades later, and are likely to be pertinent for years to come. Perhaps most importantly, in this book Franks addresses not only potential reforms to the system, but also the barriers to reform and the problems with past attempts at reform. Franks also makes use of comparisons with Britain and the United States, in order to highlight the strengths and weaknesses of the Canadian system. An important part of his argument is the observation that the Canadian parliamentary system is performing better than many critics would suggest.*

Introduction: Parliament in an Age of Reform

Ours is an age of reform. In 1979 the privy council office, in its submission to the royal commission on financial management and accountability, claimed that "during the last twenty years ... more change has occurred in the way the government orders its machinery for getting things done, and in the variety and pervasiveness of the programs it delivers, than in any comparable period in our administrative and social history." Parliament underwent more reform in those twenty years than in any previous period, and arguably more than in its entire previous existence. And the process of reform did not stop in 1979. The study of procedure of the House of Commons by a special committee in 1982 led to many important reforms. Further changes were made in 1985–6, and the special committee that proposed those reforms claimed that its recommendations were "the most ambitious attempt to pursue

Source: Excerpted from *The Parliament of Canada* by C.E.S. Franks. Toronto: University of Toronto Press, 1987. All rights reserved. Notes omitted. Reprinted by permission.

major and comprehensive reform in the more than one hundred-year history of the Canadian House of Commons." The Senate also has been the target of innumerable studies, and Senate reform remains one of the more written-about topics in Canadian politics.

The record of the reforms of the past decades is not one of unblemished success. As we shall see, many reforms have not accomplished their stated objectives, while others have had unanticipated and undesirable consequences. Reforms that are not solidly grounded in reality are not likely to succeed. Quite the reverse, they are likely to create unreasonable and unreal expectations which cannot be met. The resulting failures lead to disillusionment, pessimism, and a loss of legitimacy for the public and participants. Constant reform can become as much a habit as immobility and can be as inappropriate a response to problems.

The purpose of this book is not to make more proposals for reform. The themes of reform have not changed. The same complaints of excessive partisanship, government domination, lack of influence of the private member and the need for improved committees and account-ability, for a greater role for parliament in policy-making, and for reform of the Senate continue despite the passage of time and the many changes that have been made. Similarly, the list of proposed reforms has changed little. Rather, the purpose of this book is to place discussion of parliament and its reform solidly in its context—the Canadian society, economy, political culture—and the stresses and demands to which Canada and its political system are subject. A secondary purpose is to examine the various proposed and implemented reforms in the context of this broader look at parliamentary government and its functioning in Canada. This examination will, I hope, illuminate some of the obstacles to reform, some of the ways in which criticisms and attempts at reform have been misguided, and some of the strengths (which are often neglected and sometimes difficult to see) as well as the weaknesses of the Canadian parliamentary system.

The Canadian parliamentary system is based on the British prototype. Like the Canadian House, the British House of Commons has changed in many ways during recent years. However, in some areas, such as strengthening committees and giving MPs more independ-ence from party discipline, the British House has been more successful. The comparison of Canadian and British experience helps illuminate some of the obstacles to reform in Canada, and the importance of many underlying factors that are usually not taken into account in proposals for reform. For these reasons I have used British experience as basis for compar-ison and as an illustration in several key places in this book.

I have used the example of the U.S. congressional-presidential system less often. This sys-tem, because of its high visibility, and the power and influence of the United States, inevitably becomes a basis for comparison in the discussion of parliamentary reform in Canada. On some issues our institutions have been caught between the constraints of the basic principles of the parliamentary-cabinet system and the beguiling image of the U.S. system, with its powerful committees and highly visible and influential senators and congressmen. But the U.S. system is very different, both in terms of representation and in terms of control and use of political power. There are no positions in the U.S. system in which power and responsibil-ity are concentrated to the extent that they are in the prime minister and cabinet in Canada. Nor is there any forum in which the U.S. president and political executive are subjected to the sort of continual gruelling scrutiny that the Canadian prime minister and cabinet receive in question period and debate. The structure of elections is different in the United States, as is the role of the party. The kinds of policies that emerge from the U.S. system are different from, and not necessarily better than, those that come from the Canadian parliamentary system. I agree with the recent observation that "the U.S. model is misleading and irrelevant for Canadians."

Four essential functions of parliament in the Canadian system are: first, to make a government, that is, to establish a legitimate government through the electoral process; second, to make a government work, that is, to give the government the authority, funds, and other resources necessary for governing the country; third, to make a government behave, that is, to be a watchdog over the government; and fourth, to make an alternative government, that is, to enable the opposition to present its case to the public and become a credible choice for replacing the party in power. Parliamentary activities of legislating and policy-making are largely aspects of the function of making a government work, and parliament's role in them is not now, nor has it ever been, the dominant one. In comparison, the U.S. Congress has virtually no role in the functions of making a government and creating an alternative government, and has a very large role indeed in the function of policy-making.

There are two further functions of parliament which are so important that they deserve to be identified in their own right, though they might also be subsumed under the general rubric of making a government work. The first of these is the function of parliament as a recruiting and training ground for political leaders; the second is the function of political communication, where the processes of parliamentary discussion, in Bagehot's terms, express the mind of the people, teach society, and inform both government and citizen of grievances and problems.

In structure this book progresses from a general look at the form and rationale of parliamentary government to an examination of how the system works in Canada. Chapter 2 introduces some conceptual issues and underpinnings. After a review of some fundamental principles, it shows that discussion of reform in Canada chooses one particular way of looking at parliament, and one which, it will be argued throughout this work, is at odds with how the system actually works and with the policy orientation of successive Canadian governments. Chapters 3 to 5 consider aspects of the central and essential basis of parliamentary government, the processes of representation in the House of Commons. The role of parties and the electorate, the members of parliament, and the parliamentary workworld are examined in turn. These three chapters place the House of Commons in the context of Canadian political culture and society, and illustrate the very real problems in the role and position of the member of parliament. Chapters 4 to 9 look at how parliament operates, and its work and activities. Procedure, debates and question period, and committees are examined successively and the constraints placed on them by the realities of representation are illustrated. Chapter 9 examines the Senate; chapters 10 and 11 examine two key functions of responsible government: policy-making (or making a government work) and accountability (or making a government behave). In these functions parliament and government interact, and committees, debates and question period, cabinet ministers, opposition leaders, and private members make their impact. Here many of the strengths, as well as the weaknesses, of the parliamentary system are identified. The focus of this book, therefore, develops progressively from questions of theory, to the basis of representative government in the electorate and nation, to parliament and its workings, to the relationship of parliament to government. The final chapter returns to the question of reform, and assesses its success in fulfilling the very demanding functions it is expected to perform.

The fundamental argument in this book is that reform of parliament is not simply a technical matter of making parliament more effective and efficient, although it is often presented in those terms. Reform is also a question of the purposes for which political power is to be used in Canada and how various interests and viewpoints succeed or fail to influence political choices and outcomes. The balance between parliament and government affects the balance between an emphasis on the particular and on the general welfare. There are many collective, public goods that can only be provided by government, and will only be adequately ensured if a strong voice defending a general public interest is heard in politics. Fundamental and often competing goals of equality, freedom, justice, private and public goods, and economic growth and stability must be balanced in the political processes. The parliamentary system, with a concentration of power in the cabinet and competition between parties in parliament, provides a powerful means of asserting a collective interest over and above the particular. The rhetoric of reform argues for a parliament-centred structure of power; the reality of Canadian politics is an executive-centred system. The differences between the two are not merely questions of who has power, but of what kinds of policies we want. The executive-centred system has enabled a collectivist voice to be expressed in Canadian politics that would be diminished if the system were to become strongly parliament-centred.

The second argument is that parliament has two modes of operation, the adversarial and the consensual. The adversarial mode is most prominent in question period and debates, the consensual in committee work. Each mode has its strengths and weaknesses. The rhetoric of parliament-centred reform argues for more emphasis on the consensual. It exaggerates the strengths of this mode, and understates its weaknesses, while at the same time it ignores the real and important virtues of the adversarial elements.

The third argument is that there is a severe problem in the role and position of the member of parliament in Canada. This problem is normally discussed in terms of the constraints of party discipline. This focus is wrong. Party discipline is a product of the root problem and is not the cause. The underlying problem is that the processes of representation, of parties, of electoral attitudes and behaviour, of demographic change and many other factors, all contribute to creating a House of Commons composed of amateur and short-term members who are asked to perform a very difficult and underappreciated job. MPs generally have little political experience before being elected to the House and stay there only a brief time. Senators, in comparison, have more previous experience and longer tenure. Parliament, and the cabinet too for that matter, can be no more effective and influential than resources of manpower permit. The constraints of manpower affect all aspects of parliamentary government: the executive, in limiting the range of choices and quality of potential cabinet ministers; the opposition, in being effective critics of government and creating a plausible alternative to the government; committees of the House, in rapid turnover and sometimes ineffective chairmanship and members; the value and interest of debates and question period; the capacity of members to understand and use procedure; and the speakership. The position of the individual member in terms of career, workworld, future expectations, and personal satisfaction is crucial to the working of the parliamentary system, and to the possibilities for reform. It is also unsatisfactory.

Fourth, there is a paradox that at the same time as the parties are so influential and powerful within parliament, they are weak outside it, both in terms of gaining consistent strong allegiances within the electorate and in terms of generating ideas and policy proposals. It is a well-known and often criticized fact that the parties are the most important control over an MP's voting behaviour within parliament. Not so much appreciated is how important party is to the entire career of an MP, from election, through every aspect of parliamentary tenure, to post-parliamentary life. At the same time, the weakness of parties outside parliament is one of the reasons why MPs are amateur and transient. It is also one of the reasons why political discussion in Canada often lacks both thoughtfulness and power.

Fifth, parliament and the parliamentary system are under severe stress because of the growth of government. Where the theory of parliamentary-cabinet government postulates two systems—a parliament and a government, with the cabinet as the link between them—there are now three systems, with the emergence of a huge and in many ways autonomous bureaucracy. Ministerial control over departments and agencies is now as much an issue as parliamentary control over ministers. The role of parliament is also changing in an increasingly complex and growing system of government and government–interest-group relations. These problems are exacerbated by the increasing importance of federal–provincial relations in Canadian politics, and the domination of these relations by executive federalism, in which political argument and negotiation is between levels of government rather than between parties in parliament.

Sixth, communication through the media plays a particularly important role in explaining and interpreting parliament in Canada because of the weaknesses of the parties as policy-creating and -discussing bodies. The media tend to be superficial and critical in their presentation of government and politics. While parliament and parliamentary committees are often insightful and thorough in their studies and discussion, little of this gets reported. There is a huge gap between serious discussion of policy within government, or even in parliament, and what gets reported. As a result, public understanding and the mobilization of consent are now big problems.

The final argument is that despite its faults the parliamentary system in Canada works better than the literature would lead one to believe. The system was transplanted to this country a century and a half ago, and since then has grown and adapted in the Canadian environment. A century and a half is not a long time in the perspective of the development of parliamentary institutions, and it is not surprising that the Canadian system still suffers from growing pains. But there is a vast difference between growing pains and the death throes some observers claim to see in looking at the Canadian parliament.

Reform has focused on the obvious and easy things to change, such as parliamentary committees, procedure, and the Senate, while many of the real problems lie elsewhere, in leadership, parties, the media, and political culture. Institutions have, to a large extent unfairly, borne the brunt of dissatisfaction, while the causes and remedies lie in less structured and less malleable parts of the political system. Perhaps, too, concentration on institutional reform has misdirected too much political discussion towards administration and away from content, away from substantial issues of policy.

It would require unrealistic expectations for the possibility of perfection in human institutions to hope that parliament would completely fulfill all the demands and hopes laid upon it. Parliament has many faults. It is also central to the use of power in society. The size and scope of modern government and government's intimate involvement in the economy, society, and the lives of individuals mean that government cannot be regarded as a neutral instrument. Government harms some, benefits others, and its powers and actions are legitimated by parliament. Citizens, fully aware of how their lives are affected by government, do not regard politics or political institutions neutrally. Violent passions, including greed, aggression, hate, anger, even idealism, are intimately and understandably involved in politics, and political institutions as well as leaders are the targets of these emotions. Many of the criticisms of parliament and the parliamentary system are legitimate, and relate to procedures and structures which can and need to be improved. Others arise from unreasonable expectations of what politics and political institutions can accomplish, or from dissatisfaction with outcomes. The Canadian parliamentary system has been created and is made to work or fail by human beings, with all their warts and imperfections. Institutions are not perfect, any more than people are.

To defend parliament this way is not to imply that the institution does not need reform, but to warn that caution is needed in advocating change. Government and government institutions are inevitably going to provoke some hostility and criticism, and often the institutions bear the brunt of unreasonable criticisms, or criticisms more properly directed elsewhere, perhaps at the individuals the electorate has chosen to run those institutions. One challenge is to identify the criticisms that are reasonable, that address problems that can be corrected, and to distinguish those problems from ones that would be more properly resolved through political action and change, or that arise from the uncertainty and difficulties that are part of the human condition. Another is simply to understand and appreciate parliament and its place in the processes of representation and governance. Parliament is not just a background for an agenda of reforms. It is a lively and vital part of the living constitution.

The Rise of Court Government in Canada

15

Donald J. Savoie (1999)

EDITORS' INTRODUCTION

Donald Savoie teaches at the Université de Moncton. Since 2004, he has held the Canada Research Chair in Public Administration and Governance, and during 2004–2005, he was director of research and senior adviser to Justice John Gomery's Commission of Inquiry into the Sponsorship Program and Advertising Activities in the Government of Canada. He has published widely on questions of public policy, regional development, public administration, and federalism.

The following piece was originally presented as the presidential address of the Canadian Political Science Association (CPSA) at the Université de Sherbrooke in June 1999. It is one among many works by Savoie that address the changes to our traditional understanding of the operation of government. The Westminster tradition points to the prime minister as primus inter pares, *or "first among equals," in relation to Cabinet. As Savoie notes, however, increasingly it seems that the prime minister is simply first, while Cabinet's role has been minimized, and he suggests that this arrangement is unlikely to change in the near future.*

In 1956, C.B. Power, a senior minister in the Mackenzie King government, observed with deep concern that the war years had strengthened the prestige and power of Cabinet at the expense of Parliament.[1] Power's concerns, as history has shown, were well founded. Ned Franks has stated that "unquestionably Parliament has become a less prominent place for major political announcements and debates, and the decline is continuing."[2] In this article, I argue that Cabinet has joined Parliament as an institution being bypassed, that it is clear that effective power no longer resides with the prime minister acting in concert with his "elected Cabinet colleagues."[3] Court government has taken root in Canada. By this I mean that in the late 1990s, effective power rests with the prime minister and a small group of carefully selected courtiers. These include key advisors in his office, two or three senior cabinet ministers (notably the minister of finance), carefully selected lobbyists, pollsters and other friends in court, and a handful of senior public servants.

Source: Excerpted from *Canadian Journal of Political Science*, vol. 32, no. 4 (December 1999). Some notes omitted. Reprinted by permission.

In the latter part of the twentieth century, Canadians witnessed major changes in the way they were governed. The changes were neither sudden nor, for the most part, introduced with much fanfare. They were gradual, which may explain why they attracted little notice. The public debate in Canada since the late 1960s focused on actual or proposed constitutional changes and not on the internal machinery of government. In any event, changes to the machinery of government rarely, if ever, enjoy much media or public profile. Yet the evolution of the machinery of government, particularly within the federal government, has had far-reaching consequences for the public service, public policy, Canadian federalism and, ultimately, for Canadians themselves.

This article challenges long-established conventions or understandings about how our government works. Gordon Robertson, former secretary to the Cabinet, stated in 1971 that in our system "ministers are responsible. It is their government."[4] The Privy Council Office, in its 1993 publication on the machinery of government, argued that "we operate under the theory of a confederal nature of decision making where power flows from ministers."[5] I maintain, to the contrary, that power no longer flows from ministers, but from the prime minister, and unevenly at that.

The above speaks to the evolution of how policies are struck and decisions are made in Ottawa. J.S. Dupré argued that "institutionalized" Cabinet replaced the "departmentalized" Cabinet in the late 1960s and early 1970s. Individual ministers and their departments lost a great deal of autonomy to full Cabinet, or to shared knowledge and collegial decision making.[6] This era did not last very long before court government started to take root. To be sure, information was gathered at the centre. However, it was gathered for the benefit of the prime minister and a handful of senior advisors operating in the Privy Council Office (PCO) and the Prime Minister's Office (PMO), not for collegial decision making. Court government took root in Ottawa under Pierre Trudeau and, if anything, it grew stronger under both Brian Mulroney and Jean Chrétien. ...

The Forces

Prime Minister Pierre Trudeau established in 1975 a central agency to deal with federal–provincial relations. Ever since, federal–provincial relations have enjoyed a strong presence at the centre of Ottawa's decision-making processes. The responsibility has always been a part of the Privy Council Office or has enjoyed separate status. It has never, however, shrunk to pre-1975 days, when it had only about eight officials.

What kind of federal–provincial issue can involve the centre of government and even the prime minister? The short answer is anything, everything, and it depends. There are no set rules. All major federal–provincial issues qualify, of course, but some minor ones can too, and on a moment's notice. The level of funding for a specific programme, or whether a federal programme applies in one region but not in Quebec (or vice versa), can appear on the prime minister's radar screen. It will make it to the radar screen if it gains visibility in the mass media.

The prime minister, it will be recalled, was firmly in charge of the failed Meech Lake and Charlottetown constitutional accords. Neither initiative was born out of Cabinet's collective decision making. Similarly, Chrétien's Verdun speech on national unity in 1995, where firm commitments were made to Quebeckers, was drafted by his advisors and others at the centre. Cabinet was not consulted on its contents, let alone asked to make a contribution.[12]

Provincial premiers have direct access to the prime minister and do not hesitate to pursue an issue with him. If the prime minister decides to support a premier, then the issue is brought to the centre of government in Ottawa for resolution. Commitments are made between two first ministers, for whatever reason, and the prime minister cannot risk the system or the process not producing the right decisions. As a result, someone at the centre will monitor the issue until it is fully implemented. When that happens, ministers and their departments inevitably lose some of their power to the prime minister and his advisors. Examples bound. In the summer of 1997, Frank McKenna, premier of New Brunswick, put two proposals to Chrétien during a golf game: that the federal government support a conference on the economic future of Atlantic Canada, and that it cost-share a new highways agreement to continue with the construction of a four-lane Trans-Canada highway. The prime minister agreed and instructed his officials to make it happen. One government agency provided some funding to support the conference, and several federal ministers, including the prime minister, attended it. Officials, meanwhile, were instructed to prepare a Treasury Board submission to secure the necessary funding for the highways construction agreement. Within a few weeks, everything had been sorted out and an announcement was made on both an Atlantic Vision conference and a new Canada/Highways agreement. The prime minister did not ask Privy Council and the Treasury Board Secretariat or relevant department officials to prepare a proposal and submit it for consideration in the government's decision-making process. His instructions were clear—make these two initiatives happen. Such incidents are not daily occurrences in Ottawa, nor do all federal–provincial projects enjoy the same status. But they are revealing of what happens when the prime minister decides to get involved.[13] …

The Centre of Government

At the end of the 1990s, the centre of government remained largely intact, despite a management de-layering exercise in the early 1990s, a massive government restructuring introduced in 1993 and the programme review exercise launched in 1994. It remained intact even though the workload of central agencies should have decreased substantially, given that the PCO has far fewer cabinet committees to service than in the 1970s and the 1980s. The overall size of the government is also smaller than it was in the late 1960s: numerous crown corporations have been sold and over 50,000 permanent positions have been eliminated from the public service. Yet in 1999, the PCO employed 372 people, compared to 209 in 1969. In 1998, the PMO employed 85 people, compared with 40 people in 1968.[33]

One might well ask, then, what do officials at the centre do? When Trudeau decided to enlarge the size and scope of the PMO in the late 1960s, his first principal secretary sought to reassure critics and cabinet ministers that the office would remain essentially a service-oriented organization. He explained that it existed to "serve the prime minister personally, that its purpose is not primarily advisory but functional and the PMO is not a mini-Cabinet; it is not directly or indirectly a decision-making body and it is not, in fact, a body at all."[34] It is, of course, not possible to distinguish between a service function and a policy advisory function in this context. Drafting a letter or preparing a speech for the prime minister can constitute policy making, and many times it does. There is also no doubt that several senior officials in the PMO do provide policy advice to the prime minister, and if some in Trudeau's early PMO denied this, advisors and assistants certainly no longer do.[35]

PMO staffers have the prime minister's ear on all issues they wish to raise, be they political, policy, administrative or the appointment of a minister or deputy minister. They can also work hand-in-hand with a minister to initiate a proposal, and the minster will feel more secure knowing that someone close to the prime minister supports the proposal. They can also, however, undercut a proposal when briefing the prime minister. In short, senior PMO staff members do not consider themselves simply a court of second opinion. They are in the thick of it, and do not hesitate to offer policy advice or to challenge a cabinet minister.

The role of the Privy Council Office has also changed. Arnold Heeney, the architect of the modern cabinet office in Ottawa, wrote after his retirement that he had successfully resisted Mackenzie King's desire to make the secretary to the cabinet "a kind of deputy minister to the Prime Minister: or "the personal staff officer to the Prime Minister."[36] It is interesting to note, however, that no secretaries to the cabinet since Gordon Robertson have described their main job as secretary to the cabinet. In 1997, the Privy Council Office produced a document on its role and structure whose very first page makes it clear that the secretary's first responsibility is to the prime minister. It states that the "Clerk of the Privy Council and Secretary to the Cabinet" has three primary responsibilities:

1. As the Prime Minister's Deputy Minister, provides advice and support to the Prime Minister on a full range of responsibilities as head of government, including management of the federation.
2. As the Secretary to the Cabinet, provides support and advice to the Ministry as a whole and oversees the provision of policy and secretariat support to Cabinet and Cabinet committee.
3. As Head of the Public Service, is responsible for the quality of expert, professional and non-partisan advice and service provided by the Public Service to the Prime Minister, the Ministry and to all Canadians.[37]

The direct link between the prime minister and the secretary to the Cabinet and the Privy Council Office is made clearer still in the Office's *missions* and *values* statement. Its *mission* is "to serve Canada and Canadians by providing the best non-partisan advice and support to the Prime Minister and Cabinet." Its *values* statement makes absolutely no mention of Cabinet. It reads: "We recognize the special need of the Prime Minister for timely advice and support. We dedicate ourselves to our work and to the effective functioning of government."[38]

When asked to sum up the work of the Privy Council Office from the perspective of a line department, a former senior line deputy minister observed, "If PCO, or for that matter other central agencies, were ever asked to ice a hockey team, they would put six goaltenders on the ice."[39] To be sure, the Privy Council Office has a well-honed capacity to stop the great majority of proposals from line departments dead in their tracks, if it has to. But the Office can also make things happen and take the lead in certain areas if the prime minister so wishes. In any event, in one area—machinery of government—only PCO has the mandate to initiate change. Still, goaltenders can be extremely useful to prime ministers in their efforts to avoid or manage errors the media might pick up and to keep things on an even keel so that the centre can concentrate on carefully selected policy objectives. …

The Working of Court Government

Canadian prime ministers have in their hands all the important levers of power. Indeed, all major national public policy roads lead one way or another to their doorstep. They are elected leader of their party by party members, they chair cabinet meetings, establish cabinet processes and procedures, set the cabinet agenda, establish the consensus for cabinet decisions; they appoint and fire ministers and deputy ministers, establish cabinet committees and decide on their membership; they exercise virtually all the powers of patronage and act as personnel manager for thousands of government and patronage jobs; they articulate the government's strategic direction as outlined in the Speech from the Throne; they dictate the pace of change and are the main salespersons promoting the achievements of their government; they have a direct hand in establishing the government's fiscal framework; they represent Canada abroad; they establish the proper mandate of individual minsters and decide all machinery of government issues and they are the final arbiter in interdepartmental conflicts. The prime minister is the only politician with a national constituency, and unlike members of parliament and even cabinet ministers, the prime minister does not need to search out publicity or national media attention, since attention is invariably focused on the person, the office and even the prime minister's residence, 24 Sussex Drive.

Each of these levers of power taken separately is a formidable instrument in its own right, but when you add them all up and place them in the hands of one individual, they constitute an unassailable advantage. Other than by defeat in a general election, prime ministers can only be stopped, or slowed, by the force of public opinion and by a cabinet or caucus revolt. Even then, public opinion may not be much of a force if the prime minister has already decided not to run again in the next general election. One only has to think of Trudeau or Mulroney's final years in office to appreciate this. As well, caucus or cabinet revolts or even threats of revolts, are historically extremely rare in Ottawa, if not so rare in other parliamentary systems, as some British and Australian prime ministers can attest.

Canadian prime ministers have enjoyed these avenues of power for some time; however, other developments have served to consolidate the position of the prime minister and the prime ministerial advisors even further. Indeed this is evident even before they and their party assume office. Transition planning, a relatively new phenomenon in Canada, has become a very important event designed to prepare a new government to assume power. Transition planning also strengthens the hand of court government, given that, by definition, it is designed to serve the prime minister.[57] It is the Privy Council Office, however, that leads the process and it is clear that "transition services [are for] the incoming prime minister."[58] Indeed, the focus of the PCO transition planning process is entirely on party leaders or would-be prime ministers. In any event, it would be difficult for it to be otherwise, since in the crucial days between the election victory and formally taking power, the only known member of the incoming Cabinet is the prime minister-designate. For other potential cabinet ministers, it is a "moment of high anxiety," waiting to see if they will be invited to sit in Cabinet and, if so, in what portfolio.[59]

The central purpose of transition planning is to equip the incoming prime minister to make a mark during the government's first few weeks in office. It is now widely recognized that these early weeks can be critical in setting the tone for how the new government will govern.[60] It is also the period when the prime minister will make important decisions on the machinery of government and decide which major policy issues the government will tackle during its mandate. These and such key decisions, such as whether to try to amend the constitution or fight the deficit, are taken or set in motion during the transition period. ...

The way to govern in Ottawa—at least since Trudeau—is for prime ministers to focus on three or four priority issues while always keeping an eye on Quebec and national unity concerns. Tom Axworthy, former principal secretary to Pierre Trudeau, in his appropriately titled article, "Of Secretaries to Princes," wrote that "only with maximum prime ministerial involvement could the host of obstacles that stand in the way of reform be overcome ... [the prime minister] must choose relatively few central themes, not only because of the time demands on the prime minister, but also because it takes a herculean effort to coordinate the government machine."[86] To perform a herculean effort, a prime minister needs carefully selected individuals in key positions to push the agenda. Cabinet, the public service as an institution, or even government departments, are not always helpful. For example, Trudeau established an ad hoc group of officials at the centre to pursue his 1983 peace initiative "largely because of the skepticism of the Department of External Affairs."[87]

The result is that important decisions are no longer made in Cabinet. They are now made in federal–provincial meetings of first ministers, during "Team Canada" trade visits abroad, where first ministers can hold informal meetings, in the Prime Minister's Office, in the Privy Council Office, in the Department of Finance, in international organizations and at international summits. There is no indication that the one person who holds all the cards, the prime minister, and the central agencies which enable effective political authority to reside at the centre, are about to change things. In Canada, there is little in the way of internal institutional checks to inhibit or thwart the prime minister. Prime ministers Margaret Thatcher of Britain and Bob Hawke of Australia were tossed out of their offices before their mandates were finished. Their own parliamentary caucuses showed them the door. This would be unthinkable in Canada. Even at the depths of Mulroney's unpopularity, there was no indication that his caucus was about to boot him out of office. In any event, in Canada the caucus holds no such power. In Britain, prime ministers must still deal with powerful ministers who have deep roots in their party and well-established party policies and positions on many issues. In Australia, the prime minister must contend with an elected and independent Senate.

In Canada, national unity concerns, the nature of federal–provincial relations and the role of the mass media tend, in a perverse fashion, to favour the centre of government in Ottawa. The prime minister's court dominates the policy agenda and permeates government decision making to such an extent that it is only willing to trust itself to overseeing the management of important issues. In a sense, the centre of government has come to fear ministerial and line department independence more than it deplores line department paralysis. As a result, court government is probably better suited to managing the political agenda than is cabinet government. The prime minister decides, at least within the federal government, who has standing at court.

But this is not without significant implications for national political institutions and, ironically, for Canadian federalism. Indeed, from a long-term perspective, court government

·may not be as effective as the courtiers might assume. The fact is that the prime minister and a handful of courtiers can hardly fully appreciate, let alone accommodate, the regional factor in policy making.

Notes

1. C.G. Power, "Career Politicians: The Changing Role of the M.P.," *Queen's Quarterly* 63 (1956), 488–89.

2. C.E.S. Franks, "The Decline of the Canadian Parliament," *The Hill Times* (Ottawa), May 25, 1998, 15.

3. See Denis Smith, "President and Parliament: The Transformation of Parliamentary Government in Canada," in Thomas A. Hockin, ed., *Apex of Power: The Prime Minister and Political Leadership in Canada* (2nd ed.; Scarborough: Prentice-Hall, 1977), 114. See also David E. Smith, "Bagehot, the Crown and the Canadian Constitution," this Journal 28 (1995), 619–35.

4. Gordon Robertson, "The Changing Role of the Privy Council Office," *Canadian Public Administration* 14 (1971), 497.

5. Canada, *Responsibility in the Constitution* (Ottawa: Privy Council Office, 1993).

6. See J.S. Dupré, "The Workability of Executive Federalism in Canada," in H. Bakvis and W. Chandler, eds., *Federalism and the Role of the State* (Toronto: University of Toronto Press, 1987), 238–39.

12. See Donald J. Savoie, *Governing from the Centre: The Concentration of Political Power in Canada* (Toronto: University of Toronto Press, 1999), 152.

13. Ibid., chap. 4.

33. See Marc Lalonde, "The Changing Role of the Prime Minister's Office," *Canadian Public Administration* 14 (1971), 532.

34. Ibid., 520.

35. See Savoie, *Governing from the Centre.*

36. A.D.P. Heeney, "Mackenzie King and the Cabinet Secretariat," *Canadian Public Administration* 10 (1967), 367.

37. Canada, *The Role and Structure of the Privy Council Office* (Ottawa: Privy Council Office, October 1997), 1.

38. See the mandate discussion in Canada, *Privy Council Office 1997-98 Estimates.*

39. Quoted in Savoie, *Governing from the Centre*, 122.

57. Jean Chrétien, *Straight from the Heart* (Toronto: Key Porter, 1985), 108.

58. Ibid., 99.

59. Donald J. Savoie, "Introduction," in *Taking Power: Managing Government Transitions* (Toronto: Institute of Public Administration of Canada, 1993), 8.

60. Ibid., 1.

86. Thomas S. Axworthy, "Of Secretaries to Princes," *Canadian Public Administration* 31 (1988), 247.

87. Ibid., 262.

16

Value Clash: Parliament and Citizens After 150 Years of Responsible Government

Lisa Young (1999)

EDITORS' INTRODUCTION

Lisa Young is a member of the Political Science Department and dean and vice-provost of graduate studies at the University of Calgary. A leading scholar of Canadian politics, she specializes in political parties, election finance, and women's participation. In addition to her numerous books, she has published articles in the Canadian Journal of Political Science, *the* Journal of Elections, Public Opinion and Parties, Party Politics, *and* Political Research Quarterly.

This piece contributes to an ongoing discussion about the health of Canada's parliamentary system and the role of political parties and legislators within that system, and discusses potential reforms. Young argues that the institutions of responsible government are less appropriate for dealing with contemporary challenges than they were when they were first introduced in the Canadian system. She suggests that Canadians are more comfortable with the idea of representative government, and tend to eschew certain features of responsible government, such as party discipline.

Canadian society has undergone remarkable change since 1848. It is not surprising that the institutions and practices that emerged to govern a scattered, predominantly agrarian population in the nineteenth century have come under unfavourable scrutiny by the 30 million mainly urban, educated, affluent Canadians adapting to post-industrial economic conditions in an interdependent global economy and society. That the basic design of Canadian parliamentary institutions has changed little during a period in which there has been profound social change and the Canadian state has expanded exponentially attests to the durability of the idea of responsible government. That said, Parliament and the practices surrounding responsible government have throughout this century come under critical scrutiny from a variety of sources.

Source: Excerpted from "Value Clash: Parliament and Citizens After 150 Years of Responsible Government" by Lisa Young. In *Taking Stock of Responsible Government in Canada*, edited by Leslie Seidle and Louis Massicotte. Ottawa: Canadian Study of Parliament Group, 1999. Some notes omitted. Reprinted by permission.

The advent of responsible government in Canada created an imperative for cohesive, disciplined political parties to support stable governments. The development of political parties in Canada has reflected that imperative. As a consequence, responsible government and political parties are inextricably linked in the Canadian experience. As Canadians have grown dissatisfied with the quality of democracy in the country, they have laid the blame squarely on Parliament and the parties that structure it. Over the past three decades, Parliament and political parties have both become increasingly unpopular, as citizens' discontent with the Canadian political process has mounted.

The institutions of responsible government are less appropriate to contemporary Canadian society than they were to the social structures of 1848. The modern Canadian electorate is increasingly unwilling to accept a politics in which important decisions are made behind closed doors and a political elite that appears unresponsive to citizens' views and dismissive of their deliberative capacities. Popular discontent in the contemporary era focuses not so much on questions of governance, but rather on issues of representativeness, responsiveness and accountability of elected representatives. In the eyes of significant segments of the electorate, responsible government stands in the way of representative government.

This paper examines two dimensions of the representational crisis of responsible government. The first dimension is the failure of the political system to adequately represent the changing interests and identities of the Canadian electorate. This is, in large part, a failure of the Canadian party system but it also stems from certain aspects of party discipline and solidarity. The second dimension of this representational crisis centres on the capacity of Parliament to reflect the views of Canadians. This populist critique lays the blame on party discipline and calls for more direct citizen involvement in political decision-making.

Three arguments will be developed in this paper. First, the representational demands that have been placed on Canadian parties have become increasingly complex; the institutions and practices surrounding responsible governments in Canada have made the task of accommodating these representational demands all the more difficult. Second, responsible government (particularly in its Canadian variant) assumes a deferential populace. Such deference is, however, in short supply in contemporary Canada. As a result, serious tensions have emerged. Third, much of the popular discontent with Parliament stems from a disjuncture that is built into the Canadian practice of responsible government. Parties are the crucial unit within the political system, yet the electoral system and the formal workings of Parliament are all predicated upon the fiction that individual Members of Parliament enjoy sufficient autonomy to represent the interests and opinions of their constituents in a meaningful way. As the electorate grows less deferential, this disjuncture becomes less tenable. Although there are no easy solutions to remedy Canadians' discontent with their governing institutions, any proposed remedies must take into account and try to lessen this disjuncture between formal arrangements and political realities.

Parties and Representation

Disciplined, cohesive political parties are necessary to provide stable governance within the context of responsible government. For Canadian parties, however, the requirements of responsible government were complicated by the challenging task of nurturing and maintaining a country with Canada's complex cleavages. The Liberal and Conservative parties' response to this set of challenges was to constitute themselves as highly disciplined electoral machines that contested elections while seldom articulating firm or divisive policy stances. Above all else, Canadian parties have tried to accommodate all of the salient cleavages within the country. As the cleavage structure has become more complex, however, this task has proven increasingly difficult.

In the period just after Confederation, the country's predominant social cleavage was religious and linguistic, dividing Protestant English speakers from Catholic francophones. As parties emerged after Confederation, this potentially destructive cleavage was accommodated by including French Catholics and English Protestants in the governing Conservative coalition. To cement the coalition, the government relied heavily on patronage appointments which rewarded loyal party workers in both communities.[2] This established Canada's unusual pattern in which parties try to take both sides of a fundamental cleavage, rather than taking opposing sides.[3]

As the country expanded westward, regional cleavages were added to the existing religious and ethnic cleavages. The increasing salience of region was signalled by the rise of several Western-based protest parties: the agrarian populist Progressive party in the 1920s, and the socialist Commonwealth Co-operative Federation (CCF) and the conservative populist Social Credit party in the 1930s. For the most part, regional cleavages were accommodated within the governing party—this time the Liberals under Mackenzie King. One emerging cleavage that was not accommodated within the governing party during this period, however, was that of class. The CCF articulated a socialist critique of Canadian capitalism and sought to represent the emerging urban working class, but it had difficulty growing beyond its Western roots. Although the development came significantly later than in most West European democracies, Canadian workers gained a national political voice when the New Democratic Party was formed through a partnership between the CCF and the trade union movement in 1961. To date, the party has been unable to win substantial support in Quebec or even the support of the majority of unionized workers.

The major parties have not been as effective in accommodating regional cleavages as they have in accommodating linguistic differences, as is illustrated by the emergence of several Western-based protest parties in the past century. The Progressives, Social Credit, the CCF and, most recently, Reform can all be understood at least partially as regional protest parties, and the target of their protest was the party system that appeared to leave Western interests unrepresented. Western alienation mounted significantly in the late 1970s and early 1980s as the Trudeau government, with virtually no representation from Western Canada, pursued centralizing policies that were deeply unpopular in Western Canada. It is noteworthy that this wave of alienation did not result immediately in the formation of a new Western protest party, but rather a shift in focus toward reforming the Senate. The idea of a "Triple-E" Senate (elected, effective, and equal in its provincial representation) gained significant currency and is still being actively pursued by the government of Alberta, among others.[4] The Mulroney government included significant representation from Western Canada, but not long after the government took office many Westerners perceived the party to be sacrificing Western interests in order to appease Quebec. This prompted the formation of the Reform party, and alienated Westerners once again pursued the strategy of having their own party to represent them in Ottawa. In the aftermath of the failed constitutional rounds of the late 1980s and early 1990s, a substantial number of Quebecers adopted a similar strategy and supported the fledgling Bloc Québécois. In the 1993 election, these two regionally based parties supplanted the PCs and the NDP in the House of Commons.

Regional alienation has been a persistent source of discontent with the mainstream Canadian parties and Parliament, but alienated voters have had the opportunity to express their alienation and have it represented through the mechanism of regional parties. The same is not true for groups of Canadians who perceived themselves to be unrepresented in Parliament, but who lacked a territorial base which would allow them to register protest in an analogous manner. Until the 1970s, the two mainstream Canadian political parties were reasonably diverse in terms of their regional and linguistic composition, but homogeneous in terms of ethnicity and gender. Ethnic minorities were seldom represented within the parties and women, although active in party affairs, were relegated to an auxiliary role. As the Canadian population has become more ethnically diverse, and as women have come to insist on a voice in the government of the country, political parties—like many other organizations and institutions—have had to come to terms with a new politics of inclusion. As David Elkins has argued, the tradition of brokerage politics in Canada meant that the parties were inclined to accept the claims of newly mobilized groups for inclusion: "Without any intention to do so, traditional brokerage politics in Canada … laid the foundation for the successful demands of new groups seeking representation. People who are not 'insiders' in the newly active groups believe that certain of those groups must be represented by their own 'insiders.'"[5] As a result, an additional dimension of societal cleavage was added to the parties' representational task. In response to this, the parties engaged in a politics of limited inclusion that illustrated their constrained capacity to respond to new representational demands.

In the period after the Second World War, ongoing immigration from Britain was supplemented and eventually surpassed by significant waves of immigration from elsewhere in Europe and, later, non-European countries. All three parties responded to these waves of immigration through a uniform support for the principle of multiculturalism and efforts to win the loyalty of various ethnic groups.[6] None of the parties was entirely confident in its approach to new Canadians. Organizers charged with drumming up the "ethnic vote" found themselves repeatedly chiding others in the party not to condescend to ethnic voters, not to ignore ethnic groups until election time rolled around, and not to assume that ethnic voters could be won over en masse by appealing to their clergy or newspaper editors.

While the Conservatives were consistently able to win the support of immigrants from Northern Europe who settled in the West, and even enjoyed some short-lived success in ethnic Toronto, the Liberal party emerged as the party of recent immigrants. In government, the Liberals maintained a number of programs that helped them maintain their support from ethnic communities. The Liberal's "multicultural recruitment manual" noted that "the party is often seen to be remote, unapproachable and closed to new members. Instead it is necessary to get across the message of an active vigorous and open party."[7] The manual advocated ongoing involvement with ethnic groups, attendance at cultural events, and sponsorship of citizenship programs for recent immigrants. According to the manual, this latter initiative "serves the double purpose of encouraging Canadian citizenship and bringing potential members of the Liberal party into contact with established associations. … A meeting or reception should be held with these new citizens shortly after having received their citizenship. From there on they should be contacted on a regular basis and encouraged to become active in their associations."[8] The Liberals' efforts, although revealing a regrettable inability to distinguish party and state, were apparently effective in winning the loyalty of most new Canadian groups. However, as Stasiulis and Abu-Laban have noted, the party garnered this vote "without reflecting ethnic diversity internally, especially within the upper levels of their own organization."[9] The same criticism could be levied against the Conservatives, who pursued and to some degree won the urban ethnic vote in the 1984 election without substantially changing the ethnic composition of the party elite.

Through the 1960s and 1970s, the three major parties competed for the ethnic vote, but the communities whose votes they sought were relatively unassertive in their relations with parties. By the late 1980s, this dynamic changed, as members of the ethnic communities whose support was sought started to demand inclusion in the political elite. Prior to the 1988 election, for instance, four Toronto Liberals of Italian, Portuguese and Sikh backgrounds formed a group determined to push for a more prominent role for Canadians of non-Charter group origin. Two of the four won Liberal nominations in 1988 in hard-fought battles. They were joined by several other ethnic Liberal candidates in the Toronto area and in other major cities. The Conservatives and NDP also nominated several ethnic candidates in major urban centres.[10]

As ethnic groups became more assertive and demanded entry into the partisan political arena, the major parties took steps to practise a "politics of limited inclusion."[11] The NDP adopted an affirmative action program for candidates intended to increase the number of visible minority, Aboriginal and female candidates, and has guaranteed representation for visible minorities and Aboriginals on its federal council. The Liberals and Conservatives have both tried to recruit ethnic candidates, while coping with the perceived threat to the party's cohesion posed by potential candidates able to draw on tight-knit networks of support from their communities. In major centres such as Toronto or Vancouver, it is not uncommon for candidates from two different ethnic groups, or even from the same group, to contest nominations. The tendency for more recent immigrants to settle in certain neighbourhoods has facilitated their representation as it corresponds with the territorial basis of the electoral system.

A second significant development beginning in the late 1960s was the political mobilization of women. Prior to the emergence of the feminist movement, women's participation in Canadian party politics tended to take the form of political "housekeeping," channeled for the most part into ladies' auxiliaries which provided important support to party organizations, but which had little policy or other influence. The NDP responded to the emergence of the women's movement most rapidly, due in large part to a significant feminist mobilization within the party in the early 1970s. Subsequently, women have been an important and influential internal constituency within the party managing, among other things, to elect the first female leader of a major federal party in 1989. The Liberals responded somewhat more slowly and less enthusiastically, but nonetheless took steps to try to appeal to what appeared to be an emerging women's vote. In government, the Liberals provided considerable funding to feminist organizations, and perceived these groups as supporters of the government until 1980, when feminist organizations refused to lend their support to the government's proposed *Charter of Rights and Freedoms* unless it included more comprehensive equality rights for women. In the early 1990s, the party undertook a concerted effort to increase the number of women in its caucus. The Progressive Conservatives were far slower to respond to the mobilization of feminism. In 1981, humbled by losing office after only nine months in government, the party was trying to moderate its image, hoping to appeal to younger urban voters by jettisoning its image as a party dominated by elderly rural activists. As part of this effort, the PC Women's Bureau organized PC women's caucuses in major Canadian cities that emphasized networking and "access to power" for women. In 1983, newly-elected party leader Brian Mulroney appointed the first woman to serve as national director of the party, and once in government he appointed a woman to co-ordinate government appointments. This latter position was part of a broader strategy to pursue something approaching gender parity in government appointments, in essence returning to the traditional use of patronage for mediating cleavages in the Canadian electorate.[12]

Although they varied in their methods and enthusiasm for embracing some version of liberal feminism, all three parties adopted feminist policy stances of some sort and also undertook measures to try to involve women in partisan elites during the third party system. This was remarkably similar to their response to greater ethnic diversity. In essence, all three parties responded to the emergence of newly salient cleavages in precisely the way one would expect of brokerage parties: they tried to appeal to new groups of voters without alienating any traditional supporters of the party. The result was that the groups calling for representation were dissatisfied while, at the same time, others within and outside the parties were alienated by the parties' efforts to include this newly mobilized group.

The inclusion of women and, to a lesser extent, ethnic minorities into the partisan political arena proved difficult in part because the cleavages they represent, unlike linguistic and regional cleavages, are not territorially based. As it has emerged in Canada, responsible government has not adapted well to the representation of political identities that lack a territorial basis. This is related both to the first past the post electoral system and to the partisanship that structures the House of Commons. The best example for illustrating the dilemmas that emerge in this regard is the case of women. Unlike many of the minority groups that can and do congregate in neighbourhoods, women are more or less evenly spread across the country and tend not to congregate in geographic areas. As such, women as a political interest are geographically diffuse. While it may be incumbent upon the MP from a riding where there is a large immigrant population or gay community to take a particular interest in issues of concern to those groups, no MP faces an analogous pressure from women. Moreover, because of the diversity among women in terms of political ideology, ethnicity, geography and class, no party has emerged as the voice of women in Parliament. ...

Institutional Reform

Although the source of Canadians' dissatisfaction with Parliament and responsible government does not lie entirely with the institutions themselves, some institutional reforms warrant serious consideration. There is a clear disjuncture between the formal arrangements employed in Canadian elections, in which voters cast a ballot for an individual MP, not a party, and the organization of Parliament, in which tightly disciplined parties structure the parliamentary process. Institutional reforms designed to lessen this disjuncture may lessen the scope of citizen discontent.

Within Parliament, reforms that create a more meaningful role for individual Members of Parliament warrant serious consideration. Replicating the British practice of loosening the confidence convention so that strict party discipline is required only on the most significant pieces of legislation would be a positive move. It would adapt the practice of responsible government as it has evolved in Canada to allow for some independence of backbench MPs on policy issues of importance to their constituents. Once in place, such a practice is likely to loosen the cultural constraints of party discipline, as backbenchers become accustomed to a greater degree of independence. Such a reform would also require the governing party to consult more extensively with its backbench to ensure that legislation had the requisite support. This could, in time, increase the responsiveness of government to citizens' views. By increasing the autonomy of individual Members of Parliament, the capacity of these individuals to represent—and to be seen to be representing—the interests of their constituents or of non-territorially organized groups like women also increases. In this sense, such a reform would respond to the perceived representational deficit in the contemporary system.

The disjuncture between the electoral and parliamentary systems could be substantially resolved by adopting a different electoral system. The first-past-the-post system employed in Canada barely recognizes the existence of political parties. Citizens vote not for a political party, but for an individual candidate who, if elected, is to represent the view of all her or his constituents in Ottawa. Some form of proportional representation (PR) or hybrid of PR and single member plurality system would lessen this disjuncture. Voters would be able to cast a ballot not for an individual, but for a party, or for both an individual and a party. This would make a situation like the current parliament—a Liberal majority government elected with the support of only 38 per cent of voters—impossible. It would also lessen the highly regionalized results produced by the current system. Kent Weaver has demonstrated that even a small number of seats elected through a PR top-up system designed to ensure some measure of proportionality between the votes received and seats won would substantially decrease the regionalized character of electoral outcomes that have tended to leave some regions unrepresented in governing parties.[52] Such a reform is also likely to lend itself to the election of greater numbers of women and minority candidates.[53] In short, electoral reform would alleviate representative deficits for both territorially-based and non-territorial groups.

Conclusion

When first granted, responsible government represented a victory for the advocates of democracy who had campaigned for it. In contrast to the previous practice of representative government, responsible government was without question more democratic, as it gave the electorate's representatives genuine authority. Responsible government and the practices that emerged around it in Canada were appropriate to the social conditions and political culture of the day. Canadian society was predominantly rural, localist and hierarchically organized. Such conditions favoured a form of democracy in which local notables were sent to Parliament to represent the interests of a relatively homogenous and generally deferential community. In the contemporary era, however, citizens' expectations and demands for representation are difficult to accommodate within the confines of responsible government.

Before a coherent discussion of prescriptive reforms can begin, it is first necessary to develop a clearer understanding of the sources of citizen discontent and the growing populism that accompanies it. Further research is needed to determine to what extent this discontent is unique to Canada and related to institutional design. At present, it is difficult to determine whether the Canadians who say that they want to participate directly in policy decisions would, in fact, be willing to assume the demands of citizenship in such a regime. The research from American states which use ballot initiatives should serve a cautionary tale in this regard.

That said, it is clear that the disjuncture between the formal electoral arrangements in which voters cast a ballot for an MP, not a party, yet parties form the only meaningful structures within Parliament, must be lessened. Certain reforms would move in this direction. First, replicating the British practice of loosening party discipline on some votes would be a step in the right direction. Second, adopting a different type of electoral system would do a great deal to resolve this disjuncture.

Notes

2. Gordon Stewart, *The Origins of Canadian Politics: A Comparative Approach* (Vancouver: University of British Columbia Press, 1986), 90.

3. David Elkins, "Parties as National Institutions: A Comparative Study," in *Representation, Integration and Political Parties in Canada*, ed. Herman Bakvis (Toronto: Dundurn/Royal Commission on Electoral Reform and Party Financing (RCERPF), 1991), 12–13.

4. On October 19, 1998, the Alberta government held an election for "Senators in waiting" in the hope that this would force the federal government to implement Senate reform through the back door by appointing "elected" Senators.

5. Elkins, "Parties," 31.

6. The roots of the policy of multiculturalism are in the Report of the Royal Commission on Bilingualism and Biculturalism. In 1971, the Trudeau government adopted a policy of official multiculturalism that essentially remains intact today.

7. Liberal Party of Canada, "Multicultural Recruitment Manual," National Archives of Canada, MG 28 IV 2 vol. 646 File: Multiculturalism (1), circa 1982.

8. Ibid.

9. Daiva Stasiulis and Yasmeen Abu-Laban, "Ethnic Activism and the Politics of Limited Inclusion in Canada," in *Political Science: An Introduction to the Discipline*, ed. Alain Gagnon and James Bickerton, 1st ed. (Peterborough: Broadview Press, 1992), 583.

10. For a more detailed discussion of this, see Stasiulis and Abu-Laban, "Ethnic Activism."

11. The term is Stasiulis and Abu-Laban's.

12. See Lisa Young, *Feminists and Party Politics* (Vancouver: University of British Columbia Press, 2000).

52. Kent Weaver, "Improving Representation in the Canadian House of Commons," *Canadian Journal of Political Science* 30 (3): 473–512.

53. See Lisa Young, "Electoral Systems and Representative Legislatures," *Canadian Parliamentary Review* 21 (3): 12–14.

17 Referendum on the Future of the Senate: A Round Table

Senators Hugh Segal, Bert Brown, Lowell Murray, and Sharon Carstairs (2007)

EDITORS' INTRODUCTION

Hugh Segal was a senator for nine years, and is now the Master of Massey College at the University of Toronto. A former chief of staff to Brian Mulroney, and former president of the Institute for Research on Public Policy (IRPP), Segal was also a faculty member in the School of Policy Studies at Queen's University. He is a Member of the Order of Canada, and has published widely on a number of issues related to Canadian politics and public policy, including the Senate, Canada's welfare system, and foreign policy.

Bert Brown is a former senator from Alberta, and for years has been actively involved in advocating for a Triple-E Senate ("equal, elected, and effective"). He is the founder and chair of the Canadian Committee for a Triple-E Senate, and was elected to senate in Alberta before being appointed to the Senate of Canada in 2007 by Stephen Harper.

Lowell Murray was an Ontario senator until 2011. Appointed by Joe Clark, he later actively opposed the merger between the Progressive Conservative Party and the Canadian Alliance, and insisted on continuing to sit in the Senate as a Progressive Conservative.

Sharon Carstairs was a Liberal senator until 2011. She was appointed by Jean Chrétien and served as Leader of the Government in the Senate from 2001 to 2003. Active in politics in Western Canada for years, she was the first woman president of the Liberal Party in Alberta, the first woman leader of a major political party in Manitoba, and the first woman in Canada to hold the post of elected Leader of the Official Opposition (in Manitoba). She has published widely on the topic of women in politics in Canada.

In October 2007, a motion was introduced in the Senate, calling for a national referendum to ask Canadians whether the "red chamber" should be abolished. Senators made speeches for and against the motion, excerpts of which appear here. As it turned out, no referendum was held, although some people today continue to advocate for one, and many others support reforming the Senate in some manner.

Source: *Canadian Parliamentary Review*, vol. 31, no. 1 (Spring 2008). Reprinted by permission.

Senator Hugh Segal (October 30, 2007): Let me offer one quotation from Senator Joyal's *Protecting Canadian Democracy: The Senate You Never Knew*, in support of the proposition:

> The Senate is likely the least admired and least well known of our national political institutions. Its work attracts neither the interest of the media, the respect of elected politicians, the sympathy of the public, nor even the curiosity of academia. How paradoxical that very few Canadians have an understanding of the history, role, and operations of the Senate, and yet everyone seems to have an opinion on the institution.

I agree with my friend's comments regarding the outside view of the Senate, and I believe that this motion, if successful, will go a long way in not only educating the public about our role here but also towards legitimizing an institution that has often come under attack without any clear understanding of its function or merits.

Yes, it could also result in its abolition but, after years of "negotiating," "attempts at reforming" and seemingly endless "discussions," perhaps the time has come to allow the electorate to weigh in and settle the question politicians of all affiliations have been unable to answer since Confederation itself.

In a democracy, specifically in the key working elements of its responsible government, respect must be tied in some way to legitimacy. While questioning "legitimacy" of long established democratic institutions is usually the tactic of those seeking a more radical reform, the passage of time does not, in and of itself, confer de facto legitimacy, and seems a particularly undemocratic way of moving forward. The purpose of my motion regarding a referendum question put to the Canadian people is to focus squarely on the legitimacy issue.

There are many differences between Canada, Iraq and Afghanistan, too numerous to mention. One difference, however, relating to the basic law under which each seeks to govern itself is that those who negotiated the content of the respective basic laws in Iraq and Afghanistan over the last decade saw those constitutions put to the test in a popular referendum in which there was a high voter turnout. A referendum never happened in the Canada of the 1860s, which is not surprising. There was no universal suffrage at that time. There was not even a secret ballot. It is not surprising it did not happen then.

The *British North America Act* was never sanctioned by a popular referendum in which Canadians had the chance to legitimize the work of the Fathers of Confederation.

Today, after 39 federal elections and approximately 300 provincial and territorial elections since 1867, surely we can say that the elected assemblies that make our laws have been legitimized by millions of voters on numerous occasions. What is more, Canadians voted against constitutional change in the 1992 referendum on the Charlottetown Accord. We can therefore conclude that there has been some public input, which strengthens the legitimacy argument. But it would be going too far to include the unelected Senate in this circle of legitimacy.

Except in Alberta, which elected Stan Waters in the 1980s and Senator Bert Brown, Canadians have never voted in any way to legitimize an unelected upper house, which has potentially huge legislative powers.

The present government of Canada deserves some credit for attempting to address this legitimacy question through proposals in the House to consult the public on Senate vacancies before appointments are made, and to shorten terms, an effort launched in this place in a previous session. In this regard, Prime Minister Harper follows in a long and noble line of federal leaders who have attempted Senate reform. Since 1867, Liberals and Conservatives, there have been 17 proposals at Senate reform and not one has succeeded.

Surely, in a democracy, the more fundamental question is: Should the Senate exist at all? Is a second chamber, as presently constructed, necessary for the democratic governance of a modern Canada? Many democracies operate with only one chamber. While existing governments, legislators, public servants and constitutional scholars should have a say, as should every member of this place, is it not only appropriate that those people are consulted? Surely the people in an open and single question referendum also have the right to participate in this decision.

To make fundamental changes to our system of government, the Crown, Parliament, or the regular election cycle, the current amendment formula requires the consent of all provincial legislatures and the Parliament of Canada. It must be unanimous. Such a referendum would allow us to avoid another cycle of reform contortions until we knew whether Canadians actually wanted the Senate itself to continue in any way.

In the design of any referendum on the abolition or maintenance of the Senate, it would be of immense value if Ottawa and the provinces would simply agree that Ottawa would sign onto an amendment if 50-per-cent-plus-one majority of Canadians voted for abolition. Any premier would sign on for an amendment if 50-per-cent-plus-one majority of the people in his or her province voted for abolition as well.

The late-night, never-ending First Ministers' conferences where deals might be struck or broken, and constitutional amendments might be lost or won, would be unnecessary. Such a 50-per-cent-plus-one agreement would simply be a formula that embraces the rather dramatic notion that governments work for the people, even on issues of constitutional legitimacy, or perhaps, especially on these issues, as opposed to the other way around.

As a member of the Senate, I share the view of many that the Senate, as an institution, and many who have served within it, have done outstanding work for their country. Surely, without the legitimacy of a public and democratic expression relative to the Senate's existence itself, this work is, while interesting and even compelling, a little bit beside the point. There are wonderful, hard-working economists and social policy advisers who laboured for years in the Kremlin. Mother Russia was their only concern. They did good work, they were elected by no one in particular and they had no democratic legitimacy. Doing good work does not constitute, de facto, democratic legitimacy.

The Senate's existence via constitutional agreement in the 1860s has forced prime ministers to fill it. Many of those people who have been appointed from partisan or other careers have served with distinction, but those historical facts do not equal legitimacy. They reflect constitutional reality not particularly impacted by any legitimacy except the passage of time, surely a weak proxy for democratic legitimacy conveyed by the people through exercising of their democratic franchise.

Many of those who insist that we still need a Senate—and I am one of them—and even those who claim that an appointed Senate is better than an elected Senate, say that senators have as much legitimacy as judges, who are also appointed by the duly elected government. I submit that there is a huge difference. Judges are appointed to interpret the laws on a case-by-case basis. Senators get to change the law, make law and refine or reject laws sent to it by an elected House of Commons.

The illegitimacy of that status quo emerges from two realities, of which the government to date has tried to address only one. Canadians have no say in who sits in the Senate, and Canadians have never had a say as to whether we need a Senate.

In the most recent U.K. government proposal on reform of the Lords, a review of second chambers across the democratic world concluded that Canada's Senate was the most theoretically powerful of any in the entire world. Surely, it is the spirit of constitutional coherence and stability that we face the issue of legitimacy straight up. Canadians surely have the right to answer a simple question directly. A decent referendum period with a clear question and ample time for information, discussion and debate would facilitate such a response.

We do not need to recreate the wheel. In 1992, the Conservative government presented to Parliament, and Parliament passed, the *Referendum Act*, which authorizes the Governor-in-Council, in the public interest, to obtain by means of a referendum the opinion of electors on any question relating to the Constitution of Canada. With little fuss, it could be presented to Parliament by the present administration facilitating a referendum on the abolition of the Senate. Perhaps, circumstances willing, this work can be done before the next election.

A simple question—do you want to maintain or abolish Canada's second chamber of Parliament—could be put. The abolitionists can make their case over a period of some weeks. Those in favour of a second chamber, of which I would be one, reformed or otherwise, could make their case as well. There would be regional, demographic and other subsections to the debate, but we would have faced, as a country, the essence of the legitimacy question. For those colleagues across the way and on my own side who have talked about the wording of the question, let us follow the mechanics. If this motion were to pass, and the request went to the Governor-in-Council, the government would have decide to bring in the referendum legislation in which, if they used the 1992 model, Parliament would decide on the wording of the question. Thus, for colleagues on both sides who might be concerned about the wording of the question—some have asked me why the question should not be abolition or reform—there would be ample time for that debate.

If Canadians voted to abolish in sufficient number and with a majority, nationally and in each province, then our leaders would have clear direction to act. If they did not vote thus, then the Senate would have the basic legitimacy required to justify the effort. If the option of abolition were presented, and Canadians were to choose not to take it in sufficient number in a way that obviates and makes easy the amendment, then that would constitute a public consultation and the public would have spoken on the Senate of Canada.

Serving senators who support this proposal, and admittedly there might not be many, might be asked: How can you serve in a Senate that you feel is illegitimate? I do not feel that the Senate is illegitimate but we have a chance to seek legitimacy and have the question put to the public of Canada in an open referendum. As to why those of us who might favour that referendum are still enthusiastic about serving in this place, I, and others, would say: When asked by a prime minister, duly elected under our system to take on a task for the country, one would have to be pretty self-important to say, no. When one takes an oath of service and signs it, one has a duty to serve the institution as it exists to one's best ability.

Surely, that obligation does not imply disengagement from the democratic imperative of legitimacy—and democratic participation in the architecture of legitimacy. The motion I propose will afford parliamentarians a broad opportunity to reflect on the issue and contribute their own perspectives. Should a similar motion be introduced in the House, the debate would be enjoined more broadly still. While I would vote against abolition for reasons that relate to both the need for a chamber that reflects regional and provincial interest and some careful assessment of quickly and often badly drafted federal laws too often passed by the House too quickly, my vote is but one amongst our fellow citizens. My opposition to abolition does not weaken in any way my deeply held belief that Canadians should decide something they have never been allowed to decide before.

One of the core premises of the development of responsible government in Canada is the process of evolution. To be relevant and engaged, all aspects of our democratic institutions must be open to reflection, public scrutiny and public sanction. The Canadian Senate, venerable, thoughtful, constructive and often nonpartisan as it may be, cannot be outside the circle of democratic responsibility.

Senator Bert Brown (November 13, 2007): I will speak against this motion to abolish the Senate if a majority of Canadians, in a referendum, wish to do so.

I am not opposed because it took 24 years of work to get here and my tenure in this chamber has so far been less than two weeks. Rather my opposition takes two forms. The last time I witnessed a referendum in Canada, it was not a binding referendum. It is likely not possible for a government to enact a binding referendum; it would be like asking victims to supply the rope for their own hanging.

Over the past generation, many polls have been conducted on whether Canadians want their senators elected. The first polls gave a simple majority to the "yes" side. Only months ago, the polls were 79 per cent for the "yes" side. Brad Wall brought the province of Saskatchewan to the "yes" side the morning of November 8 with his recommendation to elect senators to future vacancies. That is my first point against the motion.

Second, the most compelling reason for this chamber to continue to exist even in its present state is the real fear of future prime ministers with a real majority in the House of Commons: There are no constitutional limitations on the powers of a prime minister with a majority in that other place. While Canadians appear to be increasingly pleased with the current government and its prime minister, Senate reform, when it takes place, is for the next century or two. It is not for the tenure of any current government.

Since World War II, we have witnessed governments of numerous parties that were a direct cause of a debt of $680 billion accumulated over a generation. This country will have paid $2.78 trillion by the time that debt is retired. That is after 25 years at 5 per cent interest and payments of $5 billion over those years.

At the end of the debt and deficit increases in 1993, this country was less than 18 months from having the International Monetary Fund tell us what we could and could not do with our federal taxes.

I believe that the function a future senator can play is as an effective counterbalance to the other place. A counterbalance with a legitimate vote to protect our country against future internal threats more than justifies the Senate's cost. For that reason I oppose the abolition of this chamber by referendum or any other means.

I want to speak about loyalty and party discipline. I was honoured to place a wreath at the regimental war museum in Calgary November 11 on behalf of the Government of Canada. I believe the cause of World War II to be blind loyalty to, first, the National Socialist German

Workers' Party, also known as the Nazi Party of Germany; second, the same blind loyalty to the National Fascist Party of Italy; and, finally, a Japanese emperor who believed he was a god. His subjects believed him and gave [him] their blind loyalty and trust. As a result of those blind loyalties to parties and to a religion, we, the human race, killed 50 million people.

In 1993, I was commissioned by the Canada West Foundation to interview former and current MLAs across Canada and former and current MPs, and my conclusions were published in the 1993-94 summer edition of the *Canadian Parliamentary Review*. Since then, I have not changed my belief that unquestioning blind loyalty to any philosophy or leader is the most dangerous thing that can happen in a democracy.

I believe that this chamber's best service to this country will occur when elected senators truly represent the wishes of the people of their home provinces, not the political philosophy of past prime ministers. Blind, unquestioning allegiance in politics or religion may again move us to problems within Canada and abroad.

Senator Lowell Murray (November 28, 2007): If this motion were passed, it would constitute advice to the government; however, as we all know, it would not be binding on the government. Even if the government were to take the advice of the Senate and hold the referendum on abolition, the referendum result would be non-binding. The government would still have to institute the process of constitutional amendment with the provinces.

The following questions then arise: Why bother with the motion? Why support Senator Segal's motion? First, abolition is clearly one of the options being considered by the government. The Leader of the Government in the House of Commons and Minister for Democratic Reform made that clear several times in his speech in the House of Commons at second reading of Bill C-19 on November 16, 2007.

Second, two Senate reform proposals sponsored by the government—Bill C-19, on term limits; and Bill C-20, on elections—are going nowhere, and the government knows they are going nowhere. Quite apart from the hurdle of getting those two bills through two Houses of Parliament in which the government is in a minority position, at least three provinces have made their view abundantly clear that one or the other or both of those bills are ultra vires the competence of the federal Parliament acting alone.

Premier Charest and Premier McGuinty have reiterated their position on that point, and they have served notice that they would challenge in court if Parliament were to pass those bills. What does that mean? In the courts of at least three provinces that I am aware of, New Brunswick, Quebec and Ontario, the challenges would wend their ways and ultimately come to the Supreme Court of Canada for final adjudication. If the government were serious about proceeding with government reform at this time, they could save a great deal of time, money and trouble by referring Bill C-19 and Bill C-20 to the Supreme Court of Canada now, which they should do.

The government could follow an alternative, with a constitutional amendment in mind: The government could draft a succinct model of Senate reform and ask Canadians, through a referendum, to pronounce on it. If the government's succinct model of Senate reform were to receive the support of enough voters in enough provinces, the Prime Minister could walk into a meeting of first ministers with a very strong hand indeed.

In my opinion, coming up with a succinct model of Senate reform would not be as complicated as it might appear to be on the surface. The government has already crunched two of the issues: First, they want an eight-year term for future senators, which they would probably make renewable in the case of an elected Senate; and second, it is fair to say that, notwithstanding this consultative election contained in Bill C-20, Mr. Harper's strong preference would be for direct election of senators. Those two issues have been crunched as far as the government is concerned, and its position is clear.

The first of two other elements that they would have to come up with is representation, for which there is not an infinity of options before the government. They could come up with some reasonable balance of regional or provincial representation in the Senate. The second element is the question of powers. There again, the government would not need to draft a lengthy blueprint of powers. The main issue the government would have to address in the form of a referendum question is the relationship of the Senate to the House of Commons and whether the Senate would have an absolute veto or a suspensive veto. The main issue is whether the House of Commons would have primacy at the end of the day. That would lend itself to a succinct question on a referendum balance.

The government is doing none of those things. I am not embarrassed at all to express the view that the federal government is ragging the puck on Senate reform. They are going on ad infinitum and, instead of taking a direct approach, they are taking an indirect, circuitous and devious approach that will end at a dead end, which they well know.

One option would be for one of the provinces to concentrate our minds by passing a proposed constitutional amendment for abolition and then start the clock ticking. Senator Segal's proposed referendum on abolition might not be anyone's first choice, but it would move us off dead centre and in a straight line. As well, it would get the attention of the country on the issue in a concrete way.

With all the loose talk that has been heard on Senate reform and the Senate, it is time to focus on first principles. We need the benefit of a thorough discussion on whether Canada wants a unicameral or bicameral Parliament. Does Canada need a Senate? Does Canada need any kind of Senate? Those who vote for abolition perhaps will have been persuaded by one or more of the following arguments: First, many other democratic countries have unicameral Parliaments. I know that most federations have bicameral Parliaments, but in none of those federations, certainly not in the United States, Australia or Germany, does the constituent parts—the provinces or states—have the constitutional and fiscal powers that our provinces have. A strong argument can be made that those states need an upper house at the centre to represent their interests and that ours do not need that.

Second, experience, sadly including fairly recent experience, shows that party solidarity almost always trumps the regional role in respect of legislative votes in this place.

Third, many of our provinces had bicameral legislatures and all of them have abolished their upper houses. In many of those provinces, in particular the bigger ones, there are still regional and other minority tensions. However, no one suggests that any of those provinces should recreate their upper houses as a way of reconciling or resolving those tensions.

Fourth, Canadians are over-governed already. We could save some money by doing away with the Senate.

Fifth, the many non-governmental organizations, policy advocacy groups, cultural and linguistic organizations, professional and occupational groups, and think tanks, all of whom now participate in the policy development and the legislative process and do so with the active encouragement of government and political parties, have become much more prom-inent and influential in setting the national agenda than the Senate is.

Sixth, our 25 years of experience with the *Canadian Charter of Rights and Freedoms* has made the Senate's role in protecting minority rights rather marginal.

Seventh, the existence at both the federal and provincial levels of various ombudsmen, human rights commissions, appeal boards, complaints committees and so forth provides a much better recourse for citizens and a redress for injustice and the capacity to overturn arbitrary decisions of government.

Eighth, the increasing tendency in the House of Commons to amend bills there, even under majority governments, and the growing practice of referring bills to committees in the House of Commons after first reading are overtaking the Senate as a revising chamber.

Ninth, a second chamber, whether its members are appointed, elected by proportional representation or on the basis of provincial or regional balance, contradicts the basic democratic principle of representation by population and to the extent it does so would be undemocratic.

Tenth, all efforts to achieve a reformed Senate having failed, it is better to abolish the present body and rebuild it from the beginning.

In a referendum campaign, some will argue that abolition of the Senate would be prefer-able to the status quo. That is the position of the government, as stated several times by Mr. Van Loan. Others will argue that abolition would be preferable to some of the more exotic models of a reformed Senate, models that would paralyze the federal government and dead-lock the federal Parliament. That has been my position.

Others, while opposed to the status quo, will also oppose abolition of the present Senate. Keep it to reform it, they say. Others in favour of a new Senate argue, as I have suggested, that the only path to reform is on the ashes of the present Senate, so abolish it and start over. Others will argue that a second chamber, as a check on the power of the executive govern-ment and of the House of Commons, is so essential that even a body as imperfect as our present Senate is better than unicameralism.

I am not making myself the advocate of any of these arguments. However, the people of Canada need to hear them and hear the counter-arguments of those who hold that Canada needs a bicameral Parliament.

I say there is nothing to fear from trusting to the judgment of the people. Let us pass Senator Segal's motion and give the government and the country something to think about.

Senator Sharon Carstairs (December 11, 2007): In my view, the most regressive thing a politician can do is to raise an expectation that is not deliverable. This is exactly what this motion proposes.

Canadians would be asked to vote on a referendum to abolish the Senate; but the expectation in the minds of most Canadians would be that if the majority of Canadians voted to abolish the Senate, then the Senate would indeed be abolished. However, this would not be the case.

The Senate could not be abolished without a constitutional amendment, and we all know how difficult such an amendment would be. Therefore, an expectation that has been set up in the minds of the citizens of this country is dashed, resulting in even greater disillusion-ment of the citizenry and further cynicism.

This motion by Senator Segal goes one step further in the development of cynicism because the person who proposes the motion does not even believe in his own motion. He has indicated that he would vote no. For me, this proposal is the ultimate in cynicism. Therefore, I believe we should vote a resounding no to this motion.

There is only one solution to Senate reform. That is for the Prime Minister of this country to show leadership. Leadership on behalf of the Prime Minister would manifest itself in calling a first ministers meeting of all the premiers of the provinces and territories to discuss Senate reform because without their support, a constitutional amendment is not possible.

It is when they have come to an agreement that a referendum should occur. ... Canadians did not reject Senate reform. They rejected a massive package of reforms on the way Canada was to be governed. We do not know how they would have voted had there been a choice only on Senate reform. They deserve the right to make a choice about this institution and this institution alone.

What are some of the questions that the premiers and the Prime Minister should discuss? The first should be the distribution of seats. Should we go to the American model and recognize all provinces as equal and, therefore, entitled to exactly the same number of seats? Should they re-examine our present regional representation and question whether the numbers need some adjustment? I favour the second option.

Clearly, the west suffers a significant disadvantage. I would recognize British Columbia as a new region and allow their number of seats to grow gradually to the full 24 seats for their region when the population of British Columbia equals the population of the region of Quebec. I would make a further adjustment that would allow the Prairie region to grow to 30 seats under a provision that would state, if a region represented more than one province, then that region would have 30 seats, thereby equalizing the seats of the Atlantic and the Prairie regions.

As to the elected nature of the Senate, a debate must begin with a discussion on how powerful they want the Senate of Canada to be. If senators in Canada are to be elected in a manner similar to members of the House of Commons, then the discussion of powers is critical. Do we want a chamber of sober second thought or do we want a chamber more powerful than the House of Commons? There are 110 seats in the Province of Ontario—the present proposal, and 24 senators. Which parliamentarians will be more powerful? I suggest, honourable senators, that the 24 senators, if elected, will be more powerful than 110 members of Parliament. I favour an indirect election process with names coming forward from the legislatures of the provinces and territories. The number of names must reflect the gender and ethnic diversity of the province and, therefore, the numbers proposed must exceed the number of vacancies. The names should be vetted through the legislatures and should require the support of all parties represented in the legislatures. The Prime Minister would then have the choice to select from these names to ensure broad representation in this place.

Other issues require debate. Should senators all sit as independent senators with no caucus loyalty? Should the Speaker of the Senate be elected? Should the Senate be totally gender balanced? Should the Senate have a special role to protect linguistic minorities? Should higher votes be required for legislation that limits minority rights? Should the Senate have quota numbers with respect to First Nations people? Many other questions probably should be debated and examined. I have given a few this afternoon.

Democratizing the Constitution: Reforming Responsible Government

Peter Aucoin, Mark Jarvis, and Lori Turnbull (2011)

18

EDITORS' INTRODUCTION

Peter Aucoin was a professor emeritus of political science and public administration at Dalhousie University. A leading theorist on public administration and governance in Canada, this is one of his many works on the topic of the reform of governance. Mark Jarvis is a doctoral student at the University of Victoria, as well as directing research on public service reform at the Mowat Centre at the University of Toronto's School of Public Policy. Lori Turnbull is an associate professor at the School of Public Policy and Administration at Carleton University. She has published work in the Canadian Political Science Review, *the* Journal of Parliamentary and Political Law, Canadian Public Administration, *and the* Canadian Parliamentary Review.

This book was only the second ever to receive both the Donner Prize, awarded to the best public policy book by a Canadian, and the CPSA's Donald Smiley Prize, awarded to the best book on the study of government and politics in Canada. In it, the authors lament "the erosion of conventions meant to guide the practice of responsible government," and propose some practical fixes. They highlight specific issues with Canada's Constitution, including the lack of written conventions, and point to problems with the regular operation of Parliament, all of which provide the prime minister—not only Stephen Harper, but several of his predecessors as well, including Pierre Trudeau—with opportunities to "run roughshod" over legislative practices, and thereby undermine Canadian democracy.

A Uniquely Canadian Problem

The Canadian system of parliamentary government faces a fundamental problem that has been allowed to undermine Canadian democracy. The prime minister wields too much power over the operations of the House of Commons. The House of Commons is the parliamentary assembly of the people's elected representatives, the pre-eminent democratic institution of representative government (Franks 1987; Smith 2007). Too much power in the hands of a prime minister over the House of Commons in a parliamentary democracy is

Source: Excerpted from *Democratizing the Constitution: Reforming Responsible Government* by Peter Aucoin, Mark Jarvis, and Lori Turnbull. Toronto: Emond Montgomery, 2011.

Structure of the Federal Government

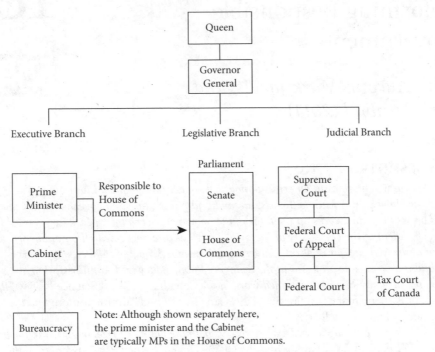

Note: Although shown separately here, the prime minister and the Cabinet are typically MPs in the House of Commons.

always a problem. Unconstrained power in any form of government invariably leads to the abuse of power. When power is abused, democracy is diminished.

The potential for unconstrained prime ministerial power has always been a risk inherent in parliamentary democracies, like Canada's, that are based on the British, or Westminster (after the name of the Gothic-style building in which the British Parliament meets in London) model. The prime minister occupies a crucial position in this structure. The prime minister is both the political head of the executive government *and* the leader of the governing party in the House of Commons. As the political head of the government, the prime minister advises the governor general to summon Parliament after an election, to prorogue Parliament for a period of time, and to dissolve Parliament in advance of an election. These decisions are not subject to the approval or consent of the House of Commons. They are separate executive powers. At the same time, the prime minister and his or her government, in order to retain office, must maintain the confidence of a majority of the members of Parliament—the people's elected representatives in the House of Commons. The tenure of the prime minister, as well as the life of the government, is thus subject to the control of the House of Commons. In this way, the constitutional system of parliamentary government is democratic.

... [W]e focus specifically on the capacity of the Canadian prime minister to control the operations of the House of Commons, including using the powers legally assigned to the governor general. Prime ministerial control of the operations of the House of Commons weakens the House's responsibilities and capacities:

- to review and approve or reject the government's legislative proposals;
- to scrutinize the government's administration of public affairs;
- to hold the prime minister and other ministers to account for their performance (collectively and individually);
- to withdraw its confidence in the prime minister and government when a majority wishes to do so; and
- to replace the prime minister and government with an alternative prime minister and government that has the confidence of a majority.

Prime ministerial control of the operations of the House risks an abuse of the basic premise of responsible government, namely, that the House be *in session* in order to carry out these responsibilities. The House cannot do so when it has not been summoned, has been prorogued, or has been dissolved.

The Canadian problem has two dimensions. One dimension is constitutional; the other is a matter of parliamentary government. The constitutional dimension concerns the capacity of the prime minister to abuse the constitutional powers to summon, prorogue, and dissolve the House of Commons to advance the partisan interests of the governing party. For example, there are no firm rules for the governor general to refer to when the prime minister has lost the confidence of the House of Commons and then wants to dissolve it. This was demonstrated following the March 25, 2011 defeat on confidence of the Harper government. As far as we are aware, Governor General David Johnston did not consult with the leaders of the opposition to see whether a new government could be formed from the opposition with the confidence of a majority. This would be standard procedure in Australia, Great Britain, and New Zealand, where it is fully accepted that the House decides who forms the government.

The parliamentary government dimension concerns the capacity of the prime minister to abuse the rules and procedures of the House of Commons that are meant to allow the government to manage the business of the House in an orderly and efficient manner. It also concerns the prime minister's powers as party leader to run roughshod over parliamentary practices meant to advance parliamentary democracy; for example, by imposing excessive party discipline on the governing party's own members of Parliament who are not ministers— the backbench MPs who sit behind the ministers in the House.

In both of these ways the prime minister governs in bad faith, allowing the government's partisan interests to subvert the opportunities for backbench government MPs and opposition MPs to perform their basic parliamentary responsibilities properly. Public opinion, at least in theory, especially the threat of electoral defeat, should induce the prime minister and MPs to act in good faith when they are inclined to act otherwise. But there is little evidence from the practices of several prime ministers in recent decades to support an assumption that public opinion and elections are sufficient constraints. ...

The Parliamentary Governance Dimension

The second dimension of the democratic problem concerns the Canadian prime minister's capacity to exercise excessive power over the day-to-day operations of the House—powers easily abused purely for partisan purposes. ...

The Prime Minister and Responsible Government

Prime ministers have always been more than first-among-equals in their Cabinet of ministers and have had the power to impose party discipline on their MPs. Canadian prime ministers have had greater control over their ministers and MPs than in Australia, Great Britain, and New Zealand ever since the Liberal, and then the Conservative parties, removed the power of their party caucus to select and dismiss their party leader. Instead, the parties, beginning with the Liberals in 1919, adopted the practice of national party conventions, with delegates from across the country, ex officio party officials, and the party's MPs, to select the party leader, including when the party leader would become prime minister after the party was in government.

Since at least the 1960s, prime ministers in all Westminster systems have become more powerful in relation to their elected parliaments and, with few exceptions, the constraints or checks on their power have weakened. Several developments have enhanced the power of the prime minister in relation to the House of Commons. Among them, two stand out.

First, the federal government has expanded its roles into almost every aspect of society and the economy. This has required an enhanced capacity for coordinating government policy-making and thus managing the government's legislative agenda in the House of Commons. This enhanced capacity is located at the centre of government under the direction of the prime minister.

Second, television had a significant effect on personalizing party leadership, with election campaigns becoming even more leader-centred and focused (Savoie 2010). In addition, the Canadian prime minister, as the government's "chief executive officer," has greater control over non-partisan public service executives and has the largest partisan political staff among the Westminster democracies. It is not surprising that Canadian prime ministers have not been inclined to reduce their powers. Why would they if the main objective is to be in power and stay there? The two most recent prime ministers, Martin and Harper, both expressed interest in reform before they gained office ... neither succeeded after he became prime minister.

In 1997, between periods in his career as an elected politician, Stephen Harper co-authored an article with his one-time adviser, Professor Tom Flanagan, entitled "Our Benign Dictatorship." They argued: "We persist in structuring the governing team like a military regiment under a single commander [the prime minister] with almost total power to appoint, discipline and expel subordinates [Cabinet ministers and members of Parliament]" (Harper and Flanagan 1997). In 1999, Professor Donald Savoie wrote a widely cited book, *Governing from the Centre: The Concentration of Power in Canadian Politics*, in which he portrayed the concentration of power under the prime minister as a governance structure resembling a powerful monarchy, with the prime minister surrounded by a cabal of courtiers, all dependent for their influence in "the king's court" on the personal whims of the prime minister (Savoie 1999). In 2001, Jeffrey Simpson, *Globe and Mail* columnist, penned a book about Liberal prime minister Jean Chrétien, whom he described as a "friendly dictator" (Simpson 2002). And, in 2010, Simpson's colleague at the *Globe and Mail*, Lawrence Martin, published a bestseller called *Harperland: The Politics of Control*, in which he describes how Stephen Harper, now prime minister, has taken prime ministerial power to even greater heights (Martin 2010).

We will argue that the abuse of these and other constitutional powers by the prime minister is more damaging to parliamentary democracy than the much publicized practice of recent prime ministers centralizing government decision making in their own office. The consequent bypassing of the structures of Cabinet government and individual ministerial responsibility has received far greater attention to date. Even Prime Minister Stephen Harper's two controversial prorogations are seen as simply part and parcel of highly centralized and tightly controlled prime ministerial government, rather than abuses of power.

We acknowledge that centralization under the prime minister and his or her political staff in the Prime Minister's Office is indirectly related to the prime minister's capacities to control the House of Commons. This centralization diminishes the likelihood that the prime minister's Cabinet colleagues, let alone his or her party's MPs, will be able to constrain the prime minister from abusing the governor general's powers or running roughshod over the parliamentary process. But centralization within the executive branch of government does not by itself lead to the abuse of the governor general's powers. Something more is required: the willingness of the prime minister to exercise these powers simply and merely to promote and protect the political interests of the governing party. In other words, the willingness to act in bad faith.

A Note on the Effect of Partisanship and the Malaise of Modern Politics

Partisanship, in and of itself, is not damaging to parliamentary democracy. Indeed, it is an integral and positive part of our system of parliamentary government. Our system is one of "party government" in several important respects. Competing political parties are freely organized by citizens. These parties structure the choices for voters at elections by nominating party candidates, offering a party platform, and identifying their party leader. After the election, they organize Parliament into two sides: the government and the opposition. The members of Parliament on the government side support the prime minister and Cabinet ministers as the political executive. By democratic convention, the prime minister and almost all other ministers are also MPs, rather than members of the Senate, the unelected house of Parliament. Since 1867, the Canadian experience has seen the government side always composed of just one party, as is the case at the time of writing, with the Conservative Party in office.[1] Since the 1920s, the opposition has comprised two or more parties. Today, it is made up of four parties—the New Democrats, the Liberals, the Bloc Québécois, and the Green Party. In all these ways, partisanship serves important democratic purposes.

However, partisans can sometimes be excessive in their partisanship. They can demonize their opponents. They can fail to listen to the arguments of the other side. They can deliberately misrepresent what their opponents have said or stand for. They can portray robust democratic competition as a war between enemies. And partisanship can go beyond simple excess. Partisanship leads to the abuse of the prime minister's conventional powers to summon, prorogue, and dissolve the House of Commons whenever they are exercised solely to protect or advance the interests of the governing party. The prime minister is constrained in the use of these powers only by public opinion and the prospects of voter disapproval in a subsequent election.

The malaise of modern politics encompasses a number of developments, some of which are easily observed but not well understood. These include a general decline of citizen engagement and interest, especially among youth, in the traditional and still basic forms of voting, asso-ciating with a political party in some manner (even if only as loosely considering oneself a partisan for one party), and generally being attentive to politics and government. When citizens become disengaged in large numbers, the likelihood of their being concerned about the state of Canadian democracy is diminished. The influence of the mass media, to which the great bulk of the population paid some attention for most of the latter half of the 20th cen-tury, has also diminished, in part because the various new electronic media have captured so many of the specialized or niche markets that these other developments themselves helped to fracture.

Citizens, pundits, scholars, and politicians themselves have singled out partisanship and political parties for special criticism. Many would like to see MPs voting more freely, based either on what their constituents want (assuming MPs could know) or the MP's personal conscience. They oppose the excessive party discipline imposed by party leaders that occurs when leaders silence the voices of their MPs and turn them into robots who merely echo the party line. All party leaders have been responsible at times for succumbing to both these temptations, although it is ironic that the Conservative Party has probably been the party most characterized by this practice, despite the fact that the core of the new party is the defunct Reform Party of Preston Manning, a party formed precisely to advance the ideals of reduced partisanship and party discipline in parliamentary government (Smith 1999).

Many—though not all—of those who support reforming how Parliament works on a day-to-day basis have set their sights on reducing, if not eliminating, partisanship. However, the entire parliamentary process is predicated on partisan politics, which sees institutional-ized adversarialism as the best means of securing democracy. Partisanship is thus an essential dynamic of public accountability in our democratic system and any efforts to improve dem-ocracy by reducing partisanship are doomed to failure. Efforts to improve democracy should instead be focused on reducing excessive party discipline.

Note

1. A possible exception was the Union government put together by the Conservative prime minister during the First World War that included some Liberal MPs in the Cabinet. But it was not a coalition because the Liberal Party, with the rest of the Liberal MPs, remained in opposition.

The Electoral System and the Party System in Canada, 1921–1965

19

Alan C. Cairns (1968)

EDITORS' INTRODUCTION

Alan Cairns was a professor of political science at the University of British Columbia from 1960 to 1995, and a visiting scholar at numerous Canadian universities. He has published many works and articles on Canadian public policy and the Constitution. He is an Officer of the Order of Canada and a Fellow of the Royal Society of Canada.

This is a revised version of a paper presented in 1967 at the 39th annual meeting of the Canadian Political Science Association. In this paper Cairns draws important links between the electoral system and party competition in Canada, pointing to the impact the system has had on the exacerbation of regional identities and discontents. He argues that, contrary to popular ideas, the electoral system has not had a nationalizing influence on Canadian party politics, but that Canada's divisions have become deeper as a result of the institutional incentives structuring party competition.

This paper investigates two common assumptions about the party system: (i) that the influence of the electoral system on the party system has been unimportant, or non-existent; and (ii) that the party system has been an important nationalizing agency with respect to the sectional cleavages widely held to constitute the most significant and enduring lines of division in the Canadian polity. Schattschneider, Lipset, Duverger, Key and others have cogently asserted the relevance of electoral systems for the understanding of party systems. Students of Canadian parties, however, have all but ignored the electoral system as an explanatory factor of any importance. The analysis to follow will suggest that the electoral system has played a major role in the evolution of Canadian parties, and that the claim that the party system has been an important instrument for integrating Canadians across sectional lines is highly suspect.

Discussion of the respective merits of single member constituency electoral systems and various systems of proportional representation is frequently indecisive because of an inability to agree on the values which electoral systems should serve. Advocates of proportional representation base their arguments on democratic fundamentalism. They simply argue that each vote should have equal weight, and that the distortion of the voters' preferences by single

Source: Excerpted from *Canadian Journal of Political Science*, vol. 1, no. 1 (March 1968). Notes omitted. Reprinted by permission.

member constituency systems is no more to be justified than the use of false scales by a butcher. This idealistic argument is countered by the opponents of proportional representation with the assertion that executive stability is a more basic consideration, and that it is well served by the propensity of Canadian type systems to create artificial legislative majorities. This controversy will not concern us further.

It may be noted, however, that critical analysis of the single member constituency system encounters a cultural bias in the Anglo-Saxon world because of the pervasive hostility shown to systems of proportional representation, and the executive instability to which they allegedly contribute. Proportional representation has not been seriously considered as a possible alternative to the existing system. It exists in a limbo of inarticulate assumptions that it is responsible for the ills of the French political system, but it is given no credit for the sophistication and maturity of the Swedish political system.

Given this bias there is, no doubt, a tendency to transform a critique of the existing system into advocacy of proportional representation. The purpose of this paper, however, is not to advocate proportional representation, but simply to take a realistic look at some of the consequences of the prevailing system which have received insufficient attention. In any case, the habituation of Canadians to the existing system renders policy oriented research on the comparative merits of different electoral systems a fruitless exercise.

The Basic Defence of the System and Its Actual Performance

If the electoral system is analysed in terms of the basic virtue attributed to it, the creation of artificial legislative majorities to produce cabinet stability, its performance since 1921 has been only mediocre. Table I reveals the consistent tendency of the electoral system in every election from 1921 to 1965 to give the government party a greater percentage of seats than of votes. However, its contribution to one-party majorities was much less dramatic. Putting aside the two instances, 1940 and 1958, when a boost from the electoral system was unnecessary, it transformed a minority of votes into a majority of seats on only six of twelve occasions. It is possible that changes in the party system and/or in the distribution of party support will render this justification increasingly anachronistic in future years.

TABLE I Percentage of votes and seats for government party, 1921–1965

	% Votes	% Seats		% Votes	% Seats
1921	40.7	49.4 (L)	1949	49.5	73.7 (L)
1925*	39.8	40.4 (L)	1953	48.9	64.5 (L)
1926	46.1	52.2 (L)	1957	38.9	42.3 (C)
1930	48.7	55.9 (C)	1958	53.6	78.5 (C)
1935	44.9	70.6 (L)	1962	37.3	43.8 (C)
1940	51.5	73.9 (L)	1963	41.7	48.7 (L)
1945	41.1	51.0 (L)	1965	40.2	49.4 (L)

* In this election the Conservatives received both a higher percentage of votes, 46.5%, and of seats, 47.3%, than the Liberals. The Liberals, however, chose to meet Parliament and with Progressive support they retained office for several months.

Note: The data for this and the following tables have been compiled from Howard A. Scarrow, *Canada Votes* (New Orleans, 1963), and from the *Report of the Chief Electoral Officer* for recent elections.

If the assessment of the electoral system is extended to include not only its contribution to one-party majorities, but its contribution to the maintenance of effective opposition, arbitrarily defined as at least one-third of House members, it appears in an even less satisfactory light. On four occasions, two of which occurred when the government party had slightly more than one-half of the votes, the opposition was reduced to numerical ineffectiveness. The coupling of these two criteria together creates a reasonable measure for the contribution of the electoral system to a working parliamentary system, which requires both a stable majority and an effective opposition. From this vantage point the electoral system has a failure rate of 71 per cent, on ten of fourteen occasions.

This unimpressive record indicates that if other dysfunctional consequences of the electoral system exist they can be only marginally offset by its performance with respect to the values espoused by its advocates. In this paper discussion of these other consequences is restricted to the effect of the electoral system in furthering or hindering the development of a party system capable of acting as a unifying agency in a country where sectional cleavages are significant. Or, to put the matter differently, the stability which is of concern is not that of the cabinet in its relations to the legislature, but the stability of the political system as a whole. Has the electoral system fostered a party system which attenuates or exacerbates sectional cleavages, sectional identities, and sectionally oriented parties?

The Effect on Major and Minor Parties

Table II indicates an important effect of the electoral system with its proof that discrimination for and against the parties does not become increasingly severe when the parties are ordered from most votes to least votes. Discrimination in favour of a party was most pronounced for the weakest party on seven occasions, and for the strongest party on seven occasions. In the four elections from 1921 to 1930 inclusive, with three party contestants, the second party was most hurt by the electoral system. In the five elections from 1935 to 1953 inclusive the electoral system again worked against the middle ranking parties and favoured the parties with the weakest and strongest support. In the five elections from 1957 to 1965 inclusive there has been a noticeable tendency to benefit the first two parties, with the exception of the fourth party, Social Credit in 1957, at the expense of the smaller parties.

The explanation for the failure of the electoral system to act with Darwinian logic by consistently distributing its rewards to the large parties and its penalties to the small parties is relatively straightforward. The bias in favour of the strongest party reflects the likelihood that the large number of votes it has at its disposal will produce enough victories in individual constituencies to give it, on a percentage basis, a surplus of seats over votes. The fact that this surplus has occurred with only one exception, 1957, indicates the extreme unlikelihood of the strongest party having a distribution of partisan support capable of transforming the electoral system from an ally into a foe. The explanation for the favourable impact of the electoral system on the Progressives and Social Credit from 1921 to 1957 when they were the weakest parties is simply that they were sectional parties which concentrated their efforts in their areas of strength where the electoral system worked in their favour. Once the electoral system has rewarded the strongest party and a weak party with concentrated sectional strength there are not many more seats to go around. In this kind of party system, which Canada had from 1921 to Mr. Diefenbaker's breakthrough, serious discrimination against

TABLE II   **Bias of electoral system in translating votes into seats**

Year	1	2	3	4	5
	Rank order of parties in terms of percentage of vote				

Rank order of parties in terms of percentage of vote

Year	1	2	3	4	5
1921	Libs. 1.21	Cons. 0.70	Progs. 1.20		
1925	Cons. 1.017	Libs. 1.015	Progs. 1.09		
1926	Libs. 1.13	Cons. 0.82	Progs. 1.55		
1930	Cons. 1.15	Libs. 0.82	Progs. 1.53		
1935	Libs. 1.57	Cons. 0.55	CCF 0.33	Rec. 0.05	Socred 1.68
1940	Libs. 1.43	Cons. 0.53	CCF 0.39	Socred 1.52	
1945	Libs. 1.24	Cons. 1.00	CCF 0.73	Socred 1.29	
1949	Libs. 1.49	Cons. 0.53	CCF 0.37	Socred 1.03	
1953	Libs. 1.32	Cons. 0.62	CCF 0.77	Socred 1.06	
1957	Libs. 0.97	Cons. 1.087	CCF 0.88	Socred 1.091	
1958	Cons. 1.46	Libs. 0.55	CCF 0.32	Socred 0	
1962	Cons. 1.17	Libs. 1.01	NDP 0.53	Socred 0.97	
1963	Libs. 1.17	Cons. 1.09	NDP 0.49	Socred 0.76	
1965	Libs. 1.23	Cons. 1.13	NDP 0.44	Cred. 0.72	Socred 0.51

Independent and very small parties have been excluded from the table.

The measurement of discrimination employed in this table defines the relationship between the percentage of votes and the percentage of seats. The figure is devised by dividing the former into the latter. Thus 1—(38% seats/ 38% votes), for example—represents a neutral effect for the electoral system. Any figure above 1—(40% seats/ 20% votes) = 2.0, for example—indicates discrimination for the party. A figure below 1—(20% seats/40% votes) = 0.5, for example—indicates discrimination against the party. For the purposes of the table the ranking of the parties as 1, 2, 3 … is based on their percentage of the vote, since to rank them in terms of seats would conceal the very bias it is sought to measure—namely the bias introduced by the intervening variable of the electoral system which constitutes the mechanism by which votes are translated into seats.

the second party in a three-party system and the second and third party in a four-party system is highly likely.

Table III reveals that the electoral system positively favours minor parties with sectional strongholds and discourages minor parties with diffuse support. The classic example of the latter phenomenon is provided by the Reconstruction party in the 1935 election. For its 8.7 per cent of the vote it was rewarded with one seat, and promptly disappeared from the scene. Yet its electoral support was more than twice that of Social Credit which gained seventeen seats, and only marginally less than that of the CCF which gained seven seats. The case of the Reconstruction party provides dramatic illustration of the futility of party effort for a minor party which lacks a sectional stronghold. The treatment of the CCF/NDP by the electoral system is only slightly less revealing. This party with diffuse support which aspired to national and major party status never received as many seats as would have been "justified" by its voting support, and on six occasions out of ten received less than half the seats to which it was "entitled." The contrasting treatment of Social Credit and the Progressives, sectional minor parties, by the electoral system clearly reveals the bias of the electoral system in favour of concentrated support and against diffused support. (There is an unavoidable problem of circular reasoning here. There is an important difference between saying that the electoral system favours parties which *are* sectional, and saying that the electoral system encourages parties to *be* sectional.) …

TABLE III   Minor parties: percentage of seats and votes

	Progressives		Reconstruction		CCF/NDP		Soc. Credit		Créditiste	
	votes	seats	votes	seats	votes	seats	votes	seats	votes	seats
1921	23.1	27.7								
1925	9.0	9.8								
1926	5.3	8.2								
1930	3.2	4.9								
1935			8.7	0.4	8.9	2.9	4.1	6.9		
1940					8.5	3.3	2.7	4.1		
1945					15.6	11.4	4.1	5.3		
1949					13.4	5.0	3.7	3.8		
1953					11.3	8.7	5.4	5.7		
1957					10.7	9.4	6.6	7.2		
1958					9.5	3.0	2.6	—		
1962					13.5	7.2	11.7	11.3		
1963					13.1	6.4	11.9	9.1		
1965					17.9	7.9	3.7	1.9	4.7	3.4

Party System as a Nationalizing Agency

The ramifications of sectional politics are highly complex. Given the paucity of literature on Canadian parties it is impossible to make categorical statements about these ramifications in all cases. Where evidence is sparse, the analysis will of necessity be reduced to hypotheses, some of which will be sustained by little more than deduction.

One of the most widespread interpretations of the party system claims that it, or at least the two major parties, functions as a great unifying or nationalizing agency. Canadian politics, it is emphasized, are politics of moderation, or brokerage politics, which minimize differences, restrain fissiparous tendencies, and thus over time help knit together the diverse interests of a polity weak in integration. It is noteworthy that this brokerage theory is almost exclusively applied to the reconciliation of sectional, racial, and religious divisions, the latter two frequently being regarded as simply more specific versions of the first with respect to French–English relations. The theory of brokerage politics thus assumes that the historically significant cleavages in Canada are sectional, reflecting the federal nature of Canadian society, or racial/religious, reflecting a continuation of the struggle which attracted Durham's attention in the mid nineteenth century. Brokerage politics between classes is mentioned, if at all, as an afterthought.

The interpretation of the party system in terms of its fulfilment of a nationalizing function is virtually universal. Close scrutiny, however, indicates that this is at best questionable, and possibly invalid. It is difficult to determine the precise meaning of the argument that the party system has been a nationalizing agency, stressing what Canadians have in common, bringing together representatives of diverse interests to deliberate on government policies. In an important sense the argument is misleading in that it attributes to the party system what is simply inherent in a representative democracy which inevitably brings together Nova Scotians, Albertans, and Quebeckers to a common assemblage point, and because of the majoritarian necessities of the parliamentary system requires agreement among contending interests to accomplish anything at all. Or, to put it differently, the necessity for inter-group collaboration in any on-going political system makes it possible to claim of any party system compatible with the survival of the polity that it acts as a nationalizing agency. The extent to which any particularly party system does so act is inescapably therefore a comparative question or a question of degree. In strict logic an evaluation of alternative types of party systems is required before a particular one can be accorded unreserved plaudits for the success with which it fulfils a nationalizing function.

Assistance in grappling with this issue comes from an examination of a basic problem. In what ways does the party system stimulate the very cleavages it is alleged to bridge? The question can be rephrased to ask the extent to which an unvarying sectionalism has an autonomous existence independent of the particular electoral and party systems employed by Canadians. The basic approach of this paper is that the party system, importantly conditioned by the electoral system, exacerbates the very cleavages it is credited with healing. As a corollary it is suggested that the party system is not simply a reflection of sectionalism, but that sectionalism is also a reflection of the party system.

The electoral system has helped to foster a particular kind of political style by the special significance it accords to sectionalism. This is evident in party campaign strategy, in party policies, in intersectional differences in the nature and vigour of party activity, and in differences in the intra-party socialization experiences of parliamentary personnel of the various parties. As a consequence the electoral system has had an important effect on perceptions of the party system and, by extension, of the political system itself. Sectionalism has been rendered highly visible because the electoral system makes it a fruitful basis on which to organize electoral support. Divisions cutting through sections, particularly those based on the class system, have been much less salient because the possibility of payoffs in terms of representation has been minimal. ...

Electoral System, Sectionalism, and Instability

Individuals can relate to the party system in several ways, but the two most fundamental are class and sectionalism. The two are antithetical, for one emphasizes the geography of residence, while the other stresses stratification distinctions for which residence is irrelevant. The frequently noted conservative tone which pervades Canadian politics is a consequence of the sectional nature of the party system. The emphasis on sectional divisions engendered by the electoral system has submerged class conflicts, and to the extent that our politics has been ameliorative it has been more concerned with the distribution of burdens and benefits between sections than between classes. The poverty of the Maritimes has occupied an honourable place in the foreground of public discussion. The diffuse poverty of the generally underprivileged has scarcely been noticed.

Such observations lend force to John Porter's thesis that Canadian parties have failed to harness the "conservative–progressive dynamic" related to the Canadian class system, and to his assertion that "to obscure social divisions through brokerage politics is to remove from the political system that element of dialectic which is the source of creative politics." The fact is, however, that given the historical (and existing) state of class polarization in Canada the electoral system has made sectionalism a more rewarding vehicle for amassing political support than class. The destructive impact of the electoral system on the CCF is highly indicative of this point. It is not that the single member constituency system discourages class-based politics in any absolute sense, as the example of Britain shows, but that it discourages such politics when class identities are weak or submerged behind sectional identities.

This illustrates the general point that the differences in the institutional context of politics have important effects in determining which kinds of conflict become salient in the political system. The particular institutional context with which this paper is concerned, the electoral system, has clearly fostered a sectional party system in which party strategists have concentrated on winning sectional appeals and conditioned-by-one-party bastions where the opposition is tempted to give up the battle and pursue success in more promising areas.

A politics of sectionalism is a politics of instability for two reasons. In the first place it induces parties to pay attention to the realities of representation which filter through the electoral system, at the expense of the realities of a partisan support at the level of the electorate. The self-interest which may induce a party to write off a section because its weak support there is discriminated against by the electoral system may be exceedingly unfortunate for national unity. Imperfections in the political market render the likelihood of an invisible hand transforming the pursuit of party good into public good somewhat dubious.

Secondly, sectional politics is potentially far more disruptive to the polity than class politics. This is essentially because sectional politics has an inherent tendency to call into question the very nature of the political system and its legitimacy. Classes, unlike sections, cannot secede from the political system, and are consequently more prone to accept its legitimacy. The very nature of their spatial distribution not only inhibits their political organization but induces them to work through existing instrumentalities. With sections this is not the case.

Given the strong tendency to sectionalism found in the very nature of Canadian society the question can be raised as to the appropriateness of the existing electoral system. Duverger has pointed out that the single-member constituency system "accentuates the geographical localization of opinions: one might even say that it tends to transform a national opinion ... into a local opinion by allowing it to be represented only in the sections of the country in which it is strongest." Proportional representation works in the opposite manner for "opinions strongly entrenched locally tend to be broadened on the national plane by the possibility of being represented in districts where they are in a small minority." The political significance of these opposed tendencies is clear: proportional representation tends to strengthen national unity (or, to be more precise, national uniformity); the simple majority system accentuates local differences. The consequences are fortunate or unfortunate according to the particular situation in each country.

20 The Higher the Fewer: Women's Participation in Major Party Organizations

Sylvia Bashevkin (1985)

EDITOR'S INTRODUCTION

Sylvia Bashevkin is one of Canada's foremost scholars on the topic of women and politics. A professor of political science at the University of Toronto, she served as principal of University College, president of the Canadian Political Science Association, and president of the Women and Politics Section of the American Political Science Association. A Fellow of the Royal Society of Canada, she has written or edited more than ten books and scores of articles and book chapters on the topic of women and gender and politics.

This excerpt from her book Toeing the Lines *is some of her earliest work, although in many ways it remains her most influential, at least in terms of the way we think about women's place in Canadian electoral politics. Bashevkin highlights women's participation in politics in a variety of roles, including local constituency activity, legislative office holding, and intra- party leadership and organization, and notes that women are involved in all capacities. However, and importantly, she argues that while women are involved in party politics, they tend to be concentrated in certain types of activities more than others. She introduces two maxims: "the higher the fewer" and "the more competitive the fewer," both of which continue to ring true today: the higher up we go in party hierarchy, and the larger the stakes, the fewer women we see.*

> *She has been working in the trenches of this party for years ...*
> *and particularly around the kitchen tables of this party.**

Writing in 1950, historian Catherine Cleverdon suggested that a brighter future would await Canadian women who sought to become active in partisan politics. Cleverdon believed there existed "some evidence that political parties are becoming increasingly aware of the need to offer women something more in the way of political activity than to do party chores and to vote for their candidates (male, of course) on election days." Cleverdon's hopeful expectations

---

* Ontario Cabinet Minister Robert Welch, nomination speech for Marg Lyon, candidate for eighth vice-president of the Ontario Progressive Conservative Association (September 1982).

Source: *Toeing the Lines: Women and Party Politics in English Canada* by Sylvia B. Bashevkin. Toronto: University of Toronto Press, 1985. Reprinted by permission.

were expressed more than three decades following the federal-level enfranchisement of Canadian women, a struggle which she documented in detail in *The Woman Suffrage Movement in Canada*. In large part, this optimism grew out of a sense that the increasing educational and employment opportunities which were available to women after World War II would serve to enhance future levels of political participation.

Despite these promising trends, however, the political involvement of Canadian women in the post-war years bore close resemblance to that of previous decades. As Rosamonde Boyd (1968) observed in a comparative American–Canadian study, "women's rise to responsible positions of decision-making and administrative leadership has been slow and sporadic." The impact of traditional role constraints, combined with what Boyd termed "an underestimation of their political potential" by North American women generally, thus contributed to an older trend whereby females were less numerous than males in positions of visible political influence. As legislators, cabinet ministers, and party leaders, women were simply few and far between.

A growing recognition of this weak numerical representation in North American political elites helped to fuel the feminist movement of the late 1960s and following. As we have argued … , feminists responded to their lack of representation in diverse ways, including through the fielding of independent candidates in federal elections, as well as by the establishment of increasingly assertive women's groups within major party organizations. Overall, the objective of such activities was fairly consistent across time and across party ideologies: namely to elevate both the numerical and substantive (i.e., policy) impact of women in Canadian politics.

The general approach which was adopted in order to achieve this goal frequently began with an examination of the problem of political candidacy. Following early research in the field of Canadian women and politics by Jill McCalla Vickers and Janine Brodie, partisan and independent feminist activists questioned how the numbers of female candidates in winnable ridings could be increased and, concomitantly, how the overall policy priority accorded to so-called women's issues could be improved.

On the level of research, one of the major difficulties with this approach has been its failure to situate women's participation within the broader context of party life at all levels. While political candidacy remains an important and highly visible form of elite-level involvement, it hardly captures the diverse and oftentimes less visible activities which generate, and regenerate, party organization in a modern democracy. Local constituency-level work, campaign activity other than candidacy for public office, participation in party women's groups, internal party office-holding, delegation to party conventions, and many other types of party involvement have generally been overlooked in Canada because of an overriding concern with female candidacy. …

The participation of women in local riding associations is generally neglected in the Canadian politics literature. One project which does consider this subject in the context of urban party organizations concludes that women form a disproportionately small segment of party insider (intermediate level) and elite (top organizational) strata, at the same time as they are relatively overrepresented in the party stalwart (routine functionary) category. According to Harold D. Clarke and Allan Kornberg (1979), the few Canadian women who are involved in urban party activities tend to work harder than their male colleagues and, at the same time, expect fewer tangible rewards for their commitment. Clarke and Kornberg suggest that these females "are in a very real sense 'survivors,'" who have reconciled themselves to the "law of increasing disproportion" within urban party organizations.

What types of activities do women perform in local constituency associations? While data collected by Kornberg, Smith, and Clarke (1979) suggest that "relatively similar proportions of men and women were members of their constituency executive committees or held poll captain and miscellaneous lower level positions," our own research points toward considerable gender differences in both the *extent* and *type* of local party activity in English Canada. More specifically, we suggest that women perform stereotypically feminine types of party work at the local level in English Canada. In addition, we propose that the competitive position of party organizations has a direct impact upon female participation, such that there are especially few women at the executive level in ridings where the power stakes are high.

An appropriate place to begin this study of local constituency association activity is the province of Ontario, where approximately 44.8% of the Anglophone population of Canada reside. With 95 (33.7%) of the nation's federal ridings, and 125 (18.0%) of its provincial seats, Ontario remains the longstanding centre of political, as well as economic and social, gravity for most of Canada.

Figures on local riding participation at the provincial level in Ontario, presented in table 3.1, document women's involvement in 125 provincial constituency associations in each of the three major parties. In terms of riding executive positions, our data indicate that, as expected, women in all three provincial parties are considerably less likely to serve as local riding presidents than men. In 1981, women comprised 14.4% of Conservative riding presidents ($N = 18$), 20.0% of Liberal riding presidents (25), and 28.8% of NDP riding presidents (36), so that overall in Ontario there were 79 female riding presidents out of a possible 375 in the three provincial parties, or 21.1%. The level of female representation in riding treasurerships was similar, except in the NDP, where male–female parity was approached (41.6%).

Comparing riding secretary and membership secretary data with these figures points toward the existence of a "pink-collar" sector in local constituency organizations in Ontario. In 1981, between two-thirds and three-quarters of riding secretaries in the three parties were

TABLE 3.1   Riding-level participation of women in Ontario, by provincial party and year[a]

	Party and year				
	Liberal	New Democratic		Progressive Conservative	
Riding position	1981	1973	1981	1977	1981
President	20.0 (25)	8.5 (10)	28.8 (36)	9.6 (12)	14.4 (18)
Treasurer / CFO	29.6 (37)	—	41.6 (52)	5.6 (7)	12.0 (15)
Recording secretary	76.8 (96)	—	67.2 (84)	62.4 (78)	66.4 (83)
Membership secretary / memb. chair	—	—	53.6 (67)	—	69.6 (87)

[a] Cell entries represent the percentage of riding positions held by women in the years and parties indicated. Figures in parentheses represent the actual number of women holding these positions. Note that percentages for 1977 and 1981 are calculated on a base N of 125 ridings, while those for 1973 are on a base of 117 ridings.

Source: Cell entries for 1981 are drawn from party records made available to the author, while 1973 and 1977 figures are from internal party studies. A dash indicates that information was not available.

female (notably, 76.8% in the provincial Liberal organization), and membership secretary positions seemed to be held disproportionately by women as well. Therefore, it would appear that the same types of executive and financial positions usually held by men in the Canadian labour force generally are also held by them in the Ontario provincial ridings. At the same time, the more clerical and generally less prestigious positions in which women are clustered in the work force are also those where they seem to be ghettoized in Ontario riding associations. It should be noted, however, that this clustering is least pronounced in the NDP riding associations, where women are better represented as presidents and particularly as financial officers than in the Liberal and Conservative organizations, and are also less likely to serve as membership secretaries than in the Conservative ridings.

What other conclusions can be drawn from these riding-level data? First, in reference to their decision-making implications, the figures would initially suggest that few women wield effective power in local party organizations. However, upon closer inspection of internal riding activity in all three cases, we would propose that large numbers of women perform critical human relations, and especially communications, functions at the local level. As secretaries and membership chairs, they help to ensure organizational continuity by keeping local riding minutes, recruiting new members, and maintaining older memberships. In cases where the riding president or treasurer is not active, these women would also appear to provide the only visible evidence of their party's presence in the riding. Therefore, while it is important to recognize the implicit and often indirect nature of "pink-collar" power in the Ontario ridings, the importance of women's contributions should not be overlooked.

Second, and parallel with this first point, our research suggests that many Ontario women who have broken out of the "pink-collar" ghetto have done so in ridings where their party is generally inactive and has little chance of electoral success. That is, a considerable number of female riding presidents in all three parties seem to hold symbolic power only, since they have little opportunity to elect members to their legislative caucus and thus cannot attract resources from the central provincial organization—which, in turn, helps to propel party activity on the local level. For example, our research shows that female NDP riding presidents in 1981 were clustered in rural Liberal and suburban Conservative-held seats, while Liberal women were frequently elected in strong Tory and New Democratic areas. In short, then, the number of women holding formal positions of power on the riding level may be less significant than the competitive position of their respective parties—a factor which seems to suggest that there is little real political power in many of the constituencies where women hold prominent executive positions.

A third conclusion which may be drawn from data in table 3.1 concerns longitudinal or cross-time change in female riding involvement. While few longitudinal figures are available, those which are suggest a significant increase in women's participation during the past decade, which corresponds with the growth of feminist activism in Ontario, and in Canada generally. In the provincial NDP, for example, only 10 women held riding presidencies in 1973, compared with 36 in 1981. This change represents an increase of more than threefold over an eight-year period. Data from Conservative ridings suggest increased involvement as well, since 19 women were presidents or treasurers in 1977, and 33 held these same positions in 1981. However, during this same four-year period women also became more numerous as Conservative riding secretaries (from 78 to 83), indicating that women continue to fill "pink-collar" positions in many Ontario riding associations.

TABLE 3.2   Riding-level participation of women in major Manitoba provincial parties, 1982[a]

Position	New Democratic	Progressive Conservative
President	14.3 (8)	12.7 (7)
Vice-president	16.1 (9)	15.1 (8)
Treasurer	41.1 (23)	43.6 (24)
Recording secretary	69.6 (39)	—
Membership sec'y	40.0 (12/30)	69.8 (37)
(N) of women	(91)	(76)

[a] Cell entries represent the percentage of riding positions held by women in the parties indicated. Figures in parentheses represent the actual number of women holding these positions. Note that Progressive Conservative entries are calculated on a base N of 53–55 ridings, and NDP entries on a base N of 56 (some of the province's 57 ridings had no executive).

Source: Party records made available to the author.

Comparable participation data from Manitoba, presented in table 3.2, indicate that fairly similar patterns obtain in a two-party provincial political system. In 1982, women comprised less than 15% of NDP and Conservative riding presidents, with figures for riding association vice-presidents only slightly higher. As in the case of Ontario, female office-holding at these levels was greater in the New Democratic than the Conservative party, but only marginally so. Once again the heavy clustering of women in "pink-collar" or clerical riding work was pronounced, with females comprising 69.6% of NDP secretaries and 69.8% of PC membership secretaries at the constituency level. ...

Legislative Office-Holding

The paucity of women as elected legislators in Canada has long been a source of frustration and challenge to observers both inside and outside the chambers of government. In the more than six decades since the election of Louise McKinney and Roberta Macadams as the first female provincial lawmakers (in Alberta) in 1917, and of Agnes Macphail as the first federal MP in 1921, approximately 100 women have held elected legislative office in Canada. Clearly, this record would dismay even the optimistic Macphail, whose biographers describe her initial entrance to the House of Commons as follows: "She thought of the women who would surely walk this corridor too. 'I could almost hear them coming,' she said later. Her ear must have been tuned to a still remote time, for in the next quarter century only four other Canadian women were elected to the federal House of Commons." In light of our discussion of female candidacies, it is not difficult to understand the direct political causes of this situation. As predominantly marginal candidates in federal and provincial elections, women are unlikely to win election, and thus few hold legislative office.

On a deeper level, a wide variety of structural and psychological explanations have been proposed in order to account for the absence of women in elected legislative office, in both Canada and other Western democracies. Perhaps the most compelling reason is one which follows from the interplay of gender role socialization and organizational processes within party politics; that is, the practice and/or expectation of masculine assertiveness, combined with the practice and/or expectation of feminine docility, have served to produce (and re-produce) a predominantly male party elite structure and a predominantly female party support base. Because they are essentially organizations of volunteers, with some careerists in their higher echelons, political parties are very dependent upon the initiative of individual activists—generally men—who until recently had little reason to seek out or encourage women elites. These organizational factors, combined with the impact of gender role social-ization, have dealt an especially hard blow to efforts toward increasing female representation within Canadian legislatures.

Many of the women who succeeded Agnes Macphail in the House of Commons shared important personal characteristics and political experiences with her: as a group, female legis-lators have tended to be unmarried, and childless or else the mothers of grown children. Like Macphail, as well, many have represented Ontario ridings; worked as teachers, journalists, or social workers (unlike their male colleagues who have legal and business backgrounds); and had pre-election political backgrounds. While the specific experiences of these women within the House of Commons have varied, it seems fair to say that all confronted a pre-dominantly masculine environment upon their entrance to Parliament. In the words of Liane Langevin (1977), "Legislatures are often compared to a men's club in that their membership is predominantly male and consequently, so are their traditions and atmosphere. A woman who enters a legislature as a member is an anomaly, a deviant in the sense that she is defying traditional limits on acceptable feminine behaviour."

The degree of gender role defiance implied by women's legislative participation has de-clined, though, with the passage of time. Since the fourteen-year tenure of Agnes Macphail as the sole female MP, and the subsequent election of at least seven women who inherited federal seats from their husbands, the social limitations upon independent political involve-ment by Canadian women have generally subsided. One important barometer of change has been the appointment of females to federal cabinet positions, beginning in 1957 with the nomination of Hamilton accountant Ellen Fairclough to the secretary of state portfolio.

Despite these notable advances, however, women continue to be vastly underrepresented in both federal and provincial legislatures in Canada. As reported in table 3.12, the percent-age of females holding elective parliamentary office in the 1980s remains less than 10%, with an overall provincial figure of 6.2% in 1982 and a federal figure of 9.6% in 1984. The record numbers of women legislators at both levels of government in the contemporary period thus represent a small handful relative to the proportion of women in the Canadian population generally.

TABLE 3.12 Female representation in Canadian federal and provincial legislatures, 1982–4

Legislature	Year	% women	(N)
House of Commons	1983	5.7	(16)
House of Commons	1984	9.6	(27)
Provinces overall	1982	6.2	(43)

Sources: Canadian Parliamentary Guide, 1983; *Chatelaine* series on Women in Provincial Politics, 1982; federal election returns reported in the *Globe and Mail*, 6 September 1984.

21 The Party System

Janine Brodie and Jane Jenson (1990)

EDITORS' INTRODUCTION

Janine Brodie teaches in the Department of Political Science at the University of Alberta. She holds a Canada Research Chair in Political Economy and Social Governance, and has published widely on questions of gender equality, political representation, citizenship, social policy, globalization, and transformations in governance. Jane Jenson is a professor of political science at the Université de Montréal, holds a Canada Research Chair in Citizenship and Governance, and is a member of l'Institut d'études européenes (IEE) at the same university. Her more recent works examine issues of citizenship and social policy.

The following excerpt examines the Canadian party system in relation to the party systems of other countries. In particular, the authors assess the role of social class (or absence thereof) in shaping the nature of party politics in Canada. They argue that it is important to go beyond the simple label of "brokerage politics" in the Canadian context in order to understand why brokerage is the dominant model of party organization (see also Reading 24 by Carty and Cross). They suggest that Canada's party system is an anomaly, in that it is not heavily based in class consciousness or class-based organization.

Canada's federal party system provides a somewhat perplexing case for students of politics in liberal democracies. Some sociological theory, drawing on western European experience in particular, predicts that as changes in social structure induced by urbanization and industrialization occur, the traditional electoral cleavages of religion, language and region are eroded by the politics of class. In so-called "modernized" party systems, a class cleavage differentiates the electoral support base of the parties as well as their major policies. From this perspective, the Canadian federal party system does not appear to have "modernized." Instead, religion, language and especially region continue to differentiate the Canadian electorate's support for political parties. Studies of federal voting behaviour consistently depict an electorate which does not divide its support for political parties according to occupational

Source: Excerpted from "The Party System" by Janine Brodie and Jane Jenson. In *Canadian Politics in the 1990s*, 3rd edition, edited by M.S. Whittington and G. Williams. Toronto: Nelson, 1990. Reprinted by permission of the authors.

position or even according to the location which voters think they occupy in a status ranking. In addition, the programs and policies of the two major parties reveal few differences in the class interests that they claim to protect and advance. Both depict themselves as guardians of the "national interest." As a result, they are most clearly distinguished by the differences in electoral support that they gain from Canada's major language groups and regions.

This is not to say that Canadian electoral politics has not witnessed at least some of the symptoms of a modernizing party system. From the earliest years, there have been social democratic or socialist parties active in the federal party system. Yet, all these parties, including the New Democratic Party, have never enjoyed anything near a majority of the support of their supposed constituency, the Canadian working class. Rather, the Liberal party gains more votes from workers than does the self-styled social democratic party, the NDP.

Students of Canadian political parties do not agree on how to explain or even describe this perplexing feature of our party system. One kind of study simply attempts to categorize the members of the federal party system so that they can be compared. For example, some typologies describe the federal party system according to the number of parties competing within it. Yet, even at this most elementary level of categorization, there is minimal agreement. Does Canada have a two-party system, since only the Liberals and Progressive Conservatives stand any reasonable chance of forming a government? Or, has there been four-party system (until 1980) because there were four competitors which consistently won seats in Parliament? Or, should we count two-and-a-half parties, acknowledging the persistence of the NDP despite its remote chance of forming a national government? These questions have all been answered in the positive by students of party politics.

Another body of literature characterizes the federal parties according to their organization and electoral orientations. Here again, there is little consensus. Most observers agree, however, that there is a noteworthy difference between the two major parties and the NDP and its predecessor, the Co-operative Commonwealth Federation (CCF). The two major parties are generally described as cadre parties, pragmatic parties, or parties seeking consensus, while the CCF/NDP is depicted as a mass party and a party of program, principle, or protest. Nevertheless, regardless of the basis of categorization, none of these typologies explains the anomalies of the federal party system, especially its apparent inability to "modernize" in predicted ways.

Party and Class in Canada

There are several popular explanations for the absence of pervasive class-based voting in federal politics. This absence has been attributed, by different authors, to the cultural cleavage between French and English Canada and the consequent lack of a sense of nation, to the conflict between central and peripheral regions, and to constitutional biases which encourage regionalism. A familiar theme, however, is the notion that Canadian politics never has been characterized by class conflict because such conflict is irrelevant. Economic and geographic conditions, it is argued, have defused potentially divisive economic cleavages by promoting population movement and social mobility. A further deduction made by such observers is that Canada is a "middle-class" society where material and social benefits are widely shared and, thus, Canadian politics need not be affected by either class conflict or ideology. Partisan debate can focus on the other issues.

Another suggestion about why class-based electoral politics has not flourished in Canada is based on observations about the nature of the federal parties themselves. Sometimes coupled with the "middle-class" view of Canadian society, this perspective describes the Liberals and Conservatives as "brokers," offering the electorate an aggregation and accommodation of the myriad of potentially conflicting interests that inevitably arise in any society. The parties' only concern, according to this analysis, is to accommodate diverse interests sufficiently to build an electoral coalition large enough to capture power. Instead of organizing the electorate around class interests, the major parties are said to engage in a politics of moderation which minimizes differences and restrains divisive tendencies. It is further argued that a beneficial consequence of such brokerage parties is that they can knit together diverse interests in a polity which is otherwise weakly integrated.

As appealing as the middle-class and brokerage theses may be, there are a number of factors which potentially challenge their validity as explanations of the absence of class voting. First, and most obviously, Canada is not and never was a "middle-class" society. In recent years, in fact, the distribution of wealth has grown even less equal. Similarly, there are ample reasons to question the accuracy of the brokerage conception of federal politics. If the major parties are solely concerned with accommodating social conflicts, then the federal party system is witness to their failures. For decades, large regionally-based third parties have occupied their own space on the partisan landscape, citing the neglect and biases of the "brokerage parties" as their reason for entering the electoral fray. Their existence suggests that not all interests are equally accommodated by the two major parties.

Finally, there is little evidence to suggest that brokerage parties are neutral and non-class-based organizations. Their major sources of campaign financing, their patterns of recruitment of members and candidates, and their policy orientations all suggest that the Liberals and Progressive Conservatives have a decidedly status quo and frankly pro-capitalist bent. Yet, paradoxically, these class parties find much of their electoral support among workers. Thus, we return to the question: why is there so little evidence of class-based voting in Canada's federal party system?

To begin answering, it is helpful to return and re-examine the original prediction about the "inevitability" of class-based electoral politics in industrial societies. The principal assumption underlying the prediction is that there is a direct relationship between economic and partisan development. This view of the organization of class relations in liberal democracies arises from economistic Marxist analyses as well as from political sociology's observation that labour or socialist parties and class-based voting emerged and endured in industrialized countries. This formulation is also predicated on a further assumption—notably, that voters' political demands, attitudes and behaviour automatically reflect their class position.

According to these assumptions, electoral politics, organized around a class cleavage, will be concerned primarily with questions of control over economic production and distribution. In this view, competition between classes will lead to the general partisan organization of the bourgeoisie, and those supporting the interests of the bourgeoisie, into one party, and workers, and those supporting the interests of workers, into another. Partisan competition is thus assumed to develop between those who have, according to the rules of the private economy, control over the production process and its profits and those who have, according to the laws of liberal democracy, some control over the production process through the state.

The deduction that workers will be organized into one party and the bourgeoisie into another, however, is not the only one possible starting from an initial assumption about the political importance of classes in liberal democratic politics. In fact, what history has demonstrated in the last century of the joint development of capitalism and liberal democracy is the following: while capitalism has proceeded in all countries in similar directions toward centralization, monopolistically large corporations, and an increase in state intervention in the economy, partisan expression of class conflict has differed widely in the several countries. Students of political sociology who have taken a rather deterministic view of the relationship between economic development and partisan organization, by and large, have been unable to explain the many variations of electoral politics in advanced capitalist countries. This is perhaps because they have tended to minimize the effects of specific national and historical contexts as well as the combined impact of elections, ideologies and political parties themselves in structuring partisan and class relations.

Historically, mass political parties came into being when franchise reform created large numbers of voters who had not previously participated in electoral politics. The way this integration occurred was important in structuring the subsequent partisan organization of class relations because parties primarily (though not exclusively) provided the electorate with a *definition of politics*. They defined the content of politics and the meaning of political activity by shaping an ideology. Most generally, *political parties have a major role in shaping the interpretation of what aspects of individuals' lives should be considered political, how politics should be conducted, what the boundaries of political discussion most properly may be, and what kinds of conflicts can be resolved through the electoral process.* From the vast array of tensions, differences, and inequalities characteristic of an society, parties are crucial to the selection of those which will be defined as political alternatives in the electoral process and thereby shape how the electorate will divide against itself. Whether a problem is considered to be a religious, economic or political question is set by this definition. This role of parties is profoundly important because *before* electoral cleavages come into being a definition of what is political must exist.

Elections are events of conflict and competition, but the substance of electoral politics is not automatically given. For example, politics may be described as the expression of conflict between classes or between ethnic groups or as the aggregation of individual preferences. Economic conditions, such as the level of industrialization, set parameters around the range of organization which is possible in any society, but they can never guarantee that particular classes will be politically active. Subordinate classes will not spontaneously recognize the political implications of their disadvantaged location in capitalist relations of production and vote according to their class position. Members of particular occupational sectors in capitalist society, whether they are farmers, blue-collar workers or office workers, do not and will not act cohesively as a class until they become aware that they are members of a class. The nurturing of this awareness demands, as a prerequisite, ideological and organizational activity. Classes as active and self-conscious social actors must be created, and, in turn, the extent to which they live politically as classes is largely the extent to which they behave as classes in elections.

At a very minimum, class-based voting must be preceded by the development of a class-based organization which challenges existing definitions of politics which interpret social and political relations in non-class terms. If the existence, characteristics and partisan implications of class conflict are exposed by the activities of a well-developed trade-union movement of a powerful and influential party of the left, then there will be evidence, at the level of voting, of class-based politics. Without these prior conditions, class cleavages will be submerged, distorted and rarely visible in voting behaviour.

Since the late nineteenth century, socialist parties have existed which have defined politics as the expression of conflict between classes and not as neutral aggregations of individual or group preferences. They have precipitated a conflict over definitions of politics as well as government policies. The existence of such a debate over definitions means that voters have been offered alternative bases for electoral alignment, and some of these threaten the very existence of one or more of the bourgeois parties. Not surprisingly, then, such parties struggle hard to maintain and recreate a definition of politics which denies the centrality of class differences and relations in capitalist systems. Time and again, confronted with a class-based definition of politics advanced by socialist parties, bourgeois parties have retorted that this definition is inappropriate and that politics is really about race or religion, and moreover that politics is not about conflict at all but about finding consensus so that the capitalist system can be managed successfully to the benefit of all.

If alternative ways of organizing the electorate are possible under the same economic conditions, and the nature of this organization affects the manner in which classes and individuals behave in electoral politics, we begin to see a way of unraveling the perplexity of the Canadian party system. The extent to which capitalist relations of production are debated politically depends in large part on how successfully either socialist or bourgeois parties organize the electorate behind their respective points of view. If politics is defined as conflict between language groups, it is more difficult to unite for partisan action members of the same class who have different linguistic backgrounds. In other words, some political cleavages are likely to be incompatible with others, as the dominance of one cleavage generally inhibits the growth of others. By examining this contest over the definition of politics, it is possible to arrive at a better understanding of the background to the contemporary Canadian party system, which is divided along lines of language and region. ...

The Contemporary Party System

During the late 1930s and war years, it appeared as if the CCF might successfully challenge, with the politics of class, the two major parties and their definition of politics. Some forty years later, however, it is apparent that neither the CCF nor its successor, the NDP, has succeeded in this goal. The Liberal Party, kept afloat by the politics of language, has won most of the federal elections since the Second World War, and it has been the Progressive Conservative Party rather than the CCF/NDP that has won the rest. Confounded by a seemingly insurmountable electoral arithmetic, the CCF first moderated its policies, later forged an organizational alliance with the trade union movement, and finally changed its name and formal structure in 1961 by reconstituting itself as the New Democratic Party. Each strategy was designed to enhance the electoral fortunes of social democracy in Canada. Yet, rather than expanding the space for class politics, they tended to close it, leaving the NDP today relatively weak and uncertain about its definition of the political.

The reorientation of the NDP's socialism began during the Second World War when the party cautiously redefined its nationalization policy goals so as to avoid alienating potential voters. This strategy of moderation accelerated until, in 1956, the party adopted a new statement of principles, the Winnipeg Declaration, which provided the theoretical foundation for the new NDP. An essential element of the NDP's moderation was its view of the state's role in social change. Departing from its earlier and more radical advocacy of state ownership of key sectors of the economy (in order to guarantee that production would reflect the public interest), the party increasingly proposed only Keynesian economic solutions. It promised to pursue anti-cyclical policies to stabilize the economy and maintain full employment as well as to provide a comprehensive net of social programs to improve the lives of the disadvantaged. The Liberals and Conservatives, as did most bourgeois parties in other countries in the post war years, also promised most of the same policies. The CCF/NDP, therefore, did not represent a position sufficiently different from either the Liberals or the Progressive Conservatives to allow the electorate to distinguish its policies from what the other parties were offering.

The CCF's, and later the NDP's, failure to impose a new definition of politics following from a distinctive strategy meant that the party did not constitute a clear alternative for the voters. With its liberal view of a basically neutral state, the NDP had only a single argument to rally support behind it: vote NDP for more honest and fair government. In consequence, the NDP had few policy alternatives to propose once full employment and investment policies came into conflict with each other. When the continued economic growth on which these policies were premised grew more and more difficult to achieve, the NDP was as confounded as the other parties. It moved from "more Keynesianism" to an "industrial policy" to state directed "investment programs," but none of these presentations appeared credible to the voters of the 1970s and 1980s. It found itself competing with the two bourgeois parties, especially the Liberals, more or less on their terms.

A second factor accounting for the failure of the NDP to inject a viable alternative definition of politics into the federal party system followed from the strategic decision to construct a particular kind of organizational base for the party. In the 1950s the CCF thought that its decline could be halted only if it followed the example of the British Labour Party and constructed a formal organizational link with the trade union movement. Together with the newly formed Canadian Labour Congress (CLC), the CCF created a new social democratic party, the NDP, in 1961. The anticipated surge of electoral support toward the NDP from Canadian workers did not materialize, however. Overall, the union links with the party remained more formal and financial than directed toward mobilization of the union membership in support of the NDP. The new party was largely a marriage of notables—designed by the leadership of the old CCF and the new CLC. Therefore, the NDP did not replicate the successes the British Labour Party enjoyed after the Second World War. The obsession with bringing about union affiliation that dominated the CCF in the 1950s also meant that the new party accepted the union movement as it was—without political class consciousness, without a history of struggle for socialism, and without partisan experience. This meant that the CCF/NDP felt compelled to moderate its program so as to gain the support of union leaders who, in turn, recognized the conservatism of their rank and file or who were politically conservative themselves.

22 The Politics of Tecumseh Corners: Canadian Political Parties as Franchise Organizations

R. Kenneth Carty (2002)

EDITORS' INTRODUCTION

Ken Carty is professor emeritus of political science at the University of British Columbia. Specializing in political parties and electoral systems, he has held a number of prestigious academic posts, including the Brenda and David McLean Chair in Canadian Studies, Distinguished Scholar in Residence at the Peter Wall Institute of Advanced Studies, director of the Centre for the Study of Democratic Institutions, and president of the Canadian Political Science Association. In 2013 he was awarded the Mildred Schwartz Lifetime Achievement Award from the American Political Science Association. Carty is a former boundary commissioner in British Columbia, and was the director of research for the BC Citizens' Assembly on Electoral Reform. Carty has published widely and deeply on the topics of political parties, electoral systems, party systems, and electoral and party system reform.

In this piece, Carty addresses the complex calculations that parties must make in balancing their national interests with local dynamics in order to compete in elections. He likens political parties to franchise organizations, maximizing efficiencies that come with size and standardization, while also taking advantage of local participation. This type of organization, Carty argues, breeds brand recognition to a mass market while still being able to meet the particular needs of local populations.

Presidential Address to the Canadian Political Science Association, Toronto, Ontario, 2002

> *People who have only witnessed gatherings such as the House of Commons at Westminster and the Senate at Washington and never seen a Conservative Convention at Tecumseh Corners or a Liberal Rally at the Concession school house, don't know what politics means.*
>
> Stephen Leacock—"The Great Election in Missinaba County"

Stephen Leacock's account of the great election in Missinaba County provides a classic analysis of electoral politics in Canada. On the one hand, we are told that this epic contest took place within the context of a major countrywide political battle over reciprocity—would

Source: Excerpted from *Canadian Journal of Political Science*, vol. 35, no. 4 (December 2002). Notes omitted. Reprinted by permission.

there be, should there be freer trade with the Americans? Leacock reports the question was thrashed out with such a patriotic spirit in Mariposa that "for a month, at least, people talked of nothing else." With the parties squaring off against one another, it appears to have been a straight fight, with voters' long-standing party loyalties interacting with a big national issue to shape the outcome. However, there is a second story line. It emphasizes the realities of the immediate world of Mariposa, Tecumseh Corners and the concession lines defining the rest of the county. That face of the election contest reveals the struggle by an established incumbent to hold his seat against an unexpected challenger. In it we see the sitting member actively sponsor an independent candidate in the hopes of splitting the opposition's vote, politicians eagerly agreeing with those on both sides of the dominant issue, casual manipulation of the local communication networks, and sophisticated vote mobilization strategies by election-day campaign organizations. At the end of the count, the insurgent Conservative candidate, Josh Smith, emerged victorious, defeating John Henry Bagshaw, the sitting Liberal MP.

In this case study, all of André Siegfried's four "arguments that tell" in Canadian elections are at work, but the most powerful are the impulses of local advantage and the appeals of national party as defined by their leaders. We see the interplay of skillful politicians, both inciting and responding to local prejudices and interests as they struggle for position. Despite 20 years of service as the incumbent, and enough resources to surreptitiously fund a third candidate, Bagshaw was out manoeuvred by Smith's campaign which told local electors what they wanted to hear, and then managed its voter turnout machine with military precision. Writing before the behavioural revolution, Leacock does not give us the final vote counts, for Tecumseh Corners or any other polling place in the county, but we know elections in the East Simcoe ridings of this period were won by only a few hundred votes, so it seems plausible that Smith's local campaign made the difference. Nevertheless, this activity was all structured by enduring national political parties, whose traditions and claims on the loyalties of the voters shaped the politics of the county. Perhaps, then, the real story is the Conservative party's decision to oppose the Liberal's reciprocity initiative, and the Tory candidates' subsequent sweep across the province. If that is the case, then all the planning and efforts of the local activists may have made no difference to the outcome. Perhaps Bagshaw, as he feared, was doomed from the moment his party leaders decided to fight the election over the tariff.

However they read this, most ordinary observers find the story deeply satisfying for it embraces both sides of a political world so familiar to the Canadian style and practice of single-member constituency politics. Political scientists, however, seem more inclined to resist Leacock's seductive pen. They are apt to ask: What is really going on here? Did candidate Smith win, or did the Liberal party lose? Can we measure the relative contributions of leaders, parties and candidates to the election results? Perhaps not surprisingly, there is comparatively little agreement on these questions. Those in the election study business use their data from rich national surveys to demonstrate that electoral success or failure is tied to parties' capacity to mobilize support around the defining issues of national campaigns. They would say Bagshaw was a goner, destined to be swept away in an anti-reciprocity party vote. Those who study constituency-level organizations argue that their evidence indicates that local campaigns often develop their own idiosyncratic issues, that riding associations depend on the energies and resources of self-starting local notables like Josh Smith, and that parties prosper as a function of their constituency organizations' efforts. So, we are left with a picture of Canadian parties as organizations that have a distinct and lively existence in both national and local political worlds. But what kind of organizations are these? How, if at all, do they attach the politics of Tecumseh Corners to those of every other corner in the country?

These are not merely questions for political scientists to ponder on sleepy afternoons in the Mariposa sun. Political parties have been described, in John Meisel's words, as "among the relatively few genuinely national forces in Canada" with their success at brokering the competing claims of the country as essential to the nation's well being. This is no small task in a country in which, more often than not, the forces of cultural difference trump the claims of class, the appeals of community override the demands of society, and the imperatives of geography overwhelm the lessons of history. Despite their perceived centrality to the democratic process, or their theoretical import for national unity, we know little about how Canadian parties actually work. Conventional wisdom says the classic Canadian party acts as a broker, presenting policy packages that accommodate the competing claims of different regions, communities and groups. In a word, national parties are to succeed by aggregating, rather than articulating, interests. This, of course, sets them off from the cleavage-based parties of most other democracies whose very raison d'être is to articulate the claims of their distinctive clienteles. It suggests that Canadian parties will be very different kinds of organizations, and that they will practise their own, unique style of politics.

Of course, parties can succeed, but not win, in Canada by appealing to more narrowly based interests along one of the many cleavage lines dividing Canadians. Given the territorial cast of the electoral system, the easiest way to do this is by playing to regional discontents. And the history of the party system has been marked by the ebb and flow of such parties. They have typically arisen when an overreaching national party collapsed under the strain of trying to accommodate the conflicting demands of too many interests gathered onto a political omnibus. It is no coincidence that each of the great party system crises in Canadian history occurred in the wake of the disintegration of the oversized party coalitions assembled by Robert Borden, John Diefenbaker and then Brian Mulroney. This suggests that if Canada's successful brokerage parties are catch-all parties, they have to be careful not to actually catch all the interests, or embrace all the Tecumseh Corners, clamoring for their care and attention.

But why should this be? Leon Epstein provided an answer years ago in a perceptive essay comparing Canadian and American parties. He noted that political parties in both countries faced the same challenge of representing the diverse interests of geographically sprawling, socially plural, economically disparate, politically federal, mobile and open, new-world electorates through a similar single-member plurality electoral system. However, while the party system in the United States managed to contain all its diversity in two parties, the smaller Canada produced a multi-party system. The reason, Epstein argued, is to be found in the systems of government and more particularly in the distinctive demands for discipline each makes on their respective parties. American parties need be disciplined on questions of office but not policy; in Canada, parties with a bent for majority government must be disciplined on both. Parliamentary norms call for a level of party discipline on policy and programme questions that simply make it impossible to contain all of the country's political diversity within two parties. Consequently, regions that feel neglected, and groups who think their interests are not being articulated, find themselves drawn to build and support new parties.

This dynamic defines the balancing act required of governing parties in Canada. They must construct a political tent large and shapeless enough to encompass the inchoate coalitions of supporters they need, but not so big as to explode, leaving a more fragmented system. The great Conservative party collapses of 1921, 1962–1963 and 1993 all produced just such a turning point. Each produced a new wave of third-party growth and increased the fragmentation of party and electoral politics. Yet, with each cycle of the party system wheel, the brokerage balancing act became more difficult as the size and breadth of the new governing party's base narrowed. And, with fewer corners of the country finding a place in the dominant coalition, popular confidence in politicians and their parties declined. More than ever, parties have come to depend upon the electoral system to deliver them parliamentary majorities. Yet, these majorities provide the very reason, and means, to create and sustain such broad-based brokerage parties. Without them, disciplined national parties might well dissolve. …

Parties as Franchise Organizations

The central linkage problem for Canadian parties is to respond to the imperatives of a competitive national system while incorporating the demands and energies of parochial supporters. The solution is an organizational form that best accommodates those tensions. Franchise systems are designed to do just that. They exist to maximize the efficiencies of scale and standardization while exploiting the advantages of local participation in the operation and delivery of an organization's product. Typically, a central organization operating under an established brand determines the products and sets standards for their production and labelling; designs and manages mass marketing and advertising strategies; and provides management help and training while arranging for the basic supplies needed by local outlets. For their part, individual franchises exist to deliver the product to a particular market. To do so, they invest local resources, both capital and personnel, in building an organization attuned to the needs and demands of the community they serve, and they are preoccupied with delivering the product to their market area. In expansive systems, there may be a range of intermediary organizational units designed both to carry out specialized functions and to mitigate the inherent tensions between the centre and the individual franchises' mutual, but oft competing, interests.

The relationships between a central organization and its local franchises can vary enormously, and indeed need not be the same for each individual franchise within a single organization. Large, rich or important units may well have a level of independence and power not shared by smaller or less vital outlets, while others may be fully owned by the central organization itself. Franchise systems can be centralized, decentralized or federalized, depending upon the efficiencies and/or philosophies of the organization and, inevitably, there will be friction between the parts as each tries to influence the other to its advantage. To structure the relationship, and institutionalize the rules ordering the system, detailed franchise contracts spelling out the rights, responsibilities and obligations of each guarantee their autonomy and mutual interdependence. They ensure that the central office can penalize a local affiliate if it fails to meet the organization's standards; it also provides mechanisms for local units to hold the central organization to its policies and responsibilities.

In principle, franchise organizations are more flexible and adaptable than monolithic, bureaucratic organizations. They have the advantage of producing a reliable, identifiable product which consumers can count on, a centrally planned communication programme that ensures they are delivering the appropriate and desired message to their clients, and a leadership free to make decisions about product lines or target markets. In addition, they also have the advantage of attracting local investment, generating a set of grass-roots participants with an incentive to build and maintain an effective organization. These local partners will be more attuned to the immediate community's perspectives, practices and demands than those in a remote headquarters, an advantage in attracting support in a volatile and competitive environment. Individual franchises can also test-market product innovations and delivery services, providing valuable ground-level feedback to the centre.

This model has been successful in a wide variety of industries and activities, providing goods and services to mass publics across national and international space. Organizations such as Canadian Tire, General Motors and McDonalds have managed to penetrate different communities and societies offering a standard product line, varied around the edges to satisfy local sensibilities (Lobsterburgers in Nova Scotia, Dr. Pepper soft drinks in Texas). Their franchise operators locate, build and operate outlets designed to capture consumers in communities they know well. Not all individual franchises are the same (some are unionized, others not), nor do all have the same relationship with the company (which for some changes over time), but thanks to a consistent labeling and advertising programme all are part of an easily recognizable organization whose brand offers an essentially familiar product to a mass public.

Without stretching the analogy too far, or suggesting that parties are nothing more than the political equivalent of a hardware or hamburger chain, it is possible to recognize in the franchise model a framework for analyzing and interpreting the organization and operation of modern political parties. Their central organizations are typically responsible for providing the basic product line—policy and leadership; for devising and directing the major communication line and appeal—the national campaign; and for establishing standard organizational management, training and financing functions. In office, the central party plays the dominant part in any governance responsibilities the party assumes. Local units, however they are defined (geographically or otherwise), more often provide the basic organizational home for most individual members, and are normally charged with delivering the product by creating organizations that can find and support candidates as well as mounting campaigns to mobilize the vote on election day. Intermediary and specialized entities can support these activities, but all units must recognize their part and accept their defined power and role trade-offs as a necessary part of the bargain required to make the party, as a whole, successful.

This simple framework provides for the functional autonomy of the organizational elements that exist within parties, while still leaving considerable room for variation between and within parties in terms of the relationships among their units, or in the locus of particular activities. It does not proscribe any particular balance of forces or pattern of influence in a party. Quite different solutions to the problems of policy development or personnel recruitment can be institutionalized in parties structured in franchise terms. In one, local organizations might play a decisive role in candidate selection processes, while in others that power could be reserved for a different level of the party machine. The role of members, and so the incentives to membership, can vary considerably depending upon the level at which individual members are attached to the party, and what part they are assigned in the life of those units. Where professionally supported national leadership roles are separated from local mobilization efforts, the party in office might dominate policy-making activity leaving local franchises free to manage the politics of the grass roots. In an environment of declining levels of party identification, that will allow the relatively autonomous elements of a franchise party to pursue an increasingly available electorate in ways that are independent, yet compatible, with one another. ...

The Franchise Party System

The franchise model helps us discern the fundamental dynamics of party organization in Canada. It also points to what are at once the basic organizational strengths and weaknesses of the system's parties. Their franchise structure allows national parties to encompass a wide variety of distinctive communities, and cope with the pressures of a complex, pluralistic society. They do this by tying their members and activists into local associations and giving them almost complete autonomy to choose their representatives and manage the affairs of their constituency party. Members work to support local politicians, but know that they have little influence on party policy. From this organizational base, party leaders can pursue an aggregation strategy designed to maximize their popular support. The difficulty is that leaders can end up constructing coalitions that contain more internal contradictions (aggregation excesses) than their party members are willing to accept. When the discipline demanded of local MPs becomes an unacceptably high franchise fee, exit (to another association, party or out of politics) becomes a more viable option than voice, and a more tolerable option than loyalty, for the volunteers who people the local party units.

This franchise party structure works best when skillful politicians can develop and nurture the informal and personal networks necessary to knit together the otherwise separate elements of a decentralized organization, but the personal factionalism that it fosters makes it inherently fragile. In periods of rapid social change that overturn the country's electoral equations, or when institutional reform makes significantly new demands, the parties and the wider party system can quickly crack apart under the strain. This happened three times during the twentieth century. After each crisis, the parties were rebuilt, always using the basic franchise model to structure their organizations, albeit with slightly altered bargains changing the relationship between members and party leaders. Each of those longer organizational cycles saw a strengthening of the leader's position vis-à-vis others, though a greater democratization of the process of leadership selection has left leaders increasingly vulnerable to the vicissitudes of an unpredictable and mobilizable membership.

Canadian parties are open and opportunistic, disciplined and fragile. The result is a less coherent or unified party structure than called for by the classic model of responsible parliamentary government. These are not organizations that can be easily counted on by governing politicians seeking to implement an agenda, nor are they an effective machinery for an engaged citizenry trying to hold its government accountable. They are nineteenth-century solutions for linking Tecumseh Corners to Ottawa. They have survived into the twenty-first century because they continue to be Canadian politicians' organizational response to their problem of connecting a diverse plural society to a set of inherited old-world governing institutions.

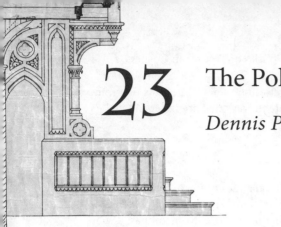

23 The Politics of Voting

Dennis Pilon (2007)

EDITORS' INTRODUCTION

Dennis Pilon is an associate professor in the Department of Political Science at York University. A scholar of Canadian and comparative politics, most of his work has been focused on democratic reform in Western democracies. He has published in the Canadian Political Science Review, *the* Journal of Canadian Studies, *and* Labour/Le Travail.

He has been an advocate of electoral system reform at various levels of government for many years, and this excerpt addresses the complex issues involved in that endeavour at the federal level. In particular, Pilon points to the political nature of both our electoral institutions and the process of reform itself. Arguing that you cannot separate politics from electoral system change, he suggests that it is important to understand the tradeoffs involved in different systems, the winners and losers under the current system, and the incentives that structure political competition in Canada. Once voters are more informed and aware of these nuances, it becomes possible, he argues, to discuss and promote a more democratic agenda.

Introducing the Politics of Voting

Consider the following election scenarios:

Scenario 1: A party that has secured considerably less than a majority of the votes has nonetheless won a majority of the seats and control of the government.

Scenario 2: The party with the most votes wins fewer seats than the second-place finisher and remains in opposition while the less popular party forms the government.

Scenario 3: The governing party gets more votes than they did in the previous election and increases its percentage of the popular vote but still loses the election.

Scenario 4: One party receives more than half a million votes but wins no seats while another wins 22 seats for a roughly similar amount of support.

Scenario 5: Of the millions of votes cast in the election, fewer than half are counted toward electing anyone.

Source: Excerpted from *The Politics of Voting: Reforming Canada's Electoral System* by Dennis Pilon. Toronto: Emond Montgomery, 2007.

These election results seem perverse, and contrary to common-sense notions of fairness and justice. They sound like just the sort of results our media report occurring in what they call tinpot dictatorships, banana republics, or unstable authoritarian regimes. But in the cases above, the seemingly irregular results are not the product of meddling by generals or apparatchiks or authoritarian leaders. All the scenarios have actually occurred in Canadian elections. Scenario 4 can be related to results in the 2004 federal election, where 582,247 votes for the Greens gained them no seats while 474,247 votes for the Liberals in the Maritime provinces alone won them 22 seats. Scenario 3 sounds like the 2006 provincial election in New Brunswick, where the governing Conservatives increased their total number of votes and their percentage of the overall vote but still won fewer seats than the rival Liberals. Scenario 2 can be linked to the 1996 and 1998 provincial elections in BC and Quebec, where in both cases the most popular party lost to the second-place finisher. And Scenarios 1 and 5 describe nearly all Canadian elections. We regularly witness election results where a "majority" government is won by a party that gains less than a majority of the votes. Meanwhile millions of votes, often representing as much as half of the total ballots cast, do not contribute to the election of any representatives at all—they are effectively "wasted."

These results run contrary to Canadian expectations about election results and indeed defy common sense. Nobody goes to vote thinking that his or her ballot won't be counted. People expect that a party with more votes should get more seats, and that parties with roughly equal levels of support should be awarded a similar number of seats. It seems reasonable that a government that gained more support in an election should be re-elected. And terms like "majority government" should mean something—in this case, that the government actually represents a majority of the people. Yet far too often our election results repudiate such common-sense assumptions. Worse still, such results are typically accepted as normal by our political elites and media, who very rarely ask any questions or draw public attention to them.

Part of the reason that election results such as these go uncontested is that Canadians are largely unaware of the details of our elections and have a poor understanding of the workings of our electoral institutions. This isn't surprising when we recognize how little effort is made by our government and media to help people understand such details. After all, most election-day coverage consists of screaming headlines about a "landslide majority" for this or that party, or a televised party leader claiming to have won a "mandate" to govern and implement his or her party's policies. But the media and the politicians seldom point out that these "majorities" rarely rest on a real majority of the votes. One key purpose of this book is to change that. The more the public is aware of how our electoral institutions work and the anomalous results they regularly produce, the greater the chance that such results will no longer be passively accepted. The point of this volume is to focus attention on the voting system as the key factor producing these distorted results and the primary institution for reform if we want to eliminate them. In drawing attention to the centrality of the voting system we will also address why this institution and its workings are typically obscured, poorly understood, and very difficult to change. …

The Politics of Voting-System Reform in Canada

It's time to pull together the various arguments in this book and apply them to the present condition of voting-system reform in Canada. In many ways, it seems like the best of times: never have so many different voting-system reform initiatives been pursued at the provincial level in Canada as in the last decade. But in other ways, it seems like the worst of times: two initiatives have failed to produce results (BC and PEI), others appear stalled (Quebec) or in limbo (New Brunswick), and another seems to be getting short shrift from the media and opinion leaders (Ontario). It is entirely possible that none of these reform initiatives will bear fruit. The way forward seems unclear. So far, reform-oriented academics and activists have focused their efforts on debating the values and performance of different voting systems, with middling to poor success. It's time to alter that strategy.

Part of the problem has been rooted in a less-than-critical approach to many problematic assertions about our political system. This book has sought to shift the terms of the debate by challenging the myths that have arisen—specifically, the allegedly key role of local representation in our political system, the pressing need for stability in government above all other values, and the so-called accountability that our present system it is supposed to deliver to voters. Additionally, the book has challenged many of the myths about the allegedly negative performance of PR systems. But more to the point, this book has demonstrated that questions of voting-system performance have not been central in decisions about choosing plurality or PR, either in the past or in contemporary settings, despite what public debate on the issue might seem to suggest. Instead, voting systems have been chosen primarily for political reasons, in order to serve the interests of mobilized political forces. Even in the most recent and more publicly deliberative reform processes, the success or failure of the reform initiatives has depended crucially on what organized political forces have done to aid or hinder making change happen.

The central argument of this book is that the institutions of voting are themselves political. Thus the reform of a voting system is a fundamentally political decision, involving a necessary appreciation of the political divisions at work in a given locale and how they are mobilized into concrete political action. The divisions are manifest in the mobilized political power we recognize as parties, and what parties want or don't want is an important factor in efforts at voting-system reform. But political divisions are not simply the creation of parties. Unlike our presently dominant populist discourse, which seems to posit a world where folks could all just get along if it weren't for meddling politicians, there are real political divisions that cut across Canadian civil society—divisions that are reflected, albeit imperfectly, in our political parties. Those seeking voting-system reform must come to grips with both these aspects of politics if they want to increase their chances of success.

This chapter will sum up the insights from this book that support the view that our electoral institutions are—and indeed, *must* be—political, and that changing them requires an appreciation of this politics and its dynamics. We will then apply that approach to understanding the politics of securing voting-system reform at the present time in Canada.

Why the Voting System Is Necessarily Political

This book began with a criticism of efforts to depoliticize discussions of voting-system reform. I argued that attempts to go "beyond politics" invariably end up somewhere that is just *differently* political, not genuinely un-political. The push to depoliticize the discussions has two forces behind it—one academic, the other public—and both are deeply problematic. The academic approach assumes that institutions should be designed outside of the sphere of political contestation and that such a process will produce institutions defined by values, not self-interest. The public approach lumps all politicians together as the problem and refashions the notion of political struggle away from party competition and toward a battle between "the politicians" and "the people." Both approaches appear to assume that there is someplace beyond politics where better or more fair decisions can be made. But both are mistaken. Ignoring politics means that when decisions emerge from these allegedly depoliticized places, they will be cast back into the conventional politicized world and will succeed or fail as a result of their ability to survive in such a contested environment. And nor will these results simply reflect the actions of self-interested politicians, as politicians and parties and the decisions they make do bear some relationship to actual divisions among people within the polity. Given this reality, we would be better off to recognize the politics going on here from the outset and, when considering voting-system change, make strategic decisions that address and incorporate them.

The historical record of voting-system change itself recommends such an approach. As recounted at various points in this book, voting systems throughout western countries were the product of political self-interest, not of values or value-driven assessments of voting-system performance. Though the rhetoric of voting-system discussion almost always takes on a value- or performance-driven discourse, these are post hoc rationalizations informed by considerations of power rather than by idealistic values. Now, some readers might object that this line of analysis veers dangerously close to the populist anti-party explanations criticized above. After all, populists claim that politicians are "in it for themselves," and I am arguing that voting systems have been designed by parties to serve their self-interests. But there are important differences dividing the two explanations. Let's explore them in more detail.

The populists use a discourse of "the people versus politicians/parties," which has the effect of denying the fact that there do exist real political differences among people. In a sense, such critics seem to be saying: "Everyone I know thinks the same, so these political problems must be the creation of politicians." It is easy to see how such views could become popular. The hallmark of modern societies, as opposed to traditional ones, is the fluidity of group membership. Within various constraints, people can associate or not with different people, allowing those who would prefer to mix only with others who share their ideas and opinions to do so. It is not a big step to move from thinking that the consensus in your group is, in fact, the consensus in the larger polity, especially when your self-selection process means that you seldom encounter anyone who disagrees with you. Thus such populists typically call for an end to parties or party discipline, or for more local representation, or even for direct democracy like referendums—all with the confidence that such changes will allow the consensus they have come to believe exists to finally emerge.

The "populist" approach to understanding politicians is very different from one that focuses on party self-interest as the animating force in institutional choice. The former assumes an undifferentiated political class whose members have more in common with each other than with the public they claim to represent. Thus institutional choices are about protecting politicians, as a group, against the interests of the public, also as a group. The latter approach, however, assumes that political self-interest differs among parties and that these differences do bear some links to real and abiding differences among the people in civil society. Furthermore, this self-interest cannot just be asserted; it must be explored concretely in order to see both what parties are trying to accomplish in taking various positions as well as how such positions may relate to what people in civil society may or may not want from politics.

Let me be clear: I am not arguing that parties are a transparent reflection of public wants, as obviously parties have considerable power to choose and shape what issues to take up from the public. But it is equally problematic to argue that parties and their policies have no links to those from whom they seek to gain votes.

Voting-system reform is an interesting case in point because, in some cases, it has emerged out of elite decisions within the party regarding strategy while, in others, it has been forced onto the agenda by party members and supporters. This is why the positions of different parties have changed throughout Canadian history and why they have even differed across the country in the same period. Thus both federal Liberals and Conservatives have supported voting-system reforms at various times, depending on what they saw as being in their self-interest. The federal NDP has both opposed and supported a switch to PR at different historical moments and, today, different branches of the provincial NDP seem to favour or oppose reform depending on their likelihood of forming a provincial administration.

Complaints about political-party behaviour notwithstanding, the populist take on politics goes further, in the end amounting to a denial of real political differences among Canadians. But the populist case against politics is both empirically wrong and normatively suspect. Let me deal with each of these issues in turn. There are numerous facts that seem to call the populist non-political idyll into question. Canadian election and survey data demonstrate that we are divided in our political opinions. Across the country—indeed, in every riding—Canadians give their support to parties across the political spectrum. Survey work demonstrates that these voting patterns are not just random, but reflect fairly clear ideological differences among us concerning the key questions of politics, from social ones involving abortion and sexual orientation to economic ones relating to the market and government regulation. Though Canadians may not be well informed on the nuances of policy, they do have a sense of where the different parties stand generally on issues that are important to them and they choose accordingly (Nevitte et al. 2000: 48–51). It is because most evidence concludes that party label is the key indicator informing individual voting decisions that this book makes the case that we need a voting system that can effectively translate those decisions into representation (Clarke et al. 1980: 102, 216, 218–9, 222; Nevitte et al. 2000: 133–4; Blais et al. 2002: 116–7). If "party" is what people are voting for, then our political institutions should reflect that as accurately as possible, and that means switching to some form of PR. Anything that interferes with registering what voters are saying they want with their votes—like most of the so-called positive features of our present plurality system—must be rejected in this analysis as undemocratic.

But just demonstrating that people *do* vote for parties is not the same as demonstrating that they *want* to. If we are talking about what voters want and about reforms to make that happen, some might argue that we should expand the discussion to include the possibility of reforming or eliminating parties. After all, there is arguably much more attention focused today on the problems of party representation than on the electoral system, particularly among populists. The political party as an institution and the practice of party discipline are often characterized by populists as illegitimate—essentially, as interlopers in the political system coming between voters and their democracy. Survey work to determine the public's view of parties has produced mixed results, with the public both criticizing and endorsing the role of political parties in our political system (Howe and Northrup 2000). Yet even if we just focus on the negative polls, the problem with such results is that they register what people think as individuals divorced from the need to address just how our political institutions must also reconcile conflicting individual desires. Such polls seldom force respondents to think through the implications of their anti-party views—issues like how an individual local representative would represent the divided local views of her area (particularly on zero-sum decisions) or why pooling votes on the basis of geographic locale makes more sense than pooling them on some other criteria (such as party affiliation). So despite what some surveys might suggest about a public antipathy toward parties, we cannot act on such recommendations because— at least in their present form—they are fundamentally un-political. They try to assume away what is demonstrably real in Canadian society: that we are divided about politics.

The anti-politics rhetoric is mirrored in a host of other "reforms" often touted by populists. Parliamentary reform, referendums, more power to individual MPs, less party discipline— these are just variations on the "denial of politics" thesis. Instead of posing "solutions" that deny politics, we need solutions that recognize and work with our political divisions. Of course, the solution proffered in this volume is proportional representation. Taking politics seriously means recognizing that Canadians are divided politically and that we must do something to reflect this fact institutionally as best we can. Recognizing political differences is arguably the first step in the democratic trinity of representation, deliberation, and deci- sion taking. We have already demonstrated that, empirically, party representation is what Canadians vote for in elections, and that, normatively, this appears to be the only practical available vehicle to represent the real, collective political divisions that exist across Canadian civil society. The basic argument of this book—backed up by insights from Canadian and comparative experience—is that PR can best reflect our political differences as mobilized by parties through (1) better representation and (2) better accountability as a result of increased competition. Indeed, public complaints about parties focus less on their illegitimacy than the fact that the parties are too similar and voters lack choice.

Of course, not all of our presently organized political forces may accept the need for this "solution" and, indeed, many of their supporters may share their view. While publicly mouth- ing platitudes about the need for stability, majority government, and the time-honoured link between the MP and her constituents, those in power will quietly note among themselves how the current system already works in their favour. This is another aspect of the "politics" of voting-system reform. Those who currently benefit from our institutional arrangements will likely use all the power they can muster to preserve them, even if that means twisting logic, distorting facts, and attempting to rig the debate in their favour. Yet between a "politics of party self-interest" and the less sharply defined political differences among the general population, there is considerable room to push an agenda of democratic reform. The gap identified by populists—that parties are imperfect reflections of their supporters—is also an opportunity, as it creates some space to marshal public support on the issue and perhaps force the parties to respond. Indeed, this was the case in New Zealand, where the public's frustration with the actions of their parties kept the voting-system reform issue alive and ultimately opened it up to a public referendum. ...

Conclusion

Voting-system reform is political. In one sense, this is so because we are a people in a particu- lar place—Canada—with divided views about "the good life"; the proper way to govern; and the values that should inform, shape, and limit public choices. There is no depoliticized space where we can go to make such decisions, much to the chagrin of academic and populist advocates of a non-partisan or depoliticized process. Given this unavoidably political world in which we live, normatively we must find a way to represent our differences as the necessary first step in a democratic trinity of representation, deliberation, and—finally—decision taking. This book has argued that such a normative understanding of political reality points us necessarily toward proportional forms of voting. Arguments against PR often amount to a denial of our politically divided reality (an empirically untenable position) or attempt to use undemocratic rationales (a normatively untenable position).

In another sense, voting-system reform is political because it touches on questions of power—specifically, the power exercised by conventionally organized political forces in civil society. The kind of voting system in place will crucially affect the kind of political competition that exists in any given polity, the accuracy of the representation achieved, and the nature of the governing process that results. Because the voting system is the gateway to power and influence for those who aspire to exercise decision-making control over the state, attempts to alter it will spark resistance from those accustomed to exercising that power. Yet the conventional political forces are themselves coalitions of interests, and these coalitions can be affected by unpredictable events and organizing within civil society.

Here lies one of the great challenges at the heart of voting-system reform initiatives: to promote a universalistic vision of democracy that respects our political pluralism—one that rises above partisan appeals and direct party self-interest—even as reformers gauge the political realities on the ground, specifically the realities informed by the *realpolitik* of party-centred voter mobilization and electoral politics. Between the self-interest of the organized political parties and the public's less-formal political commitment to party voting, there is much opportunity to promote a democratic agenda. These opportunities exist in the public's lack of knowledge about our present electoral arrangements, in the gap between party members and leaders on questions of democratic accountability, in the myriad spaces of civil society more informally, and in the "public service" discourse (if not practice) of our print and broadcast media. No one can predict when the breakthrough moment might occur for the issue of voting-system reform. But if the preparatory work has been done in the many spaces outlined here, a surprisingly minor event can sometimes blow the whole thing wide open.

Political Parties and the Practice of Brokerage Politics

R. Kenneth Carty and William Cross
(2010)

EDITORS' INTRODUCTION

Ken Carty is professor emeritus of political science at the University of British Columbia. In addition to several books on topics related to political parties, electoral systems, and representation, he has published papers in Party Politics; Journal of Elections, Public Opinion and Parties; Representation; *the* Canadian Journal of Political Science; *and* Electoral Studies, *among others.*

William Cross is the Hon. Dick and Ruth Bell Chair for the Study of Canadian Parliamentary Democracy in Carleton University's Department of Political Science. An expert on political parties and legislatures, he has written numerous articles and books on the topic of political institutions. His book with André Blais, Politics at the Centre: The Selection and Removal of Party Leaders in the Anglo Parliamentary Democracies *won the Donald Smiley Prize in 2013.*

This excerpt brings together the expertise of both scholars, as they address one of the fundamental aspects of political parties in Canada: brokerage politics. ("Brokerage politics" refers to the desire of political parties to build coalitions and support by balancing the interests of different groups or regions.)

The authors note that in comparison to other party systems, Canadian political parties are organizationally quite weak, and while the system has undergone change a number of times, the parties themselves have changed little. The authors examine the extent to which parties are able to perform their functions and act as linkages between citizens and the state.

Political parties are central to the Canadian political experience. Indeed, they are more central to the very nature and working of the country than they are in most other established liberal democracies. Canada was initially created by party politicians anxious for an institutional framework that would allow them to break existing stalemates. It was subsequently expanded and restructured, often on partisan terms, and then later constitutionally reengineered, by party leaders. And, after 125 years of electoral competition, one of the major parties in the federal Parliament is dedicated to the breakup of the country.

Source: Excerpted from *The Oxford Handbook of Canadian Politics*, edited by John C. Courtney and David E. Smith. Toronto: Oxford University Press, 2010. Notes omitted. Reprinted by permission.

Despite their part in defining Canadian political life, or the importance they play in shaping and energizing the country's democratic processes, Canadian political parties are, by comparative standards, among the most organizationally weak and decentralized of parties in established democratic party systems. Underinstitutionalized and thinly regulated, they persist remarkably unchanged from the basic cadre-style structures of the mid nineteenth century that gave them birth. The parliamentary and electoral system within which they work has changed little, but, as organizations positioned to mediate between the wider society and its governing institutions, the parties have not been immune to the enormous social, economic, and demographic changes that have continually reshaped Canadian society. This has forced them to reinvent themselves more than once, and it is possible to identify several distinct periods during which the old parties successfully reemerged in new guise (Carty et al. 2000). Those reorderings of the party system have flowed from significant institutional alterations in Canadian governance and marked realignments of the electorate. Despite these changes, much of the essence of Canadian parties would be recognizable to André Siegfried, whose 1906 descriptions still ring true.

This chapter begins by providing an account of the distinctive character of brokerage party politics practiced by Canadian parties and the organizational structures they have, of necessity, developed in response to its demands. ...

The Distinctive Character of Canadian Parties

Accounts of the parties traditionally divide them into two simple groups: the two major parties and then all the others. The major parties, the Liberals and the Conservatives, are the only parties ever to have formed a national government. These two parties have persisted throughout the life of the system, adapting as necessary, but seeking to maintain a nationwide constituency and practicing system-tending politics. For most of the twentieth century, the Liberals have dominated as the centerpiece in a system of polarized pluralism (Johnston 2008). Other parties, variously referred to as *minor parties*, *third parties*, or *protest parties*, have sought unsuccessfully to break up the cozy duopoly that has long governed electoral competition. But operating from a smaller base, and protesting existing political practice, the nature and structure of the political system, the character of the socioeconomic order, or sometimes all of these, they have typically had a limited life. Parties with a distinctive geographical base have sometimes managed to persist for decades, but their very character as regionally defined parties ultimately inhibited them from displacing either of the two large national parties.

These differences have been aggravated and exaggerated by the electoral system, which has systematically overrewarded (with a greater seat share than vote share) the largest party and made survival difficult for small parties. One consequence has been to solidify the organizational structures and practices of the large parties as the norm to which successful parties should conform. This impact of the major parties' example and experience has been particularly important in the absence of any significant legal or regulatory framework governing most aspects of party life.

Heavily influenced by the Lipset and Rokkan (1967) paradigm, most accounts of democratic party systems begin with an analysis of the social cleavages that underlie partisan divisions and define the social bases of the individual parties. Canadian parties have long been described as one of the great exceptions to this paradigm (Alford 1963; Rose 1974).

And by comparative standards, there is some truth to that interpretation. However, for all their heterogeneous character, the two large national parties are neither identical nor completely disconnected from the country's social structure. For decades, the Liberals depended on heavy support from French-speaking Catholic Quebec, but when displaced from their privileged place they quickly adapted and found an alternate base on which to construct a winning coalition. Blais (2005) has demonstrated that there remains a marked religious cleavage leading (English-speaking) Roman Catholics disproportionately to support the Liberals, and his argument suggests that support has been critical to Liberal predominance. If less powerful than in many European systems, class has also played some part in structuring partisanship, especially in providing a base and organizational dynamic for the social democratic New Democratic Party.

Nevertheless, the relative weakness of social divisions in structuring partisan conflict, and thus defining individual parties, has led scholars to recognize that the major Canadian parties are significantly different from their counterparts in most other democracies. The principal functions of the country's major parties are not those of mobilizing distinctive communities and articulating conflicting claims rooted in their interests. Canadian parties are organized to do just the opposite. In the name of accommodating the potentially destructive internal tensions of a weakly integrated national community, they work to obscure differences and muffle conflicting interests. This is the brokerage politics model of democracy. In it, *brokerage parties* are organized and operate in a way that positions them to act as principal instruments of national accommodation rather than democratic division (Carty 1995; Meisel 1963).

Thus, Canada's brokerage parties operate by denying that they should be representative of particular social groups in the national community. Their implicit position is that representative politics of that kind is an inappropriate underpinning for Canadian political life. This is not to say that the parties practice what they preach, for both the Liberals and the Conservatives have at times been quick to recognize and appeal to the interests of distinctive regional or social groups in the electorate. However, they do so claiming that national unity requires a party that can rise above such divisions and argue that only they can do so. This leaves the brokerage party as a distinctive type of party characterized by a unique mix of features.

At the core of a brokerage party's approach to democratic politics is a fierce *electoral pragmatism*. These are organizations consumed with winning and holding office, and they combine an organizational ruthlessness marked by a propensity to abandon losing leaders, with an ideological catholicity that engenders great policy flexibility. Over time, Conservatives and Liberals have shifted sides on major defining issues as well as being prepared to adopt programs only recently denounced and campaigned against. Part of the Liberal's electoral success as the party of the center appears to rest on its practice of campaigning to the Left but governing to the Right. Although the Conservatives are conventionally portrayed as on the Right, there have been periods when they have found themselves to the Liberals' Left. For both, the primary consideration is to find the place that will give them a majority government at that moment.

Brokerage parties' commitment to the broadest possible support base increases their internal diversity and fragility. In response, they are forced to magnify the importance of partisan boundary maintenance as a tool of interparty differentiation. When combined with a fixation on government seeking for its own sake, and reinforced by a self-justifying rhetoric as nation builders, the result is a deep *antipathy to coalition politics*. When the electoral system does not produce a majority (the electorate rarely provides one; it has done so just twice in the past fifty years), the parties prefer to govern alone with a parliamentary minority. In fully half (nine of eighteen) of the general elections of the past half century, the party with the largest parliamentary presence did not have a majority, but in not a single instance was an interparty coalition government formed. In those situations, the parties' basic instinct is to amplify and sharpen partisanship in the hope that the next election will return the system to "normal." This syndrome is rooted in the working of the first-past-the-post electoral system, which helps account for these parties' opposition to fundamental electoral reform.

As organizations with such comparatively ill-defined bounds, brokerage parties make unquestioning *party allegiance*, rather than some ideological test or personal loyalty, the supreme political virtue. André Siegfried (1966) noted this one hundred years ago when he described the parties as almost "sacred institutions" to which individuals owe "absolute loyalty" and could oppose "even in the smallest matters" only at the cost of their reputation and career. This inhibits easy partisan change and, thus, considerably increases the sense of turmoil in periods of party system reorganization that stimulate episodes of parliamentary floor crossing.

Party loyalty reinforces another key characteristic of Canada's brokerage parties—the preeminence of and *domination by the leader*. As chief broker, the leader is responsible for assembling and maintaining a winning coalition. To do this, leaders are given enormous personal latitude to determine and articulate policy, to craft and organize their party's electoral appeals and campaigns, and to manage the careers of even senior party personnel. So important is the position, that for most of a century now, leadership selection has been stripped from the parliamentary caucus and made the prerogative of the wider party meeting in convention. This makes for an extraordinarily strong leadership but also for a fragile one. The parties' only evaluative criteria for leaders is electoral success, and failure can lead to challenges from anywhere in the organization. The leadership is such an important prize that even electorally successful leaders who have overstayed, and so thwarted the ambitions of would-be successors, can be deposed by an internal party uprising.

Flexible brokerage parties that are politically pragmatic, office focused, and leader-centric have an enormous capacity to respond to a changing environment and shifting electoral imperatives. But, this portrait of Canadian brokerage parties raises the question as to whether they are just a North American version of Kirchheimer's (1966; see also Krouwel 2006) catch-all party. Certainly the two appear to share similar approaches to governing, to the central importance they give to leadership selection, and to the role of candidate nomination in establishing their legitimacy. But, that noted, brokerage parties differ from European catch-all parties in important ways that reflect their characteristic approach to electoral dynamics and the management of the country's political life. These differences establish them as a distinct and unique type of political party.

Catch-all parties grow out of a system of social cleavage politicization and recognize that this underlying structural reality means that, whatever their efforts to expand their base, they cannot actually hope to catch all voters. Brokerage parties reject the notion that socioeconomic dimensions of the society close off some voters to them and deny a vision of politics in which that is a determining constraint. In practice, this difference means that catch-all parties deliberately restrain their natural "expressive function" in an attempt to attract voters across existing structural divides whereas brokerage parties have the expressive function—in the Canadian case, a claim to nation building—central to their *raison d'être* and so make it a principal tool of political mobilization.

Party loyalty is understood differently in these two kinds of parties. It is a defining virtue of the brokerage party, given its importance in maintaining support, whereas the catch-all party's ambition to attract support from other parties leads it to accept the attenuation of strong partisanship as the price of success. In both, the party leader plays a central role, particularly as a focus of electoral campaigns. In the catch-all party, the leader carries the message, personifying the appeal; but, in the brokerage party, the leader has a more powerful policy-defining role as the key actor in the brokerage, generating activity that defines the party and its appeal.

One further critical feature distinguishes these parties from one another. Catch-all parties can coexist relatively easily with others of their kind in a single-party system. Indeed, Kirchheimer (1966) argues that catch-all parties emerge as a competitive response to the success of their opponents and points to cases like Great Britain and postwar West Germany as classic examples of systems with two large opposing catch-all organizations. However, the very defining characteristic of the brokerage party—its claim to encompass the entire political community—suggests that there is likely to be only one successful brokerage party in a system at a time. In the Canadian case, this has generally been the Liberals, who emerged as the country's "natural governing party" early in the twentieth century and have rarely relinquished the position. More often than not, this has left the Conservatives at a significant competitive disadvantage, playing the role of would-be national brokers. Thus, the inherent propensity of the successful brokerage party is to become a dominant party rather than just one element in a system of balanced electoral competition.

Major parties may adopt the brokerage model as the standard for national politics, but that option is not available to small parties. Since the introduction of universal suffrage after World War I, almost every Canadian Parliament has had some members from parties that explicitly reject the very premises that define brokerage politics. For the most part, those parties have represented identifiable constituencies—particularly, regional ones, given the biases of a geographically organized electoral system. Some have sought to build a mass-style organization but most soon drifted into adopting many of the organizational norms and forms of the larger parties. But in doing so, they opened themselves and made it possible for the brokerage parties to soak up their supporters and drive them from the field. Such were the successive fates of the Progressives in the 1920s, Reconstruction in the 1930s, the Bloc Populaire in the 1940s, Social Credit and the Ralliement des Créditistes in the 1960s, and Reform in the 1990s. The social–democratic Cooperative Commonwealth Federation only avoided that fate in the early 1960s by constructing an organizational partnership with the trade unions that allowed it to transform itself into the New Democratic Party.

"Stratarchical" Party Organization

Katz and Mair (1993) suggest that there are three organizational faces to political parties, and an analysis of the interrelationships among them exposes the dynamics governing their internal working. And they argue that an analysis of the evolution of the relationships between the "party in public office" (the parliamentary caucus), the "party on the ground" (local membership units), and the "party in central office" (the bureaucratic apparatus) can provide an account of the transformation of party types over time (Katz and Mair 2002). Although this has proved a powerful framework for examining party structure and organization in most western parliamentary democracies, it can be misleading in the Canadian case.

As the direct descendants of nineteenth-century cadre-style political machines, Canadian parties still bear many of the marks of their origins. Rooted in loosely connected constituency-level organizations, they did not develop a coherent single national organization with a corresponding effective party in central office. Never empowered, that face of the party was excluded from the primary business of organizing and managing election campaigns. Thus, from the beginning, Canadian parties have had an essentially dyadic structure. On the one hand, there is the party on the ground organized in a set of local constituency-focused associations; on the other, the party in central office consisting of its leader-focused parliamentary caucus. The enduring organizational challenge of Canadian parties has been to accommodate and balance these two parts with their competing and often divergent interests.

At the heart of Canadian parties' organization structure is a *stratarchical* arrangement that establishes the relationships between these two faces of the parties (on party stratarchy, see Mair 1994, 17). The core organizational bargain leaves the parliamentary party free to determine and articulate party policy whereas the locally organized membership chooses the party's key personnel—candidates and leaders. In effect, disciplined support for the party in public office is exchanged for local autonomy in the management of the party on the ground's affairs. This internal division of labor is guaranteed by a norm of mutually autonomous coexistence. But of course, if this principle is clear and simple in theory, it is inevitably less so in practice. There is an ongoing pattern of intraparty tension and rivalry as each side seeks to expand its influence over the other. The leadership would like more control over personnel recruitment and advancement; the members would like more authoritative say in party policy making (Carty and Cross 2006).

Institutionalizing this pattern of political relationships has led Canadian parties to develop a *franchise* style of organization (Carty 2002). The party center, largely dominated by the leader, determines policy, articulates strategy, and manages party communication (in franchise terms, this amounts to creating and advertising a product). In each of the hundreds of local electoral districts, individual party members come together to find candidates and to organize and manage the constituency campaigns that harvest electoral support (in franchise terms, this is about finding and delivering customers). Highly decentralized, this form allows brokerage parties to establish a presence in each of the many enormously varied constituencies that make up the country's electoral map (Carty and Eagles 2005). The loose connections between individual local associations leaves them shaped by the interests of the particular group of supporters who control them, their extraordinary permeability means that their composition may change dramatically between successive elections, and their considerable autonomy can produce neighboring associations in the same party with quite different political or social complexions.

Levitsky (2003) argues that populist parties survive best when weakly institutionalized, and much the same logic appears to hold for these franchise-style brokerage parties. Their thinly institutionalized character allows them to penetrate distinctive and divergent elements of the community, supports mechanisms of accommodation among competing values and interests, and provides a frame that facilitates their reorientation in the face of significant realignments in the electorate.

Public Opinion and Canadian Identity

25

Mildred A. Schwartz (1967)

EDITORS' INTRODUCTION

Mildred Schwartz is professor emerita of sociology at the University of Illinois at Chicago, and a visiting professor in the Department of Sociology at New York University. A pioneer of voting behaviour research (she directed the National Opinion Research Centre at the University of Chicago in the 1960s), Schwartz has published widely on both Canadian and American political behaviour, public opinion, and political parties. Her work falls at the intersection of political sociology and political science, and in addition to her numerous books, she has published in journals such as Publius, Party Politics, Comparative Sociology, *the* International Journal of Political Science, *and* Canadian Public Policy.

This excerpt, from her 1967 book Public Opinion and Canadian Identity, *comes from her substantial early work on the role of regionalism in Canadian voting behaviour and public opinion. Schwartz assesses the extent to which the different regions are homogeneous, and finds that the Atlantic provinces have the most similarities with one another, followed by the prairie provinces. She argues that the nature of party competition, including the distribution of party supporters and the stability of party loyalties across those regions, coupled with differences in attitudes and opinions, has had an influence on the development and sustenance of regional variations in Canadian identity.*

Regionalism

It has been well documented from a number of countries other than Canada that the region where people live has a bearing on their political outlook. The bases of regionalism may be related to the settlement of distinct social or ethnic groups, the development of regional subcultures through isolation, or the economic conditions peculiar to an area. These factors all have some relevance to the Canadian experience and contribute to the difficulty faced by parties in counteracting the effects of region. This generalization needs to be qualified by the observation that not all regions in Canada are equally homogeneous in opinions. Looking at regional (or cross-party) rather than intraparty Indices of Group Homogeneity, we find the Maritime provinces most homogeneous, followed by the prairie provinces, Quebec, British Columbia, and Ontario (see Table 54). …

Source: *Public Opinion and Canadian Identity.* Berkeley: University of California Press, 1967. Notes omitted. Reprinted by permission.

TABLE 54 Relation Between Party Preference and Region in Canada

	Cross-party IGH's for region	
Region	Number of possible combinations with party	Percent low IGH's across party lines
Maritimes	30	80
Quebec	30	60
Ontario	30	57
Prairies	29	62
British Columbia	29	59

	Intraparty IGH's related to region	
Party	Number of possible combinations with party	Percent low intraparty IGH's
Conservative	30	23
Liberal	30	20
CCF/NDP	28	61
Social Credit	27	56

Note: The greater the proportion of low IGH's, the greater the consensus within groups.

Party Influences

This examination of the interplay between party and region suggests several explanations for variations in the influence of party on the formation of Canada's identity; these stem from the distribution of party supporters, the stability of party loyalties, and the existence of regional climates of opinion.

Distribution of party supporters.—Parties which appeal to limited groups in the population rather than to a broad spectrum of voters are more likely to influence the opinions of their supporters in a uniform fashion. Thus the relatively strong influence of the CCF/NDP on supporters' opinions can be related to the small number of supporters it has been able to attract in the Maritimes and Quebec. It has not had to accommodate to the special interests of residents of these regions. Homogeneity of viewpoint is reinforced as well by that party's attraction of support with a limited occupational base, drawn particularly from workers and farmers. From its founding, the CCF has made a deliberate attempt to educate its followers in its policies and to allow them a role in formulating programs. It is noteworthy that CCF/NDP supporters showed greatest homogeneity across regional lines on questions of independence and political symbols, two areas where other parties failed to achieve this unanimity ... . But success in achieving a climate of opinion in this manner means also the CCF/NDP's continuity as a minor party, particularly when ... the views of its supporters are so often at variance with those of other Canadians.

The Social Credit party, although less able to cut across regional lines than the CCF/NDP, still appeared more effective than either the Liberal or Conservative parties. Again this was partly achieved by a minimal appeal in some regions, in this case Ontario and the Maritimes.

Unlike the CCF/NDP, however, in western Canada, where it has received its greatest share of the popular vote in general elections, it has attracted support from a broad occupational base. But in Quebec its support comes mainly from farmers and small shopkeepers in the smaller towns. It is perhaps surprising that under these circumstances Social Credit has been as influential as it has. Other factors affecting that party's impact on the opinions of supporters may be more important than the lack of appeal to all regions, especially since it has been making electoral inroads in Quebec. These will be discussed in relation to our other explanations.

An uneven distribution of party supporters appeared to contribute to the homogeneity of viewpoint found among those of the CCF/NDP, and perhaps to some extent of the Social Credit. The Conservatives and Liberals, as parties which historically have appealed to all regions of Canada, have thus been hindered in acquiring the united outlooks which might result from attracting supporters only from particular regions.

Stability of party loyalties.—We can also hypothesize that party influence will be weaker during a period of electoral shift when a party is expanding its social base and attracting new types of voters. This is well exemplified by the Conservatives. Until they took office in 1957 the Conservatives had been in opposition for twenty-two years. Having last served as the governing party during the depression of the early 1930s, and being associated with the dominant British Protestant group in central Canada, it was important, if the Conservatives were to attain office, that they create a new image for themselves. In doing so, they were fortunate to have as their leader a small-town western lawyer with none of the stereotyped characteristics of a Tory. But as the election of 1957 approached, it was also evident that the Conservatives would be able to benefit from the general feeling of dissatisfaction with the Liberals and the notion that it was time for a change. As a result, the Conservatives were able to capitalize on these new circumstances by appealing to more voters from all regions in Canada. This was not accompanied, however, by the creation of a party climate of opinion. Thus, between 1951 and 1956, intraparty differences across regional lines were high in 67 percent of the questions, but between 1957 and 1959, the years of greatest popularity, they had risen to 91 percent. The dropoff in voter appeal indicated in the elections of 1962 and 1963 was anticipated by a drop in high intraparty IGH's between 1960 and 1962 to 71 percent of the questions asked. Even if not too much is read into this last finding, it does still suggest that the Conservatives were best able to achieve cross-regional homogeneity when their appeal was restricted primarily to those to whom voting Conservative had become a customary practice. This tends to be further substantiated by inspection of IGH's constructed according to whether respondents were supporting the Conservatives for two elections. There was an accumulation of high 1GB's between 1956 and 1957, during a time when the electoral trend was in favour of the Conservatives. That is, the attraction of new voters is often not accompanied by their incorporation into a party point of view (see Table 55). The Liberals exhibit similar tendencies. At the time of their greatest electoral strength, they also showed the highest proportion of intraparty differences: 91 percent between 1951 and 1956. While they were in opposition between 1957 and 1959, intraparty differences were lowest, 64 percent of the questions. In 1960 to 1962, 71 percent of the IGH's were high, a proportion identical to that of the Conservatives. While the Liberals increased their share of seats in the House of Commons in the elections of 1962 and 1963, their share of the popular vote remained similar to that of the Conservatives, indicating that they had not appreciably broadened their electoral base. For Liberals, examining IGH's on party stability gives us no further insight, since these are dispersed without any apparent pattern through the years for which we have information.

Considering responses over the time span available, no trend toward greater or lesser influence could be discerned for the CCF/NDP. There was, however, some slight suggestion of greater party influence since 1956.

Generalizations must be made with caution because similar questions were not asked every year, yet the influence of Social Credit on opinions seems to have operated in a curve. It was low up to 1956, greatest between 1957 and 1960, and low again in 1962. Between the general elections of 1953 and 1957 Social Credit gained strength in Manitoba and Saskatchewan and lost slightly in Alberta and British Columbia. These changes in supporters in the West may have then contributed to a greater homogeneity of outlook. But it was in 1962 that the impact of new voters from Quebec was felt: Intraparty differences were great on all three questions asked that year: on the Commonwealth, a new flag, and a labour party. For example, prairie respondents were highly opposed to the formation of a labour party, those in British Columbia were slightly less opposed, but the majority in Quebec thought that such a new party would be good for Canada.

A further indication of the impact of new kinds of supporters comes from examining intraparty IGH's for respondents who favoured Social Credit in two elections, those who switched parties, and those who do not remember how they voted; a large share of the latter are likely to have not voted (see Table 55). Generally such IGH's on voting stability are low for all parties, but the difference between new and more stable supporters was great for Social Crediters in 1960, 1961, and 1962 on questions on independence. No control was introduced here for region, but it is most likely that new voters in Quebec were reducing party unanimity.

Regional climates of opinion.—From evidence supplied by Gallup Polls, and from scholarly observations on the course of Canada's development, it is reasonable to conclude that,

TABLE 55   Trends in Distribution of High Intraparty IGH's According to Stability of Party Preference, 1951–1962

Year of survey	Number of combinations of party preference and stability of preference	Number of high intraparty IGH's			
		Conservative	Liberal	CCF	Social Credit
1951	2	0	0	1	0
1954	5	2	1	1	2
1955	1	0	1	0	0
1956	7	4	2	1	2
1957	11	3	2	3	2
1958	2	0	1	a	a
1959	1	0	1	0	a
1960	4	2	0	1	2
1961	2	0	1	0	1
1962	3	0	0	1	1

[a] Not calculated.

Note: The greater the number of high intraparty IGH's, the greater the lack of consensus within parties.

up until now at least, sectionalism has inhibited the development of a concept of nationhood for which a political party could find wide support in all regions. If anything, traditions of the British parliamentary system have helped control much of the sectionalism inherent in Canadian life. It is a frequent and now commonplace observation that sectional interests have led to the emergence of minor parties in Canada; but these same interests have also shaped the two older parties. As a result, the older parties have favoured compromise and the avoidance of ideological consistency in an attempt to appeal to as many disparate groups as possible. When the opinions of supporters of the same party in different localities are compared, we can more truly appreciate the difficulty of achieving this wide appeal. The difficulty may be partly explained, in the modern era of rapid communication, in terms of a conflict between policies and pronouncements made on national issues and the response of provincial parties with the same name, as well as federal candidates, to local conditions. Among these local conditions are the existing political climates of opinion and the natures of the parties contending for power. For example, Ross Thatcher, leader of the provincial Liberal party in Saskatchewan and a former member of the CCF, has often publicly declared himself opposed to the mildly left-of-centre policies of the national Liberal party. In Manitoba, the provincial Liberals are considered more conservative than the Conservatives, while in Alberta the provincial Liberals are essentially a third conservative party. In the 1963 provincial election in that province, the Liberals attempted to campaign on the issue of provincial takeover of electric power in an area where some utilities are already publicly owned. This program was played down, however, in the face of opposition from those within the party—a stance which Liberals in central Canada found hard to accept. Such differences in approach by parties bearing the same label have undoubted consequences for the outcome of federal elections and the shaping of opinions. For example, in the 1957 survey on government versus private resource development, the order of preference for private enterprise by Liberal supporters was, beginning with the most favourable, British Columbia, the prairie provinces, Ontario, the Maritimes, and Quebec.

Regional differences also have implications for the minor parties. Social Credit did not begin growing as an important electoral force in Quebec until 1960 but even before that time differences in outlook were apparent between the eastern and western wings of the party. But the West itself is not homogeneous, and in most surveys where regional differences emerged, although these were largely due to the distribution of opinions in Quebec, variations also existed between British Columbia and the prairie provinces. For example, in the 1954 questions on foreign development of resources, most opposition was in Quebec, but it was also high in British Columbia. … The 1962 survey on the flag found a majority favouring the Red Ensign in British Columbia, the Union Jack in the prairies, and a new flag in Quebec. While the data used here have indicated that Social Credit has been fairly successful in controlling regional differences, this is partly related to the unevenness in sampling of Social Credit supporters. Differences which do appear suggest that there are distinct climates of opinion in each region.

If regional factors have more significance for the major parties, this is because these parties are forced, by their very nature, to cope with the problem of supplying national leadership in a diversified society. Sectionalism has restrained the growth of national parties, and with them, the development of an unambiguous public conception of the nation.

26 Party Identification and Campaign Dynamics

Richard Johnston (1992)

EDITORS' INTRODUCTION

Richard Johnston is Canada Research Chair in Public Opinion, Elections, and Representation at the University of British Columbia. He was principal investigator of the 1988 and 1992–93 Canadian Election Studies, and research director of the National Annenberg Election Study at the University of Pennsylvania in 2000–2001 and 2006–2009. Johnston has substantial expertise in both Canadian and American voting behaviour. His books include The End of Southern Exceptionalism: Class, Race, and Partisan Change in the Postwar South *with Byron Shafer, published in 2009, which won the American Political Science Association Race, Ethnicity, and Politics Prize and the Southern Political Science Association VO Key Award.*

The reading below represents some of Johnston's early work on party identification and campaign dynamics, a theme that has resurfaced in his writings throughout his career. Using data from the 1988 federal election, and the first rolling cross-section survey design, Johnston provides solid evidence that partisanship in Canada is "an unmoved mover," much like partisanship in the United States. This is contrary to the argument that "party identification" is a concept that does not travel well outside of the American context.

The dynamic impact of party commitment was noticed even before the expression "party identification" became commonplace. Our sense of campaign dynamics continues to be shaped by Berelson, Lazarsfeld, and McPhee's (1954) account of the reconstitution of the New Deal coalition in the 1948 campaign. But is the imagery of rebuilding old coalitions still appropriate in the age of media politics? Should it ever have been the dominant image? And was it ever appropriate outside the United States? This paper supplies evidence from the 1988 Canadian General Election. This seemed very much to be a television election: The daily grind of leaders' tours was contrived to manipulate news programming; a nationally televised leaders' debate was pivotal; and the aftermath of the debate brought advertising strategy and counterstrategy. As a Canadian election, the 1988 event also helps address the question of the portability of party identification as a dynamic and directive concept.

Source: "Party Identification and Campaign Dynamics." *Political Behavior*, vol. 14, no. 3. Special Issue on Party Identification (September 1992), 311–331. Notes omitted.

Commentary on Canadian elections tends to be hostile to the view that much can be gained by referring to American examples. But if this is so, the reverse must also be true: Americans have little to learn from the Canadian case. One task, then, is to substantiate that Canadians' long-term party commitments can survive the vicissitudes of a hard-fought campaign, as is true in the U.S. Once this is established we need to work through the ways in which long-term identifications can shape and constrain campaign dynamics. Finally we must ask: Net of long-term forces, what does the campaign bring that is new?

The Stakes

The 1948 event seems to haunt the study of campaigns. The fact that the campaign whose dynamics are still the best understood only brought the system back to its roots naturally makes observers wonder if this is all that campaigns ever do. Campaigns may not be important in their own right. Perhaps all they do is create enough noise to reawaken voters to their abiding interests. These interests might be captured by party identification. A campaign that is only a hollow shell ought only to bring vote intentions back in line with the longstanding distribution of identifications. There might also be some reordering of leader perceptions or of issue opinions, but in the larger scheme of things these would be only window dressing, part of a process whose outcome is predetermined. A more sophisticated account would admit the possibility that the basic alignment of votes that emerges over the campaign is controlled by more than just party identification. Indeed the work that gave party identification its name (Campbell et al., 1960) was filled with the references to short-term forces. More recent accounts of flux in aggregate outcomes makes clear that factors of a fairly short-run nature—in the macroeconomy, in overseas military or foreign-policy crises, and summarily in ratings of presidents' performance—have a powerful effect on elections.

But the effect lies outside campaigns. The drift of estimation models in this domain has been to employ information that clearly predates the campaign in making predictions to its outcome. Indeed, the case is made that advance information yields nothing in predictive power, that precampaign values on the basic variables are *better* predictors of the result than most of the information gathered in the campaign. Campaign events are distractions, essentially irrelevant to the result.

A rival view exists. Accounts that emphasize voter psychology, which consider how candidates are perceived (Popkin, 1991) and how issues are framed (Iyengar and Kinder, 1987), are open to the possibility of real campaign dynamics. These effects may be small compared with the constraints imposed by long-term identifications or with the flux induced even before the campaign begins. But they may be critical at the margin.

So far, though, the literature on campaign effects seems rather unfocused. It relies on scattered evidence, much of it experimental. By its very nature—an emphasis on short-term contingencies—it lacks the predictive power of accounts employing a handful of predetermining factors with stable coefficients of effect. Most of the time, accounts of leader perception and issue framing do not seem connected to evidence of actual campaign dynamics. Findings from actual campaigns come almost entirely from primary elections (Bartels, 1988; Brady and Johnston, 1987), ones for which party identification is irrelevant, which are maximally personalized, and in which information, especially in the critical early stages, is at a premium. The time seems ripe for a study of a general election campaign.

What should such a campaign study look for? Four questions stand out: How does party identification perform over the campaign? Do any voters change their opinions on issues or their perceptions of leaders? Does the weight attached to certain issues or perceptions shift over the campaign? What, if any, is the net effect of such shifts?

The first question to ask about party identification is: How stable is its distribution? If it is not stable then the potential for campaign effects is enormous. If it is stable then identifications may constrain the flux of campaigns, either by inhibiting it outright or by channeling it along partisan lines. If the party identification distribution is stable it is also useful to know how ubiquitous party commitments are. The larger the proportion of nonpartisans, the more potential there should be for across-the-board flux.

One form campaign flux might take is *persuasion*, on issues or on perceptions. Can a disadvantaged competitor introduce a consideration that shifts an opinion or perceptual distribution in its strategic favor? Party identification may condition susceptibility to such persuasion. Movement may be more likely if it resolves psychological tension than if it increases it. If a party leader is rehabilitated by an event, for example, the improvement in his ratings may be greatest among his own partisans.

The lesson of 1948, though, was that persuasion is less likely than priming. The key to that year's Democratic recovery was a renewed emphasis on New Deal issues, on which the party enjoyed a strategic advantage. This early finding is echoed by some of the most striking results of the later 1980s' research agenda: Iyengar and Kinder (1987) brought the psychological notion of priming into the language of political science. The idea corresponds to our own notions of social choice and of the role of agenda shifts in overturning preexisting majorities. In data, the primary manifestation of priming should be sudden shifts in the structure of regression weights in the issues-perceptions-vote nexus. Again, though, a party's own identifiers may be differentially likely to exhibit shifts toward the strategically favorable calculus.

Finally, what does all of this do to the bottom line? Does defection from party identification systematically erode over the campaign, or does it swing back and forth to mirror events? Are nonpartisans systematically more prone to swings than partisans? Indeed, do nonpartisans provide the bulk of the net movement?

The Study

The 1988 Canadian Election Study (CES) marked a departure from previous practice in Canada and elsewhere: It was the first rolling cross section survey (henceforth RCS) conducted by academics during a general-election campaign in Canada or anywhere. The campaign cross section of the 1988 CES was broken up into 47 replicates, yielding a daily average of 77 completed interviews (to a total of 3,610 respondents). To all intents and purposes, the day of interview was a random event and so daily tracking analyses are quite straightforward. The American NES offers two partial precedents: the 1984 and 1988 RCSs. But neither was conducted during the general campaign and neither produced daily densities on the scale of the 1988 Canadian study. The Canadian study sought to go back to the spirit, if not the letter, of the 1940 and 1948 Columbia studies.

Another critical departure from earlier Canadian practice lies in the measurement of party identification. Response to the traditional Canadian party identification measures has been labile, so much so that observers naturally question the rootedness of partisan dispositions.

But Johnston (1992) staked an experimentally based claim that the problem lay not so much with voters as with the measure and proposed wording that brings the item closer to the U.S. original. The proposed wording was employed in the 1988 study.

The Campaign

The 1988 sampling strategy was inspired by a sense that Canadian campaigns were growing in importance and that the dynamic potential for 1988 was especially great. The potential reflected widespread doubts in the electorate about each major party, about their leaders, and about the central policy issue. The 1988 Canadian election was fought primarily over the Canada–USA Free Trade Agreement (henceforth FTA). The FTA was very comprehensive; it was difficult to understand and thus was susceptible to symbolically charged rhetoric; both its acceptance and its rejection involved risks; and all earlier such proposals had been electoral disasters. Also critical were perceptions of the two old parties' leaders. For Brian Mulroney, Conservative leader and prime minister, the question was whether he could be trusted to negotiate commercial union; otherwise he was reasonably highly regarded as the leader of a competent team. For John Turner of the Liberals, serious doubts about his executive capacity lingered and these doubts threatened his credibility as a critic of the FTA. The potential for volatility was realized. Figures 1, 2, and 3 track each party's share of vote intentions and of party identifications. Concentrate for the moment on the vote. For each old party, the campaign brought dramatic shifts. Each surged once and declined once. Each surge and decline was sudden, a matter of three or four days.

FIGURE 1   Conservative vote and identification, 7-day moving average

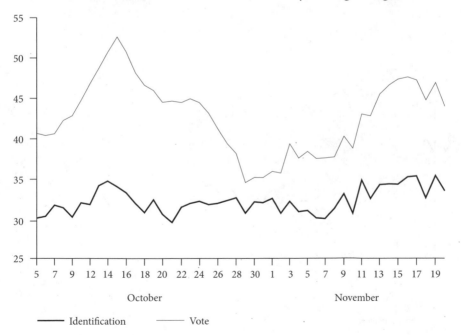

FIGURE 2   Liberal vote and identification, 7-day moving average

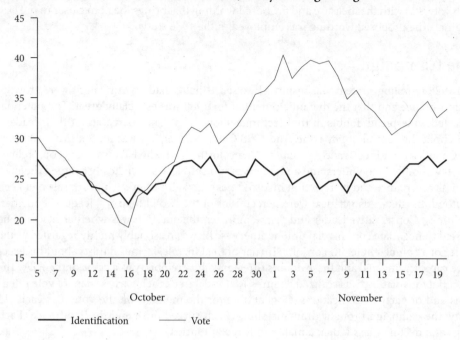

FIGURE 3   NDP vote and identification, 7-day moving average

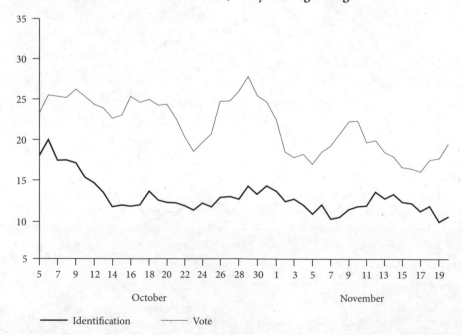

The Conservative party entered the campaign with a vote plurality sufficient, given the mechanics of the electoral system, to produce a majority of parliamentary seats; by the end of the second week, the Conservatives may have picked up an outright majority in the popular vote itself. After leaders' debates on October 24 and 25, won unexpectedly by Mr. Turner, the Conservative edge dissipated rapidly; the net loss was about 10 points. The party hit bottom about October 29, just four days after the English debate. Although the Conservative recovery began immediately, it was slow, so much so that more than a fortnight after the debates the Conservatives were still well short of the vote share necessary to secure a seat majority. The impact of the debates does not, thus, appear to have been an impulse fated to decay autonomously.

The pattern for the Liberals seems to confirm the reality of the debates' impact. The Liberals surged where the Conservatives dropped. But Liberal gains were slower to be realized than were Conservative losses and Liberal gains were not dissipated immediately. From about one week after the debates to just over one week before the end of the campaign the Liberal share oscillated in the upper 30s. This roughly level-pegged the Conservative share in this period.

Then, around the beginning of the last week, the Conservatives surged and the Liberals plummeted. Each party's initial shift, again about 10 points, overshot the final result, but when the dust settled on the last weekend the Conservatives retained a large enough share to return a majority of seats. The late shifts coincided with a furious advertising battle that most observers concede the Conservatives won.

The NDP share followed a rhythm of its own. Before the debates the NDP share oscillated in the mid-20s. There may have been a decline in NDP intentions before the debates, but the party's share appeared to resume its mid-20s standing until about October 30. Then it dropped between 5 and 10 points. The share slid some more and then recovered slightly on the last weekend. The NDP decay came later than the Liberal and Conservative shifts and proved virtually irreversible. …

Discussion

The distribution of party identification in place on the eve of the 1988 campaign was not obviously displaced by the forces that had so dramatic an impact on vote intentions. Canadians in 1988 thus satisfied a basic condition for studying the role of long-term identifications in a campaign: possession of the very identifications in question. If party identification was unmoved, was it, in its own right, a mover?

The answer is both yes and no and is so for both persuasion and priming. At midcampaign all persuasion was biased and almost all worked to resolve attitudinal or perceptual tension. Attitudinal tension was dramatically lowered for Liberals as they moved toward their party's position on the FTA, a movement they did not recant. Perceptual tension was reduced as, again, Liberals dramatically raised the rating of their leader. Reinforcing all this were late campaign shifts by Conservatives toward their party's FTA position. Also consistent with this story was the priming of the FTA: It became more important in its own right but only as respondents' own positions on the issue became more consistently partisan.

On the other hand, perceptions of John Turner never went in opposite partisan directions. All groups upgraded him after the debates and all groups downgraded him in the last week. The difference noted in the preceding paragraph was for a postdebate difference of degree. For the downward movement at the end, there was not even a difference of degree. And as perceptions of John Turner were dropping across the board, they were becoming more important in the final choice. This was true even for Liberals, who might have been expected to resolve the growing tension by suppressing the link between their leader and their vote.

All along, of course, 30 percent of those reporting a vote intention failed to report a party identification, at least not straightaway. There is a side question about how many of these were true nonpartisans but we cannot deal with this question here. Suffice it to say that a large fraction of this group could not in any meaningful sense be constrained by a specifically partisan history. On the issue, this group was more malleable than were partisans. On perceptions of John Turner, though, partisans and nonpartisans were almost equally malleable. And the basic structure of nonpartisans' issue-leader-vote calculus was much like that for partisans. But this observation can be turned around: Partisans responded to the issue and to leaders much as nonpartisans did.

Defection from party identification did *not* go systematically down over the campaign. Rather, it reflected the flow of events: When a party suffered a reverse, identifiers' defection went up; when events favored the party, identifiers' defection went down. What is more, the late-campaign swings in identifiers' defection rates were as large as swings in vote intention among nonpartisans, once overshooting by the latter was corrected. Obviously, Liberals and Conservatives were always cross-sectionally more likely to support their respective party than were nonpartisans. But as the moment of truth approached, no obvious systematic homing process was to be found.

Is there a lesson in here for students of campaigns and elections in other countries? Canadians do exhibit the partisan tendencies associated with other systems. The continued relevance of Canadian party commitments in the later 1980s suggests that the same may be true elsewhere. But the Canadian event was not only a matter of reaffirming the standing alignment; the campaign also cut through party identification barriers. This too is likely to be true elsewhere. Work on just how campaigns cut through long-term constraints has hardly begun. In the U.S., observers have been so beguiled by the predictive power of models dominated by macroeconomic variables that they have found little time to explore those models' error terms. The dynamic possibilities of the NES pre-post design lie largely unexploited. If the NES vein is tapped in the near future, analysts might start with lessons from the 1988 Canadian campaign: Look to persuasion and priming on issues and perceptions; expect to find a mixture of reinforcing and cross-cutting effects; expect some of the shifts, especially on the vote intention bottom line, to be sudden. Taking campaigns seriously does not require us to abandon what we know about long-term forces. Long-term forces powerfully condition the rules of the game, but they do not necessarily supply the margin between victory and defeat.

Women to the Left? Gender Differences in Political Beliefs and Policy Preferences

Elisabeth Gidengil, André Blais, Richard Nadeau, and Neil Nevitte (2003)

27

EDITORS' INTRODUCTION

Elisabeth Gidengil is Hiram Mills Professor of Political Science at McGill University. One of Canada's leading experts on gender and politics, she has published widely, including nearly ten books and scores of book chapters and journal articles.

André Blais is the Canada Research Chair in Electoral Studies at the University of Montreal. His work appears in the Canadian Journal of Political Science, Electoral Studies, Comparative Politics, *and* Political Behavior, *among other journals.*

Richard Nadeau is a professor of political science at the University of Montreal. A scholar of voting behaviour and public opinion, he is probably best known for his extensive work on economic voting in Canada.

Neil Nevitte is professor of political science at the University of Toronto and the principal investigator of the World Values Survey (Canada). Best known for his 1996 book The Decline of Deference, *Nevitte has published numerous works related to values, value change, and political behaviour and attitudes.*

This group of scholars ran the Canadian Election Study for over two decades, and this piece explores the gender gap in attitudes among Canadians, using data gathered for the CES. The authors provide evidence of a gender gap in Canada, with women leaning more to the left than men, following a similar gap in the United States, and argue that the gap is likely to increase over time.

Introduction

The 1993 federal election witnessed the emergence of a significant gender gap in support of the new party of the right: women were much less likely than men to vote Reform, a trend that continued in the 1997 federal election. Although the Reform party subsequently reconstituted itself as the Alliance party and sought to reshape its image, the gender gap in support persisted in the 2000 federal election. Meanwhile, in the 1997 election, a gender gap also opened up on the left, and it too appeared again in the 2000 election. In both 1997 and 2000,

Source: "Women to the Left? Gender Differences in Political Beliefs and Policy Preferences." In *Women and Electoral Politics in Canada,* edited by Manon Tremblay and Linda Trimble. Toronto: Oxford University Press, 2003.

women were more likely than men to opt for the NDP, the traditional party of the left. In this chapter, we examine whether these gender gaps in vote choice are paralleled by differences between women and men in their basic political beliefs and policy preferences.

The gender gap literature suggests that there should be significant differences in women's and men's opinions on questions relating to social welfare policy, free enterprise, and questions relating to the use of force. There is a growing body of evidence showing that Canadian women are more skeptical about the workings of the free enterprise system and more supportive of the welfare state than Canadian men (Everitt 1998b; Kopinak 1987; Terry 1984; Wearing and Wearing 1991), and women attach a higher priority to social welfare issues than do men (Everitt 2002; Gidengil 1995). There is also compelling evidence that women are more reluctant than men to resort to the use of force (Everitt 1998b; Terry 1984). By contrast, gender gaps on other issues have typically been weak or inconsistent. This is true of feminist beliefs and women's issues more generally (Everitt 1998a, 1998b; O'Neill 1995; Terry 1984) as well as issues relating to questions of morality and social mores in general.

As Pippa Norris (forthcoming) has recently reminded us, though, context matters to both the size and direction of gender gaps. The 2000 federal election provides a novel context for examining gender gaps in a variety of domains. With a federal budget surplus, the question was no longer where cuts should be made to social programmes, but where new monies should be allocated. And with the unemployment rate clearly on the decline, jobs were no longer the central issue that they had been in the two preceding elections (see Nadeau et al. 2000; Nevitte et al. 2000). Meanwhile, with the Liberals campaigning to portray the Alliance as a party of social conservatives out of step with mainstream Canadian society, and with the religious beliefs of Stockwell Day, the Alliance leader, a matter of media scrutiny, issues relating to traditional moral standards and lifestyle choices assumed a new electoral importance. ...

Opinions of Women and Men

Free Enterprise, the Welfare State, and Health Policy

Previous studies of the gender gap phenomenon have consistently found that women are less sanguine than men about the virtues of free enterprise, more supportive social welfare programs, and less open to market solutions. It turns out these differences are not just a function of hard economic times and cutbacks in the welfare state.

Even in the changed context of the 2000 federal election, women remained consistently more skeptical than men about the workings of the free enterprise system, though the degree of skepticism depends very much on which aspect of those workings is under discussion (see Table 9.1). Women are especially skeptical of the notion that "when businesses make a lot of money, everyone benefits, including the poor." On the other hand, they were clearly less persuaded than men that individual effort will be rewarded. Similarly, women were more reluctant than men to rely on market solutions. For instance, only a minority of women believed that "the government should leave it entirely to the private sector to create jobs." Still, a majority of women do seem to prefer the market solution. When these items are combined, we can clearly see that women are more ambivalent than men about the free enterprise system. The difference is fairly modest, but it is statistically significant ($p < .01$) and it exceeds the differences among income groups and across Canada's regional divides.

Similar sex differences appear when we look at views about the welfare system (see Table 9.1). First, improving social welfare programs was clearly a much more important election issue for women than for men. Of the eight issues that respondents were asked to rate, improving social welfare programs (along with health care) revealed the largest difference in the priorities of women and men. Second, women were more likely than men to believe that more should be done to reduce the gap between the rich and the poor in Canada, and they were also more likely to think that governments have a legitimate role in ensuring a decent standard of living. And finally, women were more likely than men to reject the notion that the welfare state undercuts the work ethic by promoting dependency on the state.

However, the fact that a majority of women did *not* reject this argument should temper any characterization of women's support for the welfare state. Only a minority of women rated improving social welfare programmes as being very important. And despite both their concern with income disparities and their endorsement of the government's role in providing a social safety net, women, like men, were reluctant to support an increase in welfare spending. By the same token, views about welfare spending provide little support for the notion that resentment of the welfare state is a distinctively masculine orientation.

The difference between women and men on social welfare questions should certainly not be overstated. When we combined the items to form a 0 to 1 scale (with 1 representing the highest level of support for the welfare system), the difference between women (.64) and men (.58) was statistically significant ($p < .01$) but it was clearly much smaller than the gap that separated the lowest (.68) and the highest (.55) income groups. And with mean scores ranging from a low of .54 in the West to a high of .70 in Quebec, regional differences also outstrip sex differences. The fact remains, though, that the advent of an era of federal budget surpluses has not eliminated the differences between women and men in their views about social welfare.

Opinions about health care provide further evidence that women are more inclined than men to favour state provision. Improving health care was the single most important issue in the 2000 federal election for women and men alike. But the issue was more salient for women than for men (see Table 9.1). It is easy to understand why such importance was attached to the issue and also why it was even more important for women: two-thirds of men and fully three-quarters of women believed that the quality of health care had deteriorated over the previous five years. Not surprisingly, women and men largely agreed that this was an area where spending by the federal government should be increased. Interestingly, though, a substantial number of those who perceived the quality of health care to have worsened blamed the deterioration on poor management rather than lack of money.

Even though women were more likely to think that the quality of health care had deteriorated, they were more opposed than men to market solutions, such as allowing private hospitals in Canada or allowing doctors to charge a fee for office visits. When we combined these two items into a simple additive scale that ran from 0 (favour both private hospitals and user fees) to 1 (oppose both private hospitals and user fees), women received an average score of .67, compared with .57 for men ($p < .01$). Again, the difference between women and men is hardly huge, but it rivalled the difference between the lowest (.67) and the highest (.56) income groups and it exceeded the regional differences, at least outside Quebec.

Whether we look at views about free enterprise, the welfare state, or health policy, a similar pattern of gender differences appears. Women are more ambivalent about the free

TABLE 9.1 Women's and Men's Opinions on Issues (Percentages)

	Women	Men
Free Enterprise		
Everyone benefits when businesses make a lot of money ***	28	37
People who do not get ahead have only themselves to blame***	66	71
People can find a job if they really want***	75	82
The government should leave job creation to the private sector***	40	49
Jobless should move to regions where there are jobs***	59	67
Welfare System		
Social welfare is a very important issue***	44	31
Should do more to reduce gap between rich and poor***	78	71
The government should see that everyone has a decent standard of living***	68	61
The welfare state makes people less willing to look after themselves (disagree)***	38	30
Increase welfare spending	29	26
Health Care		
Health care is a very important issue***	90	78
Health care has gotten worse***	66	6
Increase spending on health care***	89	85
Oppose allowing private hospitals***	56	50
Oppose allowing doctors to charge a fee***	70	60
Feminism and Gender-Related Issues		
Sympathetic to feminism***	60	65
The feminist movement encourages women to be independent***	80	71
The feminist movement just tries to get equal treatment for women***	63	53
Discrimination makes it extremely difficult for women***	57	46
Do not lay off women with employed husbands first	86	86
Society would not be better if women stayed at home***	50	54
Should do more for women***	66	55
Having more women MPs is the best way to protect women's interests***	56	36
Lack of women MPs is a serious problem***	41	30
Favour requiring parties to nominate 50% women**	37	31
Moral Traditionalism		
Should not allow gay marriage***	35	48
Only married women should be having children	26	30
Should not be more tolerant of different lifestyles*	25	30
Newer lifestyles contributing to societal breakdown***	45	51
Fewer problems if more emphasis on traditional family values*	69	74
Should not adapt our view of moral behaviour**	53	48
Should be difficult to get an abortion*	35	33
Crime and Punishment		
Crime is a very important issue***	76	68
Crime has gone up***	55	43
Crack down on crime***	76	72
Tougher sentences for young offenders***	43	53
Favour death penalty***	36	49
Support gun control***	65	49

Significance levels for female-male differences: *** $p < .01$ ** $p < .05$ * $p < 0.10$

enterprise system, more sympathetic to the welfare state, and more reluctant to turn to the market for solutions. But a key question remains unanswered: Is this because women tend to be more reliant on the state or is it because women in general tend to be less individualistic than men, as Gilligan's (1982) work suggests?

The welfare state dismantlement thesis implies that women will be less persuaded of the virtues of free enterprise than men because they are less likely to be among its beneficiaries. While the gap is narrower among women (.52) and men (.56) in the lowest income group ($p < .10$), women in the highest income group proved to be only slightly more pro–free enterprise (.54) than less affluent women. A similar pattern holds for views about the welfare state. If the welfare state dismantlement thesis explained the gender gap in support for the welfare state, we would expect the gap to disappear once we control for income differences. The gap between women (.69) and men (.67) did narrow in the lowest income group, but affluent women remain significantly more supportive of the welfare system (.61) than similarly affluent men (.52; $p < .01$), and income clearly made less of a difference to women's opinions than it does to men's. Differences in the material circumstances of women and men made even less difference to their views about health care. True, the gap between women (.70) and men (.64) was smaller in the lowest income category, but it still met conventional levels of statistical significance ($p < .05$), and the gap actually widened among the most affluent women (.63) and men (.51; $p < .01$). In fact, high-income women were almost as committed to universal provision as low-income men. Clearly, something other than differences in material self-interest must be driving these gender gaps.

This conclusion is reinforced when we look at the effects of sector of employment. According to the welfare state dismantlement thesis, part of the explanation for these gender gaps in views about the role of the state versus the market lies in the fact that women are more likely than men to be employed in the public sector. It turns out, though, that the gender gaps persist. Whether they are employed in the public sector or in the private sector makes little difference to women's and men's opinions about the free enterprise system. A similar pattern holds for views about welfare. Men employed in the public sector were no more supportive of the welfare system than their counterparts in the private sector, and women employed in the public sector (.64) did not score significantly higher than women employed in the private sector (.61). Furthermore, far from eliminating the gender gap in support for universal health care, the gap is actually wider among women (.72) and men (.60) in the public sector ($p < .01$).

Similarly, gendered patterns of employment more generally cannot explain these differences in the views of women and men. According to this argument, entry into the paid workforce has a radicalizing effect on women by exposing them to gender inequalities and discrimination. However, labour-force participation has little or no effect on women's (or men's) perceptions of the economic system, and women remain more supportive of universal health care whether they were in the paid workforce or not. As for views about welfare, support for the welfare system was, if anything, a little lower among women who were in paid employment, though they remain significantly more supportive (.62) than men who are employed (.55; $p < .01$).

Having children is also said to have a radicalizing effect on women by pushing them in a more liberal direction, at least on questions having to do with collective provision and the role of the state. Lise Togeby suggests that this effect will be most evident when there is only one child (1994). This gender-roles argument did not fare well, though. If anything, women with a single child were slightly more persuaded (.55) of the virtues of free enterprise. And far from having a radicalizing effect, women who had one child tended to be a little *less* positive in their views about welfare. Surprisingly, having children has no effect on women's views on health policy. The effect is confined to men; consistent with Togeby's argument, having one child has a radicalizing effect whereas having more than one child has the opposite effect.

The fact that none of these structural and situational explanations can account for the gender gaps in views about the role of the state versus the market lends plausibility to socio-psychological interpretations that emphasize gender differences in fundamental values. To the extent to which women are less individualistic than men, this cannot be explained in terms of differences in material interests or experiences in the workforce or the home.

As we noted above, though, there are a variety of differences among women themselves that need to be taken into account. First, the "women's autonomy" argument suggests that women require economic and psychological independence from men in order to express their distinctive values and priorities (Carroll 1988). To achieve psychological independence, women have to transcend traditional sex-role socialization. One of the most potent factors in encouraging such independence is higher education. Economic independence, meanwhile, is more likely to be achieved by women who are in paid employment and who are not married. As Susan Carroll notes, "economic independence is highly, although not perfectly correlated with marital status" (1988: 256).

This argument implies that skepticism about the free enterprise system should be most apparent among women who are in paid employment, who are more highly educated, and who have either never married or are separated or divorced. The same should be true of support for the welfare system and public provision of health care. However, these expectations received only mixed and weak support from our study. We have already seen that labour-force participation did not have the expected effect. The same holds for marital status: the gender gaps were not confined to those who had never married but appeared regardless of marital status. Women who had never married (.46) were a little more skeptical of the virtues of free enterprise, but married women remained significantly more skeptical (.54) than married men (.61; $p < .01$). A similar pattern held for views about welfare and health care. With one notable exception, education had little effect on women's views on all of these questions. The exception was health care: as the level of education increased, the gender gap widened. The mean score for university-educated women is .70, compared with only .54 for their male counterparts ($p < .01$). Aside from this, though, there is little to suggest that the gender gaps are more likely to occur among women who enjoy sufficient autonomy to express their difference from men.

Pippa Norris, meanwhile, has pointed to the existence of a gender–generation gap that she attributes to the impact of the second-wave women's movement on the cohorts of women who reached maturity in its wake (1999). The effect of this feminist mobilization is to make younger women more liberal in their views than both men and older women. In order to pursue this possibility, we compared opinions across four age cohorts that correspond to distinct phases in the evolution of the women's movement: the pre–second wave cohort born before 1942; the second-wave cohort born between 1942 and 1957; the post-movement cohort, born between 1958 and 1972; and finally the third-wave cohort born after 1972 (see Everitt 2001).

However, this feminist catalyst argument fared little better than the women's autonomy argument. Women who came of age during the rise of third-wave feminism were a little more skeptical of the virtues of free enterprise (.48) than women whose formative experiences predated the rise of the second-wave feminism (.56), but a parallel effect appears for men. On the other hand, there is no association between age and support for the welfare system: the gender gap cuts across age cohorts. And if exposure to the feminist movement has a radicalizing effect on women's views about health care, that effect was modest and it is confined to women who came of age during the rise of third-wave feminism (.74). The gender gap persists, regardless of age cohort; even in the pre–second wave cohort, women (.67) were significantly more opposed to market solutions than men (.58; $p < .01$).

Feminism and Gender

So far, we have been treating feminist mobilization as a possible catalyst for the expression of women's difference, but we also need to compare women's and men's orientations toward the feminist movement and indeed toward gender issues more generally. One possible explanation for the rightward tilt on the part of some men is a reaction against changes in gender roles over the past three decades, changes that have challenged their traditional position of dominance within both the public and private spheres. Given the central role of the feminist movement in instigating this challenge, we should expect to find much more negative views about feminism among men.

If we focus simply on how much sympathy respondents express with feminism, we could immediately discount the notion of an anti-feminist backlash on the part of men. If anything, it is women, not men, who are less likely to be sympathetic (see Table 9.1). However, men do tend to have less positive perceptions of the feminist movement. They were less likely than women to think that the feminist movement "just tries to get equal treatment for women" and encourages women "to be independent and speak up for themselves." Significantly, though, only a minority of men opted for the view that the feminist movement "puts men down" (27 per cent) and encourages women "to be selfish and think only of themselves" (18 per cent). And these views had less impact on men's sympathy with feminism than on women's: only 42 per cent of men who said the movement puts men down and 50 per cent of those who said it encourages women to be selfish were unsympathetic, compared with 63 per cent and 68 per cent, respectively, of women.

When the three items are combined into a pro-feminism scale, there is a statistically significant, albeit modest, difference in the mean scores of women (.72) and men (.67; $p < .01$) on a 0 to 1 scale. With average scores ranging from a low of .67 in both Ontario and the West to a high of .77 in Quebec ($p < .01$), where a person lives clearly had more of an effect on their views about feminism than whether they were a man or a woman. As the gender–generation gap thesis would lead us to expect, there was even less difference among women (.68) and men (.65) who came of age before the advent of the second-wave women's movement. That said, the differences across age cohorts in support of feminism are surprisingly modest, even among women. It is only among women who were socialized during the rise of third-wave feminism that there was much of an increase in support for feminism (.78).

O'Neill argues that religiosity acts as a countervailing force to feminism in many women's lives (2001b), and this may well be one reason why the gender gap in support for feminism is so modest. Religion is typically a more salient factor for women than for men: Canadian women are more likely to state a religious affiliation than Canadian men and they are also more likely to say that religion is personally important to them. Religiosity does indeed help to explain why the gender gap in support for feminism is so modest in our study. The gap disappears altogether among women (.64) and men (.64) for whom religion was very import-ant, and significantly more women (36 per cent) than men (26 per cent) said that religion was important in their lives. Tellingly, secularism is associated with a sizeable increase in support for feminism among women (.80) but not among men (.68).

The women's autonomy argument would predict that support for feminism would also be higher among women who enjoy economic and psychological independence from men. However, labour-force participation had virtually no effect on women's (or men's) support for feminism, and full-time homemakers in particular are no less supportive than women in general. Education, meanwhile, has only very modest effects, with support ranging from .69 among women who did not complete high school to .77 among university graduates ($p < .05$). The one dimension of the women's autonomy argument that did make a difference was marital status, with support ranging from a low of .69 among women in traditional (that is, non-common law) marriages to .81 among those who had never married ($p < .01$). There are no indications that having children has a radicalizing effect on women.

The lack of effect for labour-force participation may seem surprising given that women are more likely than men to believe that "discrimination makes it extremely difficult for women to get jobs equal to their abilities" (see Table 9.1). It turns out, though, that this belief was *less* prevalent among women (and men) who were in paid employment (53 per cent) than among those who are not (63 per cent). This poses something of a challenge to the notion that participation in the labour force radicalizes women by exposing them to gender inequalities.

As with views about feminism, opinions about gender-related issues do not lend much support to the notion of a backlash on the part of men. Women and men alike generally reject the suggestion that "if a company has to lay off some of its employees, the first workers to be laid off should be women whose husbands have jobs." Only a small minority would countenance such blatant discrimination, and they were as likely to be women (11 per cent) as they are to be men (12 per cent). And when it comes to conceptions of gender roles, women were actually a little less likely than men to reject the traditional notion that "society would be better off if more women stayed home with their children."

On the other hand, women were more likely than men to say that more should be done for women, and they were much more likely to agree that having more female MPs is the best way to protect women's interests. That said, they do not necessarily see the lack of women in the House of Commons as a serious problem and they were only a little less re-luctant than men to endorse the idea of requiring parties to nominate as many female as male candidates.

The questions on discrimination, doing more for women, and having more women MPs were combined into a scale, which revealed a significant gap between women (.62) and men (.54; $p < .01$) on attitudes toward gender-related issues. The gap may be modest but it rivals the differences to be observed across Canada's regions (ranging from a low of .55 in the West to a high of .64 in Quebec). There is little evidence, though, of any gender–generation gap. Attitudes on gender-related questions were even less affected by age cohort than was support for feminism. Whether socialized before the advent of second-wave feminism or during the rise of third-wave feminism, women on average held very similar views on these questions. And if the gender gap narrowed in the oldest cohort, it is because older men actually scored a little higher than younger men. In contrast to support for feminism, religiosity has only very minor effects on views about gender-related issues. ...

Discussion

Despite the change in the economic context and the advent of budget surpluses, women clearly remained more skeptical of the virtues of free enterprise, more supportive of the welfare system, and more reluctant to endorse market solutions than men in the 2000 federal election. The fact that these gender gaps could not be explained in terms of differences in women's and men's material interests lends weight to the socio-psychological argument that women tend to be less individualistic than men. The gender gap in views about crime and punishment also provides support for a socio-psychological interpretation of the gender gap phenomenon.

In contrast to a number of earlier studies, we also find consistent evidence of gender gaps in opinions on both feminism and gender-related questions more generally. However, these gaps do not extend to the broader domain of traditional social values, despite the fact that the 2000 election brought questions of traditional morality to the fore. There are signs that men tend to take slightly more conservative stances on these questions than women do, but with the notable exception of gay marriage, the gender gaps were small or inconsistent. And even on the issues that are explicitly gendered, the differences among women themselves exceeded the differences between women and men, as do the regional differences. Religiosity, in particular, clearly served as a conservative influence when it came to views about feminism and questions of traditional morality.

Other sources of difference among women prove to be less important. Of the factors that might enhance women's autonomy, education and marital status were the most consequential, but their effects were not uniform. There is little indication that participation in the paid workforce makes a significant difference to women's views. Meanwhile, having children either had no effect or had contradictory effects.

While the socio-psychological approach generally fared better than the structural and situational explanations, the gaps we observed would seem too modest to support the notion of a distinctive women's political culture (O'Neill 2002). That does not mean, though, that they are inconsequential. The gender gaps on free enterprise, health policy, and crime and punishment all exceeded the differences across Canada's regional divides. And because gender is the "fault line of maximum potential cleavage" (Jennings 1988: 9), even small differences between women and men can have important implications for party fortunes. Finally, to the extent that younger women, but not younger men, are more left-wing than their elders in domains like health care, feminism, and crime and punishment, we can expect these gender gaps to increase through generational turnover. Gender, in short, is a source of cleavage that must be taken seriously in any analysis of Canadian politics.

28 Accounting for the Electoral Success of the Liberal Party in Canada

André Blais (2005)

EDITORS' INTRODUCTION

André Blais is the Canada Research Chair in Electoral Studies at the University of Montreal. An expert on elections and voting, a large proportion of his work also concentrates on the impact of electoral institutions on party and voter behaviour. Blais might be Canada's most prolific political scientist, with a very long list of books and articles, usually the result of substantial international collaboration. He has published in many journals, including Comparative Political Studies, Political Research Quarterly, *and* Electoral Studies.

This excerpt is drawn from a memorable address given as president of the Canadian Political Science Association, in which he challenged Canada's political scientists to figure out what made the Liberal Party so successful (from 1963 through 2006, most elections were won by the Liberals, which led to them sometimes being described as "the natural governing party"). Blais notes that the success of the Liberal Party is not common among centrist parties in contemporary democracies, where parties of the right and left tend to be more successful. He points in particular to the links between Catholics and support for the Liberal Party, a relationship that could not be easily explained.

The Liberal party of Canada is one of the four most successful parties in contemporary democracies. It has won a plurality of the vote in 15 of the 19 elections held since 1945 and it has formed the government for 44 of the last 60 years. It belongs to a small club of very successful parties, together with the Liberal Democratic party in Japan, the Irish Fianna Fail and the Swedish Social Democrats, the three other parties on the planet that have systematically won democratic elections and formed the government since the end of the Second World War.

My task is to account for the success of the Liberal party in Canadian politics. I analyze the elections held since 1965, the starting point of the Canadian Election Studies (CES). The period covered is 40 years and it includes 12 elections and 11 Canadian Election Studies (there was no CES in 1972).

The Liberal party does not dominate everywhere. It is weak in the West, where it has received only 26 per cent of the vote, on average, since 1965. In Quebec, the party has obtained a plurality of the vote only once in the last six elections.

Source: Excerpted from *Canadian Journal of Political Science*, vol. 38, no. 4 (December 2005), 821–840. Notes omitted. Reprinted by permission.

The Liberal party is extremely successful in Ontario, where it has received, on average, 43 per cent of the vote, compared to 33 per cent for its main competitor. The situation is similar in Atlantic Canada, where the Liberals' average share of the vote is also 43 per cent, against 34 per cent for its main competitor.

It is in Ontario and Atlantic Canada that the Liberals have established their recent dominance, and this is where my inquiry starts. I offer a simple explanation for Liberal pre-eminence in those two regions. I then consider the West, and I examine whether the same reasons could explain why the Liberals have been less successful in that region. I do not extend my analysis to Quebec, which would require still another explanation (in fact two distinct explanations, one for francophones, one for non-francophones).

I am concerned with the big picture, the structural dominance of the Liberal party. I am not interested in explaining why the Liberals did better or worse in some elections than in others. Whenever possible, I pool election outcomes and/or Canadian Election Studies over the 1965–2004 period. ...

Are Catholics Different?

Without the Catholics, the Liberals would not dominate Ontario and Atlantic Canada and they would be extremely weak in the West. But why do Catholics vote Liberal?

One interpretation is that Catholics vote differently because they have different views on issues. To test that interpretation, I considered the 2004 CES questions that tapped Canadians' opinions on the issues of the day: views about government spending and taxes, health care, abortion and gay marriage, gun control and Canada's relation with the United States. I examined the link between these opinions and religion, region and ethnicity. A total of thirty issues were considered.

Table 4 summarizes the findings. I find religion to have a statistically significant effect in only nine cases out of thirty, and in all cases except one the difference of opinion between Catholics and non-Catholics was less than 10 points. Catholics are more conservative on abortion and gay marriage. But this does not explain their support for the Liberal party, since opposition to abortion and gay marriage tends to enhance support for the Conservative party. Aside from these two issues, no clear pattern emerges: Catholics are slightly more inclined to think that we should do more for women and against poverty, they are more prone to favour gun control and income tax cuts, and they are slightly less willing to spend on the environment, to approve a two-tier health system or to give Quebec the right to separate unilaterally. The bottom line is that Catholics do not systematically differ from non-Catholics.

Johnston (1985: 112; see also Johnston, 1991) has suggested that "there may be, however, a countervailing ethnic *ethos* among Catholics which produces the Catholic Liberal attachment. Growing up Catholic may produce a distinct view of the ethnic character of the Canadian nationality. To those schooled in the company of other Catholics, Canada will seem perhaps more French and almost certainly less British."

Unfortunately, I find little support for that conjecture. Catholics outside Quebec are *not* more likely to say that more should be done for Quebec, they are not more inclined to support more immigration, and they react similarly towards racial minorities.

We are thus left with a paradox. Catholics vote differently but they do not appear to differ on the issues.

TABLE 4 Attitudes, Religion and Ethnicity in English Canada

Questions	Catholic		Non-European	
	Coeff.	Impact	Coeff.	Impact
Government spending. Spend more on …				
Defence, military			−.72**	−.17
Welfare			−.98**	−.13
Health care				
Education			.74*	.12
Aid to developing countries			.75**	.13
Environment	−.23*	−.05*		
Social housing				
How much power do you think unions should have?				
How much power do you think business should have?				
How much should be done to reduce the gap rich/poor?	.40**	.07		
How much should be done for women?	.22*	.05	.66*	.12
How much should be done for racial minorities?			1.37**	.26
How much should be done for Quebec?			1.17**	.16
Quebec has the right to separate	−.32**	−.06		
Do you think Canada's ties with the United States should be closer?				
Do you favour or oppose having some private hospitals in Canada?				
People who pay should be allowed to get medical treatment sooner	−.26**	−.06	.65**	.16
Do you favour or oppose same-sex marriage?			−.72**	−.16
Gays and lesbians should be allowed to get married	−.25*	−.06	−1.09**	−.24
Do you think it should be very easy for women to get an abortion?	−.63***	−.15	−.65**	−.14
Do you think Canada should admit: more immigrants, fewer … ?			.90**	.16
Do you favour or oppose the death penalty?				
The government should leave it to the private sector to create jobs				
Only the police and the military should be allowed to have guns	.40**	.09	1.18**	.25
The gun registry should be scrapped entirely				
Should personal income taxes be increased, decreased, or … ?	.24*	.06		
Should corporate taxes be increased, decreased, or … ?			.84**	.11
Canada did not participate in the war against Iraq. Good decision?				
Free trade with the US has been good for the Canadian economy				
What is the best way to deal with young offenders who commit violent crime? (give them tougher sentences)			−.29*	−.07

Source: CES data, 2004.
*significant at the .05 level (two-tailed test)
**significant at the .01 level (two-tailed test)

Another possibility is that Catholics, especially the most religious of them, vote Liberal because they perceive the Liberal party to be "Catholic"; non-Catholics refrain from voting Liberal for the very same reason.

Canadians might view the Liberal party as Catholic because Liberal leaders are Catholic. Since 1965, all the Liberal leaders except Pearson have been Catholic, while none of the NDP, Reform or Alliance leaders, and only half of the Progressive Conservative leaders (Clarke, Mulroney and Charest) have been Catholic.

I have found no support for that interpretation. The religious cleavage was not weaker in 1965, when the Liberal party leader was not a Catholic, or in those elections where the Progressive Conservatives had a Catholic leader. Furthermore, Catholics systematically gave Conservative leaders more negative ratings even when these leaders happened to be Catholic. There is no evidence that Catholics vote for a party with a Catholic leader. This finding is consistent with those of Cutler (2002) who shows that leaders' gender, language and region matter but not their religion. I suspect that many (if not most) voters simply ignore the religious denomination of party leaders.

It is not only at the top that the Liberals are Catholic. Liberal candidates are also heavily Catholic. Sixty-three per cent of the 1988 Liberal candidates for whom we have the religious denomination were Catholic, compared to 45 per cent among Conservatives and 31 per cent among NDPers (the percentages are 51%, 29% and 15% if we exclude Quebec).

This led me to inquire whether Catholics are more prone to vote Liberal where the Liberal candidate is Catholic. The answer is no. I added a "Catholic Liberal candidate" dummy to my model for the 1988 election. That variable proved to be insignificant, as well as the interaction "Catholic respondent" × "Catholic Liberal candidate." There is no support for the hypothesis that Catholics vote Liberal only (or mostly) in constituencies where the Liberal candidate is Catholic.

Still another possibility is that Catholics vote Liberal only in those constituencies where there is some concentration of Catholics sufficient to form a significant community. The 1984 CES includes data on the percentage of Catholics in the respondent's constituency. I incorporated that variable into my model for the 1984 election, as well as the interaction "Catholic respondent" × "per cent Catholics in the constituency." Both variables came out non-significant. It seems that what matters is whether an individual is Catholic, not whether the individual lives in a Catholic environment.

The fact that Catholics systematically vote Liberal suggests that many of them have strong attachments to the party. Indeed, 37 per cent of Catholics interviewed since 1965 said they think of themselves as Liberals, compared to only 21 per cent among non-Catholics. Party identification is clearly part of the story. But it is not the whole story. As Johnston (1985) has powerfully demonstrated, a religious cleavage, or any cleavage for that matter, must be renewed in order to remain relevant. When I add party identification to my model, the Catholic coefficient is substantially reduced, by about half, but the coefficient remains highly significant. Furthermore, the Catholic variable is strongly significant when the analysis is restricted to those with no party identification. The bottom line is that Catholic support for the Liberals cannot be construed as a residue of the past, transmitted through family socialization. The religious cleavage is as strong now as it was forty years ago.

The following conclusions can be drawn from the evidence presented above. First, the religious cleavage is very important in Canadian elections; it is as strong as the regional cleavage. Second, the strong support of Catholics is a key factor in Liberal success. Third, the religious cleavage has not significantly weakened over time. Fourth, we still do not know much about why Catholics vote Liberal.

Some thirty years ago, Irvine (1974) thought he had succeeded in explaining the religious basis of the vote. His explanation was family socialization. Ten years later, Johnston (1985) showed that he was wrong. At the end of his article, Johnston offered two conjectures, about the presence of an ethnic ethos among Catholics and about contextual effects. I have examined these two possibilities but I have found no sign of a Catholic ethos and little contextual effect. Why Catholics vote Liberal is still largely a mystery, at least for me. I propose the creation of a special prize for the individual or team that solves the mystery. ...

Discussion

This journey into the sources of Liberal success has produced many nil findings. Some readers of previous drafts have expressed concerns about my remarkable ability to disconfirm hypotheses and my (equally) remarkable inability to produce "positive" results.

My typical response to such "unfair" criticisms has been that I adhere to a Popperian epistemology, according to which the goal of science is to disprove as many propositions as possible. Unfortunately, my Popperian convictions have weakened as I have grown older. I prefer writing and reading articles or books that provide compelling explanations over those that refute apparently plausible ones.

That being said, it is our task to take stock of both what we know and what we do not know about Canadian voting behaviour. We have known for a long time that Catholics and Canadians of non-European origin are among the strongest supporters of the Liberal party (see Meisel, 1956; Schwartz, 1974). My analysis shows that we still do not have a compelling explanation of why it is so.

One implication of the findings presented here is that groups matter. The Liberals are very successful among Catholics and voters of non-European origin and without the support of these two key groups they would have lost many elections.

This pattern is not peculiar to Canada. In the United States, we miss a crucial part of the picture if we do not consider the immense support that the Democrats enjoy among Black voters and the Republicans among Evangelicals (Abramson et al., 2002).

Classical studies of voting behaviour paid close attention to the link between social forces and vote choice. *The American Voter* (Campbell et al., 1960) devoted a whole section, more than 200 pages long, to the "social and economic context," with the first chapter dealing with membership in social groupings and focusing on four groups: labour unions, Negroes (sic), and (yes) Catholics and Jews. Likewise, *Political Change in Britain* (Butler and Stokes, 1960) focuses on the link between class and party, trade union influence, and (yes) the political legacy of religion.

This sociological approach is in disrepute. Perhaps the best illustration is provided by *Political Choice in Britain* (Clarke et al., 2004). The central claim of the book is that the valence model provides a more compelling explanation of vote choice than the sociological model. As the authors put it, "rather than being life-long political captives of their class locations or other ponderous social forces, British voters are capable of making effective, if 'rough and ready,' judgements regarding which party is best suited for government" (2004: 326).

I do not argue that Canadian voters are captive to their religion and/or ethnic origin or that they are incapable of ascertaining the merits and limits of the various parties. My point is rather that we miss something important if we do not examine the group bases of party support. In the Canadian case, we miss the fact that the Liberals have won most elections and that they have won in great part thanks to the strong support of Catholics and Canadians of non-European origin.

The standard interpretation is that the Liberal party has been so successful because it is centrist. There are at least two problems with this interpretation. The first is that centrist parties are not particularly successful outside Canada. I have mentioned at the outset that there are three other very successful parties in the world: two of them are generally classified as right wing, Fianna Fail in Ireland and the Liberal Democratic party in Japan, and one is on the left, the Swedish Social Democrats (see the classifications by Imbeau, 1985; Castles and Mair, 1984; and Blais and Crête, 1989). In fact, in many countries, centrist parties are among the least successful (Rabinowitz et al., 1991).

This interpretation also fails to account for the differential success of the Liberal party among segments of the electorate. Catholics and Canadians of non-European origin are *not* more centrist in their policy views than other Canadians, and so the spatial position of the Liberal party does not explain why the party is more successful among these two groups than with others.

Furthermore, the Liberal party would *not* dominate in Ontario in the absence of the strong support it enjoys among Catholics and visible minorities. In that province, the Conservatives have been, and are still, as popular as the Liberals outside Catholic and non-European circles. Outside these two groups, parties of the right have done as well as the centrist Liberal party. Outside these two groups, there is no evidence that the Liberal party has benefited from its centrist policy location. And there is no evidence that Catholics and Canadians of non-European origin vote Liberal because they like its moderate positions.

It is often argued that the Liberal party has been so successful in Ontario and Atlantic Canada because voters are repelled by its main competitor, which is perceived to be too much to the right. I question that interpretation. *Rendons à César ce qui revient à César.* The Liberal party has been successful because it has been strikingly adept at nurturing the support of two key social groups. How and why that success has been achieved remains to be explained. Natural experiments, such as those associated with the sponsorship scandal, should help us understand how and why members of different groups do or do not revisit their support for a party.

29 The Political Foundations of Support for Same-Sex Marriage in Canada

J. Scott Matthews (2005)

EDITORS' INTRODUCTION

Scott Matthews is an associate professor of political science at Memorial University. He is also director of the Canadian Opinion Research Archive and adjunct professor in the School of Policy Studies at Queen's University. Matthews specializes in voting behaviour and public opinion in Canada and the United States, and has published widely on policy attitudes, election campaigns and their effects, and voter turnout. He has published papers in the British Journal of Political Science, Electoral Studies, *the* American Journal of Political Science, *and others.*

Although work on voting behaviour in Canada abounds, there has been less focus on public opinion and attitudes about issues in Canada. This excerpt provides an example of Canadian public opinion research at its finest. Matthews points to the impact of "framing" on public opinion, demonstrating that once the Supreme Court of Canada treated the issue of same-sex marriage as a question of equality, opinion among the general population followed suit.

Introduction

Canadian public opinion moved markedly on the issue of same-sex marriage across the nineties. In 1993, roughly 37 per cent of Canadians were in favour of extending the rights and entitlements associated with marriage to gay and lesbian couples. Just seven years later, in 2000, a bare majority of Canadians—just over 50 per cent—backed the idea of gay marriage. And, in June 2003, as Canadian courts began to make same-sex marriage a legal reality, 54 per cent of Canadians, a majority, were behind them.

What accounts for this striking shift in public opinion on gay marriage? How is it that, in the span of just ten years, majority opposition can turn to majority support? The most obvious causal suspect is what is typically termed "value change." A range of sociological arguments suggest that large-scale social change in the postwar era, including rising affluence, changing work environments and the collapse of traditional family structures, have led to the rise of a new "post-industrial" politics. Characteristic of this new politics at the mass level is a distinctive value orientation, one that eschews the materialist politics of class,

Source: Excerpted from *Canadian Journal of Political Science*, vol. 38, no. 4 (December 2005), 841–866. Notes omitted. Reprinted by permission.

economic growth and national security in favour of more abstract concerns, such as the politics of cultural recognition, self-determination and environmentalism (Inglehart, 1997; Nevitte, 1996; Clark and Lipset, 2001). Applied to the domain of gay rights politics, this new value orientation implies increased support for novel rights and recognition claims, including demands for legal same-sex marriage. At the same time, particular social changes in the realm of sexuality, including the increased public visibility of gays and lesbians and, especially, of same-sex relationships, may also engender more favourable attitudes toward gay marriage and similar rights claims. Taken together, these social changes would seem to imply a substantial, long-run increase in support for same-sex marriage.

Claims like these have more than a little face validity, and this paper does not aim to challenge any such sociological account of attitude change concerning same-sex marriage. The principal aim of the present paper, however, is to emphasize the pivotal importance of the *political*, rather than the *social*, foundations of support for gay marriage in Canada. The magnitude and speed of the shift in attitudes on same-sex marriage implicitly makes this point. If sociological change were the most important force in the system, we would expect support to rise at a glacial pace, as the steady operation of the mechanism of generational replacement—the "selective politics of death" in Butler and Stokes' (1971) evocative phrasing— slowly added gay marriage supporters to the body politic at the same time as it slowly removed gay marriage opponents. But as alluded to in the opening lines of the paper, the change in support for same-sex marriage in Canada appears to be more a sudden spike than a gradual, epochal shift. A full account of opinion change on gay marriage will, thus, have to look beyond sociological change.

The argument of this paper is that such a full account must place special emphasis on the role of courts and legislatures in the formation of public opinion. Over the course of the late nineties, in a series of highly visible and politically influential decisions concerning the legal recognition of same-sex relationships, Canadian courts presented the mass public with a—then novel—interpretation of the same-sex marriage issue. For public opinion on gay marriage, the significance of these decisions was two-fold. First, the Courts *framed* the issue as one of equal rights. Although not explicitly addressing same-sex marriage, in deciding that gay and lesbian couples were entitled to equivalent regulatory treatment to that enjoyed by heterosexual couples, the Courts argued that the legal entailments of the value of equality demanded the same treatment for each kind of relationship. In other words, gays and lesbians are entitled to the same treatment as heterosexuals because that is what the principle of equality demands. Insofar as the Courts' interpretation informed a torrent of legislative activity at both the federal and provincial levels in response, this interpretation of the stakes involved in the recognition of same-sex relationships quickly became politically hegemonic. As a result, it would appear that public opinion on gay marriage shifted dramatically, as attitudes became increasingly anchored in a value with deep roots in the Canadian polity: the liberal value of equality.

At the same time, the judicial and legislative activity also appears to have had a direct, *persuasive* impact on Canadians. We have both empirical (Sniderman et al., 1991; Druckman, 2001) and theoretical (Lupia and McCubbins, 1998) reasons for suspecting that many citizens will accept the views of the courts and, to a lesser extent, legislatures on matters of public policy and incorporate these in the formation of their opinions. And so it appears to have been in the realm of same-sex marriage. Not only did Canadians accept the Courts' interpretation (its "frame") of the gay marriage issue, they also seem to have accepted the Courts' ultimate position on the matter—perhaps only by dint of the Courts' (and the legislature's) legitimacy.

Thus, it appears that the impact of the courts and legislatures on public opinion concerning gay marriage in the late nineties was double-barreled. The courts and legislatures argued that the value of equality demands equivalent treatment for same-sex and opposite-sex couples and many Canadians accepted this argument—both its premise *and* its conclusion. ...

The Courts and Legal Recognition of Same-Sex Relationships

The nineties marked a high point in judicial action on the recognition of same-sex relationships. In a series of challenges to federal and provincial statutes, lesbian, gay, bisexual and transgendered (LGBT) activists and individuals induced the courts to articulate a new legal doctrine concerning same-sex relationships that, in the end, roughly amounted to formally equivalent recognition of homosexual and heterosexual relationships (Smith, 2002: 14–5). The timeline of the legal decisions stretched across the nineties—from roughly 1993 to 1999—but the most important judicial statements and the bulk of the legislative activity did not appear until 1999 or later. As this paper aims to show, the rhythms of this legal–political timeline were reflected in the nature of public opinion across the period.

The first such important Supreme Court decision, *Canada (AG) v. Mossop*, involved a federal public servant's right to bereavement leave following the death of his same-sex partner's father. Although the Court ruled against the complaint in this case on the specific grounds presented in the claim, the decision was a significant step forward for same-sex relationship recognition. The complaint had been based on a challenge to federal human rights legislation, a challenge the Court rejected. Still, in the process of rejecting the claim, the Court indicated that its decision might have been different had the claim been made on the basis of the equality provisions of the Charter (Hiebert, 2002: 171–3).

Two decisions in 1995 confirmed the emergence of a new legal doctrine concerning same-sex relationships. The first decision, *Miron v. Trudel*, concerned spousal benefits for common-law partners in the context of provincial automobile insurance regulations. The second decision, *Egan and Nesbit v. Canada*, concerned spousal benefits for same-sex partners under the federal Old Age Security Act. Both decisions, especially *Egan*, affirmed clearly that the equal rights provisions contained in the Charter demand that gay and lesbian couples be treated the same as opposite-sex couples. However, although a significant victory for LGBT rights at the doctrinal level, the practical import of the decisions was more modest. In particular, *Egan* did not compel immediate legislative redress. Although five members of the Supreme Court affirmed that equality rights were violated by the Old Age Security provisions, one of those five, Justice Sopinka, accepted the violation as a "reasonable limit" under section 1 of the Charter. As Hiebert (2002: 177–8) writes,

> Justice Sopinka accepted the argument of government lawyers that flexibility should be afforded Parliament in the extension of social benefits within a context that recognized new social relationships. Parliament must contend with fiscal constraints and the implications of these for the scope of social programs. He characterized the recognition of same-sex spouses as a "novel

concept" and so concluded that inaction on this front did not amount to an unreasonable restriction on equality.

In concert with the four remaining members of the Court, who rejected the equality claim, Sopinka upheld the Old Age Security Act. *Egan*, thus, was a rather equivocal ruling from the perspective of LGBT rights.

A key impact of *Egan* from the perspective of this paper is that it had a cooling effect on legislative efforts to reform human rights and other legislation in the realm of same-sex relationship recognition. Hiebert writes that *Egan* was "interpreted by federal departments and ministers as removing pressure for immediate legislative reforms, and it had a similar effect for provincial jurisdictions" (2002: 178). The political logic here is easy to understand. At the federal level and in most provincial jurisdictions—save perhaps British Columbia— reform in the direction of same-sex relationship recognition posed potentially serious political risks. In 1994, for instance, the Ontario New Democratic Party (NDP) government failed to secure large-scale reforms in the interest of LGBT rights in the face of strong opposition both inside and outside the government. Thus, insofar as the courts indicated in *Egan* that legislative changes were not urgent, risk-averse politicians were keen to avoid gay rights reform.

Judicial equivocation and legislative dithering on LGBT rights in the early and mid-nineties is significant here insofar as this meant that the message of the Supreme Court on same-sex relationships—the Court's framing of and position on the issue—did not reach the Canadian public as loudly and as clearly as it might otherwise have done. In short, the Court's message was an ambiguous one, and the legislatures were loath to clarify it. In the mid-nineties, it seems fair to conclude, the equal rights frame was not hegemonic in the realm of same-sex relationship recognition.

The Supreme Court's 1999 decision in *M. v. H.* was, thus, a crucial turning point, both for gay rights and for public opinion *on* gay rights. Indeed, Smith writes that *M. v. H.* "was the most important lesbian- and gay-rights case to date" (2002: 7). The case concerned postbreak-up support in same-sex relationships. In this case, M. sought support from H., her erstwhile lesbian partner. Two features of the Court's ruling are important. First, the Court affirmed its position that the principle of equality demands that same-sex and opposite-sex couples receive the same legal treatment. Second, and most importantly for the present paper, the Court set aside the precedent in *Egan*—that violation of gay and lesbian equality rights was justified as a reasonable limit under section 1 of the Charter (Smith, 2002: 7–8).

At a stroke, the courts had made compulsory what most Canadian legislatures had hitherto understood as voluntary. A frenzy of legislative activity to implement the decision quickly followed federally and in Ontario, British Columbia, Quebec and Nova Scotia in the lead-up to the federal election in November 2000, with changes in Saskatchewan, Manitoba and Alberta not far behind. Here, then, we have an important contrast. Before *M. v. H.*, the courts and the legislatures transmitted an unclear, diffident message concerning the legal recognition of same-sex relationships. After *M. v. H.*, the message of the courts and the legislatures on gay rights was loud and clear. It seems fair to conclude, then, that by 2000 a dominant, equality-rights frame of same-sex relationship recognition had been diffused to the Canadian public. Furthermore, necessarily, the Supreme Court's position in favour of same-sex relationship recognition also likely had been diffused throughout Canada.

While the Supreme Court had not yet ruled explicitly on gay marriage, the issue was bound up routinely in discussions of same-sex relationship recognition—especially insofar as the federal Liberal government was keen to emphasize that its legislative changes did not imply anything about the nature of the institution of marriage (Smith, 2002: 14). Moreover, it seems plausible that the fine distinction between legally recognizing same-sex relationships and recognizing same-sex marriage is not a common one to Canadians. Efforts by Reform/Alliance and Liberal MPs to clarify the difference legislatively is powerful testimony to this fact (Smith, 2002: 13–4). Thus, it is likely that the dominant framing and message on same-sex relationship recognition, developed by the Supreme Court and implemented by the legislatures, informed public opinion on same-sex marriage by the end of the nineties. This, of course, is the general claim of this paper. ...

Conclusion

Support for legal recognition of same-sex marriage moved swiftly upwards over the 1990s. There is little doubt that generational shifts in fundamental values contributed something to this shift. The aim of the present paper, however, is not to probe the social foundations of gay marriage support. Rather, the aim here is to lay emphasis upon the political foundations of public opinion on this often controversial policy question. The particulars of the paper's interpretation are roughly as follows. A novel legal doctrine in relation to same-sex relationship recognition emanated from the courts in a series of important decisions across the nineties. The doctrine was based on the belief that gay and lesbian couples were entitled to equivalent legal treatment to that enjoyed by heterosexual couples, on the grounds that the principle of equality enshrined in the Charter demands non-discrimination on the basis of sexual orientation. In the early part of the decade, the courts' transmission to the Canadian people of this conception of the rights of gay and lesbian couples was diffident at best, unclear at worst. At the same time, the legislatures either were silent on or, at least in some degree, hostile to this view. After the Supreme Court's landmark decision in *M. v. H.*, however, the legislatures had little choice but to act on the Court's direction. In so doing, the courts and legislatures presented the typically ill-informed and inattentive Canadian citizen with useful cues regarding the appropriate framing of and position to take on the implicitly related same-sex marriage issue. By the end of the decade, most Canadians had received and variously acted upon these framing and persuasive cues, resulting in an increase in support for gay marriage far more sudden and striking than could be predicted on the basis of sociological change alone.

This narrative finds reasonably strong support in the present paper. Even so, the evidence is circumstantial. Any covariate of the above legal–political dynamics that is also a plausible determinant of public opinion is a candidate explanation as well. Still, consider the present argument's fit to the data. Apart from realizing relatively precise predictions about the timing and nature of changes in the psychological structure of opinion on same-sex marriage (the increased impact of equality values after 1999), other observable implications of the argument find support in the data, including the nationalization of opinion on the issue (significant regional differences disappear in 2000) and the strengthening of its psychological roots across the nineties (model fit improves by over 70 per cent between 1993 and 2000). Furthermore, it is difficult to imagine another plausible argument that could account so well for so many aspects of the empirical pattern. The increasing salience of the issue over time, for instance, seems inadequate as an explanation on its own—among other things, excepting the activity of the courts and legislatures, there is no obvious reason why increases in salience should be realized through attention to equality values and, moreover, why such increases should occur only after 1999. Nevertheless, some measure of uncertainty must attach to the paper's inferences about the dynamics of opinion on same-sex marriage. It is, thus, probably best to think of the present analysis less as a theory-testing exercise and more as a "clinical case study," *per* Eckstein (1975): an interpretation of a particular case grounded in an existing body of theory and rigorous empirical research.

What are the broader implications of the paper's argument? Clearly, the psychological basis of opinion on gay marriage has political significance for LGBT activists. One might conclude on the basis of the present analysis that support for gay marriage is, in some sense, soft. Opinion change grounded in fundamental value shifts somehow seems more sturdy, more lasting. Yet two important arguments provide a counterpoint to this view. First, as framing theory makes clear, even opinions "grounded" in fundamental values can change as the framing of issues evolves. Thus, the hard–soft opinion perspective is something of a false dichotomy. Second, and relatedly, insofar as opinion on all political issues depends on framing, the real question concerns frame stability. It is hard to imagine a major political institution more likely to offer a stable construction of a political issue than the courts. Indeed, insofar as past precedent binds future decision making, stable constructions are hard-wired into the nature of the institution itself. Thus, in a perhaps ironic way, opinion on gay marriage is not relatively soft or ungrounded—it is strongly grounded in (relatively) stable legal conceptions of the nature of equality as it applies to same-sex relationship recognition.

The psychological basis of opinion on gay marriage has other implications for LGBT activists and for the broader recognition of gay rights. It seems common practice in popular commentary on LGBT politics in Canada to infer that rising support for same-sex marriage in some way indexes attitudes toward LGBT rights and attitudes towards LGBT communities in general. Yet an important implication of the present paper is that attitudes on gay marriage can shift independently of underlying shifts in fundamental values and dispositions, including affect toward homosexuals. Straightforward inferences from gay marriage support to opinionation on gay rights in other domains, thus, are likely misleading. This is not to suggest that there is no link at all. Legal developments on same-sex marriage undoubtedly have implications for doctrine in related policy areas (adoption by LGBT individuals, for example) and may lead, ultimately, to framing and persuasion processes in these areas similar to those examined in the present paper.

Apart from the implications for LGBT politics, the conclusions of the present paper bear on our understanding of the impact of the courts on public opinion in Canada. In short, it seems fair to conclude that the impact of the courts on public opinion is conditional. Opinion on gay marriage and its underlying structure did not move until the message of the courts was clarified and picked up by the legislatures. This interpretation suggests that the impact of the courts on public opinion is limited in certain ways, the worst fears of "court party" critics (Knopff and Morton, 2000; see also Manfredi, 2001) notwithstanding. Without the legislature, for instance, the signal of the Supreme Court may not always be loud enough to reach the typical Canadian. And an ambiguous message from the Court may never register in Canadian attitudes, whether delivered with a bang or a whimper.

References

Butler, David and Donald Stokes. 1971. *Political Change in Britain*. New York: St. Martin's Press.

Clark, T. and S.M. Lipset, eds. 2001. *The Breakdown of Class Politics: A Debate on Post-Industrial Stratification*. Washington, DC: Woodrow Wilson Center Press.

Druckman, James. 2001. "On the Limits of Framing Effects: Who Can Frame?" *The Journal of Politics* 63-4: 1041–1066.

Eckstein, Harry. 1975. "Case Study and Theory in Political Science." In *Handbook of Political Science, Vol. 7: Strategies of Inquiry*, eds. F. Greenstein and N. Polsby. Reading, MA: Addison-Wesley.

Hiebert, Janet. 2002. *Charter Conflicts: What's Parliament's Role?* Montreal: McGill-Queen's University Press.

Inglehart, Ronald. 1997. *Modernization and postmodernization: cultural, economic, and political change in 43 societies*. Princeton, NJ: Princeton University Press.

Knopff, Rainer and F.L. Morton, eds. 2000. *The Charter Revolution and the Court Party*. Peterborough, ON: Broadview Press.

Lupia, Arthur and Matthew McCubbins. 1998. *The Democratic Dilemma: Can Citizens Learn What They Need to Know?* New York: Cambridge University Press.

Manfredi, Christopher. 2001. *Judicial Power and the Charter: Canada and the Paradox of Liberal Constitutionalism*. Don Mills, ON: Oxford University Press.

Nevitte, Neil. 1996. *The Decline of Deference: Canadian Value Change in Cross-national Perspective*. Peterborough, ON: Broadview Press.

Smith, Miriam. 2002. "Recognizing same-sex relationships: The evolution of recent federal and provincial policies." *Canadian Public Administration* 45-1: 1–23.

Sniderman, Paul M., Richard A. Brody and Philip E. Tetlock. 1991. *Reasoning and Choice: Explorations in Political Psychology*. Cambridge, UK: Cambridge University Press.

The Effects of Information and Social Cleavages: Explaining Issue Attitudes and Vote Choice in Canada

30

Amanda Bittner (2007)

EDITORS' INTRODUCTION

Amanda Bittner is an associate professor of political science at Memorial University. Specializing in voting behaviour and public opinion, most of her work has incorporated, in some capacity, an examination of the influence of information and knowledge on attitudes. Bittner published Platform or Personality? Understanding the Role of Party Leaders in Elections *in 2011 (Oxford University Press), and, with Royce Koop,* Parties, Elections, and the Future of Canadian Politics *in 2013 (University of British Columbia Press). Her work has been published in the* Canadian Journal of Political Science, Electoral Studies, *and the* Journal of Elections, Public Opinion, and Parties.

This excerpt is from her work that won the John McMenemy Prize for best paper published in 2007 in the Canadian Journal of Political Science. *In it, Bittner assesses the impact of political knowledge and information on the relationship between social group identity (for example, gender, region, or religion), and opinions and vote choice. She finds that political knowledge changes the influence of social group identity on attitudes, in some cases minimizing the effect on opinion, and in some cases amplifying it.*

Introduction

For years, Canadian political scientists have identified a number of social cleavages which have been thought to have a substantial impact on citizens' attitudes, opinions, and vote choice. While the origins of these social cleavages have been debated extensively, it is generally accepted that *social identities shape political values*. Some studies have suggested that "Catholics vote Liberal" (Bélanger and Eagles, 2005; Blais, 2005; Irvine and Gold, 1980; Johnston, 1985). Others have observed that individuals of non-European origin also vote Liberal (Blais, 2005; Blais et al., 2002). Others still have argued that rural Canadians tend to be more socially conservative than those living in urban areas (Cutler and Jenkins 2002); that women are more "left-wing" than men (Gidengil et al., 2003); and that "the West" tends to vote differently than "the East" (Blais et al., 2002). These observations about the impact

Source: Excerpted from *Canadian Journal of Political Science*, vol. 40, no. 4 (December 2007), 935–968. Notes omitted. Reprinted by permission.

of social group identity on political attitudes fit within a wider literature on voting behaviour which has identified the importance of the social group since the earliest election studies (Berelson et al., 1954; Lazarsfeld et al., 1944).

More recently, some scholars have argued that social group identity may do more than simply help to explain vote choice. A subset of research within the voting behaviour literature has examined citizens' reasoning processes, and in particular, how it is that individuals are able to make decisions with little or no information. Some studies have suggested that group identification may act as a shortcut, helping individuals to overcome a lack of knowledge and information when arriving at political preferences (Brady and Sniderman, 1985; Sniderman et al., 1991). In contrast, however, others have shown that with increased exposure to the media, individuals rely less upon group identity when forming preferences (Mendelsohn and Nadeau 1997).

Mendelsohn and Nadeau's (1997) results hint at a relationship between voters' social group identities and information levels that conflict with the notion of the social group as a simple shortcut, and leave us with an important and unresolved question: what is the relationship between social group identity and levels of information in explaining attitudes and vote choice? And, further, how do these two factors interact to influence the decisions made by citizens? The studies cited above allow us to hypothesize three potential outcomes of the interaction between social group identity and information. The first possibility is that information serves to bridge group differences, meaning that the differences between social groups are minimized with higher levels of information (as Mendelsohn and Nadeau found with regards to the effects of media exposure on the differences between Catholics and Protestants). The second possibility is that information may have no effect on the impact of social group identification; and the third possibility is that information may serve to reinforce differences between social groups along cleavage lines—for example, with higher levels of information, Catholic voters would become *more* likely to vote for the Liberal Party.

Using data from the Canadian Election Studies (CES), this paper investigates these possibilities empirically, and finds that information has contradictory effects for different types of cleavages. In some cases, voters' level of information reduces the role of social group identity in explaining attitudes and vote choices: information acts to bridge the differences between different social groups. In other cases, increased levels of information act to amplify the importance of the social group identity in predicting attitudes. Furthermore, these findings suggest that there are important underlying differences between so-called "old" and "new" cleavages in Canada when it comes to understanding their impact on political values. ...

The Uninformed Citizen—The Role of Information in Voting Behaviour

In one of the earliest studies of voting behaviour, Campbell and others observed the lack of interest and knowledge among the majority of voters, and found that both were closely associated with education—that is, that people with more education tended to be more interested in and knowledgeable about politics (1960: 25). These findings were reinforced by Converse's seminal work, in which he found that the mass public had little understanding of basic political concepts (for example, left/right dimensions), and that the political ideas that voters did possess lacked constraint or consistency both horizontally, across ideas, and longitudinally, over time (1964). The implications of these findings were devastating for notions of democracy which expected individuals to have some basic understanding of politics in order to be able to articulate their own interests. What is the point of democracy if citizens lack coherent attitudes and beliefs?

In the last 40 years, political scientists have made significant efforts to address this "democratic dilemma" and have responded to the problems raised by Converse's article in four main, and often related, ways. The first is the group, spearheaded by the efforts of Christopher Achen, who suggests that Converse's findings are largely a result of measurement error. Using the same data as Converse, Achen suggested that the issue was really the reliability of the measures themselves—what was the likelihood that an individual with unchanged values would give the same answer time after time (1975)? He argued that the problem was not that respondents are thick-headed, but that survey measures themselves are problematic. In contrast, a second group within the literature suggests that in fact, the lack of attitude stability seems to sort itself out at the aggregate level, that any inconsistencies that may exist at the individual level are not present at the aggregate level, thus the electoral outcomes are unaffected (Converse and Pierce, 1986; Kramer, 1971; Page and Shapiro, 1992; Wittman, 1989).

A third strand seeks to understand what constitutes citizen knowledge, and to specify what it is that citizens actually need to know (Delli Carpini and Keeter, 1996; Lupia and McCubbins, 1998). The results among this group are mixed, as some scholars argue that citizens tend not to have the information they need (Delli Carpini and Keeter, 1996), while others suggest that they have the capacity to make reasoned choice using the tools available to them (Lupia and McCubbins, 1998).

A fourth strand, closely related to the third, consists of a group of scholars seeking to understand how it is that citizens reason about politics, combining political science with social and cognitive psychology (Brady and Sniderman, 1985; Conover and Feldman, 1989; Fiske 1986; Hamill, Lodge, and Blake, 1985; Sniderman, Brody, and Tetlock, 1991). Some in this fourth tradition have attempted to ascertain whether citizens are able to overcome their information shortfalls by using a series of cognitive tools (Brady and Sniderman, 1985; Sniderman, Brody, and Tetlock, 1991). These scholars have suggested that perhaps individuals use heuristics or information "short-cuts" to come to the same decisions they would make if they were fully informed. Further, they have pointed to a key role for social group identity and affinity with different social groups, suggesting that group affiliation can in fact act as a short-cut for uninformed voters. The idea here is that the less informed are able to make the same kinds of decisions as those who are more informed by relying on identification with the social group. This points to an important link that might exist between the roles of social group and information, but the nature of the relationship is unclear: does information/ knowledge affect the role of the social group identification, or does social group identification help to overcome a lack of information? If the social group acts as a shortcut for decision making, then information should not really have a role: within a given social group, those who are less informed should behave similarly to those who are more informed. If, however, information affects the impact of social group identity, then we can realistically expect one of two outcomes, outcomes which I have labeled bridging and amplifying effects. Information may either reduce the impact of the social group, thus bridging the gap between groups as identified by both Mendelsohn and Nadeau (1997) and Cutler and Jenkins (2000), or it may amplify the effect, causing the different social groups to behave even more dramatically in opposing directions (for example, among the more informed, Catholics would vote in even larger numbers for the Liberal Party compared to non-Catholics). ...

The Effect of Information on Opinions and Attitudes, 2004

...

Catholics

Figure 2 illustrates the effect of information on opinion among Catholics. Uninformed Catholics are approximately eight percent more likely than non-Catholics to support closer ties to the United States, while informed Catholics are nearly ten percent less likely than non-Catholics to support closer ties; information results in nearly a 20 percentage point drop in support for closer ties to the US. In contrast, uninformed Catholics are not in favour of doing more for Quebec, and information results in a slight increase in the probability of support for this issue.

A similar effect is evident when it comes to support for same sex marriage. Uninformed Catholics are ten percentage points less likely than uninformed non-Catholics to support same sex marriage. With increased information, we see a ten percentage point increase; the probability of supporting same sex marriage increases and becomes positive, leaving informed Catholics not really any different from informed non-Catholics.

It is only on the issue of abortion that information serves to reinforce the divide between Catholics and non-Catholics. Informed Catholics are slightly less supportive of easier access to abortion than are uninformed Catholics; however, we should not read too much into the abortion line, as the magnitude of change is small, and the means did not achieve traditional levels of statistical significance. The importance of this graph is that taken as a whole, these data suggest that we cannot necessarily generalize about a Catholic "ethos" for the entire group: *informed Catholics hold different opinions than uninformed Catholics.*

FIGURE 2   Catholics and Issue Attitudes (2004)

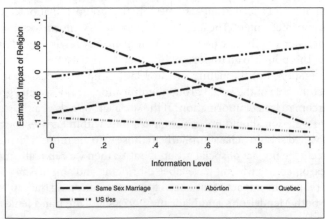

Women

Figure 3 illustrates the effect of information for women. As can be seen from the graph, the gender gap identified in Canadian politics (Gidengil et al., 2003) appears to widen on a number of issues when individuals are more informed. Women become more left-leaning when it comes to both abortion and attitudes toward same sex marriage, and the changes in both achieve traditional levels of statistical significance.

On the issue of same sex marriage, uninformed women were approximately 20 per cent more likely to support same sex marriage than were men, and information had the effect of widening that gap, bringing the probability of support up to nearly 29 per cent higher than men. Information had a similar (and larger) effect on the support for easier access to abortion. Uninformed women were approximately 5 percent less likely than men to support easier access to abortion, and information has the effect of increasing the probability of support for easier access to abortion to nearly 10 percent: *an increase of nearly 15 percentage points*.

The effect of information is equally substantial with regards to the issue of ties to the United States. As the bottom-most line indicates, uninformed women are only slightly (2 per cent) less likely to support closer ties to the US than are uninformed men, while fully informed women are 17 per cent less likely to support closer ties to the US than are informed men. A with the effect of information on attitudes towards abortion, information results in a change in probability of support for close ties to the US by approximately 15 per cent. Again, these data indicate that information has the effect of widening the gender gap: the value differences between women and men are most pronounced among the most informed.

In addition to confirming the findings of others, these results indicate that information does not only have a substantial effect for new issues (for example, same sex marriage) where there might be more uncertainty and less information overall, but also has an important effect for issues that have played a role in Canadian politics for decades. Simply put, information appears to affect the nature of opinion and decision making, regardless of how long information on a given issue has been around. …

FIGURE 3   Women and Issue Attitudes (2004)

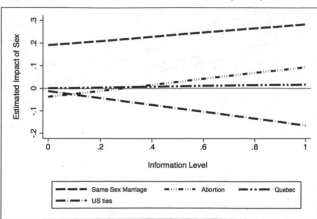

Trends Over Time? Modeling the Role of Information, 1988–2004

...

Catholics and Vote Choice

Figure 6 examines the effect of information on the relationship between Catholics and Liberal vote choice. The data support Blais' observation (2005): Catholics do indeed vote Liberal. Having said that, the data also suggest that uninformed Catholics vote Liberal in much higher proportions than do informed Catholics. In each election year, with the exception of 2000, informed Catholics are at least 15 percentage points less likely than uninformed Catholics to vote Liberal. In 1993 we see the largest information effect, where informed Catholics are over 30 percentage points less likely than uninformed Catholics to vote Liberal. Both the substantive and statistical significance of these effects strongly suggest that information has the effect of bridging the gap between Catholics and non-Catholics, in much the same way as described by Mendelsohn and Nadeau in relation to media exposure (1997). Support for the notion that Catholics behave as a voting block is substantially reduced when we consider the role that information plays.

A similar relationship between information and vote choice among Catholics can be seen when we examine vote propensity for the Reform/Alliance/Conservative Party from 1993 to 2004. While vote models for the Progressive Conservative Party during this time period were also run (including 1988), it seems more appropriate to focus on the evolution of support for the newer party, given how much there was to learn, and the potential role that information could have in explaining support for the party. Further, by excluding data from 1988 for the bulk of the analysis, greater uniformity in the information measure is maintained, both conceptually and methodologically.

FIGURE 6   Catholics and the Liberal Vote

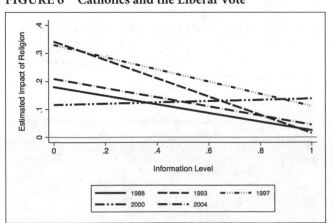

As Figure 7 illustrates, uninformed Catholics do not tend to support Reform or the Canadian Alliance, or the new Conservative Party. However, informed Catholics behave quite differently from uninformed Catholics. In every election year except for 2000, informed Catholics are both substantially and significantly more likely to vote for this party than are uninformed Catholics. The 2000 election appears to be an anomaly, and not only among Catholics. This appears to be the case across the board, regardless of social group membership. As the graphs in the following pages illustrate, when more informed, *all* groups were slightly *less* likely to vote for the Canadian Alliance. A possible explanation is that informed Catholics were not actually embracing the Liberal Party more than usual, but that instead, this may have been a reaction against Stockwell Day's Canadian Alliance Party. … In every year except for 2000, not only are informed Catholics more likely than uninformed Catholics to vote for the Reform and Conservative Party, but information actually results in a 15 to 20 percentage point jump in support for this party, and the endpoint is a positive coefficient. Thus information has the effect of substantially reducing the gap between Catholics and non-Catholics: it seems that the nature of the Catholic choice varies dramatically by level of information.

FIGURE 7   **Catholics and the Reform/Alliance/
Conservative Vote**

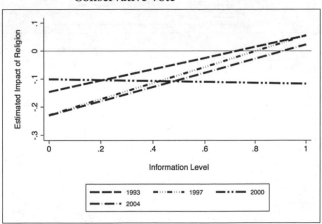

Women and Vote Choice

Consistent with 2004 data, information has the role of widening the gender gap. Women's left-leaning tendencies are strengthened, as they are less likely to support the Reform/Alliance/ Conservative Party when they are more informed. Figure 8 illustrates the information effect.

In 1993 we see the biggest information effect, where uninformed women are not very different from uninformed men. Informed women, however, behave quite differently. Information results in a 20 percentage point drop, and informed women are approximately 18 per cent less likely than informed men to vote for Reform. Similar patterns (though less drastic) can be seen for all of the other years as well. 2004 is similar to 1993 in that uninformed women are no different from uninformed men in their propensity to vote for the Conservative Party. Information results in a near ten percentage point drop, as informed women are less likely to support the Conservatives.

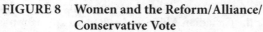

**FIGURE 8   Women and the Reform/Alliance/
                        Conservative Vote**

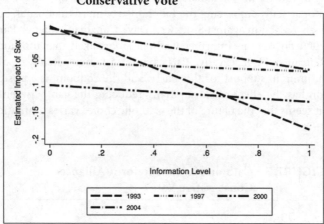

Empire and Communications

31

Harold Innis (1950)

EDITORS' INTRODUCTION

Harold Innis was a noted professor of political economy at the University of Toronto. Perhaps best known for his "staples theory" of Canadian culture, history, and economy, his work in political communication was also seminal, and has had long-lasting influence on the way we think about the shaping of cultures.

This excerpt is from his 1950 book Empire and Communications, *which was based on a series of lectures he delivered at Oxford University in 1948. Though criticized by some for an occasionally dense writing style, underneath his prose stylings lie ideas that remain vital and worthy of serious consideration more than half a century after they were written. In this selection, he argues that media and communication shape civilization and culture, and have done so from the earliest days of human society. In particular, Innis looks at aspects of time versus space, suggesting that certain mediums (such as clay and stone) emphasize an orientation toward time, while other mediums (papyrus, paper) facilitate an orientation toward space and empire building. In the latter half of this excerpt, Innis considers the repercussion of the advent of "mechanized communication" (such as newspapers) on political organization in the Western world.*

It has seemed to me that the subject of communication offers possibilities in that it occupies a crucial position in the organization and administration of government and in turn of empires and of Western civilization. But I must confess at this point a bias which has led me to give particular attention to this subject. In studies of Canadian economic history or of the economic history of the French, British, and American empires, I have been influenced by a phenomenon strikingly evident in Canada which for that reason I have perhaps over-emphasized. Briefly, North America is deeply penetrated by three vast inlets from the Atlantic—the Mississippi, the St. Lawrence, and Hudson Bay, and the rivers of its drainage basin. In the northern part of the continent or in Canada extensive waterways and the dominant Precambrian formation have facilitated concentration on bulk products the character of which has been determined by the culture of the aborigines and by the effectiveness of navigation by lake, river, and ocean to Europe. Along the north Atlantic coast the cod fisheries were exploited over an extensive coast-line; decentralization was inevitable; and political interests of Europe were

Source: Excerpted from *Empire and Communications* by Harold Innis. The Clarendon Press/Oxford University Press, 1950. Notes omitted.

widely represented. The highly valuable small-bulk furs were exploited along the St. Law-rence by the French and in Hudson Bay by the English. Continental development implied centralization. Competition between the two inlets gave the advantage in the fur trade to Hudson Bay, and after 1821 the St. Lawrence region shifted to dependence on the square timber trade. Monopoly of the fur trade held by the Hudson's Bay Company checked expan-sion north-westward from the St. Lawrence until Confederation was achieved and political organization became sufficiently strong to support construction of a transcontinental rail-way, the Canadian Pacific, completed in 1885. On the Pacific coast the discovery of placer gold was followed by rapid increase in settlement, exhaustion of the mines, and the develop-ment of new staples adapted to the demands of Pacific Ocean navigation such as timber. The railway and the steamship facilitated concentration on agricultural products, notably wheat in western Canada and, later on, products of the Precambrian formation such as precious and base metals and pulp and paper. Concentration on the production of staples for export to more highly industrialized areas in Europe and later in the United States had broad im-plications for the Canadian economic, political, and social structure. Each staple in its turn left its stamp, and the shift to new staples invariably produced periods of crises in which adjustments in the old structure were painfully made and a new pattern created in relation to a new staple. As the costs of navigation declined less valuable commodities emerged as staples—precious metals, dried fish exported to Spain to secure precious metals, timber to support defence, in the words of Adam Smith "perhaps more important than opulence," and finally wheat to meet the demands of an industrialized England. An attempt has been made to trace the early developments elsewhere but little has been done to indicate clearly the effects of the development of the pulp and paper industry. The difficulty of studying this industry arises partly from its late development and partly from the complexity of the prob-lem of analysing the demand for the finished product. Concentration on staple products incidental to the geographic background has involved problems not only in the supply area but also in the demand area, to mention only the effects of specie from Central America on European prices, the effects of the fur trade on France, of wheat production on English agri-culture, and of pulp and paper production on public opinion in Anglo-Saxon countries. The effects of the organization and production on a large scale of staple raw materials were shown in the attempts by France to check the increase in production of furs, in the resistance of English purchasers to the high price of timber ending in the abolition of the Navigation Acts, in the opposition of European agriculture to low-cost wheat, and in the attempt to restrain the sensationalism of the new journalism which followed cheap newsprint.

In this reference to the problem of attack it will be clear that we have been concerned with the use of certain tools which have proved effective in the interpretation of the economic history of Canada and the British Empire. It may seem irreverent to use these tools in a study of public opinion and to suggest that the changing character of the British Empire during the present century has been in part a result of the pulp and paper industry and its influence on public opinion, but I have felt it wise to proceed with instruments with which I am familiar and which have proved useful. The viewpoint is suggested in a comment of Constable to Murray: "If you wish to become a great author your chance will be bye and bye when paper gets cheap-er." In any case I have tried to present my bias in order that you may be on your guard.

I shall attempt to outline the significance of communication in a small number of empires as a means of understanding its role in a general sense and as a background to an apprecia-tion of its significance to the British Empire. Bryce has stated that from the time of Menes down to that of Attila the tendency is generally towards aggregation: and the history of the ancient nations shows us, not only an enormous number of petty monarchies and republics swallowed up in the Empire of Rome, but that empire itself far more highly centralized than any preceding one had been. When the Roman dominion began to break up the process was reversed and for seven hundred years or more the centrifugal forces had it their own way. … From the thirteenth century onwards the tide begins to set the other way … neither Democracy nor the principle of Nationalities has, on the balance of cases, operated to check the general movement towards aggregation which marks the last six centuries.

In attempting to understand the basis of these diverse tendencies, we become concerned with the problem of empire, and in particular with factors responsible for the successful operation of "centrifugal and centripetal forces." In the organization of large areas communication occupies a vital place, and it is significant that Bryce's periods correspond roughly first to that dominated by clay and papyrus, second to that dominated by parchment, and third to that dominated by paper. The effective government of large areas depends to a very important extent on the efficiency of communication.

The concepts of time and space reflect the significance of media to civilization. Media which emphasize time are those which are durable in character such as parchment, clay, and stone. The heavy materials are suited to the development of architecture and sculpture. Media which emphasize space are apt to be less durable and light in character such as papyrus and paper. The latter are suited to wide areas in administration and trade. The conquest of Egypt by Rome gave access to supplies of papyrus which became the basis of a large administrative empire. Materials which emphasize time favour decentralization and hierarchical types of institutions, while those which emphasize space favour centralization and systems of government less hierarchical in character. Large-scale political organizations such as empires must be considered from the standpoint of two dimensions, those of space and time, and persist by overcoming the bias of media which over-emphasize either dimension. They have tended to flourish under conditions in which civilization reflects the influence of more than one medium and in which the bias of one medium toward decentralization is offset by the bias of another medium towards centralization.

We can conveniently divide the history of the West into the writing and the printing periods. In the writing period we can note the importance of various media such as the clay tablet of Mesopotamia, the papyrus roll in the Egyptian and in the Graeco-Roman world, parchment codex in the late Graeco-Roman world and the early Middle Ages, and paper after its introduction in the western world from China. In the printing period we are able to concentrate on paper as a medium, but we can note the introduction of machinery in the manufacture of paper and in printing at the beginning of the nineteenth century and the introduction of the use of wood as a raw material in the second half of that century. …

Paper and the Printing Press

… The British Empire, which gained from a fusion of Roman law traditions and common-law traditions, has been exposed to the effects of increasing nationalization based to an important extent on language under the influence of mechanization of the printed and the spoken word as in the case of the French in Canada, the Dutch in South America, the languages of India and Pakistan, and the attempt to revive the Irish language in Eire. The common-law tradition tends to become more powerful and to reflect the influence of elements which have been decentralizing in character. "Under democratic control England must abandon all idea of influence upon the world's affairs" (Lord Salisbury).

The United States, with systems of mechanized communication and organized force, has sponsored a new type of imperialism imposed on common law in which sovereignty is preserved *de jure* and used to expand imperialism *de facto*. It has been able to exploit the tendencies toward imperialism which have emerged in members of the British Commonwealth. Canada has been used as a means of penetrating the British Commonwealth. Resistance to this influence can be made effective by adherence to common-law traditions and notably to the cultural heritage of Europe. The state and the Church have lost control in large areas of Europe as a result of successive periods of occupation, and survival in the West depends on their continual subordination and on a recognition of the cultural leadership and supremacy of Europe. States are destroyed by lack of culture (Jaeger), and so too are empires and civilizations. Mass production and standardization are the enemies of the West. The limitations of mechanization of the printed and the spoken word must be emphasized and determined efforts to recapture the vitality of the oral tradition must be made.

Large-scale political organization implies a solution of problems of space in terms of administrative efficiency and of problems of time in terms of continuity. Elasticity of structure involves a persistent interest in the search for ability and persistent attacks on monopolies of knowledge. Stability involves a concern with the limitations of instruments of government as well as with their possibilities.

Concentration on a medium of communication implies a bias in the cultural development of the civilization concerned either towards an emphasis on space and political organization or towards an emphasis on time and religious organization. Introduction of a second medium tends to check the bias of the first and to create conditions suited to the growth of empire. The Byzantine empire emerged from a fusion of a bias incidental to papyrus in relation to political organization and of parchment in relation to ecclesiastical organization. The dominance of parchment in the West gave a bias towards ecclesiastical organization which led to the introduction of a paper with its bias toward political organization. With printing, paper facilitated an effective development of the vernaculars and gave expression to their vitality in the growth of nationalism. The adaptability of the alphabet to large-scale machine industry became the basis of literacy, advertising, and trade. The book as a specialized product of printing and, in turn, the newspaper strengthened the position of language as a basis of nationalism. In the United States the dominance of the newspaper led to large-scale development of monopolies of communication in terms of space and implied a neglect of problems of time. Regional monopolies of metropolitan newspapers have been strengthened by monopolies of press associations. The bias of paper towards an emphasis on space and its monopolies of knowledge has been checked by the development of a new medium, the radio. The results have been evident in an increasing concern with problems of time reflected in the growth of planning and the socialized state. The instability involved in dependence on the newspaper in the United States and the Western world has facilitated an appeal to force as a possible stabilizing factor. The ability to develop a system of government in which the bias of communication can be checked and an appraisal of the significance of space and time can be reached remains a problem of empire and of the Western world.

Filtering the Female: Television News Coverage of 1993 Canadian Leaders' Debates

32

Elisabeth Gidengil and Joanna Everitt (2000)

EDITORS' INTRODUCTION

Elisabeth Gidengil is Hiram Mills Professor of Political Science at McGill University. Most of her work focuses on elections and voting behaviour, with a particular eye to gender in politics. In addition to her many books, her work has been published in the Journal of Women, Politics & Policy, Electoral Studies, Political Psychology, *and the* Canadian Journal of Political Science.

Joanna Everitt is professor of political science and Dean of the Faculty of Arts at the University of New Brunswick in Saint John. Everitt specializes in gender and politics, and has published numerous articles in Canadian and international journals, including Electoral Studies, Political Psychology, *and the* Journal of Canadian Studies.

These two scholars have collaborated on a number of occasions, and this excerpt showcases some of their important work on the media, gender, and politics. They assess the leaders' debates in the 1993 federal election and the news coverage of those debates, demonstrating that "gendered mediation" is alive and well in political coverage, based on the different ways in which male and female candidates are covered.

Introduction

With women leading two of the parties, the 1993 Canadian leaders' debates afford a unique opportunity to assess whether "the mediated presentation of politics is gendered" (Sreberny-Mohammadi and Ross 1996, 103). The notion of gendered mediation implies that voters will be presented with a more filtered picture of women politicians and that the filter itself will be gendered. This filtering means, first, that the behavior of women politicians will be subject to more analysis than their male counterparts and, second, that the women's coverage will reflect traditional masculine conceptions of politics. This article examines whether these propositions apply to television coverage of the two women leaders in the 1993 Canadian leaders' debates.

The concept of gendered mediation succinctly captures the current thrust of the literature on women, politics and the media. Reflecting the greater presence of women in politics, work on media coverage of women politicians has gone beyond the early preoccupation with

Source: *Women and Politics*, vol. 21, no. 4 (2000), 105–131. Notes omitted.

the lack of coverage to explore the nature of the coverage that women receive (Carroll and Schreiber 1997; Kahn and Goldenberg 1991; Kahn 1994; Norris 1997; Robinson and Saint-Jean 1991; Robinson and Saint-Jean 1995; Ross 1995). That coverage has typically dwelled on women's electoral viability, characterized their issue competencies and personality traits in stereotypically feminine terms, and involved the use of woman-specific narrative frames. As women become more visible in political life, however, they may come to be treated in more conventional terms. Certainly, the most recent empirical work has yielded a more mixed pattern of findings (Peake 1997). When Smith (1997) studied press coverage of 1994 United States statewide campaigns, for example, he found less evidence of sex-differentiated coverage than Kahn (1992, 1994) had uncovered in the 1980s.

Being covered "like a man," however, may not necessarily mean receiving gender-neutral coverage. The application of conventional political frames to women politicians can result in subtle and insidious forms of gender bias. This is the central insight of the gendered mediation argument. It rests on the assumption that electoral politics remains a male-dominated sphere that still operates very much according to masculine norms. This is mirrored in media coverage. Political reporting typically employs "a masculine narrative" (Rakow and Kranich 1991, 8), portraying election campaigns in stereotypically masculine terms, replete with images of warfare and the sports arena (see Blankenship 1976; Blankenship and Kang 1991; Gidengil and Everitt 1999; Gingras 1997). The problem with the use of conventional political frames, then, is that they treat the male as normative (see Sreberny-Mohammadi and Ross 1996). The media's resort to these seemingly sex-neutral, but profoundly gendered, frames may result in a classic "damned if you do, damned if you don't" dilemma for many aspiring women leaders. If they try to adapt to the masculine norms, the media will tend to focus unduly on the behavior that is contrary to deeply held stereotypes of feminine behavior. And yet, if women fail to conform to those norms, they can end up receiving less coverage by the media. We are not suggesting that this gendered mediation is necessarily a conscious process. What interests us is the unconscious bias that arises from the nature of the media as a "cultural looking glass" (Bridge 1995, 19), both reflecting and reinforcing society's dominant cultural values (see Peake 1997). ...

Interpretative Reporting

Was the coverage of the two women leaders more heavily mediated? As Table 1 shows, there was a marked asymmetry in the treatment of Campbell and Chrétien on CBC. Campbell's performance was more likely than Chrétien's to be interpreted as opposed to merely reported. Only 31% of the statements made about Campbell were descriptive, compared with 43% of the statements made about Chrétien. Coverage of Campbell was predominantly (62%) analytical, focusing on the *why* much more than the *what*. Chrétien did receive more evaluative coverage (22%) than Campbell (8%), but these evaluations, unlike Campbell's, were mostly positive. Of course, it could be that Chrétien simply did better in the debates than Campbell. As Robinson and Shehan (1983, 131) concede, "Reality must play a part in the press image, unless the media behave dishonestly or irresponsibly." As they go on to note, however, "Reality is almost never the whole story" (137).

This becomes clear when we compare CBC coverage with CTV coverage (see Table 1). Evaluations of Campbell on CTV were as likely to be positive as negative. The key point from

TABLE 1 Type of Coverage by Leader (French and English Debates Combined)

1. CBC

	Campbell	Chrétien	McLaughlin	Manning	Bouchard
Descriptive	31%	43%	58%	60%	56%
Analytical	62	36	33	33	25
Positive Evaluative	0	18	8	7	12
Negative Evaluation	8	4	0	0	6
N	(39)	(28)	(12)	(15)	(16)

2. CTV

	Campbell	Chrétien	McLaughlin	Manning	Bouchard
Descriptive	19%	31%	12%	71%	57%
Analytical	42	38	38	14	29
Positive Evaluative	19	22	25	0	7
Negative Evaluative	19	9	25	14	7
N	(31)	(32)	(8)	(7)	(14)

Note: Column %s may not sum to 100% due to rounding

our perspective, however, is that coverage of Campbell continued to be more mediated. On CTV, as on CBC, her participation in the debates was more likely than Chrétien's to be interpreted, as opposed to merely being described. On both networks, analytical statements about her outnumbered descriptive statements by a margin of 2 to 1.

The results are less consistent for McLaughlin. While her CTV coverage was highly mediated, her coverage on CBC tended to be more descriptive (in fact, in this respect, she was treated almost identically to Manning). We should be cautious about interpreting the percentages for McLaughlin (and Manning), however, given the small number of statements made. Indeed, what is most striking about coverage of McLaughlin on both networks is how little of it there was. Only 12 statements were made about her in the aftermath of the debates on CBC, still fewer (8) on CTV. The low numbers are the more telling in that, unlike Manning, she was a participant in both debates. For Campbell, on the other hand, the issue was not the lack of coverage, but the type of coverage she received. As the gendered mediation thesis predicted, Campbell's debate performance was indeed subject to more interpretation than the men's.

Sound Bites

Interpretative coverage is one form of mediation. A second—and related—form of mediation is editing of reported speech. Did news coverage of the English debate afford viewers as much opportunity to hear the women speaking as the men? Table 2 shows the total length of all the debate sound bites for each leader in CBC and CTV coverage of the English debate. If we compare the treatment of Campbell with Chrétien and McLaughlin with Manning, it would be hard to conclude that there was any consistent bias shown toward the men leaders. On the contrary, at least when it comes to the total time that each leader was heard speaking, the coverage of the English debate might be judged quite evenhanded. For all four of these leaders, the total length of their sound bites was roughly proportionate to their speaking time

TABLE 2   Frequency and Length of Sound Bites by Leader
(English Debate) CBC and CTV Combined

	Number	Total Length (seconds)	Average Length (seconds)	Total Length (words)	Average Length (words)
Campbell	20	171.3	8.6	528	26.4
Chrétien	15	155.2	10.3	506	33.7
McLaughlin	10	125.6	12.6	415	41.5
Manning	14	119.9	8.6	296	21.1
Bouchard	10	53.7	5.4	173	17.3

in the debate itself. It is hardly surprising that the leader of the separatist Bloc Québécois was heard speaking much more briefly in coverage of the English language debate since his party was not running candidates outside Quebec.

This apparent evenhandedness is deceptive. When we turn to the average length of the sound bites, Campbell clearly fares less well. Her sound bites were typically shorter than Chrétien's. The assumption in much of the sound bite literature has been that shorter sound bites are indicative of more heavily mediated coverage (see Hallin 1992). To judge by this criterion, then, Campbell's coverage was again more mediated than Chrétien's. The same cannot be said of McLaughlin. Her sound bites were few in number, but at least they were long enough to permit viewers to gain some sense of her argument.

It would be premature, however, to conclude that coverage of McLaughlin was less subject to gendered mediation. As noted earlier, gendered mediation goes beyond sex differences in the amount of filtering. It is also a matter of the kind of filtering that occurs. As Russomanno and Everett (1995) argue, fair coverage is as much a matter of sound bite *substance* as it is of sound bite *length*. It is the television networks, after all, not the leaders, that get to decide which sound bites are aired. If the sound bites reflect negatively on the leader, then neither more nor longer is better.

Sound bites are selected by the media to make for a more compelling narrative. The dominant narrative framework in debate coverage is conflict, with the participants typically portrayed as warriors, street-fighters, or boxers (Blankenship 1976; Blankenship and Kang 1991; Gidengil and Everitt 1999). We can, therefore, expect debate sound bites to highlight the confrontational aspects of the event (see Clayman 1995). We predicted that this tendency would be reinforced in the case of the two women leaders. To the extent that Campbell and McLaughlin did debate aggressively, they were acting contrary to deeply rooted conceptions of sex-appropriate behavior. If the gendered mediation argument is valid, the unexpectedness, and hence conspicuousness, of such behavior should combine to enhance the likelihood of its selection for a sound bite (see Bell 1991; Clayman 1995).

Table 3 presents the results of our analysis of the leaders' behavior in the English debate. McLaughlin was the most likely to address another leader by name (26 times) and second only to Reform leader Preston Manning in her use of the personal form of address "you" (54 times to Manning's 63 times). When it came to the more confrontational forms of behavior, however, she was clearly the least aggressive: she was the least likely to interrupt another speaker (22 times) or to point her finger as she spoke (24 times), and she only once used the most aggressive gesture, namely a clenched fist. Campbell, on the other hand, was the least aggressive in her use of personal forms of address, but the picture is more mixed when it comes to more aggressive forms of behavior. She rivaled Chrétien in her use of the clenched fist, clenching her fist 12 times to Chrétien's 11, but she ranked behind Chrétien (61 times) and Manning (55 times) when it came to finger-pointing (43 times) and behind Manning (67 times) and Bouchard (35 times) when it came to interruptions (31 times). Certainly, there was nothing to suggest that Campbell, still less McLaughlin, was *more* aggressive than her male counterparts. Manning interrupted other leaders more frequently than Campbell and McLaughlin *combined*.

This is not the conclusion that would be drawn by a viewer watching news coverage of the debate. Table 4 shows how often each type of behavior was shown in each leader's sound bites. Comparing Table 4 with Table 3, we see that Campbell accounted for 34% of the instances of "you" being used in the sound bites, but only 17% of instances of "you" in the debate itself. In other words, use of this personal form of address on Campbell's part was overemphasized in her sound bite coverage by a factor of 2.0 (34 divided by 17). Table 5 presents the results of similar calculations for all five leaders. A value of one indicates that the frequency of a given type of behavior in sound bites is proportionate to the leader's use of that behavior in the debate itself.

Our prediction that sound bites would highlight the women leaders' confrontational behavior is strongly confirmed. As the gendered mediation argument predicts, the women's sound bite coverage focused disproportionately on instances of aggressive behavior. This was the case for Campbell for four of the five types of confrontational behavior. Sound bites portrayed her addressing other leaders as "you" or by name, interrupting, and pointing her finger much more frequently than her behavior in the debate warranted. The contrast with sound bite coverage of Chrétien is striking. Only one behavior on his part received disproportionate coverage. He was shown addressing other candidates by name more frequently than we would predict on the basis of the debate itself. When it came to more confrontational behaviors, however, these were underemphasized. This was most evident for finger-pointing. He was the most prone to pointing his finger at other leaders during the debate, but Campbell was shown using this confrontational gesture much more frequently. In fact, viewers of the news got to see her pointing her finger (and addressing another leader as "you") more frequently than any other leader. She accounted for only 20% of the episodes of finger-pointing

TABLE 3   Aggressive Debating Behavior in the English Debate by Leader

	Use of "you"	Address by name	Interruptions	Finger-pointing	Clenched fist
Campbell	44 (17%)	4 (6%)	31 (17%)	43 (20%)	12 (48%)
Chrétien	45 (18%)	11 (16%)	23 (13%)	16 (28%)	11 (44%)
McLaughlin	54 (21%)	26 (38%)	22 (12%)	24 (11%)	1 (4%)
Manning	63 (25%)	21 (31%)	67 (38%)	55 (25%)	0 (0%)
Bouchard	46 (18%)	6 (9%)	35 (20%)	34 (16%)	1 (4%)
Total	**252**	**68**	**178**	**217**	**25**

Percentages of total occurrences appear in parentheses

TABLE 4   Aggressive Debating Behavior Shown in Sound Bites
            by Leader CBC and CTV Combined

	Use of "you"	Address by name	Interruptions	Finger-pointing	Clenched fist	N
Campbell	11 (34%)	1 (8%)	7 (24%)	10 (32%)	0 (0%)	20
Chrétien	2 (6%)	3 (23%)	2 (7%)	4 (13%)	0 (0%)	15
McLaughlin	7 (22%)	5 (38%)	5 (17%)	4 (13%)	1 (100%)	10
Manning	7 (22%)	4 (31%)	8 (28%)	6 (19%)	0 (0%)	14
Bouchard	5 (16%)	0 (0%)	7 (24%)	7 (23%)	0 (0%)	10
Total	**32**	**13**	**29**	**31**	**1**	**69**

Percentage of total occurrences appears in parentheses

TABLE 5   Emphasis on Aggressive Debating Behavior in Sound Bites
            by Leader CBA and CTV Combined

	Use of "you"	Address by name	Interruptions	Finger-pointing
Campbell	2.0	1.3	1.4	1.6
Chrétien	0.3	1.4	0.5	0.5
McLaughlin	1.1	1.0	1.4	1.2
Manning	0.9	1.0	0.7	0.8
Bouchard	0.9	0.0	1.2	1.4

The column entries are obtained by dividing the corresponding figures in Table 4 by the figures in Table 3. Results are not presented for fist-clenching because only one instance of this was shown in in the sound bites.

in the debate itself, but one-third of all the instances shown in network coverage. Similarly, she was shown interrupting almost as often as Manning, despite the fact that in the debate itself Manning interrupted other leaders more than twice as frequently as Campbell did. The only aggressive behavior on Campbell's part that was not overemphasized was fist-clenching. She was not shown engaging at all in this aggressive gesture, but then neither was Chrétien, who rivaled her when it came to clenching his fist in the debate.

The one leader shown using a clenched fist was McLaughlin. This was the *only* instance of McLaughlin using a clenched fist in the entire debate. It is striking that McLaughlin was the subject of so few bites, and yet they included this atypically aggressive behavior on her part. When it came to the less confrontational types of behavior, McLaughlin's sound bites gave them about the amount of exposure we would expect based on the debate itself. It is when we look at the more aggressive actions that the disproportionate attention begins to become apparent. Of the five leaders in the English debate, she was the least prone to interrupting other leaders or pointing her finger at them and yet her sound bites focused disproportionately on instances of such confrontational behavior. The contrast with Chrétien and Manning is particularly revealing. While McLaughlin's sound bites played up her finger-pointing and interruptions, similar displays on the part of Chrétien and Manning were downplayed.

When the sound bites are compared with a transcription of the debate itself, the asymmetrical treatment of both women is apparent. Not only are interruptions by both Chrétien and Manning edited out of some of the sound bites, but both women are shown interrupting the men when it was actually one or other of the men who had interrupted first. This occurs twice for Campbell and four times for McLaughlin. The figure for McLaughlin is particularly noteworthy since she only had ten sound bites. There is not a single instance of this asymmetry occurring for any of the men. In one edited exchange, McLaughlin is shown apparently cutting Manning off as he says "Let me finish." In fact, the transcript shows that McLaughlin let Manning continue his response before interrupting again. In another sound bite, Campbell is shown calling Chrétien a "laughing stock." This bite is introduced with the reporter saying, "When Chrétien shot back, Campbell quickly forgot her promise to avoid getting personal." What the viewer of the news coverage cannot know is that it was Chrétien who first got personal by using the very same phrase in reference to Campbell's deficit reduction plan. It is hard to avoid the conclusion that these sound bites had been edited to highlight the women's confrontational behavior.

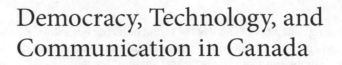

33 Democracy, Technology, and Communication in Canada

Darin Barney (2005)

EDITORS' INTRODUCTION

Darin Barney is the Canada Research Chair in Technology and Citizenship, in the Department of Art History and Communication Studies at McGill University. A political theorist by training, his work focuses on media and communication theory, democracy, and the philosophy of technology. He has published work in the Canadian Journal of Communication, *the* Canadian Journal of Cultural Studies, Party Politics, *and the* American Review of Canadian Studies.

This excerpt comes from the book Communication Technology, *which he published as part of the wide-ranging* Canadian Democratic Audit *Series. In this book, Barney examines the possibility that Internet and communication technologies (ICTs) can improve the nature of democracy in Canada, including increasing the political engagement and participation of Canadians. He is cautiously optimistic that ICTs can enhance democracy.*

The 2000 Canadian general election, understood at the time to be the country's first "Internet election," also featured the lowest voter turn out in the history of these contests at the federal level. Just 61 percent of registered voters turned out to cast ballots—when measured against the entire voting-age population, this figure drops to 55 percent (Johnston 2001, 13). Significantly, these numbers are less a blip than the continuation of a trend that has seen voter turnout in Canada drop precipitously and consistently from 75 percent of registered voters in the 1988 election to 71 percent in 1993, to 67 percent in 1997, and finally to the millennial level of 61 percent. This downward trajectory in this most basic form of political participation has occurred during the same period of time that formidable new information and communication technologies have come to occupy the Canadian political landscape and fairly saturate the Canadian political imagination. In its 1999 speech from the throne, the government of Canada articulated its goal "to be known around the world as the government most connected to its citizens" (Canada 1999); two years later it declared that it had "helped to make Canada one of the most connected countries in the world" (Canada 2001). This was no idle boast, as Canada does indeed rank highly among industrialized nations on most measures of Internet connectivity. It is also the case that, as political scientist Richard Johnston (2000, 13) has observed, recent electoral history "puts Canada near the bottom of the industrialized world turnout league tables ... No other G7 country besides the US has turnout as low as Canada's."

Source: Excerpted from *Communication Technology* by Darin Barney. Vancouver: University of British Columbia Press, 2005. Published in the series *The Canadian Democratic Audit*.

Admittedly, voter turnout is neither the only nor, arguably, even the best measure of the health of a democracy, and many factors combine to determine its level at any given time. The suggestion here is certainly not that the explosive growth of new information and communication technologies directly correlates with the decline in voter turnout in recent Canadian elections. That being said, the fact of their coincidence is provocative. One of our deepest liberal democratic intuitions is that generalized advance in our ability to gather and share information, and to communicate with one another, invigorates democratic participation. This intuition has received forceful expression in relation to the computerized and networked information and communication technologies (ICTs) that mediate an increasing array of social, political, and economic activity in Canada. Information and communication, we believe, are foundational to democracy, and therefore technologies that facilitate these contribute positively to democracy's achievement and enhancement. How could a technology such as the Internet, which provides widespread instant access to increasing volumes of politically relevant information, and which enables direct, undistorted communication among citizens (and rulers) be anything other than complementary to informed, democratic deliberation and self-government?

The coincidence of the rise of the Internet and a historic decline in voter turnout does not invalidate the hypothesis that ICTs will enhance democracy in Canada. It does, however, raise the possibility that recent technological advances in information and communication capacity are not unambiguously or automatically beneficial to Canadian democracy, nor capable of overcoming other factors that may contribute to its current condition. Indeed, one of the nasty little facts of the coincident growth of mass democracy and mass media in the twenty-first century is that despite a dramatic trajectory of technological expansion in information and communication capacity, democratic participation has not improved significantly in quantitative or qualitative terms. As Bruce Bimber has written, documenting the absence of statistical evidence linking Internet use to increased political engagement (in its various forms) in the United States:

> Opportunities to become better informed have apparently expanded historically, as the informational context of politics has grown richer and become better endowed with media and ready access to political communication. Yet none of the major developments in communication in the twentieth century produced any aggregate gain in citizen participation. Neither telephones, radio, nor television exerted a net positive effect on participation, despite the fact that they apparently reduced information costs and improved citizens' access to information (Bimber 2001, 57).

While we must be sensitive to the technical attributes that distinguish new from previous mass media, we must also acknowledge the ways in which they may be the same. Similarly, we must be as open to the possibility that politics mediated by new technologies will aggravate the disconnection between information/communication and democratic engagement as we are to our intuition that they will mediate a democratic renaissance.

This suggests that the relationship between ICTs and Canadian democracy is more of a problem to be explored than a foregone conclusion. It is a problem that exists at a very basic philosophical level, a problem that has manifested itself historically in Canada, and a problem that surfaces in particular ways in the contemporary context of new ICTs. For many reasons that will become evident through the course of this investigation, the problem of democracy, technology, and communication crystallizes broader dynamics and questions of democratic citizenship, identity, power, and the public good. In this sense, democratic questions about technology and communication are something of a crucible, especially in the Canadian context.

This exploration of the relationship between ICTs and democracy in Canada will be framed by the three criteria set out for the Canadian Democratic Audit: public participation, inclusiveness, and responsiveness. Public participation is the sine qua non of democratic politics and government. Though participation can take many forms and be enacted in a variety of venues, the degree to which citizens take part in various processes of political expression, decision making, and governance is an indispensable measure of democratic legitimacy. Participation is an important concept for assessing the politics of ICTs in several respects. Have political processes surrounding the development and regulation of these technologies been participatory or not? Do ICTs provide means for improving or expanding political participation in Canada? And do ICTs enhance, or undermine, the socioeconomic equality that supports effective political participation?

Inclusiveness is the second Audit criterion, and it too is related to the core democratic principle of equality. Exclusivity, or privilege, is anathema to a democracy, wherein political participation must be at least available to, and at best undertaken by, as many citizens as possible without prejudice. A political order that formally or practically excludes significant segments of its citizenry from effective participation will be far less democratic than one that provides for inclusion of as many people as possible in the political process. This criterion is especially important in Canada, whose population exhibits multiple diversities that often correspond to systemic forms of disadvantage and exclusion. Here again, special questions are raised about ICTs. Has decision making surrounding their development and regulation included the diversity of views and interests of relevant constituencies in Canada? Do ICTs provide a means of effectively including a greater diversity of Canadians in political life? And have these technologies contributed to, or undermined, the socioeconomic basis of inclusion and political equality in Canada?

The third Audit criterion is responsiveness. It measures the degree to which various elements of the political system actually address, and are affected by, the needs, priorities, and preferences expressed by citizens in their participatory activities. In democratic polities, a diverse range of citizens participate not simply to lend the appearance of legitimacy to processes that may not *really* take their views into account; they participate so that political outcomes will reflect, at least to some degree, their duly expressed interests. In representative systems such as Canada's, the responsiveness of political agencies and institutions is a crucial measure of the democratic acceptability of a given regime. As with the criteria of participation and inclusiveness, ICTs have a special bearing on the question of responsiveness, and vice-versa. Has the development of ICT policy in Canada been sufficiently responsive to the diversity of interests at stake in it? Has the relationship between ICTs and globalization enhanced or diminished the capacity of Canadian governments to be responsive to their citizens? And has the use of ICTs by a variety of political actors made Canadian political institutions more responsive to public participation?

Taken together, the three criteria of participation, inclusiveness, and responsiveness focus the investigation that follows on three central questions: To what extent has the development of digital communication technology in Canada been subjected to democratic political judgment and control? What effect is the increasing mediation of political communication by digital technologies having on the practices of democratic politics in Canada? How do digital technologies affect the distribution of power in Canadian society?

These questions derive from an understanding that communication technology occupies a complex position in the universe of Canadian democracy. Communication and its mediating technologies are at once an object and an instrument of democratic practice in Canada. They also affect the material context in which democratic politics and citizenship take place. …

[T]echnologies are political because they constitute widely shared social arrangements that frame a broad range of human social, political, and economic priorities and practices, and because they are artifacts in which power is embedded and through which power is exercised. Consequently, moments of technological change especially have the potential to be moments of intense democratic political contest, moments of deliberation over the character and needs of the common interest relative to the technology in question. These moments can also be sacrificed to the logic of depoliticization that is embedded in the technological spirit, which is often called forth by those who stand to benefit from insulating issues of technology from democratic political scrutiny. The history of the deployment of technologies of mass communication in Canada, and policy making surrounding this deployment, is replete with examples of this dynamic.

The political questions surrounding communication technology and policy in Canada have remained relatively consistent since at least the advent of the telegraph. They include questions about the following:

- the role of the state relative to the market in the distribution of communication resources
- the priority of either national cultural or commercial–industrial objectives, and the tension between them
- the democratic imperative to ensure universal access to communication services throughout the country and the means to achieve it
- the liberal imperative of free expression in communication
- the structure of ownership and regulation in Canadian communication industries, including the possibility of state ownership
- the need to stimulate and secure domestic production and consumption of cultural content
- the role of public consultation in communication policy making
- the importance of separating control over carriage infrastructure (i.e., the pipes) from control over content (i.e., what goes through the pipes).

What is interesting about these enduring questions of Canadian communication policy historically is that, just as they begin to reach a point of settlement in relation to one communication medium, a technological change reopens them. Just when the politics surrounding the telegraph, for example, appeared to subside into normalization, the advent of the telephone repoliticized all the same old questions. It is also interesting to note the historical regularity with which technologically determinist arguments and rhetoric surface during times of technological change in communication—arguments and rhetoric often aimed at obscuring and depoliticizing the deeply political and highly contingent character of policy in this area. This strategy extrapolates from particular characteristics of the technology to specific policy choices that are presented as necessary outgrowths of the technology itself and, therefore, non-negotiable. This tactic is most often employed by those interests that have a great deal to gain in a particular configuration of technological change and a great deal to lose in political, and especially democratic, consideration of possible options.

A stark example is the "systems integrity" arguments used by telephone companies in the early and middle decades of the twentieth century to justify structuring the telephone industry in Canada as a natural monopoly. They argued that the technology involved in the successful construction and maintenance of a high-quality telephony system simply required that the system be controlled from end to end by a single entity, and ruled out other options from political consideration. The degree to which this technologically determinist argument became policy orthodoxy is suggested in *Instant world*, the 1971 report of a federal task force on telecommunications, which conceded that telephone companies had presented "powerful technical arguments for complete control of the public networks, including terminal devices and attached equipment. To maintain a high quality of service to all users, they must be able to guard against the technical pollution of the network from other signal sources" (DOC 1971, 156).

As we will see, there is no shortage of contemporary claims regarding the necessary connection between various technical aspects of new digital information and communication technologies and particular policy outcomes that are presented as non-negotiable. Interestingly, many of these—such as the suggestion that the technical properties of digital communication technologies demand competition and minimal regulation if they are to develop to their fullest potential in Canada—contradict the substance of earlier technologically determinist arguments such as those entailed in the "systems integrity/natural monopoly" thesis. This would seem to indicate that such arguments at times of technological change are themselves deeply strategic and political, and that the extent to which they are accepted by policy makers reflects the distribution of political power in Canada more than it does any inherent technological necessity. Curiously, the surfacing of technologically determinist rhetoric in moments of technological change can be read as evidence of the essentially political character of those moments.

This is not to say that technologies do not constrain and condition political options. A strong tradition in the philosophy of technology—to which Canadians such as George Grant (1998) have made enduring contributions—asserts that something in the essence of technology prescribes a particular way of being in the world, a particular way of relating to our environment and to those with whom we share it, to the exclusion of other ways. In a society where technology is ubiquitous and technological progress is an overwhelming collective social project, certain ways of living recommend themselves, persuasively, at the expense of others. It is to this quality that Canadian political economist and theorist of communication Harold Innis (1995, xxvii) referred when he suggested that communication technologies do more than enable us to communicate, and emphasized "the importance of communication in determining 'things to which we attend.'" Innis's concern was primarily with how all communication technologies reorient the human experience of space and time, and consequently reorganize human priorities and practices. Different communication technologies accomplish this in different ways, but the fact that each of them alters our natural experience of space and time can be said to belong to their essence as technologies.

Canadian Politics in 140 Characters: Party Politics in the Twitterverse

34

Tamara A. Small (2010)

EDITORS' INTRODUCTION

Tamara Small is an associate professor of political science at the University of Guelph. She specializes in Canadian political communication and political marketing, with a particular focus on digital politics, the role of the Internet, and new information technology in politics. She has published work in the Canadian Parliamentary Review, Policy and Internet, *and* Information, Communication and Society.

The following selection reflects some of her work on the role of social media in Canadian politics. Here, Small focuses on Twitter's great potential for improving the nature of democratic discussion and involvement in Canada. She finds, however, that most politicians use Twitter to broadcast party messages rather than for discussion and debate. The potential benefits behind Web 2.0 as an additional access point between citizens and representatives are, apparently, not yet being realized.

Created in 2006, Twitter is a hybrid of social networking and microblogging. "Microblogging applications share a set of similar characteristics: (1) short text messages, (2) instantaneous message delivery, and (3) subscriptions to receive updates."[1] Worldwide, Twitter is the premier microblogging site. In February 2008, Nielsen News reported that Twitter had almost 500,000 users; within a year that number had increased 1382%.[2] However, only a very small proportion of Twitter users are Canadian. An Ipsos-Reid survey reported, "26% of online Canadians are aware of Twitter. Of those, 6% reported using the social networking tool."[3] Sysomos Inc similarly found that only 5.69% of worldwide users are from Canada.[4] This said, Canada has the third largest Twitter population according to the study.

Like other social networking sites, a user establishes an account. Twitter allows subscribers to write a 140-character status update called a "tweet." Tweets can be posted by instant or text message, cell phone, third-party applications including Facebook, email or the web. Originally, Twitter was conceived as a mobile status update service to one question: What are you doing? In November 2009, Twitter changed the official question to "What's happening?" There are two types of relationships on Twitter: "following" and "followers." Following someone on Twitter describes the list of people whose updates an individual follows, while follower describes the list of people receiving and reading an individual's tweets. Being followed and

Source: *Canadian Parliamentary Review*, vol. 33, no. 3 (Autumn 2010), 39–45. Reprinted by permission.

following can allow a reciprocal relationship between Twitter users. But unlike other social networking sites reciprocity is not required. One does not have to be a subscriber of Twitter to access someone else's page. By following others, however, their tweets are delivered directly to your own page.

Methodology

This analysis is an illustration of "supply" Internet research. Supply research employs some form of content analysis to determine the structure and content of sites. This is opposed to "demand" research, which examines how Internet users respond to such Web sites. Demand research typically employs survey data. Therefore, in order to assess how Canadian politicians twitter and the extent to which this use contributes to the creation of a virtual community, a content analysis on the Twitter accounts of parties and/or leaders with seats in the federal Parliament or provincial legislatures was conducted in July 2009. Twitter accounts were located using both the internal Twitter search engine and Google. Each page was then coded based on a scheme derived from previous studies and researcher interest. The codebook was pre-tested and refined. The content analysis focused on the overall Twitter account and individual tweets of every party and/or leader with a seat in the federal Parliament or the provincial legislatures. Each Twitter account was coded for the following categories: A total of 729 items were read and coded.

Canadian Party Politics in the Twitterverse

Based on the content analysis Table 2 shows the accounts belonging to a Canadian legislative party in July 2009. During the analysis period, a total of 30 political parties had a seat in a provincial legislature or the federal parliament. The Saskatchewan NDP was the first legislative party with a Twitter page. Its first tweet is dated August 7, 2008. During the 2008 election campaign Canadian parties used Twitter. Prior to the writ dropping, Stephen Harper established a Twitter account, making him the first federal leader to do so. Within 10 days, the other four party leaders established accounts. Most provincial party Twitter sites emerged in 2009. There are 27 Twitter accounts associated with a legislative party—both political parties *and* party leaders use Twitter.

The finding that parties and leaders have separate online presences is not new in Internet politics. Voerman and Boogers describe this as the "personalization of politics online."[5] In the 2003 Dutch election, Dutch party leaders operated Web sites different from the official party site. Voerman and Boogers concluded that leaders' sites sought to win voter sympathy by allowing them to share a little personal life of the party's leading man or women. In Canada, party leaders have never established Web sites separate from the official party site. This said, leaders tend to dominate party Web sites in terms of images and content. Personalization is also evident in the use of social networking sites. During the 2008 federal election, several major parties had two Facebook pages: one for the national party and one for the party leader. "Friends" of leaders were privy to some personalized information, such as that the Prime Minister is writing a book on the early history of professional hockey. James Stanyer argues that personalization is now a key feature of contemporary political communication systems. He writes

TABLE 1 Definitions and Methodology

Category	Description
Followers	The number of followers
Time on Twitter	The length of time online in days from the first tweet to July 31, 2009
Tweets	The number of tweets from the first tweet to July 31, 2009
Tweets per day	The average number of tweets per day, calculated by dividing the total number of tweets by the number of days online
For individual tweets, the last twenty-five tweets dating back from July 31, 2009 were coded, excluding any @replies. Each tweet was classified into one or where appropriate several of the following categories:	
Conversations	A message sent from one person to another over Twitter; distinguished by the "@reply"
Events	Tweets providing information about future political events
Hashtag	Tweets that include a hashtag; distinguished by the "hash" symbol (#) preceding the tag
Political	Tweets about policy or political issues including criticism of other parties that is not official party communication
Personal	Tweets about matters unrelated to politics
Party	Tweets about party or government related activities including policy announcements, press releases and other documents
Retweet	The re-posting of someone else's tweet; distinguished by the formulation: "RT@user"
Reporting news	Tweets about current events and news
Status update	Tweets about what one has done, is currently doing and is going to do
Other	Tweets that do not fit in any other category

The arrival of the electronic media in particular has provided the public with a regular flow of images of these main political actors as well as information. Leading politicians in the US and Britain have not only become recognizable performers but also "intimate" strangers over the twentieth century, their private lives have slowly come to be considered acceptable subject of journalistic revelation and self disclosure.[6]

Given this growing trend in political communication, it is possible that the use of Twitter by leaders will be personalized and intimate, and will differ from the tweets of the political parties they represent.

Twittering varies across Canada. In only five jurisdictions do all legislative parties and/or leaders use Twitter. With the exception of Nova Scotia, twittering is all but absent in Atlantic Canada. The digital divide provides a potential explanation. The term digital divide refers to a gap between those with access to digital technologies and those with very limited or no access. There are income, education and racial divides within many countries. Despite Canada's high rate of Internet penetration, a number of divides exist. The regional and linguistic divides are relevant here. According to Zamaria and Fletcher regional differences in Internet use are startling. Research from the 2007 Canadian Internet Project shows that while 78% of Canadians use the Internet, it varies across the regions; "While British Columbia, Alberta, the Prairie provinces and Ontario share robust levels of Internet penetration between 82% and 84%, Quebec and the Atlantic provinces have considerably fewer current users, 67% and 72% respectively."[7] In Atlantic Canada, Zamaria and Fletcher point to a lag in technical infrastructure and deployment and the difficulty in providing Internet access in a large rural territory to explain lower penetration rates. Additionally, language explains Internet penetration in Québec. In 2002, the Office of the Commissioner of Official Languages reported that there is a digital divide between Francophones and Anglophones. This divide continues; 77% of Francophones compared to 85% of Anglophones used the Internet in 2007. There appears to be a relationship between Internet penetration rates and the willingness or necessity of a politician to use Twitter.

Twitter is a popular social networking site. Some Twitter celebrities have more than 4 million followers. "As the number of followers is so visible, Twitter is disposed to give rise to a new, highly objectifiable dimension of public reputation."[8] During the 2008 presidential campaign, more than 123,000 people followed Barack Obama, making his page the number one Twitter page [of the presidential candidates] for much of 2008. For politicians being followed is crucial; "The effectiveness of using Twitter to communicate information is partially dependent on the number of 'followers' that have subscribed to an individual Twitter stream."[9] Have Canadians responded to twittering politicians? The total number of people listed as a "follower" of a legislative party or leader is just over 58,000. The average number of followers is 2,154.

There is a substantial difference in the number of people who follow a party leader versus the party as a whole. Eighty-six percent followed a party leader compared to 13% following a party. Compare the followers of the Liberal Party of Canada and their leader Michael Ignatieff. Ignatieff has more than 8,000 followers than the party he leads. This holds in other cases where a party and their leader both have accounts. This speaks to the importance of party leaders within Canadian politics. As Cross notes "Leaders dominate election campaigns, exercise considerable influence over the parties' parliamentary agendas, and fill important parliamentary positions including those of premier and prime minister."[10]

What Are Parties and Leaders Twittering About?

In determining how Canadian party communicators use Twitter, the first question is how often do they use the technology. Microblogging by nature encourages frequent posting. Since a tweet is only 140 characters, microblogging sites lower users' requirement of time and thought investment for content generation. This should make it easier for people to update frequently. Despite this, research shows that this is not the case. In their study of a random sample of 300,000 Twitter users in May 2009, Heil and Piskorski found that the "typical Twitter user contributes very rarely."[11] Among Twitter users, the median number of lifetime tweets per user is one. This translates into over half of Twitter users tweeting less than once every 74 days.[12] Sysomos reports that 85% of Twitter users tweet less than once per day.

TABLE 2 Canadian Political Parties & Leader Twitter Accounts by Jurisdictions in July 2009

Jurisdiction	Political Parties	Party Account	Leader Account
Canada	CPC	x	pmharper
	Liberal	liberal_party	M_Ignatieff
	NDP	x	Jacklayton
	BQ	x	GillesDuceppe
AB	PC	mypcmla caucus	premierstelmach
	Liberal	albertaliberals	davidswann
	NDP	x	bmasonNDP
BC	NDP	bcndp	carolejames
	Liberal	bcliberalparty	g_campbell
MB	NDP	x	x
	Liberal	x	DrJonGerrard
	PC	x	x
NB	Liberal	x	x
	PC	x	x
NL	Liberal	x	x
	PC	x	x
	NDP	x	x
NS	NDP	NSNDP	x
	Liberal	x	StephenMcNeil
	PC	nspc	x
ON	NDP	OntarioNDP	andreahorwath
	Liberal	x	x
	PC	x	timhudak
PE	Liberal	x	x
	PC	x	x
QC	PQL	x	x
	PQ	x	x
	ADQ	ADQ_Parlement	x
	QS	QuebecSolidaire	FrancoiseDavid
SK	SP	SaskParty	x
	SP	skcaucus	x
	NDP	Sask_NDP	x
Total	30	13	14

This study comes to similar conclusions on how often parties and leaders use Twitter. We use "tweets per day" to assess frequency. On average, Canadian parties and leaders update once a day (1.02). There is a considerable range in how often parties and leaders twittered. In general, most parties and leaders tweet infrequently; 70% of the parties and leaders tweet less than once per day.

What are party communicators twittering about? The tweets of political parties were focused on official party communication. Almost 50% of party tweets were of this nature. A random selection of tweets is illustrative:

Sask_NDP: #ndp Caucus News: NDP Urges Talks on Federal Visa Rules http://bit.ly/4pLPXE

liberal_party: Exclusive! 2nd Quarter Fundraising numbers are in: $3.9M! More than 4 times last year's. So far this year: $5.7M #LPC23

mypcmla: Province strengthens mental health and addiction programs with $11.8 million in funding this year. Read more: http://tiny.cc/vNC2R #ableg1

Tweets are often titles of press releases as in the case of the Sask_NDP or announcements in the case of the federal Liberals. Links to official documents and online videos were common. The final example is interesting; mypcmla is the Twitter account of the caucus of the Alberta Progressive Conservatives; all mypcmla tweets are about government business. This conflation between the caucus and the government, certainly calls into question the divide between partisan and government communication. Due to the focus on twittering official party communication, Twitter varies little from the official party site. Rather it appears that when the Web site is updated, so too is Twitter.

Personalization is evident in the use of Twitter in Canada. Leaders essentially tweet about themselves. Indeed, 63% of tweets by party leaders are personalized. Party leaders mainly use Twitter in the manner that the site was first conceived. That is, leader tweets generally answer the question: "What are you doing?" Status updates are the most prominent form of leader tweets. More than 50% of tweets by party leaders are personal tweets. For instance,

carolejames: On my way to the Comox Valley campaign office to meet NDP candidate Leslie McNabb–first stop of a whirlwind tour of the island #bcelection.

g_campbell: Saw first hand the #kelownafire. Incredible work by firefighters, pilots & volunteers. Because of them, people's spirits up.

Party leaders mostly tweeted about their job as leader. As the examples show, the tweets focus on what the leader did or was going to do, where the leader had been or was going to be. In this sense, status updates give followers an opportunity to see what politicians do on a daily basis. According to Stanyer, one aspect of personalized politics is self-disclosure; politicians are revealing aspects of their personal lives including information about their families. The following tweet by the Prime Minister is an example of self-disclosure:

pmharper: Celebrating my 50th birthday with Rachel and a crowd of 50 pink flamingos on the lawn of 24 Sussex. Twitpic: http://www.twitpic.com/4a4bz

The tweet is linked to a photo of Mr. Harper with his daughter, Rachel. This type of self-disclosure is not common on Twitter. Even though party leaders tweet about themselves;

TABLE 3 Use of Twitter by MPs, MLAs and Political Parties as of July 2009

Name	Followers	Following	Total Tweets	Tweets per day
pmharper	16,802	13,410	175	0.9
M_Ignatieff	10,617	5,142	67	0.5
jacklayton	9,193	9,587	281	2.1
g_campbell	4,089	3,798	183	1.2
liberal_party	2,181	2,164	138	0.7
GillesDuceppe	2,121	1,907	196	1.5
carolejames	1,692	1,947	79	0.5
premierstelmach	1,386	1,210	138	0.7
bcndp	1,385	1,402	135	0.6
QuebecSolidaire	1,333	1,207	1,383	5.2
bcliberalparty	1,160	1,372	187	1.2
timhudak	976	354	613	2.7
FrancoiseDavid	705	688	52	0.3
andreahorwath	687	449	124	0.5
davidswann	683	1,519	105	0.5
OntarioNDP	678	390	73	0.5
NSNDP	521	663	113	0.5
StephenMcNeil	370	169	79	0.5
albertaliberals	253	182	191	1.3
mypcmla	250	132	156	0.9
Sask_NDP	245	10	181	0.9
bmasonNDP	244	63	30	0.3
ADQ_Parlement	230	238	223	2.0
nspc	148	107	58	0.4
SaskParty	112	0	23	0.2
DrJonGerrard	56	15	135	0.6
skcaucus	43	0	76	0.5
Total	58,160	48,125		
Average			192	1.0

the tweets are very much about their activities as leader. Indeed, a small proportion of leader tweets, 7% were coded as personal. Only occasionally do leaders speak about their lives outside of party politics. Research by Glassman *et al.* on the US Congress found similar results; less than 5% of tweets by congressional members were personal in nature. Party-business and political commentary also figures little in the tweets of party leaders. Only 17% of leader tweets are about official party communication. Even in instances where a party only has one Twitter account (i.e. [Ontario Conservative leader] Tim Hudak), the leader accounts are personalized. There is a clear separation between leader and party Twitter accounts.

Both parties and leaders rarely make off-the-cuff statements about policy, political issues or other parties in their tweets. Overall less than 10% of the entire content analysis was coded as political. Much of the political twittering came from the leader of the Alberta New Democrats, Brian Mason. On June 2, 2009, Mr. Mason tweeted from the floor of the Alberta Legislature during the debate and vote on the controversial Bill 44, which gave parents the option of pulling their children out of class when lessons on sex, religion or sexual orientation are taught. Party and leader tweets are generally about official party communications or status updates about official duties of the leader.

One thing that should be evident from the aforementioned party and leader examples is the use of the hyperlink or URL. Hyperlinks featured prominently in the tweets of Canadian politicians. Almost 50% of all the tweets coded included a URL. Compressing sites, such as tinyurl.com, are used to shorten URLs to ensure that links can fit into the 140 characters. Tweets linked to party or government Web sites, Facebook, photos, videos, blogs and media stories.

There are several benefits of hyperlinking for a politician. First, microblogging is brief by definition; therefore, by posting a link, a politician can say more than 140 characters. For instance, the ADQ tweet:

ADQ_Parlement: « Arrêt des négociations entre Québec et les techniciens ambulanciers paramédics: Une autre crise signée YvesBolduc » http://bit.ly/ynCRU

links to a press release on the ADQ home page. With 303 word and 1,939 characters, the press release provides substantially more information than the original tweet. Second, URLs allow politicians to leverage existing online content. The virtual world of a Canadian political party is extensive. Since 2000, a party Web site is standard. However, with the growth of social networking, it is commonplace for parties to operate a Facebook page and YouTube channel in addition to a Twitter account. Indeed, previous research indicates that some federal parties have accounts with up to 10 different social networking sites. Another example comes from Michael Ignatieff:

M_Ignatieff: Happy Canada Day everyone. Watch my video message here: http://bit.ly/MjsW2 links to the Liberal leader's personal YouTube channel called IggyTube.

The final benefit is reinforcement of the tweet. In examining the American political blogosphere, Richard Davis found that bloggers reinforce their points by "employing sources that bolster [the] bloggers position and undermine those of the opposition." On blogs this occurs through linking to other blogs, websites or media outlets. Clearly a microblog can also be used in this way. For instance, during the 2009 Nova Scotia election, the NDP posted tweets with links to media stories favourable to the party, such as,

NSNDP: The @chronicleherald says "NDP tends to balance labour, economy" http://bit.ly/TruUnion #NSelection.

Rather than appearing simply political, appealing to neutral authorities gives credence to the tweets. By making extensive use of URLs, Canadian politicians are getting more out of Twitter.

Hashtags are an important feature of Twitter that are also evident in the aforementioned examples. A hashtag is a term assigned to a tweet that organizes discussion around specific topics or events and aids in searching. A #(hash symbol) before a word creates a tag. Hashtags can be beneficial, as they allow party communicators to extend their messages beyond followers. Indeed, one does not have to be a Twitter user to follow the conversation because hashtags are visible to anyone. Hashtags are searchable through Twitter, Google and trending sites such as What the Hashtag?! Moreover, they allow party communicators to contribute to a conversation about different topics, political or otherwise.

Despite these benefits, only 36% of tweets were coded as having a hashtag; however, most party communicators used a hashtag at some point. Only 30% of the accounts examined never used a hashtag. For some accounts, it was ritualistic; every tweet by Stephen McNeil and Ed Stelmach included a hashtag. Others used them as needed. Liberal leader Michael Ignatieff used the #lpc (Liberal Party of Canada) tag to designate party tweets, but other tweets such as his status updates were not tagged. Overall, of those that make use of hashtags, they occurred 56% of the time.

There were three main categories of hashtags used by party communicators found in this analysis. First, some hashtags were "partisan," that is, the hashtag was related to a specific political party. For example, Tim Hudak used the Progressive Conservative Party of Ontario hashtag (#pcpo) in just about every tweet, along with the #roft (Right of Twitter). Indeed, prominent Conservative blogger Stephen Taylor encouraged right-wing Canadians to use #roft in all tweets in order to create a right-wing online community. The second category of hashtags used on party and leader Twitter pages can be designated as "political." Political tags were added to tweets with a particular political topic or events that were relevant to various party actors. For instance, both Nova Scotia Liberal Leader Stephen McNeil and the Nova Scotia NDP used #nselection (Nova Scotia election) during the campaign. All Albertan parties occasionally used the hashtag #ableg (Alberta Legislature). This meant that those that search or visited these tags were able to get updates from the various party communicators in addition to others using the tag. The final category is not related to politics at all. One example of this would be when BC NDP leader Carole James tweeted a cheer for the hockey team the Vancouver Canucks, she added the tag #Canucks to her tweet. In all cases, hashtags allowed party communicators to extend their messages beyond just their followers.

Embracing Web 2.0?

Do parties and leaders engage in other ways with their followers? Key words in conceptualizing Web 2.0 are interaction, collaboration, co-production, and active contribution. As O'Reilly put it there is an "implicit 'architecture of participation' "[13] in Web 2.0. This section examines whether parties and leaders embrace Web 2.0 in their use of Twitter.

Two features of Twitter, @replies and retweets, will be used to assess Web 2.0. Although Twitter does not allow for instantaneous communications, scholars suggest Twitter can be interactive. @replies allow one user to respond publicly to a question or comment from one of their followers. Like hashtags, @replies were not originally part of the Twitter application. Early users began using the format @+username+message as a way to designate a message as a reply. Later Twitter built @replies into the application. The Nova Scotia Progressive Conservatives provide an example:

> **nspc:** @thedingler if the premier retired, he'd have told the party. We'll be sure to keep everyone posted. He will be a regular MLA for a while.

Here the nspc is responding to a question from thedingler on whether the Premier will retire.

A study by Honeycutt and Hearing examined conversationality on Twitter. They conclude that Twitter is a "noisy environment" where "successful exchanges can and do take place."[14]

Similar to forwarding e-mail, a retweet is a re-posting of the tweets of another user. According to Boyd and colleagues, retweeting contributes to a conversational ecology in which conversations are composed of a public interplay of voices. They go on to note "Retweeting brings new people into a particular thread, inviting them to engage without directly addressing them."[15] For example,

> **RT @davidswann:** http://twitpic.com/c10fg - Having fun at a CMHA kids day camp! #YEG #ablib.

Here, the Alberta Liberals are retweeting a status update of their leader David Swan. Retweeting demonstrates that a politician is reading the posts of others and sharing them with their own Twitter followers.

Since @replies are not tweets, they were not counted as one of the 25 tweets. Rather, any @reply that occurred within the 25 tweets was coded. Of 729 items coded, only 54 of them were identified as an @reply, that is 7.4%. Almost a quarter of those came from a single party, the ADQ. One interpretation of this would be that Canadians were uninterested in interacting with parties or leaders, thereby not making use of the function. Since the comments of others do not appear on the public timeline, it is difficult to rule this out as a possibility.

A second, more probable, interpretation is that most parties and leaders had disabled the @replies setting. Retweeting by Canadian party communicators is also rare. Only 51 tweets (7.5%) were coded as a retweet. Given that two accounts, Ontario NDP and Alberta Liberals, constituted 56% of those demonstrates how rarely a party or leader participated in this activity. Worse yet, the retweets of the Alberta Liberals were all from the party leader or Liberal MLAs. Indeed, 63% never retweeted. This lack of retweeting not only demonstrates a lack of interactivity, but also a failure of reciprocity and generosity. Despite the fact that Canada's party leaders are following thousands of people, the lack of retweeting calls into question what they are doing with this relationship. Retweeting depends on following and reading the tweets of others and then sharing those tweets.

Should we be surprised by these findings? Perhaps not. Studies of Canadian political actors consistently show a flouting of characteristic of interactivity. Kernaghan[16] maintains that while the use of e-mail and online polls by Canadian parliamentarians has increased, there has been little change in the use of online chats, discussion forums and electronic town hall meetings on MP web sites. Regardless of the platform, Web sites, blogs, Facebook, or

Twitter, Canadian politicians avoid online interaction with citizens. Despite the fact that participation should be implicit in the architecture of Web 2.0 sites, Canadian parties and leaders do not use Twitter in this way.

Conclusion

There is very little scholarly work on Twitter and politics. This research is a first attempt at providing a systematic understanding of Twitter politics in the Canadian context. The twitterverse of Canadian party politics is broad. Both political parties and party leaders of all stripes and levels have established Twitter accounts. Although Twitter is supposed to be a social network, it is being used by Canadian parties and leaders as a broadcasting channel. Broadcasting occurs when information follows in one direction from a single sender to the audience. For political parties, they broadcast the message of the day, whether it is a press release or a policy statement. For leaders, they broadcast their status.

While this certainly may not meet the democratic expectation of Web 2.0, does this mean there is no value for party communicators? As noted, the Internet is thought to have democratic characteristics, especially when compared to mass technologies such as radio or television. One criticism of Internet politics has been the notion that the Internet is a "pull technology"; "Unlike television or radio, it is extremely difficult for [political] organisations to push their messages onto an unsuspecting and passive audience." [17] However, with the rise of social networking sites, the Internet can be a push technology like television and radio. Once an individual chooses to follow a Canadian party or leader, political information can now be pushed on him or her. For a party communicator this is extremely beneficial, a captive and interested audience. Thus if Twitter is meant to answer the question "What's happening?" perhaps Canadian politicians are meeting the expectations of their followers.

Notes

1. B.J. Jansen, M. Zhang, K. Sobel, and A. Chowdury. Micro-blogging as online word of mouth branding. Proc. Int. Conf. on Human Factors in Computing Systems, pp. 3859–3864. ACM, 2009.

2. Michelle McGiboney. *Twitter's Tweet Smell of Success*, http://blog.nielsen.com/nielsenwire/online_mobile/twitters-tweet-smell-of-success (accessed May 1, 2009).

3. Ipsos-Reid. *What's all That Twitter About—A Lot About Nothing?* http://www.ipsos-na.com/news/pressrelease.

4. Alex Cheng, Mark Evans, and Harshdeep Singh. 2009 Inside Twitter An In-Depth Look Inside the Twitter World. http://www.sysomos.com/insidetwitter/ (May 25, 2010).

5. G. Voerman and M. Boogers. "Netherlands: Digital campaigning in the 2002 and 2003 elections" in *Making a Difference: A Comparative View of the Role of the Internet in Election Politics*, edited by Richard Davis, Diana Owen, David Taras and Stephen Ward, Lexington: Lexington Press, 2008.

6. James Stanyer. *Modern Political Communication*, Cambridge: Polity Press, 2007.

7. Charles Zamaria and Fred Fletcher. *Canada Online! The Internet, media and emerging technologies: Uses, attitudes, trends and international comparisons 2007*, Toronto: Canadian Internet Project.

8. Hans Geser. "Tweeted Thoughts and Twittered Relationships," in *Sociology in Switzerland: Toward Cybersociety and Vireal Social Relations*, Online Publications, Zuerich, 2009, http://socio.ch/intcom/t_ hgeser22.pdf.

9. Matthew Eric Glassman, Jacob R. Straus and Colleen J. Shogan. *Social Networking and Constituent Communication: Member Use of Twitter*, During a Two-Week Period in the 111th Congress, Congressional Research Service, 2010, http://www.politico.com/static/ PPM138_090922_ twitter.html (accessed October 2, 2009).

10. William Cross. *Political Parties*, British Columbia: UBC Press, 2004, p. 76.

11. Bill Heil and Mikolaj Piskorski. New Twitter Research: Men Follow Men and Nobody Tweets, http://blogs. harvardbusiness.org/cs/2009/06/new_twitter_research_ men_follo.html (accessed October 2, 2009).

12. Cheng *et al. op. cit.*, 2009.

13. Tim O'Reilly. What is Web 2.0? O'Reilly Media (September 30, 2005). Retrieved July 7, 2009 from http://www.oreillynet.com/pub/a/oreilly/tim/news/2005/09/30/what-is-Web-20.html.

14. C. Honeycutt and Susan C. Herring. "Beyond microblogging: Conversation and collaboration via Twitter," *Proceedings of the Forty-Second Hawii International Conference on System Sciences*, Los Alamitos, CA: IEEE Press, 2009.

15. Danah Boyd, Scott Golder and Gilad Lotan. (Forthcoming 2010) "Tweet Tweet Retweet: Conversational Aspects of Retweeting on Twitter," *Proceedings of HICSS-43*, Kauai, HI: IEEE Computer Society, January 5–8, 2010.

16. Kenneth Kernaghan. "Making Political Connections: IT and Legislative Life," *Digital State at the Leading Edge*, ed. Sandford Borins, Kenneth Kernaghan, David Brown, Nick Bontis, Perri 6 and Fred Thompson, Toronto: University of Toronto Press, 2007, pp. 224–52.

17. Wainer Lusoli, Stephen Ward and Rachel Gibson. "Political Organisations and Online Mobilisation: Different Media—Same Outcomes?" *New Review of Information Networking*, Volume 8, 2002, pp. 89–107.

PART 3
Governing Canada

Introduction

The *British North America Act* of 1867 outlines the powers and responsibilities of Canada's two orders of government, the federal Parliament and the provincial legislatures. If the general institutional set-up was clear to the Fathers of Confederation 150 years ago, the intents and purposes behind the creation of Canada remain an object of debate. The central government has always displayed an important capacity to intervene in the economy, but since the end of the Second World War, the provinces have become increasingly active in the realms granted to them by the Constitution (which include social affairs, municipalities, education, and health).

Nevertheless, the development of the welfare state in the post-war years has translated into higher levels of state intervention—a trend only partially undone by the electoral success over the past decade of the Conservative Party under Stephen Harper. In the post-war years, the federal government sought, successfully, to intervene in several areas considered to be exclusively provincial jurisdictions, notably in the health and social service spheres. The two orders of government now operate in nearly every domain of social, economic, and cultural activity. Many consider the initial division of powers to be obsolete. The numerous initiatives of the federal and provincial governments have become intertwined to the point where it has become difficult to differentiate the responsibilities of each—a dynamic that creates a multitude of conflicts.

This part of *Essential Readings* addresses four different but complementary themes. The first relates to the constitutional debates that began to erupt at the end of the 1960s, and the second addresses conflicts around federalism—the division of powers and their balance in the Canadian federation—and related intergovernmental politics. The repatriation of the Constitution in 1982 (without Quebec's consent); the failures of the Meech Lake and Charlottetown accords in 1990 and 1992, respectively; and the Quebec referendum in 1995 all illustrate not only the contradictory interests of political actors, but also opposing visions within the Canadian political community, and the conflicting understandings of what Canadian federalism is supposed to achieve.

The third section focuses on the role played by the judiciary in the Canadian political system. It is only since adopting a constitutional charter of rights that the study of judges and the courts has been broadly accepted as an important branch of Canadian political science. But the judiciary did play a significant role in Canadian political life well before the arrival of the Charter. Canada's highest court up until 1949 was a British court, the Judicial Committee of the Privy Council (JCPC). The JCPC's decisions interpreting the federal division of powers in the Canadian Constitution had an important influence on the functioning of the Canadian federation. The British judges who staffed the JCPC had their fans and their critics in Canada. Their vigorous protection of provincial rights found strong support in Quebec and among provincial premiers. But politicians and legal scholars in English Canada who favoured a strong central government were critical of the JCPC. It is only in 1931 that Canada formally ceased to be a colony of Great Britain. Under the terms of the Statute of Westminster, the power of the Dominions of the British Empire (Canada, Australia, South Africa, the Irish Free State, New Zealand, and Newfoundland) to make their own extra-territorial laws was confirmed.

The final section of readings addresses themes and issues relating to Canada's foreign policies, in light of the domestic constitutional framework. Having developed, over the course of the 20th century, its own international personality, the question of establishing foreign policy priorities arose with more acuity. Canada, however, had inherited a constitutional structure that saw control of foreign affairs fall under the responsibility of the federal Cabinet. This institutional design plays an important role in the way Canada's foreign policy is conducted. Not only is the prime minister the most important figure, but the scope and the depth of his relationship with other foreign leaders can have a great impact in determining the nature of Canada's international involvement. Moreover, global changes in recent decades have influenced which priorities and objectives are put forward by the Canadian state. In particular, issues such as the relative decline in America's international power, and the realities of global warming (which is leading to an opening up of Canada's North) have raised new questions about Canada's role on the international stage.

Constitutional Politics

The first section tackles the theme of constitutional politics and, specifically, the conflict between the governments of Quebec and Canada. The issue of Quebec sovereignty was the main focus of political discussion from the beginning of the 1970s to the end of the 1990s. Many political initiatives were taken either to justify or to counter, if not thwart, this political project. The first selection (Reading 35) revisits arguments put forward by the Parti Québécois, first elected in 1976, which justify the need to modify the political status of Quebec and to opt for a different form of association with the "rest of Canada." This PQ White Paper insists upon limits to the federal system and its form, which would create a new understanding between Quebec and Canada.

The next two readings deal with the political consequences, both for Canada and Quebec, of the defeat of the 1980 referendum and the 1982 patriation of the Constitution. Jean Chrétien was responsible for the federal government's referendum campaign and, as minister of justice, in charge of the constitutional negotiations that led to its patriation. In his contribution to the book *Towards a Just Society: The Trudeau Years*, he sheds light on the federal government's perspective adopted during the patriation saga, explaining why it was so important to break the last colonial link with London in order to achieve full Canadian independence. One of the objectives was to inscribe into the Constitution the federal government's views on the nature and development of Canada, and its role in stopping trends toward decentralization, providing room for minority linguistic groups, and strengthening the central government's ability to redistribute wealth. In Reading 36, Chrétien criticizes the strategies and positions of the provincial premiers and, more vehemently, the strategy of Quebec, which was working to block the federal project, and avoid a reasonable compromise.

A year after the Constitution's 1982 patriation, political scientist Donald Smiley (Reading 37) wonders whether Canadians have reason to be so grateful for the new *Constitution Act*, in light of Quebec's refusal to sign it. In fact, the Constitution had restricted the powers of Quebec's legislature and government, and was brought into being by a procedure that was opposed by that legislature and government. More importantly, Smiley was one of the first to contend that the legitimacy of the *Constitution Act* was denied because, he believed, the constitutional review—and more particularly the new amending formulas, the entrenchment of the *Charter of Rights and Freedoms*, and the absence of any substantial revision of the division of powers between the two orders of government—was flawed. As he states, "[It] has involved a betrayal of the Quebec electorate, a breach of fundamental constitutional convention, a recrudescence of Quebec nationalism, and an even more serious Quebec challenge than before to the legitimacy of the Canadian constitutional order." In other words, Smiley questions the claim that the patriation and the *Charter of Rights and Freedoms* was an appropriate instrument to foster national unity.

Among the three remaining readings in this section, two of them examine non-constitutional changes or institutional arrangements that allow Canadian federalism to evolve without modifying the fundamental law of the country. In *Unfulfilled Union*, Garth Stevenson (Reading 40) adopts a political economy approach to underline economic and social trends that had been conducive to institutional centralization in Canada. In the long run, the fragmentation of Canada's economy, coupled with the absence of any strong sense of national identity, put at risk the survival of Canada as a united federal state. Hence, the project to strengthen the central government has to be seen as a response by the central Canadian political and economic elites to prevent the negative consequences of aggressive, resource-based provincialism in Alberta and Saskatchewan, and of rising nationalism in Quebec. Finally, if mega-constitutional debates are over, Peter Russell suggests in Reading 39, recent innovations demonstrate that Canadian federalism is capable of adjusting to contemporary challenges. This would represent a return to a more pragmatic approach, in the tradition of political philosopher Edmund Burke, rather than a contractual approach à la John Locke, which is what had characterized the rhetoric of the constitutional debate.

The constitutional issue raises other concerns beyond the division of powers, institutional design, and who possesses and limits state authority. For Reg Whitaker (Reading 38), it is the fundamental concept of sovereignty that acts as a powerful reinforcement of the internal authority of the nation-state. The Canada–Quebec conundrum could be seen as a confrontation of two sovereignties, both claiming exclusivity on their own territories and people.

That raises an interesting paradox, and puts some limitations on classical and liberal conceptions of sovereignty, as they are applied to Canada. In insisting on territorial sovereignty that imposes territorial exclusivity, Quebec's political project clashes with the views of Aboriginal peoples. Not only does that project complicate any negotiations between Canada and Quebec, but it might force various political actors to revisit their obligations toward, for example, Aboriginal rights. This might lead governments to enter into a new set of arrangements for establishing joint sovereignty in, for example, Canada's North (see also Reading 56 by Michael Byers).

Intergovernmental Relations

Three of the readings in this second section examine the impact of federalism on the functioning of Canadian society. Alan Cairns (Reading 41) emphasizes that Canadian federalism is a function not of society, but of the Constitution; and more importantly, of governments that operate within the constitutional framework, looking out for their own self-interests. He wants to highlight the degree of autonomy possessed by governments and the ongoing capacity of the federal system to create the conditions necessary for its survival. He underlines that the federal government was unable to acquire new powers at the expense of the provinces, because of the fact that the Canadian political system is haunted by the question of national unity, and the system's operation reveals a bias favouring the provinces. This bias seems to have been adopted by academic and intellectual opinion, which "has been characterized by an anti-federalist mentality" and which has underestimated the autonomy of elites, the weight of government, and the effect of institutions on political behaviour.

Canadian political science literature has examined the patterns of relations between governments, attempting to shed light on the evolution of various governments' mutual interdependence. For Donald Smiley and Ronald Watts (Reading 42), it is also important to put emphasis on what they label "juristic elements of federal systems"—in other words, the ways in which regional interests and values are provided for in the structures and operations of the central governments of federations.

The relationship among governments is largely shaped by the fact that there are significant regional differences at the core of conflicts in a country as territorially large and complex as Canada. Roger Gibbins, in "Federalism and Regional Alienation" (Reading 43), asks to what extent our political institutions moderate or exacerbate regional conflicts and regional alienation. In the same vein as the previous entry, Gibbins interrogates how well the various regional communities are treated by and within the national government, and how well they fare within the national community. The main argument is that while the division of powers and the active participation of provincial governments in national politics have been relatively successful in protecting regional interests, those interests have not been successfully represented within the institutions of the national government. This partially explains the growing emphasis on *interstate federalism*—that is, the interactions between the federal and provincial governments—although this dynamic has been detrimental to the promotion of nation building. (Interstate federalism is contrasted to *intrastate federalism*, in which territorially based interests are addressed within central institutions. For example, the constitutional provision that guarantees that membership in the Senate is based on the principle of regional representation or the convention according to which there should be a regional balance in the Cabinet.)

Richard Simeon and Ian Robinson (Reading 44) insist on the fact that federalism is simultaneously a particular set of governing institutions and a characteristic of society that takes into account multiple identities. They discuss these dimensions and show how they are at the heart of many political changes and political conflicts over the past few decades.

Finally, François Rocher argues in Reading 45 that, although Canadian federalism has been analyzed from many different angles, the literature is largely characterized by two particular phenomena. First, the interpretation of the evolution of Canadian federalism differs greatly, depending on the origin of the author. On the one hand, Quebec francophone scholars have largely attempted to illustrate that the spirit that marked the adoption of a federated state in Canada has been betrayed. On the other hand, scholars from English-speaking Canada have been more interested in pragmatic issues, such as the extent to which federalism encourages (or not) citizen participation, supports state capacity to develop public policies, manages diversity, or reduces regional or territorial conflicts. He examines how the notions of autonomy and interdependence have been articulated in both traditions, and contends that students of federalism in English-speaking Canada have shown an inadequate understanding of the importance of the notion of autonomy, in favour of efficiency, while those in Quebec have largely ignored the principles of interdependence, solidarity, and participation.

The Courts and the Charter

Alan Cairns's classic overview of the decisions of the Judicial Committee of the Privy Council (JCPC) as the judicial arbiter of Canada's federal system opens this section (Reading 46). Cairns' analysis of the JCPC's critics shows that, while the critics shared a common view about the need for a more centralist approach to constitutional interpretation, they lacked a coherent theory of how judges ought to interpret a constitution. Though opinion in Canada was divided on the constitutional jurisprudence of the Judicial Committee, the debate had the effect of strengthening judicial nationalism in the country and lent support to abolishing appeals to the JCPC and making the Supreme Court of Canada the country's highest court. In 1949, the Supreme Court of Canada became supreme in fact as well as in name.

The addition of the *Canadian Charter of Rights and Freedoms* (included as an addendum to this introduction) to Canada's Constitution in 1982 resulted in a quantum leap in the political prominence of the Supreme Court of Canada. As Peter Russell's essay "The Political Purposes of the Canadian Charter of Rights and Freedoms" points out, this was not one of the intended purposes of the Charter's political sponsors (Reading 47). A constitutional charter of rights and freedoms was Pierre Elliott Trudeau's top priority for constitutional reform. He saw the Charter as a necessary antidote to the centrifugal forces of Quebec nationalism and provincial government demands for more powers. By giving expression to the shared values of Canadians, it would help to unify the country. But Russell argues that, while the Charter's capacity for unifying the country was dubious, its tendency to increase judicial power was much more certain. The selections that follow in this section bear out Russell's prediction.

As the power of courts to make decisions on controversial and politically salient matters became apparent in the Charter era, a lively political debate arose on the democratic legitimacy of this expansion of judicial power. The article by Peter Hogg and Allison Bushell (Reading 48) entitled "The Charter Dialogue Between Courts and Legislatures" was a seminal contribution to this debate. Hogg and Bushell systematically examine the various ways in which the Charter provides for interaction between the courts and legislatures. They argue that the frequency of these interactions amounts to a continuing "dialogue" in which courts rarely have the final word in accommodating legislation to the requirements of the Charter.

The considerable public support for the court's Charter decisions has not blunted attacks on the Supreme Court of Canada by academics, journalists, and right-of-centre politicians. These critics allege that the court has an "activist" approach to the Charter, and is overstepping its bounds. The intensity of these attacks is evident in Chief Justice Beverley McLachlin's discussion of the role of courts, legislatures, and executives in the post-Charter era (Reading 49). However, the chief justice emphasizes the democratic process that produced the Charter, and she rejects the suggestion that in giving force and effect to it the judiciary are usurping power. The chief justice's words would not persuade F.L. Morton and Rainer Knopff, authors of a much-discussed 2000 book, *The Charter Revolution and the Court Party*. "Judges and the Charter Revolution," the chapter excerpted from their book in Reading 50, addresses the many ways in which the Supreme Court has chosen approaches that give greater scope to the Charter's impact. Morton and Knopff view the Supreme Court justices, together with Charter enthusiasts in the academic and legal community and organizations that support Charter litigation, as forming a "court party" that uses the Charter to promote an agenda of social reform.

Canada in the World

Although Canada became a country in 1867, it took decades to develop a foreign policy independent from the United Kingdom. In 1938, R.A. MacKay and E.B. Rogers published *Canada Looks Abroad* in an effort to circumscribe the emerging role of Canada in the world. They identified the three major problems of Canada's external relations: how to reconcile the fact that Canada is located in North America, its historical association with the British Empire, and the "psychological fact" of a growing national consciousness. They also laid out the guiding principles for how Canada should operate in international society. Among them, they mention a principle that was tacitly accepted but rarely stressed: that in order to maintain friendly relations with the United States, Canada should restrain from what they termed "Oriental immigration" or "undesirable aliens"—namely, those coming from countries such as India and Japan. They also stressed the advantages of a Canadian foreign policy driven to maintain good relationships with its two most important foreign partners, the United States and the United Kingdom.

Three decades later, James Eayrs, a well-known expert in Canadian foreign policy, published *The Art of the Possible*. This book describes how institutions and practices have changed over time. In this excerpt (Reading 52), he describes the prime minister's pre-eminent role in determining domestic foreign policy, as well as the evolution of the external affairs portfolio since its establishment in 1909. He then insists on the importance of the relationship between the prime minister and his foreign minister, which "is seldom free from difficulty and may easily become tensely competitive." At the end of the day, according to Eayrs, the competition between these two figures boils down to the temperament of the prime minister.

One of the major figures of the Canadian diplomacy in the 1950s and '60s was John Holmes. Describing himself as a prudent pragmatist, he published an important essay in 1970, *The Better Part of Valour*. In Reading 53, he presents Canada as a very special case, because it is a bi-national state, and has an ambiguous sense of nationalism. He touches upon the impact of French-Canadian nationalism on Canadian foreign policy, and the relationship of the former with English-Canadian nationalism, either in identification with the empire or with the United States, presented as a "tribalism [that] has usually been a counter-national or counter-Canadian force." After the Second World War, Canada's position in the world was strengthened, though mainly by internal factors. Holmes discusses the concept of Canada as a middle power, and wonders whether this view that Canada has of itself is essentially a rationalization of the needs of Canadian nationalism, or a response to the demands of international politics. Holmes is a master in identifying the many paradoxes that Canada is continuously facing in defining itself, both on the domestic and international scenes.

The most important commercial and political partner of Canada remains the United States. Charles Doran has studied that relationship, and finds that it is composed of three dimensions: psychological-cultural, trade-commercial, and political-strategic. In Reading 54 Doran addresses the following question: How special is the special relationship? For him, Canada's major preoccupation is the development of its own unified sense of political identity, and this shapes the nature of the national agenda. Nevertheless, the Canada–US partnership is special because of its peaceful nature, the importance of bureaucratic and private sector activity, and the existence of many institutional treaties. But this cannot be taken for granted forever.

Stephen Clarkson also deals with the Canada–US relationship, but uses a political economy framework to analyze the geopolitical-economic realities of Canada's position in North America (Reading 55). He discusses the extent to which Canada could adopt an independent foreign policy while being under the umbrella of US hegemony. As a middle power, under Pierre Elliott Trudeau, Canada was capable of playing a significant role in multilateral affairs even if, for its own economic interests, bilateral relationships remained central. During the Brian Mulroney era, with the signing of the Canada–US Free Trade Agreement, a new relation was established, strengthening that US hegemony through a formal document. Clarkson notes that this policy was not questioned by Liberal Prime Minister Jean Chrétien who, when he came to power, contributed to the partial privatization of Canada's international relation industry, with private foundations offering their recommendations to government. Moreover, Canada did not hesitate to support the United States in its "War on Terror" in the years after the 2001 terror attacks. While the Chrétien government declined to send ground troops into Iraq in 2003, Canada did send its military into Afghanistan (suffering many casualties), and endorsed the Bush administration's position that Islamic terrorism was a global threat. Canada has continued to function as a subordinate to the American international superpower—a stance driven mainly by economic self-interest.

The last selection (Reading 56) deals with a different but complementary issue: Canada's sovereignty in the Arctic. In *Who Owns the Arctic?* Michael Byers examines an Arctic frontier rapidly changing as a result of climate change, with an expanding northern sea route that is facilitating the extraction of fossil fuels and other natural resources. In this new context, other coastal states, including Russia, have laid claims to the Arctic. Byers explains that the federal government, while committed to defending Canada's sovereignty in the Arctic, refused to fully recognize the immemorial presence of Inuit and the crucial role they will have to play in the Canadian strategy. Byers writes: "[The Inuit] want to work with other Canadians to forge a better future. They seek to preserve the Arctic environment, to protect our common sovereignty, and to provide their children with a quality of life equivalent to that in the rest of Canada." Byers explains why the Inuit are central to Canadian claims, and points to the need to strengthen the Inuit dimension of the Arctic in political as well as cultural and economic terms.

Further Suggested Reading

Constitutional Politics

Alan C. Cairns. "Citizens (Outsiders) and Governments (Insiders) in Constitution-Making: The Case of Meech Lake." *Canadian Public Policy* 14, 1988.

Alain-G. Gagnon and Raffaele Iacovino. *Federalism, Citizenship and Quebec: Debating Multinationalism*. Toronto: University of Toronto Press, 2007.

Guy Laforest. "The Internal Exile of Quebecers in the Canada of the Charter." In James B. Kelly and Christopher P. Manfredi, eds., *Contested Constitutionalism: Reflections on the Canadian Charter of Rights and Freedoms*. Vancouver: University of British Columbia Press, 2009.

Samuel V. LaSelva. "Federalism as a Way of Life: Reflections on the Canadian Experiment." *Canadian Journal of Political Science* 16(2), 1993.

Samuel V. LaSelva. *The Moral Foundations of Canadian federalism Paradoxes, Achievements, and Tragedies of Nationhood*. Montreal and Kingston: McGill-Queen's University Press, 1996.

W.R. Lederman. "Unity and Diversity in Canadian Federalism." *Canadian Bar Review* 53, 1975.

B. Reesor. *The Canadian Constitution in Historical Perspective*. Scarborough, ON: Prentice-Hall Canada, 1992.

François Rocher and Nadia Verrelli. "Questioning Constitutional Democracy in Canada: From the Canadian Supreme Court Reference on Quebec Secession to the Clarity Act." In A.-G. Gagnon, M. Guibernau, and F. Rocher, *The Conditions of Diversity in Multinational Democracies*. Montreal: Institute for Research on Public Policy, 2003, 207–237.

Peter H. Russell. *Constitutional Odyssey: Can Canadians Become a Sovereign People?* Toronto: University of Toronto Press, 2004.

Garth Stevenson. *Ex Uno Plures: Federal–Provincial Relations in Canada, 1867–1896*. Montreal and Kingston: McGill-Queen's University Press, 1993.

Intergovernmental Relations

Herman Bakvis, Gerald Baier, and Douglas Brown. *Contested Federalism: Certainty and Ambiguity in the Canadian Federation*. Don Mills, ON: Oxford University Press, 2009.

Herman Bakvis and Grace Skogstad. *Canadian Federalism: Performance, Effectiveness, and Legitimacy*. Don Mills, ON: Oxford University Press, 2012.

David Cameron and Richard Simeon. "Intergovernmental Relations in Canada: The Emergence of Collaborative Federalism." *Publius* 32(2), 2002.

G. DiGiacomo and M. Flumian, eds. *The Case for Centralized Federalism*. Ottawa: University of Ottawa Press, 2010.

Audrey Doerr. "Public Administration: Federalism and Intergovernmental Relations." *Canadian Public Administration* 25(4), 1982.

Government of Canada. "Social Union Framework Agreement: An Agreement Between the Government of Canada and the Governments of the Provinces and Territories." February 1999.

R. Hubbard and G. Paquet, eds. *The Case for Decentralized Federalism*. Ottawa: University of Ottawa Press, 2010.

Gregory J. Inwood, Carolyn M. Johns, and Patricia L. O'Reilly. *Intergovernmental Policy Capacity in Canada: Inside the Worlds of Finance, Environment, Trade, and Health*. Montreal and Kingston: McGill-Queen's University Press, 2011.

Claude Ryan. *Regards sur le fédéralisme canadien*. Montreal: Boreal, 1995.

Richard Simeon. *Federal–Provincial Diplomacy: The Making of Recent Policy in Canada*. Toronto: University of Toronto Press, 2006.

The Courts and the Charter

Thomas M.J. Bateman, Janet L. Hiebert, Rainer Knopff, and Peter H. Russell. *The Court and the Charter: Leading Cases*. Toronto: Emond Montgomery, 2008.

Jacques Frémont. "La face cachée de l'évolution contemporaine du fédéralisme canadien." In Gérald A. Beaudoin et al., eds., *Le fédéralisme canadien de demain : réformes essentielles/Federalism for the Future: Essential Reforms*. Montreal: Wilson and Lafleur, 1998.

Janet L. Hiebert. *Charter Conflicts: What Is Parliament's Role?* Montreal and Kingston: McGill-Queen's University Press, 2002.

James B. Kelly. *Governing with the Charter: Legislative and Judicial Activism and Framers' Intent*. Vancouver: University of British Columbia Press, 2005.

Christopher P. Manfredi. *Judicial Power and the Charter: Canada and the Paradox of Liberal Constitutionalism*, 2nd ed. Toronto: Oxford University Press, 2001.

Peter H. Russell, Rainer Knopff, Thomas M.J. Bateman, and Janet L. Hiebert. *The Court and the Constitution: Leading Cases*. Toronto: Emond Montgomery, 2008.

John Saywell. *The Lawmakers: Judicial Power and the Shaping of Canadian Federalism*. Toronto: University of Toronto Press, 2002.

Richard Sigurdson, "Left- and Right-Wing Charterphobia in Canada: A Critique of the Critics." *International Journal of Canadian Studies* 7-8, Spring-Fall 1993.

James Snell and Frederick Vaughan. *The Supreme Court of Canada: History of the Institution*. Toronto: University of Toronto Press, 1985.

Donald A. Songer. *The Transformation of the Supreme Court of Canada*. Toronto: University of Toronto Press, 2008.

Various contributors. "Charter Dialogue: Ten Years Later." Special issue of *Osgoode Hall Law Journal* 45(1), Spring 2007.

José Woehrling. "The Canadian Charter of Rights and Freedoms and Its Consequences for Political and Democratic Life and the Federal System." In Alain-G. Gagnon, ed., *Contemporary Canadian Federalism: Foundations, Traditions, Institutions*. Toronto: University of Toronto Press, 2009.

Canada in the World

Brian Bow. "Paradigms and Paradoxes: Canadian Foreign Policy in Theory, Research and Practice." *International Journal* 65(2), 2010.

Derek H. Burney and Fen Osler Hampson. *Brave New Canada: Meeting the Challenge of a Changing World*. Montreal and Kingston: McGill-Queen's University Press, 2014.

Bruno Charbonneau and Wayne S. Cox, eds. *Locating Global Order: American Power and Canadian Security After 9/11*. Vancouver: University of British Columbia Press, 2010.

Stephen Clarkson. "Canada's Secret Constitution: NAFTA, WTO and the End of Sovereignty." Ottawa: Canadian Centre for Policy Alternatives, 2002.

Ken S. Coates, P. Whitney Lackenbauer, William R. Morrison, and Greg Poelzer. *Arctic Front: Defending Canada in the North*. Toronto: Thomas Allen Publishers, 2008.

Michael Hart. *From Pride to Influence: Towards a New Canadian Foreign Policy*. Vancouver: University of British Columbia Press, 2008.

Steven K. Holloway. *Canadian Foreign Policy: Defining the National Interest*. Peterborough, ON: Broadview Press, 2006.

John Kirton. *Canadian Foreign Policy in a Changing World*. Toronto: Nelson, 2007.

James McHugh. "The Foundations of Canadian Foreign Policy: Federalism, Confederalism, International Law, and the Quebec Precedent." In Patrick James, Nelson Michaud, and Marc J. O'Reilly, eds., *Handbook of Canadian Foreign Policy*. Lanham, MD: Lexington Books, 2006.

Kim Richard Nossal, Stéphane Roussel, and Stéphane Paquin. *International Policy and Politics in Canada*. Toronto: Pearson, 2011.

Barry Scott Zellen, ed. *The Fast Changing Arctic: Rethinking Arctic Security for a Warmer World*. Calgary: University of Calgary Press, 2013.

Canadian Charter of Rights and Freedoms

Part I of the Constitution Act, 1982

Whereas Canada is founded upon principles that recognize the supremacy of God and the rule of law:

Guarantee of Rights and Freedoms

1. The *Canadian Charter of Rights and Freedoms* guarantees the rights and freedoms set out in it subject only to such reasonable limits prescribed by law as can be demonstrably justified in a free and democratic society.

Fundamental Freedoms

2. Everyone has the following fundamental freedoms:

(*a*) freedom of conscience and religion;

(*b*) freedom of thought, belief, opinion and expression, including freedom of the press and other media of communication;

(*c*) freedom of peaceful assembly; and

(*d*) freedom of association.

Democratic Rights

3. Every citizen of Canada has the right to vote in an election of members of the House of Commons or of a legislative assembly and to be qualified for membership therein.

4. (1) No House of Commons and no legislative assembly shall continue for longer than five years from the date fixed for the return of the writs of a general election of its members.

(2) In time of real or apprehended war, invasion or insurrection, a House of Commons may be continued by Parliament and a legislative assembly may be continued by the legislature beyond five years if such continuation is not opposed by the votes of more than one-third of the members of the House of Commons or the legislative assembly, as the case may be.

5. There shall be a sitting of Parliament and of each legislature at least once every twelve months.

Mobility Rights

6. (1) Every citizen of Canada has the right to enter, remain in and leave Canada.

(2) Every citizen of Canada and every person who has the status of a permanent resident of Canada has the right

(*a*) to move to and take up residence in any province; and

(*b*) to pursue the gaining of a livelihood in any province.

(3) The rights specified in subsection (2) are subject to

(*a*) any laws or practices of general application in force in a province other than those that discriminate among persons primarily on the basis of province of present or previous residence; and

(*b*) any laws providing for reasonable residency requirements as a qualification for the receipt of publicly provided social services.

(4) Subsections (2) and (3) do not preclude any law, program or activity that has as its object the amelioration in a province of conditions of individuals in that province who are socially or economically disadvantaged if the rate of employment in that province is below the rate of employment in Canada.

Legal Rights

7. Everyone has the right to life, liberty and security of the person and the right not to be deprived thereof except in accordance with the principles of fundamental justice.

8. Everyone has the right to be secure against unreasonable search or seizure.

9. Everyone has the right not to be arbitrarily detained or imprisoned.

10. Everyone has the right on arrest or detention

(*a*) to be informed promptly of the reasons therefor;

(*b*) to retain and instruct counsel without delay and to be informed of that right; and

(*c*) to have the validity of the detention determined by way of *habeas corpus* and to be released if the detention is not lawful.

11. Any person charged with an offence has the right

(*a*) to be informed without unreasonable delay of the specific offence;

(*b*) to be tried within a reasonable time;

(*c*) not to be compelled to be a witness in proceedings against that person in respect of the offence;

(*d*) to be presumed innocent until proven guilty according to law in a fair and public hearing by an independent and impartial tribunal;

(*e*) not to be denied reasonable bail without just cause;

(*f*) except in the case of an offence under military law tried before a military tribunal, to the benefit of trial by jury where the maximum punishment for the offence is imprisonment for five years or a more severe punishment;

(*g*) not to be found guilty on account of any act or omission unless, at the time of the act or omission, it constituted an offence under Canadian or international law or was criminal according to the general principles of law recognized by the community of nations;

(*h*) if finally acquitted of the offence, not to be tried for it again and, if finally found guilty and punished for the offence, not to be tried or punished for it again; and

(*i*) if found guilty of the offence and if the punishment for the offence has been varied between the time of commission and the time of sentencing, to the benefit of the lesser punishment.

12. Everyone has the right not to be subjected to any cruel and unusual treatment or punishment.

13. A witness who testifies in any proceedings has the right not to have any incriminating evidence so given used to incriminate that witness in any other proceedings, except in a prosecution for perjury or for the giving of contradictory evidence.

14. A party or witness in any proceedings who does not understand or speak the language in which the proceedings are conducted or who is deaf has the right to the assistance of an interpreter.

Equality Rights

15. (1) Every individual is equal before and under the law and has the right to the equal protection and equal benefit of the law without discrimination and, in particular, without discrimination based on race, national or ethnic origin, colour, religion, sex, age or mental or physical disability.

(2) Subsection (1) does not preclude any law, program or activity that has as its object the amelioration of conditions of disadvantaged individuals or groups including those that are disadvantaged because of race, national or ethnic origin, colour, religion, sex, age or mental or physical disability.

Official Languages of Canada

16. (1) English and French are the official languages of Canada and have equality of status and equal rights and privileges as to their use in all institutions of the Parliament and government of Canada.

(2) English and French are the official languages of New Brunswick and have equality of status and equal rights and privileges as to their use in all institutions of the legislature and government of New Brunswick.

(3) Nothing in this Charter limits the authority of Parliament or a legislature to advance the equality of status or use of English and French.

16.1. (1) The English linguistic community and the French linguistic community in New Brunswick have equality of status and equal rights and privileges, including the right to distinct educational institutions and such distinct cultural institutions as are necessary for the preservation and promotion of those communities.

(2) The role of the legislature and government of New Brunswick to preserve and promote the status, rights and privileges referred to in subsection (1) is affirmed.

17. (1) Everyone has the right to use English or French in any debates and other proceedings of Parliament.

(2) Everyone has the right to use English or French in any debates and other proceedings of the legislature of New Brunswick.

18. (1) The statutes, records and journals of Parliament shall be printed and published in English and French and both language versions are equally authoritative.

(2) The statutes, records and journals of the legislature of New Brunswick shall be printed and published in English and French and both language versions are equally authoritative.

19. (1) Either English or French may be used by any person in, or in any pleading in or process issuing from, any court established by Parliament.

(2) Either English or French may be used by any person in, or in any pleading in or process issuing from, any court of New Brunswick.

20. (1) Any member of the public in Canada has the right to communicate with, and to receive available services from, any head or central office of an institution of the Parliament or government of Canada in English or French, and has the same right with respect to any other office of any such institution where

(*a*) there is a significant demand for communications with and services from that office in such language; or

(*b*) due to the nature of the office, it is reasonable that communications with and services from that office be available in both English and French.

(2) Any member of the public in New Brunswick has the right to communicate with, and to receive available services from, any office of an institution of the legislature or government of New Brunswick in English or French.

21. Nothing in sections 16 to 20 abrogates or derogates from any right, privilege or obligation with respect to the English and French languages, or either of them, that exists or is continued by virtue of any other provision of the Constitution of Canada.

22. Nothing in sections 16 to 20 abrogates or derogates from any legal or customary right or privilege acquired or enjoyed either before or after the coming into force of this Charter with respect to any language that is not English or French.

Minority Language Educational Rights

23. (1) Citizens of Canada

(*a*) whose first language learned and still understood is that of the English or French linguistic minority population of the province in which they reside, or

(*b*) who have received their primary school instruction in Canada in English or French and reside in a province where the language in which they received that instruction is the language of the English or French linguistic minority population of the province,

have the right to have their children receive primary and secondary school instruction in that language in that province.

(2) Citizens of Canada of whom any child has received or is receiving primary or secondary school instruction in English or French in Canada, have the right to have all their children receive primary and secondary school instruction in the same language.

(3) The right of citizens of Canada under subsections (1) and (2) to have their children receive primary and secondary school instruction in the language of the English or French linguistic minority population of a province

(*a*) applies wherever in the province the number of children of citizens who have such a right is sufficient to warrant the provision to them out of public funds of minority language instruction; and

(*b*) includes, where the number of those children so warrants, the right to have them receive that instruction in minority language educational facilities provided out of public funds.

Enforcement

24. (1) Anyone whose rights or freedoms, as guaranteed by this Charter, have been infringed or denied may apply to a court of competent jurisdiction to obtain such remedy as the court considers appropriate and just in the circumstances.

(2) Where, in proceedings under subsection (1), a court concludes that evidence was obtained in a manner that infringed or denied any rights or freedoms guaranteed by this Charter, the evidence shall be excluded if it is established that,

having regard to all the circumstances, the admission of it in the proceedings would bring the administration of justice into disrepute.

General

25. The guarantee in this Charter of certain rights and freedoms shall not be construed so as to abrogate or derogate from any aboriginal, treaty or other rights or freedoms that pertain to the aboriginal peoples of Canada including

(*a*) any rights or freedoms that have been recognized by the Royal Proclamation of October 7, 1763; and

(*b*) any rights or freedoms that now exist by way of land claims agreements or may be so acquired.

26. The guarantee in this Charter of certain rights and freedoms shall not be construed as denying the existence of any other rights or freedoms that exist in Canada.

27. This Charter shall be interpreted in a manner consistent with the preservation and enhancement of the multicultural heritage of Canadians.

28. Notwithstanding anything in this Charter, the rights and freedoms referred to in it are guaranteed equally to male and female persons.

29. Nothing in this Charter abrogates or derogates from any rights or privileges guaranteed by or under the Constitution of Canada in respect of denominational, separate or dissentient schools.

30. A reference in this Charter to a Province or to the legislative assembly or legislature of a province shall be deemed to include a reference to the Yukon Territory and the Northwest Territories, or to the appropriate legislative authority thereof, as the case may be.

31. Nothing in this Charter extends the legislative powers of any body or authority.

Application of Charter

32. (1) This Charter applies

(*a*) to the Parliament and government of Canada in respect of all matters within the authority of Parliament including all matters relating to the Yukon Territory and Northwest Territories; and

(*b*) to the legislature and government of each province in respect of all matters within the authority of the legislature of each province.

(2) Notwithstanding subsection (1), section 15 shall not have effect until three years after this section comes into force.

33. (1) Parliament or the legislature of a province may expressly declare in an Act of Parliament or of the legislature, as the case may be, that the Act or a provision thereof shall operate notwithstanding a provision included in section 2 or sections 7 to 15 of this Charter.

(2) An Act or a provision of an Act in respect of which a declaration made under this section is in effect shall have such operation as it would have but for the provision of this Charter referred to in the declaration.

(3) A declaration made under subsection (1) shall cease to have effect five years after it comes into force or on such earlier date as may be specified in the declaration.

(4) Parliament or the legislature of a province may re-enact a declaration made under subsection (1).

(5) Subsection (3) applies in respect of a re-enactment made under subsection (4).

Citation

34. This Part may be cited as the *Canadian Charter of Rights and Freedoms*.

Quebec–Canada: A New Deal

Government of Quebec (1979)

35

EDITORS' INTRODUCTION

The Parti Québécois' White Paper was made public in 1979, one year before the 1980 referendum, which asked that Quebeckers provide their government with a mandate to negotiate the terms of a new agreement between Quebec and Canada. This document introduces how the Parti Québécois (PQ) presented notions of association and sovereignty to its citizens, as well as the mechanisms that would be put in place in order to realize the PQ's project. It also presented the arguments in favour of independence.

The May 1980 referendum question was aligned with the government's step-by-step strategy: the government would not ask Quebeckers to declare themselves in favour of sovereignty association; instead, it would ask for a mandate to negotiate its terms. Once the negotiation was complete, a second referendum would take place. Rather long and complex, the question read as follows:

> *The Government of Québec has made public its proposal to negotiate a new agreement with the rest of Canada, based on the equality of nations;*
>
> *this agreement would enable Québec to acquire the exclusive power to make its laws, levy its taxes and establish relations abroad—in other words, sovereignty—and at the same time, to maintain with Canada an economic association including a common currency;*
>
> *no change in political status resulting from these negotiations will be effected without approval by the people through another referendum;*
>
> *on these terms, do you give the Government of Québec the mandate to negotiate the proposed agreement between Québec and Canada?*
>
> *YES*
>
> *NO*

If we are really looking for a new agreement between Quebec and the rest of Canada, it is absolutely essential to replace federalism by another constitutional formula.

This search for a new formula must be carried out with due consideration for the fundamental, legitimate preoccupations of Quebecers, who want to communicate and talk directly and freely with their neighbours and with other nations, who do not want to destroy Canada

Source: Excerpted from the English translation of *La nouvelle entente Québec–Canada. Proposition du gouvernement du Québec pour une entente d'égal à égal : La souveraineté-association.* Quebec City: Government of Quebec, 1979.

or to be completely separate from it, who wish to improve their situation, and who are determined to see that the changes to come are made democratically and without disorder.

The Government of Quebec fully shares and endorses these preoccupations.

The Way of the Future

Thinking of the future the Government of Quebec proposes a constitutional formula which would replace the present federal system and at the same time respect the legitimate feelings of Quebecers toward Canada. This new system, while freeing Quebec from Ottawa's domination, would not break up an economic community that extends from the Atlantic to the Pacific; it would ensure for Quebec a maximum of autonomy while maintaining the natural interdependence and the historical and human links that exist between Quebec and the rest of Canada; it would enable Quebec to institute the measures that it lacks at present, without forcing the other provinces to accept responsibilities they do not feel they need. This new system would provide permanent solutions to the many problems engendered by relations between Quebec and Ottawa over the years.

Of the two roads open to Quebecers—a federalism whose fundamental renewal is to all intents and purposes impossible because it would contradict the very nature of federalism, and a new agreement between Quebec and Canada capable of reconciling political autonomy and economic interdependence—the Government of Quebec has chosen the latter, sovereignty-association, a contemporary expression of Quebec's continuity, in brief a new deal.

The Modern Phenomenon of Association

The recent history of international relations shows that federalism can no longer be regarded as the only formula capable of reconciling the objectives of autonomy and interdependence. Although it was fashionable in the past century, the federal formula must now give way to associations between sovereign countries. While no new federations are being created, economic associations are on the increase on every continent. ...

These various associations of sovereign states are distinguished from one another by the nature of their activity and the degree of their integration, as well as by the history of relations between the member states and their various characteristics: population, culture, political system, etc.

The European communities are probably the most advanced examples of economic integration. Their activity is primarily economic, but it also spills over into social policy and scientific policy, among other areas. The economic union between Belgium and Luxembourg, and the Benelux countries, which appeared before the European Economic Community, are part of the European movement toward economic integration, while preserving a certain cohesion of their own within the Nine. As for the European Free Trade Association, its economic links are rather weak.

On the other hand, the Nordic Council and the Association of Southeast Asian Nations, while not as completely integrated, have a much more diversified activity.

Basing itself firmly on the historical trend of Quebec thinking, which has always sought to redefine relations between Quebec and the rest of Canada on a more egalitarian basis, the

Government of Quebec proposes this type of modern formula of association between sovereign countries to ensure for Quebecers a better control of their own affairs, without shattering the Canadian economic framework.

Association in equality may take many forms: far more flexible than federalism, it is more easily adapted to the realities of countries that resort to it, and the degree of association will depend on whether cooperation is to be limited to certain fields or maximum advantage is to be taken of a broader economic community.

Modern economic associations are generally the result of cooperation between individual countries and entirely sovereign nations, which have agreed to pool some of their powers. In such cases, integration is based on the sovereignty of the partners. In our case, however, economic integration already exists and it is the sovereignty of the partners that must be established. The point of departure is different but the aim is identical.

The Implications of Sovereignty

The idea of sovereignty is clearly defined in international law: it is, in general terms, the power to make decisions autonomously, without being subject in law to any superior or exterior power, which implies that the sovereign state has full jurisdiction over a given territory. Sovereignty ensures complete autonomy, in the sense that the state enjoys full legal freedom in all fields; its authority is exercised to the exclusion of any other within the limits of its territory; and it can be present in the community of nations. ...

The Special Character of the Quebec–Canada Relationship

The examples cited above show the great variety in the types of association entered into by many sovereign peoples throughout the world; no less different are the historical circumstances that led these people to such varied solutions. Quebec too has evolved in circumstances that are specific to it, circumstances which, while they have certain analogies with some of the cases cited above, cannot be reduced to any one of them. The institutions and the functioning of the future association between Quebec and Canada must reflect what is specific to each of the communities.

Most of the countries now grouped in various associations enjoyed sovereignty long before they joined together, while those that associated a few decades ago did so at a time when the state did not yet occupy as large a place in the economic activity of nations. On the one hand, Quebec has not yet gained its sovereignty, while on the other hand, the institutions of the state, because of the size of their expenditures at all levels of government, play a considerable economic and social role in Quebec as well as in the rest of Canada.

Given the situation of our two communities, and because the economic space that Canada and Quebec share must be both preserved and developed, the Quebec government wants to propose to the rest of Canada that the two communities remain in association, not only in a customs union or a common market but in a monetary union as well. Thus Canada can be preserved intact as an economic entity, while Quebec can assume all the powers it needs as a nation to ensure its full development. Replacing federalism by association will, in effect, maintain economic exchange, but the nature of political and legal relations between Quebec and Canada will be changed.

The Proposal

For a proper understanding of the formula proposed by the Government of Quebec, we will describe how it will function by examining the powers that will be exercised by Quebec and specifying the extent of the association between Quebec and Canada; we will also say a word about the Quebec–Canada community structures that must be provided for.

We hasten to state that the changes described here will not occur overnight after the Referendum, but will be, can only be, the result of negotiations between Quebec and Canada, negotiations that will be started as a result of a positive answer in the Referendum. In the next chapter we will explain how the proposed formula will be gradually implemented.

A. *Sovereignty*

Through sovereignty, Quebec would acquire, in addition to the political powers it already has, those now exercised by Ottawa, whether they were assigned to the federal government under the British North America Act of 1867 or whether it assumed them since that time, directly or indirectly.

Sovereignty is the power to levy all taxes, to make all laws and to be present on the international scene; it is also the possibility to share freely, with one or more states, certain national powers. Sovereignty for Quebec, then, will have a legal impact on the power to make laws and to levy taxes, on territorial integrity, on citizenship and minorities, on the courts and various other institutions, and on the relations of Quebec with other countries.

For each of these subjects, the government wishes to define as clearly as possible the position it intends to adopt in its negotiations with the rest of Canada.

- Laws and Taxes—The only laws that will apply on Quebec's territory will be those adopted by the National Assembly, and the only taxes that will be levied will be those decreed by Quebec law. In this way, there will be an end to the overlapping of federal and Quebec services, which has been so often denounced, thereby enabling Quebec to control the totality of its fiscal resources. Existing federal laws will continue to apply as Quebec laws, as long as they are not amended, repealed or replaced by the National Assembly.
- Territory—Quebec has an inalienable right over its territory, recognized even in the present Constitution, which states that the territory of a province cannot be modified without the consent of that province. Moreover, since the agreements were reached on James Bay, there no longer is any lien on any part of the Quebec territory. In becoming sovereign, Quebec, as is the rule in international law, will thus maintain its territorial integrity. Moreover, it would be desirable for Quebec to regain the advantages that would normally come to it from its geographical position, putting an end to the uncertainties that have surrounded the issue of jurisdiction over the Gulf of St. Lawrence, Labrador and the Arctic regions.
- Citizenship—The Quebec government gives its solemn commitment that every Canadian who, at the time sovereignty is achieved, is a resident of Quebec, or any person who was born there, will have an automatic right to Quebec citizenship; the landed immigrant will be able to complete residency requirements and obtain citizenship. The Parliament of Canada will have to decide whether Canadians who become Quebec

citizens may maintain their Canadian citizenship as well. Quebec, for its part, would have no objection. Any person who is born in a sovereign Quebec will have the right to Quebec citizenship; the same will hold true for any person born abroad of a father or mother who has Quebec citizenship. Quebec citizenship will be recognized by a distinct passport, which does not rule out the possibility of an agreement with Canada on a common passport, since the two states will have close relations, of a community nature, that may cover many subjects. Canadian citizens will enjoy the same rights in Quebec as Quebec citizens enjoy in Canada. The acquired rights of foreign nationals will also be fully recognized.

- The Minorities—The government pledges that Quebec's Anglophone minority will continue to enjoy the rights now accorded it by law, and that other communities in Quebec will be given the means to develop their cultural resources. The Amerindian and Inuit communities, if they so desire, will be in full possession on their territory of institutions that maintain the integrity of their societies and enable them to develop freely, according to their own culture and spirit. As for Francophone minorities in Canada, Quebec intends to fulfil its moral responsibilities towards them, as it has started to do, for that matter, despite its limited means.
- The Courts—Naturally, the Quebec courts will be the only ones to administer justice in Quebec. All judges will be appointed in accordance with Quebec laws, and judges who are now on the bench will remain in their functions. However, a joint court, constituted through the treaty of association between Quebec and Canada, will have the power to interpret this treaty and decide on the rights that result from it.
- External Relations—Quebec will continue to be bound by the treaties to which Canada is now a signatory. It may withdraw from them should the occasion arise according to the rules of international law. Consequently, Quebec will respect the agreement on the St. Lawrence Seaway and will become a full partner in the International Joint Commission. As for alliances such as NATO and NORAD, Quebec will respect its responsibilities and offer its contributions in accordance with its aims. In order to fully play its role on the international scene and defend its interests, Quebec will ask to be admitted to the United Nations and to its specialized agencies. Finally, while developing its relations and its cooperation with Francophone countries, Quebec will consider remaining a member of the British Commonwealth.

B. Association

In today's world no nation, great or small, can live in isolation. Interdependence, considering the economic advantages that it brings, far from being as constraining as some seem to think, can on the contrary result in enriching forms of cooperation and interaction, and thus improve the present and future lot of the societies taking part.

Quebec has never wanted to live in isolation: from the start it has accepted interdependence. However, it wishes to ensure that it will be directly involved in determining the terms of this interdependence.

To this end, the Quebec government intends to offer to negotiate with the rest of Canada a treaty of community association, whose aim will be, notably, to maintain the present Canadian economic entity by ensuring continuity of exchange and by favouring, in the long run, a more rapid and better balanced development of each of the two partners.

This treaty will have an international status and will bind the parties in a manner and for a term to be determined. It will define the partners' areas of common activity and confirm the maintenance of an economic and monetary union between Quebec and the rest of Canada. It will also determine the areas where agreement on goals will be considered desirable. Finally, it will establish the rules and institutions that will ensure the proper functioning of the Quebec–Canada community, and determine its methods of financing.

Bringing the Constitution Home

36

Jean Chrétien (1990)

EDITORS' INTRODUCTION

During his political career, Jean Chrétien served as a senior minister and was minister of justice from 1980 to 1982. In 1980, he was in charge of the federal government's referendum campaign, and was the senior federal representative during the constitutional negotiations that resulted in the patriation of the Constitution in 1982. In 1990, he became the leader of the Liberal Party of Canada, and led the party to three majority governments (1993, 1997, and 2000). He resigned as prime minister in 2003.

Known as a strong opponent of the Quebec sovereignty movement, Mr. Chrétien shares in this excerpt his views on the importance of patriation for achieving complete legal independence from the United Kingdom, on the nature of Canada and the role of the federal government in defending national over provincial interests, and the process of constitutional reform itself. According to him, the 1982 Constitution was the product of compromise and negotiation. The refusal of the Quebec government to sign it was the result of a flawed strategy, whose aim was to block the federal project. Ultimately, the Constitution was a great achievement, enshrining in it a concept of Canadian citizenship that guarantees fundamental liberties, and democratic and legal rights.

Changing the Constitution confronts a society with the most important choices, for in the Constitution will be found the philosophical principles and rules which largely determine the relations of the individual and of cultural groups to one another and to the State. If human rights and harmonious relations between cultures are forms of the beautiful, then the State is a work of art that is never finished. Law thus takes its place, in its theory and its practice, among man's highest and most creative activities.

—F.R. Scott, *Essays on the Constitution: Aspects of Canadian Law and Politics* (Toronto, 1977)

Source: Excerpted from *Towards a Just Society: The Trudeau Years*, edited by Thomas S. Axworthy and Pierre Elliott Trudeau. Markham, ON: Viking, 1990.

The process of constitutional reform which culminated in the patriation of the Constitution in 1982 began not with the Trudeau government, but with the British government's Balfour Declaration in 1927. It was then that the Imperial government agreed to give full political autonomy to the self-governing dominions of its empire and that Prime Minister Mackenzie King began the process of looking for a mechanism that would allow Canada to amend its own Constitution. At that time no one would have expected that Canada would be the last part of what was then the British Empire to achieve complete legal independence. Indeed, it was not because Canadians wanted to maintain a last colonial link with London that their country was unable to achieve that independence for so long. The problem was that the federal and provincial governments could not agree on a constitutional amendment formula. ...

1968–1971: The First Trudeau Government

The Trudeau government took office with strong views on the nature of Canada and the role of the federal government. At the same time, the whole constitutional debate took a new turn as a result of the ferment in Quebec. The issue was no longer only the amending formula but the very nature of Canada. It was time for people to take a stand. Was Canada to be an extremely decentralized country of two nations or a strong country with two official languages and room for minority linguistic groups to prosper everywhere in the country? Was the role of the federal government to foster a Canada with two official languages and access for all Canadians to federal services in both languages? Was its role to be strong enough to achieve redistribution of wealth or was the federal government merely to run what Joe Clark later called a community of communities? It was this basic philosophical question that characterized the constitutional debate from 1968 through to the spring of 1982. ...

1980–1982: The Referendum and Constitutional Reform

The spring of 1980 saw the political confrontation of the century in Canada. Federalists and separatists fought a great battle. While the population saw the supreme confrontation between Trudeau and Lévesque, the daily fight for the federalist forces was led by the Quebec Liberal leader, Claude Ryan, whom I assisted as the federal lieutenant delegated by Mr. Trudeau. A campaign of almost two months touched all the extremes from the initial despair and disorganization to the almost joyous collaboration of the last weeks, from initial lack of interest to the great enthusiasm of the larger rallies, from mistakes caused by the inexperience of volunteers unused to such strong emotions, to the unexpected successes of the federalist women who called themselves "Yvettes." The result was an unequivocal expression by Quebeckers of their will to belong to Canada.

During the referendum campaign Prime Minister Trudeau and his Quebec members and ministers formally promised constitutional reform in the event of a victory for the federalist forces. The Trudeau position was clear—patriation of the Constitution, a constitutional charter of rights and freedoms which would protect the two official languages across the country, a federal government strong enough to redistribute income and to equalize opportunity among the regions of Canada and a willingness to negotiate on the distribution of powers on a functional basis while ensuring that the federal government's role of serving all Canadians was not threatened. The prime minister set out his constitutional philosophy clearly in the House of Commons on April 15, 1980, during the referendum campaign. He stated:

> The feeling of being a Canadian, that individual feeling which we must cultivate, the feeling of being loyal to something which is bigger than the province or the city in which we happen to live, must be based on a protection of the basic rights of the citizen, of an access by that citizen to a fair share of the abundance of wealth in this country and to the richness and diversity of its laws. In that sense, the national interest must prevail over the regional interest, difficult as it is for some of us sometimes to set aside our feelings as citizens of this town or inhabitants of that province, because the provincial governments and other groups are there to speak for their interests. That is their duty and that is what they are elected for. But we are elected to speak for all of Canada, and if a person cannot feel that in any part of the country he or she will get a fair share, then they will transfer their loyalty from the whole to the particular part of the country in which they choose to live. ... That concept of sharing can only be guaranteed, I repeat, if there is a national government which is prepared to state that the national interest must prevail in any situation of conflict over regional differences.

On May 21, the morning after the referendum, the prime minister asked me to visit all provincial premiers over the next seventy-two hours to begin the process of constitutional reform. With a small group of officials I travelled across the country and met each premier except the premier of Quebec, who for obvious reasons was not then open to consultation. The reception in all provincial capitals was excellent; all were prepared to proceed immediately with constitutional reform and I stressed the need for the charter of rights, for patriation, for finding an acceptable amending formula and for entrenching minority language education rights in all provinces. There was also discussion about the need to examine the division of powers and to examine reform of federal institutions such as the Supreme Court and the Senate. The charter of rights remained controversial: Premier Sterling Lyon of Manitoba, for example, was convinced that the British principle of parliamentary sovereignty was better than the American supremacy of the Bill of Rights.

The result of my trip across the country was agreement on an early federal–provincial meeting of first ministers to set an agenda for what became a summer of intensive federal–provincial constitutional negotiations. Three consecutive weeks of negotiations were scheduled for July—the first in Montreal, the second in Toronto and the third in Vancouver. They were to be followed by a break of several weeks and were to resume in mid-August in Ottawa in preparation for a final first ministers' conference at the beginning of September 1980.

In preparing for the negotiations, the federal government took to heart the lessons of constitutional negotiations learned over the previous fifteen years as well as the realities of decentralization in Canada. A decision was made that rights of individuals and the juridical independence of the country would not be traded for powers claimed by the provincial governments. The federal position from which we never wavered was that the questions of patriation, an amending formula, a preamble to the Constitution, a charter of rights and freedoms and the reform of institutions such as the Supreme Court of Canada and the Senate would be discussed at one negotiating table and that the issues dealing with division of powers, such as communications, offshore resources, family law and the Canadian economic union, international trade in natural resources and indirect taxation of natural resources, and other similar powers, would be discussed at another negotiating table.

The federal government was determined to look at rights as a package on its own—apart from negotiations over the federal–provincial power split. We were prepared to discuss what should or should not be in a charter of rights based on international covenants, provincial and federal bills of rights, the changing nature of society, the conflict between parliamentary supremacy and the supremacy of the courts, and so on. We were prepared to look at an amending formula based on how rigid a constitution should be, whether all provinces should be equal, or whether certain provinces as a function of size or linguistic composition should have vetoes and so on. In essence, the federal government was prepared to take a functional and pragmatic approach to constitutional reform and refused to be drawn into a bargaining session that would have involved giving up federal jurisdiction over powers to the provinces in return for unrelated protection of fundamental human rights. The federal government also made a basic decision that all the demands should not come from the provinces and all the concessions from the federal government. If constitutional reform was to be meaningful, it had to reflect a society that was more than a community of communities and indeed was one where the bonds of citizenship were strong. We realized the long-term dangers to Canada if we did not lay to rest the myth that Canada is a highly centralized federation. The evidence was clear that despite all the speeches to the contrary, Canada was becoming too decentralized. ...

The evening before the official opening of the conference featured a dinner hosted by the governor general. It was certainly the most unpleasant official reception I have ever had occasion to attend. Many of the premiers who had received me with such warmth and good-will the day after the referendum were now prepared to destroy the authority of both the prime minister of the country and the federal Parliament so as to make the provinces into powerful principalities. There was even an attempt to remove the prime minister of Canada from his role as chairman of the federal–provincial conferences. The atmosphere became so tense and disagreeable that the governor general had to adjourn the dinner before the end of the meal.

The conference began the next day, and it was not long before the premiers presented Mr. Trudeau with a catalogue of demands that would have left the federal Parliament with jurisdiction over little more than Parliament Hill itself. The result of the provincial demands, combined with provincial reaction to a leaked federal strategy paper, was that the goodwill that had developed over the summer had completely evaporated. The conference adjourned with the incredible declaration by Premier Peckford of Newfoundland that he preferred the Canada of René Lévesque to the Canada of Pierre Trudeau.

It became evident that some premiers were merely power hungry; others were political opponents of the federal government and were prepared to operate on the basis of the principle that the enemy of my enemy is my friend; still others genuinely disagreed with the federal vision of Canada. They had all come to the conclusion that the prime minister was so committed to patriation, an amending formula and a charter of rights that in the end he would give up important federal powers to achieve his objectives. They were wrong.

When the demands of the provinces became so extravagant, it became clear to the federal government that the only alternative was to proceed rapidly to request the British Parliament to patriate the Constitution with an amending formula and a charter of rights. On October 6, 1980, a constitutional resolution was introduced in the House of Commons. The resolution provided for patriation of the Constitution, a charter of rights with guarantees of minority language education rights and mobility rights, and two years to reach agreement on an amending formula, failing which, effect would be given to the Victoria amending formula with a provision for a national referendum to break deadlocks. Later, the resolution was amended to clarify and increase provincial jurisdiction over trade and taxation of natural resources. ...

In September 1981, the Supreme Court held that unilateral patriation was technically legal but was in violation of constitutional convention. The court held that constitutional convention required consent of more than two provinces but not necessarily of all the provinces. The court did not state how many and which provinces had to give consent; in fact, the court was implicitly telling the federal government and the provinces to get back to the negotiating table. This the federal government was prepared to do, although the British government had already indicated to the prime minister of Canada that it would accede at any time to any request from the Parliament of Canada.

It was agreed that a last effort would be made to find a broader consensus so as to satisfy the judgment of the Supreme Court with respect to constitutional conventions. This final effort started on November 2, 1981, in Ottawa. The atmosphere was better than at previous conferences because the eight dissenting provinces saw the convening of the conference as a victory in itself. The Group of Eight believed that while the Supreme Court had recognized a narrow legal right of the federal government, in fact it had given a moral victory to the opponents of unilateral patriation by finding the federal action to be unconventional. Despite the better atmosphere, however, the fundamentals had not changed.

For the federal government, the position of the Group of Eight on the amending formula and the Charter of Rights was completely unacceptable. The result of constitutional reform as propounded by the Group of Eight would do nothing to strengthen a sense of Canadian nationhood and would do nothing to confirm the value of our citizenship. Instead, it would produce a country where opting out would be rewarded with fiscal compensation. In hindsight it is evident that for most of the dissenting provinces, their April 1981 position was a negotiating one, but for Quebec there was no room for negotiation.

The prime minister could not accept what was effectively a vision of Canada as a country founded by the provinces, with the federal government existing through their will. Mr. Trudeau argued that the whole is greater than the sum of its parts and that the repository of real power in Canada is the people of the nation as a whole. Therefore he argued that an amending formula should contain a referendum provision as a deadlock-breaking mechanism. The prime minister insisted on enshrining in the Constitution a recognition of values and ideals shared by Canadians wherever they live.

In addition to the two different philosophies of Canada, another apparently insurmountable difficulty was the determination of Premier Sterling Lyon of Manitoba to oppose any charter of rights on the grounds that parliamentary supremacy is preferable to the supremacy of the courts, a position he had maintained from the very start of negotiations. ...

As minister of Justice, I too was opposed from the beginning to the idea of national referenda as institutionalized instruments of policy formulation. As the principal federal spokesman during the Quebec referendum of May 1980, I saw the way in which families, towns and cities were divided by the emotion that a referendum can produce. I feared further national division between East and West, and between English- and French-speaking Canadians. Whatever our views on the merits of a referendum, the proposal by the prime minister produced the desired effect. Seven dissident provinces recognized that a Parti québécois government dedicated to the independence of Quebec was not a trustworthy ally. The national referendum issue was the straw that broke the camel's back. ...

There was no conspiracy between the federal government and the other provinces; there was the simple reality confirmed by the author of the Quebec strategy that Quebec came to the conference of November 1981 intent only on blocking the federal project and not on finding compromise. So much for the myth of Quebec having been stabbed in the back.

The constitutional deal itself was the product of compromise and negotiation. The federal government agreed to a formula which required in most cases that seven provinces with 50 percent of the population approve constitutional amendments. Where provinces wished to opt out of constitutional change affecting their powers, except for those pertaining to education and culture, there would be no fiscal compensation and therefore no reward for opting out. As far as a charter of rights was concerned, the provinces accepted the charter that had been studied and amended by the joint parliamentary committee. There was also a provision for enshrining the principle of equalization in the constitution and for increasing provincial powers with respect to indirect taxation of resources and international trade in resources. The major and controversial change to the Charter was the inclusion of a notwithstanding clause which would apply to fundamental freedoms, legal rights and equality rights. However, there could be no opting out or derogation from the obligation of governments to provide education for French language minorities outside of Quebec and the English language minority in Quebec, nor could there be opting out of the guarantees protecting mobility rights. ...

Shared Values, Equal Rights

We sought to achieve constitutional recognition of values and ideals shared by Canadians wherever they lived. We sought to enshrine in the Constitution a concept of Canadian citizenship that not only guarantees fundamental liberties and democratic and legal rights, but also guarantees that no one shall suffer discrimination anywhere in Canada because of any law—federal or provincial—on grounds such as race, colour, religion, national or ethnic origin, sex, age, or physical or mental handicap. We sought to ensure that Canadians would be able to seek work anywhere in Canada, regardless of province of origin, and that Canadians would be able to educate their children anywhere in Canada in their own official language, be it English or French. We sought to enshrine the constitutional guarantee that Canadians could communicate with or receive services from their federal government in both English and French; and beyond the Charter of Rights, we wanted to enshrine in the Constitution the principle of sharing, or equalization which is a cornerstone of our federalism. ...

There are important lessons to be learned from the process that led to the most fundamental reform of the Canadian Constitution in history. The first lesson is that constitutional reform is very difficult to achieve and takes a long time. It requires compromise, negotiating ability, enormous political will and tenacity, and most of all, a substantial national consensus, which can come only after much debate and public discussion.

The second lesson is that the difficulty of obtaining constitutional change means that when made, it should be right or as right as possible. Changes—even improvements—cannot be made easily and flaws cannot be easily corrected. Flaws that are recognized while discussions are still going on should be corrected before they become entrenched in the Constitution as part of the basic law of the land, when they can be changed only by amendments to the Constitution.

The third lesson is that negotiations which are effectively structured on the basis of ten provinces against the federal government risk leading to a reduction of federal authority unless those representing the federal government have a strength of purpose and a commitment to principle that can overcome the tendency to be worn down by incessant "fed-bashing" by the provinces.

The final lesson, which comes from the testimony before the joint parliamentary committee and from the controversy that arose over the treatment of equality rights and native rights in the accord of November 5, 1981, is that the people of Canada want a citizenship that means holding shared values and not merely a shared passport.

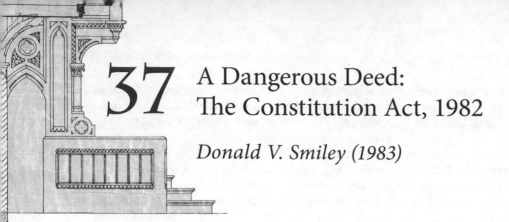

37 A Dangerous Deed: The Constitution Act, 1982

Donald V. Smiley (1983)

EDITORS' INTRODUCTION

Donald Smiley (1921–1990) taught political science at Queen's University (1954–55), the University of British Columbia (1959–70), the University of Toronto (1970–76), and York University until his death in 1990. His numerous publications focus on the party system, Canadian federalism, and constitutional politics in Canada. He was a careful observer of and commentator on the constitutional negotiations that took place in the 1970s and '80s, and was concerned with the place of Quebec within the Canadian federation.

This selection was published a year after the patriation of the Constitution. Smiley is particularly critical of the new Constitution, alleging that it had restricted the powers of the government of Quebec, and would have potentially centralizing effects. More fundamentally, he critiqued it for not having honoured, and perhaps even betraying, the constitutional reform promised to Quebec voters. For Smiley, it is the very legitimacy of the Constitution Act that might be called into question.

As the First Ministers' Conference ended on November 5, 1981 Prime Minister Trudeau and the premiers of all the provinces except Quebec preened before the television cameras in mutual congratulation. This paper is an attempt to evaluate whether other Canadians have reason to be grateful for what these self-proclaimed great and good men have done for them.

The Constitutional Developments of 1980–82: The Third National Policy and National Unity

...

The more immediate context of the constitutional developments of 1980–82 was the Quebec referendum of May 1980. In the referendum campaign, Prime Minister Trudeau and his federal Liberal colleagues made highly generalized commitments to the Quebec electorate that if a "no" verdict were returned, something unprecisely designated as "renewed federalism" would be effected. Very shortly after the referendum, there was a series of intensive

Source: Excerpted from *And No One Cheered: Federalism, Democracy, and the Constitution Act*, edited by Keith Banting and Richard Simeon. Toronto: Methuen, 1983.

intergovernmental meetings on constitutional reform, culminating in the abortive First Ministers' Conference of September 1980.

Within the framework of constitutional debate in Quebec over the preceding two decades, what could the pledge of "renewed federalism" reasonably be taken to mean? The pressures of both government and opposition parties in Quebec provincial politics from 1960 onward has been for an enhanced range of autonomy for the authorities of that province and corresponding restrictions on the powers of the federal government over Quebecers. The Constitution Act, 1982 *restricts* the powers of the Legislature and government of Quebec and was brought into being by a procedure which *was opposed* by that Legislature and government. Furthermore, the constitutional reform which was effected in the spring of 1982 was an integral part of a general initiative from Ottawa towards a more highly centralized federal system. The pledges of constitutional reform made to the Quebec electorate by the federal Liberal leaders have *not* been honoured, and it is not too much to say that this electorate has been betrayed.

One must squarely face the question whether the conventions of the Canadian constitution required Quebec assent to a request of the Parliament of Canada for an amendment altering the powers of the provinces. My conclusion is that such consent *was* required. ...

The legitimacy of the Constitution Act is thus denied not only by the government of Quebec, but also by a significant body of Quebec opinion which has not accepted the sovereignty option. The National Assembly has passed legislation which provides for a maximum use of the *non obstante* clause of section 33 of the Charter of Rights and Freedoms by Quebec, and asserts that the Quebec human rights charter is to be regarded as having primacy over the Constitution Act. While the *raison d'être* of the PQ is to remove Quebec from Confederation, the Constitution Act and the process by which it was put in place gives the separatist government an opportunity it did not have before to make a fundamental challenge to the *existing* constitutional order of which Quebec remains a part.

In general, then, an exercise in constitutional review and reform whose alleged objectives were to create more harmonious relations between Quebec and the wider Canadian community has involved a betrayal of the Quebec electorate, a breach of fundamental constitutional convention, a recrudescence of Quebec nationalism, and an even more serious Quebec challenge than before to the legitimacy of the Canadian constitutional order.

There is, of course, a contrary argument to the one I have advanced. Its general assertion is that because of the commitment of the Parti Québécois to Quebec independence, the government of the province could not reasonably be expected to participate in any but an obstructive way in efforts to reform the federal system. Certainly it appears to have become the consensus that Premier Lévesque could not be brought into agreement on any significant matters of reform acceptable to the other governments. One may also conjecture that any hesitations which the premiers of the provinces who signed the consensus may have had about the PQ's dissent were in large part overcome because the major actors in the federal government were themselves Québécois.

This line of argument has something to it. The West Germans speak of the "spirit of constitutional comity." Certainly in a political order based as largely as the Canadian is on convention, one might reasonably question the legitimacy of constitutional actors who explicitly challenge the basic elements of that order, and whose *raison d'être* is to destroy it. However, to proceed on this assumption in the Canadian context of November 1981 is in the highest degree dangerous. Certainly it is indefensible to argue, as does the PQ, that Quebec members of Parliament are not legitimate representatives of the will of Quebec. Yet it is equally indefensible to assert that these persons are the *only* representatives of that community. …

There is a counter-argument to my negative assessment of the impact of recent constitutional changes on these elements of national unity other than Canada-Quebec relations. It has been asserted that the very act of patriation—"bringing the constitution home"—has been a profoundly nationalizing experience for Canadians. More fundamentally, the Charter of Rights and Freedoms—the so-called "people's package"—has been viewed by the federal authorities as a potentially nationalizing device, weaning Canadians away from their provincialism by causing them to define themselves as possessors of certain nation-wide rights guaranteed in the final analysis by a national Supreme Court.

One must be very tentative in assessing the future consequences of the Charter of Rights and Freedoms on the political culture, and in particular the impact of the Charter on national unity. The legal philosopher Ronald Dworkin wrote in 1970, "The language of rights now dominates political debate in the United States. … It is not surprising that these questions are now prominent. The concept of rights, and particularly the concept of rights against the Government, has its most natural use when a political society is divided, and appeals to co-operation or a common goal are pointless."[14] From this perspective, the Charter is inherently a fragmenting rather than unifying measure; while one may make some rhetorical mileage by asserting that the Charter binds Canadians together in their common possession of certain rights, the defence of rights centres on conflict rather than co-operation. Furthermore, the process by which the Charter was contrived after the introduction into Parliament of the government Resolution in October 1980 centred on the claims of special interest groups. Most of the witnesses heard by the Special Joint Committee represented such interests—women, ethnic groups, religious denominations, native peoples and so on—and the action on the constitutional front between the end of the First Ministers' Conference in November 1981 and the passage of the Resolution in its final form by Parliament the next month centred on the mobilization of groups representing the claims of women and native peoples. …

Unfortunately, I think, the debate on the Charter emphasized special claims rather than those rights possessed by all Canadians, and in particular there was relatively little debate on what the Charter itself designates as "fundamental freedoms." The Charter and the procedure by which it was evolved appear to me to have limited capacities for furthering national unity. Certainly the exaggerated claims made for entrenchment by some of its supporters, including Prime Minister Trudeau, will almost inevitably lead to disillusionment as individuals and groups discover that rights cannot be guaranteed in any such sure and absolute way. …

My judgements about the implications for national unity of the Constitution Act and the procedures by which it was effected are on the whole adverse. Yet it is necessary to be quite clear about the perspectives from which the critique is made. The perspective asserts that the resources of the Canadian political system for conciliation, compromise and persuasion have not been exhausted. In pursuing the Third National Policy the federal government has clearly been willing to make compromises, and in particular, significant compromises were made by Ottawa in forging the consensus of November 5, 1981. Yet the allegedly hard-nosed view of the provinces taken by the federal government since the Liberal restoration of 1980 appears to be based on the premise that such compromises should be entered into only on the face of overwhelming pressure, and that conflict rather than conciliation is the normal condition of federal–provincial relations.[18] In an address delivered to the Law Society of Upper Canada in 1978, J.A. Corry gave a wiser counsel in conducting our common offices, based on "a meticulous constitutional morality, a mutual comity which never overlooks advance notice and consultation, always strives for accommodation." He added, "In the constitutional law of a federal state, particularly where the interests and sensitivities of minorities are involved, only in the rarest circumstances should nation-wide majorities insist on getting everything the constitution makes possible."[19] Unfortunately, this prudent advice was not taken.

Another premise of the Third National Policy is that the attachment of citizens to their respective provinces and to Canada are competing rather than complementary allegiances, and that steps must urgently be taken to strengthen national loyalties. David Elkins and Richard Simeon have presented the findings of recent survey research to the effect that, "citizens generally see no need to 'choose sides'—to renounce either their federal and provincial loyalties and identities," and go on to suggest, "We have urged that political leaders weigh carefully any actions or policies which might lead people to feel that a choice was being forced on them—a dilemma posed in terms of 'he who is not for me is against me.' We believe firmly that no such final choice is necessary or desirable."[20] The Third National Policy, of which the Constitution Act is a central element, rejects this temperate stance. ...

The Canadian Charter of Rights and Freedoms is the most radical break ever made with a constitutional and legal order hitherto characterized by continuity and incremental development. The Charter also imposes on the courts—the institutions of the governmental system most attuned towards incrementalism—the major responsibility for effecting this rupture with the past. Since April 17, 1982 Canadian law in the field of human rights has been in disarray. It will take decades, or even longer, for the courts to give authoritative meaning to the general phrases of the Charter. It is honey-combed with terms new to jurisprudence in Canada or elsewhere: "such reasonable limits prescribed by law as can be demonstrably justified in a free and democratic society," "the amelioration of the conditions of disadvantaged individuals or groups," "significant demands for communications with and services from that office in such minority official language," the "where-numbers-warrant" provisions in respect of education in the minority official languages, "proceedings which would bring the administration of justice into disrepute," "the principles of fundamental justice," "mental or physical disability," etc. Besides giving authoritative meanings to such terms, the courts must define standards of governmental conduct concerning, for example, legal rights and fundamental freedoms where hitherto Parliament and the premiers acting within their own sphere of legislative jurisdiction were supreme. It has been accurately said that the Charter will be a gold-mine for lawyers.

Lawyers are most active when the law is most uncertain, and this new source of profitable work is profoundly to be deplored by the rest of us. A defensible regime of human rights must embody not only substantive freedom and equity, but also a reasonable certainty in the definition of such rights as are protected by law. The situation vested on Canadians by the Charter demonstrably fails this second test. Admittedly, the Charter removes some of the former ambiguities in the division of powers over particular kinds of rights between Parliament and the Legislatures. Yet on balance, the Charter brings more uncertainty than it removes. In his *Quebec and the Constitution 1960–1978*, Edward McWhinney posits "digestibility" as one of his five "axioms of constitution-making."[24] Unfortunately, perhaps, Canadian decision-makers chose not to follow his prudent advice.

Both the supporters and the opponents of the Charter made regrettably weak cases for their respective positions. It was, for example, indefensible to argue, as did Premier Lyon, that constitutional entrenchment of rights would be in itself a renunciation of our monarchical and parliamentary traditions. The 1982 reforms do not constitute any change in Canada's adherence to the monarchy, and as we have seen, unanimous provincial consent is required for any amendment affecting "the office of the Queen, the Governor General and the Lieutenant Governor of a province." Several other countries which have retained the Westminster model have entrenched bills of rights. Furthermore, the British North America Act of 1867 contained a limited entrenchment of the rights of denominational minorities in education under section 93(2), and of the English and French languages in section 133.

Neither is it much of an argument to suggest that entrenchment is to be avoided by Canadians because it is an acceptance of American ways. Whatever one thinks of the general view that the devices of the United States are to be eschewed, the American constitutional traditions and circumstances in respect of human rights are so different from the Canadian that there is little correspondence between the two countries even after the Charter has come into effect: the United States Bill of Rights protects a much more limited number of claims; there is a long tradition of civil rights jurisprudence in the United States; the courts have played and continue to play a much different role in the governmental system; the American constitutional tradition is as inextricably linked with natural right and natural law assumptions as ours is not.

Also, I find unpersuasive the view that the entrenchment of rights is undemocratic because it removes final decisions about the definition and ranking of rights from elected Legislatures to appointed courts.[25] Martin Shapiro, in his spirited defence of judicial activism in the protection of First Amendment rights of free speech, argues that American opinion that judicial review is undemocratic proceeds on a very hard-nosed view of the judicial process, but that same opinion accepts a highly inaccurate and mythologized account of how Legislatures do in fact make decisions. He says "Congressional policy is today largely made in the crosscurrents of clashing committee jurisdictions, not by an orderly implementation by the will of any Congressional majorities."[26] While the Canadian parliamentary system is more closely attuned to parliamentary majorities acting in response to popular opinion, it is indefensible to argue that elected officials act almost by definition in response to such opinion. Furthermore, it is probable that the major impact of the Charter will not be on Parliament and the provincial Legislatures, but on various executive agencies, such as police forces and administrative tribunals, operating under some considerable degree of independence.

Supporters of the Charter also made a weak case. It was argued that rights could be safeguarded in an absolute fashion, but section 1 of the Charter reads, "The Canadian Charter of Rights and Freedoms guarantees the rights and freedoms set out in it subject only to such reasonable limits prescribed by law as can be demonstrably justified in a free and democratic society." No prudent consumer would buy a refrigerator with a "guarantee" subject to such imprecise qualifications. The Charter would have been more honestly and accurately entitled

"A Constitutional Enactment for the Better Protection of Certain Rights and Freedoms in Canada." The problem is not, after all, the "guaranteeing" of rights, but rather the procedures by which governmental actors are permitted by law to define, rank, modify and override certain claims of individuals and groups. If the primary objective of the Charter was the more effective protection of the rights and freedoms that this document purports to "enhance," we would have proceeded by disaggregation. It is unlikely that the procedures most efficacious in relation to, say, the protection of freedom of expression would be the same as those devised to support the claims of native peoples or the physically handicapped.

A persuasive case can be made for the entrenchment of legal rights as defined in the Charter: Canadians do have a persistent and regrettable disposition to defer to policemen; there have been many recent examples of excesses in the exercise of police powers; law enforcement and correctional officials characteristically carry out their activities largely outside public scrutiny and the control of elected officials. Because of their traditions and experience, judges may be assumed to have some capacity for wisdom in ranking the competing claims of individual freedom and effective law enforcement. There is less reason to believe that judicial procedures will be effective means of resolving intricate questions of social policy involving, for example, "equality rights," the native peoples, and the official language provisions. The fault of the process by which the Charter came into effect was not that it resulted in entrenchment *per se*, but rather the indiscriminate entrenchment of a large number of individual and group claims without sufficient discussion of the expected impact of constitutional recognition on particular kinds of rights or on the political culture more broadly.

It is trite to point out that the draftsmanship of constitutional provisions is crucial because it is subject to subsequent change only by the inflexible process of amendment. I have no credentials to judge the Constitution Act from this point of view, and at any rate whatever ambiguities, anomalies and contradictions it contains will become evident only through future judicial interpretation. However, because of the conditions under which the Act was contrived, Canadians will be almost unbelievably fortunate if the quality of draftsmanship proves to be high. ...

Conclusion

There is little cause for national self-congratulation in the Constitution Act, 1982 and the procedures by which it became a part of the constitution. There have been some gains of course—we have a wholly domestic amending process, the procedures of constitutional amendment are now in the realm of law rather than convention, there is a more secure protection of legal and democratic rights. Yet on balance, the damage done to our legal, political and constitutional order outweighs the gains. The act of changing the elements of the constitution embodying the powers of the provinces was a betrayal of the commitments made to the Quebec electorate in 1980 and created new hazards in the relations between Quebec and the wider Canadian community. The Charter imposes on the judiciary a set of responsibilities the courts are institutionally ill-equipped to deal with. And by embodying in the constitution important provisions which were hastily drafted, we have done what has been done in an inexpert and unsophisticated way.

Notes

14. Ronald Dworkin, *Taking Rights Seriously* (Cambridge, Mass.: Harvard University Press, 1977), p. 184.

18. This view is expressed in its most extreme form in the Kirby Memorandum of 1980. There is no way of knowing how close the views of that document were and are to that of the prime minister and his Cabinet colleagues, although successful courtiers seldom get out of touch with the predilections of their patrons. One is left to conclude that war-gaming federal–provincial relations are an exercise for precocious juveniles.

19. "The Uses of the Constitution," in *Law Society of Upper Canada, Special Lectures*, 1978 (Toronto: Richard de Boo, 1978), p. 3.

20. David J. Elkins and Richard Simeon, eds., *Small Worlds: Provinces and Parties in Canadian Political Life* (Toronto: Methuen, 1980), p. 308.

24. (Toronto: University of Toronto Press, 1979), p. 147.

25. There has been a long debate in the United States about whether judicial review of the constitution is inherently undemocratic. For an admirably balanced account of the controversy, see Leonard W. Levy's *Judgements: Essays on American Constitutional History* (Chicago: Quadrangle Books, 1972), pp. 24–63.

26. *Freedom of Speech: The Supreme Court and Judicial Review* (Englewood Cliffs, N.J.: Prentice-Hall, 1966), p. 18.

Sovereignties Old and New: Canada, Quebec, and Aboriginal Peoples

38

Reg Whitaker (1999)

EDITORS' INTRODUCTION

Reg Whitaker is a political scientist who taught at Carleton University, where he also served as director of the Institute of Canadian Studies, 1979–1981. In 1984, he joined the Department of Political Science at York University and, in 2001, was named Distinguished Research Professor. His fields of expertise include the study of political parties, federalism, security and intelligence, immigration policy, and the history of political thought in Canada.

In this paper, he questions the significance of the very notion of "sovereignty" in the Canadian context. Hence, "situating sovereignty in the specific context of the Canadian historical experience immediately yields a persistent incongruity," because this idea has almost never been honoured in practice. Canadian sovereignty has been exercised through wider imperial frameworks, whether located in the United Kingdom or in the United States. Quebec nationalism encounters a distinct paradox, because its concept of sovereignty has been formulated in territorial terms. For Whitaker, the problem lies in the fact that "neither the Anglophone community, nor the Allophone communities, nor Quebec's Aboriginal Peoples, have shown the slightest interest in joining forces with this admittedly liberal inclusionary nationalist project of territorial sovereignty." This raises important issues for discussing or negotiating with the Aboriginal Peoples who reside on that territory.

Sovereignty as it has commonly been understood is intimately connected to the compound concept of the nation-state. Sovereignty is an attribute of the state but it is strongest when the state is reinforced by the powerful cultural, ethnic, linguistic, and sometimes even religious identity of the nation. Conversely, sovereignty in binational or multinational states like Canada tends to be more contested. In the late twentieth century, ethnic/religious secessionist movements have erupted in many parts of the Third World and in the post-Communist states. Often these movements seek to establish successor states that more closely fuse national identity with a smaller but more ethnically or culturally "pure" state. In the process of separation, and in the suppression of other minorities that so often accompanies these breakaways, violence and authoritarianism have often been the result. We have heard a great deal in recent years about the dangers of ethnic nationalism (sometimes reformulated by Westerners

Source: Excerpted from *Studies in Political Economy*, vol. 58 (Spring 1999), 69–96. Notes omitted.

looking at the Third World as "tribalism") and we have seen the results in the horror stories of ethnic cleansing and genocide, from Bosnia to Rwanda.

Secessionist nationalisms have not been absent from the Western world. Quebec indeed represents the most successful secessionist movement in the West. Some critics assume the worst of Quebec nationalism, superficially equating it with illiberal and authoritarian movements elsewhere. I have no wish, as an English-speaking Canadian, to condemn Quebec nationalism à la Mordecai Richler or William Johnson. Despite the notorious referendum night words of Jacques Parizeau, there is no reason to believe that Quebec nationalism is particularly illiberal or culturally reactionary, and certainly not racist (or at least no more racist than English-speaking North America). Indeed I will argue that the crux of the problem lies precisely in the modernity and the liberalism of current Quebec nationalism, as it indeed has for the past twenty years or more.

My point is not really to attend to nationalism at all, but rather to its current rhetorical guise as a "sovereignty" movement. This is not rhetoric in the popular sense—a deliberately misleading verbal dressing for something else—but actually something more substantive: "sovereignty" is a concept that expresses more authentically than nationalism a contemporary, liberal striving for the recognition of national difference. Unfortunately, it also obscures far more than it illuminates, and threatens to lead us down a path that is doubtful at best and potentially destructive at worst. …

Situating sovereignty in the specific context of the Canadian historical experience immediately yields a persistent incongruity. The word and the idea have almost always been honoured in theory and rhetoric, but almost never in practice. Lip service has been paid to the dominant tradition of Bodin and Hobbes, but actual practice has belied the theory. In its external relations, Canada has in a sense never fully qualified as a sovereign state. From colonial origins, Canada moved to "Dominion" status within the British Empire without ever passing through that violent rupture and transfer of sovereignty from imperial power to new nation that characterized American development. At the formal constitutional level, this continuity was so persistent that as late as 1980–81, over a century after Confederation, the bizarre spectacle of the contested "patriation" of the Constitution through passage of a bill through the British parliament was played out: and to top absurdity with absurdity, the new "made-in-Canada" Constitution was duly proclaimed in 1982 with a ceremony in which her Majesty, Queen Elizabeth II of the United Kingdom, graciously granted her sovereign consent. For many decades, in fact well into the twentieth century, dominant schools of thought within Canada could conceive the future of the new nation only through the filter of various wider sovereignties. The Imperial Federation movement saw Canadian nationalism hitched to the star of a wider Imperial framework; others looked to a "moral federation" of the English-speaking peoples; a few to continentalist connection with the rising empire to the south. Few indeed conceived of an autonomous sovereign Canadian nation-state. Even when the linkages with Britain began to fall away, Canada moved into a new subordinate diplomatic, military and economic relationship with the US under the aegis of the Cold War. … I mention all this history not to rehearse once again the litany of left nationalist complaint, but to make what I hope is a more interesting observation: that in its external dimension, Canada has never provided even a semblance of the kind of pretence toward autonomous sovereign nation-statehood which others, even some very small states, have gone to the wall for.

The weakness of sovereignty in its external dimension has been matched, and indeed is linked to, a corresponding weakness internally. Even though the British connection implied the hegemony of Anglo-Canadians, the stubborn resistance of French Canadians prevented the formation of a unified national basis and imposed requirements for a limited but nonetheless not unimportant recognition of group difference at the institutional and representational level. ...

Unfortunately we Canadians seem strangely resistant to coming to terms with the recognition that, like Molière's *bourgeois gentilhomme*, we have actually been speaking prose all our lives. Instead, we have the spectacle of English Canadians asserting with ever-growing self-assurance that unity lies in absolute equality of individuals, provinces, groups, identities, even nations, and that any recognition of difference, any provision for special status or treatment, even measures to promote equity, as opposed to equality of treatment, are unacceptable. To make matters odder yet, this new Canadian nationalism is apparently quite innocent of any economic program. The idea of economic sovereignty was floated from marginal quarters in the 1970s but has now died. It has been replaced by a residual insistence upon something called "cultural sovereignty" that is dissociated from any economic base, indeed is even written into the continental trade agreements only to be swept away by end runs to the World Trade Organization (WTO). Or it is radically undermined by neo-liberal assaults by both federal and provincial governments on the institutional structures and funding bases of the so-called cultural industries. If the new Canadian nationalism lamely asserts a notion of a super-structural sovereignty without any economic base, the loudest and most insistent voice of sovereignty, which is of course coming from Quebec, is equally oblivious to the material base. Quebec nationalism is predominantly a liberal project, in both senses that liberalism is generally understood: politically liberal in its acceptance of pluralism and its emphasis on procedural justice as the basis of the state, rather than some overarching public Good; and economically liberal in its acceptance of markets and competitiveness as the fundamental basis for the allocation of resources. Although it has been depicted by unfriendly observers as some kind of atavistic reaction to modernity, no description could be more misleading. That characterization should be stood on its head: Quebec nationalism is a product of modernity, and is quite incomprehensible except in the frame of the familiar anxieties and dilemmas of modernity. One of the great paradoxes of the Quebec-Canada imbroglio is that the quarrel is essentially one within liberalism, or at least between variants of liberalism. ...

As part of its pervasive liberalism, the PQ has distanced itself from a narrow, exclusionary nationalism based on the core ethnic group. Instead, sovereignist thinkers have formulated a concept of territorial sovereignty. This is an inclusionary, non-ethnic nationalism that recognizes the plurality of groups within the territory. At the abstract level of principles, this is very much to be welcomed. Yet there is an enormous problem. Neither the Anglophone community, nor the Allophone communities, nor Quebec's Aboriginal peoples, have shown the slightest interest in joining forces with this admittedly liberal inclusionary nationalist project of territorial sovereignty. That is why a clear majority of Francophones has not been able to achieve an overall electoral majority for a Yes vote: all the non-Francophone minorities have voted overwhelmingly against.

There is a paradox at the heart of the sovereignty project. Liberal, pluralistic, civic nationalism—the very nationalism that all modern, right-thinking sovereignists prefer—is necessarily territorial rather than ethnic, inclusive rather than exclusionary. Sovereignty based upon a territorial nationalism of course assumes the protection of minority rights. More, it never admits a privileged ethnos or religion or national ideology, and thus a citizenship divided into first and second classes. A territorially sovereign Quebec will never be like Israel with its two distinct levels of citizenship based on ethnicity and religion, nor like the Irish Republic in its earlier days with its privileged entrenchment of Catholicism. But if territorial nationalism possesses solid, respectable pluralistic credentials, it too has its darker, intolerant side.

Sovereignty based on territoriality admits of no violation of territory; the territory of the nation is and must be sacrosanct. In this guise, nationalism can be at one and the same time pluralistic and imperialistic, inclusionary and intolerant. This comes out most decisively in relation to the claims and declarations of intention by Quebec's national minorities, the Aboriginal peoples. The sovereignists have refused, flatly, bluntly and apparently irremediably, to contemplate the notion that national self-determination is a right of first-nations resident on Quebec territory in any way comparable to Quebec's right to national self-determination. ...

Sovereignist professions of liberal intent toward minorities are sincere enough, but they do nothing to reassure those minorities, especially the Indigenous peoples as national minorities, that they are not the victims of an egregious democratic double standard. Why in the world, they ask, should anyone accept the strange assertion that the majority within a particular territorial sub-jurisdiction of the Canadian federation has a unilateral right to national self-determination to the point of definitively rupturing the federation's territorial and political integrity through secession, while at the same time declaring with an air of utter self-assurance and finality that the boundaries of this new successor state will be inviolable and ironclad proof against any further secessions? How, in short, does this particular majority, itself after all a minority within the larger existing political community, get to obviate the capacity of minorities within the minority to express their rights as local majorities? And how does this majority, constituted as it is on a territorial basis, get away with the simultaneous assertion of its own national status along with its concomitant non-recognition of the national rights of the First Nations who cohabit the same territory? Ditto for the assertion of the democratic authority of the Quebec minority-as-majority along with the refusal to recognize the democratic force of local minorities-as-majorities. It is but a short step from questions like these to the heated identification of the sovereignist project as imperialistic and authoritarian. ...

After independence, only the Quebec government will negotiate and sign self-government agreements and financial arrangements with the Aboriginal peoples who reside on Quebec territory. From the point of view of the Aboriginal peoples, this would represent not merely a loss of bargaining leverage, but far more significantly, a fundamental denial of their national rights to self-determination. They can hardly accept being swept out of one political jurisdiction and into another without their consent, without in effect abandoning any claims to national status.

The Cree and the Inuit of northern Quebec are particularly strategically placed to contest the territorial ambitions of an independent Quebec. ...

Yet perhaps it is the Aboriginal challenge that offers a way out of the impasse of sovereignty eating itself. Aboriginal concepts of self-government are not, for the most part, cast in the misleading and dangerous language of the dominant Western sovereignty tradition.

The James Bay Cree do not speak of their self-government as a rupture or a territorial secession; it is cast in opposition to such a rupture. On the other hand, their insistence on remaining part of Canada hardly stems from acquiescence to absolutist Canadian sovereignty. Self-governing Aboriginal communities will be both in and out of Canada, a different order of government, both standing alone and sharing at the same time. This suggests more creative solutions than the tedious clash of dinosaur-like sovereignties, Québécois and Canadian.

In fact, closer attention to Aboriginal voices across Canada suggests more fertile concepts of self-determination than could ever be imagined within the stolid confines of the dominant European tradition of constitutional discourse, what James Tully has called "the empire of uniformity." As Aboriginal people have begun spelling out ideas of self-determination and self-government over the past few years they have tended (of course one should not over generalize very diverse thinking) to avoid the sharp dichotomies and rigid boundaries drawn in Western thought. …

As Canadians contemplate the coming challenge of yet another Quebec referendum on sovereignty, they should consider the intriguing philosophical lesson that Aboriginal thinking poses to the fundamental idea of governance in Canadian society. Sovereignty, Aboriginal voices are telling us, is not an absolute, not a zero-sum of authority; it is something that can, and should, be shared, without one people triumphing over another. Many in the Canada of today would define sovereignty by exclusion: you are either/or, this or that, sovereign or not-sovereign. "Quebec must construct its own exclusive sovereign space through constitutional rupture" assert the sovereignists. "Quebec must submit to being simply one province among equals if it remains in Canada" assert the born-again federalists. Even the conciliators can come up with little more than controversial constitutional clauses recognizing Quebec's "distinct" or "unique" character. Not only do these ideas (perfectly fine on their own terms) tend to ignore or avoid the recognition of the rights of First Nations, but more significantly they tend to glide by the fundamental question of redefining sovereignty itself. Instead of exclusivity and uniformity, Aboriginal thinking leads toward inclusivity and diversity.

Some opinion, mainly on the neo-liberal right (with enthusiasm), but some perhaps on the left as well (with dismay), will respond to Aboriginal voices by dismissal: these are old, pre-modern, outdated concepts that will not stand up to the harsh scrutiny of a world of global marketization and relentless technological change. Perhaps. Yet it is actually the "sovereign" nation states that seem particularly incapable of coping with the contemporary changes, and with them the theorists of sovereignty in the traditional European mode. …

In this context, Aboriginal concepts of sovereignty may not appear so outdated after all. Aboriginals appear to have grasped something that the theorists of state sovereignty failed to apprehend, by and large: governance is being disengaged from territory, at least in the sense of an international order based on sovereign states with territorial monopolies. In the networked world of real-time communication, flows criss-cross territorial boundaries and this brings the global and the local into a very different form of relationship. This does not mean that territory has lost its importance, especially for traditional communities to whom the land is crucial. But in fighting to retain their ancient land and the ways of life the land sustains, new forms of political struggle are being developed that recognize that power flows across national boundaries, that local conflicts require global strategies. Not locked into the straightjacket of classical sovereignty concepts, traditional communities can seize the opportunities offered by the globally networked world—in defence of localism. …

The point is this: threatened by the enclosing networks of global capitalism (the power grid), the Aboriginal people of northern Quebec fought back by their own networking, this time networks that utilized international environmental groups and global communications. To be sure, the battle for Aboriginal rights has hardly been won in this one successful skirmish, but the strategy of resistance is interesting and offers a model for how resistance can be carried in the information age or what Manuel Castells has called the "rise of the network society." Castells has written of the Mexican Zapatista movement that it is the first "informational guerrilla movement." The Zapatista struggle is quite different from that of the Aboriginal people of northern Quebec, but the model of a movement that understands and utilizes global information networks on behalf of local resistance against globalization does apply.

Whose is the more "modern" concept of sovereignty? Is it the Quebec sovereignist movement fixated on replicating national political but not economic sovereignty over Quebec's "sacred" and indivisible territory? Or is it the Aboriginal people who speak of the self-determination of peoples, not states or territories, who network across borders to build support alliances, and who can imagine shared jurisdiction between themselves, Canada, Quebec and the wider world? I think the answer is self-evident, and is embodied in the political defeats already suffered by the péquistes at the hands of those they refuse to see as other than one more cultural minority in a Francophone nation-state, but who have shown conclusively that they are much more than that and can be politically effective operating in the real world at the end of the twentieth century.

If Quebec does separate, the challenge posed by the Aboriginal peoples of northern Quebec will demand innovative answers from all the players in the crisis. A possible way out of the impasse/catastrophe occasioned by demands for partition would be for Canada and Quebec to enter into a condominium arrangement for joint sovereignty in the north, with each government holding specified functions of sovereignty as understood presently in international law but with a much wider arrangement for Aboriginal self-government and Aboriginal jurisdiction over land and resources than exists at present. A condominium would be a distinct innovation (but one that could give flesh to the PQ's idea of a post-secession "partnership" between Canada and Quebec). …

In the event of Quebec moving toward sovereignty, the Northern Irish model offers a concept of overlapping sovereignties that could satisfy: [a] Aboriginal peoples that Canada was not abandoning its fiduciary obligations to them; [b] Quebec that "its" territory would not be partitioned in the sense that Quebec would not be expelled from the north; and [c] Canada that a secessionist Quebec could not depart except by agreement honouring Canada's existing rights and obligations as well as Quebec demands. I must reiterate that such an unusual arrangement will only work if it comprehends a very large degree of Aboriginal autonomy, but one that grants the inevitability of a continuing interest and presence of both Canada and Quebec. None of this however can easily apply to the Aboriginal peoples in the south of Quebec, where geographical separation is hardly possible, and where history does not as readily distinguish Aboriginal lands from original Quebec territory.

Constitutional Politics: In a New Era Canada Returns to Old Methods

39

Peter H. Russell (2006)

EDITORS' INTRODUCTION

Peter Russell, Professor Emeritus at the University of Toronto where he taught from 1958 to 1997, is one of Canada's most eminent writers and commentators on the Constitution. His books include Constitutional Odyssey: Can Canadians Become a Sovereign People? *now in its third edition. He was president of the Canadian Political Science Association, a director of research for the McDonald Commission on the RCMP, and a member of the Federal Task Force on Comprehensive Land Claims, and is an Officer of the Order of Canada and a Fellow of the Royal Society of Canada.*

This extract presents an insightful analysis of the nature of the Canadian constitutional crisis and its aftermath. Russell juxtaposes two constitutional styles: one understanding the system in an organic way, where change is incremental and pragmatic, in Edmond Burke's tradition; the other embracing the idea that the Constitution is a covenant among sovereign people, based on the political philosophy of John Locke. Russell contends that Canadian constitutionalism began on an organic, Burkean note, but shifted to a Lockean one, according to which the Canadian people should be sovereign and the Constitution should express their will. Since the failed exercise of amending the Constitution in the 1990s, Canadians learned that it is impossible to reach a consensus on fundamental change, which brings us back to Burke.

Quietly, almost silently, Canada's constitutional politics has entered a new era. The days when the national unity issue and attempts to resolve it dominated political life are behind us, at least for the time being. The last time we Canadians attempted a grand restructuring of our constitution was when a majority of us rejected the Charlottetown Accord in October 1992. After that, for another three years, a pending referendum on Quebec sovereignty kept the national unity issue at the top of our political agenda. Then, by the narrowest of margins, on 30 October 1995, the citizens of Quebec said no to the sovereignty option. Had a few thousand of them voted the other way we would surely have been plunged back into as deep a constitutional crisis as the country has ever known—with a Quebec premier claiming a mandate to unilaterally make Quebec an independent state, and a Canadian prime minister denying Quebec's right to do that (Russell, 2004).

Source: Excerpted from *Continuity and Change in Canadian Politics: Essays in Honour of David E. Smith*, edited by Hans J. Michelmann and Cristine de Clercy. Toronto: University of Toronto Press, 2006. Reprinted by permission.

As things turned out, the era of what I refer to as mega-constitutional politics came to an end with a whimper rather than a bang. The federal prime minister did a little bit of constitutional tinkering to honour his eleventh-hour promise in the referendum campaign. The Supreme Court laid down the constitutional rules governing secession, after which the federal parliament and Quebec's National Assembly enacted legislation staking out somewhat conflicting versions of their respective rights and roles in a secession crisis. Fortunately, after all that, the crisis didn't come. The sovereignist government in Quebec first lost its nerve, then, in April 2003, lost the provincial election.

Now some would say—and I fear this might include all too many political scientists—that with a federalist government in power in Quebec and national unity no longer a pressing matter, constitutional politics are behind us. One often hears the view expressed that since the Charlottetown Accord débâcle, Canada has fallen into "a constitutional deep-freeze." The contributors to a symposium convened by the Royal Society of Canada a year after the Quebec referendum were almost all of the view that Canada was unlikely to survive without major constitutional change, but that constitutional reform was just about impossible. In the words of Alan Cairns, "constitutional reform is a god that failed" (Cairns, 1977). At one level this view is surely correct. Constitutional reform of the mega-constitutional variety—that is, through popular agreement on a set of formal constitutional amendments on the big issues that divide us—is a god that has failed. But that doesn't mean that constitutional politics and constitutional change are dead. Quite to the contrary, it means we are now in a new era of constitutional politics when a lot is taking place, not through the stormy, crisis-ridden processes of mega-constitutional politics, but through the quieter, incremental and much sunnier ways of organic constitutionalism—the very ways in which our constitutional system evolved through its first century.

It is appropriate to write about Canada's return to this older style of constitutional politics in a contribution to a *festschrift* honouring David Smith. Though David Smith kept company with those of us who became wrapped up in the mega-constitutional game, he never made it the centre of his work. The genius of his contribution to our discipline and our country has been to teach us about the evolution and implications of the institutions and political system we have rather than engaging in efforts to radically transform them. Now that we are getting back to a more modest approach to constitutional change, his work should be more relevant than ever. This can be seen in his recently published book, *The Canadian Senate in Bicameral Perspective* (Smith, 2003). Here, instead of treating Senate reform as cure for national unity ills or a fulfillment of our democratic dreams, he invites us to think carefully about the purpose of a second legislative chamber in our federal parliament. From this perspective, we learn that there is much that could be done through the traditional methods of small "c" constitutional change to enable the Senate to better fulfil its historic purpose. I will return to David's thoughts on doable Senate reform later in this essay.

Burke to Locke and Back Again to Burke

In *Constitutional Odyssey*, I juxtaposed two constitutional styles. One is the older English view that, instead of thinking of the constitution as a single document drawn up and agreed to at a particular point of time and containing all of a society's rules and principles of government, a constitution is the collection of laws, institutions, and political practices that have survived the test of time and are found to serve the society's interests tolerably well. Daniel Elazar referred to countries practicing this type of constitutionalism as organic polities and observed that in such societies "constitution-making and constitutional change come in bits and pieces" (Elazar, 1985: 244). In constitutional systems understood in this organic way, change is incremental and pragmatic, consent is implicit and informal. When one of the "bits and pieces" is not working satisfactorily, there is an effort to fix it. Whether the repair job is satisfactory, only time can tell. The political philosopher par excellence of organic constitutionalism was Edmund Burke. Burke was sceptical about the capacity of individuals through abstract reasoning to discern fundamental political truths. "The individual is foolish, but the species is wise" (Kirk, 1953). For Burke, the social contract that forms the foundation of a society is not between individuals here and now but between generations, each handing on to the next the product of its collective wisdom.

The constitutionalism I contrasted with the Burkean is that based on the political philosophy of John Locke. This is the idea that the constitution is a covenant among a sovereign people on how they are to be governed. The constitution so conceived is indeed the Constitution, with a great big capital "C"—a supreme law representing the enduring will of a single sovereign people containing a complete statement of its fundamental principles and institutions of governance. It is Lockean constitutionalism that underlies the foundational myth of the American Constitution, which is enacted by "We the people" as an expression of their enduring will as to how they are to be governed. The reality of how the American constitution was drawn up and ratified and has evolved over time was considerably different from the Lockean ideal. Nonetheless, in the age of democracy, the ideal of the Constitution, embodying the will of a sovereign people and serving as its highest law, stands as a compelling model for societies making new beginnings after world war, the withdrawal of empire, the overthrow of tyrannies—or, in the Canadian case, responding to a crisis of national unity. In these circumstances, constitution makers are driven to work at fashioning a new Constitution that can win the consent of the people through democratic means.[1]

Canadian constitutionalism certainly did not begin on a Lockean note. At the founding of the Canadian federation and through its first century, Canadian constitutionalism was essentially organic and Burkean. The British North America Act was not regarded as containing a comprehensive statement of the country's constitutional system. Many of the most important rules and principles of government—above all, the key practices of parliamentary government—were part of the country's constitutional inheritance from Great Britain and took the form of informal constitutional conventions. Over the next century, Canada's constitutional system changed and adapted, notably becoming far more thoroughly federal than many of the Founding Fathers intended. The changes occurred incrementally and through a variety of means, including political agreements and practices, legislation establishing new institutions (like the Supreme Court), judicial decisions, and the occasional amendment of the BNA Act. There was plenty of politics in all of this, they were relatively low key and never of crisis proportions.

We began to move towards a different kind of constitutionalism when the country—or at least its leaders—became serious about ending the written Constitution's formal legal tie to the imperial Parliament. Bringing the Constitution home to Canada raised the question of who in Canada should have custody of it—that is, which governments or people should have the power to amend the Constitution? Now if the formal capital "C" Constitution is to be treated as Canada's supreme law, this question comes down to agreeing on nothing less than who or what should be the supreme Canadian law-maker or sovereign. Should it be the Parliament of Canada? Or Parliament plus all or some of the provincial legislatures? Should Quebec, as the homeland of a founding people, be given a special role? Or should it be a simple majority of the Canadian people, or some kind of special majority? There were supporters for all of these answers, each reflecting a fundamentally different vision of what kind of political society Canada is or should become. As Canadians wrestled with this difficult question, some of the participants, beginning with a now secular but very nationalist Quebec, began to insist that it wasn't enough simply to "bring the Constitution home" but while we are at it we should redo the Constitution—in effect we should make a new beginning. Of course, the dualistic vision of Canada which Quebec nationalists wanted to write into a re-written constitution was very different from other Canadians' vision of the country. And so for a generation, from the late 1960s to the early 1990s, Canadians tied themselves in knots trying to reach agreement on their constitution.

Increasingly, the endeavour took on a Lockean hue: the Canadian people should be sovereign and the constitution should express their will, with the crisis-laden corollary that if they couldn't agree, their federation might break up. The climax came with the Charlottetown Accord—a kitchen-sink-full of constitutional reforms designed to placate every possible source of constitutional discontent in the land but rejected for a host of conflicting reasons by a majority of Canadian people in a majority of provinces.

Though Charlottetown had a negative result, it was, as they used to say, quite a learning experience. Canadians learned that if they are a sovereign people they are capable of exercising their sovereignty only in a negative way. They can use their constitutional power to reject but not approve changes in anything fundamental. What is more, Canadians learned that the very effort of trying to reach a popular accord on restructuring fundamental parts of the formal, capital "C" part of their constitutional system would likely deepen their discord. The people of Quebec must surely have learned the same lesson from the 1995 referendum. They were no more able than Canadians to act positively as a sovereign people and reach a broad consensus on that jurisdiction's constitutional future. And so the Lockean constitutional god was dead—both for Canada as a whole and for Quebec. Which brings us back to Burke. ...

Note

1. I have developed this theme more fully in "Can the Canadians Be a Sovereign People?" in *Constitutional Politics in Canada and the United States*, ed. Stephen Newman (Albany: State University of New York, 2004).

Unfulfilled Union: Canadian Federalism and National Unity

40

Garth Stevenson (2009)

EDITORS' INTRODUCTION

Garth Stevenson is a professor of political science at Brock University, specializing in Canadian politics (Quebec politics, federalism) and comparative politics (nationalism, ethnic politics). He has published widely on the ways in which Canada and the United States have dealt with ethnic and religious diversity from colonial times to the present, the English-speaking minority in Quebec, the development of nationalism in Ireland and Quebec, and Canadian federalism.

This excerpt is from Unfulfilled Union: Canadian Federalism and National Unity, *now in its fifth edition. It offers a political economy analysis, putting less emphasis on cultural explanations for the strength of Canadian provincialism than on economic factors. The federal project is analyzed in terms of conflicts among different classes and class factions. Stevenson emphasizes the uneven development in Canada, which has resulted in varying political interests between regions that make up Canada. He contends that control of economic sectors, located in Canada or abroad, played an important role in the questioning of Canadian federalism in the 1970s. It is against this process of balkanization and fragmentation, which posed a threat to Canada's elites, that one should understand the constitutional reform project put forward by Pierre Elliott Trudeau.*

The Political Economy of Decentralization

> *Provincialism has paralleled the new industrialism.... Confederation as an instrument of steam power has been compelled to face the implications of hydro-electric power and petroleum.*
>
> —Harold Innis

> *... among the more or less centralized federations of the modern world, most writers would agree that Canada is about as decentralized as one can get.*
>
> —W.H. Riker

Source: Excerpted from *Unfulfilled Union: Canadian Federalism and National Unity*, 5th edition, by Garth Stevenson. Montreal and Kingston: McGill-Queen's University Press, 2009. Notes omitted.

Norman Rogers, in a pioneering article, emphasized "changes in political consciousness and sentiment" as the source of centrifugal and centripetal trends in Canadian federalism. Although this theory is impossible to support on the evidence, it seems to be widely popular, perhaps because of its reassuring implication that Canadians always get the kind of federalism they want, and will presumably continue to do so. Rogers also contended, as have a multitude of subsequent writers, that the provincial governments could not be kept in a subordinate position because there was no widespread sense of attachment to Canada as a nation. J.M.S. Careless, following in this tradition, perceived a relationship between the various "limited identities" of Canadians, identities which are ethnic and religious as well as provincial and regional.

Yet there is reason for considerable scepticism about cultural explanations for the strength of Canadian provincialism. Apart from the concentration of francophones in Quebec, ethnic and religious divisions tend to cut across, rather than to reinforce, provincial boundaries. The cultural differences between the predominantly anglophone provinces are certainly no greater than those between Texas and Massachusetts, for example, and are actually diminishing under the impact of urbanization and the mass media.

Other possible explanations that have been offered seem equally fruitless. The greater competence of provincial bureaucracies in recent years, for example, is an important fact, but it would seem more likely to be a consequence than a cause of the fact that provincial governments have gained in power and importance. For similar reasons one cannot explain very much by asserting that the subjects enumerated in Section 92 of the BNA Act proved to be unexpectedly more important than those enumerated in Section 91. Many of the tasks performed by the modern state are not explicitly enumerated in either section, and no conceivable reading of the BNA Act would support the illogical distribution of tasks, functions, and powers between the two levels of government that has actually emerged. The important question to answer is why so many matters have, in practice, been regarded as falling under provincial jurisdiction, in whole or in part, and why the central government has had to share its power with the provincial governments, or to defend it against provincial pressures, to an extent that has few if any parallels elsewhere.

The answer to this problem seems to lie in certain characteristics of the political economy of Canada, which both produced conflicts between different classes and class fractions and at the same time caused these contending forces to identify their interests with different levels of government, and vice versa. ...

Confederation, as we have seen, was largely although by no means exclusively the result of economic motives. Its effect was both to expand the geographical jurisdiction of the Canadian state and to overhaul its machinery so that economic functions both old and new could be performed more effectively. The terms of Confederation, most of which related to economic matters, represented the common denominator of agreement among a variety of economic interests and objectives in the different colonies. Confederation did not, however, end the diversity and conflict among those interests, which soon found expression through a feature of the post-Confederation state which itself was partly the result of that diversity and conflict, namely the existence of two distinct levels of government. In addition, conflict between the dominant class and other classes, particularly the farmers, also had an impact on the dynamics of Canadian federalism.

Under a federal regime, conflicting economic interests could theoretically find expression in either or both of two ways: through accommodation and compromise at the level of the central government, assuming that all were represented there to some degree; or through different governments, federal and provincial. Class fractions that perceive the central government as more sympathetic to opposing interests than to their own will tend to seek redress by strengthening the provincial level of government. This occurs, particularly if they are geographically distributed in such a way that one provincial government represents a geographical area within which one of the frustrated class fractions is particularly important and influential. In such circumstances the provincial government in question will speak for the class fraction concerned, and will carry out on its behalf the Canadian state's traditional function as the ally and supporter of private enterprise. Efforts will be made to curtail and undermine the power and authority of the unsympathetic and potentially hostile central government, usually by ideological appeals to the virtues of local autonomy, decentralization, and the cultural values allegedly embodied in the province. Any increase in the taxing, spending, and regulatory powers of the provincial level of government will be welcomed, since it will enable that level of government to perform the accumulation function more effectively on behalf of the locally dominant class fraction.

The central government, on the other hand, will be supported by those class fractions which have the most access to it and influence over it, and which can rely upon it to act in support of their economic objectives. Another reason for preferring this level of government may be the fear that overly powerful provincial governments will "balkanize" the country by pursuing policies that restrict the free flow of commodities across provincial boundaries. In addition, classes and class fractions within a province that find the provincial government hostile or unresponsive to their needs will support the strengthening of the central government as a counterweight and may call upon the central government to intervene on their behalf against the provincial government.

Considerations of this kind can lead to fairly long-term alliances between particular class fractions and different levels of government, but changing circumstances may lead to a temporary or even permanent transference of allegiance to the other level. A class fraction which enjoys some influence at both levels of government can also use each one to prevent the other from straying too far out of line, an important consideration in view of the degree of autonomy possessed by modern state apparatuses and the limited but real responsiveness of politicians to subordinate class demands expressed through the electoral process. What Lord Palmerston once said about British foreign policy could be applied to the politics of business in a federal state: its alliances are determined by its interests, not the other way around. ...

The National Policy and Its Opponents

Canada's economic development progressed rapidly in the early part of the twentieth century, but the development was unevenly distributed across the country, producing the phenomenon that would come to be known as regional disparity. The increasing concentration of ownership in the industrial and financial sectors of the economy increased the economic power of Toronto and Montreal to the detriment of smaller centres like Halifax, Saint John, and Quebec City which were gradually reduced to subordinate positions. Secondary manufacturing became concentrated in southern Ontario and the Montreal region, not because of the tariff as is often alleged, but because these locations were close to markets and raw materials. Average levels of wealth and personal income began to vary noticeably from one province to another, with the Maritime provinces, and to some extent Quebec, deteriorating in relation to Ontario and the West.

These developments affected the federal system in two ways. Maritime businessmen, never unanimously convinced that Confederation had been to their benefit, were increasingly inclined to blame federal transportation and tariff policies for the deterioration of their regional economy, and attempted to use the provincial level of government as an instrument to retain as large as possible a share of the national income. In Ontario, paradoxically, good fortune had a similar if not greater impact. The Ontario government, because of Ontario's wealth and prosperity, had the financial means to pursue economic policies that contributed to the further accumulation of wealth within the province. Ontario's vast size, as well as its wealth, equipped the Ontario government to perform an economic role that was unusual, if not unique, for a subnational state within a federation, and thus to gain the support of Ontario businessmen. Simultaneously, Ontario businessmen tended to view the federal level of government as an instrument for redistributing Ontario's wealth to the benefit of the voters in other provinces. Thus uneven development made the federal government a target for resentment in both rich and poor provinces, while causing the accumulation functions of the provincial level of government to be emphasized.

Related to uneven development, and also a consequence of the National Policy, was the emergence of three distinct sectors of the Canadian economy, each with divergent economic interests and class relationships. Of particular importance to the development of federalism was the fact that the three sectors were concentrated in different provinces and regions. Thus each provincial government tended to become the representative for a distinct set of interests, rather than a microcosm of the country as a whole.

Secondary manufacturing was one of the three sectors and, as already mentioned, it was heavily concentrated in Ontario. Confederation exposed Maritime manufacturing to Ontario competition, while the National Policy protected Ontario manufacturing from foreign competition and greatly stimulated new industrialization to substitute indigenous products for imports. ...

The second major sector of the economy was export-oriented agriculture. Ontario had originally dominated this sector as well, but after the completion of the CPR main line in 1885 the major growth of this sector occurred in the "Northwest," or the area now occupied by the provinces of Manitoba, Saskatchewan, and Alberta. Prairie wheat became Canada's major export staple and the whole east-west economy was increasingly oriented around it.

Agricultural commodities for export were produced by independent farmers who owned their land and equipment, in contrast to the wage earners who produced manufactured goods. The antagonism of the farmers was directed against the banks, the mortgage companies, the railways, and the grain merchants. The protective tariff was also a source of resentment, since it increased the farmer's expenses while offering no benefit in return. Thus the farmer's economic interests were contrary to those of the manufacturing sector. ...

The third sector of the economy consisted of the export-oriented resource industries: lumbering, mining and smelting, pulp and paper. These industries resembled the agricultural sector in their dependence on foreign rather than domestic markets, but they resembled the manufacturing sector in that they were based on large-scale enterprises employing wage labour rather than independent commodity production. Class conflict was pronounced, partly because of working conditions and partly because there was no issue that united employees and employers, as the tariff united them in the manufacturing sector. Foreign direct investment, largely American, was important from the outset in this sector. The mining industry was insignificant until about thirty years after Confederation, but grew rapidly thereafter. Forestry had been important since long before Confederation. Pulp and paper expanded rapidly after the United States removed its tariff on newsprint in 1913. The resource sector was less geographically concentrated than the other two sectors, and was important in every province apart from Alberta, Saskatchewan, and Prince Edward Island. (Alberta already produced coal and oil by 1914, but for domestic consumption only.) However, British Columbia was the only province where the resource sector predominated, producing a distinctive political culture that in many respects makes it more like an Australian state than a Canadian province. Resource-oriented areas in other provinces, such as northern Ontario, Cape Breton Island, and the Abitibi region of Quebec, developed a sense of distinctiveness and an antagonism toward other parts of their provinces, occasionally expressed in secessionist movements but more frequently in votes for provincial opposition parties. ...

However, the resource sector, like others, reinforced the centrifugal pressures in Canadian federalism. More than either of the other sectors, it was intimately associated with provincial government, because the provinces owned most of the lands and resources. This gave resource capital a weight in provincial politics that was disproportionate to its real importance in provinces like Ontario and Quebec. On the other hand, resource capital was relatively indifferent to the federal level of government, since it required neither protective tariffs nor the elaborate financial and transportation infrastructure of the wheat economy. Thus the rise of the resource sector contributed to the growing importance of provincial governments and the declining relevance of the federal level to the accumulation function of the state. This was particularly true in British Columbia, Quebec, and Ontario. ...

The Impact of Depression and War

The Depression of the 1930s produced some changes in the political economy of federalism. The agricultural sector declined catastrophically, weakening the three Prairie provinces but also weakening the federally oriented banks, railways, grain merchants, and financial institutions. The resource sector also suffered (although to a lesser extent), apart, that is, from gold mining, which was the only industry that actually expanded during this period. Manufacturing suffered least, largely because the Ottawa Agreements of 1932 increased its share of British Empire markets at the expense of its competitors in the United States. The overall effect was to strengthen Ontario and Quebec, where both gold mining and manufacturing were concentrated, and to weaken the peripheries of the country, especially the Prairie West, where the fiscal structure of provincial and local government collapsed completely. The federal level of government was called upon to rescue the peripheries, but faced increasingly determined and successful obstruction by the governments of the two central provinces. ...

The greatest expansion occurred in the resource sector of the Canadian economy, mainly in response to the depletion of American raw material supplies during the war and the preference of the United States for seeking new supplies in a country that was politically reliable and geographically proximate. ...

Ironically it was the postwar government of Louis St. Laurent, the convinced centripetal federalist, that did the most to orient the Canadian economy in this direction, thereby contributing to the increasing irrelevance of the central government and the increasing power and importance of the provincial governments.

The effect of developments in both the manufacturing and resource sectors was to integrate the Canadian economy into that of the United States. ...

The Branch-Plant Economy

Closely associated as both cause and consequence with the reorientation of Canada's trade was the increasing importance of American direct investment, particularly in the manufacturing and resource sectors of the economy. ...

As a result of these developments, the control of the Canadian economy was fragmented in a peculiar fashion. The indigenous "big bourgeoisie" controlled the banks, insurance companies, department stores, and other such enterprises extending across the country, but were poorly represented in manufacturing and the natural resource industries. A comprador fraction, in Wallace Clement's words, managed the American branch plants that predominated in the industrial sectors of the economy. A third fraction, large in numbers and political influence if not in economic power, controlled the small-scale enterprises in the service industries and those sectors of manufacturing where Canadian capital still predominated.

Of these fractions only the first still identified its interests predominantly with the federal level of government, with which many of its activities had been closely associated since Confederation. The power of this fraction, while extensive, was too narrowly based to enable it to carry out the movement toward centralization of state power that other advanced countries were then experiencing. For the comprador fraction, the Canadian federal government was in a sense the least important among three levels of government: the continental, national, and provincial. Viewing Canada as part of a North American economy (and many multinationals are organized to reflect this assumption, with the Canadian and American operations organizationally separated from those overseas), they were naturally more oriented to Washington than to Ottawa. On the other hand, the provincial level of government was significant to them because the activities of a manufacturing or resource firm were typically concentrated in a single province and because provincial government controlled their terms of access to the two major inputs of natural resources and labour. The third fraction, with essentially localized operations, was also provincially oriented, although less so in the case of manufacturing enterprises, which relied on the protective tariff, than in the case of service industries. ...

The Revival of Centripetal Forces

By the early 1970s, it appeared to some observers that the fragmentation of the Canadian economy and the absence of any strong sense of national identity had reached the point at which the survival of Canada as a united federal state could not be taken for granted. Indeed the federal government itself, faced with increasingly rambunctious provincial governments, appeared to lack either the will or the ability to resist their numerous demands, or to formulate and implement coherent policies of its own. While this impression was not entirely unwarranted, there were some countervailing forces at work whose importance would only become fully apparent in the 1980s. ...

The most credible explanation for all of these developments is that elements of the central Canadian bourgeoisie were becoming apprehensive about the consequences of aggressive resource-based provincialism in Alberta and Saskatchewan and of rising nationalism in Quebec. Western provincialism began to appear threatening in 1973 when the international price of oil and thus the potential value of the energy resources owned by Alberta and Saskatchewan, quadrupled within a few months. Significantly, both the Alberta and Saskatchewan governments soon abandoned their traditional indifference to constitutional discussions and began to demand that the constitution be revised to reflect their new economic power. Quebec nationalism … had been on the rise since 1960, but the election of a Parti Québécois government headed by Rene Lévesque in November 1976 appeared to make the secession of that province from the Canadian federation a distinct possibility. Despite the assurances of the Parti Québécois the independence would be accompanied by economic association with the rest of Canada, the business community (including the business community of Quebec itself) did not find this concept either credible or reassuring.

Ontario in particular felt threatened on two fronts. At a time of increasingly strong international competition, the secondary manufacturing industries that were the basis of its economy faced the threat of much higher prices for fuel, energy, and transportation, as well as the possible fragmentation of the Canadian market by an independent Quebec and increasingly interventionist and protectionist policies of other provincial governments. The Ontario government naturally reacted sooner to these grim possibilities than the federal government, which responded to a much broader range of interests and which for political reasons had to be cautious in dealing with Quebec, at least prior to that province's referendum on sovereignty-association. Both the Ontario government and its business allies, however, realized that only a strong federal government, responding to the large bloc of votes which Ontario represented but capable of imposing its will on the other provinces, could protect Ontario's economy against the dangers which it faced. The Ontario government thus abandoned its traditional provincialism in favour of a more pro-federal approach to intergovernmental relations. The federal government responded only gradually, but the return of the Liberals with an increased majority in 1980, and the rejection of sovereignty-association by the voters of Quebec in a referendum three months later, helped to dissolve its inhibitions. As a result, the years from 1980 to 1984 were marked by unusually acute federal–provincial conflict, with Ontario and the federal government forming an alliance against most of the other provinces with Quebec and Alberta leading the opposition.

Prime Minister Trudeau retired in 1984 and Premier Davis in 1985; and their respective parties were both defeated in the federal and provincial elections that followed soon afterward. Simultaneously the apparent eclipse of Quebec nationalism and the rapid decline in the price of oil, which undermined the economic base of western provincialism, reduced the need for the Ontario–federal alliance which Trudeau and Davis had represented. Canadian federalism thus seemed to have attained a temporary equilibrium between its centrifugal and centripetal forces in the latter part of the decade. Federal–provincial relations, which tend to be bitter and conflictual when the balance of power is shifting rapidly from one level of government or the other, were more placid and harmonious after 1984, when Brian Mulroney headed a progressive Conservative federal government. Whatever the future may hold, however, future trends in the Canadian economy are likely to have decisive impact on Canadian federalism.

41 The Governments and Societies of Canadian Federalism

Alan C. Cairns (1977)

EDITORS' INTRODUCTION

Alan Cairns was a professor of political science at the University of British Columbia from 1960 to 1995 and a visiting scholar at numerous Canadian universities. He published many books and articles on Canadian public policy and the Constitution. He is an Officer of the Order of Canada and a Fellow of the Royal Society of Canada.

An earlier version of this selection was presented as the Presidential Address to the Canadian Political Science Association in Fredericton in June 1977. Cairns takes this opportunity to discuss the interaction between government and society in Canada. He contends that political science does not yet treat government with appropriate seriousness. He states that Canadian federalism is not a function of societies but of the Constitution, "and more importantly of the governments that work the constitution." This argument is particularly important because it goes against a well-established tradition that uses a sociological perspective to study Canadian federalism. In this excerpt, Cairns recalls that the survival of provincial governments, and a renewal of their vitality, is based on their capacity to mould their environment, reflecting their own governmental purposes.

> *If you marry the Spirit of your generation you will be a widow in the next.*
>
> —Dean Inge

The Canadian political system, now in its second century, can no longer be taken for granted. It is altogether possible, some would say probable, and some would say desirable, that major institutional change, not excluding the fragmentation of Canada, is on the immediate horizon. It is therefore an opportune time to reflect on the century-long interaction between government and society in Canada. I use the word "reflect" advisedly, for this is not the type of interaction about which hard statements can be confidently made.

The impact of society on government is a common theme in the study of democratic polities. Less common is an approach which stresses the impact of government on the functioning of society. I have chosen the latter for the guiding theme of my remarks, because I

Source: Excerpted from *Canadian Journal of Political Science*, vol. 10, no. 4 (December 1977). Some notes omitted. Reprinted by permission.

am convinced that our approach to the study of Canadian politics pays inadequate attention to the capacity of government to make society responsive to its demands. ...

The reaction against traditional political science, with its alleged overemphasis on the formal, legal aspects of the polity at the expense of the social forces which worked it, was given striking emphasis for students of federalism in W.S. Livingston's famous assertion in 1956 that "Federalism is a function not of constitutions but of societies."[1] The dynamic of the system was to be sought not in government, or in features of the constitution, but in society. In the elaboration of this sociological perspective political systems are seen as superstructures devoid of autonomy, and lacking independent coercive and moulding power *vis-à-vis* their environment.

Two decades before the appearance of Livingston's seminal piece, the depression of the thirties produced a great outburst of federalist literature, or, more properly, anti-federalist literature, in English Canada, which presupposed "The Obsolescence of Federalism."[2] This literature viewed the central government as the fortunate and necessary beneficiary and provincial governments as the hapless victims of overwhelmingly powerful socioeconomic forces. In essence, it was argued that technological interdependence and the evolution of a national market made centralized leadership necessary for planning purposes, and destroyed the sociological basis for the vitality and meaningful survival of the provinces. Provincial governments, considered out of tune with fundamental requirements and urgent imperatives rooted in society and economy, apparently had no resources adequate to stay the execution decreed for them by scholars with the future in their bones.

The centralization predicted in the thirties seemed firmly and securely in place in the forties, and for much of the fifties. It was explained in 1957 by Professor J.A. Corry as a product of technological necessity. Corry, responding to prevailing interpretations of the nature and direction of socioeconomic change, produced a polished epitaph for any significant future role for provincial governments. The growth of "giant corporations, national trade associations, and national trade unions" created a nationalizing of sentiment among elites who backed the central government and thus contributed to the centralization of authority in Ottawa. The most a province could hope for, he asserted, "is freedom for minor adventure, for embroidering its own particular patterns in harmony with the national design, for playing variant melodies within the general theme. ... [I]t is everywhere limited in the distance it can go by having become part of a larger, although not necessarily a better, scheme of things."

To the distress of a later generation of liberal-left critics of federalism, Corry's prediction of a nationalization of politics and the continuing centralization of authority in federal hands proved premature. For John Porter, writing in the mid-sixties, when the centralizing impulse born of depression, war, and post-war reconstruction had faded, the federal system was little more than a pious fraud devoid of real meaning for the citizenry, and sustained by academics with a vested interest in their esoteric knowledge of the system's functioning, and by political and bureaucratic elites happy to place federal roadblocks in the way of class politics. To Porter, reiterating an argument widely employed in the thirties, the "conditions of modern industrial society and international relations ... [made] it ... almost essential that the central government acquire power at the expense of the provincial ... governments."[5] Canada, however, was relatively exempt from this necessary and beneficial trend. The cause of this regrettable backwardness was located in the political system with its exaggerated obsession with national unity, and its bias in favour of provincial rights. Reduced to essentials, Porter's position was simply that the class cleavage, based on the economic system, was the true, natural, and dynamic cleavage, while regional cleavages stimulated and fostered by the political system were fundamentally artificial, meaningless, and accordingly undeserving of respect. A well-functioning, modern political system, in marked contrast to the existing federal system, would serve, above all else, as an instrumentality for the expression of creative politics founded on the class struggle of advanced industrial society, with regional considerations shunted to the sidelines. This may be called the sociologist's ideal political system, for it awards primacy to his subject matter.

The unavoidable briefness of my remarks obviously does not do justice to the complexity and diversity of the extensive literature on Canadian federalism, and inevitably oversimplifies the views of those few writers mentioned above. What I have tried to do is to highlight their relative failure to perceive the degree of autonomy possessed by governments and the ongoing capacity of the federal system to manufacture the conditions necessary for its continuing survival. Where such is partially noted, as it is by Porter, the admission is grudging and is accompanied by pejorative adjectives which cloud the analysis.

In a sense, Livingston's plea to search for the determinants of a changing federalism in society, not constitutions, was not needed in Canada. From the mid-thirties to the present we have not lacked sociological approaches to federalism. The weakness of our understanding lies elsewhere, in a failure to treat government with appropriate seriousness. The remainder of this paper is an attempt to redress the balance by arguing, contrary to Livingston, that federalism, at least in the Canadian case, is a function not of societies but of the constitution, and more importantly of the governments that work the constitution.

The great mystery for students of Canadian federalism has been the survival and growth of provincial governments, particularly those of English Canada. Sociologically-focussed inquiries, with Quebec as an implicit model, have looked for vital, inward-looking provincial societies on which governments could be based and, finding none, have been puzzled why these governmental superstructures, seemingly lacking a necessary foundation, have not faded away.

The sociological perspective pays inadequate attention to the possibility that the support for powerful, independent provincial governments is a product of the political system itself, that it is fostered and created by provincial government elites employing the policy-making apparatus of their jurisdictions, and that such support need not take the form of a distinct culture, society, or nation as these are conventionally understood. More specifically, the search for an underlying sociological base, whatever its nature and source, as the necessary sustenance for viable provincial political systems, deflects us from considering the prior question of how much support is necessary. Passivity, indifference, or the absence of strong opposition from their environment may be all that provincial governments need in order to thrive and grow. The significant question, after all, is the survival of provincial governments, not of provincial societies, and it is not self-evident that the existence and support of the latter is necessary to the functioning and aggrandisement of the former. Their sources of survival, renewal, and vitality may well lie within themselves and in their capacity to mould their environment in accordance with their own governmental purposes.

In the analysis of contemporary party systems much has been made of the extent to which today's parties represent the historic residue of the cleavages of yesteryear. In the Canadian case the freezing of party alternatives fades into insignificance compared with the freezing by the federal system of initially five and now eleven constitutionally distinct and separate governments. The enduring stability of these governments contrasts sharply with the fluctuating fortunes of all parties and the disappearance of many. Governments, as persisting constellations of interests, constitute the permanent elements of the Canadian polity which, thus far, have ridden out the storms of social, economic, and political change.

The decision to establish a federal system in 1867 was a first-order macro decision concerning the basic institutional features of the new polity. It created competitive political and bureaucratic elites at two levels of government endowed with an impressive array of jurisdictional, financial, administrative, and political resources to deploy in the pursuit of their objectives. The post-Confederation history of Canadian federalism is little more than the record of the efforts of governing elites to pyramid their resources, and of the uses to which they have put them. Possessed of tenacious instincts for their own preservation and growth, the governments of Canadian federalism have endowed the cleavages between provinces, and between provinces and nation which attended their birth, with an ever more comprehensive political meaning.

The crucial, minimum prerequisites for provincial survival and growth have been the preservation of jurisdictional competence, and of territorial integrity. In terms of the former, it is notable that explicit change in the constitutional responsibilities of the two levels of government has been minimal, in spite of strong centralizing pressure on occasion. The division of powers has been altered to federal advantage only three times, in each of which unanimous provincial consent was obtained, and in two of which provincial paramountcy was respected. Provincial pressure has ensured the *de facto* acceptance of the principle that the concurrence of all provincial governments is necessary for any amendment which would reduce their formal constitutional authority. Even in their periods of greatest weakness provincial governments steadfastly resisted and thwarted all efforts to accord explicit constitutional recognition to a more flexible amendment procedure dealing with the division of powers. By their self-interested obstinacy they preserved their basic bargaining power for the future, and formally protected the jurisdictional integrity essential for subsequent increases in their governmental potency. ...

A federal system of governments, supported by parties and pressure groups which parallel the governmental structure, and infused with conflicting federal and provincial visions of economy and society held by competing political and bureaucratic elites, requires a language of political debate appropriate to its fundamental political concerns. Hence, the dominant political language since Confederation has been geared to the making of claims and counterclaims by the federal and provincial spokesmen for territorially-defined societies. In an indirect way, and with the passage of time, the federal language of political discourse became a vehicle for the standard normative controversies which concern modern political systems, questions dealing with equality, the socioeconomic rights of citizens, and social justice. Inevitably, however, the pressure of existing language contributed to the clothing of new controversies in federal garments and their emergence in claims on behalf of provincial communities and governments, or charter members, or founding races, or the national interest as defined by Ottawa.

Clearly, the political language of federalism, and the federal political system with which it is intertwined, have encouraged a politics in which provincial particularisms have been accorded special prominence. Provincial governments as the claimants for, and recipients of federal bounty, have acted as surrogates for the communities they govern. In the dialectical process of federal provincial controversies, the claims of provincial governments encounter the rival claims of the central government with its constitutional authority to speak for all Canadians, for the national community stretching from Bonavista to Vancouver Island. The political incentives for the federal government to couch its claims in the language of individual citizen rights and obligations engender a direct conflict with provincial claims on behalf of territorially-based communities, the reconciliation of which is worked out in the federal process.

Formerly, many of these conflicts derived sustenance from specific clauses in the British North America Act, from the terms of admission of individual provinces to the federal system, or from certain alleged intentions of the Fathers relating to the rights of particular provinces or communities. The resultant language of political debate was fundamentally stabilizing in its emphasis on rights and claims which presupposed continuing membership in an ongoing political system. Under the impact of the constitutional crisis of the past two decades, essentially precipitated by the changed objectives of Quebec political elites, and the concomitant allocation of the political decisions of 1867 to a distant and irrelevant past, the language of political debate has undergone a dramatic change. The historic, rooted language of the various versions of the compact theory has virtually disappeared, as have other backward-looking justifications which appealed to a common past. They have been replaced by a confusion of newly-developing political languages, more nakedly power-seeking, which reflect the ambitions of some political elites to refashion their position, inside or outside the federal system, as the past fades into insignificance, and the induced obligation for other elites to respond in kind. In Quebec the forward-looking language of national self-determination has replaced the traditional elite emphasis on prescriptive rights derived from history and the constitution. The new attitude was graphically expressed by Claude Morin when he was deputy minister of federal–provincial affairs in the Lesage government. "Quebec's motto is: We're through fooling around! It seems ridiculous to me to invoke the Constitution. It is like invoking St. Thomas."[68]

The destruction of a customary historical language was accelerated by the recent process of constitutional review which downgraded the Canadian constitutional heritage and promised new beginnings which it failed to deliver. The present language situation is clearly in flux as disputants talk past each other, rather than to each other. No new linguistic paradigm in which debate can be couched has emerged. Linguistic instability and federal instability reinforce each other.

The political language of federalism, a language for the conducting of political competition and cooperation between territorially-based groups and their governments, is necessarily hostile to the nation-wide politics of class. The politics and language of class assume that the conditioning effects of capitalism have washed out identities and political perspectives based on socialization into provincial frames of reference. This has not yet happened. In spite of the auspicious depression circumstances of its birth, its early antipathy to the provinces, and its long-standing attempts to create a new politics and language of class at the national level, the CCF and its successor the NDP have made only minor dents in the nonclass language of federalism.

For nearly half a century left-wing academic analysis has stressed the allegedly inexorable logic of capitalist development in producing class polarization and a modern class-based politics, described as "creative politics" by its more recent exponents. Indeed, by constant repetition this perspective has become the time-honoured traditional language of a dissenting minority which updates the old arguments and the standard predictions decade after decade. Elections and surveys have been carefully monitored since the thirties in numerous attempts to detect the always imminent emergent trend of class mobilization and polarization, the assumed hallmarks of a maturing economy. The failure of reality to conform to the canons of this version of social science has evoked fulminations against federalism, and an adroit use of the concept of false consciousness. These have had minimal impact on the nonclass world view of elites and masses involved in the political world of federalism. The political language of territorially-based group competition derived from the federal system, and socialized into the consciousness of political actors since Confederation, has prevailed over the twentieth-century challenge from the weakly-developed language of class based on the economy. ...

By implication this paper has suggested that to look at the literature of Canadian federalism historically makes clear how much has been a response to particular climates of academic and intellectual opinion, how much has been characterized by an anti-federalist mentality, and how the wish has too frequently fathered the thought. Studies of Canadian politics have suffered from a disciplinary mobilization of bias which grossly underestimates the autonomy of elites, the weight of government, and the moulding effect of institutions on political behaviour. A form of sociological reductionism common to North American political scientists has stressed society at the expense of the polity and either devalued, ignored, or denied an autonomous role for government. Democratic assumptions have elicited analyses which focus on the popular impact on government and neglect the reverse. Egalitarianism has had similar effects by undervaluing and underweighting the extent, significance, and unavoidability of elite discretion. Further, the search for class politics has entailed a stress on elections, an excessive interest in parties, and a deflection of attention from the overriding reality of government.

Developments in comparative politics have played a part in our miseducation. The evanescence and crumbling of political systems in the post-independence states of the Third World have contributed to a brutal awareness of the fragility of political structures incompatible with the historic social systems they confront. The study of the latter and their impact on the polity has elicited a strong sociological thrust in Third-World studies. However, the sociological perspective appropriately applied to the "soft states" of Africa, Asia, and Latin America has been uncritically and inappropriately extended to the study of the highly-institutionalized political systems of the western world. Finally, the weakly-developed idea of the state in the English-speaking world has reduced the visibility of government, and, no doubt, contributed to the academic underestimation of its central political role. Accordingly, the enterprise of assessing the creative, formative, and coercive capacities of government, authority, and institutions requires us to overcome the biases of sociological reductionism, democratic mythology, egalitarian levelling, incorrect Third-World analogies, and the disciplinary errors to which they contribute. Success in the enterprise will provide much-needed understanding of "the reality of structures, the extent of their 'grip' over society, and the true importance of constitutions in shaping behaviour."

Notes

1. *Federalism and Constitutional Change* (Oxford: Clarendon Press, 1956), 4.

2. The title of a famous 1939 article by Harold J. Laski, reprinted in A.N. Christensen and E.M. Kirkpatrick (eds.), *The People, Politics, and the Politician* (New York: Holt, 1941).

5. *The Vertical Mosaic* (Toronto: University of Toronto Press, 1965), 380.

68. Cited in Donald V. Smiley, *The Canadian Political Nationality* (Toronto: Methuen, 1967), 80.

Intrastate Federalism in Canada

Donald V. Smiley and Ronald L. Watts (1985)

42

EDITORS' INTRODUCTION

Donald Smiley (1921–1990) taught political science at Queen's University (1954–55), the University of British Columbia (1959–1970), the University of Toronto (1970–1976), and York University until his death in 1990. He is considered to be one of the most distinguished specialists in constitutional politics and Canadian federalism. Ronald Watts is Principal Emeritus and Professor Emeritus of Political Studies at Queen's University. He is an internationally recognized scholar of comparative federal systems.

In this study, originally written for the Royal Commission on the Economic Union and Development Prospects for Canada in 1982, they present a discussion of different definitions of federalism, and recall that "a federal political system involves the protection of regional units in the structures and operations of the governmental systems within a sovereign state." They also look at the extent to which the Canadian federal system can accommodate any territorially based interests within its central institutions (this is known as intrastate federalism).

The Intrastate Dimension of Federalism

Students commencing the study of political science are usually instructed that there are three alternative ways of organizing governmental power in a state which is sovereign in the sense that its processes of decision making are not subject to any external legal authority. These modes are unitary federal and confederal. The last of these is uncommon in the modern world, and the student will probably learn no more than that the United States adopted this form in 1781, found it unsatisfactory, and moved to federalism under the Constitution of 1787. The alternatives generally focussed upon are therefore the unitary and federal, and the United Kingdom and the United States are the respective prototypes.

A.V. Dicey in his classic *Introduction to the Study of the Law of the Constitution*, whose first edition was published in 1885, describes the "three leading characteristics of completely developed federalism" as

> the supremacy of the constitution—the distribution among bodies with limited and co-ordinate authority of the different powers of government—the authority of the Courts to act as interpreters of the constitution.

Source: Excerpted from *Intrastate Federalism in Canada*. Toronto: University of Toronto Press, 1985. Notes omitted.

294 / ESSENTIAL READINGS

Dicey derives this juristic definition of federalism from the American experience. In somewhat similar fashion, K.C. Wheare more recently enunciates "the federal principle" as

> the method of dividing powers so that the general and regional governments are each, within a sphere, co-ordinate and independent.

The Dicey-Wheare definition of federalism has rightly been faulted by contemporary scholars for giving undue emphasis to the mutual independence of the central and regional authorities within the spheres of jurisdiction allocated to them by the constitution. It has been additionally criticized for neglecting the interdependence of these governments and the complex pattern of intergovernmental relations that are so prominent in all existing federations. Although the United States is often regarded as the prototype of federations, the research of Daniel Elazar and the late Morton Grodzins has shown that, from the very early days of the Republic onward, there developed an intricate pattern of cooperative interactions between the national and state governments. Apart from the research of Christopher Armstrong and H.V. Nelles on federal-Ontario relations, there has been little systematic investigation of the relations between Ottawa and the provinces prior to the 1930s, although it is perhaps possible that such investigation may turn up evidence similar to that of Elazar and Grodzins. At any rate, students of contemporary federations are very much aware of the intricate pattern of relations between governments as they attempt to cope with the circumstances of their mutual interdependence. At times, this preoccupation with intergovernmental relations, with what Canadians have come to call "executive federalism," has come almost completely to displace the former emphasis on the juristic elements of federal systems. One recent book, for example, on United States government, entitled *Pragmatic Federalism*, is organized around six pairs of intergovernmental relations.

Yet even an approach which goes beyond the Dicey-Wheare formulation to take into account the interactions among governments in contemporary federations makes us oblivious to a very crucial dimension of the federal experience. This dimension is the way in which regional interests and values are provided for in the structures and operations of the central governments of federations. In a recent book, Preston King emphasizes this element and writes:

> We propose that any federation be regarded as an institutional arrangement, taking the form of a sovereign state, and distinguished from other such states solely by the fact that its central government incorporates regional units into its decision procedure on some constitutionally entrenched basis.

King's definition of the distinctive character of federations as the constitutional entrenchment of regional power at the centre is a valuable corrective to formulations which exclusively or almost exclusively focus on the division of powers between the national and the state/provincial/cantonal governments and the relations between these governments. Significantly, in the founding of the American, Canadian and Australian federations, it was not the constitutional distribution of powers which proved to be the most intractable issue but rather conflicts between larger and smaller constituent units about the composition and power of the second chamber of the national legislature. The "Connecticut Compromise" as reported to the Philadelphia convention on July 5, 1787, is generally believed to have saved that convention from failure. This compromise, involving a bicameral solution, reconciled the conflicting demands for representation according to population and for equality of state representation in Congress. This provided that states would be allowed one member in the lower house for each 40,000 inhabitants, that all bills for the revising or appropriating of public money would originate in the lower house and not be subject to amendment by the upper chamber, and that each state would have an equal number of representatives in the upper house whose members could be elected by the legislatures of the states. At the Quebec Conference of 1864, the British North American politicians gave over six of the fourteen days devoted to the discussion of the Confederation scheme to consideration of the composition of the second chamber with *their* version of the Connecticut Conference—namely, equal representation of Ontario, Quebec and the Maritime provinces in the Senate. In the events leading up to the foundation of the Commonwealth of Australia, it was early decided that the upper house should be directly elected by residents of the states and that each state should have the same number of members; but the most intractable issue that emerged was one relating to the powers of the Senate to amend financial legislation. R.L. Watts writes more generally:

> Because control of the central legislature is a major element in the control of central power, the organization of the central legislature has proved a contentious issue during the creation of every federation.

Other institutional elements besides the second chamber of the national legislature have served to protect the interests of regions in the operations of the central governments of federations. In an article published in 1955, Herbert Wechsler analyzed "the political safeguards of federalism" in terms of the roles of the American states in the procedures by which members of the national government were chosen. Subject to certain constitutional provisions, the state legislatures controlled the qualifications of voters in national elections and also, within certain judicially determined guidelines, the delineation of the boundaries of congressional districts. Presidential electors were appointed by the states in the manner determined by their respective legislatures, and these legislatures also controlled the procedures for nominating party candidates for national office. Wechsler argued that these political safeguards have been more important in protecting the states against intrusive national action than the activities of the Supreme Court in invalidating manifestations of Washington's power. In the Canadian case, the decisions made by the British North American politicians at the Westminster Conference of 1866 about the size and composition of the Dominion cabinet were an essential element of the Confederation settlement.

According to those decisions, there was to be a single prime minister rather than, as in the United Provinces of Canada, two political heads of government. In the first cabinet, Ontario was to have five members including the prime minister, Quebec four, and Nova Scotia and New Brunswick two each. Regional representation in the federal cabinet was from the first and continues to be an important device for sensitizing the government of Canada to regional interests, values and grievances.

A federal political system involves the protection of regional units in the structures and operations of the governmental systems within a sovereign state. Such protection may be either of the governmental authorities of the provinces/states/cantons or of the people who reside within the territorial boundaries of those sub-national jurisdictions. There are two sets of choices.

First, there is the distribution of authority between the general and regional governments whereby jurisdiction, with respect to those matters about which the regional units differ most markedly or which they insist are essential to preserving their distinctiveness, is conferred by the constitution on the states or provinces. In this study, we designate the distribution of powers and financial resources between the federal and provincial governments as well as the relations between those two orders of government as "interstate federalism."

Secondly, there are arrangements by which the interests of regional units—the interests either of the government or of the residents of these units—are channelled through and protected by the structures and operations of the central government. We call this "intrastate federalism."

The founding and subsequent experience of federations is characterized by a complex relation between interstate and intrastate elements. Thus we view interstate and intrastate strategies as partly complementary and partly contradictory and, because of this aspect of complementarity, we reject both the interstate definitions of Dicey and Wheare and the intrastate definition of King as being the exclusive differentiating characteristics of federal political systems. ...

Intrastate Federalism in Canada: Critiques and General Perspectives

There is a consensus among students of Canadian affairs that there are fundamental deficiencies in the structures and processes of governmental decision making, particularly as these relate to economic matters. This consensus is reflected in the mandate given to this Royal Commission. ...

Although there is consensus that the Canadian system of governmental decision making is inadequate, there is no agreement on the precise nature of those deficiencies or the desirable and possible ways to overcome them. A number of generalizations can be made about this system.

First, in comparison with other western democracies, the institutional infrastructure for aggregating and articulating interests both governmental and non-governmental is weak and fragmented. Canada is the least likely candidate for corporatism, if corporatism is defined as a regime in which representatives of government, business, labour and agriculture collaborate in the making of macroeconomic decisions. The fact is, each of these "estates" is fragmented: that of government between federal and provincial jurisdictions; the private business sector among domestic and foreign-controlled industries, manufacturing and resource development, importers and exporters, large and small business, and so on; and the labour union movement between national and international unions, French-speaking and English-speaking groups of unions. In response to this fragmentation in the non-governmental sector, the federal authorities have from time to time given financial and organizational support to private groups: native peoples, consumers, women associations in the cultural and athletic fields, and so on. However, with respect to fundamental economic choices, there is a relative absence of institutions for gathering together and articulating these interests.

Secondly, Canadian political parties by and large play a very restricted role in committing government decision makers to particular policies. The lack of ideological distinction between the two major national parties denies the voters the opportunity to make choices related to fundamental directions of policy in general elections. Unlike their counterparts in many other western democracies, the extra-parliamentary elements of the Liberal and Progressive Conservative parties are not decisively involved in policy formulation, and their research capabilities are very much underdeveloped. This gives the parliamentary leaders of the parties almost unfettered discretion in committing those parties—and when in office, the government—to particular policies. Consequently, Canadian voters are denied the opportunity to choose among distinct complexes of policy alternatives in general elections. It is not true of course that the Liberal and Progressive Conservative parties are non-ideological; rather they are not in a significant sense ideologically distinct from one another. The ongoing organizational separation of the national parties and their provincial wings means that the parties as such have negligible capacity for effecting federal–provincial harmonization in policy matters.

Thirdly, the federal and provincial governments are locked into an unending struggle for jurisdiction and money which extends to an ever-increasing number of areas of public policy. The phenomenon is well recognized among observers of Canadian affairs and requires no further comment. The intergovernmental struggle has crucial consequences for the articulation of non-governmental interests. There is a very fragmentary structure for the aggregation of spatially delineated interests not coincident with the boundaries of provinces, for example, for urban agglomerations and for transprovincial and sub-provincial regions. Richard Simeon also demonstrates that, when certain matters get into the arena of federal–provincial negotiation, non-governmental interests tend to be locked out.

Intrastate reformers are concerned with a particular kind of institutional deficiency, the perceived failure of the institutions of the central government to be representative of and responsive to regional interests and values.

One of the basic tenets of intrastate thinking, particularly in its centralist variant, is that the federal government is weak and that the weakness is overwhelmingly attributable to its lack of regional representatives. …

A federal government determined to exercise all the legal powers it possessed could find the jurisdiction to do what none of its peacetime predecessors has done through reservation and disallowance, the declaratory power, the aggressive use of the spending power, the extension of jurisdiction over the criminal law in respect to economic regulation, the exercise of peacetime emergency powers in economic matters, and so on. The fact that recent governments have not used their constitutional powers in effect to destroy federalism does not demonstrate Ottawa's weakness. …

The existing circumstances of federal–provincial conflict are not primarily a reflection of the unrepresentativeness of federal institutions. Rather, this is a manifestation of the clash of interests between two orders of government with both the will and the capacity to press their interests against each other. Increasingly, too, this struggle is waged with reference to conflicting premises about what kind of political community Canada is and should be. Various kinds of intrastate reform would alter the relative strength of the combatants and change the arenas in which the combatants meet. Yet it is unrealistic to expect, as does the McCormick-Manning-Gibson report, that such reforms would radically reduce the level of federal–provincial conflict and replace this with "a regionally sensitive national consensus" on major federal policies.

In general, then, intrastate thinking has exaggerated the influence of the regional unrepresentativeness of central institutions in determining the federal–provincial balance as well as the capacity of intrastate reforms to shape a new balance. Further, intrastate analysts have neglected the executive side of the federal government and concentrated on reforms of the second chamber, the electoral system, the House of Commons and the Supreme Court of Canada. On this basis, we argue later in this study that, if the federal apparatus is to be made more responsive to regional interests and values, there will have to be changes in the structure and operation of federal executive power.

Strengthening Central Decision Making

There is an elemental problem in the Canadian constitutional and government order. This problem relates to the difficulty if not the impossibility of reconciling the majoritarian dispositions of the Westminster model of parliamentary responsible government with the pluralistic and anti-majoritarian impulses that—in Canada as elsewhere—made federalism necessary in the first place and sustain federalism today.

Federal government concerns the protection and articulation of spatially delineated values and interests within a more comprehensive political community. For this protection, there are two possible strategies. The first is that of interstate federalism, which confers on the states or provinces the constitutionally protected jurisdiction over matters which members of some or all of the constituent communities believe to be most crucial to their welfare and survival. The second, the intrastate strategy, provides for the protection of these territorial particularisms within the structure and operations of the central government itself. The formation and subsequent development of federations indicate that generally these strategies have been considered complementary rather than contradictory. …

In the past 20 years or so, two broad developments have occurred to alter the interstate-intrastate blend adopted at Confederation, which subsequently gave the federal system a relatively high degree of stability and popular legitimacy. On the interstate side, there has been a breakdown in the division of powers and responsibilities specified by the constitution and subject to the ongoing process of judicial review. In retrospect, the Fathers of Confederation appear to have been somewhat naive in their general belief that there was a clear-cut and easily recognizable distinction between those matters which were national and those which were in the parlance of the day "local." In recent decades, the federal authorities have through various devices and strategies involved themselves in a very large number of activities which were within the scope of provincial legislative jurisdiction. And increasingly, the provincial governments have asserted their right to influence policies which are within Ottawa's jurisdiction, according to the constitution as judicially interpreted. No longer does the constitutional distribution of powers, as subject to ongoing delineation by the courts, separate out the functions of government between two relatively autonomous orders.

On the intrastate side, we argue that major national institutions—the executive, the House of Commons, the Senate and the political parties—have been relatively ineffective in assembling and speaking out on specifically regional interest. With respect to two of the national institutions where regional advocacy is most effective—the cabinet and the parliamentary caucuses of the parties—such advocacy for the most part takes place within a context of secrecy. This makes the central political system appear less responsive to regional interests and values than in fact it is.

Federalism and Regional Alienation

43

Roger Gibbins (1998)

EDITORS' INTRODUCTION

Roger Gibbins taught political science at the University of Calgary from 1973 to 2002, and is a Senior Fellow at the Canada West Foundation, where he also held the position of president and CEO (1998–2012). A prolific author, he has published on a range of subjects including federalism, Canadian politics, constitutional reform, the West, regionalism, public policy, Aboriginal affairs, societal issues, and social change.

In this reading, he asks: to what extent do our political institutions moderate or exacerbate regional conflict and regional alienation? For him, regional communities provide the societal foundation of federalism, and resist homogenizing pressures from the national community. They can protect themselves through interstate federalism—that is, the constitutional division of powers, the participation of provincial governments in national politics, and the leadership of their premiers who can speak on behalf of their provinces. On the other hand, regional influence can be exercised through intrastate federalism, within the institutions of the national government and, more particularly, within Parliament. Gibbins discusses the extent to which Parliament and other federal institutions have been sensitive to regional differences in interests, values, and beliefs.

It is important to begin with the obvious: regional differences and hence regional conflict are inevitable in a country of Canada's size and complexity. The regions—be they provinces, the northern territories, or more abstract amalgamations such as the West and Atlantic Canada—differ substantially in the economic foundations, socio-demographic composition, and political cultures. Therefore regionalism—the intrusion of territorially based interests, values, and identities into national life—is unavoidable. We can no more purge regionalism from the political system than we can purge conflict among classes or between linguistic communities; regionalism and some measure of regional conflict are facts, although by no means simple facts, of political life. However, we can and should ask to what extent our political institutions *moderate* or *exacerbate* regional conflict and regional alienation. Have those institutions been reasonably successful in handling and containing regional conflict?

Source: Excerpted from *Challenges to Canadian Federalism*, edited by Martin Westmacott and Hugh Mellon. Toronto: Prentice-Hall, 1998, 40–52. Notes omitted.

Or have they exaggerated and intensified such conflict? In short, have our political institutions been part of the solution or part of the problem?

To answer these questions we must turn to the relationship between federalism and regional alienation, a relationship that takes on a unique coloration in the Canadian experience, reflecting the particular way in which parliamentary government and federalism have been institutionally married in this country. Therefore, in order to come to grips with the manner in which Canadian federal institutions moderate and sometimes foster regional alienation, we need first to understand the more generic relationship between federalism and regionalism.

Regionalism and Federalism

...

Regional communities provide the societal foundation for federalism and for the provincial governments that in turn protect and promote regional communities in the face of homogenizing pressures from the national community. Just as regional divisions led to the adoption of federalism in the first place, the provincial governments which were thereby created go on to sustain and sometimes even to promote regional divisions in the national society. Citizens think politically in provincial terms because their lives are structured largely by provincial institutions and surrounded by provincial symbols such as drivers' licences, car plates, flags, and distinctive forms of social services. Politically, we come to see ourselves as British Columbians or New Brunswickers rather than in terms of class, ethnicity, or gender because our political institutions push us in this direction. This also means, and not incidentally, that regional communities lacking governmental structures are less significant than those that have governments to support and promote them. The "West," for example, or for that matter even the prairie West, lacks institutional or governmental structures—there are no *regional* political offices or bureaucracies, networks of social services, or elections and there is no flag, driver's licence, or car plate. The West is a "region of the mind" rather than one knit together by political institutions and public services. True, there are the Western Canada Summer Games, the annual meeting of the western premiers, and the Canada West Foundation, but these are small potatoes indeed compared with the institutional, programmatic, and symbolic resources of the region's constituent provincial governments. As a consequence, the West is a less significant factor in citizen identities and regional conflict than are the individual western provinces. The whole in this case is much less than the sum of its parts.

There is a broader point to make here, and that is that federalism recognizes and sometimes even celebrates a particular form of diversity. It is the recognition and protection of *territorial diversity* that are central to the federal creed. Thus we find in Canada today an acceptance that patterns of public policy will inevitably vary, indeed should vary, across provincial boundaries. We expect provinces to differ one from another, and would be disappointed if they did not. Social programs are molded, at least to a degree, to fit idiosyncratic provincial conditions, and economic programs are expected to reflect the nuances and needs of the provincial economy. The contemporary push for greater decentralization, the continued existence of interprovincial trade barriers, and the nationalist movement in Quebec all reflect federalism's respect for diversity, or at least for diversity that is territorially defined. At the same time, it is by no means clear that federal states are any more respecting of *non-territorial diversity* than are unity states. National minorities that are also minorities in the provinces or states: minorities such as African-Americans, aboriginal peoples in both Canada and the United States, and the gay and lesbian communities, may find that federalism per se works to their disadvantage. Certainly this was the case in the United States in the 1960s when state governments in the South sheltered policies of racial discrimination from civil rights legislation emanating from Washington, D.C.

In a more innocuous fashion, federalism may crowd out the mobilization of non-territorial forms of political identity by strengthening the centrality of regional identities in the political realm. We can only take on so many political identities at a time, and the omnipresent nature of regional identities provides stiff competition for other identities based on class, gender, ethnicity, or even ideology. Canadian socialists have often argued, for instance, that the fragmentation of social classes by provincial boundaries and the salience of regional identities have made the orchestration of class-based political action difficult. (Some, of course, might see this as one of the virtues of federalism amid the regionalism it sustains.) Only regional identities, or at least provincial identities, have governments dedicated to their maintenance. Transboundary identities, such as those associated with feminism and environmentalism, lack similar forms of governmental support. ...

Yet the constitutional division of powers alone cannot meet the integrative aspects of federalism. A critical question remains: how well are the various regional communities treated by and within the national government *in areas of federal jurisdiction*? In short, how well do they fare within the national community? If regional alienation is to be moderated and contained, regional communities must have not only protection through the constitutional division of powers; they also must have an effective voice within national political institutions. The real test here comes not from the largest of the regional communities, such as Ontario, for they have sufficient economic and electoral clout to ensure their interests are heard; formal protection within the institutions of the national government is seldom an issue. The test comes instead from the regional communities to the west of Ontario, to the east of Quebec, and, in a complex way, from Quebec itself. Do these communities feel sufficiently protected from the political weight of the national majority?

To summarize the discussion to this point: federalism provides two basic forms of protection for regional communities and the territorial diversity they are thought to embody. The first comes from the constitutional division of powers, and through the provincial governments created by that division of powers. This basket of protections is generally referred to as *interstate* federalism. The second form of protection comes from the design and operating principles of national institutions such as Parliament. Protections embedded within national institutions are generally referred to as *intrastate* federalism. A closer look at these two forms reveals some of the problems Canadians have had in dealing with regional alienation and discontent.

Interstate Federalism

The term *interstate federalism* encompasses two forms of protection that federal systems provide to regional communities. The first and most fundamental protection comes from the federal division of powers between, in the Canadian case, the national and provincial governments. This division of powers is sketched in by sections 91 to 93 of the 1867 Constitution

Act. The legislative domain of the provinces is protected from the political weight of the national majority by the division of powers, provided of course that those matters of concern to the regional community fall within the provincial legislative domain. The importance of this proviso can be seen in the different regional experiences of Quebec and the West. ...

The protection of regional interests through the constitutional division of powers never worked particularly well for western Canadians, or at least failed to do so until quite recently. The primary interests of the West, particularly in the early period of agrarian settlement, were economic rather than social or cultural. More importantly, they were not ones that could be assigned logically to the legislative domain of the provinces. For example, western Canadians in general and particularly those involved in the prairie grain economy were very concerned with international trade, interprovincial trade, interprovincial transportation, national tariff policy, regulation of the financial sector, and national fiscal policy relating to interest rates. Legislative powers in these respects could not be delegated to the provinces, and thus the central issue for western Canadians was how to achieve effective influence *within the national government*. The founding slogan of the Reform Party—"The West Wants In"—nicely captured this long-standing western Canadian quest. Interstate federalism through the constitutional division of powers was of little relevance in addressing the region's traditional basket of economic grievances. Unfortunately, and as we will discuss in a moment, intrastate federalism offered little more by way of assistance. ...

Support for interstate federalism is now enjoying growing support in western Canada. In part, this revival may simply reflect the lack of headway with respect to intrastate reform. Interstate reform may not be the preferred option, but it appears to be the only option in play, which is to say the only option acceptable to soft nationalists in Quebec who have no interest in strengthening the legitimacy of parliamentary institutions in Ottawa. However, the growth of regional support for interstate federalism also reflects the dramatic transformation that has recently taken place in the economic sphere. The implementation of the North American Free Trade Agreement (NAFTA) and the larger context of economic globalization have meant that the federal government's powers with respect to international trade and monetary policy are becoming increasingly constrained. If globalization means anything, it means that national governments are less able to shield their economies from international market forces. As a consequence, regional power at the centre becomes less important as the national government's power to shape the economy diminishes. Thus, as control over tariffs international trade, monetary policy, and investment drifts more and more to international agreements, or drifts out of the hands of governments altogether and into the hands of markets, decentralization and interstate federalism make more sense. Here we see, then, a potential convergence between western Canadian visions of the federal state and nationalist sentiment in Quebec. Both favour decentralization, although by no means to the same degree or with the same ends in mind.

As mentioned above, a second and important interstate line of regional defence comes through the participation of provincial governments in national politics. Of particular note here is the role played by provincial premiers. This role has been enhanced by the constraints that party discipline places on intrastate representation by MPs (discussed below), and by the fact that senators are not taken seriously as regional representatives. Although MPs and even senators may be effective advocates for regional interests behind the closed doors of caucus and cabinet, they are not *seen* to be effective. As a consequence, premiers often have the stage to themselves when it comes to vigorously defending regional interests *in the public forum.*

The premiers' federal role is strengthened by the nature of parliamentary governments, which concentrates political power in the hands of the executive, and more specifically, in the hands of premiers and prime ministers. Because premiers control their cabinets, and because cabinets seldom face any effective challenge from provincial legislatures, the premiers can speak with authority on behalf of their province on the national stage. They can wheel and deal with other premiers, and with the federal governments, and can do so with the confident expectation that any agreement they might conclude will be supported by their cabinet and, if necessary, ratified by the provincial legislature. This expectation is not always met, as the Meech Lake debacle showed. However, Meech was truly an exception to the general rule that premiers, and for that matter the prime minister, command the loyalty of their cabinet and caucus, and therefore encounter few if any significant legislative constraints. This combination of *federal division* of legislative powers and the *parliamentary concentration* of legislative powers has produced a unique brand of executive interstate federalism, a brand epitomized by the first minsters' conference.

Intrastate Federalism and Parliamentary Government

The intrastate routes of regional influence are to be found *within* the institutions of the national government, and particularly within Parliament. It is, therefore, the representative performance of MPs and senators that is of particular importance; although the methods by which justices are appointed to the Supreme Court has also been a matter of debate, the representative *behaviour* of those justices has been less at issue. The general argument that has emerged in the Canadian political science community, especially among political scientists in western Canada, is that intrastate federalism often works poorly, and that in this respect parliamentary institutions are maladapted for the regional nature of the country. In short, parliamentary institutions do more to cause regional alienation than to resolve it. ...

The central, defining role of party discipline in the Canadian House of Commons has had important repercussions for regional representation. If, for example a western Canadian MP on the government side of the House disagrees with a cabinet decision, if he or she concludes that its regional impact is unwarranted, the MP can only voice that disagreement behind the closed doors of cabinet or caucus. Within the House itself, the MP has no alternative but to toe the party line. As a result, voters back home have no evidence that their MP understands their concerns or has spoken out on their behalf. Instead, they see their elected representative faithfully following a party line that might well reflect the regional interests of central Canada rather than their own. A House divided on party lines, and operating according to strict party discipline, has difficulty providing for the public expression of regional differences and regional discontent.

The House, of course, was not designed to be a *federal* institution, although it does accommodate federalism at the margins. For example, smaller provinces tend to have more seats in the House than they would be entitled to by population alone. Nova Scotia has one more, New Brunswick two, Prince Edward Island three, Saskatchewan three, and Manitoba two. The northern territories have three seats in the House, although their total population amounts to less than that for a single riding in southern Canada. However, these departures from strict representation by population have not been the subject of serious critical debate in Canada. …

The cabinet, which is drawn almost exclusively from the House, is considered to be the most important *federal* institution in Parliament. Generally, all provinces are represented within the cabinet, provided there are elected MPs from each province on the government side of the House. When there are not, senators are sometimes appointed to the cabinet to fill in the provincial holes. The cabinet, therefore, is chosen to look like a territorial microcosm of the national population; all provinces are in, the larger provinces have greater cabinet representation than do the smaller provinces, and even regions within the larger provinces are represented. …

Frustration with the public face of regional representation in the House and cabinet has frequently been mobilized by western Canadian protest parties. In the early 1920s, much of the electoral appeal of the Progressive Party of Canada stemmed from the Progressives' adamant opposition to party discipline, and to what they saw as the nefarious influence of political parties broadly defined. More recently, the Reform Party has campaigned on the need to relax party discipline, and to make MPs more accountable to their constituencies and less accountable to their party. However, none of this protest has had any effect; party discipline in the House and secrecy in cabinet are as strict today, if not stricter, than they have ever been. While loosening party discipline in order to provide more effective, or at least more visible, regional representation in the House has long been a staple of opposition rhetoric, it has never been of any appeal to governing parties even at times when regional alienation has been a matter of acute concern, as it was in the late 1970s and early 1980s.

Given that the House is designed only at the margins to reflect federal principles, and that regional representation within cabinet takes place behind closed doors, the Senate assumes great *potential* importance as a federal institution. It was in the Senate that the 1867 marriage of parliamentary government and federalism was to be consummated. In the initial design of the Senate, furthermore, Canadians were not constrained by British institutional precedence. We could not have replicated the British House of Lords even if we had wanted to do so because Canada lacked a landed aristocracy, and therefore we were able to use the Senate as a federal body to represent the regional communities. In this instance, and in this instance alone, we opted for American rather than British precedence. Unfortunately, from the outset the Senate was badly designed as a federal chamber, and it only got worse with time. Equal representation of the provinces (the American model, and subsequently the Australian model) was rejected in favour of regional equality for the Maritimes, Quebec, and Ontario. …

It should be stressed that the distribution of Senate seats has been the subject of less critical commentary than has been the method by which senators are selected. Senators are appointed rather than elected, and therefore their legitimacy as regional representatives has been fatally eroded in a mature, democratic society. Perhaps worst of all, senators, who are supposedly regional representatives, are appointed not by the provincial governments but by the federal government. Thus, in virtually all respects, the Senate fails as a *federal* institution. …

Looking Ahead

As we noted at the outset … regional differences in interests, values, and beliefs are inevitable in a country of Canada's size and complexity. So too are regional identities, conflicts, and alienation. It would be unrealistic to hope that regionalism could be banished from Canadian political life, and indeed our political life would be poorer as a consequence. Rather, the central question to ask is whether Canadian political institutions do a reasonable job in maintaining the federal balance between the protection of regional interests and the promotion of national integration. Is the level of regional alienation in *political life* greater than we should expect given the territorial diversity of Canadian life?

If an answer is to be found, it is to be found in the nature of federal institutions. In trying to address the regional dimensions of political life, Canadians have relied upon federalism as the master solution. More specifically, they have relied upon the federal division of powers, the active participation of provincial governments in national politics, and the representation of regional interests within the institutions of the national government. Of these three solutions, the third has clearly been the least successful, and weakness in this respect has contributed to a growing emphasis on interstate federalism. This shift from the search for intrastate reforms to a reliance on interstate federalism is reinforced by the nationalist movement in Quebec, which is emphatically interstate in its orientation to the Canadian federal state.

In the years ahead, the growth of interstate federalism should ensure that one side of the federal challenge, the protection of territorial diversity, is met. If there is less and less that Ottawa can do, then there is less and less harm it can inflict on regional interests. What remains to be seen is whether the other side, the promotion of national integration, will also be met. Here there may be greater cause for concern as the Canadian federal state enters the twenty-first century.

44 The Dynamics of Canadian Federalism

Richard Simeon and Ian Robinson
(2004)

EDITORS' INTRODUCTION

Richard Simeon (1943–2013) taught political studies at Queen's University (1968–1991) where he also served as director of the Institute of Intergovernmental Relations (1976–1983), and joined the University of Toronto in 1991 as a professor of political science and law. From 1983 to 1985, he was a research coordinator (institutions) for the Royal Commission on the Economic Union and Canada's Development Prospects (the Macdonald Commission). He also served with several government of Ontario advisory groups. His interests have focused on comparative and Canadian federalism, public policy, and decentralized governance. Ian Robinson teaches at the Residential College, University of Michigan in Ann Arbor. He works on issues related to labour and globalization, with a particular focus on North America.

In 1990, Simeon and Robinson published State, Society and the Development of Canadian Federalism. *In this earlier book, in which they first present the themes of the 2004 essay excerpted below, they explore several meanings of federalism and present a number of models to explain how the Canadian federal system works, and how it changes over time. They conclude that federalism should be understood as a process, rather than a steady state.*

Introduction

Federalism is the most visible and distinctive element in Canadian political life. More than in most other advanced industrial countries, our politics have been conducted in terms of the conflicts between regional and language groups and the struggles between federal and provincial governments. Many of our most important political issues—from the building of the postwar welfare state to the energy wars in the 1970s to the constitutional wars of the 1980s and 1990s to the crisis in health care in this decade—have been fought in the arena of federal–provincial relations and shaped by the institutions of the federal system. The very structure of Canadian federalism, with its ebb and flow of power between federal and provincial governments, has been at the heart of our political debates. Indeed, for many observers, what makes Canada distinct is the highly decentralized character of its federal system.

We can think of federalism in several ways. Federalism refers, first, to a particular set of governing institutions (the classic definition comes from Wheare 1964). It is a system in

Source: Excerpted from *Canadian Politics*, 4th edition, edited by James Bickerton and Alain-G. Gagnon. Peterborough, ON: Broadview Press, 2004. Reprinted by permission.

which political authority is divided between two or more constitutionally distinct orders or levels of government. Each has a set of constitutional powers; each has an independent base of political legitimacy in the electorate. In Canada, we talk of federal and provincial governments. Municipal governments are also important in the lives of Canadians, but they do not have independent constitutional status. On the other hand, Aboriginal governments may one day constitute a "Third Order of Government," parallel to federal and provincial governments (Royal Commission on Aboriginal Peoples 1993).

Several other elements are central to the design of federal institutions (Watts 1996). There is the *constitution*, which sets out *the division of powers* and the relationships among the governments. In the Canadian context, there has been increasing debate about whether it is necessary for all provinces to have identical powers ("symmetrical federalism") or whether powers can either formally or informally vary according to the needs and characteristics of individual provinces, as in the case of Quebec ("asymmetrical federalism") (Smiley and Watts 1985). Most federal constitutions also create a Supreme Court, one of whose central purposes is to act as umpire between levels of government, and an *amending formula* establishing procedures for altering the division of powers. Since one of the central characteristics of all federal systems is the wide range of shared and overlapping responsibilities ("*interdependence*"), federal institutions also include a set *of mechanisms of intergovernmental relations* (first ministers' conferences and the like) through which the governments deal with each other. Associated with these mechanisms is a complicated set *of fiscal arrangements*, dividing up the revenue pie, financing shared responsibilities, and assisting the poorer provinces through equalization payments. Almost unique among federal countries, Canada is largely lacking in one other institution—that is, a *second chamber* in the national Parliament explicitly designed to represent the states or provinces within central decision-making. Unlike the American Senate or the German Bundesrat, the Canadian Senate has conspicuously failed to play this role, thus forcing struggles within our federal system to be worked out in relations between governments which sometimes take on the character of international negotiations or "federal–provincial diplomacy" (Simeon 1972).

Federalism, then, is at heart an *institutional structure*. Along with Westminster-style cabinet government and, since 1982, the Charter of Rights and Freedoms, it is one of three institutional pillars of Canadian government. Each of these pillars embodies a somewhat different conception of democracy; they coexist in a dynamic tension.

Second, federalism can be seen as *a characteristic of the society*. We talk of Canada as a "federal society" (Livingston 1956). By that we mean the salience of differences that are organized and expressed largely on the basis of region or territory. Such differences may be rooted in language, history, and culture or in differences of economic interest. They interact strongly with the institutional dimension of federalism: Canada has federal institutions largely because of the initial differences in interest and identity among the founding provinces. But federal institutions, in turn, perpetuate these regional differences and reinforce Canadians' tendency to see politics in regional terms.

Third, federalism is underpinned by *multiple identities*. Citizens are members of both the national community, embodied in the national government, and of provincial communities reflected in their provincial governments. If the balance falls too far to one side, there remains little to hold the system together in the face of demands for provincial independence; if it falls too far the other way, there is little to prevent the aggrandizement of federal power and movement towards a unitary state. Federalism is thus about the coexistence of multiple loyalties and identities; it is about divided authority, "national standards" and provincial variation, "self-rule" and "shared rule," "coming together" and "coming apart." Finding the right balance between these is the trick. Much survey evidence confirms that Canadians are, indeed, federalists in this sense, valuing both their national and their provincial identities (Graves *et al.*, 1999; Cutler and Mendelsohn 2001).

Federalism is often justified as a means by which different regional/linguistic communities can live together in a single state. On the one hand, it helps preserve local communities by assuring them the opportunity to manage their own affairs through their provincial government; on the other hand, it allows them to pursue their common interests through the federal government. Federalism thus combines "*shared rule* through common institutions and *regional self rule* for the governments of constituent units" (Watts 1996: 7).

Other ideas have also been used to justify federalism. In the American political tradition, federalism is seen, along with the Bill of Rights and the separation of powers between president and legislature, as a way to check and limit excesses of governmental power. ...

In this chapter, we will talk about all three dimensions of Canadian federalism. Our focus is primarily on what drives the federal system and what accounts for the changes that we have seen over time. In this sense, for the most part we treat federalism as a *dependent variable*. What explains, for example, the relative balance of power and influence between federal and provincial governments? What explains the nature and level of conflict or disagreement among them? What accounts for the ways they manage their interdependence?

Relative to other federations, Canada is one of the most decentralized, in terms of political authority, powers, and financial resources. The relationship between governments is more often seen as an equal partnership than as a hierarchy. It is also more competitive and adversarial than in most other federations.

We can also look at federalism as an *independent variable*. Here we focus on the consequences of federalism. Does federalism make a difference? What are its effects on public policy or the structure of identities? Do some groups or interests benefit by federalism; are others weakened? How does federalism structure our party system or the role and strategies of interest groups? ...

To see federalism as an independent variable quickly shades into a third kind of question: evaluation or judgement. Does federalism contribute to the quality of Canadian democracy? To making public policy that is timely and effective? To the successful management of the diverse social groups that make up the Canadian population?

On all these dimensions, federalism seems to point in two directions. It offers the democratic virtues of government closer to the people and to local needs, but the closed nature of much intergovernmental decision-making has led many to complain of a "democratic deficit" (Simeon and Cameron 2002). It suggests effective ways to balance national and regional concerns in public policy, but again it can be criticized for slowing policy responses in areas where the responsibilities of governments overlap—the "joint decision trap" (Scharpf 1988). Finally, federalism does provide valuable tools for accommodating differences, providing regional and linguistic minorities with provincial governments they can use to pursue their own interests and resist control by the national majority. But, at the same time, federal institutions help institutionalize and perpetuate these same divisions (Simeon and Conway 2001).

Evaluative questions quickly spill over into questions about reform. Many elements of the federal system have been and remain hotly contested in Canadian politics. And the stakes have been high: at some times even the very survival of the country. Traditionally, reform efforts stressed the operation of federal structures such as fiscal arrangements, the division of powers, and the amending formula. Since the 1960s, however, the issues have become more fundamental: the place of Quebec in the federal system and whether it should have distinct status or powers; Senate reform to accommodate better in Ottawa the interests of the smaller provinces; self-government for Aboriginal peoples in the federal system; and the implications of federal arrangements for disadvantaged groups such as women and the disabled, many of whom have felt neglected by one or another aspect of federalism (Russell 1992).

Explanatory Models

Scholars have used a number of models or theories to explain how the federal system works and how it changes over time. *Societal* explanations view political institutions and policies as fundamentally shaped by the social and economic environment in which they are embedded. The "causal arrow" runs from society to the state. Within this category, there are further subdivisions. *Political economy* sees economic factors as the primary driving forces of political phenomena. There are many variants of this idea, some emphasizing international economic forces, others domestic factors (Stevenson 1977). Scholars point to such things as the economic imperatives that drove the impulse to unite in a federal system in the first place, the variations in regional economies as central sources of conflict, the impact of the Great Depression of the 1930s on the federal system, and the *need* to reshape federalism in order to build the postwar Keynesian welfare state. Contemporary exponents of these approaches stress how changes in the global political economy, especially the economic integration of North America, reshape domestic economic and political forces, including federalism (Courchene 1992).

Societal explanations also explore the social and cultural foundations of federalism, including French-English relations and the relations between the different regions and provinces. Thus, the presence of Quebec ensured that the Canadian union would be federal, and the political effects of its "Quiet Revolution" in the 1960s fuelled the debates of the 1970s and 1980s. Western alienation was exacerbated by the "energy wars" of the 1970s, leading to demands for greater provincial power and greater provincial constraints on national decision-making.

Along with these regional and linguistic divisions are other divisions in Canadian society that are not necessarily territorially concentrated. Class conflicts play an important role, as the federal system needed to respond to the policy agenda (greater recognition of trade unions, a stronger welfare state) of workers, unionists, and political parties such as the Co-operative Commonwealth Federation and the New Democratic Party (Porter 1965). More recently other identities, for example, women and ethnic Canadians, have gained greater political prominence and in so doing have mounted major challenges to the functioning of Canadian federalism, with its institutions predicated largely on territory (Cairns 1991).

All these approaches argue that the federal state is a product of underlying social forces. In recent years many writers, especially Alan Cairns (1977, 1979), have turned that model around. The causal arrow, they argue, runs the other way: the state and its leaders shape, mould, and manipulate society. What governments do is not a product simply of external pressures, but of the ambitions, skills, resources, and ideologies of the bureaucratic and political authorities who occupy formal positions. Again, there are variants of this institutional, or "state-centred," approach. Some emphasize the interests of political elites, especially their desire to preserve and enhance their own power. Public criticism of the Meech Lake Accord in 1987 and the Charlottetown Accord in 1992 as illegitimate deals concocted behind closed doors by self-serving first ministers reflected this idea. The conduct of intergovernmental relations is often criticized as being more concerned with governments protecting their turf, and winning political credit while shifting blame, than it is with the substantive issues of public policy.

A more benign institutional explanation is simply that all institutions, including federalism, enshrine their own internal logic and thus help structure political life—empowering some groups and weakening others, making some kinds of strategies successful and others unsuccessful (Simeon 1975). Thus, in Canada, federalism entrenches and institutionalizes the territorial divisions and blurs and weakens other divisions, such as class. It leads to a politics especially preoccupied with linguistic and regional conflict and with intergovernmental relations.

No single approach can possibly account for the evolution of the federal system over more than a century. We bring together elements of both societal and state-centred approaches, and we focus on the *interaction* between them. The causal arrow flows both ways. In particular we emphasize the impact of economic and social forces in setting the basic context within which federalism operates. But how these forces are channelled and expressed, and how successful they will be, is in turn greatly influenced by the federal structure and by the choices made by individual leaders.

We begin with the Confederation settlement, then trace the period from 1867 to the 1920s, showing how centralized federalism, based in part on the extension to Canada of the British colonial model, was replaced by a more province-centred and classical form of federalism. Then we look at the crises that faced Canadian federalism in the Great Depression and World War II, followed by the development of the Keynesian welfare state through *cooperative federalism*. The period from 1960 to 1982 saw the intensification of federal–provincial conflict, driven first by Quebec nationalism and later by the resurgence of provincialism, especially in the West. We call this *competitive federalism*. Following 1982, we trace the conflicting pressures on federalism engendered on the one hand by the continuing need to resolve regional and linguistic tensions and on the other by the need to respond to newly mobilized social forces, armed with the Charter of Rights and Freedoms, which challenged many aspects of federal politics. This was the period of *constitutional federalism*. Woven through these social divisions were profound economic changes, which also challenged many elements of contemporary federalism. By the late 1990s, after the failures of constitutional federalism, attention turned to alternative ways to adapt and modernize the federation and to the development of new ways for provincial and federal governments to work collaboratively on economic and social issues (Lazar 1998). We call this emerging pattern *collaborative federalism*. As we shall see, change is seldom moving in one direction, and the economic and social pressures are not always synchronized. ...

Conclusion

Federalism, it has been said, is a "process" rather than a steady state. This has been abundantly true of Canadian federalism throughout its history, as the governments and institutions that make it up have responded to changing circumstances and shifting policy agendas. We conclude with a few of the current and future challenges that the system faces.

1. *Alleviating the "democratic deficit."* How can intergovernmental relations be rendered more open and transparent to citizens? This could involve opening the process to more citizen participation or strengthening the role that parliaments and legislatures play in debating and scrutinizing the conduct of intergovernmental relations.

2. *Alleviating the "policy deficit."* Here the concerns are: how to shift federal–provincial debates from often sterile debates over turf and status to a greater concern for the substance of issues. Behind that is the question of how to find the right balance between "national standards" that will apply across the whole country, and the variations in policy that federalism is designed to encourage. And there is the further question of whether effective policy is more likely to emerge from close collaboration between governments or through more vigorous and open competition and debate between them.

   Another continuing challenge is getting the roles and responsibilities—and the financial resources to pay for them—right. Provinces have recently complained of a "fiscal imbalance," arguing that the chief areas of growing government spending lie largely in their jurisdiction, while Ottawa has more access to revenues. The solution, they say, is not in greater use of the federal spending power to act in areas of provincial jurisdiction, but to move more taxing powers to the provinces.

3. *Accommodating difference.* Many of the difficulties in reconciling East and West, French- and English-speakers in Canada lie not in federalism itself, but in larger elements of our institutional structure discussed elsewhere in this book: an ineffective Senate; an electoral system that exaggerates regional differences; a regionally fragmented party system; and a parliamentary system that is dominated by the executive, leaving little room for individual MPs to speak for their local interests. This analysis suggests that simply improving the institutions of intergovernmental relations is insufficient. With respect to Quebec, the continuing question is how much "asymmetry"—whether formal or informal—is possible or desirable in the Canadian federation.

4. *From federalism to multilevel governance.* Traditionally, Canadians have seen federalism as concerning federal and provincial governments. But Canadians are also greatly affected by two other orders of government—local or municipal government and Aboriginal governments. Local governments provide a vast array of services, yet are constitutionally subordinate to the provinces. Local governments—especially the large urban areas that are the centres of economic growth and multiculturalism—are now calling for greater recognition and authority, for greater financial resources, and for seats at the intergovernmental table. Whether, and how, they will be integrated into the Canadian pattern of multilevel governance is an important question for the future. The same is true for Aboriginal governments. The idea that they would constitute a "Third Order" of government in Canada was included in the 1993 Charlottetown Accord and was a central recommendation of the Royal Commission on Aboriginal Peoples (RCAP), but it has not been enacted. Nevertheless court decisions and political negotiations are moving towards self-government, and critical questions remain about how they will relate to both federal and provincial governments in the future.

45   The Quebec–Canada Dynamic *or* the Negation of the Ideal of Federalism

François Rocher (2009)

EDITORS' INTRODUCTION

François Rocher is a professor of political science at the University of Ottawa who specializes in Canadian and Quebec politics, federalism, citizenship and identity politics, and nationalism.

This reading outlines the different conceptions of federalism that have marked key moments of Canadian political history and reveals the manner in which federal principles have been understood or misunderstood. The aim is less to determine whether Canada has conformed to federal principles, than to examine how federalism has generally been conceived of by Canadian political and intellectual elites. He argues that the Quebec tradition of federalism has insisted on the respect of the "spirit" that preceded the foundation of the Dominion of Canada, and the principle of provincial autonomy, paying little attention to the principle of interdependence and collaboration. Conversely, federalism within English-Canadian literature is mainly presented as a formula or an arrangement relative to the exercise of power, informed by a pragmatic, managerial, and functional approach. All in all, both traditions fall short of properly embracing the complexity of the normative principles of federalism, which seek to find a balance between the notions of autonomy, heterogeneity, and non-subordination on one hand; and interdependence, solidarity, and participation on the other hand.

Canadian federalism has been analyzed from many different angles, but the literature on the subject is characterized by two particular phenomena. First, even the least attentive observer would note that the interpretation of the evolution of Canadian federalism differs greatly depending on the origin of the author. Quebec francophone scholars have, in large measure, attempted to illustrate that the spirit that marked the adoption of a federated state in Canada has been betrayed. They have accused various federal governments of using the federal spending power to interfere in provincial jurisdiction and of attempting to centralize power, most recently through the 1982 patriation of Canada's Constitution and the enactment of the Canadian Charter of Rights and Freedoms. Federal initiatives are invariably judged by these authors to be contrary to the initial division of powers. Conversely, scholars from English-speaking Canada have dealt with more pragmatic questions. Their approach to

Source: Excerpted from *Contemporary Canadian Federalism*, edited by Alan Gagnon. Toronto: University of Toronto Press, 2009, 81–131.

political institutions has been influenced by three dominant questions: (1) They have studied the links between federalism and democracy including the opportunity for citizen participation, the multiplication of political entry points, the establishment of counterweights to the respective power of each government, and the reduction of tyrannical behaviour; (2) they have explored the capacity of governments to develop public policies responsive to the needs of their citizens and have searched for the possibility of policy learning between diverse governments; and (3) English-speaking Canadian authors have focused on federalism as a way to manage Canada's diversity and reduce tensions by giving territorially concentrated minorities control of institutions that would allow them to protect and promote their distinctive traits—first Quebec and, more recently, First Nations.[1]

The second phenomenon I wish to point out about the literature on federalism in Canada is a perspective that has been *absent* from it. Generally, the analyses of Canadian federalism have been too descriptive, and federalism has been depicted first and foremost as a mode of organization and a sharing of jurisdiction. With the exception of a few authors,[2] the principles and normative dimensions of federalism are rarely discussed, at least when compared with studies on federalism's political and institutional dimensions.

Even if the analysis of the evolution of Canadian federalism has long been the subject of numerous studies,[3] the modes of representation of federalism and its ideals have not solicited much attention. Without suggesting that the idea of federalism should determine its practice, it is important to recognize that representations are crucial bases for the evaluations that we make. For example, the studies that examine the decentralized character of federalism rest on a particular conception, often implicit, of a mode of political organization that is optimal for Canada. Similarly, focusing on results and efficiency (e.g., what federalism produces by way of public policy in the areas of health care, environmental protection, human rights, skills training, education and justice) presupposes a certain conceptualization, again often implicit, not only of federalism but as well of the community in which it is embedded. This community is rarely identified because it is usually taken for granted: the general government[4] acts in the name of the Canadian nation, and the Quebec government performs the same function for the Quebec nation. …

The Evolution of the Canadian Political System or the Negation of the Federal Ideal

The interpretation of the Canadian federal regime differs greatly depending on its source. The Quebec tradition has insisted the federal system should reflect the spirit that preceded the foundation of the Dominion of Canada, but that multiple perversions and distortions have followed since this initial compact. The interpretation outside of Quebec has focused on the public policies that the federal regime has produced. This section will examine the principal elements that motivate these two interpretations, the conclusions that follow from them, and the prescriptions formulated to assure the continuance of the Canadian federation. Our attention will be focused both on the institutional aspects explored in the literature and the representation of the federal ideal on which rest value judgements concerning the origin and nature of, as well as the solutions to, the problems by which Canada is confronted.

Contemporary representations of federalism have been consistently articulated for several decades. In Quebec, the dominant understanding of federalism and federal institutions has its origins in the Tremblay Report, named for the chairman of the Quebec government's Royal Commission on Constitutional Problems, published in 1956. Since then, while evidently being adapted for particular political conjunctures, the Quebec–Canada debate has taken place almost exclusively within the argumentative framework set out in the report. Similarly the literature in English on Canadian federalism, as well as the practice of federalism by the general government, follows the argumentation advanced by the Rowell-Sirois Commission, informally so named for its co-chairmen, in the *Report of the Royal Commission on Dominion–Provincial Relations*, published in 1940.

Without reducing the complexity of the history of the Canadian federal regime to these two documents, it is clear that they have shaped the manner in which intergovernmental relations and citizens–state relations are understood in Canada. The reasoning that we find in these reports has nurtured the way in which political actors and intellectuals have understood the evolution of the Canadian federal system and have interpreted the key events, such as putting in place of the Canadian welfare state, the constitutional debate that culminated in the patriation of the Constitution of Canada, which included a Charter of Rights and Freedoms and an amending formula, the saga of the Meech and Charlottetown Accords, the creation of the North American Free Trade Agreement (NAFTA)—inspired by the recommendations of the Macdonald Commission (published in 1985)—and more generally, the diminishing role of the general government, which paralleled the increasing power of the provinces. It is my argument that the representations of federalism contained in the Rowell-Sirois and Tremblay reports, as well as the understanding that flow from these reports does not respect the ideal and normative federal project—articulated within the above triptychs—that have as their central element the twin notions of autonomy and interdependence. To summarize my central argument in a few words: the dominant understanding of the English-language literature on Canadian federalism pays no heed to the notion of autonomy but emphasizes the notion of efficiency, while Quebec francophone scholars and the practices of the Quebec government have not adequately taken into account the notion of interdependence. If the institutional problems concerning the functioning of the federal system that are raised in the literature are often pertinent, the understanding of such problems is embedded in a mode of thought that leaves little place for a federal conception of the nature of relations that should characterize a federation.

A Double Obsession: Pact and Autonomy

The work on the evolution of federalism emanating from francophone Quebec emphasizes the Canadian federal system's invariably centralizing character and desires the rehabilitation of the original federative idea.[5] This interpretation must recognize the fact that the political regime put in place in 1867 was not completely federal and, in fact, subordinated the provinces to the general government. The political regime of 1867 did not respect the principle of autonomy of the provinces; nor did it permit the provinces to participate in the decisions taken by the general government. Essentially, the above interpretation follows the principle arguments of the Tremblay Commission and adapts them to contemporary realities. The Tremblay Commission systematized the definition of both the place of Quebec within Canada and the form conditions that interprovincial and intercommunity relations should respect within the Canadian federation. ...

While the Tremblay Commission's report is almost entirely devoted to the philosophical, historical, judicial, and institutional justification of the principle of provincial autonomy—and therefore the principles of heterogeneity and non-subordination—it devotes only six pages to the matter of how the principle of interdependence should be materialized. Of course, the notion of collaboration is invoked on several occasions, but there is never a reflection on how to incorporate the concept of collaboration into federal practices. The question of the coordination of policies, which is nonetheless essential to respecting federal principles, merits only superficial consideration in the Commission's report. Paradoxically, the reasoning developed in these six pages of the report, under the pretext of the normative and institutional justification of the principle of interdependence, only contributes to reinforcing "the federalist spirit" that is summarized by the respect for autonomy.

The Tremblay Commission emphasized that within democracy the divergence of opinions is a fact and is not necessarily negative. Such divergence calls for a certain coordination of policies that should nevertheless be clearly distinguished from the policies aimed at imposing uniformity. When discussing coordination, the Tremblay Report states firmly that the general government should not be held up as the sole guarantor of the collective well-being. In a system that is both federalist and democratic, the solution to the problem of coordination of policies is not the suppression or weakening of provincial authorities but the persuasion and putting in place of common organisms that respect the dignity and liberty of provinces. While coordination does bring about certain difficulties, the disadvantages are largely compensated for by the virtues of the federal regime (such as the respect for differences). In the end, the Tremblay Report proposes the creation of permanent organisms of collaboration that would function in a true federal spirit.[6] ...

It is not surprising that the Tremblay Commission, having so strongly insisted on the first principle (autonomy), was almost completely silent with regard to the second principle (interdependence). This imbalance constitutes no less than the distortion of the federal ideal, a distortion that subsequently had a profound influence on the way political discourse was articulated around the question of the Quebec–Canada dynamic. ...

From the point of view of political institutions and the normative project of federalism, the dominant approach in Quebec is problematic in many ways. First, the emphasis on notions of pluralism, autonomy, and non-subordination is clearly disproportionate to the scant attention paid to the concept of interdependence. This imbalance was present in the work of the Tremblay Commission and has since been consistently reproduced. The desire to construct a "complete" Quebec society has privileged the expansion of the spheres of sovereignty of the Quebec state and sought disassociation from the Canadian political space. In this context, the necessity of a double loyalty within the federal space proves impossible to articulate. Although the Quebec approach is not resistant to all modifications of the sharing of jurisdiction, the constitutional preoccupations of the political elites aimed at the construction of a "complete" Quebec society and were not sympathetic to the possible need to participate in the building of Canadian political community. Instead, the Quebec political elite has rejected all "pragmatic" evolution of Canada's Constitution that would lead to the "decompartmentalization" of jurisdiction or the intervention by the general government in jurisdictions initially attributed to the provinces. ...

A Double Preoccupation: Performance and Legitimacy

The interpretation of the federal regime within English-Canadian literature emphasizes the transition from a highly centralized system, in which the general government could intervene in provincial jurisdiction using declaratory powers of reservation and disallowance, to one of the most decentralized federations in the world.[7] The narrative is generally the following: The recourse to unitary mechanisms has diminished over time to the point where the power of disallowance has not been exercised since 1943. Responding to the demands of the provinces, including Ontario, the Judicial Committee of the Privy Council (JCPC) in London rendered several decisions that contributed to the "federalization" of the Canadian political regime through the forcing of the general government to respect the original division of powers. Therefore, the authority of the provinces was confirmed and their subordination to the general government was reduced. The compartmentalization of jurisdictions imposed by the JCPC, and qualified by K.C. Wheare as constrained and rigid, limited the possible actions of the general government and prevented it from responding in an effective manner to the economic and social challenges posed by the Great Depression. However, by the middle of the 1940s, mechanisms of intergovernmental cooperation had rendered possible the construction of a welfare state; these changes and this level of cooperation were realized without having to modify the text of the constitution (the BNA Act).

Ultimately, the growth of the Canadian state made the compartmentalized model of federalism obsolete. The increase in the size of the Canadian state was accompanied by an interpretation of the federal regime that aimed less at accommodating its constitutive communities and more at a "pragmatic" approach to the sharing of jurisdictions. The increase in state interventionism was not limited to the federal government, as provinces themselves became more active in the areas of health care, education, social services and economic development. The development of state interventionism made the two orders of government compete with each other for the loyalty of their citizens.[8] Postwar federalism was characterized by a dense overlapping of jurisdictions, an interdependence of policies, and a greater level of intergovernmental competition. Thus, several mechanisms of "intergovernmental collaboration" were put into place through the increased practice of executive federalism.

In summary, federalism within English-Canadian literature is presented first, foremost, and above all as a *formula* or an *arrangement* relative to the exercise of power. Viewed through the lens of functionality, the overall evaluation of the Canadian political regime is generally positive despite the inevitable tensions it creates. ...

This pragmatic, managerial, and functional approach corresponds to what Simeon and Robinson call "modern" federalism. It traces its origins to the gradual construction of the welfare state that led to a decompartmentalization of jurisdictions. Far from realizing greater decentralization, the modernization of Canadian federalism in the postwar era was achieved through the growth of both orders of government, the overlapping of jurisdictions, and the establishment of cooperation mechanisms. While the notion of decentralization is never clearly defined, it is implicitly understood as the augmentation of the influence of provincial governments (which is measured through the growth of provincial public expenditures and bureaucracy in relation to the central government's increase in expenditures and bureaucracy) and the resistance of provincial governments to the exclusive consolidation of the authority of the general government. In this perspective, it is not important if the division of powers is respected or not. The proliferation of public policy has increased considerably the level of interdependence between the orders of government to the point where the initial division of powers is no longer referenced. Such interdependence has also limited the capacity of the general government to act unilaterally, due to the decentralization associated with the growth of state intervention and the practical obligation for the central government to take into account provincial interests: "Increasingly, the federal government found itself in the position of having to consult, coordinate and, inevitably, compromise in the face of mounting federal–provincial conflict; the declining efficacy of a federal system that increasingly required intergovernmental good will to function coherently."[9]

This mode of understanding Canadian federalism with its insistence on efficiency, transparency, legitimacy and, more specifically, the capacity to deepen democracy, is not new. Already in 1940, the Rowell–Sirois Report displayed a political discourse in which the concepts of efficiency, rationalization, (fiscal) equity between the two "orders" of government, constitutional flexibility, and national unity occupied a central place.[10] Indeed, the quest for efficiency and the rebalancing of federal–provincial relations was at the heart of the mandate of the Rowell–Sirois Commission. However, since the publication of the report, observers have noted the absence of deep reflection on the underlying principles of the Canadian federal system.[11] Nonetheless, similar to the Tremblay Commission, the Rowell–Sirois Commission played a determining role in the understanding of federalism throughout Canada. ...

What remains of the normative federal political project as defined by the literature? Honestly, very little. The principles of autonomy, non-subordination and heterogeneity are contradictory to the managerial approach that has gradually taken over since the work of the Rowell–Sirois Commission emphasized notions of efficiency, performance and formal equality in 1940.[12] Even the normative principle of interdependence, which arises from the multiple mechanisms of federal–provincial collaboration, only seeks participation as part of the quest for efficiency. In the process of federal–provincial collaboration, it is not inevitable that the most efficient solutions come from the central government. However, the dominant conviction holds that the most efficient response to problems lies in a triple combination of provincial initiatives, inter-provincial cooperation and "federal" leadership (read: Ottawa).[13] In the same manner, institutional reforms that may have long-lasting effects (reform of the electoral system, the Senate, the nomination process for judges, etc.) are solely evaluated according to democratic principles (without being combined with federal principles) and by the political stability that they will buttress or undermine.

The legitimization of the Canadian political regime does not rest in its conformity with federal principles, but instead in the connection between public policy outcomes and the needs expressed by citizens. In other words, from the point of view of the dominant approach in Canada, federal legitimacy is no longer essential to the stability of the Canadian political system. Of course, there remain those who cling to an idealist representation of the federation critiqued for its mythical and nostalgic character; they are subsequently ignored.[14]

Notes

1. Richard Simeon, "Criteria for Choice in Federal Systems," *Queen's Law Journal*, vol. 8 (1983), p. 131–151 and by the same author, *Considerations on the Design of Federations* (IIGR, Queen's University, Working Paper (2), 1998), p. 4. See as well Jennifer Smith, *Federalism* (Vancouver, UBC Press, 2004).

2. David J.Elkins, *Beyond Sovereignty: Territory and Political Economy in the Twenty-First Century* (Toronto, University of Toronto Press, 1995); Thomas O. Hueglin, *Early Modern Concepts for a Later Modern World: Althusius on Community and Federalism* (Waterloo, Ont., Wilfrid Laurier University Press, 1999) and "Federalism at the Crossroads: Old Meanings, New Significance," *Canadian Journal of Political Science*, vol. 36, no. 3 (2003), p. 275–294; Dimitrios Karmis and Wayne Norman, "The Revival of Federalism in Normative Political Theory," in D. Karmis and W. Norman, eds., *Theories of Federalism. A Reader* (New York, Palgrave Macmillan, 2005), p. 3–21.

3. Maurice Lamontagne, *Le fédéralisme canadien: évolution et problèmes* (Québec, Presses universitaires Laval, 1954); Richard Simeon et Ian Robinson, *State, Society, and the Development of Canadian Federalism* (Toronto, University of Toronto Press, 1990).

4. Throughout this text, I will use the term general state or general government in place of what most authors refer to as the federal government or the central government. The notion of federal state denotes the ensemble of the orders of government that compose a state. In the same manner, I will not use the term levels of government because it presupposes a hierarchy of governments.

5. For a representative work of this type, consult Eugénie Brouilland, *La négation de la nation. L'identité culturelle québécoise and le fédéralisme canadien* (Sillery, Éditions du Septentrion, 2005), p. 379–385; See as well Réjean Pellandier, "Constitution and fédéralisme," in Manon Tremblay, Réjean Pellandier and Marcel R. Pellandier, eds., *Le parlementarisme canadien*, 3rd édition (Québec, Presses de l'Université Laval, 2005), p. 37–79.

6. Québec (province), *Rapport de la Commission royale d'enquête sur les problèmes constitutionnels*, vol. 2 (Québec, Commission royale d'enquête sur les problèmes constitutionnels, 1956; our translation), p. 327–332.

7. Herman Bakvis and Grace Skogstad, "Canadian Federalism: Performance, Effectiveness, and Legitimacy," in Herman Bakvis and Grace Skogstad, eds., *Canadian Federalism*, p. 4–5; Ronald L. Watts, *Comparing Federal Systems*, 2nd Edition (Kingston, Institute of Intergovernmental Relations, Queen's University, 1999).

8. K.C. Wheare, 1963, p. 216–217; William S. Livingston, "Canada, Australia and the United States: Variations on a Theme," in Valerie Earle, ed., *Federalism*, p. 124–125; R. Simeon and I. Robinson, 1990.

9. R. Simeon and I. Robinson, 1990, p. 126.

10. Alain-G. Gagnon and Daniel Latouche, *Allaire, Bélanger, Campeau and les autres. Les Québécois s'interrogent sur leur avenir* (Montréal, Québec / Amérique, 1991), p. 49–50.

11. S.A. Saunders and Eleanor Back, *The Rowell–Sirois Commission. Part II. A Criticism of the Report* (Toronto, The Ryerson Press, 1940), 1–2.

12. Richard Simeon and Martin Papillon, "Canada," in Akhtar Majeed, Ronald L. Watts and Douglas M. Brown, eds., *Distribution of Powers and Responsibilities in Federal Countries. A Global Dialogue*, Vol. 2 (Montreal & Kingston, McGill-Queen's University Press, 2006), p. 114–115.

13. D. Weinstock, 2005, p. 218.

14. A. Burelle, 2005, p. 439–449.

The Judicial Committee and Its Critics

46

Alan C. Cairns (1971)

EDITORS' INTRODUCTION

In 1971, Alan Cairns, one of Canada's leading political scientists, wrote this analysis of the work of the Judicial Committee of the Privy Council (JCPC) in interpreting the Canadian Constitution. Although Privy Council appeals had been terminated in 1949 and the Supreme Court of Canada was now truly supreme, there remained a good deal of interest in assessing its performance as the judicial umpire of the Canadian federation. Cairns's penetrating analysis of the JCPC's critics, both in politics and in law, shows that they lacked a clear and coherent understanding of how judges should carry out the responsibilities of constitutional interpretation.

The interpretation of the British North America Act by the Judicial Committee of the Privy Council is one of the most contentious aspects of the constitutional evolution of Canada. As an imperial body the Privy Council was unavoidably embroiled in the struggles between imperialism and nationalism which accompanied the transformation of Empire into Commonwealth. As the final judicial authority for constitutional interpretation its decisions became material for debate in the recurrent Canadian controversy over the future of federalism. The failure of Canadians to agree on a specific formula for constitutional amendment led many critics to place a special responsibility for adjusting the BNA Act on the Privy Council, and then to castigate it for not presiding wisely over the adaptation of Canadian federalism to conditions unforeseen in 1867.

Given the context in which it operated it is not surprising that much of the literature of judicial review, especially since the depression of the thirties, transformed the Privy Council into a scapegoat for a variety of ills which afflicted the Canadian polity. In language ranging from measured criticism to vehement denunciation, from mild disagreement to bitter sarcasm, a host of critics indicated their fundamental disagreement with the Privy Council's handling of its task. Lords Watson and Haldane have been caricatured as bungling intruders who, either through malevolence, stupidity, or inefficiency channelled Canadian development away from the centralized federal system wisely intended by the Fathers.

This article will survey the controversy over the performance of the Privy Council. Several purposes will be served. One purpose, the provision of a more favourable evaluation of

Source: Excerpted from *Canadian Journal of Political Science*, vol. IV, no. 3 (September 1971). Notes omitted. Reprinted by permission.

the Privy Council's conduct, will emerge in the following discussion. This, however, is a by-product of the main purpose of this article: an assessment of the quality of Canadian jurisprudence through an examination of the most significant, continuing constitutional controversy in Canadian history. The performance of the Privy Council raised critical questions concerning the locus, style, and role of a final appeal court. An analysis of the way in which these and related questions were discussed provides important insights into Canadian jurisprudence.

Varieties of Criticism

Criticisms of the Privy Council can be roughly separated into two opposed prescriptions for the judicial role. One camp, called the constitutionalists in this essay, contained those critics who advocated a flexible, pragmatic approach so that judges could help to keep the BNA Act up to date. Another camp, called the fundamentalists, contained those who criticized the courts for not providing a technically correct, logical interpretation of a clearly worded document.

According to the fundamentalists the basic shortcoming of the Privy Council was its elementary misunderstanding of the act. The devotees of this criticism, who combined a stress on the literal meaning of the act with a widespread resort to historical materials surrounding Confederation, had four main stages in their argument. Naturally, not all critics employed the full battery of arguments possible.

1. The initial requirement was the provision of documented proof that the Fathers of Confederation intended to create a highly centralized federal system. This was done by ransacking the statements of the Fathers, particularly John A. Macdonald, and of British officials, for proof of centralist intent. Given the known desire of some Fathers for a "legislative union," or the closest approximation possible in 1867, a plethora of proof was readily assembled.

2. The next logical step was to prove that the centralization intended was clearly embodied in the act. This was done by combing the act for every indication of the exalted role assigned to Ottawa and the paltry municipal role assigned to the provinces. This task required little skill. Even the least adept could assert, with convincing examples, that the division of powers heavily favoured Ottawa. If additional proof seemed necessary the dominance of the central government could also be illustrated by referring to the provisions of the act dealing with the disallowance and reservation of provincial legislation, and with the special position of the lieutenant governor as a federal officer.

    Once concordance was proved between what the Fathers intended and what they achieved in the act the critics could then delve into a vast grab bag of pre-Confederation sources for their arguments. This greatly increased the amount of material at their disposal, and strengthened their claim that a prime reason for Privy Council failure was its unwillingness to use similar materials.

3. The third feature of this fundamentalist approach was a definition of the judicial role which required of judges no more and no less than the technically correct interpretation of the act to bring out the meaning deliberately and clearly embodied in it by

the Fathers. Where necessary the judges were to employ the methods of historical research in performing this task. ...

4. Proof that the Fathers had intended and had created a centralized federal system in the terms of the BNA Act, coupled with the transformation of the judge into a historian, provided conclusive evidence of the failure of the Judicial Committee. This was done by contrasting the centralization intended and statutorily enacted with the actual evolution of the Canadian polity towards a more classical decentralized federalism, an evolution to which the courts contributed. Since the judges were explicitly directed to apply the act literally it was obvious that they had bungled their task. As W.P.M. Kennedy phrased it, their "interpretations cannot be supported on any reasonable grounds. They are simply due to inexplicable misreadings of the *terms* of the Act." The same point was made in more polemical fashion by J.T. Thorson in a parliamentary debate on the Privy Council's treatment of the Bennett New Deal legislation:

> ... they have mutilated the constitution. They have changed it from a centralized federalism, with the residue of legislative power in the dominion parliament, to a decentralized federalism with the residue of legislative power in the provinces—contrary to the Quebec resolutions, contrary to the ideas that were in the minds of the fathers of confederation, contrary to the spirit of confederation itself, and contrary to the earlier decisions of the courts. We have Lord Haldane largely to blame for the damage that has been done to our constitution.

In summary, the fundamentalists simply asserted that the Privy Council had done a bad job in failing to follow the clearly laid out understandings of the Fathers embodied in the BNA Act. O'Connor, the author of the most influential criticism of the Privy Council, viewed their decisions as indefensible interpretations of a lucidly worded constitutional document. He felt that the act was a marvellous instrument of government, the literal interpretation of which would have been perfectly consonant with the needs of a changing society. ...

Underlying the specific criticisms of the Privy Council there was the overriding assumption that a powerful central government endowed with broad ranging legislative authority and generous financial resources was an essential requirement of modern conditions. "The complications of modern industry and of modern business," asserted W.P.M. Kennedy in 1932, "will sooner or later demand national treatment and national action in the national legislature." ...

Thus the critics, particularly the constitutionalists, were convinced that both domestic and foreign policy requirements necessitated the dominance of the central government in the federal system. Their opposition to the Privy Council on grounds of policy was backed by a growing Canadian nationalism. Even some of the early supporters of the Privy Council had recognized that in the fullness of time the elimination of appeals was inevitable. Nationalist arguments had been used by Edward Blake when the Supreme Court was established in 1875. They were later to form a staple part of John S. Ewart's long campaign for Canadian independence in the first three decades of this century. To Ewart the appeal was "one of the few remaining badges of colonialism, of subordination, of lack of self-government." A later generation of critics reiterated Ewart's thesis. In 1947 F.R. Scott stated that the continuation of appeals "perpetuates in Canada that refusal to shoulder responsibility, that willingness to let some one else make our important decisions, which is a mark of immaturity and colonialism."

The nationalist argument was incorporated in the official justifications of the Liberal government when appeals were finally abolished in 1949. ...

The nationalist attack on the Privy Council was fed by the special pride with which many Canadian writers asserted the superiority of Canadian over American federalism. The centralized variant of federalism established north of the "unguarded frontier," in reaction to the destructive effects of a decentralized federalism which the American civil war allegedly displayed, was for many critics part of the political distinctiveness of Canada which they prized. In these circumstances for a British court to reverse the intentions of the farsighted Fathers was doubly galling. This helps to explain the bitterness with which Canadian writers frequently contrasted the divergent evolutions of the American and Canadian federal systems away from their respective points of origin.

Explanations of the Judicial Committee

Critics of the Privy Council attempted to explain, as well as condemn, the results they deplored. In addition to explanations in terms of incompetence critics offered specific interpretations of the Privy Council's conduct. ... A legal explanation of the Privy Council's conduct has been given recent support by Professor Browne's attempted justification of the claim that the act was in fact properly interpreted in the light of its evident meaning.

Occasionally critics suggested that Privy Council decisions were influenced by political considerations inappropriate to a court. While the nature of these considerations was seldom made clear, the most frequent accusation was that imperial interests were best served by a weak central government. This explanation was consistent with the political bias most frequently attributed to the court, the protection and enhancement of the position of the provinces in Canadian federalism. Proof of this was found in cases favouring the provinces, or restricting federal legislation, and in the provincialist statements which these cases frequently contained. Critics also pointed to the several occasions on which the Privy Council referred to the BNA Act as a compact or a treaty. Further proof could be found in the speeches by Lord Haldane explicitly noting a protective attitude to the provinces, especially by his predecessor Lord Watson. Haldane's candid admissions are of special significance because of the propensity of Canadian critics to single out these two judges for particularly hostile treatment. Haldane stated of Watson:

> ... as the result of a long series of decisions, Lord Watson put clothing upon the bones of the Constitution, and so covered them over with living flesh that the Constitution of Canada took a new form. The provinces were recognized as of equal authority co-ordinate with the Dominion, and a long series of decisions were given by him which solved many problems and produced a new contentment in Canada with the Constitution they had got in 1867. It is difficult to say what the extent of the debt was that Canada owes to Lord Watson ...

Haldane was also explicit that a judge on the Privy Council had "to be a statesman as well as a jurist to fill in the gaps which Parliament has deliberately left in the skeleton constitutions and laws that it has provided for the British colonies." In view of these overt indications of a policy role favouring the provinces there can be no doubt that Watson and Haldane consciously fostered the provinces in Canadian federalism, and by so doing helped to transform the highly centralist structure originally created in 1867.

An alternative policy explanation deserves more extensive commentary. This was to identify the court with more or less subtlety as defenders of free enterprise against government encroachments. Spokesmen for the Canadian left, such as Woodsworth and Coldwell, were convinced that "reactionary interests have sought to shelter and to hide" behind the BNA Act. F.R. Scott asserted that the "large economic interests" who were opposed to regulation sided with the provinces who would be less capable of their effective regulation than would the federal government. The courts, as both Scott and Professor Mallory noted, responded favourably to the protection from control which business sought.

Mallory's description is apt: "The force that starts our interpretative machinery in motion is the reaction of a free economy against regulation ... In short the plea of *ultra vires* has been the defence impartially applied to both legislatures by a system of free enterprise concerned with preventing the government from regulating it in the public interest." ... The tactics of business and labour were pragmatic reflections of self-interest. A necessary consequence of a federal system is that each organized interest will seek to transform the most sympathetic level of government into the main decision-maker in matters which concern it. The evaluation to be put on these tactics, and the responses of the courts to them, however, is another matter. Regardless of the groups which align themselves with different levels of government at different times, it is far from clear that support for provincial authority is necessarily reactionary and support for federal authority necessarily progressive. ...

In brief, collectivism, in Canada as elsewhere, had to be fought out in a variety of arenas, before mass electorates, in parliaments, and in courts. In each arena there were supporters and opponents of the emerging transformation in the role of public authority. The real question is not whether courts were embroiled in the controversy, or whether some judges sided with "reactionary" forces. It would be astonishing if such were not the case.

The important questions are more difficult and/or more precise. Were the courts more or less receptive than other elite groups to collectivism? Where did they stand in the general trend to the welfare, regulatory state? What were the links between judges and courts and the various influential groups that appeared before them? How did the Privy Council compare with other final appeal courts, or with lower Canadian courts, in its response to collectivism? Research on these questions would be extremely informative in pinning down the role of courts in the transition from the night watchman state to the era of big government.

Supporters of the Judicial Committee

Depression criticism, followed in the next decade by the elimination of appeals, had the effect that the period in which the Privy Council was under strongest attack has probably had the greatest effect on contemporary attitudes to it. Some of the most influential academic literature dealing with judicial review comes from that period and its passions. As a consequence the Privy Council has typically received a very bad press in numerous influential writings by historians, political scientists, and lawyers in the past forty years.

In these circumstances, it is salutary to remember that if its critics reviled it, and turned Watson and Haldane into almost stock figures of fun, the Privy Council nevertheless did have a very broad body of support. Many highly qualified and well-informed analysts gave it almost unstinting praise. Indeed, if its critics reviled it too bitterly, its supporters praised it too generously. Often they wrote in fulsome terms, replete with awe and reverence for this most distinguished court.

It was described as "this splendid body of experts," as "one of the most unique tribunals in the world," as a body of judges which "possesses a weight and efficiency as a supreme Judicial tribunal unequalled in the history of judicial institutions ... a tribunal supremely equipped for the task—equipped for it in unexampled degree." In 1914 Sir Charles Fitzpatrick, the chief justice of Canada, claimed that "amongst lawyers and Judges competent to speak on the subject, there is but one voice, that where constitutional questions are concerned, an appeal to the Judicial Committee must be retained." ...

The defenders and supporters of the Judicial Committee typically intermingled judicial and imperial arguments. The alleged contribution of the board to uniformity of law between Britain and her colonies and dominions straddled both arguments while the general assertion that the court was a link of empire was explicitly imperial. It was also from this vantage point—that of a British citizen across the seas—that appeals were viewed and defended as a birthright, and much sentiment was employed over the right to carry one's appeals to the foot of the throne.

A reading of the eulogies of the Privy Council prior to 1930 makes it clear that its most important source of Canadian support was imperial, and only secondarily judicial. The bulk of its supporters regarded it as an instrument of empire. Rather than viewing its dominant position in the judicial structure as a symbol of Canadian inferiority, they derived pride and dignity from the empire of which it was a part. ...

Sociological Justification of the Judicial Committee

The defence of the Privy Council on grounds of its impartiality and neutrality is, however, difficult to sustain in view of the general provincial bias which ran through their decisions from the 1880s. This was the most consistent basis of criticism which the Judicial Committee encountered. A defence, therefore, must find some support for the general provincialist trend of its decisions.

It is impossible to believe that a few elderly men in London deciding two or three constitutional cases a year precipitated, sustained, and caused the development of Canada in a federalist direction the country would otherwise not have taken. It is evident that on occasion the provinces found an ally in the Privy Council, and that on balance they were aided in their struggles with the federal government. To attribute more than this to the Privy Council strains credulity. Courts are not self-starting institutions. They are called into play by groups and individuals seeking objectives which can be furthered by judicial support. A comprehensive explanation of judicial decisions, therefore, must include the actors who employed the courts for their own purposes.

The most elementary justification of the Privy Council rests on the broad sociological ground that the provincial bias which pervaded so many of its decisions was in fundamental harmony with the regional pluralism of Canada. The successful assertion of this argument requires a rebuttal of the claim of many writers that the Privy Council caused the evolution of Canadian federalism away from the centralization of 1867.

From the vantage point of a century of constitutional evolution the centralist emphasis of the Confederation settlement appears increasingly unrealistic. In 1867 it seemed desirable and necessary to many of the leading Fathers. "The colonial life had been petty and bitter and frictional, and, outside, the civil war seemed to point to the need of binding up, as closely as it was at all possible, the political aspirations of the colonies." Further, it can be argued that what appeared as overcentralization in the light of regional pluralism was necessary to establish the new polity and to allow the central government to undertake those nation-building tasks which constituted the prime reasons for union.

It is, however, far too easily overlooked, because of the idolatry with which the Fathers and their creation are often treated, that in the long run centralization was inappropriate for the regional diversities of a land of vast extent and a large, geographically concentrated, minority culture. The political leaders of Quebec, employing varying strategies, have consistently fought for provincial autonomy. The existence of Quebec alone has been sufficient to prevent Canada from following the centralist route of some other federal systems. In retrospect it is evident that only a peculiar conjuncture of circumstances, many of them to prove ephemeral, allowed the degree of central government dominance temporarily attained in 1867. ...

It would be tedious and unnecessary to provide detailed documentation of the relative appropriateness of the decisions of the Judicial Committee to subsequent centrifugal and centripetal trends in Canadian society. It can be generally said that their decisions were harmonious with those trends. Their great contribution, the injection of a decentralizing impulse into a constitutional structure too centralist for the diversity it had to contain, and the placating of Quebec which was a consequence, was a positive influence in the evolution of Canadian federalism. Had the Privy Council not leaned in that direction, argued P.E. Trudeau, "Quebec separatism might not be a threat today: it might be an accomplished fact." The courts not only responded to provincialism. The discovery and amplification of an emergency power in section 91 may have done an injustice to the intentions of Macdonald for the residuary power, but it did allow Canada to conduct herself virtually as a unitary state in the two world wars in which centralized government authority was both required and supported.

The general congruence of Privy Council decisions with the cyclical trends in Canadian federalism not only provides a qualified sociological defence of the committee but also makes it clear that the accusation of literalism so frequently levelled at its decisions is absurd. Watson and Haldane in particular overtly and deliberately enhanced provincial powers in partial defiance of the BNA Act itself. The Privy Council's solicitous regard for the provinces constituted a defensible response to trends in Canadian society. ...

The Weakness of the Judicial Committee

The Judicial Committee laboured under two fundamental weaknesses, the legal doctrine which ostensibly guided its deliberations, and its isolation from the setting to which those deliberations referred.

The basic overt doctrine of the court was to eschew considerations of policy and to analyse the BNA Act by the standard canons for the technical construction of ordinary statutes. The objection to this approach is manifold. Numerous legal writers have pointed out that the rules of statutory construction are little more than a grab bag of contradictions. It is also questionable whether a constitution should be treated as an ordinary statute, for clearly it is not. In the British political system, with which judges on the Privy Council were most acquainted, it is at least plausible to argue that the doctrine of parliamentary supremacy, and the consequent flexibility of the legislative process, provides some justification for the courts limiting their policy role and assigning to parliament the task of keeping the legislation of the state appropriate to constantly changing circumstances. The BNA Act, however, as a written constitutional document, was not subject to easy formal change by the amending process. Consequently, the premise that the transformation of the act could be left to law-making bodies in Canada, as in the United Kingdom, was invalid. A candid policy role for a final appeal court seems to be imperatively required in such conditions.

Even in the absence of this consideration it is self evident that no technical analysis of an increasingly ancient constitutional document can find answers to questions undreamt of by the Fathers. The Privy Council's basic legal doctrine was not only undesirable, therefore, it was also impossible. In reality, as already indicated, the Privy Council obliquely pursued a policy of protecting the provinces. The clear divergence between the act as written and the act as interpreted makes it impossible to believe that in practice the Privy Council viewed its role in the narrow, technical perspective of ordinary statutory construction. The problem of the court was that it was caught in an inappropriate legal tradition for its task of constitutional adjudication. It partially escaped from this dilemma by occasionally giving overt recognition to the need for a more flexible, pragmatic approach, and by covertly masking its actual policy choices behind the obfuscating language and precedents of statutory interpretations.

The covert pursuit of policy meant that the reasoning process in their decisions was often inadequate to sustain the decision reached. This also helps to explain the hypocritical and forced distinguishing of previous cases which was criticized by several authors. Further, the impossibility of overt policy discussion in decisions implied the impossibility of open policy arguments in proceedings before the court. Inevitably, the court experienced severe handicaps in its role as policy-maker. ...

The second main weakness of the Privy Council was its isolation from the scene to which its judgments applied. Its supporters argued otherwise by equating its distance from Canada with impartiality. Judges on the spot, it was implied, would be governed or influenced by the passions and emotions surrounding the controversy before them. British judges, by contrast, aloof and distant, would not be subject to the bias flowing from intimate acquaintance.

The logic of this frequently espoused position was curious. The same logic, as J.S. Ewart satirically observed, implied the desirability of sending British cases to the Supreme Court at Ottawa, but no such proposals were forthcoming. "Local information and local methods," he continued, "are very frequently essential to the understanding of a dispute. They are not disqualifications for judicial action."

The critics were surely right in their assertions that absence of local prepossessions simply meant relative ignorance, insensitivity, and misunderstanding of the Canadian scene, deficiencies which would be absent in Canadian judges. "The British North America Act," Edward Blake had asserted in 1880, "is a skeleton. The true form and proportions, the true spirit of our Constitution, can be made manifest only to the men of the soil. I deny that it can be well expounded by men whose lives have been passed, not merely in another, but in an opposite sphere of practice …" The same argument was reiterated by succeeding generations of critics until the final elimination of appeals.

The weakness flowing from isolation was exacerbated by the shifting composition of the committee which deprived its members of those benefits of experience derived from constant application to the same task. "The personnel of that Court," stated a critic in 1894, "is as shifting as the Goodwin Sands. At one sitting it may be composed of the ablest judges in the land, and at the next sitting its chief characteristic may be senility and general weakness." This instability of membership contributed to discontinuities in interpretation as membership changed. It also allowed those who sat for long periods of time, as did Watson and Haldane, to acquire disproportionate influence on Privy Council decisions. …

The single opinion of the court, while it possibly helped to sustain its authority and weaken the position of its critics, had serious negative effects. Jennings pointed out that "the absence of a minority opinion sometimes makes the opinion of the Board look more logical and more obvious than it really is. The case is stated so as to come to the conclusion already reached by the majority in private consultation. It is often only by starting again and deliberately striving to reach the opposite conclusion that we realize that … there were two ways of looking at it." The absence of dissents hindered the development of a dialogue over the quality of its judgments. Dissents provide a lever for the critic by their indication of a lack of judicial unanimity, and by their provision of specific alternatives to the decisions reached. …

The Confusion of the Critics

For the better part of a century the performance of the Judicial Committee has been a continuing subject of academic and political controversy in Canada. Even the elementary question of whether its work was basically good or fundamentally bad has elicited contrary opinions. The distribution of favourable and critical attitudes has shifted over time. From the turn of the century until the onset of the depression of the thirties informed opinion was generally favourable. Subsequently, English-Canadian appraisals became overwhelmingly critical. …

In the period up to and subsequent to the final abolition of appeals in 1949 there was a consistent tendency for opposed evaluations of the Judicial Committee to follow the French-English cleavage in Canada. This divergence of opinion was manifest in French-Canadian support for the Judicial Committee, with opposition on grounds of nationalism and its provincial bias largely found in English Canada. Many English-Canadian writers hoped that the Supreme Court, as a final appeal court, would adopt a liberal, flexible interpretation, eroding at least in part the debilitating influence of *stare decisis*. In practical terms, their pleas for a living tree approach presupposed a larger role for the central government than had developed under the interpretations of the Judicial Committee. In essence, one of the key attitudes of the predominantly English-Canadian abolitionists was to view a newly independent Supreme Court as an agent of centralization. The very reasons and justifications which tumble forth in English-Canadian writings caused insecurity and apprehension in French Canada which feared, simply, that if English-Canadian desires were translated into judicial fact the status and influence of the provinces which had been fostered by British judges would be eroded. The American-style supreme court sought by the constitutionalist critics of the Privy Council was justifiably viewed with apprehension by French-Canadian observers. They assumed, not unfairly, that if such a court heeded the bias of its proponents it would degenerate into an instrument for the enhancement of national authority. These contrary English and French hopes and fears are closely related to the present crisis of legitimacy of the Supreme Court.

An additional significant cleavage in Canadian opinion was between those fundamentalist critics who opposed the Judicial Committee for its failure to provide a technically correct interpretation of a clearly worded document, and the constitutionalists who castigated it for its failure to take a broad, flexible approach to its task.

The fundamentalist approach, already discussed, imposed on the courts the task of faithfully interpreting a document in terms of the meanings deliberately embodied in it by the Fathers of Confederation. This approach was replete with insuperable difficulties. ...

In brief, if the performance of the Privy Council was, as its critics suggested, replete with inconsistencies and insensitivity, the confused outpourings of the critics displayed an incoherence completely inadequate to guide judges in decision-making. To contrast the performance of the Judicial Committee with the performance of its opponents is to ignore the dissimilarity of function between artist and critic. It is however clear that the Judicial Committee was much more sensitive to the federal nature of Canadian society than were the critics. From this perspective at least the policy output of British judges was far more harmonious with the underlying pluralism of Canada than were the confused prescriptive statements of her opponents. For those critics, particularly on the left, who wished to transform society, this qualified defence of the Judicial Committee will lack conviction. However, such critics have an obligation not only to justify their objectives but also the role they advocated for a non-elected court in helping to attain them.

Whether the decline in the problem-solving capacity of governments in the federal system was real or serious enough to support the criticism which the Privy Council encountered involves a range of value judgments and empirical observations of a very complex nature. The purpose of this paper has been only to provide documentation for the minimum statement that a strong case can be made for the Judicial Committee, and to act as a reminder that the basic question was jurisprudential, a realm of discussion in which neither the Privy Council, its critics, nor its supporters proved particularly illuminating.

The Abolition of Appeals and an Inadequate Jurisprudence

It is valid, if somewhat perverse, to argue that the weakness and confusion of Canadian jurisprudence constituted one of the main justifications for ending appeals to the Privy Council. The attainment of judicial autonomy was a prerequisite for a first class Canadian jurisprudence. Throughout most of the period of judicial subordination the weaknesses in Canadian legal education produced a lack of self-confidence and a reluctance to abolish appeals. As long as the final court of appeal was an alien body the jurisprudence which did exist was entangled with the emotional contest of nationalism and imperialism, a mixture which deflected legal criticism into side issues. In these circumstances the victory of nationalism was a necessary preliminary to the development of an indigenous jurisprudence which has gathered momentum in the past two decades.

It is also likely that the quality of judicial performance by Canadian courts was hampered by subordination to the Privy Council. The existence of the Privy Council undermined the credibility of the Supreme Court and inhibited the development of its status and prestige.

The Supreme Court could be overruled by a superior, external court. In many cases it was bypassed as litigants appealed directly from a provincial court to the Privy Council. Finally, the doctrine of *stare decisis* bound the Supreme Court to the decisions of its superior, the Privy Council. The subject status of the Supreme Court and other Canadian courts was further exacerbated by the absence of dissents which reduced the potential for flexibility of lower courts in subsequent cases. In spite of the quality of its performance the dominant position of the Privy Council in the Canadian judicial hierarchy was an anomaly, incompatible with the evolving independence of Canada in other spheres, and fraught with too many damaging consequences for its elimination to be regretted.

The inadequate jurisprudence, the legacy of nearly a century of judicial subordination, which accompanied the attainment of judicial autonomy in 1949, has harmfully affected the Supreme Court in the last two decades. The Supreme Court, the law schools, the legal profession, and the political élites have been unable to devise an acceptable role for the court in Canadian federalism. Shortly after the court attained autonomy the institutional fabric of the Canadian polity, the court included, began to experience serious questioning and challenges to its existence. The Diefenbaker Bill of Rights was succeeded by the Quiet Revolution with its confrontation between rival conceptions of federalism and coexistence. Additional uncertainty has been generated by the proposed Trudeau Charter which, if implemented, will drastically change the significance of the judiciary in our constitutional system. In the unlikely event that a significantly different BNA Act emerges from the present constitutional discussions the court will face the task of imparting meaning to a new constitutional document delineating a division of powers different from the existing division. To these factors, as indications of the shifting world of judicial review, can be added the possibility that the court may be reconstituted with a new appointment procedure, with a specific entrenched status, and perhaps even as a special court confined to constitutional questions.

It would be folly to suggest that the above problems would not exist if Canadian jurisprudence had been more highly developed. Their source largely lies beyond the confines of the legal system. On the other hand, the confused state of Canadian jurisprudence documented in this article adds an additional element of difficulty to their solution.

47

The Political Purposes of the Canadian Charter of Rights and Freedoms

Peter H. Russell (1983)

EDITORS' INTRODUCTION

Peter Russell, a political scientist with a long-standing interest in the judiciary, was invited by the editors of the Canadian Bar Review *(CBR) to write this article on the political purposes of the Charter for a special issue of the CBR on the* Charter of Rights and Freedoms, *published shortly after the Charter came into force. Russell's article aimed at preparing Canadians for the main political consequence of adopting a constitutional bill of rights. Although the Charter's principal political sponsors thought that the Charter's main purpose was to serve as an instrument of national unity, Russell predicted that its main effect would be to increase the role of the judiciary in making decisions on the nature and extent of Canadians' rights and freedoms.*

Discussion of Canada's new constitutional Charter of Rights and Freedoms should not overlook the broad political purposes which inspired Canadian politicians to propose it and induced so many Canadian citizens to support it. In the long run, it is in terms of these broad political purposes that the Charter should be, and probably will be, judged.

The political purposes of the Charter can be thought of as falling into two general categories. These two kinds of purposes are, as I shall show, closely related, although analytically distinct. The first has to do with national unity and the Charter's capacity to offset, if not reverse, the centrifugal forces which some believe threaten the survival of Canada as a unified country. This national unity function of the Charter is most relevant to explaining why politicians, especially those who led the federal government, pushed so hard for a charter. The second kind of purpose is the conviction that a charter will better protect, indeed will even "guarantee," fundamental rights and freedoms. Belief in this purpose is most relevant to explaining the widespread public support for the Charter. In this article I will examine each of these purposes in turn and the prospects of their being fulfilled by the Charter.

Source: Excerpted from *Canadian Bar Review*, vol. 61 (1983). Notes omitted. Reprinted by permission.

I. National Unity

To understand the national unity rationale of the Charter, it is necessary to recall the context in which the federal government made a charter its number one priority for constitutional reform.

In the mid-1960s right up to the Confederation of Tomorrow Conference organized by the Premier of Ontario, John Robarts, in the fall of 1967, the Liberal Government in Ottawa was not interested in constitutional reform of any kind. Patriation with an amending formula had been very nearly achieved in 1964. Since then only Quebec had been pushing for constitutional change. But Quebec had drastically raised the stakes. The Lesage Liberals followed by Daniel Johnson's Union Nationale administration insisted that the price of Quebec's support for patriation of the Canadian Constitution would be agreement on substantive constitutional reform giving Quebec more recognition and power as the French Canadian homeland. This demand of Quebec provincial leaders for major constitutional change reflected a wholly new phase in Quebec nationalism. Historically the constitutional position of Quebec leaders had been profoundly conservative. Their prime concern had been to preserve the rights they believed had been acquired for Quebec and French Canada in the constitution of 1867. But now, under the impetus of Quebec's "quiet revolution," the province's leading politicians had become constitutional radicals. So long as these Quebec demands for radical change were the central preoccupation of constitutional debate, it was not in the federal government's interest to encourage the process of constitutional reform. The proposals likely to dominate such a debate, if they went far enough to placate Quebec nationalism, would either go too far in weakening the involvement of the federal government in the life of Quebec or else give Quebec representatives in federal institutions such a privileged place as to alienate opinion in the rest of the country. So the Pearson government at first tried to respond to Quebec through pragmatic adjustments in fiscal and administrative arrangements and took a dim view of Premier Robarts' constitutional initiative.

However, the very success of the Confederation of Tomorrow Conference in raising national expectations about both the necessity and the possibility of responding creatively to Quebec's constitutional discontents seemed to convince the Prime Minister and his Justice Minister, Pierre Trudeau, who was soon to succeed him, that a different strategy was needed. The constitutional issue could no longer be kept on the back burner. But if constitutional reform was to be seriously pursued, it was essential that Quebec's demands be countered by proposals designed to have a unifying effect on Canada. It was at this point that the federal government urged that a charter of rights be at the top of the constitutional reform agenda.

After the Confederation of Tomorrow Conference, Prime Minister Pearson suggested to the provincial governments "that first priority should be given to that part of the Constitution which should deal with the rights of the individual—both his rights as a citizen of a democratic federal state and his rights as a member of the linguistic community in which he has chosen to live." This was the position his government took at the Constitutional Conference in February 1968. Prime Minister Trudeau took exactly the same position. His government's paper prepared for the February 1969 Constitutional Conference repeated the commitment to a charter of rights as the first priority in constitutional change. "To reach agreement on common values," Trudeau argued, was "an essential first step" in any process of constitutional renewal. From this point until the final enactment of the Constitution Act,

1982, giving constitutional expression to fundamental rights including language rights was the Trudeau government's first constitutional priority. ...

The Charter's attractiveness to the leaders of the federal Liberal Party as the centrepiece of their constitutional strategy was decisive in improving the political fortunes of the project of entrenching rights and freedoms in the Canadian constitution. Since World War II there had been a great deal of discussion of the Bill of Rights idea both within and outside Parliament. The prime stimulus of this discussion was international—the concern for human rights arising from the war against fascism and Canada's obligations under the United Nations Declaration of Human Rights. Domestic events also stimulated interest in a Bill of Rights. At the federal level, there was regret concerning the treatment of Japanese Canadians during the war and the denial of traditional legal rights in the investigation of a spy ring following the Gouzenko disclosures in 1946. At the provincial level the persecution of Jehovah's Witnesses by the Duplessis administration in Quebec, the treatment of Doukhabors and other religious minorities in the west and the repression of trade unionism in Newfoundland were major *causes célèbres*. There was also a touch of the national unity theme in the submissions made on a number of occasions to parliamentary committees on the implications of post-war immigration. The addition of such large numbers of new Canadians with no education or experience in liberal democratic values, it was argued, meant that Canada could no longer rely on the British method of protecting civil liberties. For such a heterogeneous population a written code was needed. Liberal leaders were not moved by these arguments for a Canadian Bill of Rights. The C.C.F. was the only national party to commit itself to establishing a Bill of Rights. And it was under a Progressive Conservative government led by John Diefenbaker that a statutory Bill of Rights affecting only the federal level of government was enacted in 1960.

Pierre Trudeau, before he entered politics and joined the Liberal Party, expressed interest in a constitutional Bill of Rights. In 1965, as a legal academic writing a background paper on how to deal with the Quebec agitation for constitutional change, he placed a Bill of Rights in first place on his list of constitutional reform proposals. But the main thrust of his paper was to dissuade Quebecers from relying on constitutional reform to solve their problems of political and social modernization. His constitutional reform proposals were for "some day" in the future. ... In any event, by 1967 that distant day when constitutional reforms should be undertaken had suddenly arrived. Speaking to the Canadian Bar Association as Justice Minister in 1967 Trudeau announced his government's conclusion that a constitutional Bill of Rights proposal was "the best basis on which to begin a dialogue on constitution reform between the federal government and provincial governments," and he emphasized that in taking this approach: "Essentially we will be testing—and, hopefully, establishing—the unity of Canada." ...

Aside from the political and strategic advantages of the Charter, it may also have had some purely intellectual or even aesthetic attractions for Mr. Trudeau and some of his colleagues. Federal government position papers put forward the view that the rational approach to the constitution was to begin with a statement of the fundamental values of the Canadian political community. This notion of constitutional rationality, of the constitution as a logical construct built on an explicit formulation of first principles, may be a manifestation of French rationalism and the civil law tradition with its penchant for deduction from codified principles in contrast with English empiricism and the inductive nature of common law.

Even if there is some validity in this kind of ethnic stereotyping, it surely cannot account for the strength of the Trudeau government's political commitment to the Charter.

That commitment proved to be very strong indeed. A version of a constitutional Bill of Rights took pride of place in the Victoria Charter which Mr. Trudeau came so close to negotiating successfully with the provincial Premiers in 1971. Again in 1978 when, in response to the electoral victory of the separatists in Quebec, the federal government embarked on another serious programme of constitutional reform, a constitutional charter, albeit one which at first would not bind the provinces, was given a prominent position. But it was the inclusion of a constitutional Charter of Rights binding on the provinces in the package of constitutional change which Mr. Trudeau threatened to achieve, if necessary, unilaterally without provincial support that demonstrates how deeply he and his government believed in its benefits. At this point, when federal–provincial negotiations on the constitution were at an impasse, it would have been ever so much easier, from a political point of view, for the federal government to have proceeded simply with patriation and an amending formula. The insistence on coupling a consitutional charter with patriation shows how strongly the Trudeau government believed in the nation-building potential of a constitutional charter. They would risk dividing the country in order that it might become more united. This nation-building aspect of the Charter was the central thesis of Mr. Trudeau's final parliamentary speech on the Charter:

> Lest the forces of self-interest tear us apart, we must now define the common thread that binds us together.

Will the Charter fulfill the expectations of its political sponsors in promoting national unity? In the context of the immediate exigencies of Canada's constitutional debate the Charter did provide a useful counterpoise to demands for greater provincial powers. But the national unity benefits of such a manoeuvre were discounted, if not eliminated by Mr. Trudeau's unilateralism and by the failure, in the end, to secure the Quebec government's assent to the constitutional package. The thirst for more provincial power or more effective representation in national institutions evident in Quebec and western Canada has not been quenched by "the people's package." In the long run, the Charter's efficacy in contributing to national unity will depend not on its utility to federal politicians at a particular stage in the constitutional debate but on its real potential for strengthening the Canadian political community.

The most frequently and widely acclaimed unifying effect of a charter is its capacity to serve as a unifying symbol. The symbolic function of a constitutional charter was, for instance, emphasized by the Canadian Bar Association's Committee on the Constitution:

> A clear statement in the Constitution of the fundamental values all Canadians share would, we think, have an important unifying effect. It would inculcate in all citizens, young and old, a consciousness of the importance of civil liberties and an authoritative expression of the particular rights and liberties our society considers fundamental.

Lawyers and politicians seem very confident about the Charter's symbolic impact. And they may be right! Social scientists have stressed the important role that symbols play in shaping political attitudes and beliefs. Murray Edelman, for example, in his classic study of

The Symbolic Uses of Politics goes so far as to suggest that all political constitutions are "large-ly irrational, in genesis and in impact." But exactly how the emotional chemistry of laws as political symbols operates, in precisely what kind of circumstances a particular set of symbols (for instance a constitutional charter of rights) will have a particular effect (for instance strengthening national unity), has not been established. ...

There are certain parts of the Charter which are clearly intended to be unifying not only symbolically but also in terms of their real effects on government policy and citizens' rights. These are the sections dealing with mobility and language rights. The mobility rights in section 6 aim at overcoming the "balkanization" of Canada by giving citizens the right "to take up residence and to pursue a livelihood anywhere in Canada without discrimination based on the previous province of residence." The language clauses, by giving formal constitutional recognition, for the first time, to English and French as Canada's Official Languages, by extending the constitutional right to use these languages to dealings with the executive branch of the federal government and with all branches of government in New Brunswick and, most importantly, by establishing minority language education rights for the English in Quebec and the French outside of Quebec, aim at giving greater reality to the ideal of the whole of Canada being a homeland for French-speaking as well as English-speaking Canadians.

For the Liberal government these sections were the heart of the Charter. Their importance is underlined by the fact that section 33 which permits the federal and provincial legislatures to override sections of the Charter does not apply to these rights. In his speech introducing the Charter to the House of Commons, Mr. Chretien, the Minister of Justice, referred to these rights as "fundamental to what Canada is all about." They express the pan-Canadian nationalism which, at the level of ideology, is the counter to the nationalism of Quebec separatism. Since entering politics in the 1960's Mr. Trudeau had, in a sense, been engaged in a rival programme of nation-building to that of Quebec independentistes. At the centre of this programme was the task of persuading the Québécois that they could best fulfill themselves by enjoying the opportunities flowing from membership in a Canadian community wider than Quebec. It was for this reason that these nationalist provisions of the Charter, especially the language rights, were of such great importance to Mr. Trudeau and his Quebec colleagues. They were also the only part of the whole constitutional package which, by any stretch of the imagination, Mr. Trudeau and his federalist allies could point to as fulfilling the commitment they had made during the Quebec Referendum campaign to "constitutional renewal."

What is the potential of these sections for realizing their nationalist objectives? So far as mobility rights are concerned, section 6 is not likely to make any great inroads on the economic balkanization of Canada. To begin with it deals only with labour mobility and not with other major obstacles to a Canadian common market such as discriminatory tax and government purchasing policies. Moreover, section 6's impact on labour mobility was severely curtailed by the qualification introduced as part of the November Accord between the federal government and nine provinces. This proviso will shield from the Charter the protective employment policies of provinces experiencing above average unemployment. Still, section 6 may turn out to be an important check on provinces like Alberta endeavouring to preserve their relative prosperity by denying provincial services to Canadians from other provinces.

The language rights relate to a more intractable dimension of the national problem—the question of identity. Here, section 23, the language of education clause, makes a more significant contribution than sections 16 to 20 which deal with the language of government.

The latter do little more than elevate statutory rights into constitutional rights. Any symbolic gains for national unity that may flow from such a change are largely offset by the persistence of the government of Ontario, the province with the largest Francophone minority, in refusing to give constitutional status to bilingualism in the public life of that province. The language of education section is bound to spark controversy in the short run. In Quebec it collides directly with educational policies emanating from Franco-Quebec nationalism that deny English Canadians who move to Quebec access to the province's English schools. This collision was softened by a last minute concession that makes the rights of new Canadian citizens whose English education was obtained outside of Canada to send their children to Quebec's English schools conditional on the agreement of the Quebec legislature. The rights which section 23 extends to the small francophone minorities in the western provinces will do nothing to reduce alienation in the west where there is little respect for the fundamental nature of French-English dualism in the Canadian experience.

Nevertheless it could turn out that these divisive effects were only short term and that in the longer run were worth risking if the Charter's recognition of bilingualism makes it more likely that Canada will survive as a common homeland for English and French-speaking North Americans. But the rights contained in the Charter, even when added to all that has been done to promote bilingualism outside of the Constitution, may be too little too late to overcome the legacy of political and judicial policies which in the late 1800's and early 1900's gave priority to provincial rights over minority cultural rights and thereby prevented the building of a dualistic society on the new Canadian frontier. I suspect that if Canada overcomes Quebec separatism, it will be not so much because recognition of bilingualism in the "new" Canadian Constitution is decisive in the battle for the hearts and minds of the Québécois but because of the exhaustion of nationalist politics brought on by more compelling economic concerns.

But it is neither through the Charter's nationalist provisions nor its symbolic force that the Charter is likely to have its strongest centripetal effect on the Canadian polity. I think the Charter's nationalizing influence will be felt most through a process scarcely mentioned by its political sponsors—the process of judicial review. It is primarily through judicial decisions interpreting the Charter—applying its general terms to particular laws and government activities—that the Charter will come to play an important part in the on-going political life of Canada.

Now it may seem rather perverse to think of judicial interpretation of the Charter as a unifying process. Judicial decisions based on the Charter will frequently be concerned with sensitive political issues and are therefore bound to be controversial. Consider, for instance, the sharp divisions of opinion within Canadian society on such issues as censoring pornography, school prayers, abortion, police powers, compulsory retirement and affirmative action. Judicial decisions on claims made under the Charter will touch on all of these issues. American experience demonstrates that judicial decisions in these areas are bound to anger the losers as much as they please the winners. Given the political sparks that judicial interpretation of the Charter will set off, why do I ascribe unifying consequences to the process of judicial review?

Judicial decisions on the Charter will be unifying in that the very debates and controversies they produce will be national and on issues that transcend the regional cleavages which are usually a feature of national political controversy in Canada. Court cases on the Charter

336 / ESSENTIAL READINGS

normally will not pit region against region or the provinces against the "feds." Instead the principal protagonists will be interest groups and aggregations of individuals from all parts of Canada. For instance, litigation dealing with police powers (the first major policy field in which judicial interpretation of the Charter is likely to be of political importance) will find small "c" conservatives aligned against small "l" liberals all across the country. Although the controversy will be intense, it will be waged on a national level in the arena of national politics and on grounds that do not call into question the legitimacy of Canada as a national political community. It is in this sense that the Charter may well turn out to be a nation-building instrument.

There is an even more direct sense in which judicial interpretation of the Charter will be a nationalizing process. In interpreting the Charter, the Supreme Court of Canada, at the top of the judicial structure, will set uniform national standards—often in policy areas which otherwise would be subject to diverse provincial standards. Film censorship, school prayers and discrimination in employment practices are all clear examples. In contrast to the executive and legislative power, the judicial power in Canada is essentially unified. Policy directives flowing from Supreme Court decisions on the Charter are transmitted through a single hierarchy of appeals that binds all the courts in the land, and shapes the rights of all Canadians and the powers of all who govern.

It is true that section 33 by permitting legislatures to override certain sections of the Charter—for five years at a time—modifies judicial supremacy. However, because of the adverse political consequences that a government would usually risk in using this power, I very much doubt that it will be frequently used. In the case of Quebec, where the P.Q Government has already purported to have used the section on a blanket basis, it has been invoked not to protect provincial policies from the impact of judicially established standards but as part of a campaign challenging the legitimacy of changes in the constitution made without the consent of Quebec's provincial government. ...

In selling the Charter, the federal government tended to ignore this dimension of the Charter. Federal representatives were at pains to point out that the Charter involves "no transfer of powers from the provinces to the federal government." These disavowals of any centralizing implications of the Charter are entirely valid providing one interprets "government" narrowly to exclude the judicial branch. However, in this day and age, it is only on the basis of a blind, and most anachronistic view of the judicial process that the policy making role of the judiciary, above all in interpreting the broad language of a constitutional Bill of Rights, could be denied. Once the discretion and choice necessarily involved in interpreting that language is recognized, the centralizing tendencies of judicial review must be acknowledged. As the Supreme Court's capacity to function as a kind of national Senate reviewing the reasonableness of provincial laws and policies becomes evident, the reality of judicial power will overtake the rhetoric of federal politicians. Among other things, this will mean that the federal government's monopoly of the power to appoint judges, not only to the Supreme Court of Canada but to all of the higher provincial courts, will be increasingly questioned. ...

Such a development assumes a widening recognition of the importance of judicial power in determining the actual policy consequences of a constitutional charter. Public awareness of that power is still in the making. The popularity of the Charter was based primarily on a belief that one basic policy would flow automatically from the Charter—the better protection of fundamental rights and freedoms. It is to the analysis of that belief and the likelihood of the Charter's fulfilling it that I now turn.

II. Protecting Rights and Freedoms

"Protecting rights and freedoms" is a deceptively simple idea. Those who accept such a slogan as a fair summary of what a constitutional Bill of Rights is all about could hardly be expected to be anything other than enthusiastic about adding a charter to the Canadian Constitution. As Yvon Pinard, the government's House Leader, echoing so many of his colleagues, put it, "what is wrong with the fundamental freedoms of Canadian citizens being protected forever by the Canadian constitution?" What indeed could possibly be wrong with such a project if that was basically all there was to it? Surely all of us would be mad to reject or even to question a proposal that is guaranteed to protect our individual rights and freedoms forever.

While this simplistic language undoubtedly assisted in winning public support for the Charter, it is not very helpful in understanding the real political consequences of such an instrument. The trouble with this language is that it tends to reify fundamental rights and freedoms, by treating them as things which people either possess in their entirety or not at all. But in our actual civic experience we do not encounter these rights and freedoms in such a zero-sum fashion. We enjoy more or less of them. What we have to settle about these rights and freedoms is not whether or not we will "have" them but what limits it is reasonable to attach to them and how decisions about these limits should be made.

Those parts of the Charter which deal with what might be termed universal rights and freedoms (as opposed to rights and freedoms based on the particular circumstances of Canadian history) are related to core values or ideals of all contemporary liberal democracies: political freedom, religious toleration, due process of law and social equality. In Canada for some time now there has been no serious debate about the *minimum* extent to which each of these values should be realized in the laws and practices of our state. The right to criticize the government and to organize non-violent opposition to it has been basically unquestioned since the middle of the last century. Since the Quebec Act of 1774, it has been accepted that individuals should not suffer civil disabilities because of their religious beliefs nor be forced to subscribe to the tenets of any religion. At least since the advent of legal aid, Canadians charged with a criminal offence have had access to a fair trial. As in other liberal democracies, social equality has been the last of the core values to gain effective recognition. But now there is wide-spread acceptance of the ideal that each person should be treated as an individual on his or her merits and not penalized or denied opportunities by the state because of gender, skin colour, ethnic background or other distinguishing characteristics of birth.

As we move out from the central core of these values, we encounter restrictions and limits on each, and considerable controversy about the right limits. Have we gone far enough in removing restrictions on political speech or should we go further and narrow the civil wrong of defamation when politicians are the targets of criticism, or perhaps eliminate the crime of inciting race hatred? Should the protection of political speech extend to the public exhibition of all kinds of sexual activities? Is it right to limit the freedom of broadcasters in order to nurture our national culture? Should religious freedom be extended to the point where no one should suffer an economic penalty (like closing a business on Sundays) in order to comply with a law originally introduced for religious reasons, or to the point where no one is obliged to obey a law that offends his religious or philosophic beliefs—no matter how eccentric those beliefs? How far back in the pre-trial proceedings of our criminal justice system should we extend the right to counsel? Should it apply (and in the case of indigent persons, be paid for by the state) to all offences however minor—even to infractions of parking by-laws? Should the police be able to use evidence from private premises only when they have obtained it through a judicially authorized search warrant? What about evidence they come upon by chance in effecting an arrest or responding to a citizen's complaint? Should we begin to make amends for inequalities suffered in the past by adopting laws that discriminate against males and Caucasians? Should the premises of private clubs that practice racial discrimination receive police protection? Should our courts enforce wills that discriminate on the basis of religion or race or gender? How far should we go in ensuring that all of our public facilities are fully accessible to the physically handicapped?

It is in the way we deal with these questions that the Charter will have its main effect. A constitutional charter guarantees not that there will be no limits to rights and freedoms but that a change will be made in the way our society makes decisions about these limits. At the initial level, decisions on these limits will still be made, for the most part, by the legislature and executive, although where common law remains important—for instance, contempt of court, the law of libel and the law of evidence—even the initial decisions will be judge-made rules of law. A charter introduces a second level of decision making in which decisions made at the first level are subjected to a process of judicial review triggered by litigants who claim that a particular limit is excessive or unreasonable. Not only that, but what is most dramatic about this process when it is based on a constitutional as opposed to a statutory charter—and accounts, of course, for the language of "entrenchment" and "guarantees"—is that the results of this second level of decision-making, especially when they issue from the highest court, are very difficult to change. These judicial decisions can only be altered by the difficult process of constitutional amendment, by a change in judicial outlook (resulting, perhaps, from a change in the composition of the bench) or through the exercise of that unique Canadian option—the legislative override power.

Considered from this point of view, the legislative override is not as contradictory a feature of the new Canadian Charter as some of its detractors have claimed. Section 33 has been denounced as incompatible with the Charter's basic purpose:

> The whole object of a charter is to say, you never opt out, they're inalienable rights. If you believe in liberty, if you believe in rights, the rights are not inalienable. (Edward Greenspan)

But note how this objection assumes the zero-sum, absolute nature of rights and freedoms. Once the fallaciousness of that assumption is recognized, and the hard issues concerning the proper limits of rights are acknowledged, the legislative override appears in a more acceptable light. The legislative override simply enables a legislature to put off for five years judicial review of its decision to accept a particular limit on a right or freedom.

In treating the Charter as primarily affecting the way we make decisions about the limits on fundamental rights and freedoms, I do not mean to call into question beliefs about the fundamental nature of certain rights or principles of government. I believe that the right to government based on the consent of the governed rather than on coercion, freedom from the theocratic enforcement of a particular religious creed, the right to be secure from arbitrary and unlawful deprivations of one's personal liberty or property, and recognition of the essential dignity of every human being regardless of race, colour, creed or gender are basic requirements of good government that derive from man's nature. For countries in the liberal democratic tradition these principles constitute fundamental purposes of government. As general principles, I cannot see that they are any less fundamental to liberal democracies without constitutional charters—for example, Australia, pre-charter Canada, and the United Kingdom—than they are in countries with constitutional charters—for example, Ireland, Japan, the United States and West Germany. What I am insisting upon is the difference between a right stated as a general principle and operative rules of law affecting that principle. ...

The expectation of those who supported a constitutional charter on the grounds that it would guarantee rights and freedoms might be more realistically phrased as a belief that a charter will at least work against tightening existing limits on rights and freedoms and might even lead to the reduction of some restrictions. In this way, it might be argued, a constitutional charter will preserve and possibly expand fundamental rights and freedoms.

There can be no doubt that the Charter will promote a more systematic review of public policies in terms of the rights and freedoms included in the Charter. At least initially, this review will involve more than the judiciary. Already police officials have been taking steps to bring police practices into line with the standards of due process set out in the Charter. Ministries of the Attorney General have been scouring statute books for possible breaches of the Charter. The three-year postponement of the coming into force of the equality rights in section 15 is designed to facilitate an intensive review of discriminatory aspects of law and policy so that potential conflicts with the Charter can be minimized. Even though the Charter does not contain an equivalent of section 3 of the Canadian Bill of Rights which required the Minister of Justice to scrutinize draft regulations and Bills for inconsistencies with the Bill of Rights, still it is likely that at both the federal and provincial levels legal advisers to the government will examine legislative proposals in the light of the new Charter's provisions.

But the judicial branch will be the most important forum for the systematic application of Charter standards. Judicial opinions will be authoritative on the specific meanings to be given to the Charter's general principles. In most instances judicial decisions will be final and definitive on the proper limits of rights and freedoms. Moreover, initiation of the judicial review process is essentially independent of the executive and legislative branches of government. Where constitutional rights and freedoms rather than the division of powers are at issue, the process of judicial review will normally be "turned on," so to speak, by individuals and groups, not by governments. As a result the spectrum of interests that can influence the agenda of law reform is considerably widened. ...

This opening up of the law reform process may be the major democratizing consequence of a constitutional charter. But what are the substantive results of this process likely to be? There can be no doubt that old and new restrictions on rights and freedoms are more apt to be challenged under a charter. But will the results of these challenges necessarily expand rights or freedoms or prevent their contraction? Here we must acknowledge a great deal of uncertainty. The political orientations and legal philosophies of the judiciary are not static. If American experience with constitutional "guarantees" teaches us anything it is that over the decades or even centuries of judicial interpretation we should expect periods of both judicial conservatism and judicial liberalism. Because politicians play the crucial role in the selection of judges it is unlikely that the ideological profile of the judiciary will differ dramatically from that of the countries' dominant political elite. Changes in judicial attitudes may lag behind changes in the political culture, but in the long run these attitudes will reflect major shifts in popular political orientations.

Even if Canada does experience a relatively liberal period of judicial review under the Charter, it does not follow that all of the consequences for fundamental rights and freedoms will be positive. To begin with rights and freedoms conflict with one another. A freedom may be expanded at the expense of another right. It is not difficult to think of possibilities: review of our laws concerning contempt of court may expand free speech while adversely affecting the right to a fair trial; contraction of police powers through interpretation of legal rights may better protect the rights of criminally accused while diminishing the effective protection to the right to life and personal security of the victims of crime. Nor can it be said that the rights of minorities are bound to be beneficiaries of a liberally interpreted charter. Leaving aside the question of why in a democratic society the views of minorities should be systematically favoured on basic policy questions over the view of the majority, there is the difficulty of identifying the relevant minority on the legislative issues which will be the subject of judicial review. On the pornography issue, for instance, which is the preferred minority—the conservatives who believe present restrictions provide insufficient protection of human dignity or radicals who regard these same restrictions as an illegitimate encroachment on free expression? On many of the issues to be decided under the Charter the interested public consists not of a majority and *the* minority but of a number of minorities some of which will feel benefited by and others which will feel offended by the outcome of judicial review.

Lawyers are too prone to think of rights and liberties entirely in legal terms. They are apt to ignore the possibility that judicial decisions which remove or narrow legislative restrictions on rights and freedoms can have the effect of expanding social or economic constraints. The issues raised by the Kent Commission on corporate concentration of the press provide a good illustration. It is possible that the courts will find legislation enacted in response to the Kent Commission to be an unconstitutional violation of "freedom of the press and other media of communication." If this occurs, it would mean the continuation of restrictions on the expression of political opinion stemming from the concentration of ownership of the means of mass communication. Harold Innis warned Canadians some years ago of the bias which results from viewing freedom of speech through the prism of an excessive legalism. It would be a pity if adoption of a constitutional charter of rights blunted our capacity to recognize that the state is not the only centre of power in our society capable of restricting freedom or equality or of abusing rights.

Here again we encounter the complexity of rights and freedom issues. Rights and freedoms do not form a simple piece of whole cloth which by some new constitutional mechanism can be made to expand in a single direction. Around any civil liberties issue there will likely be a cluster of rights and social interests some of which will be affected positively and others of which will be affected negatively by contracting a legal restriction on a particular right or freedom. This does not mean that we must be agnostic about what is the right way to treat an issue or that there is no better way than that embodied in the existing legislative arrangements. But it does suggest how facile it is to regard a broad liberal construction of a guarantee as always yielding the most reasonable balance—the result which provides the fairest treatment of rights and freedoms.

There is also the possibility that the courts will render conservative decisions—that is decisions that uphold existing laws and practices as not violating rights and freedoms or at least as not constituting unreasonable limitations on these rights and freedoms. The libertarian enthusiast of a charter of rights may think that while such decisions will be disappointing in that they represent missed opportunities for expanding rights and freedoms, still such decisions cannot reduce rights and freedoms. Conservative decisions, it might be contended, may not push out the limits on rights and freedoms but neither will they push those limits in. But this argument overlooks the way in which a decision upholding existing arrangements as constitutional can legitimize the status quo. There may be a tendency under a constitutional charter of rights and freedoms to accept as a corollary of the proposition that "if it is unconstitutional it must be wrong" the proposition that "if it is constitutional it must be right." There is an element of this in American constitutional history. The Supreme Court decision in *Plessy v. Ferguson* did not establish racial segregation in American schools, but by putting the constitutional seal of approval on separate but equal facilities it created an additional obstacle for proponents of integration. ...

The point in questioning libertarian expectations of the constitutional Charter is not to renew the debate on whether Canada should "entrench" rights. For all practical purposes that debate is over. Canada has a constitutional charter and all of us, its former opponents and supporters alike, must learn to live with it intelligently. To do this it is necessary to discard the rhetoric of the Charter's political salesmen and adopt a more realistic appraisal of the Charter's potentialities. Such an understanding requires that we bear in mind the Charter's consequences not only for policy results but also for the policy process.

The principal impact of a charter on the process of government can be neatly summarized as a tendency to judicialize politics and politicize the judiciary. The political leaders who led the campaign for the Charter gave little attention to this consequence of a charter. When they did refer to it, they did so in a very optimistic vein. Mr. Chrétien, for instance, in acknowledging the important policy questions which judges will have to decide in interpreting the language of education section of the Charter, said:

> I think we are rendering a great service to Canada by taking some of these problems away from the political debate and allowing the matter to be debated, argued, coolly before the courts with precedents and so on.

Unquestionably Canada can benefit from the rationality which a thoroughly researched, well reasoned judicial decision can bring to the resolution of a difficult question of social or political justice. Such benefits will contribute to national unity if cogent judicial decisions help build a stronger national consensus on such historically divisive issues as language rights. But, while acknowledging these possible benefits, we should not lose sight of the possibility that excessive reliance on litigation and the judicial process for settling contentious policy issues can weaken the sinews of our democracy. The danger here is not so much that non-elected judges will impose their will on a democratic majority, but that questions of social and political justice will be transformed into technical legal questions and the great bulk of the citizenry who are not judges and lawyers will abdicate their responsibility for working out reasonable and mutually acceptable resolutions of the issues which divide them.

Mitigation of this danger to Canadian democracy will require, on the part of both judges and the public, a sensitivity to the hazards of a judicial imperium. It would be a tragic self-delusion for judges to believe that they can escape the dilemmas of the new power which the Charter has thrust upon them by resorting to a kind of knee-jerk conservatism. An automatic upholding of virtually everything challenged under the Charter would bestow the mantle of constitutionality on all manner of legislation, government practice and police activity. It would be equally unfortunate if Canadian judges were to go to the other extreme of "government by judiciary" and become guilty of what an American critic of the United States judiciary refers to as "a kind of moral arrogance and judicial imperialism in undertaking to solve social problems for which they lack the competence, wisdom, or, for that matter, charter to undertake."

No simple recipe for avoiding these extremes can be written. But there is one change in the methodology of judicial decision making that Canadian judges should consider. That is softening, if not discarding, the taboo against the use of legislative history in interpreting the general language of the Charter. There was an extensive parliamentary discussion of the Charter. If counsel and judges mine the record of this discussion, I think there is less danger of the Canadian judiciary constituting itself a constituent assembly fabricating constitutional law without reference to the expectations of the original framers. No doubt the light which the historical record casts on some points will be scant and uncertain. The trouble with such a massive constitutionalization of rights as was undertaken in the new Canadian Charter is that, despite many days of discussion in the Joint Parliamentary Committee on the Constitution and debate in the House of Commons and the Senate, some difficult points were glossed over lightly or settled in last minute, private negotiations. Still there are sections which were extensively discussed in Parliament. The concepts and purposes embodied in some of these sections evolved through well reported political negotiations outside of Parliament. A good example is section 23 on the language of education. Examination of this legislative and political background material may rarely, if ever, uncover the full range of meaning which it was intended should attach to a constitutional guarantee, but it may often be a reliable guide to what was *not* included in the intentions of the constitution makers.

A new discipline will also be required by the public that evaluates the work of judges. If Canadians are to enjoy the cool rationality which Mr. Chrétien and others believe should result from the adjudication of disputes about constitutional rights, there must be a wider public capacity for giving consideration to judicial reasons. If for the public it is only the judicial outcome—"the bottom line"—that counts, our judges will tend to become simply another group of politicians and we will realize little of the distinctive benefits to be derived from expanding the judiciary's policy-making responsibilities. On the other hand, public debate and discussion of judicial decisions must not be muted by awe of the judicial office. It must be remembered that what is at stake in applying the norms of a constitutional charter of rights to the ever-changing details of our public life is the balance to be struck among our fundamental political values. In a democracy the public should not be disenfranchised from this area of decision-making. Unfortunately, the political rhetoric of "guarantees," "entrenchment" and "inalienable rights" used to promote the Charter has left the Canadian public ill-prepared for life under the Charter.

The Charter Dialogue Between Courts and Legislatures *or* Perhaps the Charter of Rights Isn't Such a Bad Thing After All

48

Peter W. Hogg and Allison A. Bushell (1997)

EDITORS' INTRODUCTION

This 1997 article on Charter dialogue by Peter Hogg, one of Canada's leading constitutional law scholars, and his Osgoode Hall colleague Allison Bushell has become a centrepiece in debates about the Charter. Hogg and Bushell mapped the various ways that courts and legislatures can interact in applying the Charter to legislation. These modes of interaction they call a "dialogue" between courts and legislatures. In their view, recognizing that judicial decisions on the Charter may trigger legislative responses shows that courts often do not have the last word on how the Charter should apply to legislation. This dynamic, they argue, should help meet concerns that, under the Charter, courts have usurped the role of elected legislators.

I. Introduction: The Charter of Rights as a "Bad Thing"?

A. *The Legitimacy of Judicial Review*

The subtitle of this article is "Perhaps the Charter of Rights Isn't Such a Bad Thing After All." The view that the Charter is a "bad thing" is commonly based on an objection to the legitimacy of judicial review in a democratic society. Under the Charter, judges, who are neither elected to their offices nor accountable for their actions, are vested with the power to strike down laws that have been made by the duly elected representatives of the people.

The conventional answer to this objection is that all of the institutions of our society must abide by the rule of law, and judicial review simply requires obedience by legislative bodies to the law of the constitution. However, there is something a bit hollow and unsatisfactory in that answer. The fact is that the law of the constitution is for the most part couched in broad, vague language that rarely speaks definitively to the cases that come before the courts. Accordingly, judges have a great deal of discretion in "interpreting" the law of the constitution, and the process of interpretation inevitably remakes the constitution into the likeness favoured by the judges. This problem has been captured in a famous American aphorism: "We are under a Constitution, but the Constitution is what the judges say it is."

Source: Excerpted from *Osgoode Hall Law Journal*, vol. 35, no. 1 (1997). Notes omitted. Reprinted with permission.

B. *The American Experience*

In the United States, the anti-majoritarian objection to judicial review could not be ignored. The long history of the American Bill of Rights revealed massive shifts in the judicial view of the meaning of the Bill—shifts that could not be explained except as changes in the attitudes of the judges to social and economic policies. The decisions of the Warren Court (1953–1969), starting in 1954 with *Brown v. Board of Education* and ending in 1973 with *Roe v. Wade* (a case that was actually decided after Warren C.J.'s retirement), wrote a whole new chapter of American constitutional law, and one that was openly a departure from earlier jurisprudence. There had been similar shifts in judicial interpretation before, especially the overruling of *Lochner v. New York* in 1937, but the decisions of the Warren Court coincided with the existence of a large class of full-time law professors whose academic duties required that they provide thoughtful analysis of new developments in the Supreme Court of the United States. Most law professors shared the civil libertarian values of the Warren Court and approved of the outcomes, but they could not ignore the widespread unpopularity of the decisions, and they had to face up to the anti-majoritarian objection to judicial review.

A small beleaguered minority of professors simply said that the Warren Court had departed from the original meaning of the constitutional text, and that the Court was wrong to do so. This was a courageous solution to the theoretical problem, but it was not particularly helpful, since it did not make the decisions go away. The great bulk of the academic commentary was devoted to advancing ingenious theories to justify judicial review, and each new theory provoked a further round of criticism and new theories until the literature reached avalanche proportions. Most of the ideas are somewhat relevant to Canada as well as the United States, and some Canadian law professors joined the debate and attempted to apply the ideas to judicial review in Canada.

II. Dialogue: Why the Charter May Not Be Such a "Bad Thing"

A. *The Concept of Dialogue*

The uninitiated might be excused for believing that, given the deluge of writing on the topic, everything useful that could possibly be said about the legitimacy of judicial review has now been said. However, one intriguing idea that has been raised in the literature seems to have been left largely unexplored. That is the notion that judicial review is part of a "dialogue" between the judges and the legislatures.

At first blush the word "dialogue" may not seem particularly apt to describe the relationship between the Supreme Court of Canada and the legislative bodies. After all, when the Court says what the Constitution requires, legislative bodies have to obey. Is it possible to have a dialogue between two institutions when one is so clearly subordinate to the other? Does dialogue not require a relationship between equals?

The answer, we suggest, is this. Where a judicial decision is open to legislative reversal, modification, or avoidance, then it is meaningful to regard the relationship between the Court and the competent legislative body as a dialogue. In that case, the judicial decision causes a public debate in which Charter values play a more prominent role than they would if there had been no judicial decision. The legislative body is in a position to devise a response that is properly respectful of the Charter values that have been identified by the Court, but which accomplishes the social or economic objectives that the judicial decision has impeded. Examples of this will be given later in this article.

B. How Dialogue Works

Where a judicial decision striking down a law on Charter grounds can be reversed, modified, or avoided by a new law, any concern about the legitimacy of judicial review is greatly diminished. To be sure, the Court may have forced a topic onto the legislative agenda that the legislative body would have preferred not to have to deal with. And, of course, the precise terms of any new law would have been powerfully influenced by the Court's decision. The legislative body would have been forced to give greater weight to the Charter values identified by the Court in devising the means of carrying out the objectives, or the legislative body might have been forced to modify its objectives to some extent to accommodate the Court's concerns. These are constraints on the democratic process, no doubt, but the final decision is the democratic one.

The dialogue that culminates in a democratic decision can only take place if the judicial decision to strike down a law can be reversed, modified, or avoided by the ordinary legislative process. Later in this article we will show that this is the normal situation. There is usually an alternative law that is available to the legislative body and that enables the legislative purpose to be substantially carried out, albeit by somewhat different means. Moreover, when the Court strikes down a law, it frequently offers a suggestion as to how the law could be modified to solve the constitutional problems. The legislative body often follows that suggestion, or devises a different law that also skirts the constitutional barriers. Indeed, our research, which surveyed sixty-five cases where legislation was invalidated for a breach of the Charter, found that in forty-four cases (two-thirds), the competent legislative body amended the impugned law. In most cases, relatively minor amendments were all that was required in order to respect the Charter, without compromising the objective of the original legislation.

Sometimes an invalid law is more restrictive of individual liberty than it needs to be to accomplish its purpose, and what is required is a narrower law. Sometimes a broader law is needed, because an invalid law confers a benefit, but excludes people who have a constitutional equality right to be included. Sometimes what is needed is a fairer procedure. But it is rare indeed that the constitutional defect cannot be remedied. Hence, as the subtitle of this article suggests, "perhaps the Charter of Rights isn't such a bad thing after all." ...

C. Our Definition of Dialogue

In order to examine how the dialogue between Canadian courts and legislatures has unfolded, we surveyed a total of sixty-five cases in which a law was struck down for a breach of the Charter. These include all of the decisions of the Supreme Court of Canada in which a law was struck down, as well as several important decisions of trial courts and courts of appeal which were never appealed to the Supreme Court of Canada. The breakdown of the cases we looked at is depicted below.

For each case, we searched the regulations and statute books for evidence of a response to the declaration by a court that a law was of no force or effect. These "legislative sequels" are the basis for the discussion of dialogue which follows.

Accordingly, the "dialogue" to which this article refers consists of those cases in which a judicial decision striking down a law on Charter grounds is followed by some action by the competent legislative body. In all of these cases, there must have been consideration of the judicial decision by government, and a decision must have been made as to how to react to it. This may also have occurred in cases where a decision was not followed by any action by the competent legislative body. However, we have not essayed the difficult task of documenting all of the occasions when Charter cases were discussed within government but were not followed by legislative action.

III. Features of the Charter That Facilitate Dialogue

A. *The Four Features That Facilitate Dialogue*

Why is it usually possible for a legislature to overcome a judicial decision striking down a law for breach of the Charter? The answer lies in four features of the Charter: (1) section 33, which is the power of legislative override; (2) section 1, which allows for "reasonable limits" on guaranteed Charter rights; (3) the "qualified rights," in sections 7, 8, 9 and 12, which allow for action that satisfies standards of fairness and reasonableness; and (4) the guarantee of equality rights under section 15(1), which can be satisfied through a variety of remedial measures. Each of these features usually offers the competent legislative body room to advance its objectives, while at the same time respecting the requirements of the Charter as articulated by the courts.

1. SECTION 33 OF THE CHARTER

Section 33 of the Charter is commonly referred to as the power of legislative override. Under section 33, Parliament or a legislature need only insert an express notwithstanding clause into a statute and this will liberate the statute from the provisions of section 2 and sections 7–15 of the Charter. The legislative override is the most obvious and direct way of overcoming a judicial decision striking down a law for an infringement of Charter rights. Section 33 allows the competent legislative body to re-enact the original law without interference from the courts.

In practice, section 33 has become relatively unimportant, because of the development of a political climate of resistance to its use. Only in Quebec does the use of section 33 seem to be politically acceptable. And even in Quebec there is only one example of the use of section 33 to overcome the effect of a judicial decision. This was a response to the decision of the Supreme Court of Canada in 1988 in *Ford v. Quebec (A.G.)*, which struck down Quebec's law banning the use of languages other than French in commercial signs. After that decision, Quebec enacted a new law that continued to ban the use of any language but French in all outdoor signs (while allowing bilingual indoor signs), and the province protected the new law with a section 33 notwithstanding clause. ...

2. SECTION 1 OF THE CHARTER

Section 130 of the Charter subjects the rights guaranteed by the Charter to "such reasonable limits prescribed by law as can be demonstrably justified in a free and democratic society." In principle, all the guaranteed rights, and certainly all those couched in unqualified terms, can be limited by a law that meets the standards judicially prescribed for section 1 justification. Those standards, which were laid down in 1986 in *R. v. Oakes*, are as follows: (1) the law must pursue an important objective; (2) the law must be rationally connected with the objective; (3) the law must impair the objective no more than necessary to accomplish the objective; and (4) the law must not have a disproportionately severe effect on the persons to whom it applies. Experience with section 1 indicates that nearly all laws meet standards (1), (2), and (4). The dispute nearly always centres on standard (3)—the minimal impairment or least restrictive means requirement. Therefore, when a law is struck down for breach of the Charter, it nearly always means only that the law did not pursue its objective by the means that would be the least restrictive of a Charter right. If it had done so, then the breach of the Charter right would have been justified under section 1.

When a law that impairs a Charter right fails to satisfy the least restrictive means standard of section 1 justification, the law is, of course, struck down. But the reviewing court will explain why the section 1 standard was not met, which will involve explaining the less restrictive alternative law that would have satisfied the section 1 standard. That alternative law is available to the enacting body and will generally be upheld. Even if the court has a weak grasp of the practicalities of the particular field of regulation, so that the court's alternative is not really workable, it will usually be possible for the policymakers to devise a less restrictive alternative that is practicable. With appropriate recitals in the legislation, and with appropriate evidence available if necessary to support the legislative choice, one can usually be confident that a carefully drafted "second attempt" will be upheld against any future Charter challenges. ...

In *RJR-MacDonald Inc. v. Canada (A.G.)* (1995), the Supreme Court of Canada struck down a federal law that prohibited the advertising of tobacco products. In its discussion of the least restrictive means standard, the Court made clear that it would have upheld restrictions that were limited to "lifestyle advertising" or advertising directed at children. Within two years of the decision, Parliament enacted a comprehensive new Tobacco Act. The new Act prohibits lifestyle advertising and restricts advertising to media which is targeted at adults, but allows tobacco manufacturers to use informational and brand-preference advertising in order to promote their products to adult smokers. ...

3. QUALIFIED CHARTER RIGHTS

Several of the guaranteed rights under the Charter are framed in qualified terms. Section 7 guarantees the right to life, liberty, and security of the person, but only if a deprivation violates "the principles of fundamental justice." Section 8 guarantees the right to be secure against "unreasonable" search or seizure. Section 9 guarantees the right not to be "arbitrarily" detained or imprisoned. Section 12 guarantees against "cruel and unusual" punishment. There is some uncertainty in the case law as to whether the qualified rights are subject to section 1, although the dominant view is that they are. But, even if section 1 has no application to the qualified rights, by their own terms they admit of the possibility of corrective legislative action after a judicial decision has struck down a law for breach of one of the rights.

For example, section 8 does not prohibit search and seizure, but only "unreasonable" search and seizure. ...

4. EQUALITY RIGHTS

Section 15(1) of the Charter prohibits laws which discriminate on the basis of nine listed grounds, namely race, national or ethnic origin, colour, religion, sex, age or "mental or physical disability," or laws which discriminate on the basis of any ground that is analogous to the listed grounds. Typically, where a law is declared to be unconstitutional for a violation of section 15(1), the problem is that the law is underinclusive, such that persons in the applicant's position, who have a constitutional right to be included, suffer the disadvantage of being excluded. A judicial decision under section 15(1) does force the legislature to accommodate the individual or group that has been excluded. Nevertheless, there are a number of different ways of complying with section 15(1) that allow the competent legislative bodies to set their own priorities.

The most obvious solution is to extend the benefit of the underinclusive law to the excluded group. For example, when the Nova Scotia Court of Appeal held that a law extending family benefits to single mothers, but not to single fathers, was unconstitutional, the Family Benefits regulations of that province were promptly modified to allow equal access to family benefits for single parents of both genders. The Nova Scotia legislature obviously considered that the provision of family benefits was of sufficient importance that the program should be extended rather than eliminated. However eliminating (or reducing) a government benefit is another option which is open to a legislature where a law has been held to be underinclusive. After all, it is not the applicant's right to a government cheque, but rather his or her right to equality, that the Court has affirmed. ...

IV. Barriers to Dialogue: Some Charter Decisions May Not Be "Open for Discussion"

A. *Three Situations Where Dialogue Is Precluded*

While it is generally the case that Charter decisions leave some options open to the competent legislative body, and allow a dialogue to take place between the courts and legislatures, we must acknowledge that there may be some circumstances where the court will, by necessity, have the last word. There appear to be three situations where this will be the case: (1) where section 1 of the Charter does not apply; (2) where a court declares that the *objective* of the impugned legislation is unconstitutional; and (3) where political forces make it impossible for the legislature to fashion a response to the court's Charter decision.

1. WHERE SECTION 1 DOES NOT APPLY

It is possible that some of the rights protected under the Charter are framed in such specific terms that there is no room for Parliament or a provincial legislature to impose "reasonable limits" on those rights. This was the position taken by the Supreme Court of Canada, with respect to minority language education rights, in the very first Charter case considered by the Court. That case was *Quebec (A.G.) v. Quebec Protestant School Boards* (1984). It concerned provisions in Quebec's Charter of the French Language, which restricted admission to English-language schools in Quebec to those children whose parents had been educated in the English language *in Quebec*. ...

2. WHERE THE OBJECTIVE OF THE LAW IS UNCONSTITUTIONAL

Even where a court has been willing to entertain arguments under section 1 of the Charter, a decision striking down a law for a breach of the Charter will be virtually impossible to overcome if the court determines that the law fails the first test of section 1 justification: the requirement that the law have a "pressing and substantial purpose" that justifies limiting a Charter right. In practice, the courts have rarely declared that a law does not meet this initial threshold. However, there are a few exceptions in the case law, particularly for laws in which the purpose of the law, as opposed to the law's *effects*, are found to violate the Charter.

The first example is *R. v. Big M Drug Mart Ltd.* (1985), in which the Supreme Court of Canada struck down the federal Lord's Day Act. In that case, the Court determined that the purpose of the Act was "to compel the observance of the Christian Sabbath." This was a violation of the guarantee of freedom of religion under section 2(a) of the Charter. Moreover, because the Court held that the Lord's Day Act's primary objective was contrary to the Charter, there was no possibility of advancing the same objective through a subsequent amendment of the Act. Accordingly, the Court had the last word when it struck down the Lord's Day Act. The Act was never repealed, but was simply dropped from the next consolidation of federal statutes. ...

3. WHERE POLITICAL FORCES PRECLUDE LEGISLATIVE ACTION

A third situation that may obstruct dialogue between courts and legislatures is where an issue is so controversial that it seems to preclude a legislative response to a judicial decision striking down a law for a breach of the Charter. An example of this is the situation which arose after the decision in *R. v. Morgentaler* (1988). In *Morgentaler*, the restrictions on abortion in the Criminal Code were struck down as unduly depriving pregnant women of liberty or security of the person, contrary to section 7 of the Charter. In *obiter*, the Court added that a less restrictive abortion law could possibly be upheld. In 1990, a bill which would have implemented a less restrictive abortion law was introduced into Parliament. However that law was defeated on a tied vote in the Senate, and the divisive issue of abortion has never been revisited, either in terms of a new law, or even in terms of the formal repeal of the law that was declared unconstitutional in 1988. While neither the Charter nor the Court precluded a legislative response to the *Morgentaler* decision, the abortion issue is so politically explosive that it eludes democratic consensus. Accordingly, the Court's decision, striking down Canada's old abortion law, remains the last word on this issue.

Where political forces, as opposed to the judicial decision itself, are the reason for a lack of response from the competent legislative body after a law is struck down on Charter grounds, it can hardly be said that unelected judges are stifling the democratic process. Quite the opposite is true, in fact; the Charter decision forces a difficult issue into the public arena that might otherwise have remained dormant, and compels Parliament or a legislature to address old laws that had probably lost much of their original public support. If a new law is slow to materialize, that is just one of the consequences of a democratic system of government, not a failing of judicial review under the Charter.

V. The Nature of Dialogue Between Canadian Courts and Legislatures

A. *Most Decisions Have Legislative Sequels*

The decisions which have just been discussed, in which a dialogue between the court and the competent legislative body has not been possible, are truly exceptional. As we alluded to earlier in this article, we have found that the majority of cases in which laws have been struck down on Charter grounds have given rise to a dialogue between the court and Parliament or the provincial legislature. This trend is reflected in the accompanying table.

Table I

Type of Legislative Sequel

	Fed.	BC	AL	SK	ON	QUE	NS	‡Oth.	Tot.
†Mod.									
Before	9	1	0	0	1	0	0	0	11
Repeal	3	1	1	0	1	0	0	1	7
Mod.									
After	21	2	0	0	4	3*	2	1	33
Used									
s. 33	0	0	0	1	0	1	0	0	2
Did									
Nothing	10	0	0	0	1	0	1	1	13

* There were two sequels to the case of *Ford v. Quebec (A.G.)*, [1988] 2 S.C.R. 712: (1) use of legislative override; and (2) modification of the original law. Both of these are reflected in this table. Thus, the total number of cases is 66.

† Denotes a law that was modified before a final decision was rendered by the highest reviewing court.

‡ Other denotes delegated legislation, specifically municipal by-laws and Rules of the Alberta Law Society.

Legislative action of some kind has followed all but thirteen of the sixty-five cases we surveyed; fully 80 per cent of the decisions in this survey have generated a legislative response. Of the thirteen cases without sequels, at least two have been the subject of proposed legislation, and another three have only been decided within the last two years, making it premature to discount the possibility of a legislative sequel in the future.

Are all legislative sequels examples of dialogue? We have taken the position that any legislation is dialogue, because legislative action is a conscious response from the competent legislative body to the words spoken by the courts. However, there may be room for debate about exactly what counts as dialogue. For example, in seven of the cases we surveyed, Parliament or a provincial legislature simply repealed the provision that was found to violate the Charter. In those cases, the competent legislative body simply acquiesced in the decision of the court, and it might be argued that no true "dialogue" took place. Similarly, in several cases where competent legislative bodies amended their laws, the remedial legislation merely implemented the changes the reviewing court had suggested. No effort was made to avoid the result reached by the court, and in at least one case there was no possibility of doing so. Consequently, those cases, too, might be excluded from the meaning of dialogue.

But it is probably casting the notion of dialogue too narrowly to discount those remedial measures that have merely followed the directions of the Court, either by repealing or amending an unconstitutional law. After all, it is always possible that the outcome of a dialogue will be an agreement between the participants! ...

B. *Legislative Response to Decisions Is Generally Prompt*

Another finding that emerged from our survey is that Canadian legislators typically respond promptly to decisions in which a law has been struck down on Charter grounds. The accompanying table displays the response time for the cases we considered.

Table II

Timing of Legislative Response

	Fed.	BC	AL	SK	ON	QUE	NS	Oth.	Tot.
Before Final	9	1	0	0	1	0	0	0	11
Dec'n									
<2 yrs	13	3	1	1	4	2	2	2	28
3–5 yrs	8	0	0	0	1	0	0	0	9
>5 yrs	3	0	0	0	0	1	0	0	4

Out of the fifty-two cases in which Parliament or a provincial legislature has implemented corrective legislation, in thirty-nine cases (or 75 per cent), the legislative response came within two years. In nine cases, the legislative response took more than two years, but less than five. In only four cases did a legislative response take more than five years to be enacted. ...

C. *Legislators Are Engaging in "Charter Speak"*

The nature of the Charter dialogue between Canadian courts and legislatures is not reflected in numbers alone. The language of post-Charter laws themselves, particularly in statutory preambles and purpose clauses, suggests that Canadian legislators are engaging in a self-conscious dialogue with the judiciary. Where laws closely skirt the boundaries of the Charter, and particularly where new laws are enacted to replace those that have been struck down on Charter grounds, it is not uncommon for the preamble to a statute to explain how the measures taken in the legislation are directed at a "pressing and substantial" objective, and are intended to "reasonably limit" rights and freedoms. ...

D. *Dialogue May Occur Even When Laws Are Upheld*

This article has focussed primarily on the legislative changes that have followed decisions striking down laws for a breach of the Charter. However, it should be noted that judicial decisions can occasionally have an impact on legislation even when the court does not actually strike down any law.

An example of this is the aftermath of the 1995 judgment in *Thibaudeau v. Canada*. The case concerned provisions in the Income Tax Act which allowed a non-custodial parent to deduct child-support payments from (generally his) income, and which required a custodial parent to include child support payments in (generally her) income. The applicant, a custodial parent, claimed that her obligation to pay income tax on the child-support payments she received from the non-custodial parent infringed section 15(1) (the equality guarantee) of the Charter. However, a majority in the Supreme Court of Canada rejected her claim, holding that there was no breach of section 15(1). Ms. Thibaudeau's case attracted a great deal of media attention, and exposed the fact that the Income Tax Act could sometimes lead to hardship for custodial parents. Consequently, even though the Attorney General of Canada had prevailed in the courts, he announced shortly after the *Thibaudeau* decision that Parliament would change the inclusion-deduction scheme for child support payments in the Income Tax Act. Amendments to the Act were enacted in 1997, under which child support payments are no longer deductible by the non-custodial parent, and are no longer taxable as income of the custodial parent.

Parliament's response to the *Thibaudeau* decision emphasizes that it is a mistake to view the Charter as giving non-elected judges a veto over the democratic will of competent legislative bodies. Canada's legislators are not indifferent to the equality and civil liberties concerns which are raised in Charter cases, and do not always wait for a court to "force" them to amend their laws before they are willing to consider fairer, less restrictive, or more inclusive laws. The influence of the Charter extends much further than the boundaries of what judges define as compulsory. Charter dialogue may continue outside the courts even when the courts hold that there is no Charter issue to talk about.

VI. Conclusion

Our conclusion is that the critique of the Charter based on democratic legitimacy cannot be sustained. To be sure, the Supreme Court of Canada is a non-elected, unaccountable body of middle-aged lawyers. To be sure, it does from time to time strike down statutes enacted by the elected, accountable, representative legislative bodies. But, the decisions of the Court almost always leave room for a legislative response, and they usually get a legislative response. In the end, if the democratic will is there, the legislative objective will still be able to be accomplished, albeit with some new safeguards to protect individual rights and liberty. Judicial review is not "a veto over the politics of the nation," but rather the beginning of a dialogue as to how best to reconcile the individualistic values of the Charter with the accomplishment of social and economic policies for the benefit of the community as a whole.

Courts, Legislatures and Executives in the Post-Charter Era

49

Beverley McLachlin (1999)

EDITORS' INTRODUCTION

In the Charter era, chief justices of the Supreme Court of Canada have felt compelled to speak out and explain the Court's role, especially in interpreting the Charter of Rights and Freedoms. *This essay by Beverley McLachlin, the first woman jurist to head Canada's highest court, is a good example. When chief justices engage in this kind of public discourse they must avoid defending or explaining any particular decision. Were they to break this rule, their words might be taken by lawyers as additional reasons for the court's decision. Here we can see that the chief justice, in responding to criticisms that the court has made itself a self-appointed legislature, emphasizes the courts' responsibility to take seriously constitutional laws made by democratically accountable political leaders.*

> *Courts striking down laws is nothing new in Canada, as a review of both the* Persons Case *in the 1920s and the* Alberta Press Case *in the 1930s makes clear. The Charter of Rights and Freedoms has clearly given impetus to the assertion of rights and to the pursuit of equality. But the courts have not shown undue "activism" or radically re-made law, and have not generally taken it upon themselves to find the social compromises that remain the appropriate domain of legislatures.*

In 1982, on a cold, windy day on Parliament Hill, the Queen signed the *Canadian Charter of Rights and Freedoms* into law. It marked a momentous step in Canadian constitutional history. Some, including many in England, viewed the step with grave apprehension. Today, it seems much less singular. Now the British have passed their own written Bill of Rights. In Africa, in Asia, in Europe—everywhere—people seem to have or to be getting constitutional bills of rights. New Zealand has a charter. Australia does not, but its High Court is nevertheless prepared to strike down laws on the basis of unwritten constitutional conventions. People vehemently defend their own particular charter versions. The British, for example,

---

Source: Excerpt from *Policy Options* (Institute for Research on Public Policy), vol. 20, no. 5 (June 1999). This is the text of a speech she delivered in Ottawa in April 1999 at a conference entitled "Guiding the Rule of Law in the 21st Century." Reprinted by permission.

make much of the fact that their Bill of Rights does not automatically invalidate offending legislation, instead giving Parliament one year to amend the law. But whatever the mechanism for ensuring compliance of the law with the basic charter principles, in the end it is a safe guess that substantial compliance there will be.

All over the world, people are subjecting their parliaments to a higher constraint, that of the written constitution. This may be the short answer to the debate that fills so many Canadian newspaper columns about whether we should or should not have a charter. It is increasingly difficult to imagine any modern democracy without a charter that sets out agreed-upon principles governing the conduct of parliament. Constitutional, rights-based democracy is swiftly becoming the international norm, if it has not already so become. It seems fair to suppose that sooner or later Canada, whose Parliament and legislatures were from their inception subject to the constraints of the *British North America Act*, would have entrenched in a constitutional form the fundamental principles upon which our democracy and legal order are based, just as so many other countries have done or are poised to do.

This is the background against which we must set the Canadian Charter—a world that increasingly accepts that legislatures may properly be limited by the need to conform to certain basic norms—norms of democracy, norms of individual liberties like free expression and association, norms governing the legal process by which the state can deprive people of their liberty and security, and norms of equal treatment. No longer is democracy synonymous with naked populism. The world increasingly accepts that while the will of the people as expressed through their elected representatives must be paramount, that will should always respect the fundamental norms upon which the very notion of democracy and a civil society repose, and upon which the legitimacy of the legislative assemblies themselves is founded.

In one sense, the reordering of democracy necessitated by the entrenchment of constitutional rights norms is merely an evolutionary adjustment of the Canadian democratic landscape. Anyone who supposes that, prior to the Charter, Parliament and the legislatures were not constrained by basic constitutional principles, including fundamental democratic rights, has not studied our history closely enough. And anyone who supposes that the courts pre-Charter did not hear and decide on challenges to legislative powers is equally mistaken. From the beginning of Canadian democracy, courts have had the task of deciding whether laws challenged as going beyond the powers of the legislature that enacted them were valid or not. Moreover, even without a written bill of rights, courts required legislatures to conform to the basic principles of democratic government and equality. They did this through interpretation and in some cases—and this surprises some people—through striking laws down. Let me cite an example of each.

The first example is interpretative. It shows how, 50 years ago, the courts used the process of interpretation to recognize equality rights in Canada. Canada, of course, was founded amid the patriarchal notions prevalent in the mid-nineteenth century. Professions, governance—indeed, everything outside domestic work and a little teaching and nursing—was strictly reserved for men. When Emily Murphy was sworn in as a police magistrate in 1916 in Alberta, she was met on her second case with a challenge to her jurisdiction. The challenge went this way: Only "persons" are entitled to sit as judges. "Persons" means men. You are not a man. Therefore you cannot sit as a judge. Or to put it in the quaint but precise terms of Edwardian legalese: "Women are persons for pains and punishments, but not for privileges. Sitting as a judge is a privilege. Therefore, you, a woman, cannot sit as a judge."

To us this argument sounds ridiculous. But in the early 1900s it was not. Courts in England and in various parts of Canada had repeatedly ruled that laws enabling persons to do certain things—be they to practice law or medicine or sit as judges—applied only to men. Outside the criminal law, which applied regardless of sex, the word "persons," interpreted legally, meant "men." So the lawyer who challenged Emily Murphy's jurisdiction to sit as a police magistrate was on sound legal ground. But Emily Murphy refused to accept the legal status quo. She believed the law to be fundamentally unjust and decided to seek its change. She brought a case before the Supreme Court of Alberta and obtained a ruling, revolutionary at the time, that "persons" in the Judges' Act included women.

But that was not the end of the story. The federal government did not accept the view of the Supreme Court of Alberta that "persons" included women. It continued to deny women the right to sit in the Senate of Canada on the ground that women were not "persons" within the meaning of those provisions of the *British North America Act* dealing with the constitution of the Senate. Emily Murphy and four cohorts in Alberta sued again, this time for an order that "persons" included women. The government fought them all the way. They pursued their claim to the Supreme Court of Canada, which ruled against them. So they raised more money and took their case all the way to the Judicial Committee of the Privy Council in London, which was then Canada's court of last resort. There, finally, in a decision that has come to be known as the "Persons Case," they prevailed.

The Privy Council, in a landmark ruling that affected the law not only in Canada but in Britain and throughout the Commonwealth, held that contrary to previous law, "persons" should be read to include women. Viscount Sankey proclaimed that the Constitution of Canada was "a living tree, capable of growth and expansion within its natural limits. The object of the Act was to grant a Constitution to Canada … Their Lordships do not conceive it to be the duty of this Board—it is certainly not their desire—to cut down the provisions of the Act by a narrow and technical construction, but rather to give it a large and liberal interpretation …"

In the course of interpreting the Constitution this way, two important things occurred: The law was altered, indeed fundamentally reversed; and women were accorded vast new rights they had not enjoyed before. Many people didn't like the ruling, and many people, we can safely speculate, muttered darkly about judicial activism. Sound like the Charter? Indeed, yes. Of course, at the time, it would have been open to Parliament to pass a new law saying expressly that women could not sit as senators. But reading the history books, one gets the sense that parliamentarians were not keen to remove from women what the Privy Council had found to be a fundamental right: the right to participate in the governance of the nation.

The second example illustrates how pre-Charter courts could and did require legislatures to conform to the fundamental principles of justice by striking down offending legislation. I refer to the 1938 *Alberta Reference*. The times were hard, people were desperate, and extreme ideas held great appeal. One of the strongest majoritarian governments Canada had ever known, the Aberhart government in Alberta, determined that for the good of the people, it must restrict the press' criticism of the government's economic policies. So it passed an act, modestly entitled "An Act to Ensure the Publication of Accurate News and Information," requiring critical comment to be submitted to the government for advance inspection.

Canada then possessed no bill of rights or Charter. It had only the *British North America Act*, setting forth the division of powers between the federal and provincial governments. Nowhere did that Act mention free speech. Yet the Supreme Court of Canada struck the bill down. Although the result was ultimately based on the fact that the entire scheme was beyond the legislative competence of the provinces, the Court commented on the impact of this particular Act. It held that there was an implied guarantee in the Canadian Constitution that protected free expression about the conduct of government. Free speech was one of the pillars upon which the very notion of democracy itself existed. Free speech, said Chief Justice Duff, was "the breath of life for parliamentary institutions." As such, the legislature of Alberta was bound by it, even though it did not formally appear in the *British North America Act*.

These are but two examples. There are many others. In the area of criminal law and evidence, for example, pre-Charter courts modified and adapted the common law and interpreted legislation in a way that ensured that the fundamental liberties of the individual were maintained. Thus, Charter rights did not spring, full-grown from the head of Zeus. Canadians had rights long before the Charter and the courts served as the guardians of those rights. The Charter accepted this tradition and entrenched the role of judges as interpreters and guardians of the rights it guaranteed. Once we came to realize as a community that some rights were fundamental, there was really no alternative. As former Supreme Court Justice Bertha Wilson wrote in the April 1999 issue of *Policy Options*, "You cannot entrench rights in the Constitution without some agency to monitor compliance. The judiciary was the obvious choice."

So in one sense, the Charter is old news. Yet in another, it has changed things, indeed, changed them profoundly. On a micro level, it has forced us to update our laws of criminal evidence and procedure. It has given impetus to the move to require governments to treat their citizens equally, without discrimination, regardless of factors like race, religion, sex or age. It has forced examination of electoral practices, like manipulative riding boundaries and bans on polling. And it has required us to consider again precisely where we should draw the line between the individual's right of free expression and the need to protect the community from harmful expression.

On the macro level, change has been equally important. I accept the frequently-made charge that the Charter has changed the way Canadians think and act about their rights. The Charter has made Canadians realize on a profoundly personal level what perhaps they had formally recognized only in a detached, intellectual sense: that their rights belong to them, that these rights are a precious part of their personal inheritance, and that they must exercise them and vigilantly protect them if they are to keep them healthy and strong.

If this is a culture of rights, then I welcome it. The debate we see every day on the editorial pages of our newspapers about the ambit of our rights and where lines should be drawn between conflicting rights and between the rights of the individual and the interest of the community, can only strengthen our society and our sense of being partners in this Canadian venture. It is the mark of a civil society, of a healthy mature democracy, that such things are debated in the newspapers and on the talk shows of our country, and not swept under the rug or, worse yet, fought out in back alleys and trenches.

The second general way the Charter has changed Canadian society is that it has increased the profile of the judicial branch of government. Before we had a Charter, judges were marking boundaries between rights, changing the law to reflect settled and emergent conceptions of rights, and occasionally even striking down laws that violated fundamental rights. However, the Charter, by putting the people's rights up front and centre, has accelerated the process. It is easier to challenge a law on the ground that it violates a fundamental right when you have in your hand a document that specifically proclaims your entitlement to that right. Compared to the task faced by Emily Murphy and her cohorts, for example, it is easier to change a legal interpretation that produces inequality, like the traditional interpretations of the word "persons," when you possess a document that commits the government to equal treatment. Moreover, people's new awareness of their rights has led individuals and interest groups—and they are to be found on both sides of virtually every issue—to come together and mobilize to protect their conception of a particular right. So the Charter has increased the challenges to laws on the basis of rights and thus incidentally increased the profile of courts called upon to resolve these issues.

This brings us to the current debate over whether the formal realignment in powers that the Charter has brought about has left too much power in the hands of judges. Depending on how the commentator views the issue, it is put in different terms. Some common variants include:

- "Judges have used the Charter to effect a giant power-grab."
- "Unelected judges are running the country."
- And simply, "Judges are too activist."

The idea of an overt power grab is easily dismissed. There is no evidence that judges, individually or collectively, particularly wanted the Charter or that, once it arrived, they decided to use it to entrench their power at the expense of Parliament and the elected legislatures. Equally easily dismissed is the idea that unelected judges are running the country. True, judges are unelected, and I believe should remain unelected, having considered the conflicts of interest and related problems an elected judge system presents. But that does not mean they cannot properly act as referees between conflicting rights and interests and as interpreters of the Constitution and the law. Nor does it mean that they are running the country.

Anyone seriously putting forth such a charge must confront the existence of Section 1 of the Charter, which permits the legislatures to trench on guaranteed rights to the extent that such a course can be shown to be justified in a free and democratic society.

Should s. 1 fail to confirm a law, Section 33 is also available to permit the elected representatives of the community to override the courts' assessment of what the rights of the individual require.

At this point the proponents of the theory that the judges are running the country shift to pragmatic arguments. It's too hard to justify infringements under s. 1 or to use s. 33 to override judicial decisions, they argue. There is something in this. It is true that, as a practical matter, it is not easy for legislatures to say to the people, or even a small unpopular sub-group of the people, "Notwithstanding your rights, we are going to violate them." But that, I believe, is as it should be. Individual rights have substance and they should not lightly be cast aside. But the fact remains that, in some circumstances, Parliament and the legislatures can override judicial decisions on the Charter if the considered sentiments of the community make it politically feasible to do so. We must therefore reject the arguments that the judges of Canada have used the Charter to effect a power grab and are running the country.

This leaves the charge of judicial activism. Judges, it is said, are too eager to overturn laws, too ready to strike statutes down, too apt to "rewrite" laws enacted by Parliament and the legislatures. I note at the outset that there is not much hard evidence that judges are inappropriately activist, whatever that may mean. A recent study by Professor Patrick Monahan of Osgoode Hall Law School concludes on the basis of considerable statistical analysis that the Supreme Court of Canada, far from being activist, as many have charged, is rather inclined to be judicially conservative and deferential to the elected arms of government. The same study suggests that it is very hard to find instances of the Court "rewriting" laws. Given the absence of any contrary studies of similar depth, this should at least give the critics pause.

Beyond this, it seems to me that if we are to talk sensibly about judicial activism, we must define our terms. Judicial activism means almost as many things to its critics as did the parts of the elephant to the blind men in the old parable.

Some people equate judicial activism with any judicial decision that changes the law. The theory here is that it is the job of judges to apply the law as it is found to exist, never to change or update it. This theory betrays a misapprehension of what judges have always done under both the common law and the civil law of this country. The venerable tradition of developing the law through an accumulation of precedent lies at the heart of our legal system, and is the lifeblood of a socially responsive body of law. New circumstances are brought before the courts. In applying the law, be it a previous case or a provision of the Charter, judges examine the law and the circumstances to see whether the old law should apply or whether it now seems unjust to do so. If a careful analysis reveals that the old law no longer reflects what is considered to be fair and appropriate, it is modified. This involves changing the law. But if changing the law is judicial activism, then judicial activism is neither new nor undesirable.

Ah, the critic says, but judicial activism is not merely changing the law, but changing the law too much. There is some truth in this. Radical changes of the law can be considered "activist" by definition. However, this does not get us any closer to answering the question of whether the Charter has made judges activist. We are left with many difficulties. The first problem is whether the fact that a change is radical necessarily means it is bad. Was it necessarily bad that the Privy Council in 1929 ruled that the word "persons" included women, thereby opening public life and the professions to women? The change was radical, but most would argue, desirable and long overdue.

The second difficulty lies in defining "radical." One person's "sensible incremental development" is another's "radical alteration of the law." Judicial activism in this sense thus often reduces itself to a debate about whether one likes or does not like a particular judicial decision. This does not bring us much closer to answering the question of whether the Charter has made judges inappropriately activist.

This concept of judicial activism is closely related to what I call the "political mirror" model of judicial activism. On this view, a decision is "activist" if it does not accord with one's political or legal viewpoint. This has led to the situation where both conservatives and liberals accuse the courts under the Charter of being too activist. Conservatives assail liberal, rights-affirming decisions as "activist." Liberals, on the other hand, assail as "activist" those decisions in which, rather than setting aside the law, the courts ignore or read down Charter provisions. Thus, as Professor Lorraine Eisenstat Weinrib wrote in the April 1999 issue of *Policy Options*, "It is the deferential, conservative justices who have been impermissibly activist. They have consistently ignored the values of the Charter text, its political history and its stated institutional roles." With the fire coming from both quarters, what, one might be forgiven for asking, is a judge to do?

Another version of judicial activism equates it with result-oriented, agenda-driven judging. I am the first to say that if it could be shown that Canadian judges were engaging in this kind of judging it would be bad. Judges must be impartial. They must not be biased. Their job is to study the law and the facts, listen to all the arguments pro and con, and after due deliberation, rule as their intellect, informed conscience, and training dictate. The spectre of agenda-driven judging is, to the best of my knowledge, just that—a spectre. If established, it would be a terrible thing and could not be tolerated. But it is not established.

It seems to me that people too often confuse agenda-driven judging, which would be bad, with judicial consistency, which is good. In the course of their work, judges may have developed fairly firm views about what a particular Charter provision means or where lines should be drawn between conflicting rights and interests. It is the task of the judge, at the beginning of each new case, to suspend those views and reconsider them in light of the submissions of the parties in that particular case. Yet if the judge, after considering all the submissions, arrives at a conclusion similar to that which he or she arrived at before, that is no cause for alarm. Indeed, it suggests a rational, carefully considered approach to the task of judging.

I am left with the feeling that the vague term "judicial activism," to the extent that it is used as more than merely a proxy for decisions the critic does not like, has to do with the fear that judges will depart from the settled law—that they will take advantage of the fact that no one, except for Parliament or the legislatures under s. 33, can override them, to foist unwarranted and unjustified laws on the people. The fear is well-known to jurists and not confined to rights litigation. Long before charters of rights were dreamed of, the English spoke ominously of "palm tree" justice, evoking the image of a colonial magistrate, seated under his judicial palm tree, meting out whatever decisions happened to seem right to him in the particular cases at hand.

The opposite of palm tree justice, or what we may call judicial activism in the Charter era, is justice rooted in legal principle and appropriate respect for the constitutional role of Parliament and the legislatures. The law has developed rules and ways of proceeding to assist judges in avoiding the evils of unprincipled, inappropriately interventionist judging. The first rule is that judges must ensure that their decisions are grounded in a thorough understanding of the Charter provisions at issue and the jurisprudence interpreting it. Where previous authority exists, changes should follow incrementally—absent the rare case of where manifest error is demonstrated, such as, for example, in the *Persons Case*. While the language of the Charter is open-textured and leaves room for judicial discretion in certain areas, it provides more guidance to those who study its language and values than is often realized. To quote Professor Weinrib again: "The Charter itself provides significant guidance for judicial interpretation."

It is still very early days for the Canadian Charter. But already we have a significant body of jurisprudence fleshing out its guarantees. Future decisions will build on this. The first time a Charter pronouncement is made that seems to change the law, it may strike many as "activist."

But as a body of principle develops, the foundation of court decisions on the words of the Charter and the stable nature of the jurisprudence will become more apparent.

The second rule judges should follow is that they should be appropriately respectful of the role of Parliament and the legislatures and the difficulty of their task. While always important, this rule assumes particular significance in cases where the Charter or law at issue permits two or more interpretations or authorizes the judge to exercise discretion. "Appropriate respect" presupposes an understanding of the role of the legislative branch of government as the elected representative of the people to enact laws that reflect the will and interests of all the people.

To state this role is to acknowledge the difficulty of its execution. In a society as diverse and complex as ours, enacting laws is rarely a simple process of codifying the will of the people. It is rather a delicate task of accommodating conflicting interests and rights. Compromise is the watchword of modern governance. Judicial decision-making, on the other hand, is necessarily a blunt instrument, incapable of achieving the balances necessary for a workable law acceptable to society as a whole (on this point see Professor Rainer Knopff's paper in the April 1999 issue of *Policy Options*).

This is not to say that, where an individual's constitutional rights are at stake, the courts must always accept the compromises the legislators work out. Where laws unjustifiably violate constitutional rights, it is the clear duty of the courts to so declare, with the result that the offending law is to that extent null and void under Section 52 of the Charter. Slavish deference would reduce Charter rights to meaningless words on a scrap of paper. It is to say, however, that judging should be grounded in principle and an appropriate respect for the different roles of the elected representatives of the people and the courts.

Thus far in our Charter's short history, the courts have repeatedly countenanced respect for the choices of Parliament and the legislatures. They have repeatedly affirmed that it is not the court's role to strike the policy compromises that are essential to effective modern legislation. The role of the courts is the much more modest but nevertheless vital task of hearing constitutional claims brought by individuals, identifying unconstitutional legislative acts where such can be demonstrated, and applying the Charter we have all agreed upon.

Judges and the Charter Revolution

F.L. Morton and Rainer Knopff (2000)

50

EDITORS' INTRODUCTION

Frederick Lee ("Ted") Morton was on the faculty of the political science department at the University of Calgary (1981–2004), was elected as a Progressive Conservative member of the Alberta Legislature in 2004, and is a former cabinet minister in the Alberta government. He is currently an Executive-in-Residence and Senior Fellow at the School of Public Policy at the University of Calgary. Rainer Knopff is also professor of political science at the University of Calgary and a well-known expert on the areas of public law, public policy, and political thought, with a particular focus on Canadian issues.

Morton and Knopff have been two of the Supreme Court's sternest critics. Their central argument is captured in the title of the book from which this extract is taken, The Charter Revolution and the Court Party. *They see the Charter as amounting to a revolutionary change in Canada's system of government, a change brought about by a coalition of like-minded social reformers on the bench, in the legal profession, the law schools, and special-interest groups. Together these groups constitute the Court Party. It is not so much the policy agenda of the Court Party that they object to, but the undemocratic means it uses to achieve its objectives. In the chapter we have excerpted below, Morton and Knopff identify the procedural and interpretative moves whereby the Supreme Court has advanced the Court Party's agenda.*

> *People have been taught to believe that when the Supreme Court speaks it is not they who speak but the Constitution, whereas, of course, in so many vital cases, it is they who speak and not the Constitution.*
>
> US Supreme Court Justice Felix Frankfurter in a
> letter to President Franklin D. Roosevelt.

The Charter does not so much guarantee rights as give judges the power to make policy by choosing among competing interpretations of broadly worded provisions. Judges often deny that they make policy, insisting that they are simply applying the Charter, and thus implementing established legal policy. In *Vriend*, for example, the Supreme Court spoke of judges

Source: Excerpted from *The Charter Revolution and the Court Party* by F.L. Morton and Rainer Knopff. Peterborough, ON: Broadview Press, 2000. Notes omitted. Reprinted by permission.

as "trustees" of the Charter whose job it was to scrutinize the work of the other branches of government in the name of the "new social contract" it represented. The hollowness of these denials is evident whenever some of the trustees disagree with others about how to interpret the Charter, as members of appeal court panels regularly do. During the Charter's first decade, for example, fewer than 60 per cent of the Supreme Court's Charter decisions were unanimous, compared with an average of over 80 per cent for its non-Charter rulings. From 1991 to 1998 the rate of unanimous Supreme Court Charter decisions dropped further, to less than 50 per cent—to the dismay of lower court judges, who are supposed to follow Supreme Court precedents.

When judges disagree, each one indulges in the legal fiction that his understanding of the Charter is correct and that his colleagues are mistaken. In fact, there are usually several plausible interpretations and no obviously correct answer. The Charter, in short, is largely indeterminate with respect to the questions that arise under it. Does the section 2 guarantee of freedom of expression prevent the censorship of pornography or hate literature, or do the section 15 equality rights justify—perhaps even require—such censorship? Does section 7, which guarantees "everyone's" right to "life, liberty, and security of the person," protect the life of a fetus or the liberty of a woman to have an abortion? No clear answer to these questions can be found in the broadly worded text of the Charter, and judges are thus free to choose.

Judicial policymaking requires more than interpretive discretion, however. The traditional barriers that restrict access to the courts, and thus limit the scope of the courts' policy review powers, must also be removed. The classic adjudication-of-disputes function of courts places many such restrictions on both litigants and courts: the rules of standing, mootness, intervener (third-party) participation, and others. Step by step, these have been removed by the Supreme Court. The result is that many policy decisions that offend well organized interest groups can now be directly challenged. In a dazzling exercise of self-empowerment, the Supreme Court has transformed itself from an adjudicator of disputes to a constitutional oracle that is able and willing to pronounce on the validity of a broad range of public policies. ...

Judicial Discretion

Judicial discretion tends to be most vigorously denied when it is most flagrantly employed. In a democratic age, those who use or benefit from the power of appointed and unaccountable offices typically deny the reality of that power lest they undermine its legitimacy. In the case of judges, the denials will not withstand scrutiny.

There are three main ways in which judges might deny the claim that the Charter revolution is caused chiefly by judicial discretion: (1) that the Charter gives effect to certain obvious or core values that are beyond the discretion of judges to transform; (2) that some parts of the Charter revolution are clearly required by the Charter's text; and (3) that where the text is unclear, judges can find objective guidance for their decisions in such non-textual sources as the original intent, traditional understanding, or essential purpose of Charter rights.

Upon inspection, none of these constraints on judicial discretion turns out to be significant. Some of them, especially the claims of original intent or traditional understanding, might indeed tie judicial hands. However, they have been rejected by the interpretive community of judges and Charter experts. The other constraints either impose no limits of practical significance or actually enhance judicial discretion.

Core Values Do Not Constrain Judicial Discretion

The Charter is not completely malleable; it is not a blank cheque made out to judicial power. On the contrary, its provisions clearly give effect to a number of unchallenged and uncontested core values. Virtually everyone in contemporary Canada would agree, for example, that a theocratic religious establishment would violate freedom of religion; that prohibiting the political participation of women or racial minorities would infringe equality and democratic rights; and that hanging pickpockets would constitute cruel and unusual punishment.

The Charter is perfectly clear about such questions. And perfectly useless. The core values guaranteed by the Charter were already legally established in common law and statutory form well before its entrenchment in 1982. More importantly, they were solidly embedded in the beliefs and habits of Canadian citizens. Precisely because there *is* a consensus about the core values of the Charter, however, they will not arise as questions for judicial determination.

There are, of course, plenty of questions that do arise for judicial determination, which is to say that there is widespread, and often passionate, disagreement about the meaning of the Charter. But do these disagreements really go to the core of Charter values? How could it be that "we find ourselves arguing, so vehemently and so often, about the very core of what we have, as participants in a democratic polity, long since presumably agreed upon?" How can a society simultaneously agree upon and endlessly dispute its foundational norms?

The answer is that our disagreements about the Charter—the questions we actually litigate—involve not the well established core but the indeterminate peripheral meaning of Charter rights. While the core meaning of a right may be widely agreed upon, its outer-limits are inherently contestable. Religious freedom is certainly infringed by theocratic establishments, but what about laws that criminalize the use of certain drugs? Do religions that make sacramental use of those drugs have a fundamental right to an exemption not available to others? Some claim such a right to be exempted on religious grounds from otherwise valid laws, but John Locke, universally recognized as a friend of religious freedom, argued against it. This is not a disagreement that pits tyrants against the true friends of liberty; it is a disagreement that divides liberal democrats of good standing. ...

Canada in short, would remain a member in good standing of the liberal democracies of the world regardless of the outcome of such Charter issues as whether Sikhs in the RCMP are allowed to wear turbans or the legal definition of spouse is read to include homosexuals. The "wrong" answer to such questions does not turn the country into a tyranny, though that is precisely what rights claimants tend to argue. Rights claiming under the Charter, in other words, often represents the attempt to enhance the normative appeal of a debatable policy claim by casting the other side in the debate as evil and tyrannical. Exaggerating policy claims is, of course, a natural and ineradicable feature of political life, but healthy polities seek ways of moderating the bellicose tendency to exaggerate. Charter-based rights talk fuels this dangerous tendency rather than checking it. ...

To summarize, legal indeterminacy and judicial discretion emerge not with respect to core values, about which consensus exists, but with respect to second-order questions, about which dissensus prevails. Canadians may agree that the Charter prohibits theocracy or grossly discriminatory laws, but they certainly do not agree about what it implies for mandatory retirement or the public funding of religious schools. No one nowadays advocates the hanging of pickpockets, but many people support capital punishment for the most heinous crimes.

The Charter supplies few obvious answers to the second order questions that actually come before the courts. The text rarely settles such issues of reasonable disagreement; judges do. The Charter's core values—those matters that the text *does* settle—are not responsible for the Charter revolution.

Textual Innovation Has Not Constrained Judicial Discretion

While the text of the Charter rarely mandates significant policy change in areas of reasonable disagreement, it does so in a few instances. A second line of defense against the charge of unbridled judicial law-reform is thus to point to those sections of the Charter which clearly do effect legal change. For example, section 24(2) of the Charter creates an exclusionary rule where none had existed before. Whether or not to exclude perfectly reliable evidence because of improprieties in the way it was collected remains much more controversial than the hanging of pickpockets, yet the Charter unmistakably mandates such exclusion in certain circumstances.

Similarly, whereas the equality provision in the 1960 Bill of Rights guaranteed only "equality before the law," section 15 of the Charter contains the additional guarantees of "equality under the law" and "equal benefit of the law." The history of section 15 shows that these phrases were added, at the behest of feminist lobbying, to overrule the *Lavell* and *Bliss* decisions, two Bill of Rights decisions from the 1970s. In *Lavell*, the Supreme Court held that "equality before the law" required only equal application of the laws, not equal laws; it thus upheld a provision of the Indian Act that blatantly discriminated against Native women because it discriminated against all of them in the same way. In *Bliss*, the Court suggested that government benefit programs, such as unemployment insurance, were exempt from equality requirements. The new wording of section 15 directed the courts to give a more substantive meaning to equality under the Charter.

Another example is section 10(b) of the Charter, which not only replicates the Bill-of-Rights guarantee of a right to counsel upon detention or arrest, but adds an American-style requirement for police to inform detainees of this right. In its 1964 *Miranda* decision, the American Supreme Court added such a requirement to the pre-existing right to counsel in the US Constitution. The Canadian Supreme Court refused to add a similar requirement to the 1960 Bill of Rights in the 1978 case, *Hogan v. The Queen*. In effect, section 10(b) of the Charter overrules *Hogan*.

Section 23 of the Charter provides yet another example. It imposes on provincial governments new obligations to provide primary and secondary education to official language minorities in their own language.

Such exceptions notwithstanding, relatively little of the Charter revolution can be explained by textually mandated change. Despite a few textual innovations in the Charter, Canadians did not go to bed on April 17, 1982 with a substantially new set of rights and freedoms. For the most part, the Charter simply constitutionalized concepts—religious freedom, freedom of expression, fair trial, the right against self-incrimination, etc.—that had a long history of legal protection in this country. Common law and statute, including the 1960 statutory Bill of Rights, had protected them. Although the legal *status* of many of these concepts changed through constitutional entrenchment in 1982, there was generally no textual indication that their *content* was also to change. The fact that the Charter revolution is more a judicial than a legal revolution is evident in the many cases that brought about dramatic legal change without any textual warrant for such change.

For example, nowhere does the Charter explicitly give suspects the right to remain silent during pre-trial investigation. Indeed, civil libertarians' requests to place this right in the Charter were rejected by the framers. This did not stop the Supreme Court from reading in such a right as a necessary corollary of both the Charter's right to counsel and its requirement of "fundamental justice." Nor did it stop the Court from extending the Canadian version of this right to blood-sample and lineup evidence gathered in the absence of counsel, something that not even the American version requires. ...

Even where clear textual changes exist, the legal transformations undertaken in their name are often anything but obvious. As noted earlier, the Charter does explicitly provide for the exclusion of evidence if it has been "obtained in a manner that infringed or denied" Charter rights. However, unlike the American rule, which tended toward automatic exclusion, the new Canadian exclusionary rule was explicitly conditional. Only if a judge deemed that "its admission would bring the administration of justice into disrepute" was evidence to be excluded. During the framing process, the government defended this new wording on the grounds that it would allow exclusion only in extreme, and therefore rare, circumstances.

In the hands of the Supreme Court, however, exclusion has become anything but rare. In a series of rulings, the most important of which is *R. v. Collins*, the Supreme Court has progressively lowered the threshold for exclusion of evidence. Given this low threshold, the Court has chosen to exclude evidence 45 per cent of the time; when the evidence takes the form of confessions or other incriminating statements, the exclusion rate jumps to 60 percent.

Critics claim that the Court has "produced [an exclusionary] rule which bears little resemblance to the text of the section." Even those who applaud this development concede that "neither the rigour of the exclusionary rule nor its extension ... were anticipated by the framers of the Charter. Both are due to the Court's willingness to give its provisions a purposive interpretation." By 1996 Crown prosecutors had become so frustrated with the judges' frequent exclusion of reliable evidence, including involuntary police line-up identification and blood samples, that the attorney-general of Canada asked the Supreme Court to formally overrule the *Collins* precedent. The Court not only refused, but extended the list of prohibited forms of self-incrimination to include involuntary DNA samples.

The equality rights provision of the Charter—section 15—provides a second example of how judicial innovations have gone well beyond those mandated by the text. As noted above, the framers expanded the traditional wording of the right to force judges to scrutinize the substance of laws as well as their application and administration. However, the opening words of section 15 refer to these expanded rights as belonging to "every individual." Despite such textual clarity, the Supreme Court has interpreted equality rights in a manner that extends them mainly to members of so-called disadvantaged groups. ...

In sum, while the Charter does include some textual innovation, this innovation explains relatively little of the Charter revolution. Most of the important questions arising under the Charter have been settled by judges exercising policymaking discretion, not by its text.

Original Intent, Traditional Understanding, and Purposive Analysis Do Not Constrain Judicial Discretion

Does the inability of the naked text to settle the kinds of questions typically raised under the Charter necessarily mean that they are settled by judicial discretion? When laws fail to settle questions arising under them, it used to be common to look behind the unclear text and consult the intention of the law's framers. And when the original intent was unclear or ambiguous, judges often fell back on the well-established or traditional understanding of the relevant legal language. Reliance on either original intent or traditional understanding provides a strong *prima facie* answer to the charge of judicial policymaking. Judges who can plausibly claim to be giving effect to the framers' intent or to longstanding understandings are indeed applying the law, not their personal policy predilections. A currently popular alternative to original intent and traditional understanding is "purposive analysis," which seeks to deduce answers to interpretive questions from the broader purposes of the legal provision. Can Canada's judges rely on original intent, traditional understanding, or purposive analysis to avoid the charge that they, more than the Charter itself, are responsible for the Charter revolution?

They certainly can't rely on the concept of traditional understanding, which can act only as a brake on policy innovation. ... But, while the courts have occasionally used the Charter to protect existing practice against legislative innovation, they have often used it to initiate new policy themselves. In effect, the Supreme Court, inspired by its academic chroniclers, has inverted the traditional understanding of constitutionalism and judicial review as conserving forces, and transformed them into instruments of social reform. Rather than serving as a prudent brake on political change, the judiciary has become a catalyst for change.

If traditional understanding cannot explain the Charter revolution, can original intent do so? Where the text does not clearly require a policy innovation, in other words, might the framers nevertheless have intended that innovation? It seems improbable. Because the questions that arise under the Charter are contentious, second-level questions, about which no consensus exists, it is unlikely that the framers would have come down clearly on one side or the other. To have done so, moreover, would arguably have been inappropriate. The relative permanence and loftiness of constitutional law, one might think, should be used to enshrine principles of deep consensus, not to settle ongoing matters of reasonable disagreement. If the framers had nevertheless intended to settle a highly contested issue, wouldn't they have been absolutely clear about it in the text, rather than leaving it to the discretion of judges? One cannot escape the conclusion that when the text is unclear, judicial policy innovation undertaken in its name cannot be justified in terms of the original intent of the framers.

This conclusion is borne out when one actually looks for evidence of original intent on some of the more contentious questions that have been answered by the courts. Original intent is admittedly a slippery concept. For instance, different framers might intend to achieve very different things with precisely the same legal wording. Still, the evidence we do have makes it difficult for the Supreme Court to claim that its substantive policy innovations are grounded in original intention rather than judicial discretion.

We have already noted, for example, that the Court ran counter to the expectations of many of the framers when it created a pre-trial right to silence for criminal suspects and operated the exclusionary rule in a manner that makes exclusion of evidence the rule rather than the exception. The same is true of Henry Morgentaler's successful Charter challenge to the abortion provisions of the Criminal Code. During the framing process, the Trudeau government rejected numerous petitions from both pro-choice and pro-life groups to entrench their respective positions in the Charter. There was strong evidence that influential framers intended to leave abortion entirely to the regular political process, beyond the scope of judicial review. This evidence was cited by the two dissenting judges in *Morgentaler*, who argued vigorously in favour of a hands-off approach by the Court. Not surprisingly, the five-judge majority in *Morgentaler* did not appeal to original intent to justify their activism; indeed, they ignored the issue of original intent altogether. ...

The issue of gay rights provides another example of the disjunction between framers' intent and judicial policymaking. During the period of Chartermaking, the Trudeau government and the Parliamentary Committee on the Constitution rejected repeated requests by gay rights activists to insert protection for sexual orientation in the Charter. As with the abortion issue, the lack of any societal consensus on these issues counselled against addressing them in the Charter. Trudeau's advisors feared that anticipated public controversy might swamp their entire package of constitutional reform. As recently as 1992, sexual orientation was not included in the Charlottetown Accord, despite symbolic mention of all the other Charter groups. Nevertheless, in its 1995 *Egan* ruling the Supreme Court added sexual orientation to the list of prohibited grounds of discrimination in section 15.

True, there is evidence that some framers, such as Jean Chrétien (then the justice minister), were prepared to leave the matter of gay rights to future judicial discretion. Indeed, Patrick Monahan contends that Chrétien's view was common among the framers. "They had," says Monahan, "a relatively sophisticated and realistic view of the nature of the adjudication process," one that recognized "the significant degree of discretion available to courts interpreting constitutional texts." The framers, in this view, undoubtedly had "substantive intent" about particular policy issues, but they did not necessarily regard "those substantive views as conclusive." If one wants to be "really serious about fidelity to the intention of the drafters," argues Monahan, one must acknowledge their intent to hand over considerable policymaking discretion to the judiciary. The drafters, he contends, "saw their task as making educated guesses as to how the courts might interpret particular constitutional language, and choosing the language which was most likely to secure for them the results they desired," while accepting that their expectations might be upset by "inevitable" judicial originality. In other words, what might be called the framers' general intent to confer broad policy discretion on the courts takes precedence over their specific or substantive intent about particular policy questions that might arise for judicial determination.

This kind of claim has become a regular feature in judicial defences of the Charter revolution. In the 1985 *British Columbia Motor Vehicle Reference*, for example, Justice Lamer confronted the charge that the Charter had created a "judicial 'super-legislature' beyond the reach of parliament, the provincial legislatures and the electorate." To the extent that this is true, Lamer reminded his readers, critics should blame not the courts but "the elected representatives of the people of Canada. It was those representatives who extended the scope of constitutional adjudication and entrusted the courts with this new and onerous responsibility." ...

Surely a general intent to permit judicial discretion cannot be used to escape the charge that it is precisely this discretion, not the intent of the framers, that accounts for particular, substantive policy innovations undertaken in the name of the Charter. Framers who intend judicial *discretion* necessarily leave judges free to take different paths on controversial policy questions. If the general intent underlying the Charter truly gives judges policy discretion, then they can just as plausibly defer to the other branches of government as oppose them. Commentators who claim that deferential judgments themselves violate the Charter by ignoring "the values of the Charter text, its political history and its stated institutional roles" cannot simultaneously embrace a general intent of judicial *discretion*; they must be claiming an activist substantive intent to transform particular policies. One cannot have it both ways.

In fact, as we have seen, it is exceedingly difficult to explain judicial policy innovations in terms of the substantive intent of the framers. Understanding this difficulty, the Supreme Court itself rejected substantive intent as a significant standard of interpretation early in its Charter jurisprudence in the *British Columbia Motor Vehicle Reference*, the very case in which Justice Lamer embraced the general intent to confer policymaking power on the courts. *BC Motor Vehicles* confronted the Court with the question of whether section 7 of the Charter— the right not to be deprived of life, liberty or security of the person except in accordance with the principles of fundamental justice—was to be given a substantive or procedural meaning. On a procedural reading, governments could infringe the rights to life, liberty, and security of the person, as long as they did so in a manner that was procedurally fair. On a substantive reading, even procedural fairness could not justify some violations of the section 7 rights. There was ample documentary evidence that many of the most influential framers intended the narrower, procedural reading.

Such evidence did not deter Justice Lamer. Characterizing indications of substantive intent as "inherently unreliable" and "nearly impossible of proof," Lamer declared that, "it would be erroneous to give these materials anything but minimal weight." If the Court bound itself to substantive intent, he warned, the Charter's rights and freedoms would "in effect become frozen in time to the moment of adoption, with little or no possibility of growth and adjustment to changing societal needs." The preferred alternative, Lamer concluded, is to approach the Charter as "a living tree … [capable] of growth and adjustment over time." …

If neither original intent nor traditional understanding provide objective support for the judicial policy innovations undertaken in the name of the Charter, can such support be found in purposive analysis? Can Charter decisions be more objectively rooted in the broader purposes of the Charter's language than in the original intent of its framers? Our judges certainly think so. As the Supreme Court downplayed substantive original intent in its early Charter jurisprudence, it enthusiastically embraced purposive analysis as a way of justifying its policy innovations.

According to purposive analysis, judges should be guided by the essential purpose of a Charter right, or by the set of interests that the right is designed to protect. To discern the relevant purpose, judges are to look not to the intentions (or purposes) of the framers but to the evolving traditions of our society. The emphasis here is not on tradition simply, but on *evolving* tradition. Purposive analysis is forward looking. It draws on the past, but does so selectively, and only to discern a trend whose perfection or end point can be achieved by judicial policymaking. The point is not to maintain tradition against legislative policy innovation, but to justify judicial policy innovation. As we have argued elsewhere, "purposive analysis generally means the selective abstraction of highly general concepts from the tradition of liberal democracy in order to transform actual practice." The problem is that almost anything can be abstracted from the past in this way. In Peter Russell's words, "The history and philosophy of liberal democracy do not exactly form an open book containing clear definitions of the activities and interests" to be protected by the Charter. Russell concludes that purposive analysis "is an approach which may not yield the same results for all who apply it." In purposive analysis we confront yet another recipe for judicial discretion rather than a source of objectivity. Combined with the living tree approach, purposive analysis of rights enhances the ability of courts to act as agents of policy reform. It gives them free rein to discover new meaning in broadly conceived constitutional principles and to establish new rights if societal need, as appointed judges understand it, calls for them.

In sum, none of the defences against the charge of judicial discretion and policymaking work. ...

The attempt to deny or hide this truth can lead to a certain mendacity in judicial decision-making. In other words, to the extent that judges labour to camouflage their discretionary choices as the inescapable commands of the Charter, their overt reasons for deciding as they do may not be their real reasons. Consider the revelations provided in an interview given by Chief Justice Lamer on the fifteenth anniversary of the Charter in 1997. Lamer sought to defend what he admitted was one of the Supreme Court's most controversial Charter decisions, the *Morgentaler* abortion ruling. While claiming that he was "personally" against abortion, he added that he also believed that, "I should not impose upon others my personal beliefs." What then was the basis for his decision? Instead of pointing to a section of the Charter or some other conventional source of legal authority, Lamer invoked public opinion. Arguing that Canadians were split about 50–50 on the issue of abortion, he said "you should not make a crime out of something that does not have the large support of the community ... Who am I to tell 50 per cent of the population that they are criminals?'

For all the talk of living trees and purposive analysis, what Justice Lamer is really up to, it appears, is surveying public opinion and ensuring that public policy has "the large support of the community." Presumably, this is the kind of thing he had in mind when he said in a 1999 interview that in some of its controversial rulings, the Court was "just keeping in sync with society." Even if we accepted this as a legitimate judicial role, we might wish that Lamer would get his facts straight. Canadian public opinion toward abortion had not changed significantly since Parliament's 1969 abortion reform law and a plurality of Canadians have always supported the kind of policy compromise the 1969 law represented. ...

It is certainly true that policymaking discretion is inherent in the interpretive enterprise. Judicial policymaking, as we have ourselves argued many times, is quite unavoidable. But legislatures can overrule judicial interpretations of the common law or legislation much more easily than they can overrule Charter rulings, the section 33 override clause to the contrary notwithstanding. Although legislative majorities also cannot overrule the jurisprudence of federalism, it is more limited in scope. Deciding under the Charter *whether* government as such may (or must) do something, goes far beyond deciding *which* government may do it. As Ian Hunter has aptly put it, "It may be true that elephants and chipmunks are both mammals, but to fail to acknowledge the difference between them is wilful deception."

While it is true, in other words, that judicial discretion under the Charter is just one example of unavoidable judicial discretion, it is disingenuous to say that there is nothing new or different about it. Recall Chief Justice Lamer's comment that, with the advent of the Charter, the courts have been "drawn into the political arena to a degree unknown prior to 1982." Surely this would not have been the case if there was really nothing new going on. In fact, not only does the Charter provide broader scope for judicial policymaking, but the judges' embrace of the living tree and purposive analysis has significantly enhanced their policymaking potential. The sheer scope of judicial policy involvement under the Charter is certainly new, as are such innovations as judges rewriting legislation themselves rather than simply striking it down and allowing legislatures to decide how (or whether) to rewrite it.

Oracularism

If newly created judicial standards are to have widespread effect on public policies, they must apply well beyond the confines of the particular case before the court. Thus, encouraged and applauded by the advocacy scholarship of Court Party academics, the Supreme Court has transformed the judiciary from an adjudicative institution, whose primary purpose is to settle concrete disputes between individuals or between individuals and the state, into an oracle of the constitution, whose primary purpose is to solve social problems by issuing broad declarations of constitutional policy. Accompanying the substantive revolution described above, in other words, has been an equally important procedural revolution. The Court has swept aside traditional common law rules that restricted access to the courts and limited the scope of judicial influence.

Traditionally, the defining characteristic of courts was their dispute adjudication function. Yes, judges also interpret, and thus add to, the law, but such judicial law making was strictly confined by the adjudicative context. This meant that constitutional rights were understood to be not just "for" but also "by" individuals. Individual litigants raised rights claims in the course of settling legal disputes with the state. Among other things, this meant that the dispute came first, the constitutional issue second. The corollary to this was that the courts might never address many important constitutional questions. This was perfectly acceptable because constitutional interpretation and enforcement was not a monopoly of judges.

The Supreme Court of Canada has abandoned this view. It now sees itself as the authoritative oracle of the constitution, whose main job is to develop constitutional standards for society as a whole, rather than just for the litigants before it. The establishment of constitutional policy now comes first, the concrete dispute second. Indeed, with the important exception of criminal cases involving legal rights, the individual litigant is vanishing in Charter litigation. Corporations bring cases, and for policy charged cases, interest groups are increasingly prominent carriers of Charter litigation, if not as litigants, then as financial backers or interveners.

The Supreme Court has expedited interest group use of litigation, and thus its own policy-review role, by eliminating two of the three most significant barriers to access to the courts: standing and mootness. (The third barrier, costs, has been removed by government subsidies of Charter litigation. ...)

The doctrine of standing required the existence of a real-world legal dispute before a court could take jurisdiction. This prevented lawsuits by individuals who objected to a law for policy reasons but were not directly affected by it. As recently as 1981, Chief Justice Laskin articulated the rationale for standing in the first *Borowski* appeal when he wrote that "mere distaste [for a policy] has never been a ground upon which to seek the assistance of a Court." This restriction on citizen access limited the opportunities for judges to review legislation, but protected the courts from constantly being forced into confrontations with Parliament by disgruntled losers in the political arena. But Laskin spoke in dissent. A majority of the

Supreme Court voted to grant Joe Borowski standing to challenge Canada's abortion law despite the fact that he was not directly affected by it.

Similarly, the doctrine of mootness restricted access to the courts by requiring that a legal dispute still be a "live" dispute. If the original parties had resolved their differences, gone away or died, judges were barred from pronouncing on the legal questions raised. The Supreme Court began chipping away at this restriction in its very first Charter ruling. … Most recently, the Court ruled that homosexual couples were entitled to spousal-support protections upon the breakup of their relationships despite the fact that the couple who brought the case—known to the public as M. and H.—had reconciled. …

The Supreme Court has further facilitated interest group litigation by adopting a new, open-door policy for non-government interveners. Interveners are not parties to the dispute, but may be affected by or have an interest in the resolution of the legal questions raised. They thus seek to intervene in the appeal to signal their interest and present their opinions on the issue to the court. Historically, the Supreme Court had been stingy in granting intervener status to citizens or interest groups, precisely because the latter were not parties to the actual dispute, the Court's primary focus.

Initially the Court was wary about allowing interest groups to intervene in Charter decisions. Groups such as LEAF and the CCLA quickly realized that without access as interveners, they would be deprived of direct participation in the interpretive development of Charter law in the critical early cases. Beginning in 1984, they mounted a furious public relations campaign in law journals, at academic conferences, and by private and public letters to persuade the Court to loosen the rules on intervention. In 1986, the Court relented and adopted what amounts to an open-door policy on interveners. In 1987, it accepted 95 per cent of the intervener applications it received, up from 20 per cent in 1985. The acceptance rate has remained in the 80 to 90 per cent range.

Drawing on the American experience of systematic litigation strategies, a new breed of Canadian interest groups seized the opportunity offered by the Court's change of heart. Applications from non-government interveners tripled from 1986 to 1987. In the first three years of Supreme Court Charter decisions there were only 17 non-government interveners. By 1990, more than 100 interest-group interveners participated in over half of all the Supreme Court's Charter cases. By the end of 1993, the number had risen to 229. …

Interest groups intervene out of policy concerns that may be quite different from the more practical concerns of the immediate parties. In such cases, they have benefited from the Court's willingness to address issues not actually raised by the factual situations of the parties. In *Big M Drug Mart*, the Court struck down the Lord's Day Act as a violation of freedom of conscience despite the fact that the litigant challenging the law, a corporation, could not have a religious conscience. …

The Court has further empowered itself by changing the status of its own *obiter dicta*. Literally, "words spoken in passing," *obiter dicta* are those portions of a judgment that are outside the reasons—the *ratio decidendi*—that actually determine the outcome of a case. They are asides, or digressions. In common law jurisdictions, the *obiter dicta* of appeal courts have never been considered binding on lower courts. In Canada, the Supreme Court changed this in a 1980 decision in which it ruled that its own judicially considered *obiter* have the force of law. Baar points out that this is what bound lower courts to apply the Supreme

Court's "6 to 8 month *Askov* rule" to all cases. In *Askov*, the Supreme Court had found that nearly two years of delay between committal and trial amounted to a Charter violation, and then, in obiter, opined that anything over six to eight months was similarly unreasonable. When lower courts began applying this standard, over 40,000 cases were stayed, dismissed or withdrawn in Ontario alone, prompting the Supreme Court later to complain that it had been misunderstood. As Baar notes, "The binding force of judicially considered *dicta* in Canada gives its Supreme Court much more leverage than its American counterpart."

Although the Canadian Supreme Court occasionally surpasses its American counterpart, in many respects the high courts of both countries have undertaken the same kind of institutional retooling. Prodded and encouraged by the new generation of Canadian legal academics who had studied American constitutional law—many of them at US law schools—the Canadian Court has gone down much the same path taken by its American counterpart a generation earlier. As a prelude to its own rights revolution of the 1960s, the Warren Court (named after its Chief Justice, Earl Warren) began by sweeping aside the traditional restrictions on access such as mootness and standing. ... If, as Laurence Tribe observes, the approach to such issues as standing and mootness describes "an institutional psychology: an account of how ... the Justices of the Supreme Court view their own role," then the Warren Court clearly viewed its role as "that of an active partner with the executive branch in the transformation of American politics." Our own Supreme Court's institutional retooling under the Charter indicates that it aspires to a similar role.

Conclusion

The Charter provides the occasion for judicial policymaking, but the document itself is not the most important explanation for that policymaking. Judges themselves have chosen to treat the Charter as granting them open-ended policymaking discretion. They do not always admit their discretion; indeed, they often try to camouflage it. But their attempts to do so cannot withstand close inspection and are contradicted by the judges' own, more frank off-the-bench observations.

In addition, the Supreme Court has multiplied the opportunities for judicial policymaking by substantially redesigning itself—changing its rules of evidence, relevance, standing, mootness, and intervener status—from a constitutional adjudicator to a constitutional oracle. This institutional retooling, combined with the new sophistication of Canadian interest groups in using litigation, means that few major government policy initiatives are likely to escape a Charter challenge. Judicial intervention in the policymaking process is no longer *ad hoc* and sporadic, dependent upon the fortuitous collision of individual interests and government policy; it has become systematic and continuous. The Supreme Court now functions more like a *de facto* third chamber of the legislature than a court. The nine Supreme Court justices are now positioned to have more influence on how Canada is governed than are all of the parliamentarians who sit outside of cabinet.

Canada Looks Abroad

R.A. MacKay and E.B. Rogers (1938)

51

EDITORS' INTRODUCTION

R.A. MacKay was a renowned professor of political science at Dalhousie University and E.B. Rogers received a master's degree from the London School of Economics and participated in a study group of the Royal Institute of International Affairs.

Canada Looks Abroad is a contribution by the Canadian Institute of International Affairs to the discussion of Canadian external policy. In his foreword, J.W. Dafoe presented the book in these terms: "It is not devoted to the advocacy of a preconceived theory; and it is not propagandist in its methods. It is a detailed, objective and detached survey of the whole field for the purpose of putting within the possession of the Canadian reader the facts—geographic, economic, historical, political, and constitutional—which will enable him to reach an individual judgment as to the course which it is most advisable for Canada to pursue." In these excerpts from Chapter 17, the authors discuss how Canada should deal with conflicting loyalties and interests, and which principles should inform the emerging Canadian foreign policy.

Policy—Past and Present

It is sometimes asserted that Canada has no foreign policy. If by this is meant that no Canadian government has announced a comprehensive platform of foreign policy, the statement is largely true. But the historical survey of Canada's relations with the world outside … discloses a continuity of development in policy which perhaps few Canadians suspect. Despite Canada's short experience in world affairs policy tends to follow paths already charted by precedent and worn smooth by experience.

The problem of Canada's external relations, especially since the Great War, has been at bottom that of reconciling the geographical fact that Canada is situated on the North American continent, the historical fact of association with the British Empire, and the psychological fact of a growing national consciousness. The geographical fact is unalterable. The historical association was supported, and is no doubt still supported; but it has had to be adjusted to meet the newer sentiments of nationhood and the hard facts of geography. In the adjustment of conflicting loyalties and interests certain principles of policy have evolved, principles which may or may not stand the pressure of historic forces now operating in international society.

Source: Excerpted from *Canada Looks Abroad* by R.A. MacKay and E.B. Rogers. Toronto: Oxford University Press. 1938. Notes omitted.

Relations with the United States

There can be no doubt that the first principle of Canadian foreign policy now is the maintenance of friendly relations with the United States. This is dictated by many considerations, not the least of which is political security, though perhaps few Canadians are conscious of this problem. Yet the situation that Canada is strategically defenceless against the United States, especially since the development of mechanized armaments, must be frankly faced. Fortunately, the use of force has long been abandoned as an element of policy both by Canada and the United States in their mutual relations; instead both have come to rely on diplomacy and judicial or arbitral procedure for the protection of rights and interests as against each other. As has been pointed out elsewhere, the use of judicial or arbitral procedure for the settlement of disputes has placed Canada on a footing of equality with the United States as reliance on force never could have done, while the establishment of direct diplomatic relations between Washington and Ottawa has placed squarely upon the shoulders of the Canadian government the responsibility for the conduct of diplomatic relations with the United States. As far as her own affairs are concerned Canada has now no reason to anticipate any difficulties with the United States which cannot be solved without resort to force or threat of force. ...

Membership in the British Commonwealth of Nations

A second principle of policy generally accepted is that of continued membership in the special association of British countries which has come to be called the British Commonwealth of Nations. There can be little doubt that this is supported by the great majority of Canadians—by Canadians of British origin because it corresponds with their traditional loyalty to the Crown and to the mother country, by French Canadians who have come to look upon continuance of the British connection as a guarantee of their minority rights. And there are obvious material advantages to be gained from membership in the market for Canadian produce, and other member-states of the Commonwealth and the dependent empire are becoming more important markets. The extension of imperial preference following the Ottawa Conference of 1932 has probably enlarged these markets and in any case has made them more secure. In a world of unstable tariff barriers, of exchange restrictions, of quotas and subsidies in foreign trade, security of markets is of substantial importance to Canada. Were Canada to withdraw from the Commonwealth she would probably lose these preferential advantages and perhaps suffer a considerable loss in export trade to these markets. ...

The terms of membership in the Commonwealth are somewhat vague, and appear to have been left so by mutual consent. But Canadian policy towards the Commonwealth in the matter of defence and foreign affairs has become relatively clear. For convenience the summary made in a previous chapter is here repeated:

1. The policy of no commitments in advance to participate in the defence of the Commonwealth, enunciated more than thirty years ago by Laurier, appears now to be the very sheet anchor of Canadian policy.
2. In order to avoid being morally committed to support by arms or other means imperial foreign policy in general, Canada now takes no pat in the control of imperial foreign policy except where her interests are definitely at stake

3. Canada is prepared to consult and co-operate with Great Britain and other member-states of the Commonwealth in the formulation of foreign policy where Canadian interests are directly at stake. In such cases, the decision whether Canadian interests are at stake rests with Canada.

4. Canada has now control, in fact if not in form, of matters of foreign policy of interest to herself alone. In such matters she is, however, under obligation to keep other member-states fully informed in order that their interests may be safeguarded.

As has been pointed out elsewhere, these principles of autonomy in external affairs have been attained by changes in the conventions, not the law, of the constitution; and if our reasoning is correct, Canada and the United Kingdom are still legally one for purposes of war and peace because of the unity of the Crown. In short, Canada has not yet secured the legal right to be neutral in a British war. And indeed she has not yet made up her mind whether she wishes to have this right or not, a situation which might compromise her freedom of action in the event of war.

Membership in the League of Nations

A third principle of policy now generally accepted by all parties is that of membership in the League of Nations. As we have seen, membership was accepted at the outset of misgivings by some political leaders because it might involve Canada in other peoples' wars. From the first Canada opposed an interpretation of the Covenant which would make participation in military activities to protect other members an automatic obligation, and she has steadily resisted any strengthening of the League in this direction. Yet in the only test of coercive action by economic pressure by league members against an aggressor nation Canada was not remiss in co-operating with other members to preserve the Covenant, though she did draw back from taking any initiative lest it morally commit her to military measures as well. But it is significant that although after the incident of sanctions showed that there are real risks in membership in the League, even on the qualified terms on which Canada has insisted, no leader of any party in the federal arena openly advocated withdrawal from the League. Indeed, at the Assembly of 1936 after the fiasco of sanctions, the Canadian Prime Minister declared that Canada desired to reaffirm adherence to the fundamental principles of the Covenant, and desired no change in the Covenant itself, though he was careful to explain Canada's understanding of the nature of the League and of her obligations under the Covenant. …

Oriental Immigration

A fourth principle of policy tacitly accepted, though rarely stressed (except perhaps in British Columbia), is that Canada should remain a white man's country. Canada has long discriminated against Oriental immigration and now prohibits it entirely except for a very small number of Japanese (150) admitted yearly under "a gentleman's agreement" with Japan; and Canadians of Oriental origin are in law and in fact discriminated against in certain provinces. Canada's policy in these respects is similar to that of the other Anglo-Saxon countries of the Pacific basin. However sound the social reasons for this policy may appear to be to those Canadians most concerned with Oriental immigration, there can be little doubt that the policy tends to provoke the ill-will of Oriental peoples and that it may be laying up trouble for the future—trouble not alone for Canada and other Anglo-Saxon countries of the Pacific, but perhaps for the British Commonwealth as well. Indian peoples, no less than Canadians, are subjects of the King; but Canada treats them as undesirable aliens. But whether or not the policy of prohibiting Oriental immigration were supported by Canadian opinion, the necessity of maintaining friendly relations with the United States would perhaps require drastic restriction of Oriental immigration. …

Defence

A fifth principle of policy is that Canada assumes full responsibility for local defence while reserving complete freedom of action for defence of other interests.

Defence has been discussed elsewhere in detail, and no extended treatment is needed here. It is sufficient to recall the salient points of Canadian defence policy. This has been based on two assumptions: first, that Canada is relatively immune from invasion, and consequently would have ample warning and ample time to prepare to meet an invasion in force should it come; second, that no armed defence is now needed as against the United States because of established traditions of peace between the two countries and the development of habits and the institutions of peaceful settlement of all disputes between the two. Under these conditions Canada has been able to keep her armament bill at an extraordinarily low figure. …

Commercial Policy

Finally, Canada's commercial policy has been one of compromise between the conflicting interests of producers for export and producers for the domestic market. This arises largely from the peculiarly dual nature of the Canadian economy. On the one hand, Canada throughout her history has been a producer of staple commodities in large quantities for foreign markets. On the other, for some sixty years Canada has consistently protected the domestic market for Canadian producers. For the most part, this has meant protection for manufacturing industries, rather than for primary producers who have had little to gain by protection against foreign competitors. … Thus foreign markets are a vital necessity for Canada if her present economy is to continue. Especially is Canada dependent on two markets, that of the United Kingdom and that of the United States. …

Advantages

"Canada, like Belgium," says André Siegfried, "remains a precarious creation." The conflicting loyalties of French- and English-speaking, and of Protestant and Roman Catholic, and the conflicting interests of primary producers and manufacturers, of eastern and central Canada, and of western and central Canada, are ever with us, and the difficulties of creating or maintaining a united Canada in the face of these divisions are very great. Perhaps the strongest argument in support of our traditional external policy is that it does not accentuate these divisions and that on the contrary it represents the highest common factor of agreement between conflicting interests and conflicting loyalties. A more positive policy in support of the League or the Empire or a more definite swing towards isolation would in all probability accentuate internal differences and particularly those between the two racial groups. The pressure of events may sometime or other impel a decision in one direction or another, as events did in 1914. But so long as no decision need be taken Canadian national unity is not in danger. Meantime it is possible that the sense of Canadian nationality is a growing one and that if and when the decision must be made it will be supported by a more united people than any decision made now or in advance of a crisis. ...

The political reason for our traditional policy rests on less idealistic grounds. It is probably the only policy which any party in Canada can follow in normal times if it hopes to remain in power or get into office. No party can expect to be successful at the polls and capture enough seats to form a government at Ottawa if it antagonizes Protestants or Catholics, English-speaking or French-speaking, agriculturists or industrialists, western Canada or eastern Canada. A political party, if it is to be successful, must be all things to all men, perhaps even more in foreign policy than in domestic policy because foreign policy touches traditional loyalties at so many points. Our traditional policy is thus largely a policy of political expediency, which is perhaps unavoidable because of the nature of Canadian politics.

And it is a policy of political expediency in the face of external conditions. It is in effect the policy of a buffer state, a role which the combined forces of geography and history have elected Canada to play. Strategically Canada is something of a buffer state in the Pacific balance of power, a Switzerland compelled to arm, because of the rising armaments of either flank, lest she become a Belgium. She is perhaps even more a buffer state in the Anglo-American balance of power though in a political, and perhaps economic, sense rather than a military, and as a buffer state she must avoid being drawn too closely into the American or the Empire camp lest her own national interest be thereby imperilled. And she is scarcely less a buffer state between the United States and the league, compelled on the one hand to avoid far-reaching commitments to a collective system which might embroil her with her neighbour, and on the other hand to avoid becoming solely a North American power over-shadowed by the United States and without any direct influence whatever in organizing the kind of world which would best suit her interests as a great commercial nation.

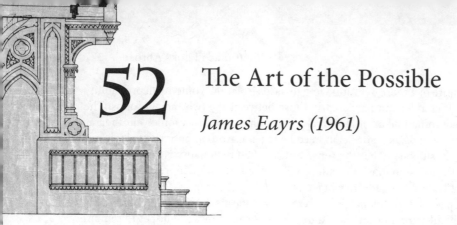

52   The Art of the Possible

James Eayrs (1961)

EDITORS' INTRODUCTION

James Eayrs is a former professor at the University of Toronto, professor emeritus at Dalhousie University, and a pioneer in the study and teaching of Canadian military-political history.

The Art of the Possible (the title is a reference to Otto von Bismarck's famous definition of politics) studied how institutions, agencies, and servants of government conduct Canada's external affairs. In the first chapter, it describes the role played by the executive, and particularly the prime minister (he examines the prime ministers from Wilfrid Laurier to John Diefenbaker), in the formulation and execution of foreign policy. According to Eayrs, both the context and the "style" of a prime minister determine, to a large extent, the way in which external relations would be conducted and the level of collegiality (or the lack thereof) with members of the Cabinet regarding the Canadian foreign policy.

The Political Executive

The Prime Minister

Politics in Canada have produced governments of extraordinary longevity. They have also produced small and feeble oppositions, to the debility of Parliament and the aggrandizement of the Executive. The Cabinet stands supreme, and within his Cabinet (his, for he makes it and may break it) the Prime Minister enjoys a pre-eminence other parliamentary systems seldom provide.

The greater prestige of his office and the greater power of his person are most obviously accounted for by the lesser lustre of his colleagues in Cabinet, and this in turn by a convention of cabinet-making wherein the political Executive becomes a miniature of the Canadian community. Regions, provinces, races and creeds are represented in the Ministry with as exact fidelity to the original as may be allowed by the sometimes competing considerations of securing tolerable efficiency in administration, and having to reward friends and punish foes. No wonder that cabinets of all the talents are rare in Canadian political life: what is more remarkable is that powerful and able ministries occasionally emerge. But the general result is the elevation of the Prime Minister over all the other ministers. Those whose claims to the office derive principally from the accidents of geography or the imperatives of the party stand

Source: Excerpted from *The Art of the Possible: Government and Foreign Policy in Canada* by James Eayrs. Toronto: University of Toronto Press, 1961. Notes omitted.

on a lower level of competence; while his equals in political sagacity and administrative ability can never forget that it is to the Prime Minister they owe their portfolios and at his pleasure continue to hold them. The usual description of the Prime Minister's relationship to his ministerial colleagues as *primus inter pares* is even less accurate in Canadian than in British parliamentary practice. "He cannot be first among equals because he has no equals."

All this applies with very special force to foreign affairs. The Prime Minister bears inevitably a unique responsibility for his country's external policy even if by taste and temperament he has little interest in it; and circumstances make it likely that he will have too much interest rather than too little. Important officials concerned with the formulation and execution of foreign policy are appointed on his recommendation; ambassadors, generals and deputy ministers are alike beholden to him for their positions. To him are normally addressed important communications from the political heads of foreign governments, and with the technically non-foreign governments of the Commonwealth of Nations consultation proceeds conventionally on a Prime Minister-to-Prime Minister basis. To him are referred important foreign policy communications received in the Departments of External Affairs, National Defence, Trade and Commerce and others. Visiting dignitaries, wishing to exchange impressions of the international scene, will want to confer with the Prime Minister rather than with any of his colleagues. Goodwill tours in foreign lands add further to his range of influential contacts, providing sources of private information long after the journey's end, as do excursions into the increasingly fashionable realm of "summit diplomacy." It is the Prime Minister's task to shape the recommendations of his foreign policy technicians (among whom the Secretary of State for External Affairs may or may not be numbered) to the requirements of domestic politics and to impart to them the correctives deemed necessary for partisan advantage. And in times of crisis, when the nation is roused from its accustomed private preoccupations to apprehensive awareness of external danger, it is the Prime Minister who through press and radio and television must play the father figure, providing reassurance and guidance and hope. Foreign policy is his prerogative; the range and intimacy of his concern are rarely matched by any of his colleagues, even by his foreign secretary.

Prime Minister and Cabinet

The extent to which the Prime Minister allows members of his Cabinet to share in the mysteries of foreign policy is as much a matter of individual temperament and style as it is a matter of constitutional law, perhaps a good deal more. A Prime Minister may resemble in this the Duke of Plazo Toro, leading "his regiment from behind"; another may prefer the vanguard. Some have been possessive, even secretive, in their conduct of foreign affairs; others have taken their colleagues into their confidence and looked to them for counsel. To state with any precision the nature of a Prime Minister's relations with his Cabinet in matters of foreign policy or any other kind of policy is not easy; a strict convention prescribes that Cabinet proceedings are secret and must remain secret. (As an illustration of the severity of this convention, one may note that a resigning Minister is not allowed to disclose the differences with his colleagues that have led to his resignation without the authorization of the Prime Minister as the custodian of Cabinet secrets.) But from available private papers and certain other evidence (which cannot, however, include Cabinet minutes), some impression may be gained of how various prime ministers have gone about their foreign policy business in relation to their Cabinet colleagues. ...

Prime Minister and Foreign Minister

The authority of the Prime Minister in foreign affairs has been potentially circumscribed by the assumption in recent years of the External Affairs portfolio by a member of his Cabinet other than himself.

When the Department of External Affairs was created in 1909 it was the expectation of its first Under Secretary, Joseph Pope, that the new portfolio should be held by the Prime Minister; and, as the individual more than any other responsible for its creation, he was vexed when the Department was placed instead under the Secretary of State. This, he wrote at the time, was "a *great* mistake. It should be under the Prime Minister." Despite the assignment of responsibility to the Secretary of State by the Act of 1909 bringing the Department into being, it was Sir Wilfrid Laurier as Prime Minister rather than Charles Murphy as Secretary of State who assumed effective control of the Department of External Affairs. In 1912 legislation of the Borden Government corrected this anomaly by bringing the Department legally as well as practically within the Prime Minister's authority:

> 2. There shall be a Department of the Government of Canada to be called the Department of External Affairs, over which the Secretary of State for External Affairs shall preside.
> 3. The Member of the King's Privy Council for Canada holding the recognized position of First Minister shall be the Secretary of State for External Affairs.

After two years of wartime leadership, Sir Robert Borden found himself increasingly unable to do justice to both positions. His remedy was not to divest himself of the External Affairs portfolio but to create the new post of Parliamentary Under Secretary of State for External Affairs. The Order-in-Council by which this was accomplished (P.C. 1719 of July 15, 1916) recited the following "orders and regulations" in connection with the position:

> 2. The Parliamentary Under Secretary shall, with respect to the Department of External Affairs, perform such parliamentary duties as may from time to time be assigned to him by the Governor in Council.
> 3. The Parliamentary Under Secretary shall, subject to such instructions as may from time to time be issued by competent authority assist the Prime Minister in administering the Department of External Affairs, and may, subject to the approval of the Prime Minister, conduct such official communications between the Government of Canada and the Government of any other country in connection with the external affairs of Canada, and perform such other duties in the said Department as from time to time may be directed.
> 4. In the absence of the Prime Minister, the Parliamentary Under Secretary shall, subject to the direction and approval of the Acting Prime Minister for the time being, preside over and administer the Department of External Affairs; and in such case he shall have authority to report to and make recommendations to the Governor in Council through the Acting Prime Minister.

The terms of the Order-in-Council permitted the Parliamentary Under Secretary of State for External Affairs to assume considerable responsibility. The first occupant of the position, Colonel Hugh Clark, whom Borden appointed in October 1916, did little more, however, than answer questions in the House of Commons, and Francis Keefer, who took over from Clark in 1918, did not enlarge its scope. The office had been authorized only "during the continuance of the war," and was soon afterward allowed to lapse. In 1943 the position of Parliamentary Assistant to the President of the Privy Council was created. ...

In 1946 Canada acquired for the first time a Secretary of State of External Affairs who was not also Prime Minister. This was Mr. L.S. St. Laurent, who for a few months after his appointment continued to hold the Justice portfolio as well as External Affairs. Since then it has been the rule rather than the exception for the External Affairs portfolio to be the sole responsibility of a member of the Cabinet other than the Prime Minister. Mr. St. Laurent held it until becoming Prime Minister in 1948, when Mr. Lester Pearson became Secretary of State for External Affairs, remaining in that capacity until the defeat of the Liberal Government in June 1957. The new Prime Minister, Mr. John Diefenbaker, was his own foreign minister until in September 1957 he brought Sidney Smith into his administration and handed the External Affairs portfolio over to him. When Sidney Smith's new career was tragically ended by his death in March 1959, the Prime Minister again assumed responsibility for the External Affairs Department, relinquishing it in July of that year to the then Minister of Public Works, Mr. Howard Green. For a time Mr. Green retained, while Secretary of State for External Affairs, not only his old portfolio but also his position as House Leader; there was some criticism in the House of Commons at this piling on of responsibilities, and within a few months Mr. Green was left free to devote all his time and energy to foreign affairs.

The relationship between a Prime Minister and his foreign minister, "the most fateful … of all imposed by the machinery of government" (Kenneth W. Thompson), is seldom free from difficulty and may easily become tensely competitive. Where a Prime Minister is wise enough and generous enough to allow an able colleague sufficient scope for judgment and initiative, or where a foreign minister is content with a technician's role, a harmonious and productive partnership may result. But this rarely happens. "The relations of subordination that bind them together," an authority has written, "the care taken by the minister of foreign affairs in order to keep his own autonomy, the fear of the prime minister that this collaborator may carry him too far towards a policy of which the parliament disapproves … , the general tendency to hold numerous international meetings at the highest level, all this creates between these two men, even when they belong to the same political party, a fatal competition." Whether they contrive a mutually profitable division of labour, or whether their energies are dissipated in rivalry, will depend mainly upon their temperaments; especially will it depend upon the temperament of the Prime Minister. …

Prime Minister and Governor General

Half a century ago, when the conduct of Canadian external policy was both theoretically and practically the concern of the British Government, the Governor General as its representative played as great a part in the external affairs of the dominion as his own temperament and that of his Prime Minister would allow; and they could allow a great deal. …

The appointment of Mr. Vincent Massey in 1952 and that of his successor, Major General Georges Vanier in 1959, have to a considerable extent rehabilitated the office. Both had wide experience of Canadian affairs (Mr. Massey indeed having been a member of the Canadian Government) and in particular of Canadian diplomacy, so that their Prime Ministers could not with much plausibility hold aloof on the ground that their Governors' knowledge and judgment of events were too slight to make their counsel worth acquiring. Nor would an increasing number of informed Canadians have been content with a cypher's role. The prestige of the Governor General's office has, for the first time in thirty years, been noticeably enhanced.

53 The Better Part of Valour

John W. Holmes (1970)

EDITORS' INTRODUCTION

John Holmes (1910–1988) was national secretary of the Canadian Institute of International Affairs (CIIA) (1941–1943) and joined the Department of External Affairs in 1943. He served successively in London, Moscow, and New York, becoming Assistant Under-Secretary of State for External Affairs in 1953 until his retirement in 1960. He then became president of the CIIA and professor of international relations at York University, Glendon College (1971–1981).

In this excerpt from The Better Part of Valour, *he discusses the place of Canada in the world and the significance of being a middle power. When he wrote this essay in 1970, Canada was coping with an identity crisis fuelled by the rise of Quebec neo-nationalism. Holmes touches upon the impact of French-Canadian nationalism on Canadian foreign policy, which directly called into question the "tribalism of Anglo-Saxon Canadians associated either with an imperial clan or now, more often, with the idea of the natural superiority of English-speaking peoples." He argues that there is a relationship between nationalism and independence, since without a sense of identity, the citizen becomes too susceptible to external influences to sustain a national foreign policy.*

Nationalism in Canadian Foreign Policy

Canada is a very special case. It is a bi-national state where the term "nationalism" is used ambivalently. Rather than pursue definitions, I propose to treat both uses as valid. For the most part I am concerned with the nationalism of the entity Canada, which one might call "Canadian-ism" or less aptly but more fluently "Canadianism," begging the question whether a bi-national state is a nation. (One virtue of its nationalism can, of course, be pride it its bi-nationalism.) I shall also touch upon the impact of French-Canadian "nationalism" on our foreign policy. As for English-Canadian nationalism, it is doubtful if it exists at all apart from Canadian nationalism. One ought not, however, to ignore the tribalism of Anglo-Saxon Canadians associated either with an imperial clan or now, more often, with the idea of the natural superiority of English-speaking peoples. Either in identification with the empire or

Source: Excerpted from *The Better Part of Valour: Essays on Canadian Diplomacy* by John W. Holmes. Toronto and Montreal: McClelland and Stewart, 1970. Notes omitted.

with the United States this tribalism has usually been a counter-national or counter-Canadian force. That fact does not necessarily make it discreditable. In its considerable influence on Canada's foreign relations, however, it has always had more of the sectarian characteristics of "nationalism" than has strictly Canadian nationalism which, whether it is constructive or merely competitive, is normally harmless.

The central problem of pan-Canadian nationalism has been the need to find a reason for the country's existence. The disadvantage of the synthetic state such as Canada is that it lacks a visceral drive to achievement. Its advantage is that it is more likely, although not predestined, to find a rational justification for its existence. Canada was the product of a resistance movement. From 1791 to 1871 the evolution of the Canadian state was a sheltering together of those northerly North Americans who, for varying reasons, did not want to be absorbed into the United States. Some, like the Quebeckers, wanted to preserve their culture; others, like the British Columbians, wanted to stay in the British empire. The idea of Canada was to come later. Resistance to the active and passive pressures of the United States was a rational enough foreign policy for the first century or two. However, it has not alone been sufficient since the transformation of the United States from an ogre into a benign ally and since the identification, in the past half century, of distant devils who are less known and feared more. The nationalism of Canadians is not now stimulated by the threat of military aggression. Their anxiety about national survival is attributable to fear of their own failure of will. ...

It is hard to understand why it was half a century after Confederation and the establishment of the Canadian Idea before control over external relations was seriously sought. Control over things that mattered to a pioneer community, such as commerce and border problems, was assumed, and Canada had neither the resources nor the will to seek a role in world politics. The hallucinations of Jubilee imperialism distracted those few Canadians with enough imagination to notice the world beyond the triangle. Concern for external relations was largely directed to questions of status within the empire. The nationalism which followed the First World War was ambivalent about whether the Canadian destiny, of which all Canadians were more conscious, should be primarily imperial or national. Mackenzie King, who dominated the era, rejected the former, and in so doing absentmindedly created the Commonwealth of Nations, with himself as its prophet. He was not, however, genuinely interested in his creation. Fortunately he left the scene in time for his successors to recognize in the Commonwealth a useful instrument of Canadian national policy. Unfortunately, the legacy of the long argument between unsound but imaginative imperialists and sound but unimaginative nationalists has been a public opinion which, confused by old shibboleths, has lagged behind its government (Liberal or Conservative) in appreciating the Commonwealth as a Canadian sphere of interest. ...

Canada's position in the world was strengthened, furthermore, by internal factors. The old schizophrenic pull between the imperialists and the continentalists was tranquillized by the new partnership of Britain, France, and the United States in NATO Isolationism was dead in North America. As a result, domestic tensions over Canada's external associations subsided. When Canadians next went overseas to fight—in Korea—there were more volunteers from Quebec than from the other provinces. As strongly entrenched government had for a decade an unprecedented consensus behind it in support of a vigorous Canadian foreign policy. From the perspective of 1965, the consensus may seem more apparent than real because of the quiescence of French Canada. Yet this foreign policy was designed by English and French

Canadians who together nourished a policy positive enough to appeal to most varieties of Canadian nationalism without offending unduly the susceptibilities and prejudices of either of the major elements in the country. Only fanatical minorities—from the British, French, and Slavic communities—were at odds with a policy in which a new Canadian nationalism found its outlet in active inter-nationalism.

The United Nations has been a boon to Canadian nationalists. As an international rather than a supranational organization, it satisfied the Canadian predilection for a cautious mixture of pragmatism and idealism, and it avoids the principle of collective security of which they have always been sceptical. It has also provided a stage on which Canada could emerge from the shadow of the great powers, which gives it complexes, and could establish an unmistakable identity. It has given Canada the chance to prove itself, to gain a reputation in the world. In the past decade it has offered also a congenial military role which has given the country a sense of purpose for its armed forces not so readily felt for the more subordinate role of lesser military allies—important and essential though the role may be. Pride in the mediatory role has given a certain style to Canadian diplomacy. The reputation for objectivity is sought. Comment on world events is muted, and emphasis is placed on maintaining contact even with international malefactors. ...

This concept of the distinct vocation of states was at the root of the so-called "functional theory," which Canadians advocated at the end of the Second World War. It was a rationalization of the new nationalist approach, an attempt to find a sensible and possible occupation for Canada in a world in which, Canadians fully recognized, the most important thing was that the great powers should combine to keep the peace. As Mr. King defined the theory on July 9, 1943, it was a recognition that in international institutions effective representation could not be restricted to the great powers or extended to all states. It must be determined on a functional basis, according membership to "those countries, large or small, which have the greatest contribution to make to the particular object in question." Although Canada got the principle written into one article of the United Nations Charter, it cannot be said to have dominated world organization ever since. Canada as one of the three original atomic partners, did become the only non-great power to sit on the United Nations' Energy Commission, by inheritance, on subsequent bodies seeking disarmament questions did much to establish the Canadian position in world affairs and satisfy Canadian nationalism. At the same time it created exaggerated notions of Canada's permanent place in the galaxy. This illusion has led to frustration and, at times, to a self-defeating concern for status rather than function (since Canada's position among middle powers suffered a relative and natural decline because of postwar readjustments). Nevertheless, functionalism has provided Canadian nationalism with a frame of reference that encourages it to seek an impact proportionate to its energy and resources, without exhausting its zeal in futile effort and making itself ridiculous by universalist fantasies. ...

The concept of the middle power as a constructive force in world politics is one for the recognition of which Canada can claim some credit. Whether it was essentially a rationalization of the needs of Canadian nationalism or a response to the requirements of international politics may be argued. Probably it was both. That it can be the basis of our continuing foreign policy is, however, a question that should be constantly under review. The danger is that Canadians will be impelled to seek this kind of fulfilment whether or not it is required; that an aggressive determination to middlepowermanship will offend or amuse the international community, thereby dissipating the reputation for sense and judgement on which the success of the role depends. ...

The kind of Canadian nationalism that finds its outlet in effective middle-power diplomacy may wither because it does not appeal to a restless public. Many people are impatient of its moderation and sobriety and, above all, of this "quietness." They want to fight real devils, nuclear weapons, and segregationists, with which there can be no compromise. Although English- or French-speaking youth are to some extent united by such sentiments, they are separated by the preoccupation of French Canadians with their own problems and the preoccupation of English Canadians with other people's. Politically-conscious English Canadians are often obsessed by a humanitarianism which, almost as a matter of principle, removes their attention from the issue which threatens to tear their own country apart; it is as if such concern would be evidence of nationalism and, therefore, less virtuous than intervention in other countries' problems. Those who demand a strongly nationalist Canadian foreign policy—of resistance to the United States or Vietnam or the Caribbean—are not always nationally conscious enough to realize that they are foreigners to Alabama. To suggest to them that priority might be given to their own country's problems is rejected as offensive to the brotherhood of man. One is tempted to ask, however, whether involvement in the Canadian issue is less attractive because it requires ratiocination, and possibly sacrifice and commitment, in place of heady emotion and adventure from which withdrawal is easy. One is reminded of what Daniel Webster described as "that wandering and vagrant philanthropy" which heated "the imagination on subjects distant, remote, and uncertain." It is the kind of comfortable internationalism that saves Canadians from the noisome and intractable issues that confront them, and warms their hearts with noble sentiments and apocalyptic visions. It is not in the better tradition of Canadian foreign policy, which has sought to exploit the peculiar advantages of the Canadian position in the general interest. ...

There is a relationship between nationalism and independence. One of the requisites for Canada's playing any distinctive role, other than that of satellite, is the maintenance of a considerable degree of independence. The strength and vitality of its rationalism is an important element of its independence. Without a sense of identity, pride, attachment to his own group, the citizen becomes too susceptible to external influences to sustain a national foreign policy. Nationalism itself is a function in part of what a nation accomplishes in international society. So the foreign policy of Canada must be designed to bolster Canadian nationalism and, in so doing, to bolster Canadian independence. Otherwise, Canadians perish, or at least are diminished. However misguided the public restlessness may seem, for the most part it represents frustrated idealism that needs an outlet. It is infinitely preferable to the cynicism about the Canadian role in the world which is all too common. If it is too often directed towards telling Washington what to do, that may be because it has not felt able to communicate with Ottawa. ...

The strength and flexibility of Canadian foreign policy could, however, be unfortunately affected by certain interpretations of bi-nationalism. In such fields as human rights Canada's voice in international circles has always been muffled by the limitations of the federal system, the fact that the federal government, which must speak for Canada abroad, cannot commit the provinces on subjects reserved for them. Canada could probably go quite a long way in allowing provinces the right to deal with foreign governments on subjects within their jurisdiction including, of course, cultural matters. On political, economic, or security matters national foreign policies should rest on a consensus of all Canadians, and French Canadians have a case to argue that their views have had less weight than they merited. They will, of course, inevitably carry more weight if and when French Canada turns its attention from domestic to international problems. Proposals, however, which imply that there is or should be a separate French-Canadian consensus and that Canadian policies should somehow or other be the product of negotiation between Quebec and Ottawa threaten Canada with paralysis. There never has been any such thing as an English-Canadian or a French-Canadian view of foreign relations, although there are, as I have said, identifiable differences in emphasis. There has been no consequential issue of foreign policy since the last war on which the division of opinion within the country has been specifically between English and French. It is not in the national interest to create the machinery or encourage the assumptions that could lead to separate foreign policies. It is not in the interest of French Canada to do so, for the inevitable result would be the surrender of the determination of federal foreign policy, the one that counts, to the sole control of English Canadians. An effective foreign policy cannot be evolved in a provincial capital because it is divorced from the international life of diplomacy, conference, negotiation, secrets, and confidences. French Canada has a significant role to play in the world, one which could be pursued in an independent state of five million people; but it is more likely to be effective through a state of twenty million—only if French Canada sees its role as a partner in a national indigestible lump of opposition. ...

Let me say, in conclusion, that I am aware that my definitions of Canadian foreign policy and my comments on the powers and international bodies are less an analysis of facts than the imposition of a framework and a justification for Canadian nationalism. How otherwise does one devise a foreign policy? Canadians cannot argue that they have a divine or racial mission, that they were created for a predestined purpose. They exist; therefore they think. If what they think up for themselves to do is good for them and serves their ultimate interest in a peaceful and prosperous world, let them rejoice in it. Even the gloomiest denouncers of nationalism claim that the "phenomenon" of "nationalism" is not dead. In Canada, however, it can be tamed and civilized.

Forgotten Partnership: US–Canada Relations Today

54

Charles F. Doran (1984)

EDITORS' INTRODUCTION

Charles Doran is the Andrew W. Mellon Professor of International Relations, director of the Global Theory and History Program, and director of Canadian Studies at Johns Hopkins University.

In his book Forgotten Partnership, *he attempts to understand relations between Canada and the United States. In this excerpt, he discusses the special nature of this relationship which, because of both its scope and depth, has a great influence on the fabric of Canadian society. In this section, he draws our attention to the many features of this special relationship, its peaceful nature, the extensive nature of bureaucratic and private sector activities, and the existence of many institutional buffers (in particular, a huge number of bilateral treaties). This close partnership is marked by the fact that Canada sought and obtained exemptions from the external impact of US economic policies. It also has a significant impact on security issues. Doran wonders, however, if this special relationship has begun to erode.*

How Special Is the Special Relationship?

Part of the confusion that surrounds the special relationship idea stems from definition and content. One can conceptualize the special relationship in essentially two ways: either as structure or as policy. Although policy can generate structure and structure may facilitate policy, the two theoretical categories do not overlap.

At the structural level, the U.S.–Canada relationship can be thought of as special because of the scope and depth of the interactions between the two countries. Scope refers to the number and variety of activities that emerge in one polity and impinge upon the other. These encompass the entire range from cultural and linguistic activities to economic and military-strategic activities. Not only is the scope broad, but the interactions are usually not trivial. They reach down into the fabric of each society, especially the Canadian. This depth of interaction makes bilateral relations all the more difficult, because of the intervulnerability of the two political systems. Scope combined with depth means that large sectors of the populations of both countries are affected by these interactions all of the time. …

Source: Excerpted from *Forgotten Partnership: US–Canada Relations Today* by Charles Doran. Baltimore: Johns Hopkins University Press, 1984.

Another structural aspect of the special relationship is the pacific nature of the relations. …
It would be difficult to assert that no other pair of proximate countries has enjoyed as long
a period of nonviolent interaction. The range of candidates, however, is probably limited to
South America. Although South America has, in general, a magnificent record of peaceful
coexistence among countries, its record of orderly governmental procedure within countries
is just the opposite. Canada and the United States have combined peaceful relations between
the governments with orderly internal governmental procedures, although the U.S. record,
based on its own cultural and social peculiarities, is marred by the Civil War and one other
factor: the United States has suffered one of the worst records of presidential assassinations
and assassination attempts of any modern country. …

In terms of cross-border violence, U.S.–Canada relations have not been marred by any
significant use of force since 1812. Although Mackenzie King may have been right to challenge
the authenticity of the "undefended border" as envisioned in the Rush–Bagot Agreement of
1817, few immediate neighbors can demonstrate such a degree of political openness.

A further structural justification for the label *special* is the extensiveness of bureaucratic
and private-sector activity. The political significance of this extensiveness is that a large
portion of the decisions that are normally funneled to the top of the governmental decision
hierarchy are dealt with instead, in the Canadian–American context, either by lower-level
governmental officials or by the private sector on both sides of the border. This means that
fewer disputes come to the attention of the Cabinet or the White House. It also means that the
prime minister and the president must share, implicitly, some of their decision-making authority with the private sector and with career civil servants. …

Finally, at the strategic level, the relationship is special because of the existence of so many
institutional buffers. By institutional buffer I mean the more than 180 bilateral treaties that
regulate every manner of trans-boundary exchange and the dozen or so commissions, working groups, and committees that serve to protect the sovereignty of the two countries while
providing a continuum of discourse. The most famous of these buffers, the International
Joint Commission (IJC) (1909) is also among the oldest and most institutionalized. But other
functionally specific buffers with greater or lesser degrees of permanence have also emerged:
International Pacific Halibut Commission (1923); International Boundary Commission
(1925); International Pacific Fisheries Commission (1937); Committee on Trade and Economic Affairs (1953); North American Defence Command (1958); Senior Committee on
Defence Production/Development Sharing (1958); Balance of Payments Committee (1963);
and the Canada–U.S. Interparliamentary Group (1959); as well as a number of others.

At least two principles seem to underlie the creation of these buffers, as epitomized by
the International Joint Commission. First, the tasks of these institutions are narrowly defined
and limited to a single functional area. The objective is not to try to create superagencies that
encompass broad areas of jurisdiction with major legislative powers. Second, Canada and
the United States have legal and operational equality on these boards and commissions. This
is important because the recommendations have a voluntary character and must reflect accurate and fair assessments of problems and solutions. …

At the structural level these four elements lend a special quality to the Canadian–American
milieu. Change affects structure slowly. These structural elements are the constants, or
"givens," that theoretically set the relationship apart from other seemingly comparable bilateral associations.

At the policy level, a cluster of government behaviours further supports the claim that something within the U.S.–Canadian relations warrants the adjective *special*. These behaviours are really governmental expectations about how the relationship ought to work. The expectations are not held equally by both actors; nor are they as little subject to change as the prior structural considerations. On the other hand, analysts have in general been more prone to justify the term *special* when assessing these policy expectations than when discussing structural considerations. In this view, the specific policy expectations about how the relationship is to be managed are special.

First among these policy expectations is that of consultations. Much of the institutional machinery that has been tested in the postwar period has had the objective of improving consultation. For consultation to be effective, each government must keep the other informed of policy changes. Once this information is in place, the governments have the responsibility of discussing policy alternatives and the implications of policy choices with counterparts. Consultation implies prior discussion of policy choices, with at least the potential that contrary recommendations from the opposite government will be considered in making policy decisions. Otherwise, consultation amounts merely to selective, ex post facto notification of policy decisions, notification perhaps made prior to the time that such information appears in the newspapers. …

The key question remains, however, Is the quality and the frequency of consultation better between Canada and the United States than between other partners? I doubt that on issues of high priority Canada consults less with Britain than the United States or that in security matters, for example, the United States consults less with the German Federal Republic and Japan than with Canada. On medium- and low-level issues, the amount of consultation between Canada and the United States is probably unparalleled. But the quality and frequency of consultation varies enormously with the personnel at the head of each government and with the historical interval. Overall, consultation in the post–World War II period has been far greater than was true in the prewar period; consultation was more consistent in the 1976–80 interval than in the 1970–76 interval, for a variety of reasons both internal and external to the relationship. It must also be remembered that consultation is not the equivalent of compromise; and compromise does not automatically translate into effective policy. This is perhaps the most recent lesson to have been learned regarding consultation in Canadian-American relations.

A second major set of policy expectations descriptive of the relationship has been identified as exemptionalism. In the post–World War II period, Canada repeatedly sought and obtained exemptions from the external impact of U.S. economic legislation. That such exemptions were requested and received was considered special because other countries did not obtain such favoured treatment; the grounds for granting the exemptions were that the two economies were inextricably intertwined. …

What this American view failed to recognized, however, was that Canada continued to think of itself, not in terms of this broader, global comparative view, but in terms of its bilateral relationship with the United States. And what appeared from America's global perspective to be justifiable treatment appeared from the Canadian view to be the "selling-out" of America's closest friend and ally when the economic going got tough for the United States.

Thus, in summarizing this conception of the "special relationship" at least two considerations ought to be kept in mind. First, if exemptionalism was all that the special relationship involved, then MacEachen and Kissinger appeared to be right that the special relationship was dead. But because the term *special relationship* probably meant, and means, much more than the granting of exemptions, others were correct to challenge the meaning of Nixon's New Economic Policy as it applied to Canada. In other words, the special relationship continued to thrive in ways other than exemptionalism.

Second, subsequent behavior called into question whether, even in the narrowest policy sense, the special relationship was indeed dead. This behavior involved the convention-tax issue. The decision of the Carter administration and Congress (which was supported by the incoming Reagan administration) to unilaterally reinstate these conventions-tax privileges, thereby making the Canadian hotel industry again competitive for the U.S. convention business, is in fact a partial return to the practice of exemptionalism. Mexico is the only other government to have received this exemption. Whether such exemptions will occur as broadly as before, and whether the United States will expect more quid pro quos from Canada in return, perhaps in other areas, remains to be seen. But even in the narrow sense of exemptions from the external impact of American economic legislation and in spite of official statements of the contrary, some aspects of the special relationship seem to live on.

Finally, the special relationship may be conceptualized at the policy level in terms of investment security. Just as Canadians have conceived of the label *special* largely as a promise of exemption from the impact of the U.S. economic policy, Americans have conceived of *special* largely as a guarantee of a safe and secure arena for U.S. private foreign investment. Americans have imagined Canada as a country uniquely hospitable to investment from abroad, especially American investment. …

In short, two answers seem to arise in response to the question, How special is the special relationship? At the structural level, the Canadian–American relationship continues to appear unique or special, because no other pair of countries can demonstrate the combination of close governmental interaction, institutional ties and buffers, pacific conflict resolution and extensiveness of cross-border bureaucratic and private sector activity. On the other hand, at the policy-making level, the factors that have made the relationship special in the past—consultation, preferential economic treatment for Canada, and a secure, hospitable atmosphere for U.S. investment—have all begun to erode. The analytical problem is not so much to explain why the special relationship is considered special; the problem is to determine where the trend in bilateral foreign policy is taking the two countries. If the special relationship deteriorates sufficiently in terms of policy, change will occur at the structural level as well. A close, complex structural relationship between the two countries may not alone have the capacity to offset the deterioration at the level of policy. Some indications exist that neither government is prepared to contend with the domestic political inconvenience of perpetuating policies of advanced and detailed consultation. Some indications also exist that the decline in the U.S. sympathy for special exemptions for Canada in the economic sphere has paralleled the Canadian unwillingness to treat U.S. private foreign investment much differently than many other countries have treated it. None of these trends are consciously interactive; indeed, government leaders themselves may not be fully aware of the history of the relationship or of the encompassing nature of current trends. But the negative impact on the notion of the special relationship is the same; Canada and the United States, despite scattered evidence to the contrary, seem to be drifting apart for a variety of reasons, some of which are at the heart of the way the special relationship has traditionally been regarded.

Uncle Sam and Us

Stephen Clarkson (2002)

55

EDITORS' INTRODUCTION

Stephen Clarkson was professor of political science at the University of Toronto and a prolific author on, among other issues, the political economy of Canada's relationship with the United States.

In Uncle Sam and Us, *he analyzes the impact of globalization on Western states' power and security. He examines the rise of American neo-conservatism, and its effect on Canada's foreign policy (including sending troops to fight in Afghanistan in 2001, which became the longest war in Canadian history). Clarkson describes Canada as being part of a "globally networked, continentally implemented anti-terrorist state."*

Global governance and proximity to the United States obscure the role of Canada's domestic political actors, and have a tremendous impact on the ability of the Canadian government to conduct an independent foreign policy. Clarkson argues that in the context of the American war on terror, and despite being under continuing US hegemony, Canada still has the potential to change its foreign policies, and could pursue an activist policy that is more multilateral than bilateral in nature.

The Diplomatic State: Lockstep Under Hegemonic Dominance

In the late 1930s, when the hitherto unthinkable threat to North America from Nazi Germany and imperial Japan was becoming thinkable, the elected leaders of the United States and Canada set the template for the way they would cope with common security threats. In a speech in Kingston, Ontario, on August 18, 1938, Franklin Delano Roosevelt declared that his country "would not stand idly by" if Canada were attacked. Two days later, William Lyon Mackenzie King responded with his own declaration from the sleepy town of Woodbridge, Ontario, to the effect that "enemy forces should not be able to pursue their way either by land, sea or air to the United States across Canadian territory."

Source: Excerpted from *Uncle Sam and Us: Globalization, Neoconservatism, and the Canadian State* by Stephen Clarkson. Toronto: University of Toronto Press, 2002. Notes omitted.

Thus defined as a willing American protectorate, Canada's military relationship with the United States passed through various phases—most notably, active economic and later military co-operation during the final four years of the Second World War. Mobilization for that total war made it easy for the two countries to move towards more complete military and economic integration during the Cold War that followed. Blending Canada into a single military system was institutionally effected by the Permanent Joint Board of Defence (PJBD) and the North American Air Defence Command (NORAD). After the Pentagon indirectly aborted Canada's production of the Avro Arrow—a military aircraft far superior to any American plane on the drawing board—Washington helped resolve the resulting crisis in the Canadian aerospace industry by signing the Defence Production Sharing Agreements, which allowed Canadian-based firms to bid on Pentagon contracts.

For the next four decades, Canadian governments endorsed successive strategic doctrines on nuclear retaliation issued by the Pentagon in response to new circumstances and adopted new technologies using constantly improved missiles and satellites. Canadians may have been uncomfortable living under the flight path of bombers and missiles that might be shot down in any U.S.–USSR exchange. None the less, most of them were squarely on the American side in the Cold War, and they accepted the calculus of permanent risk of total annihilation.

A number of understandings completed this picture of happy continental co-operation. If Canadians didn't want the Americans taking over their airspace, they had to practise the policy of "defence against help"—do it to the Pentagon's satisfaction, or have the job done for them. Eager to oblige, the Canadian armed forces lobbied for equipment to participate within U.S.-defined parameters. In order to produce the requisite weapon systems using leading-edge technology, Ottawa negotiated with U.S. contractors to offset the huge costs by sourcing and producing many of their components in Canada.

Another subtext in the dyad's dialogue was American leaders pressing a cost-conscious Ottawa to spend more on weapons. Canadian prime ministers periodically returned the compliment, counselling moderation on their more aggressive American counterparts. Pearson experienced the dangers inherent in offering unsolicited advice to the hegemon when early in 1965, during a speech at Temple University, he suggested a pause in U.S. bombing of North Vietnam to encourage Hanoi to negotiate a peace treaty. President Lyndon Johnson was so enraged that he summoned his Canadian counterpart to the presidential retreat at Camp David on April 3, 1965. Taking Pearson out on the verandah, Johnson shook him by the lapels and shouted in his face, "Don't piss on my carpet!"

The moral was clear. Washington was deaf to Canada's voice when it believed its vital interests to be at stake. Ottawa's vaunted "special relationship," which generally exempted Canadians from damaging U.S. measures against foreign competitors, was premised on a "quiet diplomacy" that forbade public expressions of divergent views such as those Pearson had ventured.

Trudeau's Variations in Diplomatic Autonomy

When Pierre Trudeau succeeded Pearson at 24 Sussex Drive in 1968, he shared some of these positions, though not out of anti-Americanism. For Canada's self-defined rationalist prime minister, foreign policy autonomy was a matter not of economics over politics but, as he liked to put it, of reason over passion. In his view, the Canadian fear of offending the hegemon next door was part of an attitudinal problem located in its diplomats' excessive involvement with the excitement of high politics and their consequent disconnection from more mundane realities at home. No longer should the Department of External Affairs expend so much energy trying to impress the major powers. It should direct its diplomatic efforts at a hard-nosed defence of Canada's national interests.

In the review of Pearsonian diplomacy that the new prime minister caused External Affairs to produce, he pushed his bureaucrats to reappraise Canada's emphasis on supporting U.S. leadership in the Cold War, as compared to other priorities. Circumstances had changed. After a decade of detente, Canada had, of course, to support a U.S.-defined approach to *international peace and security*, but it had other interests to pursue. It needed *economic prosperity* to build the Just Society that Trudeau had envisioned during his leadership campaign. And— most important to him, given the mounting threat of separatism in Quebec, which had been key to his electoral success—the country had to defend its *national unity*.

It could pursue only one of these three objectives free of American constraint. As code for combating separatism, *national unity* in foreign policy meant counteracting Gaullist support for Quebec's campaign to achieve international recognition. Since Washington was also concerned about French intervention in Quebec, which it considered its own backyard, and because it had its own problems with France's obstreperousness, the U.S. State Department did not get in the way of the national unity component of Trudeau's foreign policy. ...

A backward glance over the main features of Canadian foreign policy in the late Keynesian era showed a middle power of some international substance. On *national unity* it had successfully contained the effects of Gaullist support for international recognition of Quebec. In the early 1980s, under the socialist president François Mitterrand, Paris finally normalized relations with Ottawa.

Regarding *international peace and security*, its diplomats' intellectual contributions earned Canada a significant role in multilateral affairs as a member of the G7 and many other international organizations. Like his predecessor, Trudeau developed gravitas as a senior, experienced, and skilled head of government who intervened with verve, if not always with success, in the great issues of the Commonwealth, the Francophonie, the Third World, and the Cold War. With East–West tensions escalating in 1983, Trudeau had argued against the sabre-rattling of Margaret Thatcher and Ronald Reagan, who were sharpening their rhetoric against a still-dangerously nuclear, even "evil," Soviet Union. Whatever Reagan's displeasure about Trudeau's peace initiative or his Third World advocacy, nobody shook him by the lapels, and he had not kowtowed to those "pipsqueaks in the Pentagon" who derided his concerns about the accidental triggering of a global holocaust.

In Canada's pursuit of its own economic interests, the bilateral relationship remained central. Efforts under the "Third Option" in the late 1970s to diversify by expanding economic relations with Europe and Japan bore no significant fruit. Tensions with Washington escalated when Trudeau espoused energy nationalism just as his friend and confidant, the Democrat Jimmy Carter lost the White House to Ronald Reagan and his neoconservative Republicans. Although the Trudeau Liberals did not directly bend to the Reaganites' (and Alberta's) insistence that they axe the National Energy Program of 1980, the collapse of world petroleum prices sounded its death knell in 1982.

Foreign policy thinking throughout the whole Diefenbaker-Pearson-Trudeau era had been dominated by the ideas of the Western diplomatic mainstream, which saw Canada's role as a self-effacing adjunct to a benign American mission in the world. Sniping from the academic sidelines, Canadian nationalists had questioned the benevolence of a hegemon run amok and urged a noisy diplomacy to resist its dangerously misguided policies. The foreign policy trajectories of Lester Pearson and Pierre Trudeau largely reflected the diplomatic corps' response to an evolving balance of forces within the East–West confrontation. Only on selected high-profile issues such as China and nuclear arms did Trudeau intervene to give Canadian diplomacy his personal touch. In sum, Canada's interests abroad were defined by the Department of External Affairs, with occasional tweaking from the Prime Minister's Office.

Room for Manoeuvre Within Continental Integration: The Mulroney Years

The interplay between internal and external forces of change and, within these categories, between idea- and interest-driven pressures, should have been clear in the mid-1980s for three reasons. Brian Mulroney came to power in 1984 with a dismissive critique of Trudeau's alleged anti-Americanism and promised to restore the special Canada–U.S. relationship from the St. Laurent and Pearson eras. As the head of a self-defined conservative party, he next negotiated agreements on trade liberalization that introduced supraconstitutional constraints on economic policy makers. The third factor was the collapse of the Soviet bloc which transformed the basic paradigm of post-1945 international relations. Despite these new and powerful impulses for change, Canadian foreign policy showed marked continuity with its recent past. …

Mulroney's capacity for limited autonomy within the American imperium emerged from the fact that the leaders of the U.S. and Canada shared similar worldviews. Although the keystone of this foreign policy was recreating Pearson's special relationship, the practice of quiet diplomacy in the 1980s and 1990s would have required more self-restraint than the boy from Baie Comeau could command. For its part, Washington was not inclined to offer Ottawa the exemptionalism—making exceptions to U.S. international economics policies—that would have contradicted CUFTA's mission of imposing strict rules on Canada. A new relationship had been established, to be sure, but it was special in a different sense. U.S. hegemony was exercised not through unwritten conventions but through a formal document.

The question raised by free trade was whether institutionalizing the periphery-hegemon relationship would diminish or enhance Canada's diplomatic independence. …

Room for Manoeuvre Within Global Governance: The Chrétien Years

The Mulroney government's preoccupation with negotiating trade liberalization both continentally with NAFTA and globally with the GATT left it little energy with which to test the limits of its new geopolitical freedom before the American voters ousted George Bush in 1992 and the Canadian electorate demolished the Conservatives in 1993. This apparent sea change masked a basic continuity. Jean Chrétien was, practically speaking, as conservative as Mulroney, and Bill Clinton was to the right of most of his fellow Democrats. In short, the changing of the guards in Washington and Ottawa set the scene for another harmonious relationship between two right-of-centre governments keen on globalization.

Though anxious to distance himself from Mulroney's reputation as an American lapdog, Jean Chrétien, as the little guy from Quebec's resource hinterland, was comfortable with continentalism. Unobtrusively, he set about developing a collegial rapport with the U.S. president based on repeated encounters at summits and long walks together along the quiet fairways of their countries' greenest golf courses. Their mutual accommodation established the context for Ottawa's redefinition of its foreign policy in the post–Cold War era.

RETHINKING FOREIGN POLICY

The Liberals set out to review their foreign policy options in the time-honoured fashion of new governments. The difference this time lay in the partial privatization of Canada's international relations industry and the new strength of the public's input.

"Privatization" is usually about business takeovers of public corporations. The privatization of Canadian foreign policy consisted of private foundations' contributing funds from the study of certain international issues and offering the resulting reports as recommendations to government. ...

A LOCAL POLITICIAN GOES GLOBAL

...

The tension between the low road of Canada's economic interests and the high road of its humanitarian values had been institutionalized under Trudeau 1982, when he "economized" Canadian diplomacy by shifting the trade commissioners from Industry, Trade and Commerce to External Affairs. By 1985, when the Mulroney government opted for free trade negotiations with Washington, this small band of trade-policy interlopers achieved ideational dominance within their new home. When the Chrétien Liberals rechristened it the Department of Foreign Affairs *and International Trade*, they were formally recognizing its schizophrenic essence.

It was widely understood, when the prime minister offered the left-wing nationalist Lloyd Axworthy this plum, that he was not to reopen the wounds of the NAFTA debate. Ministers of international trade, whether Roy MacLaren (1994–6), Sergio Marchi (1996–9), or Pierre Pettigrew (1999–), would negotiate ever-more-intrusive economic agreements undisturbed by Axworthy's deeply felt reservations about trade liberalization. He was to find the niches elsewhere. He could pull an occasional feather from the American eagle's tail. But any resulting contretemps with the United States had to be on the high road of multilateralism, not on the low roads along which the continental political economy travelled. ...

Trade liberalization paradoxically provided the second reason why Axworthy enjoyed a degree of freedom in carving out a distinctive role for Canadian foreign policy. The new economic regime set commonly accepted and impartially enforced rules. For Canadian foreign policy, the more relations were governed by rules, the less susceptible Canada was to finger twisting by an unhappy hegemon. When, for instance, Axworthy suggested denuclearizing NATO's forces, critics feared that Washington would retaliate at such lèse-majesté. But economic sanctions taken by Washington against Canada, which were not legitimated by the supraconstitutional norms in NAFTA or the WTO, would be overturned by the dispute panels that Ottawa would request under these organizations' aegis. In short, the institutionalization of the Canadian–American relationship gave Ottawa a security blanket permitting it some autonomy in its foreign policy.

Beyond the conjunctural (congruity between the Canadian and American political leadership) and the institutional (economic integration based on rules) there has long been a multilateral element in Canada's foreign policy strategy vis-à-vis the United States. Canadian diplomats have traditionally preferred international sites for dealing with Washington other than on bilateral issues. During the Cold War, NATO was not just a military shield in Ottawa's view, but a forum in which Canada could air positions critical of American views with the likelihood that they would be supported by other alliance members. But as NATO's strategic importance deflated with the collapse of communism, so did much of its political utility to Canada.

In the light of Canada's loss of leverage through NATO, a revived United Nations provided the basic focus for its multilateral actions. For this reason, *Canada in the World* paid special attention to this venerable experiment in global governance, making a four-fold pledge—to strengthen the UN's capacity for preventive action; to conduct a review of the organization's activities so that it reflected a broader definition of global security; to improve the functioning of its decision-making bodies; and to help put it on a sound financial basis. Canada's proposal for a rapid-reaction force to respond more quickly to crises and conflicts received broad support at the UN Security Council, and the initiative was implemented. ...

Furthermore, Canada's actual behaviour revealed values that were closer to those of other rich, English-speaking countries than to those of struggling Latin American nations. Most notably, its zealous advocacy of a neoconservative economic agenda often made Ottawa appear more an advocate of Washington's stances than a counterweight to them. ...

LIFE AFTER LLOYD

The election of a Republican U.S. president and the eighteen-month tenure of a conservative foreign minister in Ottawa did not erase popular support for a human security agenda. Opinion polls consistently find that Canadians are passionate about world affairs. Far from being parochial, they have generous convictions about most international issues. It may be in response to this sentiment that Manley expressed reservations about the U.S. proposal to build a nuclear missile shield that would weaponize an already militarized space. Nor was it accidental that the prime minister intervened to ensure that Canada kept its distance from the Bush administration's rejection in 2001 of the Kyoto protocol on environmental warming; he instructed his negotiators to sign on to the successor agreement negotiated in Brussels in the face of Washington's continuing boycott. The luxury of cultivating such small differences came to an end on September 11, 2001, when the world's geopolitical contours were redrawn.

DEFENCE AGAINST TERROR

Suddenly Ottawa reverted to the Cold War template of a global struggle between the forces of light and those of an evil, if invisible, empire. The stunning catastrophe suffered directly by New York and the Pentagon dragged Canada, which had been languishing far off the Bush administration's cognitive horizon, back to being centrally located on the U.S. defence perimeter.

At the level of *strategy*, Ottawa endorsed the Bush administration's analysis of Islamic terrorism as a world threat. Prime Minister Chrétien immediately seconded Bush's declaration of total war against terrorism and offered Canada's armed forces to support its first phase. But replacing the Soviet Union with al-Qaeda changed not just the nature but the location of the combat. Terrorism was a threat to be fought not only abroad but at home. No longer the air space between the USSR and the United States, Canada had become a territorial buffer for U.S. homeland defence against infiltration by fanatical enemies. The implications were grave. If Washington defined its front line of defence as a Fortress America by blockading its territorial boundaries along the 49th parallel, Canada's NAFTA-integrated economy would collapse.

Ottawa's practical military and security responses to the Americans' extreme reaction after September 11 were driven as much by economic self-interest as Pearson's had been in the Vietnam War. It needed the U.S. to feel that the traffic of goods and people across its Canadian border was safe. The decision to put 750 Canadian soldiers under U.S. command in Afghanistan was something other than symbolic of Canada's good standing in the multi-lateral alliance. Ottawa chose not to offer its expertise in peacebuilding, which concentrates on reconstructing a civil society from the devastation of war. In volunteering to do Washington's dirty or—as it turned out when four Canadian soldiers were killed by an American bomb—deadly work in the mopping-up phase after its high-tech bombing war, the Chrétien government sent an unmistakable signal that Canada was fully on side, fully trustworthy.

More to the point, the federal government proceeded to strengthen Canada's internal defences against terrorism, not just to its own satisfaction but to that of its edgy neighbour. It knew Washington must feel its security was not jeopardized at its northern border crossing points, or in Canada's airports from which agents of *jihad* could fly into the United States, or at its seaports from which miniaturized weapons of mass destruction might be trans-shipped, or even in its embassies abroad where visas could be issued to potentially hostile immigrants.

The known infiltration of terrorist networks through all liberal capitalist societies re-quired not so much new policies as tightening a number of existing laws and putting more state resources behind their implementation. …

Measures announced to satisfy the government's two audiences—its own electorate and Washington—raised the perennial question of Canadian sovereignty. Certainly, if Ottawa negotiated its entry as junior partner into a continental homeland defence it would forgo sovereignty, as it had in NORAD and NAFTA, in return for a security and economic payoff. If the Canadian public wanted the same heightened security as Uncle Sam, its loss of sover-eignty would not entail a sacrifice of autonomy. …

Conclusion

Canada's lurch from Lloyd Axworthy's human security agenda towards a globally networked, continentally implemented anti-terrorist state was sudden, but not necessarily permanent. By mid-2002, the Bush White House was already having difficulty maintaining the political solidarity at home necessary to shift public spending from welfare to warfare. Though it had succeeded surprisingly well in the first stage of its war on al-Qaeda, it could not continue as well for a second stage, when Israel-Palestine bloodshed broke the tenuous Arab coalition Washington had assembled. Mere intelligence advisories of further terrorist acts could not indefinitely maintain the mix of paranoia and patriotism needed to support a state of permanent alert against the unknown. If reason forced Americans to accept less than 100 per cent security, Canada would regain some degree of international freedom.

Were the causes of anti-American *jihads* to be addressed, the international system would again present a variety of opportunities suited to middle-sized countries capable of seeking out these niches. These policy options create choices for Canadian foreign policy even in conditions of economic integration. Whether this scenario becomes again the basis of Canadian foreign policy depends on whether civil society continues to be cultivated as a source of soft power to create both external and internal change. Once the American war on terror subsides, Canada could again pursue an activist foreign policy in multilateral, if not in bilateral, relations under continuing U.S. hegemony—if its various leaders in the PMO and DFAIT, notably its unproven new foreign minister, Bill Graham, feel so inclined. But if the Middle East continues to be a war zone, Canada will continue to function as subordinate to the American commander.

Who Owns the Arctic?

Michael Byers (2009)

56

EDITORS' INTRODUCTION

Michael Byers is a professor of political science at the University of British Columbia, and holds a Canada Research Chair in Global Politics and International Law. His work focuses on issues of Arctic sovereignty, climate change, the law of the sea, and Canadian foreign and defence policy. His book International Law and the Arctic *won the 2014 Donner Prize for best book on Canadian public policy.*

This excerpt from Who Owns the Arctic? *explores the extent to which indigenous peoples, and more particularly the Inuit, play a significant and increasing role in strengthening Canadian presence and sovereignty in the North. He explains that there is a clear connection between sovereignty and the Nunavut Land Claims Agreement. He also contends that "the Inuit's role in international diplomacy extends beyond their contribution to Canada's sovereignty claims," in that they are at the forefront of the climate change crisis. In this context, the international influence of the Inuit is likely to increase significantly.*

Sovereignty and the Inuit

"Canada has a choice when it comes to defending our sovereignty in the Arctic: either we use it or we lose it." Stephen Harper's July 2007 statement was bold and succinct, but it did not impress Lorne Kusugak. "What the hell is he talking about?" the mayor of Rankin Inlet, Nunavut, asked me. "We've been using 'it' for thousands of years, and we're not going anywhere."

The feeling of chagrin is heaviest in Canada's two northernmost communities. The Inuit call Resolute Bay "Qausuittuq" (the place where the sun never sets) and Grise Fiord "Auyuittuq" (the place where the ice never melts). These Inuktitut names reflect the fact that, historically, the Inuit did not live this far north.

The Canadian government's decision to relocate seventeen families to the Queen Elizabeth Islands in 1953 and 1955 was motivated by concerns about possible Danish or American claims. The Inuit, whom government officials identified by numbers rather than their names, were essentially treated as flag poles. They were subsequently utilized as a resident source of cheap labour for RCMP detachments and at the Royal Canadian Air Force Base at Resolute

Source: Excerpted from *Who Owns the Arctic? Understanding Sovereignty Disputes in the North* by Michael Byers. Vancouver: Douglas & McIntyre, 2009.

Bay. There was, to be fair, some talk about the need to relieve the overpopulation of Inukjuak, the source Inuit community in northern Quebec. But if the interests of the Inuit were paramount, why move people more than 1,500 km northward to a High Arctic desert that bore little resemblance to their home? …

In 1996, more than forty years later, the Canadian government finally agreed to a $10 million compensation package. But it ignored the recommendations of three different bodies—the House of Commons Standing Committee on Aboriginal Affairs and Northern Development, the Canadian Human Rights Commission and the Royal Commission on Aboriginal Peoples—by refusing to apologize. The refusal was described by Amagoalik as a "real slap in the face for us."

Although the compensation agreement recognized Inuit "pain, suffering and hardship," it also stated that "government officials of the time were acting with honourable intentions in what was perceived to be the best interests of the Inuit." The Inuit who signed the 1996 agreement felt they were doing so under duress. Their overriding concern was for the financial well-being of the surviving elders, who were running out of time.

Much has happened since 1996. Climate change has vaulted Arctic sovereignty to the top of Canada's agenda, prompting, as we have seen, a series of promises designed to strengthen our military presence in the North. But the prime minister has failed to consult or cooperate with the Inuit, as was unfortunately illustrated when he ignored Inuit views on the appropriate site for an Arctic port and chose uninhabited Nanisivik over Iqaluit. Insult was added to the injury when Harper failed to invite Premier Paul Okalik to the announcement in Resolute Bay, failed to stop in Iqaluit on his way back to Ottawa, and even failed to mention the Inuit in his speech. As John Amagoalik later told the Standing Senate Committee on Fisheries and Oceans, "That's not going to work."

The Inuit know the clock cannot be turned back. They want to work with other Canadians to forge a better future. They seek to preserve the Arctic environment, to protect our common sovereignty, and to provide their children with a quality of life equivalent to that in the rest of Canada. But the Inuit also want respect. For a prime minister who really cares about sovereignty, apologizing to the High Arctic exiles would be an excellent next step. …

Upholding the Bargain

In the 1993 Nunavut Land Claims Agreement, the Inuit transferred their claim to aboriginal title over one-fifth of Canada's area. In doing so, they explicitly sought to strengthen the country's sovereignty there. It was the Inuit negotiators who suggested the inclusion of a paragraph that reads: "Canada's sovereignty over the waters of the Arctic archipelago is supported by Inuit use and occupancy."

The ability of nomadic peoples to acquire and transfer sovereignty rights was affirmed by the International Court of Justice in the 1975 *Western Sahara Case*. However, any argument based on a transfer of rights is weakened if the recipient fails to uphold the bargain, or to address other basic grievances held by the transferees. And the Canadian government made a number of commitments in the Nunavut Land Claims Agreement that have not yet been fulfilled. For instance, Article 23 requires that the percentage of government jobs held by Inuit match their share of the population. Today, the Inuit account for 85 per cent of the population in Nunavut—and hold only 45 per cent of the jobs. …

Sovereignty and the Nunavut Land Claims Agreement

Working with the Inuit, investing in social programs, building infrastructure, creating economic opportunities—all of these things are important from a fairness perspective, since northern Canadians are as entitled to Ottawa's support as the rest of us. But they are critically important for another reason, too.

The Inuit have been central to Canada's sovereignty claims since 1910, when the federal government invoked Inuit interests to deny a Norwegian request for commercial access to the Sverdrup Islands. In 1986, the proclamation of straight baselines around the Canadian Arctic Archipelago was justified partly on the basis that these were consolidated by Inuit use and occupancy. When I speak about the Northwest Passage at universities and foreign ministries around the world, the thousands of years of Inuit use and occupancy of the sea-ice is the only dimension of our legal position that resonates with non-Canadians.

The Inuit are, however, becoming increasingly frustrated with the federal government. In December 2006, after Stephen Harper's newly elected government refused even to meet with conciliator Thomas Berger, Nunavut Tunngavik Inc. launched a lawsuit aimed at forcing Ottawa to uphold its obligations under the Nunavut Land Claims Agreement. The federal Department of Justice has spent millions of dollars fighting the case on every conceivable ground. And by so doing, it is putting Canada's legal position in the Northwest Passage at risk.

Inuit leaders see a clear connection between Canadian sovereignty and the Nunavut Land Claims Agreement. Indeed, Paul Kaludjak of Nunavut Tunngavik Inc. told the Standing Senate Committee on Fisheries and Oceans: "We are now in court because the Government of Canada has failed to implement an agreement which, given full force and effect, would strengthen Canada's Arctic sovereignty." Some Inuit are so upset with the federal government that they are even discussing the possibility of withdrawing support for Canada's claim. It is not a step the Inuit want to take, given the environmental risks that would flow from the Northwest Passage becoming an international strait. But the mere fact that the possibility is being discussed should set off alarm bells in southern Canada. We cannot take the Inuit for granted: if we wish to maintain their support, we have to keep our promises.

John Amagoalik describes the Nunavut Land Claims Agreement as the Inuit's "entrance into Confederation." As Arctic expert Terry Fenge explains, implementing the agreement is "an ongoing expression of a negotiated partnership between the Government of Canada and the Inuit of Nunavut and could be an important component of a strategy to assert, affirm and express Canada's Arctic sovereignty."

Fenge is correct: Canada should be thinking about how to strengthen the Inuit dimension of our Northwest Passage claim. Hiring Inuit in the Coast Guard is one way; another is to devolve some of the federal government's existing powers to Nunavut and give it the status of a province.

In international law, as noted, the term "internal waters" refers to those maritime areas located within straight baselines that are subject to the full control of the coastal state. "Internal waters" also have a particular status in Canadian domestic law. In the 1984 *Georgia Strait Reference*, the Supreme Court of Canada was asked about the status of the seabed between Vancouver Island and mainland British Columbia. The court held that, since the western boundary of the Colony of British Columbia was the Pacific Ocean off the west coast of Vancouver Island, the waters to the east belonged to the colony. British Columbia kept the same boundaries when it joined Canada and became a province, which means that the seabed under those "internal waters" belongs to B.C.

The same is true on the Atlantic coast, where Canada has drawn a straight baseline across the mouth of the Gulf of St. Lawrence between Newfoundland and Nova Scotia. In 2002, Nova Scotia and Newfoundland asked an arbitration panel to delimit the maritime boundary between their respective jurisdictions in the internal waters created landward (i.e., to the west) of the straight baseline. The same kind of provincial rights would, logically, flow to Nunavut once devolution to provincial status was achieved.

Before becoming prime minister, Stephen Harper promised that the three northern territories would be the primary beneficiaries of natural resource revenues in any devolution deal with a Conservative government. Although it took three years, progress toward such a deal has now begun. In September 2008, the federal minister of Indian Affairs and Northern Development met with the premier of Nunavut and the president of Nunavut Tunngavik Inc. The three of them—Chuck Strahl, Paul Okalik and Paul Kaludjak—signed a Devolution Negotiation Protocol.

The preamble to the Protocol recognizes that "the Inuit of Nunavut are largely a coastal people who have a deep attachment to both the land and the marine areas of Nunavut." It makes reference to the 1993 Nunavut Land Claims Agreement, which "gave the Inuit of Nunavut certain specific rights and responsibilities in respect of Inuit Owned Lands and a role in the territory's overall resource management regime."

More pointedly, the Protocol specifies: "The parties acknowledge that it is the position of the GN and NTI that the ultimate objective of devolution is the transfer of administration and control in respect of Crown lands and resources in all areas, both onshore and in the seabed." It also specifies: "The parties further acknowledge that it is the position of the GN and NTI that a devolution agreement should make no distinction between resource management regimes onshore and in the seabed in and adjacent to Marine Areas."

None of this implies that the federal government agrees with the position of the Government of Nunavut and Nunavut Tunngavik Inc. Even if it did, the Protocol is non-binding. The Protocol also explicitly postpones the issue of the seabed: "The parties acknowledge that, owing to, among other factors, the need of the GC to consider national consistency and coherency in seabed resource management, the GC is not prepared to negotiate seabed resource management during the initial phase of devolution negotiations." The parties did, however, agree "to discuss the management of onshore and seabed oil and gas resources as an integrated unit in a future phase of devolution negotiations."

The fact that discussions are taking place is a step toward strengthening Canada's sovereignty. As Suzanne Lalonde has concluded, devolving rights over the seabed within the Archipelago would, by reinforcing the role of Inuit use and occupancy, carry weight in international law:

> Devolution of legislative jurisdiction over the land resources and marine bed resources in the Territory of Nunavut to its Government could be a further and important exercise of Canada's exclusive authority over the waters of the Arctic Archipelago. Particularly should such action draw no notice or protests from foreign governments, it would undoubtedly strengthen Canada's claim under the historic waters doctrine.

Recognizing Inuit control of oil and gas resources would also facilitate the development of Nunavut's economy and generate much-needed income for the Government of Nunavut.

The territorial government faces monumental challenges in providing basic services to thirty thousand people scattered across one-fifth of Canada without having its own tax and royalty base. At the moment, the plight of the Inuit undermines the credibility of Canada's Northwest Passage claim, since it is not as if other countries are unaware of the hypocrisy of holding forward Inuit use and occupancy as a central component of our legal position while allowing the same people to suffer so badly. ...

International Influence

The Inuit's role in international diplomacy extends beyond their contributions to Canada's sovereignty claims. The Inuit Circumpolar Council, an international organization that draws the Inuit of Alaska, Canada, Greenland and Russia together into a unified political force, has proven itself an international actor of consequence. In the 1990s, the ICC played a decisive role in the negotiation and adoption of the Stockholm Convention on Persistent Organic Pollutants. These toxic chemicals, which include DDT and PCBS, were produced and mostly used in the industrialized regions of the world. Disproportionate amounts were, and still are, being carried to the Arctic by a process of global distillation involving volatilization at low latitudes and condensation at high latitudes, also known as the "grasshopper effect." After being deposited in the Arctic, these toxins move up the food chain, accumulating in the fatty tissues of predators such as seals, bears and ultimately humans.

One of Canada's most effective politicians, Sheila Watt-Cloutier, represented the Inuit during the negotiation of the Stockholm Convention. Throughout the negotiations, she made a point of educating everyone involved about the fact that the Inuit are the world's most affected victims of persistent organic pollutants, to the point where Inuit women should think twice about breastfeeding their babies. During a particularly critical stage in the talks, Watt-Cloutier presented a soapstone carving of an Inuit woman and child to Klaus Toepfer, the executive director of the United Nations Environmental Programme. Her efforts paid off: the Stockholm Convention adopted in 2001, requires states to take specific steps to reduce or eliminate the production of persistent organic pollutants and to dispose safely of existing stocks. So far, 162 countries have ratified the convention, including Canada, China, the European Community, India and Japan. In May 2009, the Convention was amended to include nine new chemicals, some of which are still widely used as pesticides and flame retardants and will now be phased out.

The Inuit are also helping to alert southerners to the immediacy of the climate change crisis, something greatly facilitated by the fact that they are, collectively and individually, very much on the front line. Their traditional way of life has become more difficult, even dangerous, to sustain, as temperatures rise, weather patterns change, snow and ice conditions become less predictable, and populations of their food animals decline.

In 2005, Sheila Watt-Cloutier and sixty-two other Inuit from Canada and Alaska filed a petition with the Inter-American Commission on Human Rights in Washington, D.C. They argued that the United States, by failing to reduce its massive emissions of carbon dioxide and other greenhouse gases, has violated the cultural and environmental rights of the Inuit. Although the Commission declined to hear the petition for jurisdictional reasons, the effort was successful in raising media and public awareness about climate change in the United States. In 2007, Watt-Cloutier was a nominee for the Nobel Peace Prize in recognition of her work on international environmental issues.

The international influence of the Inuit is likely to grow as Greenland acquires more autonomy from Denmark and cooperates more closely with Nunavut. It is even possible to imagine an eventual federation of sorts between Greenland and Nunavut—perhaps following the model of the Mohawk nation of Akwesasne, which straddles the border of Canada and the United States—as the Inuit on both sides of Baffin Bay seek to increase their influence and benefit from economies of scale.

For the Inuit, cooperation and adaptation have always been prerequisites for survival. It took centuries of field expeditions before European explorers learned to wear clothes made out of skins, eat seal blubber (which contains the Vitamin C necessary to prevent scurvy) and use dogs to pull sleds. That history has made it all the more difficult for Inuit leaders to accept their exclusion from inter-state negotiations, especially their exclusion from the summit of foreign ministers held in Ilulissat, Greenland, in May 2008.

One year later, in April 2009, the Inuit Circumpolar Council responded by issuing a declaration on sovereignty just a day before a summit meeting of Arctic Council foreign ministers in Tromso, Norway. The declaration indicated a specific concern about the exclusion of the Inuit from the Ilulissat meeting:

> In spite of a recognition by the five coastal Arctic states (Norway, Denmark, Canada, USA and Russia) of the need to use international mechanisms and international law to resolve sovereignty disputes (see 2008 Ilulissat Declaration), these states, in their discussions of Arctic sovereignty, have not referenced existing international instruments that promote and protect the rights of indigenous peoples. They have also neglected to include Inuit in Arctic sovereignty discussions in a manner comparable to Arctic Council deliberations.

The declaration goes on to argue that the Inuit have rights as a people under international legal instruments such as the 2007 UN Declaration on the Rights of Indigenous Peoples. The argument overreaches a bit by failing to acknowledge that the UN Declaration is not a binding treaty, has not yet achieved the status of customary international law, and is actively opposed by the Canadian, New Zealand and U.S. governments. But the Inuit were right to conclude that "issues of sovereignty and sovereign rights in the Arctic have become inextricably linked to issues of self-determination in the Arctic. Inuit and Arctic states must, therefore, work together closely and constructively to chart the future of the Arctic."

John Amagoalik, as the former president of the Inuit Tapirisat of Canada, recalls attending a meeting at the United Nations where a foreign diplomat blithely stated that "nobody lived in the Arctic." Amagoalik approached the diplomat afterwards, held out his hand and said, "Hi, I'm nobody."

Another Amagoalik anecdote demonstrates even more poignantly the damaging disconnect between southerners and northerners. In 1969, he says, after the Canadian government failed to persuade Exxon and the U.S. government to request permission for the Northwest Passage voyage of the SS Manhattan, two Inuit hunters took matters into their own hands. As the super-tanker ploughed through the ice of Lancaster Sound, the two drove their dogsleds into its path. The vessel stopped, a short discussion ensued, and then the hunters—having made their point—moved aside.

The story is credible. The incident happened only four decades ago, and Inuit oral history is accurate over many generations. But the Canadian government, instead of using the incident to Canada's legal and diplomatic advantage, denies it ever occurred. "Nobody," it seems, was on the ice that day.

PART 4

Canadian Society: Identities and Diversities

Introduction

Canada has a worldwide reputation for diversity, tolerance, and multiculturalism. Legislation and numerous policies at all levels of government protect our rights as citizens of Canada, and seek to prevent discrimination based on race, ethnicity, gender, sexual orientation, and ability. Canada is also often seen as having a robust set of social policies and programs that enhance socio-economic equality, embolden Canadians' national pride and identity, and promote trust and solidarity between social groups and regions.

However, Canadian society is not without its divisions and social problems. The anti-discrimination legislation described above, and those norms of pluralism and egalitarianism we enjoy, are the products of political struggles. They are the culmination of long processes in which racial and ethnic minorities, women, sexual minorities, and Aboriginal peoples have fought to attain the full rights of citizenship. Canadian history is marked by political events that have been instrumental in the creation of a society in which all people—no matter what race, ethnicity, gender, or sexual orientation—are protected from unequal treatment. And yet, racism, sexism, and other forms of discrimination undoubtedly still exist in Canada. While it is true that Canada does not suffer from the same levels of economic inequality as the United States, the gap between wealthy and impoverished Canadians is real and growing (as noted in Reading 74 by Armine Yalnizyan). And though Canadians profess a clear sense of pride in their national identity, regional identities and interests outside of Quebec challenge our ability to make generalizations about English-speaking Canada without taking into account the unique patterns of politics in different parts of the country. To what extent do these cleavages divide us, and what is the glue that holds us together? Bearing

405

these questions in mind, the selections in this part demonstrate both how far we have come in addressing the politics of identity and diversity and the challenges that remain.

Gender and Sexuality

The first section of readings in Part 4 considers the evolution of the rights of women and sexual minorities, which have come a long way in Canada. In the first third of the 20th century, women fought for the right to vote, to hold public office, and to even be considered "persons" under the law. The latter third of the century began with the Royal Commission on the Status of Women's landmark recognition of the pervasiveness of gender inequality in Canadian society. As the first selection (Reading 57, an excerpt from the commission's report) demonstrates, the commission's inquiry examined the disadvantaged status of women and recommended steps to be undertaken by the federal government to alleviate gender discrimination in society. This disadvantage can manifest itself in a number of ways. In the realm of the formal institutions of legislatures and the judiciary, women remain underrepresented and face unique challenges in gaining access to what has historically been considered an "old boys' club."

Formal politics is also supplemented by unofficial politics—interest groups, social movements, and the ways in which the everyday lives of women are affected by gender disadvantage. It is important to recognize, however, that the category of "women" is problematic—we cannot and should not assume that all women mobilize for the same reasons, or face the same kinds of discrimination. Mary Ellen Turpel's article (Reading 58), written in response to the 20th anniversary of the Report of the Royal Commission on the Status of Women, criticizes the mandate and recommendations of the report as being conceptually and culturally inappropriate for First Nations women. Similarly, Himani Bannerji's deconstruction of Canadian multiculturalism (Reading 59) suggests the extent to which women of colour are excluded and marginalized.

Readers are also referred to several readings in Part 2 (Canada's Institutions and Representation) that further explore themes relating to women and politics in Canada: Reading 20 by Sylvia Bashevkin; Reading 27 by Elisabeth Gidengil et al.; and Reading 32 by Gidengil and Joanna Everitt).

This group of readings would certainly not be complete without reference to the struggles of gay, lesbian, and transgender people for equality in Canada. The legalization of same-sex marriage in 2005 was a major victory, and made Canada a global leader in gay rights, but it only came about after decades of uphill struggles and strategic lobbying for full citizenship rights, some of them still ongoing. Legal battles have been fought in order for sexual orientation to be included as grounds of discrimination under section 15 of the *Canadian Charter of Rights and Freedoms*, to permit same-sex couples to adopt children, to have equal access to social benefits (such as pensions plans), and even to allow a gay high school student to bring his partner to the prom. The excerpt by Miriam Smith (Reading 60) details the status, victories, and challenges of gay, lesbian, and transgender political activism in Canada from the 1990s and into the early 21st century.

Aboriginal Peoples

The second group of readings in this part concerns Canada's relationship with its First Peoples. The history of this relationship is largely characterized by government coercion, colonization, and subjugation. Section 91(24) of the *British North America Act* gave the federal government jurisdiction over "Indians and lands reserved for Indians," and in 1876 the government consolidated all legislation concerning Native peoples into the *Indian Act*—the first element of a massive regulatory regime designed to manage Aboriginal peoples' lives from cradle to grave.

Reading 61 is Canada's 1969 Statement on Indian Policy, presented to the House of Commons by then minister of Indian affairs, Jean Chrétien. Influenced by the civil rights movement in the United States that demanded equality for all, this policy proposed the eradication of "special treatment" for Aboriginal peoples, which in the government's view was the ultimate cause of their disadvantage. The White Paper, as it is commonly called, proposed eliminating the *Indian Act*, abolishing Indian status, dismantling the Department of Indian Affairs, and handing control of Indian affairs to provincial governments in order to create a more equal and just society. The unintended consequence of the White Paper was the mass mobilization of Aboriginal peoples against any attempt to demolish the special historical relationship they had with the Crown. Within a matter of weeks of the tabling of the White Paper, Harold Cardinal had published *The Unjust Society*, Reading 62 in this part. Cardinal's book attacks the Trudeau government's betrayal of Aboriginal peoples after months of supposed consultation. This book, along with the "Red Paper" that Native Peoples published in response to the government's White Paper, helped create intense political pressure from Aboriginal peoples, which eventually forced the government to retreat from its position.

Though Aboriginal policy has undeniably come a long way—from attempts at forced assimilation (such as the notorious and abusive residential school system for Aboriginal children), to the recognition many decades later of Aboriginal people's inherent right to self-government—there is still much work to be done. The last two readings in this section (63 and 64) provide a clear critique from Aboriginal scholars regarding current government policies in Aboriginal affairs, and the challenges their communities face on the road ahead. In the first of these two selections, Taiaiake Alfred calls for indigenous resistance against an inherently colonial Canadian state. This acclamation is echoed in Glen Coulthard's 2014 book, *Red Skin, White Masks*, which argues that the so-called politics of recognition that characterize the relationship between First Nations and the Canadian government has worked to ensure that indigenous people remain colonial subjects, rather than equal partners. The excerpt from Coulthard's book also includes a detailed overview of the Idle No More social movement that in 2012 and 2013 brought national attention to indigenous peoples' struggle for sovereignty and environmental protections.

Readers are also referred to several other relevant readings in this book, including Reading 10, from the Royal Commission on Aboriginal Peoples; Reading 38, by Reg Whitaker; and Reading 58, by Mary Ellen Turpel.

Race, Ethnicity, and Multiculturalism

The third section of this part considers the evolution of attitudes and policies toward racial and ethnic minorities in Canada. It begins with a selection from *Strangers Within Our Gates* by J.S. Woodsworth (Reading 65), a quintessential example of the anti-immigrant sentiment that characterized decades of Canadian history, from the imposition of a head tax on Chinese immigrants in 1885, to the immigration policies that restricted non-white immigration between 1924 and 1962.

The next three selections situate the birth of Canadian multiculturalism within the French–English cleavage of Canadian society between the 1960s and 1980s. First, the Royal Commission on Bilingualism and Biculturalism's investigation into the status of French Canadians and the use of the French language in Canadian society (Reading 66) spurred many important political developments, such as the *Official Languages Act* of 1969. However, it also had to answer to "other" ethnic Canadians, who felt their contributions to the development of Canada were overlooked within the French–English debate. These concerns were directly addressed in the 1971 "Statement on Multiculturalism" by Prime Minister Pierre Trudeau (Reading 67). In this speech to the House of Commons, Trudeau advocated the official recognition of Canadian multiculturalism within a bilingual framework, eloquently arguing that diversity and pluralism were part of Canadian identity, not opposed to it. However, some Quebeckers perceived this move as an attempt to diminish their claim to being a distinct society within Canada. This perspective is explored in Guy Rocher's piece (Reading 68), which is a direct response to Trudeau's statement.

Though we have clearly improved upon the mistakes and injustices of the past, this is not to say that racism, discrimination, and intolerance have been eradicated from Canadian society. The next selection comes from *Building the Future: A Time for Reconciliation*, the 2008 report on accommodation practices in Quebec by Charles Taylor and Gérard Bouchard (Reading 69). Commissioned in response to growing hostilities toward racial and ethnic minorities in Quebec, the report attempts to come to terms with an increasingly diverse population and the ways that this diversity collides with Quebec's distinct, secular society. The final selection considers the meaning of race in Canadian political and social life, which has always been something of a taboo topic. In Reading 70, Debra Thompson examines the intersection of race and politics, and asks why Canadian political scientists have ignored race as a viable topic of research. Thompson suggests that Canadian identity and society tend to presume a race-neutral version of multiculturalism and insist that political institutions are colour-blind. Together, these interpretations have worked to keep the politics of race off the country's radar.

Class

In many ways, class distinctions are relatively muted in Canada, which has rarely been viewed as a country characterized by class conflict. Since the protests of Occupy Wall Street in 2011 and the echo movements around the globe, however, issues of income inequality, poverty, and the growing gap between the rich and the poor have taken centre stage in many advanced industrialized societies, including Canada. The readings in this section consider the origins of the ideological left–right divide in Canada, the necessity of examining wealth disparities in Canadian society, as well as measuring the scope and breadth of economic inequality at the turn of the 21st century.

One of the best-known articulations of an explicitly socialist political agenda occurred in the 1930s with the rise of the Co-operative Commonwealth Federation, which was the predecessor to today's New Democratic Party. Reading 71 is an excerpt from the CCF's Regina Manifesto, which articulated clear goals about the need to replace capitalism with a social order not based on class exploitation. This statement included many of the national policies that Canada would eventually adopt and which Canadians now cherish, including universal health care, unemployment insurance, and old age pensions. In the second and third excerpts (Readings 72 and 73), John Porter and Leo Panitch challenge the idea that Canada lacks the class divisions that characterize political culture in Great Britain and (to a lesser extent) the United States. While Porter argues that elite-level power in Canada is largely concentrated in the hands of those of British origin, Panitch contends that political scientists must begin to make class a central part of their analytical frameworks in order to fully understand the material inequalities that permeate the Canadian social fabric.

The final excerpt in this section (Reading 74) concerns income inequality in Canada. Much has been said over the past few years about the American "one percent," which controls a disproportionate amount of wealth and power compared with the rest of the population. Are these same dynamics present in Canada, which is often considered a more egalitarian society with values that include the redistribution of wealth? In this selection, Armine Yalnizyan presents compelling evidence for the existence of a persistent and growing gap between the rich and the poor in Canada.

Regional Interests and Identities

Canada is a vast and diverse country, with many political cultures and traditions that vary substantially from coast to coast. A proper understanding of Canada requires an examination of the patterns of politics that characterize distinct regions of the country. The final four readings explore the importance of place, and the value of regional identities and loyalties in constituting Canada as a whole. These readings also illustrate how these regional differences can catalyze and define distinct political ideologies.

Nelson Wiseman's 1981 essay on politics in the prairie provinces (Reading 75) offers a challenge to, and refinement of, Gad Horowitz's thesis that political culture in English Canada is unique from the United States in that it combines a liberal tradition with a "tory touch" brought by the Loyalists to Canada around the time of the American Revolution. Instead, Wiseman urges scholars to pay closer attention to regional political cultures that appear at the level of provincial political parties. With regard to another region of Canada, Robert Finbow considers in Reading 77 whether the four eastern provinces—Nova Scotia, New Brunswick, Newfoundland and Labrador, and Prince Edward Island—can legitimately be classified together as "the Atlantic region" of Canada. He provides an overview of the provinces' similarities and differences, as well as the challenges faced by these provinces that could spur either conflict or cooperation.

Meanwhile, Canada continues, year after year, to become an ever more urban nation. Reading 76 by Caroline Andrew argues that Canada's cities, which have long been considered no more than "creatures of provincial governments," should be recognized as important sites of governance and policy-making, where many major social issues, such as diversity and ideological polarization, are played out.

We conclude with Reading 78, which relates to the growing importance of Western Canada in federal politics, a trend perhaps best illustrated by the longevity of Stephen Harper's Conservative government. Clearly, it is indicative of a shift in regional political influence—specifically, a brand of conservatism that originated in Western Canada with the Reform Party in the 1980s, and the appearance of the Canadian Alliance shortly thereafter. This movement culminated in the reshaping of the federal Conservative Party of Canada. This revamped party, firmly rooted in the west (and no longer known as the "Progressive" Conservatives), went on to achieve a decade of electoral success, including a majority victory in the 2011 election. The last excerpt of this section, from a 2009 article by William Johnson, traces the rise to national prominence of a movement in Canadian conservatism that has, under Harper's leadership, grown from a regional protest movement and entered the Canadian political mainstream.

Further Suggested Reading

Gender and Sexuality

Sylvia Bashevkin. *Welfare Hot Buttons: Women, Work and Social Policy Reform*. Toronto: University of Toronto Press, 2002.

Alexandra Dobrowolsky. *The Politics of Pragmatism: Women, Representation, and Constitutionalism in Canada*. Toronto: Oxford University Press, 2000.

Edwards v. Canada (Attorney General), [1930] AC 124 (the "Persons" case).

Egan v. Canada, [1995] 2 SCR 513 (concerning sexual orientation).

Joyce Green. *Making Space for Indigenous Feminism*. Blackpoint, NS: Fernwood Press, 2007.

R v. Morgentaler, [1988] 1 SCR 30 (concerning abortion rights).

David Rayside. *Queer Inclusions, Continental Divisions: Public Recognition of Sexual Diversity in Canada and the United States*. Toronto: University of Toronto Press, 2008.

Reference Re: Same Sex Marriage, [2004] 3 SCR 698, 2004 SCC 79.

Women's Legal Education and Action Fund (LEAF). *Equality and the Charter: Ten Years of Feminist Advocacy Before the Supreme Court of Canada*. Toronto: Emond Montgomery, 1996.

Lisa Young. *Feminists and Party Politics*. Vancouver: University of British Columbia Press, 2000.

Aboriginal Peoples

Chris Andersen. *Métis: Race, Recognition, and the Struggle for Indigenous Peoplehood*. Vancouver: University of British Columbia Press, 2014.

John Borrows. *Recovering Canada: The Resurgence of Indigenous Law*. Toronto: University of Toronto Press, 2002.

Alan Cairns. *Citizens Plus: Aboriginal Peoples and the Canadian State*. Vancouver: University of British Columbia Press, 2000.

Glen Coulthard. "Subjects of Empire: Indigenous Peoples and the 'Politics of Recognition' in Canada." *Contemporary Political Theory* 6(4), 2007.

Delgamuukw v. British Columbia, [1997] 3 SCR 1010 (concerning Aboriginal title).

Tom Flanagan. *First Nations? Second Thoughts*. Montreal and Kingston: McGill-Queen's University Press, 2000.

Martin Papillon. "Aboriginal Quality of Life Under a Modern Treaty: The Experience of the James Bay and Northern Quebec Agreement." *Choices* 14(9). Montreal: Institute for Research on Public Policy, August 2008.

Daniel Salée. "The Quebec State and Indigenous Peoples." In Alain-G. Gagnon, ed., *Québec: State and Society*, 3rd edition. Peterborough, ON: Broadview Press, 2004.

Audra Simpson. *Mohawk Interruptus: Political Life Across the Border of Settler States*. Durham, NC: Duke University Press, 2014.

Leanne Simpson. *Dancing on Our Turtle's Back: Stories of Nishnaabeg Re-Creation, Resurgence and a New Emergence*. Winnipeg: Arbeiter Ring Press, 2011.

Truth and Reconciliation Commission of Canada. *TRC Findings*. Released June 2, 2015. Available at: http://www.trc.ca/websites/trcinstitution/index.php?p=893 (documents relating to the commission's hearings and findings relating to Canada's residential school system for Aboriginal children).

Race, Ethnicity, and Multiculturalism

Yasmeen Abu-Laban and Christina Gabriel. *Selling Diversity: Immigration, Multiculturalism, Employment Equity and Globalization*. Peterborough, ON: Broadview Press, 2002.

Constance Backhouse. *Colour-Coded: A Legal History of Racism in Canada, 1900–1950*. Toronto: University of Toronto Press, 1999.

Keith Banting and Will Kymlicka. "Canadian Multiculturalism: Global Anxieties and Local Debates." *British Journal of Canadian Studies* 23(1), 2010.

Neil Bissoondath. *Selling Illusions: The Cult of Multiculturalism in Canada*. Toronto: Penguin, 1994.

Irene Bloemraad. *Becoming a Citizen: Incorporating Immigrants and Refugees in the United States and Canada*. Berkeley: University of California Press, 2006.

Linda Cardinal. "Language and the Ideological Limits of Diversity in Canada." *Journal of Multilingualism and Multicultural Development* 26(6), 2005.

Eve Haque. *Multiculturalism Within a Bicultural Framework: Language, Race, and Belonging in Canada*. Toronto: University of Toronto Press, 2012.

Genevieve Fuji Johnson and Randy Enomoto, eds. *Race, Racialization, and Antiracism in Canada and Beyond*. Toronto: University of Toronto Press, 2007.

Will Kymlicka. *Finding Our Way: Rethinking Ethnocultural Relations in Canada*. Oxford: Oxford University Press, 1998.

Jeffrey Reitz and Rupa Banerjee. "Racial Inequality: Social Cohesion and Policy Issues in Canada." In Keith G. Banting, Thomas J. Courchene, and F. Leslie Seidle, eds. *Belonging? Diversity, Recognition, and Shared Citizenship in Canada*, 489–546. Montreal: Institute for Research on Public Policy, 2007.

Charles Taylor. "The Politics of Recognition." In Amy Gutmann, ed., *Multiculturalism: Examining the Politics of Recognition*. Princeton, NJ: Princeton University Press, 1994.

Class

Keith Banting and John Myles, eds. *Inequality and the Fading of Redistributive Politics*. Vancouver: University of British Columbia Press, 2013.

H.D. Forbes. "Hartz-Horowitz at Twenty: Nationalism, Toryism and Socialism in Canada and the United States." *Canadian Journal of Political Science* 20(2), 1987.

Nicole Fortin, David Green, Thomas Lemieux, Kevin Milligan, and Craig Riddell. "Canadian Inequality: Recent Developments and Policy Options." *Canadian Public Policy* 38(2), 2012.

Gad Horowitz. "Conservatism, Liberalism, and Socialism in Canada: An Interpretation." *Canadian Journal of Economics and Political Science* 32(2), 1966.

Richard Johnston, Keith Banting, Will Kymlicka, and Stuart Soroka, "National Identity and Support for the Welfare State." *Canadian Journal of Political Science* 43(2), 2010.

Krishna Pendakur and Ravi Pendakur. "Colour by Numbers: Minority Earnings in Canada, 1995–2005." *Journal of International Migration and Integration* 12(3), 2011.

Regional Interests and Identities

Roger Gibbins. "Political Action on Stage West." *The Mark News*, September 29, 2009.

Ailsa Henderson. "Regional Political Cultures in Canada." *Canadian Journal of Political Science* 37(3), 2004.

Warren Magnusson. "Are Municipalities Creatures of the Provinces?" *Journal of Canadian Studies* 39(2), 2005.

Nelson Wiseman. *In Search of Canadian Political Culture*. Vancouver: University of British Columbia Press, 2007.

Royal Commission on the Status of Women in Canada

57

Royal Commission Report (1970)

EDITORS' INTRODUCTION

Commissioned by the government of Lester B. Pearson in 1967, the mandate of the Royal Commission on the Status of Women was to examine the situation of women in Canadian society and make policy recommendations to the federal government. These recommendations concerned a wide range of issues, such as equal pay, maternity leave, family law, the Indian Act, *and pensions. The commission's report in 1970 catalyzed the creation of Status of Women Canada (which became a departmental agency of the federal government in 1976), and is widely considered to be a landmark in the struggle for women's equality in Canada.*

Criteria and Principles

In a dozen succinct words the Universal Declaration of Human Rights has clarified the issue of the rights of women: "All human beings are born free and equal in dignity and rights."

Canada is, therefore, committed to a principle that permits no distinction in rights and freedoms between women and men. The principle emphasizes the common status of women and men rather than a separate status for each sex. The stage has been set for a new society equally enjoyed and maintained by both sexes.

But practices and attitudes die slowly. As we travelled across the country, we heard of discrimination against women that still flourishes and prejudice that is very much alive. It became abundantly clear that Canada's commitment is far from being realized.

We have been asked to inquire into and report upon the status of women in Canada and we have done so in the light of certain principles. A general principle is that *everyone is entitled to the rights and freedoms proclaimed in the Universal Declaration of Human Rights.* We have examined the status of women to learn whether or not they really have these positive rights and freedoms both in principle and in practice. Some of our recommendations should establish a measure of equality that is now lacking for men as well as for women.

Explicit in the Terms of Reference given us by the Government is our duty to ensure for women equal opportunities with men. We have interpreted this to mean that equality of

---

Source: Excerpted from *Final Report of the Royal Commission on the Status of Women in Canada.* Ottawa: Government of Canada, 1970. Notes omitted.

opportunity for everyone should be the goal of Canadian society. The right to an adequate standard of living is without value to the person who has no means of achieving it. Freedom to choose a career means little if the opportunity to enter some occupations is restricted.

Our Terms of Reference also imply that *the full use of human resources is in the national interest.* We have explored the extent to which Canada develops and makes use of the skills and abilities of women.

Women and men, having the same rights and freedoms, share the same responsibilities. They should have an equal opportunity to fulfil this obligation. We have, therefore, examined the status of women and made recommendations in the belief that *there should be equality of opportunity to share the responsibilities to society as well as its privileges and prerogatives.*

In particular, the Commission adopted four principles: first, *that women should be free to choose whether or not to take employment outside their homes.* The circumstances which impede this free choice have been of specific interest to our inquiry. Where we have made recommendations to improve opportunities for women in the work world, our goal has not been to force married women to work for pay outside of the home but rather to eliminate the practical obstacles that prevent them from exercising this right. If a husband is willing to support his wife, or a wife her husband, the decision and responsibility belong to them.

The second is that *the care of children is a responsibility to be shared by the mother, the father and society.* Unless this shared responsibility is acknowledged and assumed, women cannot be accorded true equality.

The third principle specifically recognizes the child-bearing function of women. It is apparent that *society has a responsibility for women because of pregnancy and child-birth, and special treatment related to maternity will always be necessary.*

The fourth principle is that *in certain areas women will for an interim period require special treatment to overcome the adverse effects of discriminatory practices.* We consider such measures to be justified in a limited range of circumstances, and we anticipate that they should quickly lead to actual equality which would make their continuance unnecessary. The needs and capacities of women have not always been understood. Discrimination against women has in many instances been unintentional and special treatment will no longer be required if a positive effort to remove it is made for a short period.

With these principles in mind, we have first looked at women in Canadian society. Within this perspective we have gone on to consider the position of women in the economy, the education they receive, their place in the family and their participation in public life. We have considered the particular implications of poverty among women, conditions of citizenship and aspects of taxation, and the Criminal Code as it affects the female offender. ...

Canadian Women and Society

Social Change

The democratization of education has greatly affected the aspirations and expectations of Canadian women. Little by little, the doors of nearly all educational institutions have been opened to them over the last hundred years. In 1967, female graduates made up about a third of the 27,533 Canadian graduates in arts, pure science and commerce, and more than half the 7,590 graduates in education, library science and social work. And yet many fields of learning still remain substantially male preserves with only token female representation; fewer than five per cent of the 1,796 graduates in law and theology, fewer than 12 per cent of the graduating medical doctors and about six per cent of the graduating dentists in 1967 were women. Moreover, institutions of higher learning have yet to adapt their general plans and structures to the needs of married women.

In the face of deep-rooted functional change, marriage and the family persist as an institution of particular importance to women. The importance of family is due to the need of human beings, whether children or adults, to "belong" in a close social relationship with others. Functions of the family, however, which wives used to perform—such as the education of children, treatment of illness and care of the aged—are now undertaken increasingly by private or public institutions. Today 90 per cent of Canadian women marry and live in families and, because of the longer life span, may remain married for an average of 40 years. Divorce is now increasing and many divorced women remarry.

The Cultural Mould

… [Many philosophers and most theologians] postulated the existence of an inferior feminine "nature," in opposition to that of man. Aristotle's theory that a women's role in conception is purely passive was accepted for centuries. It was not until the second half of the nineteenth century that scientists demonstrated that both parents made equivalent contributions to a child's biological inheritance.

The three principle influences which have shaped Western society—Greek philosophy, Roman law, and Judeo-Christian theology—have each held, almost axiomatically, that woman is inferior and subordinate to man and requires his domination. This attitude still persists today; for example, in most religions, a woman cannot be ordained or authorized to be a spiritual leader.

On the basis of ancient concepts, it has been all too easy to divide assumed male and female functions and psychological traits into separate, opposing categories. These categories, or stereotypes, have by no means disappeared from popular belief and thinking about the nature of women and men. Women are expected to be emotional, dependent and gentle and men are thought to possess all the contrary attributes: to be rational, independent and aggressive. These are the qualities assumed to be suitable for women in the closed world of the home, husband and children, and for men in the outside world of business, the professions or politics. The stereotypes and the models of behaviour derived from this assumption do not necessarily correspond to the real personalities of a great number of men and women. …

In Canada as elsewhere, the cultural mould has been imposed upon and accepted by many women and tends to confuse discussions on the subject of the status of women. Several briefs pointed this out: "Women, too, in large part still believe that a woman's place is in the home, at least while her children are young." "The all-too-prevalent opinion, common amongst women as well as men, that women with the odd exception are less ambitious, timid, less capable, and less well-organized than men, is fallacious, if closely examined."

During the 1968 public hearings of the Commission, two Canadian daily newspapers published questionnaires "for Men Only" in order to obtain a sampling of men's opinions on the question of women. Such surveys are usually affected by different kinds of bias: for example, the sampling might not be representative of the whole population. Nevertheless they are not meaningless even though the results have to be interpreted with care. In these samplings the results showed, generally, traditional opinions. Many of the respondents declared that women tended to find more discrimination than in fact existed and that Canada did not need a Royal Commission on the Status of Women. More than half the replies received by the *Toronto Star* declared that woman's place is in the home. In the survey by *Le Devoir*, majority opinion favoured a male rather than a female superior on the job. Most respondents were of the opinion that women lack the emotional control demanded for combining a career with marriage and motherhood. On the other hand, the young men who responded to *Le Devoir*, and the husbands of working wives who replied to the *Toronto Star*, wanted greater liberty for Canadian women. Answers received by the *Toronto Star* were almost unanimous in their view that gainfully employed women should be legally responsible for the support of their families, and that they should be required, if necessary, to pay alimony in cases of divorce.

The feeling that women who have equal financial resources should have responsibilities equal to those of men may mark an important evolution of attitudes. The stereotype of the man as the sole family breadwinner yields to the new picture of the wife as his economic partner. Yet woman remains mainly identified with her old role as housewife. When people try to reconcile these two different images—the traditional woman and the actual woman who is many-faceted, as a man is, and who often works for pay—the stereotype is not always discarded. …

The stereotype of the ideal woman has its effect upon Canadian women. It appears that many women have accepted as truths the social constraints and the mental images that society has prescribed, and have made these constraints and images part of themselves as guides for living. This theory could partly explain why some women are little inclined to identify themselves with the collective problems of their sex and tend to share the conventional opinions of society. Social scientists have noted a similar phenomenon in their study of certain minority groups, or people treated as inferior. Their members often fail to identify with their own group. This is particularly true of individuals who cross the border separating them from the majority and who then adopt its attitudes and standards.

The concept of the psychological minority offers one possible interpretation of the effects upon women of stereotyping. Women do not, in fact, constitute a social group since they are found everywhere and in all classes. They cannot be isolated, as a collectivity, from the other members of society with whom they live in close relation. They cannot, moreover, be described as a demographic minority in society as a whole, though they are often a minority in the world of work and politics. But, according to some writers, a psychological minority group is an aggregation whose collective destiny depends on the good will or is at the mercy of another group. They—the members of a psychological minority—feel and know that they live in a state of dependency, no matter what percentage they may be of the total population.

Stereotypes are perpetuated by the mass media. Day after day, advertising reinforces and exploits stereotypes to achieve greater sales by repeating the idea that the "real" woman and the "real" man use this or that product. Although men as well as women are stereotypes, the results may be more damaging for women since advertising encourages feminine dependency by urging women not to act but to be passive, not to really achieve but to live out their aspirations in the imagination and in dreams.

Woman is often presented as a sex object, defined as a superficial creature who thinks only of her appearance, who sees herself mainly in terms of whether she is attractive to men. She conforms to the beauty and youth standards which men are said to want of her. In a study prepared for the Commission, it was found that over 89 per cent of the women pictured in Canadian newspapers and magazines are less than 35 years of age. As presented by the advertiser, women are hardly ever associated with intelligence, sincerity, culture, originality or talent. Instead, they are depicted as being young, elegant and beautiful. "The mass media must in some way be encouraged to change their emphasis. ..."

At least 30 of the briefs received by the Commission protested against the degrading, moronic picture of woman thus presented. These briefs objected to woman, in advertisements, being shown as fragile, without depth or reality, and obsessed by her desire to please masculine hero-figures as artificial as herself. Repetition is a "hidden persuader" in advertising, an especially effective tool influencing children and young girls to aspire to constraining models and low ideals. When women are shown in active pursuits, these activities are in the order of polishing furniture and preparing food. Some women's magazines contribute to the exaltation of housework as a fine art and very often persuade women that to conform to the image of housewife *par excellence* is a duty and that not to conform signifies inadequacy. Housework is rarely viewed in these publications, and in advertising, for what it is: a necessary task that is performed in order to make the family comfortable.

Stereotypes pass naturally from one generation to the next. Whatever sex-linked biological determinants of personality there may be, no one yet seems to have isolated them clearly, or surely. However, the standards and models of behaviour taught either explicitly or by example in the family begin to affect boys and girls from their earliest childhood. ...

Expressed opinion is one thing—actual behaviour may be another. Despite their traditional point of view, as shown by these studies, young people are living lives that increasingly differ from those of their parents. Well over half the Canadian population is under the age of 30 and not all are conforming to all the old patterns. Some of them commonly express dissatisfaction with—and freely question—customs and institutions long taken for granted. And it cannot be assumed that the once accepted roles of men and women will be exempt. The behaviour of many young people, for example, in their choice of dress, music and lifestyle, may tell as much about their attitudes as their responses to formal surveys.

The role of women will necessarily change as society itself evolves. In making our recommendations, we have tried to take into account what may be in store for Canadians in the years to come. Predictions about what life will be like in the future are increasingly being used as tools for better understanding of changes in present society. ...

The future of our country will be determined substantially by the direction we Canadians choose to take now. If women are to be able to make full use of their capabilities, help is needed from the whole society. Even so, women themselves must work for change: "... women are the best helpers of one another. Let them think; let them act; till they know what they need. We only ask of men to remove arbitrary barriers. Some would like to do more. But I believe it needs that Woman show herself in her native dignity to teach them how to aid her; their minds are so encumbered by tradition."

Plan for Action

Conclusion

Even in the interval since the establishment of this Commission, there have been signs of change in public attitudes toward many of the problems with which we have been concerned. But the pace is not sufficiently rapid, and there is little public awareness of the extent to which an improvement in the status of women is required or of the over-all impact on society which such a change would bring. At issue is the opportunity to construct a human society free of a major injustice which has been part of history.

The extension of "woman's place" to all areas of society is part of the world-wide process of democratization. What we have recommended deals only with a few pressing and immediate problems. But what we have in mind is a releasing of positive and creative forces to take on still larger human tasks. Men, as well as women, would benefit from a society where roles are less rigidly defined.

To set the stage for this better employment of human capacities, equality of opportunity for women is a fundamental first step. The effect of our recommendations is likely to be more far-reaching than any one recommendation would indicate. The total impact will be considerably greater than the sum of the changes we propose. But the Commissioners are aware that true equality of opportunity for women and men can only result from radical changes in our way of life and in our social organization and probably must go as far as an equal sharing by parents in the care of their children and a complete reorganization of the working world.

The nine-to-five working day and full-time employment are neither sacred nor are they guarantees of efficiency. Productive efficiency may indeed have to yield its place as the sole criterion of employment practices. Human values may assume greater importance. Many rigid constraints that are part of today's economic world may be relaxed, to the benefit of all.

We may begin to question why banks, the post office, doctors and dentists are available only during the hours when everyone else is at work. Why is employment so rigidly structured that additional education is almost inaccessible? Should not the educational system stress the need to adapt to a changing society rather than to conform to the habits of yesterday? Flexibility may be introduced in many aspects of social organization as a consequence of the need to establish equality for women. Canada can afford to experiment boldly.

Women, as they seek equality, must contend with a society conceived and controlled by men. They require a high degree of resolution to disregard present barriers and to attain the positions which best reflect their ability. But existing structures are not sacrosanct; women must be aware that they are entering a world that can be changed. And men, as they recognize women's claim to equality, may welcome an opportunity to examine Canada's institutions in a new light.

We have indicated some of the characteristics of the society that could emerge. The magnitude of the changes that must be introduced does not dismay us, but we are dismayed that so much has been left undone. In terms of Canada's commitments and the principles on which a democracy is based, what we recommend is no more than simple justice.

Patriarchy and Paternalism: The Legacy of the Canadian State for First Nations Women

Mary Ellen Turpel (1993)

EDITORS' INTRODUCTION

In this reading, Mary Ellen Turpel (Aki-Kwe) assesses the report of the Royal Commission on the Status of Women in Canada 20 years later, criticizing it for failing to address the unique circumstances of First Nations women. Today, more than two decades after Turpel wrote this article, Aboriginal women still face higher instances of poverty, discrimination, and domestic violence. In 2014 an RCMP investigation into missing and murdered Aboriginal women revealed that between 1980 and 2012 there were 164 unresolved cases involving missing Aboriginal women and 1,017 homicides, numbers that are disproportionately high. Turpel, now a judge on the Saskatchewan Provincial Court, challenges other feminists to question the extent to which their goals and aspirations are truly universal.

Reflections on the Royal Commission Report: Equality Is Not Our Starting Point

The underlying thesis behind the mandate for the Royal Commission of 1967 was a commitment to ensure that women enjoy equal opportunities with men in Canadian society. The central idea in this thesis, while arguably appropriate and supportable for non-aboriginal women in Canada, is inappropriate conceptually and culturally for First Nations women. First Nations communities, and in particular the communities of my heredity, the Cree community, are ones which do not have a prevailing ethic of equal opportunity for men and women in this sense. It is important in the Cree community to understand the responsibilities of women and of men to the community. Equality is not an important political or social concept. Other First Nations people have the same attitude toward equality.[11] As Skonaganleh:rá, a Mohawk woman, explains of her perspective:

> I don't want equality. I want to go back to where women, in aboriginal communities, were complete, where they were beautiful, where they were treated as more than equal—where man was helper and woman was the centre of that environment, that community. So, while I suppose

Source: Excerpted from *Canadian Journal of Women and the Law*, vol. 6, no. 1 (1993). An earlier version of this article was presented at the conference "Women and the Canadian State" in Ottawa, November 1, 1990. Some notes omitted. Reprinted by permission.

equality is a nice thing and while I suppose we can never go back all the way, I want to make an effort at going back to at least respecting the role that women played in communities.

As Osennontion, another Mohawk woman, adds:

To me, when these women, who call themselves "feminist" or get called "feminist," talk about equality, they mean sameness. They appear to want to be the *same* as a man. They want to be treated the same as a man, make the same money as a man ... and, they consider all women, regardless of origin, to be the same, to share the same concerns. I, for one, maintain that aboriginal women are *different*, as are the women who are burdened with such labels as immigrant women, or visible minority women. I certainly do not want to be a "man!"

Equality is simply not the central organizing political principle in our communities. It is frequently seen by our Elders as a suspiciously selfish notion, as individualistic and alienating from others in the community. It is incongruous to apply this notion to our communities. We are committed to what would be termed a "communitarian" notion of responsibilities to our peoples, as learned through traditional teachings and our life experiences. I do not see this communitarian notion as translating into equality as it is conventionally understood.

In this regard, I should note that the traditional teachings by our Cree Elders instruct us that Cree women are at the centre of the Circle of Life. While you may think of this as a metaphor, it is in fact an important reality in terms of how one perceives the world and how authority is structured in our communities. It is women who give birth both in the physical and in the spiritual sense to the social, political, and cultural life of the community. It is upon women that the focus of the community has historically been placed and it was, not surprisingly, against women that a history of legislative discrimination was directed by the Canadian State. Our communities do not have a history of disentitlement of women from political or productive life. This is probably the most important point for feminists to grasp in order to appreciate how State-imposed gender discrimination uniquely affected First Nations women. I have found that it is difficult for white feminists to accept that patriarchy is not universal. ...

Because of the special position of Cree women, discrimination by the Canadian State through the Indian Act, and other initiatives, has been potentially lethal. Gender discrimination was cleverly directed (in a Machiavellian sense) against First Nations women because the legislators identified that if they could assimilate women, First Nations peoples would be most easily and effectively assimilated. In so attempting to assimilate us, the State introduced the norm of discrimination on the basis of sex: it was exported from your culture to our culture. Fortunately, we have resisted the attempt to assimilate the First Nations, although we now face a situation in which we must fight against patriarchy both inside and outside of our communities. That legislation has had the continued effect of dividing our communities, dividing our families, dividing our homes. It has broken down our matriarchal tribal support network. A First Nations woman cannot necessarily look to her mother, grandmother, or older aunties to help her because she may have been forced to leave the community through discrimination. Moreover, she may now have trouble reconnecting because of her experiences in a foreign culture, because poverty has led her to equate being a First Nations person with being worthless, and because of lost self-esteem due to racism commonly experienced outside the community. She may also be excluded because her Indian Act–elected government will not let her return.

Our family structures have been systematically undermined by the Canadian State in every way imaginable—forced education at denominational residential schools, imposed male-dominated political structures, gender discrimination in determining who is to be recognized as an "Indian," and the ongoing removal of First Nations children by child welfare authorities. It is difficult for us to look to this State for any change when the presence of the State has been synonymous with a painful dividing of our houses. We have had to struggle against these State-imposed or sanctioned initiatives. At the same time, we have had to react to and struggle with the internal imprint of State-enforced patriarchy on our men and on our political structures. Some of our men have lost touch with their sense of responsibility to women. They have been taught that patriarchy is the ideology of the civilized, and they have tried to act accordingly. However, this cannot mean we abandon our men. They too have been abused and oppressed by the Canadian State.

Some aboriginal leaders now believe that it is a sign of advancement not to have women involved in political discussions because, after all, that is the lesson they have learned by observing how the Canadian State operates. Women are to be relegated to a "private" sphere; men are public actors. This is a great community challenge for us. However, this challenge is not synonymous with the challenge of equal opportunity with men. As Osennontion shares:

> In addition to all of the responsibilities ... perhaps the most daunting for women, is her responsibility for the men—how they conduct themselves, how they behave, how they treat her. She has to remind them of their responsibilities and she has to know when and how to correct them when they stray from those.
>
> At the beginning, when the "others" first came here, we held our rightful positions in our societies and held the respect due us by the men, because that's the way things were then, when we were following our ways. At that time, the European woman was considered an appendage to her husband, his possession. Contact with that European male and the imposition of his ways on our people, resulted in our being assimilated into those ways. We forgot our women's responsibilities and the men forgot theirs.

Despite the imposition of patriarchy on our communities, our teachings still instruct us that the responsibility of men is, first and foremost, to be the woman's helper, to be the supporter of women (not in an economic sense of division of labour), because this means being the supporter of the people. A commitment to this role in our communities is not translatable into the world of equal opportunity of women with men. These are different paths, different conceptions of cultural and genderal identity we are attempting to "walk" ("walk" means to follow or exemplify).

It is essential that you separate two concepts which are at the foreground here so as not to be confused. On the one hand, it is important to understand the position that First Nations women occupy both historically and in the real contemporary sense, in some of our communities, particularly those which are matriarchal, and to appreciate how this position was attacked by the Canadian State. On the other hand, it is essential not to confuse First Nations women's suppressed status as a result of Canadian State policy of State-imposed legal definitions and institutional structures in the Indian Act, with a reaction translatable into a desire to have what White women or men have in this society. The former is patriarchy, the latter is paternalism. Both were imposed upon us as communities and individuals. We do not want continued patriarchy nor do we want paternalistic prescriptions for our future paths. We want to extricate ourselves from these debilitating forces. At the same time, it is wholly distracting and irresponsible for us to place the blame for First Nations women's experiences at the feet of First Nations men.

From our perspective, just as there are a variety of First Nations peoples, so too are there a variety of cultural perspectives in our teachings on men and women. The perspective of First Nations women is one which does not enable one to look at equal opportunity without looking at the larger political climate for our beliefs, our existence within (or at the margins of) Canadian society. In other words, before we can consider these debates about gender equality, what about our claims to cultural equality? What about your role in our problems and, more importantly, what is your role in developing solutions to the problems faced in First Nations communities? Before imposing upon us the logic of gender equality (with White men), what about ensuring for our cultures and political systems equal legitimacy with the Anglo-Canadian cultural perspective which dominates the Canadian State?

In a speech to the Conference on Women and the Canadian State, the Honourable Mary Collins, Minister Responsible for the Status of Women and the Association of National Defence, suggested that women must work to eliminate the "culture of violence" by men against women. In this regard, she was referring specifically to domestic violence. To First Nations people, the expressions "culture of violence" and "domestic violence" not only have their customary connotation of violence by men against women but also mean domestic (that is, Canadian State) violence against the First Nations. A "culture of violence" also conjures up for a First Nations person the image of a dominant Canadian culture that tolerates and even sanctions State violence against First Nations peoples. To have lived through the summer of 1990, with the spectacle of police and army intervention in Mohawk communities (with the arguably full complicity of the federal government) is to have a real sense of the other signification of "domestic violence."

What violence has this State done to the First Nations? More importantly for the feminist movement, is this violence connected to the culture of violence men exhibit toward women? Can a State which uses violence in this way preach about eliminating violence in the home? These interpretations and concerns we have obviously cannot be boxed into the category of "gender." Gender as an isolated category is useful, primarily, to women who do not encounter racial, cultural, or class-based discrimination when they participate in Canadian society. Moreover, to look only to an objective of equality with men is clearly insufficient for First Nations women's struggles and continued identities because this cannot encompass our aspirations as cultures. I cannot separate my gender from my culture. I am not a woman sometimes and Cree at others. I am both because both are intertwined in the way I experience and understand the world. It is only for the purposes of preparing papers like this one that, in trying to grasp the category of gender, I even reflect upon separating one from the other.

My interpretation of the objective of ensuring equal opportunity with men as expressed in the Royal Commission mandate implies equal opportunity for First Nations women with non-aboriginal (so-called White) men. I would suggest that this is an inappropriate starting point because, as I have been suggesting, First Nations women have different roles and responsibilities *vis-à-vis* men. Moreover, I do not see it as worthwhile and worthy to aspire to, or desire, equal opportunity with White men, or with the system that they have created. The aspirations of White men in the dominant society are simply not our aspirations. We do not want to inherit their objectives and positions or to adopt their world view. To be perfectly frank, I cannot figure out why non-aboriginal women would want to do this either. Maybe I have missed something in the discussions, and ask you to help me understand why this could be construed as what you want. I realize that your desires are probably quite diverse. However, I was troubled by my participation in the Conference on Women and the Canadian State because I did not hear women vigorously challenge this assumption in the mandate of the Royal Commission *Report*. I do not want to look to White men as the starting point to define an agenda or to assess our predicament. Is there somewhere else to look? I think there is another place, at least for First Nations communities.

The Royal Commission *Report* adopted, in its criteria and principles section, an interpretation of the Commission's mandate to mean that "equality of opportunity for everyone should be the goal of Canadian society." In fairness to the Commissioners who prepared the 1970 document, there was a statement in the *Report* that throughout the hearings, First Nations peoples urged that the Commission not adopt a view of their aspirations as defined by non-aboriginal people living somewhere else in Canada, (i.e., the South), that their aims and goals should not be established by outside authorities or those who are not part of their culture. Unfortunately, the Commissioners did not take this demand seriously enough, nor did they consider its implications in light of their mandate or conclusions. Consequently, they were not capable of understanding the significance of First Nations women's different positions on equality, and the set of concerns regarding the State which went beyond gender.

What are the implications of the mentality which suggests that the goal for society is equality with (White) men? To me, to be a First Nations person in Canada means to be free to exist politically and culturally (these are not separate concepts): to be free to understand our roles according to our own cultural and political systems and not according to a value system imposed upon us by the Indian Act for over 100 years, nor by role definition accepted in the Anglo-European culture. This means that men are not, and therefore cannot be, the measure of all things.

As noted earlier, the First Nations community of my heredity never viewed women as naturally inferior, or, with a little help, equal to a certain status which men have already achieved. For the *Report* to look at us with the assemblage of assumptions of the dominant society is to ignore our existence as peoples with distinct cultural viewpoints and political aspirations. It does violence to our understanding of the central role of women in our communities. Moreover, it does violence to us by marginalizing us and relegating our place to somewhere outside of your conceptions of meaningful membership in Canadian society. It makes us feel as though if we reject what White men have "achieved," we reject being part of this society.

The Royal Commissioners were evidently trying to help, particularly by making certain findings such as those relating to poverty as a lifestyle for First Nations women in Canada. In this regard, it is distressing to look back on the generation since the *Report*, and to realize that First Nations women live in the same cycle of poverty today that they lived in 20 years ago, if not worse. Even the Supreme Court of Canada has recently pronounced that in light of the constitutional position of First Nations peoples in Canada, First Nations women living on a reserve may not have (and in reality do not have) protection for matrimonial property.

At least one Royal Commissioner was genuinely concerned with the extent to which he was capable of understanding the situation of First Nations women. In a separate submission he suggested that:

The privations endured by these people [First Nations people] in many areas—health, education, standards of living—are shocking. Undoubtedly, we all feel that every means should be taken to improve conditions for this neglected group of Canadians. However, the subject is outside the Commission's terms of reference. Furthermore, the Commission is not qualified to deal with the complex problems which arise when attempting to introduce social and economic changes in cultures which are so very different from ours. *Goodwill in these matters is often, and sometimes quite rightly, interpreted as a form of paternalism or as a more or less conscious attempt to destroy these cultures.* I very much fear that some of the recommendations (Nos. 90–97) advanced by the Commission in this section may have been drawn up a little too hastily.

There were no First Nations people who sat as Royal Commissioners for this study. While the Royal Commission *Report* is laudable to some women, it was inadequate in that it was unable to seriously consider First Nations women's concerns. A separate study was, and is, definitely required. However, as Paulo Freire notes, "we cannot enter the struggle as objects in order to later become subjects." We must not be objects in the study and objects in the solutions to our problems. I often feel, particularly as a law teacher interacting with materials involving First Nations peoples written by those without direct knowledge, that our problems have been studied enough, especially in the object-mode of analysis. We need to turn our minds to a mutually-agreed upon framework within which to resolve our relations with the State. We no longer need to be objects, nor do we need well-intentioned paternalism or projections of what we should become. First Nations women's concerns were marginalized in the *Royal Commission Report on the Status of Women in Canada.* The few findings which were made regarding First Nations women lacked context or vision as to a future path for meaningful change. They were not by us, for us. They were a projection of an assessment of our needs, yet they did not take up in earnest the context of patriarchy and paternalism which are our shackles. …

Gender discrimination against First Nations women in the Indian Act is clearly more significant when juxtaposed against the cultural backdrop of First Nations history and State oppression. The Royal Commission *Report* confirms to me how White men and women have constructed a concept of gender equality which denies the experience of First Nations peoples' lives and which cannot grasp the magnitude of our experience of gender discrimination. We need to start a discussion which does not include a pre-conceived notion of gender equality. We need dialogue on cultural equality and an openness to other views on the roles and responsibilities of people to their communities. Perhaps on the 20th anniversary of the *Report*, we can identify how the feminist agenda, as defined and exemplified by this *Report* and accepted by the feminist movement, was insensitive to First Nations women and how this is a problem to be met in the future.

Note

11. In the Mi'kmaq language, the term for equality means to bring one down to the level of other people. This is an interesting juxtaposition with Canadian legal formulations.

The Dark Side of the Nation

Himani Bannerji (2000)

EDITORS' INTRODUCTION

Situated within feminist Marxism, Himani Bannerji, an author and sociology professor at York University, provides a critical perspective on Canadian identity and the place of non-white women in the Canadian social fabric. In particular, Bannerji questions the extent to which discourses of multiculturalism and diversity can alleviate circumstances of racial and gendered inequality. This excerpt is an example of "third wave" feminist scholarship, which emphasizes that conceptions of a universal experience of womanhood are unrepresentative of the experiences of women of colour, women of the Global South, and queer women.

The Paradox of Diversity: The Construction of a Multicultural Canada and "Women of Colour"

The Name of the Rose, or What Difference Does It Make What I Call It

The two ways in which the neutral appearance of the notion of diversity becomes a useful ideology to practices of power are quite simple. On the one hand, the use of such a concept with a reference to simple multiplicity allows the reading of all social and cultural forms or differences in terms of descriptive plurality. On the other, in its relationship to description it introduces the need to put in or retain a concrete, particular content for each of these seemingly neutral differences. The social relations of power that create the difference implied in sexist-racism, for example, just drop out of sight, and social being becomes a matter of a cultural essence (Bannerji, 1991). This is its paradox—that the concept of diversity simultaneously allows for an emptying out of actual social relations and suggests a concreteness of cultural description, and through this process obscures any understanding of difference as a construction of power, Thus there is a construction of a collective cultural essence and a conflation of this, or what we are culturally supposed to be, and what we are ascribed with,

Source: Excerpted from *The Dark Side of the Nation: Essays on Multiculturalism, Nationalism, and Gender* by Himani Bannerji. Toronto: Canadian Scholars' Press, 2000. Some notes omitted. Reprinted by permission.

in the context of social organization of inequality. We cannot then make a distinction between racist stereotypes and ordinary historical/cultural differences of everyday life and practices of people from different parts of the world. Cultural traits that come, let us say, from different parts of the third world are used to both create and eclipse racism, and we are discouraged from reading them in terms of relations and symbolic forms of power. The result is also an erasure of class and patriarchy among the immigrant multi-cultures of others, as they too fall within this paradox of essentialization and multiplicity signified by cultural diversity of official multiculturalism. In fact, it is this uncritical, de-materialized, seemingly de-politicized reading of culture through which culture becomes a political tool, an ideology of power which is expressed in racist-sexist or heterosexist differences. One can only conclude from all this that the discourse of diversity, as a complex systemically interpretive language of governing, cannot be read as an innocent pluralism.

The ideological nature of this language of diversity is evident from its frequent use and efficacy in the public and official, that is, institutional realms. In these contexts its function has been to provide a conceptual apparatus in keeping with needs which the presence of heterogeneous peoples and cultures has created in the Canadian state and public sphere. This has both offset and, thus, stabilized the Canadian national imaginary and its manifestation as the state apparatus, which is built on core assumptions of cultural and political homogeneity of a Canadianness. This language of diversity is a coping mechanism for dealing with an actually conflicting heterogeneity, seeking to incorporate it into an ideological binary which is predicated upon the existence of a homogeneous national, that is, a Canadian cultural self with its multiple and different others (see Bannerji, 1997). These multiple other cultural presences in Canada, interpreted as a threat to national culture which called for a coping, and therefore for an incorporating and interpretive mechanism, produced the situation summed up as the challenge of multiculturalism. This has compelled administrative, political and ideological innovations which will help to maintain the status quo. This is where the discourse of diversity has been of crucial importance because this new language of ruling and administration protects ideologies and practices already in place. It is postulated upon pluralist premises of a liberal democratic state, which Canada aspires to be, but also adds specific dimensions of legitimation to particular administrative functions. ...

The Essence of the Name, or What Is to Be Gained by Calling Something Diversity

In order to understand how the concept of diversity works ideologically, we have to feed into it the notion of difference constructed through social relations of power and read it in terms of the binaries of homogeneity and heterogeneity already referred to in our discussion on multiculturalism. It does not require much effort to realize that diversity is not equal to multiplied sameness, rather it presumes a distinct difference in each instance. But this makes us ask, distinctly different from what? The answer is, obviously, from each other and from whatever it is that is homogeneous—which is an identified and multiplied sameness, serving as the distinguishing element at the core in relation to which difference is primarily measured. The difference that produces heterogeneity suggests otherness in relation to that core, and in social politics this otherness is more than an existential, ontological fact. It is a socially constructed otherness or heterogeneity, its difference signifying both social value and power. It is not just another cultural self floating non-relationally in a socio-historical vacuum. In the historical context of the creation of Canada, of its growth into an uneasy amalgam of a white settler colony with liberal democracy, with its internally colonized or peripheral economies, the definitions and relations between a national self and its other, between homogeneity and heterogeneity, sameness and diversity, become deeply power ridden.[17] From the days of colonial capitalism to the present-day global imperialism, there has emerged an ideologically homogeneous identity dubbed Canadian whose nation and state Canada is supposed to be.

This core community is synthesized into a national we, and it decides on the terms of multiculturalism and the degree to which multicultural others should be tolerated or accommodated. This "we" is an essentialized version of a colonial European turned into Canadian and the subject or the agent of Canadian nationalism. It is this essence, extended to the notion of a community, that provides the point of departure for the ideological deployment of diversity. The practice is clearly exclusive, not only of third world or non-white ethnic immigrants, but also of the aboriginal population. Though often described in cultural linguistic terms as the two nations of anglophones and francophones, the two nations theory does not include non-whites of these same language groups. So the identity of the Canadian "we" does not reside in language, religion or other aspects of culture, but rather in the European/North American physical origin—in the body and the colour of skin. Colour of skin is elevated here beyond its contingent status and becomes an essential quality called whiteness, and this becomes the ideological signifier of a unified non-diversity. The others outside of this moral and cultural whiteness are targets for either assimilation or toleration. These diverse or multicultural elements, who are also called newcomers, introducing notions of territoriality and politicized time, create accommodational difficulties for white Canadians, both at the level of the civil society, of culture and economy, and also for the ruling practices of the state. An ideological coping mechanism becomes urgent in view of a substantial third world immigration allowed by Canada through the 1960s up to recent years (see Eliott & Fleras, 1992). This new, practical and discursive/ideological venture, or an extension of what Althusser has called an ideological state apparatus, indicates both the crisis and its management. After all, the importation of Chinese or South Asian indentured labour, or the legally restricted presence of the Japanese since the last century, did not pose the same problems which the newly arrived immigrants do (see Bolaria & Li, 1988). As landed residents or apprentice citizens, or as actual citizens of Canada, they cannot be left in the same limbo of legal and political non-personhood as their predecessors were until the 1950s. Yet they are not authentic Canadians in the ideological sense, in their physical identity and culture. What is more, so-called authentic Canadians are unhappy with their presence, even though they enhance Canada's economic growth. Blue ribbon Hong Kong immigrants, for example, bring investments which may be needed for the growth of British Columbia, but they themselves are not wanted. But they, among other third world immigrants, are here, and this calls for the creation of an ideology and apparatus of multiculturalism (with its discourse of a special kind of plurality called diversity) as strategies of containment and management. ...

In the very early 1980s, Prime Minister Pierre Trudeau enunciated his multicultural policy, and a discourse of nation, community and diversity began to be cobbled together. There were no strong multicultural demands on the part of third world immigrants themselves to force such a policy. The issues raised by them were about racism, legal discrimination involving immigration and family reunification, about job discrimination on the basis of Canadian experience, and various adjustment difficulties, mainly of child care and language. In short, they were difficulties that are endemic to migration, and especially that of people coming in to low income jobs or with few assets. Immigrant demands were not then, or even now, primarily cultural, nor was multiculturalism initially their formulation of the solution to their problems. It began as a state or an official/institutional discourse, and it involved the translation of issues of social and economic injustice into issues of culture (see Kymlicka 1995). Often it was immigrant questions and quandaries *vis à vis* the response of the so-called Canadians that prompted justificatory gestures by the state. These legitimation gestures were more directed at the discontented Canadians than the discriminated others. Multiculturalism was therefore not a demand from below, but an ideological elaboration from above in which the third world immigrants found themselves. This was an apparatus which rearranged questions of social justice, of unemployment and racism, into issues of cultural diversity and focused on symbols of religion, on so-called tradition. Thus immigrants were ethnicized, culturalized and mapped into traditional/ethnic communities. Gradually a political and administrative framework came into being where structural inequalities could be less and less seen or spoken about. Antiracism and class politics could not keep pace with constantly proliferating ideological state or institutional apparatuses which identified people in terms of their cultural identity, and converted or conflated racist ascriptions of difference within the Canadian space into the power neutral notion of diversity. An increase in threats against third world immigrants, the rise of neo-nazi white supremacist groups and ultra conservative politics, along with a systemic or structural racism and anti-immigration and anti-immigrant stances of political parties, could now be buried or displaced as the immigrants' own cultural problem. Politics in Canada were reshaped and routed through this culturalization or ethnicization, and a politics of identity was constructed which the immigrants themselves embraced as the only venue for social and political agency. ...

Through the decades from the 1960s, political developments took place in Canada which show the twists and turns in the relationship between third world immigrants and the state.[22] With the disarray of left politics in the country and growth of multicultural ideology, all political consciousness regarding third world immigrants has been multiculturalized. These cultural/ethnicized formulations were like chemical probes into a test tube of solution around which dissatisfactions and mobility drives of the others began to coalesce. Wearing or not wearing of turbans, publicly funded heritage language classes, state supported islamic schools modelled on the existence and patterns of catholic schools, for example, provided the profile of their politics. They themselves often forgot how much less important these were than their full citizenship rights, their demand for jobs, non-discriminatory schools and work places, and a generally non-racist society. Differentiated second or third class citizenships evolved, as a non-white sub-working class continued to develop. Their initial willingness to work twice as hard to get a little never materialized into much. Instead a mythology developed around their lack of success, which spoke of their shifty, lazy work habits and their scamming and unscrupulous use of the welfare system. This is especially ironic since they often came from countries, such as those in the West Indies, from which Canada continues to bring substantial profits. But this story of neo-colonialism, of exploitation, racism, discrimination and hierarchical citizenship never gains much credibility or publicity with the Canadian state, the public or the media. This reality is what the cultural language and politics of diversity obscures, displaces and erases. It is obvious that the third world or non-white immigrants are not the beneficiaries of the discourse of diversity. ...

Multiculturalism as an official practice and discourse has worked actively to create the notion and practices of insulated communities. Under its political guidance and funding a political-social space was organized. Politically constructed homogenized communities, with their increasingly fundamentalist boundaries of cultures, traditions and religions, emerged from where there were immigrants from different parts of the world with different cultures and values. They developed leaders or spokespersons, usually men, who liaised with the state on their behalf, and their organizational behaviour fulfilled the expectations of the Canadian state. New political agents and constituencies thus came to life, as people sought to be politically active in these new cultural identity terms. So they became interpellated by the state under certain religious and ethnically named agencies. Hardheaded businessmen, who had never thought of culture in their lives before, now, upon entering Canada, began using this notion and spoke to the powers that be in terms of culture and welfare of their community. But this was the new and only political playing field for "others" in Canada, a slim opportunity of mobility, so they were/are willing to run through the multicultural maze. What is more, this new cultural politics, leaving out problems of class and patriarchy, appealed to the conservative elements in the immigrant population, since religion could be made to overdetermine these uncomfortable actualities, and concentrated on the so-called culture and morality of the community. Official multiculturalism, which gave the conservative male self-styled representatives *carte blanche* to do this, also empowered the same male leaders as patriarchs and enhanced their sexism and masculinism. In the name of culture and god, within the high walls of community and ethnicity/women and children could be dominated and acted against violently because the religions or culture and tradition of others supposedly sanctioned this oppression and brutality. And as politically and ideologically constituted homogenized cultural essences which are typed as traditional, such as muslim or sikh or hindu communities, violence against women could go on without any significant or effective state intervention. ...

The result of this convergence between the Canadian state and conservative male representatives or community agents has been very distressing for women in particular. Between the multicultural paradigm and the actuality of a migrant citizen's life in Canada, the gap is immense. Among multiculturalists of both the communitarian and the liberal persuasion Canada is a nation space which contains different "races" and ethnicities, and this presence demands either a "politics of recognition" (Taylor, 1992) or a modified set of individual and group rights. But for both groups this diversity of others or difference between Canadian self and other has no political dimension. It speaks to nothing like class formation or class struggle, of the existence of active and deep racism, or of a social organization entailing racialized class production of gender. The history of colonization is also not brought to bear on the notions of diversity and difference. So, the answer to my original question—what is to be gained from a discourse of diversity and its politics of multiculturalism?—lies in just what has actually happened in Canadian politics and its theorization, what I have been describing so far, namely in the erasure and occlusion of social relations of power and ruling. This diversified reification of cultures and culturalization of politics allows for both the practice and occlusion of heterosexism and racism of a narrow bourgeois nationalism. This means the maintenance of a status quo of domination. Many hard socio-political questions and basic structural changes may now be avoided. People can be blamed for bringing on their own misfortunes, while rule of capital and class can continue their violence of racism, sexism and homophobia. …

Conclusion

Diversity as discourse, with its constellation of concepts such as multiculturalism, ethnicity, community, and so forth, becomes an important way in which the abstract or formal equality of liberal democracy, its empty pluralism, can gain a concreteness or an embodiment. Through it the concept of citizenship rids itself of its emptiness and takes on signals of a particularized social being or a cultural personhood. The sameness implied in the liberal notion citizenship is then stencilled onto a so-called diverse culture, and offers a sense of concrete specificity. This purported plurality with pseudo-concreteness rescues class democracy, and does not let the question of power relations get out of hand. Differences or diversities are then seen as inherent, as ontological or cultural traits of the individuals of particular cultural communities, rather than as racist ascriptions or stereotypes. This helps the cause of the status quo and maintains ascribed and invented ethnicities, or their displaced and intensified communal forms. The discourse of diversity makes it impossible to understand or name systemic and cultural racism, and cultural racism, and its implication in gender and class.

When concreteness or embodiment is thus ideologically depoliticized and dehistoricized by its articulation to the discourse of diversity, we are presented with many ontological cultural particularities which serve as markers of ethnicity and group boundaries. Since these ethnic communities are conceived as discrete entities, and there is no recognition of a core cultural-power group, a dispersion effect is introduced through the discourse of diversity which occludes its own presumption of otherness, of being diverse, and which is predicated upon a homogeneous Canadian identity. It is with regard to this that diversity is measured, and hides its assumptions of homogeneity under the cover of a value and power neutral heterogeneity. Thus it banishes from view a process of homogenization or essentialization which underpins the project of liberal pluralism.

Ultimately then, the discourse of diversity is an ideology. It has its own political imperatives in what is called multiculturalism elaborated within the precincts of the state. It translates out into different political possibilities within the framework of capitalism and bourgeois democracy, and both communitarian liberals and liberals for individual rights may find it congenial to their own goals. Politics of recognition, an ideology of tolerance, advocacy of limited group rights, may all result from adopting the discourse of diversity, but what difference they would actually make to those people's lives which are objects of multicultural politics, is another story.

Notes

17. On the racialized nature of Canada's political economy as a white settler colony, and its attempts to retain features of this while installing itself as a liberal democracy, see Bolaria and Li (1988).

22. For example, the change in immigration policy from the "family reunification" programme to a primarily skills based one shifts the demography of Canada. It brings a kind of immigrant, perhaps from Eastern Europe, who does not pose the problem of "race."

Identity and Opportunity: The Lesbian, Gay, Bisexual and Transgender Movement

Miriam Smith (2014)

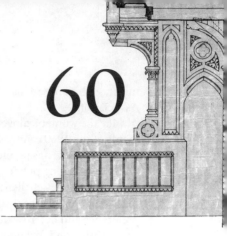

60

EDITORS' INTRODUCTION

Miriam Smith is a professor in the Department of Social Science at York University. In this examination of the recent history of lesbian, gay, bisexual, and transgender politics in Canada, Smith describes how the legal, political, and social status of LGBT people has evolved since the 1960s—a time when homosexuality was still considered a crime of "gross indecency." Most advances in LGBT rights in recent years, including Charter protections, same-sex marriage, and custody rights, can be directly linked to lobbying efforts and the legal mobilization of the LGBT movement, which seeks to challenge laws and policies that are explicitly discriminatory, as well as the heteronormative structures of social, political, and economic life.

The status of LGBT people in Canadian law, society, and politics has changed fundamentally since the 1960s. In 2002–03, courts in Quebec, British Columbia, and Ontario ruled in favour of same-sex marriage, and, as these rulings were followed by courts in other provinces and territories, the Liberal government of Paul Martin legalized same-sex marriage in 2005. Discrimination on the basis of sexual orientation is prohibited in all Canadian jurisdictions and discrimination on the basis of gender identity and expression [is] prohibited in Ontario and the Northwest Territories. Lively gay villages exist in Montreal, Toronto, and Vancouver. Huge Pride festivals in Canadian cities have brought queer life out into the open. Courts no longer routinely bar lesbian mothers from custody of their children, and, in most Canadian jurisdictions, same-sex couples have gained the right to adopt (including the right of second-parent adoption) and to enjoy a range of partner benefits. In Quebec and British Columbia, lesbian partners enjoy full filiation rights, meaning that same-sex parents can be listed together on the birth certificate, obviating the need for second-parent adoption. In an important tribunal decision, the Ontario Human Rights Tribunal ruled in 2012 that trans people do not have to have had surgery in order to register their gender identity of choice on their birth certificate, opening up the possibility of reform of passport regulations to permit the recognition of trans identities. Queer student organizations exist on most Canadian university campuses, and professional associations have recognized lesbian and gay networks in their

---

Source: Extracted from *Group Politics and Social Movements in Canada*, 2nd edition, edited by Miriam Smith. Toronto: University of Toronto Press, 2014. Notes omitted.

midst, such as the Sexual Orientation and Gender Identity Conference of the Canadian Bar Association.

Like the women's movement, the environmental movement, and other new social movements of the 1960s and 1970s, the LGBT movement challenges dominant social norms. As Alberto Melucci has pointed out, social movements do not always primarily dedicate themselves to changing public policies but also to changing the dominant "codes" of society. The LGBT movement challenges heteronormative norms or social codes. "Heteronormativity" means that social organization is structured around the assumption that heterosexual sexual preference and heterosexual coupling is the dominant mode of sexual, intimate, and family organization and that homosexuality is deviant. Even when dominant norms are not openly homophobic or hostile towards homosexuality, lesbian, gay, and bisexual people are outside of the "norm." So, for example, people are usually assumed to be heterosexual unless they state or are shown to be otherwise, an assumption that is an example of "heteronormativity." Some lesbian, gay and bisexual people label themselves "queer"—traditionally a hostile epithet aimed at them—in part to call attention to the power of "naming" as a means of enforcing social expectations and defining "normalcy." Heteronormativity is not confined to social attitudes, norms, and values but is also enshrined in public policies. Until very recently, same-sex couples were not entitled to benefits provided to heterosexual couples, such as pensions or medical benefits provided by private or public sector employers. Such policies are "heteronormative" because they assume that heterosexual couples are the only form of couple or the only form of the couple that is worthy of the social and economic support they provide. By the same token, emerging trans identities challenge the gender binary and the assumption that biological gender determines gender identity and expression. Trans people have pushed for the recognition of gender variance in Canadian social and political life. ...

The 1990s and 2000s: The Charter and Beyond

Over the course of the 1990s and 2000s, LGBTQ organizing occurred in many different institutions and organizations of Canadian society and across a broad range of issues ranging from the use of queer-positive reading materials in the education system to the issue of same-sex marriage. The Charter provided an important opening for lesbian and gay litigation. In keeping with the political process model, the movement was able to take advantage of this opportunity and to secure public policy change through the courts in areas ranging from discrimination in employment to same-sex marriage. The movement was able to achieve this despite the fact that its main organization in federal politics—Egale, a national charity promoting LGBT rights—was poorly resourced.

One of the major areas of public policy change has been that of freedom from discrimination based on sexual orientation in areas such as employment and housing. With regard to government policies, this was the main goal of gay liberation groups of the 1970s, although in most cases this type of discrimination is covered by provincial and federal human rights legislation. The Charter itself does not directly regulate relationships between private citizens (such as the relationship between landlord and tenant), although it indirectly shapes human rights legislation at both federal and provincial levels. Human rights campaigns in the provinces focused on amending provincial human rights legislation to include sexual orientation as a prohibited ground of discrimination, while at the federal level lobbying and litigation focused on the addition or "reading in" of section 15 to include sexual orientation and the amendment of the federal human rights act along the same lines. Citizen-to-citizen discrimination is governed by a patchwork of provincial and federal human rights legislation, including the Charter itself, which governs state-to-citizen relationships. While Quebec's human rights legislation was amended in 1977 and Ontario's in 1986, at the federal level, a Charter challenge by litigants Haig and Birch resulted in the *de facto* addition of sexual orientation to the federal human rights code in 1992. However, even then, the Liberal government of Jean Chrétien prevaricated on the formal amendment of the federal Human Rights Act to include sexual orientation by 1996. The Alberta government only included sexual orientation in its human rights legislation when forced to do so by the Supreme Court decision in *Vriend* in 1998. Most provinces had amended their human rights legislation to include a formal ban on sexual orientation discrimination in provincial/territorial jurisdiction by the early 1990s.

The recognition of same-sex relationship and parenting rights is another important area of social movement mobilization. After several early cases such as *Mossop* and *Veysey*, the Supreme Court of Canada ruled that sexual orientation was included in section 15 in the 1995 *Egan* case on same-sex spousal benefits under the Old Age Security program. However, the court ruled that the "reasonable limits" clause of the Charter provided grounds on which to deny benefits to same-sex couples. In the late 1990s, two important cases were decided, one on the right of same-sex couples to access spousal benefits in employer pensions under federal tax rules (*Rosenberg*) and the other on the constitutionality of Ontario's *Family Law Act*, which denied spousal support to same-sex partners upon the break-up of their relationship (*M v. H*). In the latter case, the most important ruling on same-sex spousal rights to date, one of the former partners, "M," pursued "H" for support upon the break-up of their relationship, arguing that the family law of Ontario discriminated against same-sex couples in preventing former same-sex couples from making claims of spousal support. In ruling that Ontario's family law discriminated against same-sex couples and violated their equality rights under the Charter, the Supreme Court of Canada moved away from the logic of the *Egan* case and indicated that it would not accept anything less than full equality under the law for same-sex couples and, in so doing, set the stage for the next step, which was the move to same-sex marriage. At the same time, grass roots campaigns by same sex parents in Ontario, B.C. and Quebec led to recognition of parenting rights for same sex couples, ranging from second parent adoption in Ontario and B.C. to filiation rights in Quebec. These reforms were achieved through litigation and, in the case of Quebec, through legislative change enacted by the government in 2002.

Therefore, litigation and lobbying in response to litigation have constituted important political strategies for the movement. In this context, once again, we can see the impact of the structure of political opportunity in social movement politics. The movement was not particularly well resourced during this period and did not have the means of bringing political pressure to bear on the Liberal government, except through the courts. It is highly unlikely that the Liberal government would have recognized lesbian and gay rights if it had not been for these court decisions. Provincial governments were reluctant to recognize parenting rights with the exception of the NDP government in British Columbia in 2000-2001 and the PQ government in Quebec in the early 2000s. An earlier effort by the NDP government of Bob Rae in Ontario to recognize same-sex couples went down to defeat in

1994 after Rae permitted a free vote in the legislature. In the mid-1990s, Parliament voted on several occasions against spousal recognition for same-sex couples, and it was only in response to the Supreme Court decision in *M v. H* (which recognized the constitutional necessity of equality in spousal support laws) that the federal government passed the *Modernization of Benefits and Obligations Act* of 2000, which extended most benefits (except immigration rights) to same-sex couples in federal jurisdiction, short of marriage. Similarly, the move from relationship recognition in common law (or *union de fait*) relationships to the recognition of same-sex marriage was also sparked by a series of court decisions in the early 2000s and not by the pressure brought to bear by the movement on the Liberal government. Therefore, with few exceptions, the pressure of litigation has played a major role in policy change over the 1990s and the first half of the 2000s.

Same-sex marriage litigation took place across Canada. In 1998, a Quebec gay couple brought a legal challenge to the heterosexual definition of marriage in Quebec's civil law. In 2000, the first of what would eventually be two sets of couples began their litigation on same-sex marriage in British Columbia. In 2001, four couples were married in Metropolitan Community Church in Toronto after the publication of banns, in a challenge to Ontario's laws governing marriage. Evangelical Christians and their supporters have been forceful opponents of such measures, arguing that recognizing same-sex benefits will undermine the traditional family or that such recognition will "condone" a "lifestyle" that leads to AIDS and other diseases. A wide range of religious organizations and lesbian and gay organizations spoke to the courts through the litigation in British Columbia, Quebec, Ontario, and other provinces which led to the key set of court decisions in 2002–03. The first decision, in British Columbia, rejected the same-sex couples' claims for the right to access to legal marriage. The judge argued that marriage had always been heterosexual and that the Charter did not require marriage equality for same-sex couples. However, this decision was appealed to the provincial Court of Appeal, which ruled that barring same-sex couples from same-sex marriage was unconstitutional but that the legislature should have the right to devise a solution. At the same time, in Quebec, a long battle for parenting and partnership rights, led by a wide range of social movement organizations including the labour movement, resulted in the recognition of parenting rights and the creation of a new civil union regime in Quebec, one that included same-sex partners. Nova Scotia passed domestic partnership legislation in 2001. For a time, therefore, it looked as though civil unions might emerge as the dominant policy in this area. However, this was brought to an end by the Court of Appeal decision in Ontario in 2003 in the case of *Halpern v. Ontario*, in which the Ontario Court of Appeal not only agreed with the British Columbia court that same-sex marriage was constitutional but ruled that marriage licences had to be issued immediately. Quebec followed with a decision in favour of same-sex marriage in 2004. Rather than appealing these decisions, the Chrétien government developed legislation to legalize same-sex civil marriage and then referred the question of its constitutionality to the Supreme Court. The Court (*Reference* 2004) indicated that the government's same-sex marriage was constitutional and that it did not infringe on religious freedom. Under the Liberal government of Paul Martin, the same-sex marriage legislation became law in June 2005. Although the Conservative government elected in January 2006 opposes same-sex marriage, it did not roll back the measure, despite holding a vote on the possibility of doing so in December 2006.

A number of voices within the lesbian and gay communities questioned the extent to which same-sex marriage was a worthwhile expenditure of movement resources. Some opposed relationship recognition as a co-optation of the original goals of the gay liberation movement—sexual freedom—and as marking the conservatization of the movement while others were critical of relationship recognition because they shared the feminist critique of family as a patriarchal institution. Despite this, lesbian and gay rights–seeking organizations are caught up in a political dynamic that demands the articulation of a clear-cut, almost "ethnic" identity in order to make their rights claims legible to the Canadian public, the media, the courts, the governing caucus, and policy-makers. In this dynamic, it was very difficult for the movement(s)—especially as decentred networks of activism and community—to counter the dynamic generated by the course of litigation. In this sense, then, opportunities not only shaped the success of the movement but also its priorities, claims, and demands.

In the post-marriage period, the LGBT movement has moved on to other political issues, including the age of consent, the full recognition of transgender human rights, the fight against homophobia (especially in schools), and health care for LGBT people, specifically ensuring that health research and health care delivery reflect the health needs of the communities. Activism on behalf of trans people has become a major issue in the movement in the 2000 and 2010s. A campaign for inclusion of trans people in the Canadian Human Rights Act took place in the early 2010s with the support of the federal NDP. In March 2013, a bill passed the House of Commons providing for the inclusion of gender identity as a prohibited ground of discrimination in the Canadian Human Rights Act. While gender expression was not included in the legislation, this was an important milestone. Trends in litigation in the U.S. and Canada suggest that the ways in which gender is expressed in outward appearance (e.g. clothing and hairstyles) will eventually receive explicit protection, along with gender identity. Campaigns continue to ensure that trans people are fully protected in all Canadian jurisdictions.

With regard to the age of consent, many groups of queer youth and others contested the Harper government's move to increase the age of consent to sixteen in 2008 and its failure to equalize the age of consent for anal sex. Sexual freedom is an issue that has the potential to openly challenge the line between "good sex" and "bad sex," and between sexual order and sexual chaos, in Gayle Rubin's terms. While relationship recognition has the potential to (in part) fit lesbian and gay couples into an acceptable "family" model (precisely the point of the feminist and gay liberationist critiques of "family" in the lesbian and gay communities), the political issues surrounding sexuality and sexual expression such as pornography threaten this cozy picture of middle-class and monogamously coupled respectability by pushing at the line between "good" and "bad."

Another important arena of contestation by the lesbian and gay rights movement is the area of education and social policy. The legal advances of the movement at the level of public policy cannot obscure the fact that, at the local level, life is still very difficult for some LGBTQ people, especially youth. There are still tremendous social sanctions and dangers in coming out, especially in Canada's smaller communities. Queer youth face bullying and harassment in school, and the stresses caused by facing such harassment are surely one of the factors behind the higher suicide rate for queer teens than for straight youth. In some parts of Canada, notably Toronto, Vancouver, and the lower mainland of British Columbia, LGBT activists, including youth activists in high schools, have challenged school board policies. A sustained and concerted effort by activists in the Toronto boards of education (merged into the Toronto District School Board) over the course of the 1990s resulted in the adoption of equity policies on sexual orientation and gender identity, although there are still important problems with the implementation of these policies, especially because of budget cuts. In the lower mainland of British Columbia, the province's lesbian and gay educators group, Gay and Lesbian Educators of British Columbia, has worked to create a social and support space for teachers and school administrators. From this effort came the campaign led by James Chamberlain and Murray Warren to introduce gay- and lesbian-positive reading materials into the elementary school grades in the Port Coquitlam and Surrey school districts. Chamberlain and Warren sought to use books that depicted families with same-sex parents for young children. This sparked a backlash from the evangelical movement, which had undertaken a concerted campaign to control school boards in the "bible belt" of the province. The Surrey School Board banned the gay- and lesbian-positive books from the elementary school classroom and was immediately challenged by parents, teachers (including Chamberlain and Warren), and others who undertook a successful Charter challenge to this censorship of reading materials (*Chamberlain v. Surrey School Board*, 2002).

In the 2000s, Egale commissioned a study that provided evidence for LGBTQ claims about the need for queer-friendly education policies in Canadian schools. The study, which was carried out by researchers from the University of Winnipeg, surveyed 1,700 high school students online and through in-school focus groups. The researchers provided evidence of extensive exclusion and bullying of LGBTQ queer and trans students and also documented the lack of administrative response on this issue. This evidence was important to debates over the passage of anti-bullying legislation in Ontario in 2012, after Catholic school boards resisted the establishment of Gay–Straight Alliances (GSAs) in their schools. The Liberal legislation guarantees access to GSAs in all Ontario schools as well as establishing anti-bullying programs to ensure a welcoming environment for LGBTQ youth. Similarly, in Quebec, there has been a major campaign against homophobia involving LGBTQ parent groups as well as researchers. As a result a policy against homophobia in schools was instituted in 2010. These developments represent in part a turn to evidence-based policy and demonstrate the need for social movement organizations to produce and present different forms of evidence as a basis for policy claims.

New forms of local and pan-Canadian organizing have arisen recently in the area of lesbian and gay health policy. The Canadian Rainbow Health Coalition, founded in Saskatoon, has been paralleled by local organizations across Canada, which centre on the health needs of lesbian and gay people with regard to issues including sexual health, breast cancer, domestic violence, mental health, sex reassignment surgery, and other health needs of trans people. In most major cities, queer youth projects have sprung up, in some cases funded by local government and public health agencies; these provide health and social services for queer youth, as well as facilitating organizing and community-building by them. To date, efforts to politicize social and economic policy to highlight the situation and needs of lesbian and gay youth communities have not succeeded. For example, queer and trans youth are at greater risk of homelessness than straight youth. Yet, social services for youth and the homeless do not clearly recognize how sexuality is intertwined with other bases of social and economic inequality. ...

Conclusions: Lesbian and Gay Politics and Social Movement Theories

Social movement theories from sociology and political science provide a useful perspective on some aspects of lesbian and gay social movement challenges in Canadian politics. As discussed in the introduction to this volume, resource mobilization theory stresses the idea that movements arise when they are able to obtain economic and political resources, the political process model stresses that movements must have political opportunities in order to achieve success, and new social movement theory stresses the cultural dimension of movement challenges which lead to the formation of collective identity.

All three of these dimensions may be seen at work in the evolution of lesbian and gay organizing described here. Without a sense of political identity and without a mass exit of lesbian and gay people from the closet, the modern LGBTQ movement in Canada would not exist. …

The political process model offers a more convincing account of the recent history of the LGBTQ movement. In particular, the political and legal opportunities afforded by the Charter have provided an opening for lesbian and gay organizations and individual litigants to use the courts to force public policy changes on reluctant governments. These Charter challenges have also disrupted the normative status of straight life by calling media and public attention to issues ranging from censorship and discrimination to same-sex marriage. In LGBTQ rights cases, the material consequences of changes to public policy such as the right of same-sex couples to spousal benefits are intertwined with the symbolic and cultural challenge to the traditional norms of Canadian (and other) societies. The Charter has proven to be a potent and effective weapon for lesbian and gay litigation and organizing and has forced governments to act where, otherwise, they were clearly unwilling to touch the "gay rights" hot button. The result has been a dramatic period of change in Canadian politics and one of the few success stories for progressive social movements in the neoliberal era.

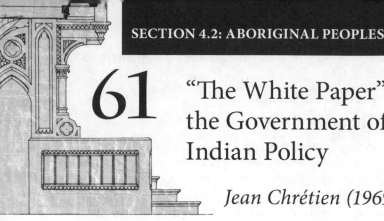

61 "The White Paper": Statement of the Government of Canada on Indian Policy

Jean Chrétien (1969)

EDITORS' INTRODUCTION

In a 1969 speech about the government's proposed White Paper, Prime Minister Pierre Trudeau summed up the government's stance with the following statement:

> *[A]boriginal rights, this really means saying, "We were here before you. You came and you took the land from us and perhaps you cheated us by giving us some worthless things in return for vast expanses of land and we want to re-open this question. We want you to preserve our aboriginal rights and to restore them to us." And our answer—it may not be the right one and may not be one which is accepted but it will be up to all of you people to make your minds up and to choose for or against it and to discuss with the Indians—our answer is "no."*

The statement was presented in the Commons by the minister of Indian affairs in Trudeau's Cabinet, Jean Chrétien. Recommending the elimination of Indian status and the Indian Act, the dissolution of the Department of Indian Affairs within five years, the conversion of reserve land to private property, and the transfer of responsibility for Indian affairs to the provinces, the White Paper inadvertently catalyzed the "Red Power" activism of the late 1960s and early 1970s that forced the government to abandon the proposal in 1971.

Presented to the First Session of the Twenty-eighth Parliament by the Honourable Jean Chrétien, Minister of Indian Affairs and Northern Development, June 1969.

Foreword

The Government believes that its policies must lead to the full, free and non-discriminatory participation of the Indian people in Canadian society. Such a goal requires a break with the past. It requires that the Indian people's role of dependence be replaced by a role of equal status, opportunity and responsibility, a role they can share with all other Canadians.

This proposal is a recognition of the necessity made plain in a year's intensive discussions with Indian people throughout Canada. The Government believes that to continue its past course of action would not serve the interests of either the Indian people or their fellow Canadians.

Source: Excerpted from *Statement of the Government of Canada on Indian Policy*. Department of Indian Affairs and Northern Development. Ottawa: Government of Canada, 1969.

The policies proposed recognize the simple reality that the separate legal status of Indians and the policies which have flowed from it have kept the Indian people apart from and behind other Canadians. The Indian people have not been full citizens of the communities and provinces in which they live and have not enjoyed the equality and the benefits that such participation offers.

The treatment resulting from their different status has been often worse, sometimes equal, and occasionally better than that accorded to their fellow citizens. What matters is that it has been different.

Many Indians, both in isolated communities and in cities, suffer from poverty. The discrimination which affects the poor, Indian and non-Indian alike, when compounded with a legal status that sets the Indian apart, provides dangerously fertile ground for social and cultural discrimination.

In recent years there has been a rapid increase in the Indian population. Their health and education levels have improved. There has been a corresponding rise in expectations that the structure of separate treatment cannot meet.

A forceful and articulate Indian leadership has developed to express the aspirations and needs of the Indian community. Given the opportunity, the Indian people can realize an immense human and cultural potential that will enhance their own well-being, that of the regions in which they live and of Canada as a whole. Faced with a continuation of past policies, they will unite only in common frustration.

The Government does not wish to perpetuate policies which carry with them the seeds of disharmony and disunity, policies which prevent Canadians from fulfilling themselves and contributing to their society. It seeks a partnership to achieve a better goal. The partners in this search are the Indian people, the governments of the provinces, the Canadian community as a whole and the Government of Canada. As all partnerships do, this will require consultation, negotiation, give and take, and co-operation if it is to succeed.

Many years will be needed. Some efforts may fail, but learning comes from failure and from what is learned success may follow. All the partners have to learn; all will have to change many attitudes.

Governments can set examples, but they cannot change the hearts of men. Canadians, Indians and non-Indians alike, stand at the crossroads. For Canadian society the issue is whether a growing element of its population will become full participants contributing in a positive way to the general well-being or whether, conversely, the present social and economic gap will lead to their increasing frustration and isolation, a threat to the general well-being of society. For many Indian people, one road does exist, the only road that has existed since Confederation and before, the road of different status, a road which has led to a blind alley of deprivation and frustration. This road, because it is a separate road, cannot lead to full participation, to equality in practice as well as in theory. In the pages which follow, the Government has outlined a number of measures and a policy which it is convinced will offer another road for Indians, a road that would lead gradually away from different status to full social, economic and political participation in Canadian life. This is the choice.

Indian people must be persuaded, must persuade themselves, that this path will lead them to a fuller and richer life. Canadian society as a whole will have to recognize the need for changed attitudes and a truly open society. Canadians should recognize the dangers of failing to strike down the barriers which frustrate Indian people. If Indian people are to become full members of Canadian society they must be warmly welcomed by that society.

The Government commends this policy for the consideration of all Canadians, Indians and non-Indians, and all governments in Canada.

Summary

1. Background

The Government has reviewed its programs for Indians and has considered the effects of them on the present situation of the Indian people. The review has drawn on extensive consultations with the Indian people, and on the knowledge and experience of many people both in and out of government.

This review was a response to things said by the Indian people at the consultation meetings which began a year ago and culminated in a meeting in Ottawa in April.

This review has shown that this is the right time to change long-standing policies. The Indian people have shown their determination that present conditions shall not persist.

Opportunities are present today in Canadian society and new directions are open. The Government believes that Indian people must not be shut out of Canadian life and must share equally in these opportunities.

The Government could press on with the policy of fostering further education; could go ahead with physical improvement programs now operating in reserve communities; could press forward in the directions of recent years, and eventually many of the problems would be solved. But progress would be too slow. The change in Canadian society in recent years has been too great and continues too rapidly for this to be the answer. Something more is needed. We can no longer perpetuate the separation of Canadians. Now is the time to change.

This Government believes in equality. It believes that all men and women have equal rights. It is determined that all shall be treated fairly and that no one shall be shut out of Canadian life, and especially that no one shall be shut out because of his race.

This belief is the basis for the Government's determination to open the doors of opportunity to *all* Canadians, to remove the barriers which impede the development of people, of regions and of the country.

Only a policy based on this belief can enable the Indian people to realize their needs and aspirations.

The Indian people are entitled to such a policy. They are entitled to an equality which preserves and enriches Indian identity and distinction; an equality which stresses Indian participation in its creation and which manifests itself in all aspects of Indian life.

The goals of the Indian people cannot be set by others; they must spring from the Indian community itself—but government can create a framework within which all persons and groups can seek their own goals.

2. The New Policy

True equality presupposes that the Indian people have the right to full and equal participation in the cultural, social, economic, and political life of Canada.

The government believes that the framework within which individual Indians and bands could achieve full participation requires:

1 that the legislative and constitutional bases of discrimination be removed;
2 that there be positive recognition by everyone of the unique contribution of Indian culture to Canadian life;
3 that services come through the same channels and from the same government agencies for all Canadians;
4 that those who are furthest behind be helped most;
5 that lawful obligations be recognized;
6 that control of Indian lands be transferred to the Indian people

The Government would be prepared to take the following steps to create this framework:

1 Propose to Parliament that the Indian Act be repealed and take such legislative steps as may be necessary to enable Indians to control Indian lands and to acquire title to them.
2 Propose to the governments of the provinces that they take over the same responsibility for Indians that they have for other citizens of their provinces. The take-over would be accompanied by the transfer to the provinces of federal funds normally provided for Indian programs, augmented as may be necessary.
3 Make substantial funds available for Indian economic development as an interim measure.
4 Wind up that part of the Department of Indian Affairs and Northern Development which deals with Indian Affairs. The residual responsibilities of the Federal Government for programs in the field of Indian affairs would be transferred to other appropriate federal departments.

In addition, the Government will appoint a Commissioner to consult with the Indians and to study and recommend acceptable procedures for the adjudication of claims.

The new policy looks to a better future for all Indian people wherever they may be. The measures for implementation are straightforward. They require discussion, consultation, and negotiation with the Indian people—individuals, bands, and associations—and with provincial governments.

Success will depend upon the co-operation and assistance of the Indians and the provinces. The Government seeks this co-operation and will respond when it is offered.

3. *The Immediate Steps*

Some changes could take place quickly. Others would take longer. It is expected that within five years the Department of Indian Affairs and Northern Development would cease to operate in the field of Indian affairs; the new laws would be in effect and existing programs would have been devolved. The Indian lands would require special attention for some time. The process of transferring control to the Indian people would be under continuous review.

The Government believes this is a policy which is just and necessary. It can only be successful if it has the support of the Indian people, the provinces, and all Canadians.

The policy promises all Indian people a new opportunity to expand and develop their identity within the framework of a Canadian society which offers them the rewards and responsibilities of participation, the benefits of involvement and the pride of belonging.

62 The Unjust Society

Harold Cardinal (1969)

EDITORS' INTRODUCTION

Harold Cardinal (1945–2005) was a long-time leader of the Indian Association of Alberta and a founding member of the National Indian Brotherhood (the predecessor of the Assembly of First Nations). Only 24 years old when he wrote The Unjust Society, *he was also the principal author of the "Red Paper"—also known as "Citizens Plus"—which was the Aboriginal response to the government's White Paper. Arguing that the White Paper was an assimilationist program that betrayed the spirit and intent of the historic treaties between First Nations and the Canadian government, the Red Paper has been widely credited with forcing the government to abandon its proposed policy. The title of Cardinal's book is a direct reference to Prime Minister Trudeau's earlier promise of a "Just Society," a term he commonly invoked in his 1968 campaign speeches as he rose to power.*

The Indian-Problem Problem

The history of Canada's Indians is a shameful chronicle of the white man's disinterest, his deliberate trampling of Indian rights and his repeated betrayal of our trust. Generations of Indians have grown up behind a buckskin curtain of indifference, ignorance and, all too often, plain bigotry. Now, at a time when our fellow Canadians consider the promise of the Just Society, once more the Indians of Canada are betrayed by a programme which offers nothing better than cultural genocide.

The new Indian policy promulgated by Prime Minister Pierre Elliott Trudeau's government, under the auspices of the Honourable Jean Chrétien, minister of Indian Affairs and Northern Development, and Deputy Minister John A. MacDonald, and presented in June of 1969 is a thinly disguised programme of extermination through assimilation. For the Indian to survive, says the government in effect, he must become a good little brown white man. The Americans to the south of us used to have a saying: "The only good Indian is a dead Indian." The MacDonald-Chrétien doctrine would amend this but slightly to, "The only good Indian is a non-Indian."

The federal government, instead of acknowledging its legal and moral responsibilities to the Indians of Canada and honouring the treaties that the Indians signed in good faith,

Source: Excerpted from *The Unjust Society: The Tragedy of Canada's Indians*. Edmonton: Hurtig, 1969.

now proposes to wash its hands of Indians entirely, passing the buck to the provincial governments.

Small wonder that in 1969, in the one hundred and second year of Canadian confederation, the native people of Canada look back on generations of accumulated frustration under conditions which can only be described as colonial, brutal and tyrannical, and look to the future with the gravest of doubts.

Torrents of words have been spoken and written about Indians since the arrival of the white man on the North American continent. Endless columns of statistics have been compiled. Countless programmes have been prepared for Indians by non-Indians. Faced with society's general indifference and a massive accumulation of misdirected, often insincere efforts, the greatest mistake the Indian has made has been to remain so long silent.

As an Indian writing about a situation I am living and experiencing in common with thousands of our people it is my hope that this book will open the eyes of the Canadian public to its shame. In these pages I hope to cut through bureaucratic doubletalk to show what it means to be an Indian in Canada. I intend to document the betrayals of our trust, to show step by step how a dictatorial bureaucracy has eroded our rights, atrophied our culture and robbed us of simple human dignity. I will expose the ignorance and bigotry that has impeded our progress, the eighty years of educational neglect that have hobbled our young people for generations, the gutless politicians who have knowingly watched us sink in the quicksands of apathy and despair and have failed to extend a hand.

I hope to point a path to radical change that will admit the Indian with restored pride to his rightful place in the Canadian heritage, that will enable the Indian in Canada at long last to realize his dreams and aspirations and find his place in Canadian society. I will challenge our fellow Canadians to help us; I will warn them of the alternatives.

I challenge the Honourable Mr. Trudeau and the Honourable Mr. Chrétien to reexamine their unfortunate policy, to offer the Indians of Canada hope instead of despair, freedom instead of frustration, life in the Just Society instead of cultural annihilation. ...

With Forked Tongue

Everyone who has watched a late late movie on television sooner or later has found himself half-sleeping through one of the old-time westerns. Inevitably, at some point in the thriller a beaten travesty of Indian leadership draws his blanket around his shoulders and solemnly intones, "White man speaks with forked tongue." Even Indians laugh at a cliché like that, but their laughter is a little strained; the truth the phrase still tells, still rankles.

Our people believe very little the white man says, even today, because the white man continues to speak with forked tongue. Individual white men may not have to lie; they may, like the minister for Indian Affairs, his deputy minister, even our prime minister, be pedantically consistent in their own public statements about Indian policy. But when the position they have taken is a complete denial of promises the Canadian government once made to us and has always upheld (though never fulfilled), then their position, their statements represent an entire society's lie—the betrayal of the Indian people.

Our people no longer believe. It is that simple and it is that sad. The Canadian government can promise involvement, consultation, progressive human and economic development programmes. We will no longer believe them. The Canadian government can guarantee the

444 / ESSENTIAL READINGS

most attractive system of education. We will not believe them. They can tell us their beautiful plans for the development of local self-government. We will shrug our disbelief. The government can create a hundred national Indian advisory councils to advise us about our problems. We will not listen to them. We will not believe what they say. The federal bureaucrats can meet with us one thousand times a year, but we will suspect their motives. We will know they have nothing new to say. We will know they speak with forked tongue.

After generations of endless frustration with the Canadian government, our people are tired and impatient. *Before* the Canadian government tries to feed us hypocritical policy statements, more empty promises, more forked tonguistics, our people want, our people, the Indians, demand just settlement of all our treaty and aboriginal rights. Fulfillment of Indian rights by the queen's government must come before there can be any further cooperation between the Indians and the government. We demand nothing more. We expect nothing less.

Yes, the prime minister roused our hopes with his talk of a compassionate and just society. Then his minister for Indian Affairs told us our problems would vanish if we would become nice, manageable white men like all other Canadians. Just recently, the prime minister himself flicked the other fork of his tongue. In a speech in Vancouver, Mr. Trudeau said, "The federal government is not prepared to guarantee the aboriginal rights of Canada's Indians." Mr. Trudeau said, "It is inconceivable that one section of a society should have a treaty with another section of a society. The Indians should become Canadians as have all other Canadians."

Have other Canadians been led to this citizenship over a path of broken promises and dishonoured treaties?

To the Indians of Canada, the treaties represent an Indian Magna Carta. The treaties are important to us, because we entered into these negotiations with faith, with hope for a better life with honour. We have survived for over a century on little but that hope. Did the white man enter into them with something less in mind? Or have the heirs of the men who signed in honour somehow disavowed the obligation passed down to them? The Indians entered into the treaty negotiations as honourable men who came to deal as equals with the queen's representatives. Our leaders of that time thought they were dealing with an equally honourable people. Our leaders pledged themselves, their people and their heirs to honour what was done then.

Our leaders mistakenly thought they were dealing with an honourable people who would do no less than the Indians were doing—bind themselves, bind their people and bind their heirs to honourable contracts.

Our people talked with the government representatives, not as beggars pleading for handouts, but as men with something to offer in return for rights they expected. To our people, this was the beginning of a contractual relationship whereby the representatives of the queen would have lasting responsibilities to the Indian people in return for the valuable lands that were ceded to them.

The treaties were the way in which the white people legitimized in the eyes of the world their presence in our country. It was an attempt to settle the terms of occupancy on a just basis, legally and morally to extinguish the legitimate claims of our people to title to the land in our country. There never has been any doubt in the minds of our people that the land in Canada belonged to them. Nor can there have been any doubt in the mind of the government or in the minds of the white people about who owned the land, for it was upon the basis of white recognition of Indian rights that the treaties were negotiated. Otherwise, there could have been nothing to negotiate, no need for treaties. In the language of the Cree Indians, the Indian reserves are known as *the land that we kept for ourselves* or *the land that we did not give to the government*. In our language, *skun-gun*.

When one party to an agreement continually, ruthlessly breaks that agreement whenever it suits his purpose, the other partner cannot forever be expected to believe protestations of faith that accompany the next peace offering. In our society, a man who did not keep his part of a fair bargain, a man who used tricks and shady deals to wriggle out of commitments, a man who continually spoke with a forked tongue became known as a crook. Indians do not deal with cheats.

Mr. Chrétien says, "Get rid of the *Indian Act*. Treat Indians as any other Canadians." Mr. Trudeau says, "Forget the treaties. Let Indians become Canadians." This is the Just Society? To the Indian people, there can be no justice, no just society, until their rights are restored. Nor can there be any faith in Mr. Trudeau, Mr. Chrétien, the government, in white society until our rights are protected by lasting, equitable legislation.

As far as we are concerned our treaty rights represent a sacred, honourable agreement between ourselves and the Canadian government that cannot be unilaterally abrogated by the government at the whim of one of its leaders unless that government is prepared to give us back title to our country.

Our rights are too valuable to surrender to gallic or any other kind of rhetoric, too valuable to be sold for pieces of gold. Words change; the value of money fluctuates, may even disappear; our land will not disappear.

We cannot give up our rights without destroying ourselves as people. If our rights are meaningless, if it is inconceivable that our society have treaties with the white society even though those treaties were signed by honourable men on both sides, in good faith, long before the present government decided to tear them up as worthless scraps of paper, then we as a people are meaningless. We cannot and we will not accept this. We know that as long as we fight for our rights we will survive. If we surrender, we die.

Currently, this lack of faith in our government, this feeling that our government speaks with a forked tongue is called a credibility gap. The credibility gap between white society and Indian, between our government and our people must be closed. Our lack of faith in the federal government has far-reaching implications. As long as our rights are not honoured, and as long as the government continues to make it clear it has no intention of honouring them, then we must continue to be apprehensive about new plans such as the Chrétien policy to abolish the *Indian Act* and to do away with the Indian Affairs branch of the government. We will be fearful of any attempt by the federal government to turn over to provincial governments responsibility for Indian Affairs. We will be certain that the federal government is merely attempting to abandon its responsibilities. Provincial governments have no obligations to fulfill our treaties. They never signed treaties with the Indians. We could not expect them to be concerned with treaty rights. In our eyes, this new government policy merely represents a disguised move to abrogate all our treaty rights. This is our government speaking once again with forked tongue.

Until such time as the federal government accepts and protects our rights with abiding legislation, we will oppose and refuse to participate in any federal–provincial schemes that affect our rights.

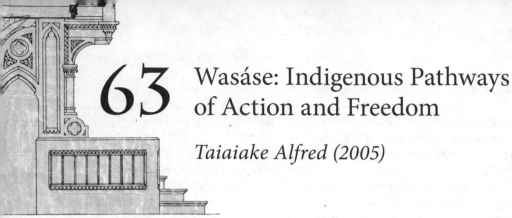

63 Wasáse: Indigenous Pathways of Action and Freedom

Taiaiake Alfred (2005)

EDITORS' INTRODUCTION

Taiaiake Alfred is a professor of indigenous governance at the University of Victoria. In this book, published several years before the Idle No More movement, Alfred rejects the current relationship between the Canadian state and Aboriginal peoples, which he argues continues to reproduce colonial hierarchies and power relations. He writes that "Wasáse" is an ancient war ritual, a ceremony of unity, strength, and commitment to action. It is through the ethical and political vision of the Wasáse that the Onkwehonwe, the original peoples, can regenerate themselves and reconnect with their cultures and communities.

First Words

There are many differences among the peoples that are indigenous to this land, yet the challenge facing all Onkwehonwe is the same: regaining freedom and becoming self-sufficient by confronting the disconnection and fear at the core of our existences under colonial dominion. We are separated from the sources of our goodness and power: from each other, our cultures, and our lands. These connections must be restored. Governmental power is founded on fear, which is used to control and manipulate us in many ways; so, the strategy must be to confront fear and display the courage to act against and defeat the states power.

The first question that arises when this idea is applied in a practical way to the situations facing Onkwehonwe in real life is this: How can we regenerate ourselves culturally and achieve freedom and political independence when the legacies of disconnection, dependency, and dispossession have such a strong hold on us? Undeniably, we face a difficult situation. The political and social institutions that govern us have been shaped and organized to serve white power and they conform to the interests of the states founded on that objective. These state and Settler-serving institutions are useless to the cause of our survival, and if we are to free ourselves from the grip of colonialism, we must reconfigure our politics and replace all of the strategies, institutions, and leaders in place today. The transformation will begin inside each one of us as personal change, but decolonization will become a reality only when we

Source: Excerpted from *Wasáse: Indigenous Pathways of Action and Freedom* by Taiaiake Alfred. Peterborough, ON: Broadview Press, 2005. Reprinted by permission.

collectively both commit to a movement based on an *ethical* and *political* vision and consciously reject the colonial postures of weak submission, victimry, and raging violence. It is a political vision and solution that will be capable of altering power relations and rearranging the forces that shape our lives. Politics is the force that channels social, cultural, and economic powers and makes them imminent in our lives. Abstaining from politics is like turning your back on a beast when it is angry and intent on ripping your guts out.

It is the kind of politics we practise that makes the crucial distinction between the possibility of a regenerative struggle and what we are doing now. Conventional and acceptable approaches to making change are leading us nowhere. Submission and cooperation, which define politics as practised by the current generation of Onkwehonwe politicians, are, I contend, morally, culturally, and politically indefensible and should be dismissed scornfully by any right-thinking person and certainly by any Onkwehonwe who still has dignity. There is little attention paid in this book to the conventional aspects of the politics of pity, such as self-government processes, land claims agreements, and aboriginal rights court cases, because building on what we have achieved up until now in our efforts to decolonize society is insufficient and truly unacceptable as the end-state of a challenge to colonialism. The job is far from finished. It is impossible to predict what constraints and opportunities will emerge, but it is clear that we have not pushed hard enough yet to be satisfied with the state's enticements. Fundamentally different relationships between Onkwehonwe and Settlers will emerge not from negotiations in state-sponsored and government-regulated processes, but only after successful Onkwehonwe resurgences against white society's entrenched privileges and the unreformed structure of the colonial state.

As Onkwehonwe committed to the reclamation of our dignity and strength, there are, theoretically, two viable approaches to engaging the colonial power that is thoroughly embedded in the state and in societal structures: armed resistance and non-violent contention. Each has a heritage among our peoples and is a potential formula for making change, for engaging with the adversary without deference to emotional attachments to colonial symbols or to the compromised logic of colonial approaches. They are both philosophically defensible, but are they both equally valid approaches to making change, given the realities of our situations and our goals? We need a confident position on the question as to what is the right strategy. Both armed resistance and non-violent contention are unique disciplines that require commitments that rule out overlapping allegiances between the two approaches. They are diverging and distinctive ways of making change, and the choice between the two paths is the most important decision the next generation of Onkwehonwe will collectively make.

This is the political formula of the strategy of armed resistance: facing a situation of untenable politics, Onkwehonwe could conceivably move toward practising a punishing kind of aggression, a raging resistance invoking hostile and irredentist negative political visions seeking to engender and escalate the conflict so as to eventually demoralize the Settler society and defeat the colonial state. Contrast this with the strategic vision of nonviolent contention: Onkwehonwe face the untenable politics and unacceptable conditions in their communities and confront the situation with determined yet restrained action, coherent and creative contention supplemented with a positive political vision based on re-establishing respect for the original covenants and ancient treaties that reflect the founding principles of the Onkwehonwe-Settler relationship. This would be a movement sure to engender conflict, but it would be conflict for a positive purpose and with the hope of recreating the conditions of coexistence. Rather than enter the arena of armed resistance, we would choose to perform rites of resurgence.

These forms of resurgence have already begun. There are people in all communities who understand that a true decolonization movement can emerge only when we shift our politics from articulating grievances to pursuing an organized and political battle for the cause of our freedom. These new warriors understand the need to refuse any further disconnection from their heritage and the need to reconnect with the spiritual bases of their existences as Onkwehonwe. Following their example and building on the foundation of their struggles, we have the potential to initiate a more coordinated and widespread action, to reorganize communities to take advantage of gains and opportunities as they occur in political, economic, social, and cultural spheres and spaces created by the movement. There is a solid theory of change in this concept of an indigenous peoples' movement. The theory of change is the lived experience of the people we will encounter in this book. Their lives are a dynamic of power generated by creative energy flowing from their heritage through their courageous and unwavering determination to recreate themselves and act together to meet the challenges of their day.

A common and immediate concern for anyone defending the truth of their heritage is the imperative to repel the thrust of the modern state's assault against our peoples. The Settlers continue to erase our existences from the cultural, social, and political landscape of our homelands. Onkwehonwe are awakening to the need to move from the materialist orientation of our politics and social reality toward a restored spiritual foundation, channelling that spiritual strength and the unity it creates into a power that can affect political and economic relations. A true revolution is spiritual at its core; every single one of the world's materialist revolutions has failed to produce conditions of life that are markedly different from those which it opposed. Whatever the specific means or rationale, violent, legalist, and economic revolutions have never been successful in producing peaceful coexistence between peoples; in fact, they always reproduce the exact set of power relations they seek to change, rearranging only the outward face of power. ...

Outright assaults and insidious undermining have brought us to the situation we face today, when the destruction of our peoples is nearly complete. Yet resurgence and regeneration constitute a way to power-surge against the empire with integrity. The new warriors who are working to ensure the survival of their people are not distracted by the effort to pass off as "action" any analysis of the self-evident fact of the defeat of our nations. They don't imagine that our cause needs further justification in law or in the public mind. They know that assertion and action are the urgencies; all the rest is a smokescreen clouding this clear vision.

The experience of resurgence and regeneration in Onkwehonwe communities thus far proves that change cannot be made from within the colonial structure. Institutions and ideas that are the creation of the colonial relationship are not capable of ensuring our survival; this has been amply proven as well by the absolute failure of institutional and legalist strategies to protect our lands and our rights, as well as in their failure to motivate younger generations of Onkwehonwe to action. In the face of the strong renewed push by the state for the legal and political assimilation of our peoples, as well as a rising tide of consumerist materialism making its way into our communities, the last remaining remnants of distinctive Onkwehonwe values and culture are being wiped out. The situation is urgent and calls for even more intensive and profound resurgences on even more levels, certainly not moderation. Many people are paralyzed by fear or idled by complacency and will sit passively and watch destruction consume our people. But the words in this book are for those of us who prefer a dangerous dignity to safe self-preservation.

People have always faced these challenges. None of what I am saying is new, either to people's experience in the world or to political philosophy. What is emerging in our communities is a renewed respect for indigenous knowledge and Onkwehonwe ways of thinking. This book hopes to document and glorify this renewal, in which Onkwehonwe are linked in spirit and strategy with other indigenous peoples confronting empire throughout the world. When we look into the heart of our own communities, we can relate to the struggles of peoples in Africa or Asia and appreciate the North African scholar Albert Memmi's thoughts on how, in the language of his day, colonized peoples respond to oppression: "One can be reconciled to every situation, and the colonized can wait a long time to live. But, regardless of how soon or how violently the colonized rejects his situation, he will one day begin to overthrow his unliveable existence with the whole force of his oppressed personality."[1] The question facing us is this one: For us today, here in this land, how will the overthrow of our unliveable existence come about? ...

Wasáse is spiritual revolution and contention. It is not a path of violence. And yet, this commitment to non-violence is not pacifism either. This is an important point to make clear: I believe there is a need for morally grounded defiance and non-violent agitation combined with the development of a collective capacity for self-defence, so as to generate within the Settler society a reason and incentive to negotiate constructively in the interest of achieving a respectful coexistence. The rest of this book will try to explain this concept (an effort the more academically inclined reader may be permitted to read as my theorizing the liberation of indigenous peoples).

My goal is to discover a real and deep notion of peace in the hope of moving us away from valuing simplistic notions of peace such as certainty and stability for these are conceptions that point only to the value of order. Some readers may find themselves confused by the seeming contradictions in my logic and question how "peace" can be the orienting goal of this warrior-spirited book, wondering if perhaps a concept like "justice" may be more to the point and truer to the spirit of a book that takes a war dance as its emblem. But justice as a liberatory concept and as a would-be goal is limited by its necessary gaze to the politics, economics, and social relations of the past. However noble and necessary justice is to our struggles, its gaze will always be backward. By itself, the concept of justice is not capable of encompassing the broader transformations needed to ensure coexistence. Justice is one element of a good relationship; it is concerned with fairness and right and calculating moral balances, but it cannot be the end goal of a struggle, which must be conceived as a movement from injustice and conflict through and beyond the achievement of justice to the completion of the relationship and the achievement of peace.

The old slogan, "No justice, no peace," is a truism. We must move from injustice, through struggle, to a mutual respect founded on the achievement of justice and then onward towards peace. Step by step. Lacking struggle, omitting respect and justice, there can and will be no peace. Or happiness. Or freedom. These are the real goals of a truly human and fully realized philosophy of change.

Peace is hopeful, visionary, and forward-looking; it is not just the lack of violent conflict or rioting in the streets. That simple stability is what we call order, and order serves the powerful in an imperial situation. If peace continues to be strictly defined as the maintenance of order and the rule of law, we will be defeated in our struggle to survive as Onkwehonwe. Reconceptualized for our struggle, peace is being Onkwehonwe, breaking with the disfiguring and meaningless norms of our present reality, and recreating ourselves in a holistic sense. This conception of peace requires a rejection of the state's multifaceted oppression of our peoples simultaneously with and through the assertion of regenerated Onkwehonwe identities. Personal and collective transformation is not instrumental to the surging against state power, it is the very means of our struggle.

Memmi, who was so powerful in his exposure of colonial mentalities at play during the Algerian resistance against French colonialism, spoke of the fundamental need to cure white people, through revolution, of the disease of the European they have collectively inherited from their colonial forefathers. I believe his prescription of spiritual transformation channelled into a political action and social movement is the right medicine. ...

The thoughts and vision I am offering through these words are rooted in the cultural heritage of Anówarakowa. And proudly so! They are not compromises between indigenous and non-indigenous perspectives; nor are they attempts to negotiate a reconciliation of Onkwehonwe and European cultures and values. These words are an attempt to bring forward an indigenously rooted voice of contention, unconstrained and uncompromised by colonial mentalities. A total commitment to the challenge of regenerating our indigeneity, to rootedness in indigenous cultures, to a fundamental commitment to the centrality of our truths—this book is an effort to work through the philosophical, spiritual, and practical implications of holding such commitments.

These commitments require the reader to challenge critically all of his or her artificial and emotional attachments to the oppressive colonial myths and symbols that we have come to know as our culture. I know that this is asking people to wander into dangerous territory; disentangling from these attachments can also feel like being banished, in a way. But stepping into our fear is crucial, because leaving the comfort zone of accepted truth is vital to creating the emotional and mental state that allows one to really learn.

It is a new approach to decolonization. Less intense, or less threatening, ideas about how to make change have proven ineffective from our perspective. I believe it is because they are bound up in and unable to break free from the limiting logic of the colonial myths that they claim to oppose. The myths' symbols and embedded beliefs force aboriginal thinking to remain in colonial mental, political, and legal frameworks, rendering these forms of writing and thinking less radical and powerless against imperialism. The reflections, meditations, teachings, and dialogues that form the core of this book are indigenous and organic: they emerge from inside Onkwehonwe experiences and reflect the ideas, concepts, and languages that have developed over millennia in the spaces we live, among our peoples. I want to bring the heritage and truth of Anówarakowa to a new generation and to engage passionately with indigenous truths to generate powerful dynamics of thought and action and change. I did not write this book *about* change, I wrote it from *within* change. I wrote it with the plain intent of instigating further contention. My hope is that people who read these words will take from them a different way of defining the problem at the core of our present existence, one that brings a radically principled and challenging set of ideas to bear on how to remake the relationship between Onkwehonwe and Settler.

A big part of the social and political resurgence will be the regeneration of Onkwehonwe existences free from colonial attitudes and behaviours. Regeneration means we will reference ourselves differently, both from the ways we did traditionally and under colonial dominion. We will self-consciously recreate our cultural practices and reform our political identities by drawing on tradition in a thoughtful process of reconstruction and a committed reorganization of our lives in a personal and collective sense. This will result in a new conception of what it is to live as Onkwehonwe. This book is my contribution to the larger effort to catalyze and galvanize the movements that have already begun among so many of our people. Restoring these connections is the force that will confront and defeat the defiant evil of imperialism in this land. We need to work together to cleanse our minds, our hearts, and our bodies of the colonial stain and reconnect our lives to the sources of our strength as Onkwehonwe. We need to find new and creative ways to express that heritage. I wrote this book as an Onkwehonwe believing in the fundamental commonality of indigenous values; yet I wrote it from within my own experience. I aim to speak most directly to other Onkwehonwe who share my commitments and who are travelling the same pathway. These words are offered in the spirit of the ancient Wasáse, which was so eloquently captured by my friend Kahente when I asked her to tell me how she understood the meaning of the ritual:

> There is a spiritual base that connects us all, and it is stimulated through ceremony. The songs and dances that we perform are like medicine, *Ononkwa*, invoking the power of the original instructions that lie within. In it, we dance, sing, and share our words of pain, joy, strength, and commitment. The essence of the ancestors' message reveals itself not only in these songs, speeches, and dances but also in the faces and bodies of all who are assembled. This visual manifestation shows us that we are not alone and that our survival depends on being part of the larger group and in this group working together. We are reminded to stay on the path laid out before us. This way it strengthens our resolve to keep going and to help each other along the way. It is a time to show each other how to step along that winding route in unison and harmony with one another. To know who your friends and allies are in such struggle is what is most important and is what keeps you going.

If non-indigenous readers are capable of listening, they will learn from these shared words, and they will discover that while we are envisioning a new relationship between Onkwehonwe and the land, we are at the same time offering a decolonized alternative to the Settler society by inviting them to share our vision of respect and peaceful coexistence.

Note

1. Albert Memmi, *The Colonizer and the Colonized* (Boston, MA: Beacon Press, 1991) 120.

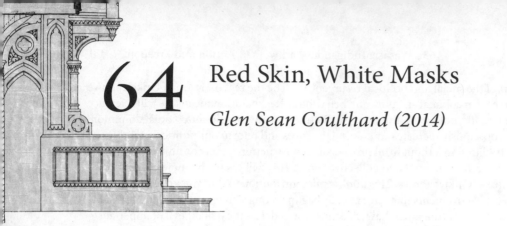

64 Red Skin, White Masks

Glen Sean Coulthard (2014)

EDITORS' INTRODUCTION

Glen Coulthard is a member of the Yellowknives Dene First Nation and an assistant professor in the First Nations and Indigenous Studies Program and the Department of Political Science at the University of British Columbia.

The title of Coulthard's book, Red Skin, White Masks, *is a play on the title of Franz Fanon's seminal work in post-colonial theory,* Black Skin, White Masks. *Coulthard defines the "politics of recognition" as the current political approach to reconciling indigenous peoples' assertions of nationhood with the sovereignty of the Canadian state through negotiated settlements over issues such as land, economic development, and self-government. He argues that this recognition-based approach is highly detrimental to indigenous peoples in that it maintains and supports colonial structures and asymmetrical power relations. In the second half of this excerpt, Coulthard also gives a history of the Idle No More movement, which provides what he sees as an example of what a resurgent decolonial politics looks like.*

Over the last forty years, the self-determination efforts and objectives of Indigenous peoples in Canada have increasingly been cast in the language of "recognition." Consider, for example, the formative declaration issued by my people in 1975:

> We the Dene of the NWT [Northwest Territories] insist on the right to be regarded by ourselves and the world as a nation.

> Our struggle is for the recognition of the Dene Nation by the Government and people of Canada and the peoples and governments of the world. ...

> And while there are realities we are forced to submit to, such as the existence of a country called Canada, we insist on the right to self-determination and the recognition of the Dene Nation.

Now fast-forward to the 2005 policy position on self-determination issued by Canada's largest Aboriginal organization, the Assembly of First Nations (AFN). According to the AFN, "a consensus has emerged ... around a vision of the relationship between First Nations and

Source: Excerpted from *Red Skin, White Masks: Rejecting the Colonial Politics of Recognition* by Glen Sean Coulthard. © 2014 by the Regents of the University of Minnesota. Courtesy of the University of Minnesota Press.

Canada which would lead to strengthening recognition and implementation of First Nations' governments." This "vision," the AFN goes on to explain, draws on the core principles outlined in the 1996 Report of the Royal Commission on Aboriginal Peoples (RCAP): that is, recognition of the nation-to-nation relationship between First Nations and the Crown; recognition of the equal right of First Nations to self-determination; recognition of the Crown's fiduciary obligation to protect Aboriginal treaty rights; recognition of First Nations' inherent right to self-government; and recognition of the right of First Nations to economically benefit from the use and development of their lands and resources. Since 2005 the AFN has consistently reasserted and affirmed these guiding principles at its Annual General Assemblies and in the numerous resolutions that these gatherings have produced.

These demands have not been easy to ignore. Because of the persistence and dedication of countless Indigenous activists, leaders, communities, and organizations, we have witnessed within the scope of four decades the emergence of an unprecedented degree of recognition for Aboriginal "cultural" rights within the legal and political framework of the Canadian state. Most significant on this front was Canada's eventual "recognition" of "existing aboriginal and treaty rights" under section 35(1) of the *Constitution Act* of 1982. This constitutional breakthrough provided the catalyst that led to the federal government's eventual recognition, in 1995, of an "inherent right to self-government," as well as the groundswell of post-1982 court challenges that have sought to both clarify and widen the scope of what constitutes a constitutionally recognized Aboriginal right to begin with. When considered from the vantage point of these important developments, it would certainly appear that "recognition" has emerged as the dominant expression of self-determination within the Aboriginal rights movement in Canada.

The struggle for recognition has become a central catalyst in the international Indigenous rights movement as well. As the works of Will Kymlicka, Sheryl Lightfoot, Ronald Neizen, and others have noted, the last three decades have witnessed the emergence of recognition-based approaches to Indigenous self-determination in the field of Indigenous–state relations in Asia, northern Europe, throughout the Americas, and across the South Pacific (including Australia, New Zealand, and the Pacific Islands). Although varying in institutional scope and scale, all of these geopolitical regions have seen the establishment of Indigenous rights regimes that claim to recognize and accommodate the political autonomy, land rights, and cultural distinctiveness of Indigenous nations within the settler states that now encase them. Although my primary empirical focus in *Red Skin, White Masks* is Canada, I suspect that readers will find many of my conclusions applicable to settler-colonial experiences elsewhere.

On a more discursive plane, the increase in recognition demands made by Indigenous and other marginalized minorities over the last forty years has also prompted a flurry of intellectual activity that has sought to unpack the complex ethical, political, and legal questions that these types of claims raise. To date, much of this literature has tended to focus on a perceived relationship between the affirmative recognition and institutional accommodation of societal cultural differences on the one hand, and the freedom and autonomy of marginalized individuals and groups living in ethnically diverse states on the other. In Canada it has been argued that this synthesis of theory and practice has forced the state to dramatically reconceptualize the tenets of its relationship with Indigenous peoples; whereas before

1969 federal Indian policy was unapologetically assimilationist, now it is couched in the vernacular of "mutual recognition."

In the following chapters I critically engage a multiplicity of diverse anti-imperialist trad-itions and practices to challenge the increasingly commonplace idea that the colonial rela-tionship between Indigenous peoples and the Canadian state can be adequately transformed via such a politics of recognition. Following the work of Richard J.F. Day, I take "politics of recognition" to refer to the now expansive range of recognition-based models of liberal pluralism that seek to "reconcile" Indigenous assertions of nationhood with settler-state sovereignty via the accommodation of Indigenous identity claims in some form of renewed legal and political relationship with the Canadian state. Although these models tend to vary in both theory and practice, most call for the delegation of land, capital, and political power from the state to Indigenous communities through a combination of land claim settlements, economic development initiatives, and self-government agreements. These are subsequently the three broad contexts through which I examine the theory and practice of Indigenous recognition politics in the following chapters. Against this variant of the recognition ap-proach, I argue that instead of ushering in an era of peaceful coexistence grounded on the ideal of reciprocity or mutual recognition, the politics of recognition in its contemporary liberal form promises to reproduce the very configurations of colonialist, racist, patriarchal state power that Indigenous peoples' demands for recognition have historically sought to transcend.

To demonstrate the above claim, *Red Skin, White Masks* will theoretically and empirically map the contours of what I consider to be a decisive shift in the *modus operandi* of colonial power following the hegemonization of the recognition paradigm following the release of the federal government's infamous Statement of the Government of Canada on Indian Policy—also known as the "White Paper"—in 1969. In the two centuries leading to this historic policy proposal—which called for the blanket assimilation of the status Indian population by unilaterally removing all institutionally enshrined aspects of legal and political differen-tiation that distinguish First Nations from non-Native Canadians under the *Indian Act*—the reproduction of the colonial relationship between Indigenous peoples and what would even-tually become Canada depended heavily on the deployment of state power geared around genocidal practices of forced exclusion and assimilation. Any cursory examination into the character of colonial Indian policy during this period will attest to this fact. For example, this era witnessed Canada's repeated attempts to overtly uproot and destroy the vitality and autonomy of Indigenous modes of life through institutions such as residential schools; through the imposition of settler-state policies aimed at explicitly undercutting Indigenous political economies and relations to and with land; through the violent dispossession of First Nation women's rights to land and community membership under sexist provisions of the *Indian Act*; through the theft of Aboriginal children via racist child welfare policies; and through the near wholesale dispossession of Indigenous peoples' territories and modes of traditional governance in exchange for delegated administrative powers to be exercised over relatively minuscule reserve lands. All of these policies sought to marginalize Indigenous people and communities with the ultimate goal being our elimination, if not physically, then as cultural, political, and legal peoples distinguishable from the rest of Canadian society. These initiatives reflect the more or less unconcealed, unilateral, and coercive nature of col-onial rule during most of the nineteenth and twentieth centuries.

Although Indigenous people and communities have always found ways to individually and collectively resist these oppressive policies and practices, it was not until the tumultuous political climate of Red Power activism in the 1960s and 70s that policies geared toward the recognition and so-called "reconciliation" of Native land and political grievances with state sovereignty began to appear. Three watershed events are generally recognized as shaping this era of Native activism in Canada. The first was the materialization of widespread First Nation opposition to the previously mentioned 1969 White Paper. Instead of serving as a bridge to passive assimilation, the White Paper inaugurated an unprecedented degree of pan-Indian assertiveness and political mobilization. The National Indian Brotherhood (now the Assembly of First Nations) issued the following response to the federal government's proposed initiative: "We view this as a policy designed to divest us of our aboriginal ... rights. If we accept this policy, and in the process lose our rights and our lands, we become willing partners in cultural genocide. This we cannot do." Although designed as a once-and-for-all solution to Canada's so-called "Indian Problem," the White Paper instead became a central catalyst around which the contemporary Indigenous self-determination movement coalesced, "launching it into a determined [defence] of a unique cultural heritage and identity." The sheer magnitude of First Nations' resistance to the White Paper proposal forced the federal government to formally shelve the document on March 17, 1971.

The second watershed event occurred following the partial recognition of Aboriginal "title" in the Supreme Court of Canada's 1973 *Calder* decision. This landmark case, which involved a claim launched by Nisga'a hereditary chief Frank Calder to the unextinguished territories of his nation in north-western British Columbia, overturned a seventy-five-year precedent first established in *St. Catherine's Milling and Lumber Company v. The Queen* (1888), which stated that Aboriginal land rights existed only insofar and to the extent that the state recognized them as such. Although technically a defeat for the Nisga'a, the six justices that rendered substantive decisions in *Calder* all agreed that, prior to contact, the Nisga'a indeed held the land rights they claimed in court. The question then quickly shifted to whether these rights were sufficiently extinguished through colonial legislation. In the end, three justices ruled that the Aboriginal rights in question had not been extinguished, three ruled that they had, and one justice ruled against the Nisga'a based on a technical question regarding whether this type of action could be levelled against the province without legislation permitting it, which he ruled could not. Thus, even though the Nisga'a technically lost their case in a 4–3 decision, the Supreme Court's ruling in *Calder* left enough uncertainty around the question of existing Aboriginal rights that it prompted a shift in the federal government's policy vis-à-vis Native land interests. The result was the federal government's 1973 Statement on Claims of Indian and Inuit People: A Federal Native Claims Policy, which effectively reversed fifty-two years (since the 1921 signing of Treaty 11 in the Northwest Territories with the Sahtu Dene) of state refusal to recognize Indigenous claims to land where the question of existing title remained open.

The third event (or rather cluster of events) emerged following the turbulent decade of energy politics that followed the oil crisis of the early 1970s, which subsequently fueled an aggressive push by state and industry to develop what it saw as the largely untapped resource potential (natural gas, minerals, and oil) of northern Canada. The federal government's holding of 45 percent equity in Panarctic Oils led Indian Affairs minister Jean Chrétien to state that "it is very seldom in public life that a minister of a government presides over that kind of profit." The proposed increase in northern development was envisioned despite concerns raised by the Métis, Dene, and Inuit of the Northwest Territories regarding Canada's proposal to sanction the development of a huge natural gas pipeline to be carved across the heartland of our traditional territories, as well as the resistance mounted by the Cree of northern Quebec against a similarly massive hydroelectric project proposed for their homeland in the James Bay region. The effectiveness of our subsequent political struggles, which gained unprecedented media coverage across the country, once again raised the issue of unresolved Native rights and title issues to the fore of Canadian public consciousness.

In the following chapters I will show that colonial rule underwent a profound shift in the wake of these important events. More specifically, I argue that the expression of Indigenous anticolonial nationalism that emerged during this period forced colonial power to modify itself from a structure that was once primarily reinforced by policies, techniques, and ideologies explicitly oriented around the genocidal exclusion/assimilation double, to one that is now reproduced through a seemingly more conciliatory set of discourses and institutional practices that emphasize our *recognition* and *accommodation*. Regardless of this modification, however, the relationship between Indigenous peoples and the state has remained *colonial* to its foundation. ...

Idle No More: A History

Below I want to turn our attention to the Idle No More movement that burst onto the Canadian political scene in the late fall/early winter of 2012/13. To my mind, Idle No More offers a productive case study against which to explore what a resurgent Indigenous politics might look like on the ground. Before I turn to this analysis, however, providing a bit of context to the movement is required.

On December 14, 2012, the Canadian senate passed the Conservative federal government's controversial omnibus Bill C-45. Bill C-45, also known as the *Jobs and Growth Act*, is a four-hundred-plus-page budget implementation bill that contains comprehensive changes to numerous pieces of federal legislation, including, but not limited to, the *Indian Act*, *Fisheries Act*, the *Canadian Environmental Assessment Act*, and the *Navigable Water Act*. From the perspective of many Indigenous people and communities, the changes contained in Bill C-45 threaten to erode Aboriginal land and treaty rights insofar as they reduce the amount of resource development projects that require environmental assessment; they change the regulations that govern on-reserve leasing in a way that will make it easier for special interests to access First Nation reserve lands for the purposes of economic development and settlement; and they radically curtail environmental protections for lakes and rivers.

Indigenous opposition to Bill C-45 began in the fall of 2012 as a grassroots education campaign initiated by four women from the prairies—Jessica Gordon, Sylvia McAdam, Sheelah McLean and Nina Wilson—under the mantra "Idle No More." The campaign's original aim was to provide information to Canadians about the impending impacts of Bill C-45 on Aboriginal Rights and environmental protections before the legislation was passed by the Canadian senate. Then, on December 4, Chief Theresa Spence of the Attawapiskat Cree Nation announced that she would begin a hunger strike on December 11 to bring attention to the deplorable housing conditions on her reserve in northern Ontario, to raise awareness about the impacts of Bill C-45, and to demonstrate her support for the emerging Idle No More movement. ...

By the second week in December the movement had exploded on social media under the Twitter hash tag #IdleNoMore (or #INM for short), with the first national "day of action" called for December 10th. Protests erupted in cities across the country. At this point, the tactics favoured by Idle No More participants involved a combination of "flash mob" round-dancing and drumming in public places like shopping malls, street intersections, and legislature grounds, coupled with an ongoing public education campaign organized through community-led conferences, teach-ins, and public panels. On December 21 an Idle No More protest involving thousands of Indigenous people and their supporters descended on Parliament Hill in Ottawa. During roughly the same time, Idle No More tactics began to diversify to include the use of blockades and temporary train and traffic stoppages, the most publicized of which involved a two-week railway blockade established in late December by the Aamjiwnaag First Nation near Sarnia, Ontario.

By late December it was clear that something truly significant was underway with the Idle No More movement. Indeed, Canada had not seen such a sustained, united and coordinated nationwide mobilization of Indigenous nations against a legislative assault on our rights since the proposed White Paper of 1969. What had begun in the fall of 2012 as an education campaign designed to inform Canadians about a particularly repugnant and undemocratic piece of legislation had erupted by mid-January 2013 into a full-blown defence of Indigenous land and sovereignty. By early January the momentum generated by Idle No More, in combination with the media attention paid to Chief Spence's hunger strike, had created such a national stir that the Prime Minister's Office was forced to respond by calling a January 11 meeting with the Assembly of First Nations, although the prime minister never explicitly stated that his decision to call the meeting was a result of pressure mounted by the escalating protests. ...

As with any grassroots political movement, the diversity at the heart of Idle No More resulted in debates and disagreements over what types of strategies and tactics to use in our efforts to forge meaningful change. These debates intensified in the days leading up to the January 11 meeting. On the one side, there was the perspective among many Native people working within mainstream Aboriginal organizations that saw the January 11 meeting as an important space to get Aboriginal issues and concerns on the federal government's political agenda. On the other side of the debate, however, were the voices emanating up from the communities (with some chiefs following suit), that saw the turn to high-level political negotiations as yet another attempt by the state and Aboriginal organizations, in particular the Assembly of First Nations, to coopt the transformative potential of the movement by redirecting it in a more moderate and reformist direction. Longtime Secwepemc activist and leader Arthur Manuel gets to the core of the debate when he writes that "one thing is clear: that certain Indigenous leaders only know how to meet with government and not fight with government. In situations like Friday [January 11], they say that it is important to 'engage' with government when they open the door to discussion. The real problem is that you get sucked into basically supporting the government's position unless you walk out. In this case it is just another 'process' and not 'change in policy' that the AFN left the room with." There is much historical evidence to support Manuel's concern. If we take a step back and look at the history that led to our present juncture, especially since the late 1960s, the state has always responded to increased levels of Indigenous political assertiveness and militancy by attempting to contain these outbursts through largely symbolic gestures of political inclusion and recognition. Indeed, this was precisely the manner in which the federal government attempted to address the fallout of the decade-long escalation of First Nations' militancy that culminated in the Meech Lake Accord and the conflict at Kanesatake in 1990. And if we push our view back a bit further yet, we see a similar strategy used by the federal government to quell the upsurge of struggle that eventually defeated the White Paper of 1969. It was at this time that the entire policy orientation of Canada's approach to solving the "Indian problem" began to shift from willfully ignoring Aboriginal peoples' rights to recognizing them in the manageable form of land claims and eventually self-government agreements. I suggest that Idle No More is an indication of the ultimate failure of this approach to reconciliation. After forty years the subtle lure of Canada's vacuous gestures of accommodation have begun to lose their political sway.

All of this is to say that the January 11 meeting did not transpire without major controversy. One of the most significant points of contention involved the refusal of Prime Minister Stephen Harper to include the participation of Governor-General David Johnston in the meeting, thwarting the demand of Chief Spence and a growing number of First Nations leaders and Idle No More supporters. As the Crown's official representative in Canada, the governor-general's roles and responsibilities are today largely symbolic in nature. However, from the perspective of treaty First Nations, securing a meeting with the governor-general would have emphasized the nation-to-nation character of the relationship between First Nations and the Crown. This is especially important given the manner in which Canada has failed to live up to the spirit and intent of these historic agreements. Prime Minister Harper's refusal to concede to Chief Spence's demand on this point signified a refusal by Canada to take the treaty relationship seriously more generally, which was the central point of demanding a meeting with the governor-general's participation to begin with. …

By the last week in January media speculation was beginning to circulate about the possibility of Chief Spence ending her hunger strike after securing a "Declaration of Commitment" by the executive committee of the Assembly of First Nations, the Native Women's Association of Canada, and the caucuses of two of Canada's federal opposition parties, the New Democrats and the Liberals. On January 23 it was confirmed that Chief Spence (along with Raymond Robinson of Cross Lake, Manitoba, who was also on a hunger strike) would be ending her strike the following day. The "Declaration of Commitment" that ended the two hunger strikes was the culmination of a week's worth of negotiations led by Native leader Alvin Fiddler and interim Liberal Party leader Bob Rae. Among the thirteen points of the declaration is a call for a "national inquiry" into the hundreds of cases of murdered and missing Aboriginal women that have gone unsolved in Canada; improving Aboriginal education and housing; fully implementing the United Nations Declaration on the Rights of Indigenous Peoples; reform of the federal government's comprehensive land claims policy; the establishment of an implementation framework for First Nations' treaty rights; and, of course, a comprehensive review of Bill C-45, undertaken with meaningful consultation with Aboriginal peoples.

As I was a close observer of the movement in general and a regular participant in the Idle No More events and teach-ins in the Vancouver area in particular, by late January it had become clear to me that a relative decline in Idle No More's more overt and thus publicly conspicuous forms of protest was underway. Somewhat predictably, this was interpreted by many outlets of Canada's corporate media as a decline in the movement itself. In newspeak, Idle No More had "lost its legs." At that time, I sensed that a moment of pause and critical reflection was underway, yes, but this should not be interpreted as a deterioration of the movement's spirit and resolve. Prime Minister Stephen Harper has stated that, despite the outcry of informed concerns emanating from Indigenous communities and their allies through spring 2013, Bill C-45 is not up for negotiation. Business, in other words, will proceed as usual. As long as the land remains in jeopardy, supporters of movements like Idle No More will continue the struggle. "We're in this for the long haul," explains Pamela Palmater. "It was never meant to be a flashy one month, then go away. This is something that's years in the making. ... You'll see it take different forms at different times, but it's not going away anytime soon." Indeed, the recent escalation and increased public visibility of Indigenous anti-fracking protests in places like Elsipogtog, New Brunswick, along with the ongoing anti-oil sands activism led by Native communities in northern Alberta, and the unrelenting anti-pipeline campaigns mounted by First Nations communities across British Columbia, are a clear demonstration of Indigenous peoples' continued resolve to defend their land and sovereignty from further encroachments by state and capital.

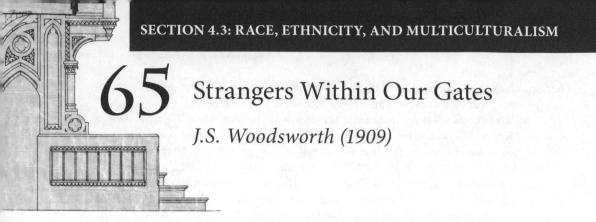

65 Strangers Within Our Gates

J.S. Woodsworth (1909)

EDITORS' INTRODUCTION

James Shaver Woodsworth (1874–1942) was a leading Methodist social reformer and the first leader of the Co-operative Commonwealth Federation (CCF), which would later become the NDP. Though he spent most of his life as an advocate for the poor, the working class, and farmers, his attitudes toward non-whites and Natives were representative of many British Canadians of the time: Asians and blacks were "essentially non-assimilable elements [that] are clearly detrimental to our highest national development, and hence should be vigorously excluded."

Through a variety of legal mechanisms such as legislation and orders in council, non-European immigrants were largely excluded from gaining admission to Canada during the first half of the 20th century, until the introduction of the immigration points system in 1967.

The Problem of Immigration

Immigration and transportation are the two questions of greatest importance to Canada. From the situation, extent and character of the country, transportation must always be one of the leading factors in industrial and commercial development. But as men are greater than things, so immigration is greater than transportation. Canada has many problems, but they all dwindle into insignificance before the one great, commanding, overwhelming problem of immigration. Of vital importance to us are the character, the welfare and the development of the peoples who are to be the people of Canada. …

Just at this stage Canada becomes a field for immigration. Just when restriction leagues are being formed in the United States and rigid immigration laws are being enacted, Canada adopts a "progressive immigration policy," and puts forth every effort to secure immigrants. It is true that our relations with the Mother Land are such that we are receiving a large number of Britishers. But we are also receiving immigrants from all parts of Europe—that is, we are taking our place side by side with the United States as the Old World's dumping ground. As the sluices are closed there, the flood will be diverted to Canada, whatever the policy of

Source: Excerpted from *Strangers Within Our Gates, or Coming Canadians* by J.S. Woodsworth. Toronto: Doreen Stephen Books, 1909.

the Government may happen to be. As the free lands are taken in the United States, and the pressure of population begins to be felt, the flood will flow in upon us as surely as water finds its level. ...

When it is considered how slow is the natural increase in a nation—that is, the excess of births over deaths—it becomes evident what an enormous strain is being put upon our institutions. We, as Canadians, must do in one year what under normal conditions would be spread over many years. Fancy a mother with her own baby to care for adopting half a dozen other babies—some of them, too, of very uncertain tempers!

Fancy a family increased suddenly by the presence of several strange children! What a problem to feed and clothe them—to train them and educate them—to instill into them the family traditions and impart to them the family spirit!

English and Russians, French and Germans, Austrians and Italians, Japanese and Hindus— a mixed multitude, they are being dumped into Canada by a kind of endless chain. They sort themselves out after a fashion, and each seeks to find a corner somewhere. But how shall we weld this heterogeneous mass into one people? That is our problem. ...

Restriction of Immigration

But if we had provision for thorough examination, what standard should we require? In addition to those already in the list of the prohibited, persons of poor physique, persons mentally deficient, the hopelessly incapable, the morally depraved—these surely should be excluded. In this matter our sympathies are divided. We pity the poor man or woman or child who cannot come up to the standard. There may be exceptional cases in which such people would "do well" in Canada. But we cannot but think that we must protect the highest interests of our own land. Each country should be forced to care for its own criminals, paupers and diseased. To relieve any country of the burden is only to delay the application of measures that will abolish the conditions which produce these classes.

But there is here a larger question—the advisability or the justifiability of excluding not merely certain individuals, but certain classes. There is the live question of the Orientals on the Pacific Coast. The Chinese, Japanese and Hindus are—or the majority of them are— physically and mentally "fit." They are in no sense paupers or incapables. Indeed, one of the most frequent and serious charges against them is that they are able to drive out other labour. Should they be excluded—if so, on what grounds? Much has been said on both sides. There is, no doubt, a national prejudice that should be overcome. On the other hand, the expression, "This is a white man's country," has deeper significance than we sometimes imagine.

The advocates for admission argue that we ought not to legislate against a particular class or nation, and that the Orientals are needed to develop the resources of the country. Their opponents believe that white labourers cannot compete with Orientals, that the standard of living will be lowered, and white men driven out, and they claim that a nation has the right to protect itself.

Needless to say, the economic aspects are those that really divide men on this subject, for, generally speaking, capitalists and employers are ranged against the labour party. Perhaps in the early stages of development, Chinese labour was necessary. Perhaps, for some time, the presence of a limited number of Orientals may be advantageous. But it does seem that the exclusionists are right in their contention that labourers working and living as the Orientals do, will displace European labourers. It is generally agreed that the two races are not likely to "mix." Ultimately, then, the question resolves itself into the desirability of a white caste and a yellow, or black caste, existing side by side, or above and below, in the same country. We confess that the idea of a homogeneous people seems in accord with our democratic institutions and conducive to the general welfare. This need not exclude small communities of black or red or yellow peoples. It is well to remember that we are not the only people on earth. The idealist may still dream of a final state of development, when white and black and red and yellow hall have ceased to exist, or have become merged into some neutral gray. We may love all men and yet prefer to maintain our own family life. ...

We, in Canada, have certain more or less clearly defined ideals of national well-being. These ideals must never be lost sight of. Non-ideal elements there must be, but they should be capable of assimilation. Essentially non-assimilable elements are clearly detrimental to our highest national development, and hence should be vigorously excluded.

Royal Commission on Bilingualism and Biculturalism

66

A. Davidson Dunton and André Laurendeau (1967)

EDITORS' INTRODUCTION

The Royal Commission on Bilingualism and Biculturalism, often referred to as "The B&B Commission," was established in 1963 by Prime Minister Lester B. Pearson with an original mandate "to inquire into and report upon the existing state of bilingualism and biculturalism in Canada and then recommend what steps should be taken to develop the Canadian Confederation on the basis of an equal partnership between the two founding races." However, partly as a result of pressure from Ukrainian Canadians, the commission also examined "the contribution made by other ethnic groups to the cultural enrichment of Canada and the measures which should be taken to safeguard that contribution." The commission's report was delivered in several stages between 1965 and 1970. The excerpt below is from the 1967 book entitled The Official Languages.

Equal Partnership or "Le Principe d'Égalité"

The languages and cultures of this country can be thought of in many different ways. However, our mandate clearly states the problem in terms of equality: it postulates an "equal partnership between the two founding races" ("le principe de l'égalité entre les deux peuples fondateurs"). As we understand our mandate, this equality should be the equal partnership not only of the two peoples which founded Confederation but also of each of their respective languages and cultures. What we are aiming for, then, is the equal partnership of all who speak either language and participate in either culture, whatever their ethnic origin. For us the principle of equal partnership takes priority over all historical and legal considerations, regardless of how interesting and important such considerations may be. ...

Equality from the Individual Point of View

Just as the equality of all before the law cannot do away with all inequalities (notably those of intelligence, courage, health, and education), equality between the two dominant languages and cultures cannot mean absolute equality of the members of both groups. The point at issue is essentially equality of opportunity, but a *real equality of opportunity*—an equality

Source: Excerpted from *Royal Commission on Bilingualism and Biculturalism*. Ottawa: Government of Canada, 1967.

ensuring that the fact of speaking English or French would be neither a help nor a handicap to a person seeking entry into the institutions affecting our individual and collective life.

We have deliberately outlined this ideal in absolute terms, which some people will consider over-simplified, in order to emphasize the great gap which separates the cultural groups. The members of a privileged group living under almost perfect conditions are tempted to take their situation for granted and not to stop to consider what others are missing. Members of the underprivileged group may reach a greater or lesser degree of alienation, and so become unaware of their cultural underdevelopment or of the hybrid nature of their culture, not to mention the inferiority complex which so often inhibits them and makes them feel inadequate.

Some analyses in this Report will show that cultural equality, as understood here, hardly exists between Canada's two main language groups. Indeed, if the facts are examined in the light of the norms that we have suggested, one may be tempted to despair of establishing the conditions for equality which form the main theme of this Report. At the very least, we must be realistic. We have no intention of proposing the impossible; it will never be possible for the members of the two main cultural groups to enjoy the advantages described above throughout the country on an equal footing. We first must see to what extent the wide gulf between current reality and an ideal cultural equality can be reduced. Inevitably in some areas there will be a striking gap between the state of affairs described and the recommendations offered for its reform. Political decisions cannot rapidly or radically change a long-standing state of affairs or old ways of thinking. We are sufficiently aware of this fact not to propose arbitrary measures based on abstract theory rather than on realities. A realistic approach avoids the possibility of unrealistic expectations among members of the minority; it also invites breadth of vision from the majority, which should be more aware than before that it will in any case always be in a privileged position. ...

The principle of equality implies respect for the idea of minority status, both in the country as a whole and in each of its regions. Within the provinces or small administrative entities, both Anglophones and Francophones live in some cases as a majority, in some cases as a minority. Since the English-speaking population is larger across the country, its members are less often in the minority; but they are the minority in some areas, especially in the province of Quebec. The Francophones are usually in the minority outside Quebec. In either case, however, the principle of equality requires that the minority receive generous treatment.

This proposal may seem Utopian, but is it really so? Recognizing the rights of a linguistic minority does not reduce those of the majority: with a little good will, the rights of both can be exercised without serious conflict, as is clearly demonstrated by the examples of Switzerland and Finland. In other words, a majority does not abdicate when it resolves to take a minority into consideration; it remains the majority, with the advantages its situation implies, while at the same time demonstrating its humanity.

This is political wisdom too. The history of countries with more than one language and culture shows how often rigid attitudes held by majorities have made common life difficult, if not impossible. The use of force, in any circumstances, results in either revolt or submission. Besides, for the majority to hold back from acts within its power or to allow events it would be able to prevent, out of respect for the minority, is not a product of weakness but a step forward in civilization. In this spirit too will we approach the matter of the other minorities.

We must work to develop and consolidate existing situations where they provide the possibility of establishing a certain equilibrium between the two communities. We know that Anglophones form the majority in nine of the ten provinces of Canada; Francophones the majority in Quebec. This is a state of affairs which should be turned to account. Indeed, the concentration of more than 4,000,000 Francophones in a single province is the only factor which gives some reality, at the outset, to the concept of equal partnership. Quebec constitutes an environment where the aspirations and the needs of four out of five Francophones in Canada can be satisfied. The mere fact of this concentration leads to a spontaneous French way of life and makes that way of life easier to organize. This is why we believe the place of the Québécois in the French fact in Canada will in practice have to be recognized much more than it is today; we are thinking particularly of the world of work, in the federal public sector and in the private sector. But there is also a political aspect: Quebec is the only province where French-speaking Canadians are in the majority and the English-speaking in the minority. Here the weight of numbers favours the Francophones, and it is a powerful lever. They can exercise a preponderant influence in their own province; they can also make themselves heard by the rest of the country, especially in the federal Parliament, and thus take an active part in the life of Canada. Of course there are risks involved. The problem can be succinctly formulated. How can we integrate the new Quebec into present-day Canada, without curbing Quebec's forward drive and, at the same time, without risking the breaking up of the country?

All these facts combine to give Quebec a leading role in promoting the French language and culture in Canada, whatever may be the political solution finally adopted. This conclusion is in the nature of things; it is not the outcome of ideology or some messianic notion. In this sense it is an obvious and incontrovertible fact that Quebec is not "a province like the others."

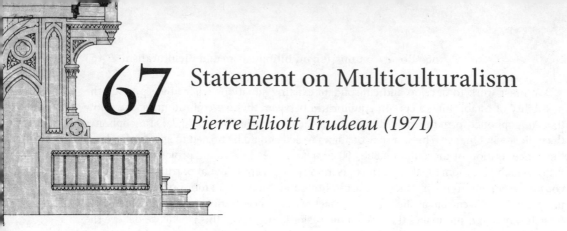

67 Statement on Multiculturalism

Pierre Elliott Trudeau (1971)

EDITORS' INTRODUCTION

Many attribute the birth of multiculturalism to Prime Minister Pierre Trudeau. In this speech to the House of Commons in 1971, Trudeau advocates the official recognition of Canadian multiculturalism for the first time, suggesting that diversity and pluralism are integral parts of Canadian identity. Coming on the heels of the Royal Commission on Bilingualism and Biculturalism, some scholars contend that Trudeau introduced Canadian multiculturalism in order to counter the "compact thesis" of Quebec nationalists that Canada is a compact between two founding peoples. Though some government programming followed this statement, the Canadian government did not pass the Multiculturalism Act until 1988. However, this original invocation of the idea of a multicultural Canada had powerful symbolic value.

House of Commons

Friday, October 8, 1971

ROUTINE PROCEEDINGS
Canadian Culture

Announcement of Implementation of Policy of Multiculturalism Within Bilingual Framework

Right Hon. P.E. Trudeau (Prime Minister): Mr. Speaker, I am happy this morning to be able to reveal to the House that the government has accepted all those recommendations of the Royal Commission on Bilingualism and Biculturalism which are contained in Volume IV of its reports directed to federal departments and agencies. Hon. members will recall that the subject of this volume is "the contribution by other ethnic groups to the cultural enrichment of Canada and the measures that should be taken to safeguard that contribution."

Volume IV examined the whole question of cultural and ethnic pluralism in this country and the status of our various cultures and languages, an area of study given all too little attention in the past by scholars.

It was the view of the royal commission, shared by the government and, I am sure, by all Canadians, that there cannot be one cultural policy for Canadians of British and French

Source: *House of Commons Debates*, 3rd Session, 28th Parliament, vol. VIII. Ottawa: Government of Canada, 1971.

origin, another for the original peoples and yet a third for all others. For although there are two official languages, there is no official culture, nor does any ethnic group take precedence over any other. No citizen or group of citizens is other than Canadian, and all should be treated fairly.

The royal commission was guided by the belief that adherence to one's ethnic group is influenced not so much by one's origin or mother tongue as by one's sense of belonging to the group, and by what the commission calls the group's "collective will to exist." The government shares this belief.

The individual's freedom would be hampered if he were locked for life within a particular cultural compartment by the accident of birth or language. It is vital, therefore, that every Canadian, whatever his ethnic origin, be given a chance to learn at least one of the two languages in which his country conducts its official business and its politics.

A policy of multiculturalism within a bilingual framework commends itself to the government as the most suitable means of assuring the cultural freedom of Canadians. Such a policy should help to break down discriminatory attitudes and cultural jealousies. National unity if it is to mean anything in the deeply personal sense, must be founded on confidence in one's own individual identity; out of this can grow respect for that of others and a willingness to share ideas, attitudes and assumptions. A vigorous policy of multiculturalism will help create this initial confidence. It can form the base of a society which is based on fair play for all.

The government will support and encourage the various cultures and ethnic groups that give structure and vitality to our society. They will be encouraged to share their cultural expression and values with other Canadians and so contribute to a richer life for us all.

In the past, substantial public support has been given largely to the arts and cultural institutions of English-speaking Canada. More recently and largely with the help of the royal commission's earlier recommendations in Volumes I to III, there has been a conscious effort on the government's part to correct any bias against the French language and culture. In the last few months the government has taken steps to provide funds to support cultural educational centres for native people. The policy I am announcing today accepts the contention of the other cultural communities that they, too, are essential elements in Canada and deserve government assistance in order to contribute to regional and national life in ways that derive from their heritage yet are distinctively Canadian.

In implementing a policy of multiculturalism within a bilingual framework, the government will provide support in four ways.

First, resources permitting, the government will seek to assist all Canadian cultural groups that have demonstrated a desire and effort to continue to develop a capacity to grow and contribute to Canada, and a clear need for assistance, the small and weak groups no less than the strong and highly organized.

Second, the government will assist members of all cultural groups to overcome cultural barriers to full participation in Canadian society.

Third, the government will promote creative encounters and interchange among all Canadian cultural groups in the interest of national unity.

Fourth, the government will continue to assist immigrants to acquire at least one of Canada's official languages in order to become full participants in Canadian society. ...

In conclusion, I wish to emphasize the view of the government that a policy of multiculturalism within a bilingual framework is basically the conscious support of individual freedom of choice. We are free to be ourselves. But this cannot be left to chance. It must be fostered and pursued actively. If freedom of choice is in danger for some ethnic groups, it is in danger for all. It is the policy of this government to eliminate such danger and to "safeguard" this freedom.

The Ambiguities of a Bilingual and Multicultural Canada

68

Guy Rocher (1972)

EDITORS' INTRODUCTION

In awarding him the Molson Prize in the Social Sciences and Humanities, the Canada Council said this of Guy Rocher of the Université de Montréal:

> *[He] is a scholar, a teacher, a visionary and a builder. As a scholar, he has been a pioneer in the sociology of education, law and medical ethics both nationally and internationally. His extra-ordinary scientific production continues to grow with each passing year. As a teacher, he has trained tens of thousands of sociology students in Canada and throughout the world through his teachings and publications of an exemplary lucidity and clarity of thought. As a visionary and builder, he was an instigator and designer of the educational, social and cultural modernization of contemporary Quebec.*

> *In the following excerpt from a 1972 article, Rocher analyzes the consequences of the Trudeau government's unveiling of its multiculturalism policy in October 1971. He argues that multiculturalism is a new vision for Canada and a significant departure from the traditional historical-sociological interpretation that the country originated in two communities— anglophone and francophone. Given this shift in the national conception of Canadian society, Rocher warns that there are several unforeseen dangers that multiculturalism poses to the future of the country.*

This official stand of the Canadian government constitutes an important innovation: it breaks with the image of a unitary country as well as with that of a bicultural one. Moreover, it is an innovation which has substantial practical consequences, realized in the form of the investment of millions of dollars in various programs designed to support Canadian cultural diversity.

Source: Excerpted from Guy Rocher, "Les ambiguïtés d'un Canada bilingue et multicultural," *Revue de l'Association canadienne d'éducation de langue française*, vol. 1, no. 3 (septembre 1972). Translated in *Cultural Diversity and Canadian Education: Issues and Innovations*, edited by John R. Mallea and Jonathan C. Young. Ottawa: Carleton University Press/McGill-Queen's University Press, 1984. Reprinted by permission.

The Bases for This New Position

Let us attempt to pursue in somewhat greater depth the analysis of this evolution of the Canadian government's view. Apart from the political, or even electoral, aims which were imputed to the Trudeau government, how does the government justify its innovation?

It seems to me that, in contrast to the Pearson government and the Commission on Bilingualism and Biculturalism, the image of Canada put forward by the Trudeau government has a new foundation or a new base. The Laurendeau-Dunton Commission and the Pearson government position was based on a point of view which was both historical and sociological. The concept of two nations was supported by two facts, one historical and the other sociological. First, it was seen that, historically, the country originated in two communities—anglophone and francophone—which provided the principal social and political structures still in evidence. Secondly, it was recognized that new Canadians integrate with one or the other of these two communities, both from the linguistic and from the cultural standpoint, even though they may maintain links with the culture of the country from which they or their forefathers emigrated.

In contrast, the Trudeau government's position relies on what I would call psycho-sociological foundations. The document of October 8, 1971 expresses it as follows:

> One of man's fundamental needs is a feeling of belonging, and much of our contemporary social malaise—among all age groups—exists because this need has not been met. Ethnic groups are by no means the only means of satisfying this need to belong, but they have played a very important role in Canadian society. Ethnic pluralism can help us to overcome or to avoid the homogenization or depersonalization of a mass society. Vital ethnic groups can give second-, third- and later-generation Canadians the feeling that they are linked to the traditions and peoples of various parts of the world and various periods of time.

The ethnic community thus appears to the Trudeau government as one of the primary groups able to fulfill contemporary man's need for identity and security, and to counter the anonymity and anomie of the mass society.

It is also through an appeal to social psychology that the document explains how multiculturalism can simultaneously serve Canadian unity; "The greater our feeling of security in a given social context, the more we are free to explore our identity outside this context. Ethnic groups give people a feeling of belonging which enables them to face society better than they could as isolated individuals. Fidelity to one's own culture does not necessarily, and does not usually, diminish the even greater fidelity towards the collectivity and towards the country."

This distinction between the historico-sociological foundations and the psycho-sociological foundations of an image of Canada may seem theoretical. However, it does indeed appear to be at the source of two very different concepts of Canada. The first emphasizes the central role of two original communities, to which is grafted the cultural impact of all the other ethnic groups. The second emphasizes instead the multiplicity of the ethnic groups, their absolute cultural as well as political equality, within the framework of Canada's official bilingualism.

The Dangers Inherent in This Position

I now wish to develop the reasons why I feel this concept of Canadian society to be ambiguous, faulty and dangerous in its longer-term implications. I have three principal objections:

Bilingualism

First, the distinction between language and culture constitutes one of the most debatable basic implications of the Trudeau government's position. Official bilingualism for Canada is thus detached from the cultural support upon which it relied up to now. In particular, official bilingualism, which as is known only too well, has practically no sociological roots since the majority of Canadians, whether anglophone or francophone, are not bilingual, takes on a very artificial character. Within the new context of multiculturalism, the fragile Canadian bilingualism likely risks being only a vestige of a past which can easily be abandoned or possibly denied. Bilingualism could have had some meaning inasmuch as it symbolized the marriage of two linguistic and cultural communities within Canadian Confederation. But when this idea of two cultural communities is abandoned in favour of Canada's multicultural nature, bilingualism becomes an abstraction, the symbol of a past which no longer corresponds to the present. Under these conditions, it can be foreseen that maintaining a bilingualism with such shallow roots will be found to be more and more difficult. In setting aside the historical basis for biculturalism, one will soon find no reason to maintain an artificial bilingualism. It may then be that Canada can be defined just as well as a unilingual country, or as a country where four, five or six languages are official.

It is not necessary to go far afield to find the ambiguities of bilingualism in a multicultural context; they appear in the Trudeau government statement of October 8, 1971. While proclaiming the distinction between language and culture, the Trudeau government announced that it would "take measures with a view to supplying educational materials for a non-official language. ... Acquiring the language of one's forefathers is an important part of the development of a cultural identity." Here we see the Trudeau government recognize the link between language and culture, after denying this same link when it was a question of biculturalism and bilingualism. Furthermore, the federal government announced that it would do something for non-official languages which it has never done in establishing French in education outside Quebec. The logical outcome of the policy set out by the Trudeau government is the imminent establishment of multilingualism to replace bilingualism.

In Montreal, there already exists the kind of bilingualism which the policy of multiculturalism will lead to. Among new Canadians, the bilingualism currently practised is English–Greek, English–Italian, English–German bilingualism; English–French bilingualism is almost non-existent.

National Identity

The second important reservation which I have with respect to multiculturalism is that I do not believe it constitutes the basis for a nation. The Canadian nation, as defined by the Trudeau government, no longer has a central cultural core which is clearly identifiable. Canada would be a sort of microcosm or meeting-place for all the nations of the world, represented here by groups of greater or lesser numerical size, all having an equal right to recognition and financial support of the Canadian government. Canada probably could have been greatly enriched if it had been able to maintain the idea of two cultural communities serving as poles for groupings of the other ethnic groups. Instead of this, there is proposed to us a nebulous sort of image constituted by an undefined number of different cultures, which the Trudeau government would wish to see interact but to which it proposes no common denominator.

I perceive a sense of failure in this stance taken by the Trudeau government: it is recognized that there is no Canadian culture, either anglophone or francophone. Whereas the idea of biculturalism put forward the image of a Canada with a certain internal structure, the concept of multiculturalism offers us the absence of a national culture as its program. I wonder what kind of nation can really exist on a basis which is so fluid and so noncommittal.

The Francophone Community

Finally, I wish to emphasize very briefly that, for the French-Canadian community, this new multicultural policy is a large step backwards which has as yet, I think, gone unrecognized by French Canadians. For several generations, French Canadians have struggled to gain a recognition of a bilingualism which would not only be a recognition of French as an official language, but at the same time a recognition of the French-Canadian community as the counterpart of the English-Canadian community in the Canadian sociological structure. By detaching bilingualism from biculturalism, the Trudeau government betrays all the hopes which French Canadians could have placed in bilingualism as they perceived it; that is, closely linked to the biculturalism of which it was both a symbol and an essential condition.

Of the two main linguistic and cultural communities, anglophone and francophone, it is obviously the francophone community which will suffer the most from this new multicultural policy, and which can feel threatened by it. In reality, since the anglophone community is predominant everywhere but in Quebec, and even there is also very powerful, it will necessarily remain the centre of attraction for all the other ethnic cultures. On the other hand, in this new context the francophone community will see its position and its status decline rapidly. With economic forces already acting to its disadvantage, it will become more and more secondary in the midst of all the other cultures which will compose the new Canadian mosaic.

It is my personal belief that, as French Canadians become aware of this new situation, the Quebec separatist option will appear to be a desirable solution to an increasing number of French Canadians. I fear that the cultural fragmentation proposed to us by the October 1971 declaration of the Canadian government will in fact prove a plan for destroying Canadian Confederation. A multicultural Canada offers too few chances for the future survival and flourishing of the French-Canadian culture. The creation of an independent francophone Quebec will then appear to be the one final chance for a North American francophone nation whose future is inevitably uncertain.

Bouchard-Taylor Report on Accommodation Practices in Quebec

Gérard Bouchard and Charles Taylor
(2008)

EDITORS' INTRODUCTION

After a series of politically charged events in Quebec that brought the relationship between multiculturalism and secularism into question, the Consultation Commission on Accommodation Practices Related to Cultural Differences was established by the province in February 2007. It had a mandate that included taking stock of accommodation practices in Quebec, conducting extensive consultations, and formulating recommendations to the government to ensure that accommodation practices conform to the pluralistic, democratic, and egalitarian values of Quebec society.

As the report authors noted in their introduction, "As was readily apparent in the fall of 2007, Quebecers are divided. This is the very first observation arising from the public and private consultations that we conducted. It is also apparent from the findings of surveys conducted in recent years. Quebecers are divided over accommodation but also over most of the questions pertaining to it." They add that "[we] well know that not everyone will agree with our conclusions," but stress that "the time has come for reconciliation."

Summary of the Full Report

I. Mandate and Investigation

A. MANDATE

On February 8, 2007, Québec Premier Jean Charest announced the establishment of the Consultation Commission on Accommodation Practices Related to Cultural Differences in response to public discontent concerning reasonable accommodation. The Order in Council establishing the Commission stipulated that it had a mandate to: *a)* take stock of accommodation practices in Québec; *b)* analyse the attendant issues bearing in mind the experience of other societies; *c)* conduct an extensive consultation on this topic; and *d)* formulate recommendations to the government to ensure that accommodation practices conform to Québec's values as a pluralistic, democratic, egalitarian society.

Source: Excerpted from *Building the Future: A Time for Reconciliation*. Report for the Consultation Commission on Accommodation Practices Related to Cultural Differences. Quebec City: Government of the Province of Quebec, 2008.

We could have broached the Commission's mandate in two ways, i.e. in a broad sense or in a narrow sense. The narrower sense would consist in confining the Commission's investigation to the strictly legal dimension of reasonable accommodation. The second approach would be to perceive the debate on reasonable accommodation as the symptom of a more basic problem concerning the sociocultural integration model established in Québec since the 1970s. This perspective called for a review of interculturalism, immigration, secularism and the theme of Québec identity. We decided to follow the second course in order to grasp the problem at its source and from all angles, with particular emphasis on its economic and social dimensions. The school-to-work transition and professional recognition, access to decent living conditions and the fight against discrimination are indeed essential conditions for ensuring the cultural integration of all citizens into Québec society.

B. OUR INVESTIGATION

The Commission had at its disposal a budget of $5 million, which enabled it to carry out a number of activities. We commissioned 13 research projects carried out by specialists from Québec universities. A number of research instruments were developed, including a typology designed to classify the arguments in the briefs submitted and the e-mails that we analysed. We organized 31 focus groups with individuals from different milieus in Montréal and the regions. We held 59 meetings with experts and representatives of sociocultural organizations. We also set up an advisory committee comprising 15 specialists from various disciplines.

As for the public consultations, we commissioned four province-wide forums, organized by the Institut du Nouveau Monde, in which over 800 people participated. The Commission held sessions in 15 regions, in addition to Montréal, for a total of 31 days of hearings. The public responded very generously to our appeal by submitting more than 900 briefs. We read all of these texts and discussed them with their authors during 328 hearings, during which we heard testimony from 241 individuals. In the centres where hearings were held, we organized 22 evening citizens' forums open without restriction to the public and broadcast live or pre-recorded by a number of television networks, which attracted a total of 3 423 participants. Each forum, which lasted for nearly three hours, afforded, on average, 40 participants from all social backgrounds to take the floor and express their opinions. Between August 2007 and January 2008, the Commission also operated a Website that afforded the public opportunities to engage in exchanges (over 400,000 visits). ...

II. Sources of the Accommodation Crisis

A. A CRISIS OF PERCEPTION

After a year of research and consultation, we have come to the conclusion that the foundations of collective life in Québec are not in a critical situation. Our investigation did not reveal to us a striking or sudden increase in the adjustments or accommodation that public institutions allow, nor did we observe that the normal operation of our institutions would have been disrupted by such requests, which is eloquently confirmed by the very small number of accommodation cases that ends up before the courts.

We also observed a certain discrepancy between practices in the field, especially in the education and health sectors, and the feeling of discontent that has arisen among Quebecers. An analysis of debate on the question of accommodation in Québec reveals that 55% of the cases noted over the past 22 years, i.e. 40 cases out of 73, were brought to the public's attention during the period March 2006 to June 2007 alone. The investigation of the cases that received the most widespread media attention during this period of turmoil reveals that, in 15 of 21 cases, there were striking distortions between general public perceptions and the actual facts as we were able to reconstitute them. In other words, the negative perception of reasonable accommodation that spread in the public often centred on an erroneous or partial perception of practices in the field. Our report describes several cases that confirm this conclusion.

B. ANXIETY OVER IDENTITY

Sudden media enthusiasm and rumours contributed to the crisis of perception, although they alone cannot explain the current of dissatisfaction that spread among a large portion of the population. The so-called wave of accommodation clearly touched a number of emotional chords among French-Canadian Quebecers in such a way that requests for religious adjustments have spawned fears about the most valuable heritage of the Quiet Revolution, in particular gender equality and secularism. The result has been an identity counter-reaction movement that has expressed itself through the rejection of harmonization practices. Among some Quebecers, this counter-reaction targets immigrants, who have become, to some extent, scapegoats. What has just happened in Québec gives the impression of a face-off between two minority groups, each of which is asking the other to accommodate it. The members of the ethnocultural majority are afraid of being swamped by fragile minorities that are worried about their future. The conjunction of these two anxieties is obviously not likely to foster integration in a spirit of equality and reciprocity.

We can conclude that Quebecers of French-Canadian ancestry are still not at ease with their twofold status as a majority in Québec and a minority in Canada and North America. However, we should also point out that a number of Western nations are experiencing malaises that resemble those expressed during debate on accommodation. A comparison of the situation in Québec with that in several European countries reveals that a number of fears that may be warranted elsewhere are not necessarily justified here.

III. Social Norms

One of the key sources of anxiety mentioned during our consultations concerns the putative absence of guidelines to handle accommodation or adjustment requests. However, over the years, Québec society has adopted an array of norms and guidelines that form the basis of a "common public culture." In our report, we allude to these reference points that must guide the process of evaluating requests, with particular emphasis on the social norms that would benefit from clarification, more specifically as regards integration, intercultural relations and open secularism.

A. REASONABLE ACCOMMODATION AND CONCERTED ADJUSTMENT

The field of harmonization practices is complex and there is more than one way to define and delineate it. Among the criteria, we have decided to give priority to the framework for handling requests, which leads us to distinguish between the legal route and the citizen route. Under the legal route, requests must conform to formal codified procedures that the parties bring against each other and that ultimately decree a winner and a loser. Indeed, the courts impose decisions most of the time. The legal route is that of reasonable accommodation. Requests follow a much different route under the second path, which is less formal and relies on negotiation and the search for a compromise. Its objective is to find a solution that satisfies both parties and it corresponds to concerted adjustment.

Generally speaking, we strongly favour recourse to the citizen route and concerted adjustment, for several reasons: *a)* it is good for citizens to learn to manage their differences and disagreements; *b)* this path avoids congesting the courts; and *c)* the values underlying the citizen route (exchanges, negotiation, reciprocity, and so on) are the same ones that underpin the Québec integration model. In quantitative terms, we have noted, moreover, that most requests follow the citizen route and only a small number rely on the courts.

Moreover, our investigation revealed that, in the case of both the citizen route and the legal route, the fear of a domino effect is unfounded. Indeed, several criteria allow us to evaluate accommodation or adjustment requests. Such requests may be rejected if they lead to what jurists call undue hardship, i.e. an unreasonable cost, a disruption of the organization's or the establishment's operations, the infringement of other people's rights or the undermining of security or public order. A number of public institutions have already sought inspiration in the legal guideline of undue hardship to define evaluation methods that take into account their distinctive features. We also observed that many milieus have acquired solid expertise in the realm of intercultural relations and harmonization practices.

B. INTERCULTURALISM

Often mentioned in academic papers, interculturalism as an integration policy has never been fully, officially defined by the Québec government, although its underlying principles were formulated long ago. This shortcoming should be overcome, all the more so as the Canadian multiculturalism model does not appear to be well adapted to conditions in Québec.

Generally speaking, it is in the interests of any community to maintain a minimum of cohesion. It is subject to that condition that a community can adopt common orientations, ensure participation by citizens in public debate, create the feeling of solidarity required for an egalitarian society to function smoothly, mobilize the population in the event of a crisis, and take advantage of the enrichment that stems from ethnocultural diversity. For a small nation such as Québec, constantly concerned about its future as a cultural minority, integration also represents a condition for its development, or perhaps for its survival.

That is why the integrative dimension is a key component of Québec interculturalism. According to the descriptions provided in scientific documentation, interculturalism seeks to reconcile ethnocultural diversity with the continuity of the French-speaking core and the preservation of the social link. It thus affords security to Quebecers of French-Canadian origin and to ethnocultural minorities and protects the rights of all in keeping with the liberal tradition. By instituting French as the common public language, it establishes a framework in society for communication and exchanges. It has the virtue of being flexible and receptive to negotiation, adaptation and innovation.

C. OPEN SECULARISM

Liberal democracies, including Québec, all adhere to the principle of secularism, which can nonetheless be embodied in different systems. Any secular system achieves some form of balance between the following four principles: 1. the moral equality of persons; 2. freedom of conscience and religion; 3. the separation of Church and State; and 4. State neutrality in respect of religious and deep-seated secular convictions.

Certain systems impose fairly strict limits on freedom of religious expression. For example, France recently adopted restrictive legislation governing the wearing of religious signs in public schools. There are three reasons why we believe that this type of restrictive secularism is not appropriate for Québec: a) it does not truly link institutional structures to the outcomes of secularism; b) the attribution to the school of an emancipatory mission directed against religion is not compatible with the principle of State neutrality in respect of religion and non-religion; c) the integration process in a diversified society is achieved through exchanges between citizens, who thus learn to get to know each other (that is the philosophy of Québec interculturalism), and not by relegating identities to the background.

Open secularism, which we are advocating, seeks to develop the essential outcomes of secularism (first and second principles) by defining institutional structures (third and fourth principles) in light of this objective. This is the path that Québec has followed historically, as witnessed by the Proulx report, which also promotes open secularism.

IV. Harmonization Practices: Elements of a Policy

In light of the social norms that we delineate in our report, we are proposing a number of general key directions aimed at guiding the interveners and individual Quebecers concerned by harmonization practices. However, it is important to note that adjustment requests must be evaluated on a case-by-case basis and that there may be exceptions to general rules.

1. Pursuant to the norms and guidelines that we are formulating, adjustment requests that infringe gender equality would have little chance of being granted, since such equality is a core value in our society. In the health care sector as in all public services, this value disqualifies, in principle, all requests that have the effect of granting a woman inferior status to that of a man.

2. Coeducation is an important value in Québec society but it is not as fundamental as gender equality. As a general guideline, coeducation should, however, prevail everywhere possible, for example when students are divided into classes, in swimming classes, and so on.

3. As for prayer rooms in public establishments, our position reflects the opinion that the Commission des droits de la personne et des droits de la jeunesse adopted on February 3, 2006. The opinion states that educational establishments are not obliged to set up permanent prayer rooms. However, it is entirely in keeping with the spirit of adjustments to authorize for the purpose of prayer the use of rooms that are temporarily unoccupied. Certain exceptions are made in the case of penitentiaries, hospitals or airports since the individuals who must remain there are not free to visit a church if they so desire.

4. Still in keeping with the notion of the separation of Church and State, we believe that the crucifix must be removed from the wall of the National Assembly, which, indeed, is the very place that symbolizes the constitutional state (a reasonable alternative would be to display it in a room devoted to the history of Parliament). For the same reason, the saying of prayers at municipal council meetings should be abandoned in

the many municipalities where this ritual is still practised. On the other hand, the installation of an erub does not infringe the neutrality of the State and thus may be authorized provided that it does not inconvenience other people.

5. The same reasoning leads to respect for dietary prohibitions and to allow in class the wearing of an Islamic headscarf, a kippah or a turban. The same is true of the wearing of the headscarf in sports competitions if it does not jeopardize the individual's safety. It should be noted that all of these authorizations promote integration into our society.

6. Applicants who are intransigent, reject negotiation and go against the rule of reciprocity will seriously compromise their approach, e.g. this would be true of a student who refused any compromise concerning dress to participate in a swimming class.

7. Requests must seek to protect or restore a right. Thus, we believe that non-Christian religious holidays are legitimate since they rectify an inequality. Conversely, requests must not infringe other people's rights. This criterion forbids the exclusion of certain scientific works in a classroom library or opposition by a parent to a blood transfusion necessary for his child's survival.

8. In keeping with the aim of the education system, students must not be exempted from compulsory courses. However, a student may be authorized to abandon a music course for another equivalent course in the case of an optional activity.

V. An Evolving Québec

Regardless of the choices that our society makes to meld cultural differences and contemplate a common future, such choices will be largely doomed to failure if several conditions are not present.

1. Our society must combat underemployment, poverty, inequality, intolerable living conditions and various forms of discrimination.

2. French-speaking Québec must not succumb to fear, the temptation to withdraw and reject, nor don the mantle of a victim. It must reject the scenario of inevitable disappearance, which has no future.

3. Another mistake would be to conceive the future of pluriethnicity as so many juxtaposed separate groups perceived as individual islets, which would mean replicating in Québec what is the most severely criticized in multiculturalism.

4. French-Canadian Quebecers have unpleasant memories of the period when the clergy wielded excessive power over institutions and individuals. It would be unfair that this situation leads them to direct at all religions the painful feeling inherited from their Catholic past.

5. Quebecers of French-Canadian origin must also be more aware of the repercussions on minority groups of their anxieties. Minority groups have undoubtedly been alerted recently by the image of an ethnocultural majority that is apparently unsure of itself and subject to outbursts of temper.

However, several factors seem to bode well for the edification of a promising future. The upcoming generations are displaying considerable openness in their way of perceiving and experiencing intercultural relations. A number of recent surveys have not revealed a clear rift between Montréal and the regions from the standpoint of perceptions of accommodation. Reliable studies reveal that, contrary to certain perceptions, the Montréal area is not ghettoized. We believe that the process of edifying a common identity is firmly under way in numerous areas that must be emphasized, i.e. the use of French, the sharing of common values, the promotion of a Québec collective memory, intercommunity initiatives, civic participation, artistic and literary creation, and the adoption of collective symbols. In keeping with the rule of law and the imperatives of pluralism, the identity that we are edifying must be able to develop as a citizen culture, and all Quebecers must be able to invest in it, recognize themselves in it and develop in it.

VI. Priority Recommendations

To conclude, our recommendations focus on five key themes:

1. First of all, they call for a definition of new policies or programs pertaining to interculturalism (legislation, a declaration or a policy statement) and secularism (a proposed white paper).
2. Several recommendations are linked to the central theme of integration and focus primarily on: *a)* recognition of immigrants' skills and diplomas; *b)* francization programs; *c)* the need for more sustained efforts to regionalize immigration; and *d)* the need for enhanced coordination between government departments.
3. From the standpoint of intercultural practices and mutual understanding, our recommendations highlight: *a)* the need for broader training of all government agents in public institutions, starting with the schools, because of the role they play in socialization and *b)* the need to further encourage community and intercommunity action projects.
4. In keeping with the harmonization policy formulated in our report, our recommendations are intended to foster the accountability of interveners in the citizen sphere (public and private agencies) by ensuring that they have received adequate training. We are asking the government to ensure that the practical knowledge acquired in institutions be recorded, promoted and disseminated in all of the milieus concerned.
5. Another priority field is the fight against inequality and discrimination. Our recommendations in this respect focus primarily on: *a)* the under-representation of ethnic minorities in the government; *b)* the urgency of combating the numerous forms of discrimination, Islamophobia, anti-Semitism and the racism to which racialized groups, especially Blacks, are subject; *c)* the support to be offered immigrant women; *d)* the need to increase the resources of the Commission des droits de la personne et des droits de la jeunesse; and *e)* the strengthening of economic and social rights in the Québec Charter.

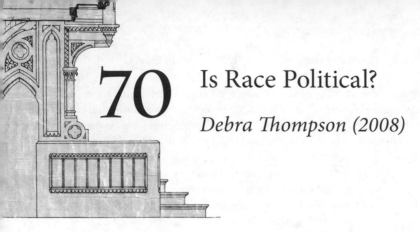

70 Is Race Political?

Debra Thompson (2008)

EDITORS' INTRODUCTION

Debra Thompson is an assistant professor of African American studies at Northwestern University. Her primary research interests are racial and ethnic politics, Canadian politics, and American political development. The article excerpted here won the 2008 John McMenemy Prize for best article published in the Canadian Journal of Political Science.

Though it is commonly accepted that the concept of race is a social construction—that is, that race is a social and historical product of human cognition, with little or no biological basis—this excerpt examines the ways in which the laws and policies of the Canadian state, both historically and contemporarily, have created and reproduced the idea of race over time.

Given that race is a political construction, Thompson asks, why then do scholars of English-Canadian political science so rarely include it as a focus of their research? She suggests that there are dominant orthodoxies in political science, and norms in Canadian society, that often prevent a more serious, sustained, and substantial engagement with the politics of race, both within the academic world, and in the world at large.

Race[1] is one of the most powerful social signifiers of identity and difference in Canada, a country reputed for diversity, multiculturalism and tolerance worldwide. Demographic trends indicate that our racial diversity can only continue to increase in the coming years and decades, holding important implications for social, political, and economic life in Canada. In spite of the increasing relevance of race in Canadian society, analyses concerning the relationship(s) between race and politics have been, at best, tangential in mainstream English Canadian political science. Kenneth McRae suggests that we can understand what constitutes the "mainstream" at least partially because of evidence that other streams, "lesser channels, eddies, backwaters, or even swamps, where different and possibly more interesting forms of life may be discovered," exist simultaneously alongside dominant paradigms and narratives (1979: 685). Research on race, which has usually been conceptualized as an apolitical force, exemplifies such a marginalized "other stream" as several political scientists have noted. A fundamental disconnect exists between Canadian demographic and social reality,

Source: Excerpted from *Canadian Journal of Political Science*, vol. 41, no. 3 (September 2008), 525–547. Some notes omitted.

which illustrates the significance of race, and the disciplinary silence of English-Canadian political science on both the conceptualization of race as a political production and the incorporation of race as a compelling explanatory variable in the analysis of political phenomena. This contradiction raises an important question for the core of our discipline: Is race political? ...

What's Political About Race?

In one sense, domestic politics concerns the relationship between the state and society. In Canada, the state is far from a monolithic entity; rather, it comprises separate levels and branches of government, formal institutions, constitutions and legal instruments such as legislation, statutes, and policies. This official realm is further complemented by an entire informal network of political agents, organizations, and social movements. Though a comprehensive or unidirectional notion of society at large may be difficult to pinpoint, political agents such as the media, interest groups, and even individual citizens have the ability to influence the trajectory of political life in Canada. The relationship between state and society is multifaceted, complex, and simultaneously mutually constitutive and fragmenting; both may act as independent or dependent variables, depending on context and interpretation.

In another sense, the definition of "the political" need not be limited to the state. Feminist, Marxist, and critical race theorists have long argued that the superstructures of patriarchy, capitalism, and white supremacy infiltrate and exist beyond the state arena, permeating all aspects of social and political life—and as such, everything is political. However, no matter which of these interpretations of the political is used, society is involved—at least to some extent—in the manifestation of politics.

But just who is implicated in the notion of Canadian society? Demographic data on the composition of Canadian society demonstrate that Canada is indeed racially diverse. According to 2001 census data, "visible minorities" represent 13.4 per cent of the Canadian population, with the three most populous groups being Chinese (3.5 per cent), South Asian (3.1 per cent) and Black (2.2 per cent). These groups are heavily concentrated in urban areas, especially Vancouver and Toronto, where the proportion of visible minorities is over 36 per cent. Between 1996 and 2001, the visible minority population increased by 24.6 per cent; compared with an increase of the overall Canadian population of just under 4 per cent (Canada, 2001), this demographic trend is significant. This trend is even more significant when Aboriginal peoples are considered; the 2001 census reported that nearly a million people identified themselves with one (or more) of the constitutionally recognized Aboriginal groups of Indian, Inuit and Métis, a 22.2 per cent increase from the 1996 count. ...

On one level the fact that racial minorities represent a significant and rapidly growing portion of the Canadian population is important in and of itself. As an analytically generous interpretation of the political concerns the relationship between state and society, and since the demography of Canadian society includes racial minorities, race is, to some degree, political. However, such analytical stretching is not necessary to determine the political nature of race in Canada. Keith Banting and others have recently argued that Canada's social, economic, and political environments are highly racialized (2007). Examples include the continuation of immigrant "entrant status" in the labour market, gang-related violence in urban centres, second-generation immigrants arrested on terrorism charges in Toronto, and the sharp debate about the role of *sharia* law in Ontario. Reitz and Banerjee relate that 35.9 per cent of racial minorities report experiences of discrimination (2007). Conceptual stretching is not necessary to consider what state arenas are implicated in these debates: criminal codes, the incarceration system, immigration policies and integration programs, human rights protections, family law, antiterrorism legislation—the list goes on.

Though the idea that discrete, separate, and hierarchically ordered races exist as a matter of biological fact was the dominant ideology in the not-so-distant past, it is now generally acknowledged that race is a social construction—though it has undoubtedly been construct-ed with incredible permeating power and longevity. However, ample evidence points not just to the social construction of race, but to the instrumental role the state itself has played in the creation of racial identities. Anthony Marx's comparative analysis of the United States, Brazil, and South Africa demonstrates that states *made* race (1998), and Ian Haney Lopez's book *White by Law* examines the central role played by law in the construction of race in the United States (1996). More recently, Melissa Nobles has demonstrated the political con-struction and consequences of race in American and Brazilian census categorizations (2000) while Jill Vickers considers the ways in which settler states such as Canada, the United States, and Australia established and relied on "race regimes" to maintain political and social order (2002a). Aside from these notable exceptions, however, race remains an under-researched and under-theorized subject within comparative political science. Moreover, Vickers (2002a) is one of the few authors to consider race in comparative political science while using Can-ada as a case study.

This disciplinary neglect has also been problematized in the context of American political science. Rogers Smith argues that we must examine "how elite political actors, institutions and public politics have not simply been reflecting, expressing, or 'enacting' racial identities through much of US history, but instead have been creating and transforming them," in order to illuminate how strongly race is tied to other manifestations of political power, including divisions and structures of government, the construction of criminal justice systems, edu-cation, social assistance, and the like (2004: 45). The point that race is political both in production and in consequence can be readily applied to Canada, where many aspects of historical and contemporary politics are, or have been, racialized. One need only think of the various and changing ways the *Indian Act* has defined Aboriginal identity to confirm the active role of the state in defining the boundaries of racial identities: "status" and "nonstatus" distinctions are part of a massive regulatory regime whose original aim was the assimilation of Aboriginal identities and cultures. In addition to the state's role in making race its redis-tributive function—combined with the undeniable connection between class and race—means that state action or inaction can alter, maintain, or solidify existing racial hierarchies. The state is relatively autonomous in deciding "who counts as a political actor, what is a political interest, and how the broad state-society relationship is to be organized" (Omi and Winant, 1994: 83). This is not to say that social actors are powerless and without agency. However, the state's influence over social life—and especially racialized social life—is un-paralleled. Politics in Canada has historically concerned both the regulation of subjects *inside* Canada (for example, the reserve system) and keeping other racialized subjects *outside* of Canada (for example, preferential immigration policies pre-1967). The central point, therefore, is that race is more than a mere and amorphous social construction; it is fundamentally a *political* one. ...

What Accounts for the Absence of Race in English Canadian Political Science?

There are a myriad of factors that can potentially explain the sustained neglect of race in political science. To begin with, scholars (V. Wilson, 1993; Vickers, 2002b) have argued that the dominant narrative of Canadian society and politics is one in which there are no major racial problems. The ideational power of this narrative manifests not simply in the social sciences, but also in prevailing attitudes of the population. Reitz and Banerjee demonstrate that there is a "prevailing view that racism is marginal in Canada," and that "only a minority of the White population think that prejudice is something that the Canadian government should address with more determination" (mis)perceptions that are unlikely to change given the elevated mythological status of multiculturalism and its solidified place in the narrative of Canadian identity (2007: 11).Yet, race and racism are undeniable elements of Canadian society. The general denial that race matters in Canada is summarized well by V. Seymour Wilson: "The point in all this is that a tradition of racism and ethnocentrism amongst Canada's founding groups is either seldom acknowledged, often denied, sometimes conveniently ignored, soft-peddled or suppressed" (1993: 667).

This dominant narrative that neither race nor racism is a serious issue in Canada is complemented by characteristics of political science that perpetuate and manipulate this myth. In his presidential address to the Canadian Political Science Association, Kenneth McRae argued that "Western political thought in general has shown little understanding or respect for the cultural diversity of mankind and has made scant allowance for it as a possible concern of government" (1979: 685). Vickers furthers this line of argumentation by examining several assumptions in Western political thought that have led to a misperception of diversity, especially as it pertains to race. Specifically, she contends that Euro-American political theory is based on a norm of a homogenous people or nation that renders it unable to conceptualize the experiences of supplanting societies, which invariably were racially heterogeneous (2002b: 19). Moreover, Vickers argues that the categories and tools utilized by Western political thought posits the white (heterosexual, able-bodied) male at the centre of history, thereby advancing an exclusive epistemic privilege that is inaccessible to those deemed "too different" because of race or gender (2002b: 23). Like Charles Mills these authors demonstrate that theoretical ideas about race are embedded in political philosophy and theory at a deep level (1997), and, as Vickers insightfully notes, the absence of race from "core texts in political theory and from political science paradigms is our clue that they are not sufficient for understanding the politics of 'race'" (2002b: 20).

This insufficiency is evidenced not only by the relative dearth of literature on race in English Canadian political science, but also by the manner in which race is examined in the discipline on those occasions when it surfaces. When analyses in political science do consider race, it is rarely acknowledged as a political production and thus the marginal disciplinary status of race remains unchanged. For example, though Canadian political theorists have invented and driven the discourse on multiculturalism (Kymlicka, 1995, 1998; C. Taylor, 1994; Carens, 2000), these debates largely concern the ability of liberalism to accommodate minority rights, especially when minority rights are synonymous with illiberal practices. Far from contributing to the centrality of race within Canadian political science, discourses of multiculturalism (somewhat ironically) perpetuate disciplinary myths that actually prevent any kind of meaningful analysis of the political production or consequences of race in Canada. In her assessment of the discursive impact of multiculturalism on women of colour, Bannerji questions the extent to which multiculturalism actually makes a difference in the lives of racial minorities who suffer from racism and systemic discrimination (2000). Taylor's central claims of the paramountcy of the "recognition" of identities "speaks to nothing like class formation or class struggle, the existence of active and deep racism, or of a social organization entailing racialized class productions of gender". (Bannerji, 2000: 554). Discourses of multiculturalism and diversity, Bannerji argues, simultaneously hide and enshrine power relations (2000: 555).

The evidence points to the importance of race and the dearth of literature on race in English Canadian political science indicates that our discipline is missing an important aspect of the real world of the political. The danger of disciplinary lag—whereby political science becomes disconnected from the society it purports to analyze—is an important concern. Though the dominant narrative in Canadian society generally denies the relevance of race, political science has internalized this myth to a greater extent than other disciplines in the social sciences which, we may recall, have better incorporated discussions and analyses of race. Not only does this suggest that political science has failed to seriously consider a topic that has been identified as important by other scholars and disciplines, but also that the difficulty of analyzing race and racial consequences of politics may be a problem specific to political science. V. Seymour Wilson, for example, argues that Canadian political science's traditional focus on institutional federalism directs our attention to only territorially based groups, while the majority of racial minorities inhabit the country's eight largest metropolitan areas (1993: 648). Similarly, I contend that there are several dominant methodologies, approaches and ideas in the discipline itself that may result in neglect both of using race as an explanatory variable and considering race to be a political production. ...

Approaches in mainstream political science concern more than a focus on elites and decision makers; analytical framing is also important. Though Dawson and Wilson have found that scholarship concerning race in the United States pays insufficient attention to the importance of theoretical modelling, they also acknowledge that the dominant theories and models of American political science—specifically, the individualistic nature of social/rational choice theory—is ill-equipped to consider the collective desires or beliefs of racial minorities (1991: 193, 212). In English-speaking Canada, political science has largely focused on institutions, "often conceptualizing political developments such as province-building, Quebec nationalism, Aboriginal nationalisms, and multiculturalism in terms of political institutional reform" (Miriam Smith, 2005: 101). The focus on the state suggests a particular colour-blindness inherent in the liberal idea of equality and social justice. Institutions are designed to treat all citizens alike, regardless of colour. However, as Constance Backhouse has indicated, Canada's legal institutions have historically been colour-coded rather than colour-blind:

Proponents of "race-neutrality" neglect to recognize that our society is not a race-neutral one. It is built upon centuries of racial division and discrimination. The legacy of such bigotry infects all of our institutions, relationships, and legal frameworks. To advocate "colour-blindness" as an ideal for the modern world is to adopt the false mythology of "racelessness" that has plagued the Canadian legal system for so long ... [that] it will only serve to condone the continuation of white supremacy across Canadian society. (1999: 274).

In effect, institutions that avoid race according to the principles of colour blindness serve to solidify existing social hierarchies. Furthermore, as the legal discourse surrounding formal versus substantive equality has demonstrated, colour blindness can never lead to equality while the social and economic playing field is not level.

A colour-blind approach to politics is not manifest in Canada's legal and political institutions alone; take the paradigmatic approaches to the study of Canadian political culture as an example. The Hartzian fragmentation thesis argues that New World societies can best be conceived as "fragments" with the ideological underpinnings of their former homelands that congealed into a dominant political culture (Hartz, 1955). Attempting to explain why socialism exists in Canada but not in the United States, Gad Horowitz adapted Hartz's original theory and argued that the fragments brought to French and English Canada are ideologically different than the liberal idealism of the United States; Canadian political culture "is touched by toryism and thus naturally produces and welcomes socialist ideas" (quoted by Forbes, 1987: 298). In the Hartz-Horowitz formulation, the Loyalist immigrants to British North America following the American Revolution were instrumental in formulating the political culture of English Canada. Here, the colour-blind emphasis on elite political actors and the subsequent erasure of racial minorities is apparent. Race is nowhere to be found in these theories, though the Loyalist migration included approximately 3,000 free blacks who had been emancipated in exchange for their loyalty to the British Crown during the American Revolution (Jhappan and Stasiulis, 1995: 107–08). ...

Finally, a general point must be made about the impact of dominant ideas in English Canadian political science on the study of politics and the dearth of scholarship on race. There are two aspects of Canadian politics that are continually implicated: first, the myth of two founding nations and the status of Quebec and language politics, and second, Canadian identity and anti-Americanism. Each of these contains an ideational power that has permeated Canadian society and perhaps even the discipline of political science as a whole, yet each serves, albeit in distinct ways, to eradicate race from politics. The idea that Canada was founded by two nations "obliterate[s] the history, role and claims of Aboriginal peoples" and has served to "exclude other identities and trivialize their contributions to the development of the country" (Jhappan and Stasiulis, 1995: 110, 127). While Quebec's contentious relationship with English Canada and the Canadian state is undeniable, the access to power that comes with being identified as a formal political entity in a federation is a privilege that has historically been denied to other minorities. This includes Aboriginal peoples, whose self-government agreements with federal and provincial governments will never result in the same amount of jurisdictional power and control guaranteed by Section 92 of the *Constitution Act, 1867*.

Secondly, the elusive search for a Canadian identity is continually defined against American nationalism and identity. The classic melting pot-versus-mosaic metaphor, inaccurate though it may be, has firmly implanted a utopian myth about the presence and potential of multiculturalism in the national psyche. Canada is constructed as the original promised land sought by fugitive slaves along the Underground Railroad, contrasted always, of course, with the oppressive and discriminatory realities of American politics and society. However, a fact check is in order: slavery was not officially abolished in Upper and Lower Canada until it was abolished throughout the entire British Empire in 1833. The Underground Railroad, the subject of many a heritage minute commercial, was originally created to smuggle slaves *out* of Canada and into the free northern United States (Cooper, 2006: 103). Further, upon arriving in Canada many ex-slaves found the only difference between the two countries was that in Canada they could not be re-enslaved (Malinda Smith, 2003: 117); that is, discrimination and segregation were just as prevalent in Canada as in the US. In contemporary times, racism is clearly a facet of Canadian society, whether it be indicated by under-representation of racial minorities in the House of Commons, the entrance status of highly educated and skilled new immigrants into the Canadian labour market, or the informal racial boundaries that permeate social life in Canada. For example, Reitz and Banerjee's research indicates that "while most Canadians deny harbouring racist views, they maintain a 'social distance' from minorities—they prefer not to interact with members of other racial groups in certain social situations" (2007: 12). Yet, to admit that racism exists in Canada, or to acknowledge the implicitly political nature of race, as most refuse to do, would be to admit that the moral superiority Canada holds over the United States in terms of race relations is unfounded and misleading. This is not to say that racism operates in absolutes, but rather to suggest that the comparison of racism in Canada to the more overt racism existing within the United States allows Canadians to deny the reality of racism in this country. This denial is made easily in Canada, for explicit race production or racism named and acknowledged as such is difficult to find. As Backhouse points out, colour blindness is a Canadian mechanism for responding to racial issues, allowing Canadians to maintain a "stupefying innocence ... about the enormity of racial oppression" (1999: 278).

It is both surprising and disturbing that while race has so clearly been implicated in the practice of politics in Canada, English Canadian political science remains cautiously silent. As V. Seymour Wilson cautioned, this silence holds the dangerous potential of becoming disciplinary lag, an option that political scientists cannot—and should not—entertain (1993: 650). However, at least part of this research gap in our discipline may be symptomatic of a larger denial in Canadian society and the academy of the existence of racial discourses and racism in Canada. Recall that while both Canadian history and sociology incorporated race to a greater extent than political science, none of the three disciplines considered had higher than 10.7 per cent of articles pertaining to race in any given time period. Ideas—especially those that concern national narratives or mythologies—are powerful forces. But time will tell; racial minorities are a quickly growing population in Canada. If current demographic trends remain constant, it is estimated that both Toronto and Vancouver will be minority-majority cities by 2012. The status quo in political science may soon prove to be inadequate; demographic realities will eventually force the hand of the dominant approaches and ideas.

Note

1. From the outset, it is important to distinguish race from ethnicity, though the two terms are often conflated. Li (1999) writes that "the important aspect of an ethnic group is that its

members share a sense of peoplehood or identity based on descent, language, religion, tradition, and other common experiences" (1999: 6). Race, on the other hand, is far more controversial, as it is often incorrectly equated with biological subspecies based on a common genetic constitution. Some sociologists advocate the use of the term "racialization" to demonstrate that social processes are the means by which certain groups are singled out for unequal treatments on the basis of real or imagined phonological differences (Li, 1999: 8).

References

Backhouse, Constance. 1999. *Colour-Coded: A Legal History of Racism in Canada: 1900–1950*. Toronto: University of Toronto Press.

Bannerji, Himani. 2000. "The Paradox of Diversity: The Construction of a Multicultural Canada and 'Women of Color.'" *Women's Studies International Forum* 23: 536–60.

Banting, Keith, Thomas J. Courchene and F. Leslie Seidle. 2007. "Ties That Bind? Social Cohesion and Diversity in Canada." In *Belonging? Diversity, Recognition, and Shared Citizenship in Canada*, ed. K. Banting, T. Courchene and F.L. Seidle. Montreal: Institute for Research on Public Policy.

Canada. Statistics Canada. 2001. *Ethno-Cultural Portrait of Canada: Visible Minority Groups*. (March 5, 2007).

Carens, Joseph H. 2000. *Culture, Citizenship, and Community: A Contextual Exploration of Justice as Evenhandedness*. Oxford: Oxford University Press.

Cooper, Afua. 2006. *The Hanging of Angelique: The Untold Story of Canadian Slavery and the Burning of Old Montreal*. Toronto: HarperCollins.

Dawson, Michael C. and Ernest J. Wilson, III. 1991. "Paradigms and Paradoxes: Political Science and African-American Politics." In *Political Science: Looking to the Future*, vol. 1, ed. William Crotty. Evanston: Northwestern University.

Forbes, H.D. 1987. "Hartz-Horowitz at Twenty: Nationalism, Toryism and Socialism in Canada and the United States." *Canadian Journal of Political Science* 20: 287–315.

Hartz, Louis. 1955. *The Founding of New Societies*. New York: Harcourt, Brace.

Jhappan, Radha and Daiva Stasiulis. 1995. "The Fractious Politics of a Settler Society: Canada." In *Unsettling Settler Societies: Articulations of Race, Ethnicity and Class*, ed. Daiva Stasiulis and Nira Yuval-Davis. London: Sage Publications.

Kymlicka, Will. 1995. *Multicultural Citizenship: A Liberal Theory of Minority Rights*. Oxford: Clarendon Press.

Li, Peter S. 1999. "Race and Ethnicity." In *Race and Ethnic Relations in Canada*, ed. Peter S. Li. Oxford: Oxford University Press.

Lopez, Ian Haney. 1996. *White by Law: The Legal Construction of Race*. New York: New York University Press.

Marx, Anthony W. 1998. *Making Race and Nation: A Comparison of the United States, South Africa and Brazil*. Cambridge: Cambridge University Press.

McRae, Kenneth. 1979. "The Plural Society and the Western Political Tradition." *Canadian Journal of Political Science* 12: 675–88.

Mills, Charles. 1997. *The Racial Contract*. Ithaca and London: Cornell University Press.

Nobles, Melissa. 2000. *Shades of Citizenship: Race and the Census in Modern Politics*. Stanford, CA: Stanford University Press.

Omi, Michael and Howard Winant. 1994. *Racial Formation in the United States: from the 1960s to the 1990s*. New York: Routledge.

Reitz, Jeffrey G. and Rupa Banerjee. 2007. "Racial Inequality, Social Cohesion and Policy Issues in Canada." In *Belonging? Diversity, Recognition, and Shared Citizenship in Canada*, ed. K. Banting, T. Courchene and F.L. Seidle. Montreal: Institute for Research on Public Policy.

Smith, Malinda S. 2003. "'Race Matters' and 'Race Manners.'" In *Reinventing Canada: Politics of the 21st Century*, ed. J. Brodie and L. Trimble. Toronto: Prentice Hall.

Smith, Miriam. 2005. "Institutionalism in the Study of Canadian Politics: The English-Canadian Tradition." In *New Institutionalism: Theory and Analysis*, ed. André Lecours. Toronto: University of Toronto Press.

Smith, Rogers M. 2004. "The Puzzling Place of Race in American Political Science." *PS: Political Science & Politics* 37: 41–45.

Taylor, Charles. 1994. "The Politics of Recognition." In *Multiculturalism: Examining the Politics of Recognition*, ed. Amy Gutmann. Princeton, NJ: Princeton Univ Press.

Vickers, Jill. 2002a. *The Politics of "Race": Canada, Australia and the United States*. Ottawa: Golden Dog Press.

Vickers, Jill. 2002b. "No Place for 'Race'? Why Pluralist Theory Fails to Explain the Politics of 'Race' in 'New Societies.'" In *The Challenge of Cultural Pluralism*, ed. Stephen Brooks. Westport, CT: Praeger.

Wilson, V. Seymour. 1993. "The Tapestry Vision of Canadian Multiculturalism." *Canadian Journal of Political Science* 26: 645–69.

The Regina Manifesto

CCF (Co-operative Commonwealth Federation) (1933)

71

EDITORS' INTRODUCTION

Led by Tommy Douglas, the CCF emerged as a national party in the midst of the Great Depression in 1930s. In contrast to the federal Conservative and Liberal parties, the CCF was explicitly socialist in its ideology, although democratic rather than revolutionary in its recommended means to achieve its policy goals. The Regina Manifesto is the CCF's policy program adopted at its first national convention in Regina, Saskatchewan in July 1933. It remained the official CCF program until 1956, at which time the CCF adopted the more rhetorically moderate and Keynesian Winnipeg Declaration.

The CCF's Regina Manifesto articulates the party's aim "to replace the present capitalist system, with its inherent injustice and inhumanity, by a social order from which the domination and exploitation of one class by another will be eliminated." Ironically, many of the CCF's specific policy recommendations, such as publicly organized health, hospital and medical services, a national central bank "to control the flow of credit and the general price level," and a national labour code including "insurance covering illness, accident, old age, and unemployment," were adopted by other parties in subsequent decades, and became core national policies.

Programme of the Co-operative Commonwealth Federation, Adopted at First National Convention (Regina, Saskatchewan, July 19–21, 1933)

The CCF is a federation of organizations whose purpose is the establishment in Canada of a Co-operative Commonwealth in which the principle regulating production, distribution and exchange will be the supplying of human needs and not the making of profits.

We aim to replace the present capitalist system, with its inherent injustice and inhumanity, by a social order from which the domination and exploitation of one class by another will be eliminated, in which economic planning will supersede unregulated private enterprise and competition, and in which genuine democratic self-government, based upon economic equality will be possible.

Source: Saskatchewan NDP Provincial Office.

The present order is marked by glaring inequalities of wealth and opportunity, by chaotic waste and instability; and in an age of plenty it condemns the great mass of the people to poverty and insecurity. Power has become more and more concentrated into the hands of a small irresponsible minority of financiers and industrialists and to their predatory interests the majority are habitually sacrificed. When private profit is the main stimulus to economic effort, our society oscillates between periods of feverish prosperity in which the main benefits go to speculators and profiteers, and of catastrophic depression, in which the common man's normal state of insecurity and hardship is accentuated. We believe that these evils can be removed only in a planned and socialized economy in which our natural resources and principal means of production and distribution are owned, controlled and operated by the people.

The new social order at which we aim is not one in which individuality will be crushed out by a system of regimentation.

Nor shall we interfere with cultural rights of racial or religious minorities. What we seek is a proper collective organization of our economic resources such as will make possible a much greater degree of leisure and a much richer individual life for every citizen.

This social and economic transformation can be brought about by political action, through the election of a government inspired by the ideal of a Co-operative Commonwealth and supported by a majority of the people. We do not believe in change by violence.

We consider that both the old parties in Canada are the instruments of capitalist interests and cannot serve as agents of social reconstruction, and that whatever the superficial differences between them, they are bound to carry on government in accordance with the dictates of the big business interests who finance them.

The CCF aims at political power in order to put an end to this capitalist domination of our political life. It is a democratic movement, a federation of farmer, labour and socialist organizations, financed by its own members and seeking to achieve its ends solely by constitutional methods. It appeals for support from all who believe that the time has come for a far-reaching reconstruction of our economic and political institutions and who are willing to work together for the carrying out of the following policies:

1. Planning

The establishment of a planned, socialized economic order, in order to make possible the most efficient development of the national resources and the most equitable distribution of the national income.

The first step in this direction will be the setting up of a National Planning Commission consisting of a small body of economists, engineers and statisticians assisted by an appropriate technical staff. …

The Commission will be responsible to the Cabinet and will work in co-operation with the Managing Boards of the Socialized Industries.

It is now certain that in every industrial country some form of planning will replace the disintegrating capitalist system. The CCF will provide that in Canada the planning shall be done, not by a small group of capitalist magnates in their own interests, but by public servants acting in the public interest and responsible to the people as a whole.

2. Socialization of Finance

Socialization of all financial machinery—banking, currency, credit, and insurance, to make possible the effective control of currency, credit and prices, and the supplying of new productive equipment for socially desirable purposes.

Planning by itself will be of little use if the public authority has not the power to carry its plans into effect. Such power will require the control of finance and of all those vital industries and services, which, if they remain in private hands, can be used to thwart or corrupt the will of the public authority. Control of finance is the first step in the control of the whole economy. The chartered banks must be socialized and removed from the control of private profit-seeking interests; and the national banking system thus established must have at its head a Central Bank to control the flow of credit and the general price level, and to regulate foreign exchange operations. A National Investment Board must also be set up, working in co-operation with the socialized banking system to mobilize and direct the unused surpluses of production for socially desired purposes as determined by the Planning Commission.

Insurance Companies, which provide one of the main channels for the investment of individual savings and which, under their present competitive organization, charge needlessly high premiums for the social services that they render, must also be socialized.

3. Social Ownership

Socialization (Dominion, Provincial or Municipal) of transportation, communications, electric power and all other industries and services essential to social planning, and their operation under the general direction of the Planning Commission by competent managements freed from day to day political interference.

Public utilities must be operated for the public benefit and not for the private profit of a small group of owners or financial manipulators. Our natural resources must be developed by the same methods. Such a programme means the continuance and extension of the public ownership enterprises in which most governments in Canada have already gone some distance. Only by such public ownership, operated on a planned economy, can our main industries be saved from the wasteful competition of the ruinous overdevelopment and over-capitalization which are the inevitable outcome of capitalism. Only in a regime of public ownership and operation will the full benefits accruing from centralized control and mass production be passed on to the consuming public.

Transportation, communications and electric power must come first in a list of industries to be socialized. Others, such as mining, pulp and paper and the distribution of milk, bread, coal and gasoline, in which exploitation, waste, or financial malpractices are particularly prominent must next be brought under social ownership and operation.

In restoring to the community its natural resources and in taking over industrial enterprises from private into public control we do not propose any policy of outright confiscation. What we desire is the most stable and equitable transition to the Cooperative Commonwealth. It is impossible to decide the policies to be followed in particular cases in an uncertain future, but we insist upon certain broad principles. The welfare of the community must take supremacy over the claims of private wealth. In times of war, human life has been conscripted.

Should economic circumstances call for it, conscription of wealth would be more justifiable. We recognize the need for compensation in the case of individuals and institutions which must receive adequate maintenance during the transitional period before the planned economy becomes fully operative. But a CCF government will not play the role of rescuing bankrupt private concerns for the benefit of promoters and of stock and bond holders. It will not pile up a deadweight burden of unremunerative debt which represents claims upon the public treasury of a functionless owner class. ...

4. Agriculture

Security of tenure for the farmer upon his farm on conditions to be laid down by individual provinces; insurance against unavoidable crop failure; removal of the tariff burden from the operations of agriculture; encouragement of producers' and consumers' cooperatives; the restoration and maintenance of an equitable relationship between prices of agricultural products and those of other commodities and services; and improving the efficiency of export trade in farm products.

The security of tenure for the farmer upon his farm which is imperilled by the present disastrous situation of the whole industry, together with adequate social insurance, ought to be guaranteed under equitable conditions.

The prosperity of agriculture, the greatest Canadian industry, depends upon a rising volume of purchasing power of the masses in Canada for all farm goods consumed at home, and upon the maintenance of large scale exports of the stable commodities at satisfactory prices or equitable commodity exchange.

The intense depression in agriculture today is a consequence of the general world crisis caused by the normal workings of the capitalistic system resulting in: (1) Economic nationalism expressing itself in tariff barriers and other restrictions of world trade; (2) The decreased purchasing power of unemployed and under-employed workers and of the Canadian people in general; (3) The exploitation of both primary producers and consumers by monopolistic corporations who absorb a great proportion of the selling price of farm products. ...

5. External Trade

The regulation in accordance with the National plan of external trade through import and export boards.

Canada is dependent on external sources of supply for many of her essential requirements of raw materials and manufactured products.

These she can obtain only by large exports of the goods she is best fitted to produce. The strangling of our export trade by insane protectionist policies must be brought to an end. But the old controversies between free traders and protectionists are now largely obsolete. In a world of nationally organized economies Canada must organize the buying and selling of her main imports and exports under public boards, and take steps to regulate the flow of less important commodities by a system of licenses. By so doing she will be enabled to make the best trade agreements possible with foreign countries, put a stop to the exploitation of both primary producer and ultimate consumer, make possible the coordination of internal processing, transportation and marketing of farm products, and facilitate the establishment of stable prices for such export commodities.

6. Co-operative Institutions

The encouragement by the public authority of both producers' and consumers' cooperative institutions.

In agriculture, as already mentioned, the primary producer can receive a larger net revenue through cooperative organization of purchases and marketing. Similarly in retail distribution of staple commodities such as milk, there is room for development both of public municipal operation and of consumers' cooperatives, and such cooperative organization can be extended into wholesale distribution and into manufacturing. Cooperative enterprises should be assisted by the state through appropriate legislation and through the provision of adequate credit facilities.

7. Labour Code

A National Labour Code to secure for the worker maximum income and leisure, insurance covering illness, accident, old age, and unemployment, freedom of association and effective participation in the management of his industry or profession.

The spectre of poverty and insecurity which still haunts every worker, though technological developments have made possible a high standard of living for everyone, is a disgrace which must be removed from our civilization. The community must organize its resources to effect progressive reduction of the hours of work in accordance with technological development and to provide a constantly rising standard of life to everyone who is willing to work. A labour code must be developed which will include state regulation of wages, equal reward and equal opportunity of advancement for equal services, irrespective of sex; measures to guarantee the right to work or the right to maintenance through stabilization of employment and through unemployment insurance; social insurance to protect workers and their families against the hazards of sickness, death, industrial accident and old age; limitation of hours of work and protection of health and safety in industry. Both wages and insurance benefits should be varied in accordance with family needs.

In addition workers must be guaranteed the undisputed right to freedom of association, and should be encouraged and assisted by the state to organize themselves in trade unions. By means of collective agreements and participation in works councils, the workers can achieve fair working rules and share in the control of industry and profession; and their organizations will be indispensable elements in a system of genuine industrial democracy.

The labour code should be uniform throughout the country. But the achievement of this end is difficult so long as jurisdiction over labour legislation under the B.N.A. Act is mainly in the hands of the provinces. It is urgently necessary, therefore, that the B.N.A. Act be amended to make such a national labour code possible.

8. Socialized Health Services

Publicly Organized Health, Hospital and Medical Services.

With the advance of medical science the maintenance of a healthy population has become a function for which every civilized community should undertake responsibility. Health services should be made at least as freely available as are educational services today. But under a system which is still mainly one of private enterprise the costs of proper medical care, such as the wealthier members of society can easily afford, are at present prohibitive for great masses of the people. A properly organized system of public health services including medical and dental care, which would stress the prevention rather than the cure of illness, should be extended to all our people in both rural and urban areas. This is an enterprise in which Dominion, Provincial and Municipal authorities, as well as the medical and dental professions, can cooperate.

9. B.N.A. Act

The amendment of the Canadian Constitution, without infringing upon racial or religious minority rights or upon legitimate provincial claims to autonomy, so as to give the Dominion Government adequate powers to deal effectively with urgent economic problems which are essentially national in scope; the abolition of the Canadian Senate.

We propose that the necessary amendments to the B.N.A. Act shall be obtained as speedily as required, safeguards being inserted to ensure that the existing rights of racial and religious minorities shall not be changed without their own consent. What is chiefly needed today is the placing in the hands of the national government of more power to control national economic development. In a rapidly changing economic environment our political constitution must be reasonably flexible. The present division of powers between Dominion and Provinces reflects the conditions of a pioneer, mainly agricultural, community in 1867. Our constitution must be brought into line with the increasing industrialization of the country and the consequent centralization of economic and financial power. ...

The Canadian Senate, which was originally created to protect provincial rights, but has failed even in this function, has developed into a bulwark of capitalist interests, as is illustrated by the large number of company directorships held by its aged members. In its peculiar composition of a fixed number of members appointed for life it is one of the most reactionary assemblies in the civilized world. It is a standing obstacle to all progressive legislation, and the only permanently satisfactory method of dealing with the constitutional difficulties it creates is to abolish it.

10. External Relations

A Foreign Policy designed to obtain international economic cooperation and to promote disarmament and world peace.

Canada has a vital interest in world peace. We propose, therefore, to do everything in our power to advance the idea of international cooperation as represented by the League of Nations and the International Labour Organization. We would extend our diplomatic machinery for keeping in touch with the main centres of world interest. But we believe that genuine international cooperation is incompatible with the capitalist regime which is in force in most countries, and that strenuous efforts are needed to rescue the League from its present condition of being mainly a League of capitalist Great Powers. We stand resolutely against all participation in imperialist wars. Within the British Commonwealth, Canada must maintain her autonomy as a completely self-governing nation. We must resist all attempts to build up a new economic British Empire in place of the old political one, since such attempts readily lend themselves to the purposes of capitalist exploitation and may easily lead to further world wars.

Canada must refuse to be entangled in any more wars fought to make the world safe for capitalism.

11. Taxation and Public Finance

A new taxation policy designed not only to raise public revenues but also to lessen the glaring inequalities of income and to provide funds for social services and the socialization of industry; the cessation of the debt-creating system of Public Finance.

In the type of economy that we envisage, the need for taxation, as we now understand it, will have largely disappeared. It will nevertheless be essential during the transition period, to use the taxing powers, along with the other methods proposed elsewhere, as a means of providing for the socialization of industry, and for extending the benefits of increased Social Services. ...

We propose that all Public Works, as directed by the Planning Commission, shall be financed by the issuance of credit, as suggested, based upon the National Wealth of Canada.

12. Freedom

Freedom of speech and assembly for all; repeal of Section 98 of the Criminal Code; amendment of the Immigration Act to prevent the present inhuman policy of deportation; equal treatment before the law of all residents of Canada irrespective of race, nationality or religious or political beliefs.

In recent years, Canada has seen an alarming growth of Fascist tendencies among all governmental authorities. The most elementary rights of freedom of speech and assembly have been arbitrarily denied to workers and to all whose political and social views do not meet with the approval of those in power. The lawless and brutal conduct of the police in certain centres in preventing public meetings and in dealing with political prisoners must cease.

Section 98 of the Criminal Code which has been used as a weapon of political oppression by a panic-stricken capitalist government, must be wiped off the statute book and those who have been imprisoned under it must be released. An end must be put to the inhuman practice of deporting immigrants who were brought to this country by immigration propaganda and now, through no fault of their own, find themselves victims of an executive department against whom there is no appeal to the courts of the land. We stand for full economic, political and religious liberty for all.

13. Social Justice

The establishment of a commission composed of psychiatrists, psychologists, socially minded jurists and social workers, to deal with all matters pertaining to crime and punishment and the general administration of law, in order to humanize the law and to bring it into harmony with the needs of the people.

While the removal of economic inequality will do much to overcome the most glaring injustices in the treatment of those who come into conflict with the law, our present archaic system must be changed and brought into accordance with a modern concept of human relationships. The new system must not be based as is the present one, upon vengeance and fear, but upon an understanding of human behaviour. For this reason its planning and control cannot be left in the hands of those steeped in the outworn legal tradition; and therefore it is proposed that there shall be established a national commission composed of psychiatrists, psychologists, socially minded jurists and social workers whose duty it shall be to devise a system of prevention and correction consistent with other features of the new social order.

14. An Emergency Programme

The assumption by the Dominion Government of direct responsibility for dealing with the present critical unemployment situation and for tendering suitable work or adequate maintenance; the adoption of measures to relieve the extremity of the crisis such as a programme of public spending on housing, and other enterprises that will increase the real wealth of Canada, to be financed by the issue of credit based on the national wealth.

The extent of unemployment and the widespread suffering which it has caused, creates a situation with which provincial and municipal governments have long been unable to cope and forces upon the Dominion government direct responsibility for dealing with the crisis as the only authority with financial resources adequate to meet the situation. Unemployed workers must be secured in the tenure of their homes, and the scale and methods of relief, at present altogether inadequate, must be such as to preserve decent human standards of living.

It is recognized that even after a Cooperative Commonwealth Federation Government has come into power, a certain period of time must elapse before the planned economy can be fully worked out.

During this brief transitional period, we propose to provide work and purchasing power for those now unemployed by a far-reaching programme of public expenditure on housing, slum clearance, hospitals, libraries, schools, community halls, parks, recreational projects, reforestation, rural electrification, the elimination of grade crossings, and other similar projects in both town and country. This programme, which would be financed by the issuance of credit based on the national wealth, would serve the double purpose of creating employment and meeting recognized social needs. ...

Emergency measures, however, are of only temporary value, for the present depression is a sign of the mortal sickness of the whole capitalist system, and this sickness cannot be cured by the application of salves. These leave untouched the cancer which is eating at the heart of our society, namely, the economic system in which our natural resources and our principal means of production and distribution are owned, controlled and operated for the private profit of a small proportion of our population.

No CCF Government will rest content until it has eradicated capitalism and put into operation the full programme of socialized planning which will lead to the establishment in Canada of the Cooperative Commonwealth.

The Vertical Mosaic

John Porter (1965)

72

EDITORS' INTRODUCTION

John Porter (1921–1979) was on the faculty of Carleton University, the University of Toronto, and Harvard University. Although known as a prominent Canadian sociologist, his most important work, The Vertical Mosaic, *was influential in political science circles as well.*

Canada's cultural mosaic of different cultural, linguistic, and ethnic groups that all contribute to a pluralistic society is often contrasted to the American melting pot, wherein immigrants are expected to assimilate into a dominant American way of life. In The Vertical Mosaic, *Porter was interested in challenging the notion of Canada as being a "classless society" in which non-elites faced no barriers to opportunity. Porter demonstrates that certain ethnic, religious, and linguistic groups had more advantages in terms of numerous socio-economic indicators, including education, income levels, and health. The metaphor of the mosaic, therefore, is more accurately an ethno-racial hierarchy, with British-origin Canadians at the top, and other ethnic groups, including francophones and Aboriginals, distinctly disadvantaged in terms of access to elite-level power in bureaucratic, political, and economic spheres. He concludes his book by stating that "Canada is probably not unlike other western industrial nations in relying heavily on its elite groups to make major decisions and to determine the shape and direction of its development. … [But] if power and decision-making must always rest with elite groups, there can at least be open recruitment from all classes into the elite."*

The Canadian Middle Class Image

One of the most persistent images that Canadians have of their society is that it has no classes. This image becomes translated into the assertion that Canadians are all relatively equal in their possessions, in the amount of money they earn, and in the opportunities which they and their children have to get on in the world. An important element in this image of classlessness is that, with the absence of formal aristocracy and aristocratic institutions, Canada is a society in which equalitarian values have asserted themselves over authoritarian values. Canada, it is thought, shares not only a continent with the United States, but also a democratic ideology which rejects the historical class and power structures of Europe. Social images are one thing and social realities another. Yet the two are not completely separate.

Source: Excerpted from *The Vertical Mosaic*. Toronto: University of Toronto Press, 1965. Notes omitted. Reprinted by permission.

497

Social images are not entirely fictional characters with only a coincidental likeness to a real society, living or dead. Often the images can be traced to an earlier historical period of the society, its golden age perhaps, which, thanks to the historians, is held up, long after it has been transformed into something else, as a model way of life. As well as their historical sources, images can be traced to their contemporary creators, particularly in the world of the mass media and popular culture. When a society's writers, journalists, editors, and other image-creators are a relatively small and closely linked group, and have more or less the same social background, the images they produce can, because they are consistent, appear to be much more true to life than if their group were larger, less cohesive, and more heterogeneous in composition.

The historical source of the image of a classless Canada is the equality among pioneers in the frontier environment of the last century. In the early part of the present century there was a similar equality of status among those who were settlers in the west, although, as we shall see, these settlers were by no means treated equally. A rural, agricultural, primary producing society is a much less differentiated society than one which has highly concentrated industries in large cities. Equality in the rural society may be much more apparent than real, but the rural environment has been for Canada an important source of the image of equality. …

That there is neither very rich nor very poor in Canada is an important part of the image. There are no barriers to opportunity. Education is free. Therefore, making use of it is largely a question of personal ambition. Even university education is available to all, except that it may require for some a little more summer work and thrift. There is a view widely held by many university graduates that they, and most other graduates, have worked their way through college. Consequently it is felt anyone else can do the same.

In some superficial respects the image of middle class uniformity may appear plausible. The main values of the society are concerned with the consumption of commodities, and in the so-called affluence that has followed World War II there seem to have been commodities for everybody, except, perhaps, a small group of the permanently poor at the bottom. Credit facilities are available for large numbers of low income families, enabling them, too, to be consumers of commodities over and above the basic necessities of life. The vast array of credit facilities, some of them extraordinarily ingenious, have inequalities built into them, in that the cost of borrowing money varies with the amount already possessed. There are vast differences in the quality of goods bought by the middle income levels and the lower income levels. One commodity, for instance, which low income families can rarely purchase is privacy, particularly the privacy of a house to themselves. It is perhaps the value of privacy and the capacity to afford it which has become the dividing line between the real and the apparent middle class.

If low income families achieve high consumption levels it is usually through having more than one income earner in the household. Often this is the wife and mother, but it may be an older child who has left school, and who is expected to contribute to the family budget. Alternatively, high consumption levels may be achieved at a cost in leisure. Many low income family heads have two jobs, a possibility which has arisen with the shorter working day and the five-day week. This "moonlighting," as it is called in labour circles, tends to offset the progress which has been made in raising the level of wages and reducing the hours of work. There is no way of knowing how extensive "moonlighting" is, except that we know that trade unions denounce it as a practice which tends to take away the gains which have been obtained for workers. For large segments of the population, therefore, a high level of consumption is obtained by means which are alien to a true middle class standard. In a later chapter where we shall examine closely the distribution of income we shall see what a small proportion of Canadian families were able to live a middle class style of life in the middle 1950's, the high tide of post-war affluence. At the high end of the social class spectrum, also in contrast to the middle level image, are the families of great wealth and influence. They are not perhaps as ostentatious as the very wealthy of other societies, and Canada has no "celebrity world" with which these families must compete for prestige in the way Mills has suggested is important for the very rich in American society. ...

The idea of class differences has scarcely entered into the stream of Canadian academic writing despite the fact that class differences stand in the way of implementing one of the most important values of western society, that is, equality. The fact, which we shall see later, that Canada draws its intellectuals either from abroad or from its own middle class, means that there is almost no one producing a view of the world which reflects the experience of the poor or the underprivileged. It was as though they did not exist. It is the nature of these class differences and their consequences for Canadian society that the following chapters seek to explore.

Closely related to differences in class levels are differences in the exercising of power and decision-making in the society. Often it is thought that once a society becomes an electoral democracy based on universal suffrage power becomes diffused throughout the general population so that everyone participates somehow in the selection of social goals. There is, however, a whole range of institutional resistances to the transfer of power to a democratic political system. ... [I]t is necessary to keep in mind that class differences create very great differences in life chances, among which are the chances of individuals' reaching the higher levels of political, economic, and other forms of power. ...

The Experience of Social Class

If in reducing classes to artificial constructions we have argued them out of existence, it is necessary to bring them back. Social images about the lack of a class structure to the contrary, there is little doubt that class is something which is experienced in everyday life and hence becomes real. Class may not impinge on all people equally, but for some it may be felt intensely. This subjective aspect of class experience was aptly described in a further remark by Schumpeter: "The difference between intercourse within the class and outside the class is the same as the difference between swimming with and against the tide."

Even though they might not want to admit it or think about it very often, most people are aware of differences in levels of living, ways of earning a living, and life chances. We make judgments about people's class on the basis of the clothes they wear, the place they live, the church they attend, the kind of jobs they have, or the size of their families. We have an extensive repertoire of class labels: the other side of the tracks, white collar, nouveau riche, the workers, and so forth. In all our cities there are residential areas which have prestige and whose names are known. Similarly the run-down and cramped areas have their appropriate names.

When a well-to-do and successful resident of "Crestwood Heights," an upper class suburb in Toronto, complains that "the Loyalist club is the only one that is really tough to get into," he is aware that he is still swimming against the tide. At the lower end of the social spectrum, class differences are experienced in a different way as the following quotation from W.E. Mann's study of a Toronto slum shows:

> Social distance between the slum and the non-slum in Toronto is reflected in the expressions, "up there" and "down here." The usage "down here" reflects the residents' concept of their lowered status. Hostility to the population "up there" is indicated by the following statement of one resident, "Up there a lot of people are trying for something—I don't know what. At least 'down here' there's a sort of truth and basic reality. ... there's no use putting on the old BS down here, because if you haven't got it, you ain't got it, and that's all there is to it."

Class becomes real as people experience it. ...

Class as Functional Inequality: The Conservative Ideology

There are two important theories about the function or purpose of classes in social structure. One, which follows directly from the idea that the reality of class is subjective, is called the "functional theory" of stratification. The second, and much better known, is Marxian theory, which is based on objectively defined classes, but classes none the less which develop a high level of class consciousness. The functional theory of stratification reflects the American conservative ideology that inequality is necessary and that people more or less arrive at the class positions which they deserve. Because of its simplicity the theory also has a popular appeal. ...

The Post-Marxian Industrial World

Concentration of Economic Power

In the Marxian view the power which goes with ownership and control of industry spills over, because of the primacy of economic affairs in social life, to all other major institutions, government, the legal system, the church, the army, education, the mass media, and so forth. The economic masters become the master class of the whole society. If it is true that the corporate elite is a relatively smaller and more coherent group than the nineteenth-century bourgeoisie, does its power extend beyond the economy? The answer can come only after empirical investigation. However, structural changes which have taken place in modern societies reduce the possibilities for complete control by a master class of economic overseers.

Institutional Specialization

The fundamental structural change which has come with modern industry is the increasing differentiation and functional specialization of social institutions. The most obvious change is the vast increase in the role of government since the turn of the century when Herbert Spencer and others were denouncing with apoplectic fervour the growth of "gas and water socialism." Government interference in economic and social life has grown to mammoth proportions and, in the process, has created a new institution in its agencies of administration. So specialized and extensive have government operations become that the bureaucracy created to undertake them assumes an independent life with its own values, norms, and career systems. The growth of the armed forces has required their concomitant professionalization in place of private military dilettantism. Modern nations do not leave their military activities to the kind of arrangements with which Britain fought in the Crimea.

Political institutions, such as legislatures and political parties, have also become more specialized. Legislatures now sit for much longer and pass an enormously increased volume of legislation. This change has had the effect in most modern societies of making their members full-time rather than part-time politicians. It was possible at one time for Donald Smith, when head of the Canadian Pacific Railway, to be, as well, a member of Parliament, but it is unlikely that corporate officials could divide their time in that way now. Nor would it be desirable for them to be so closely tied in with the political system. The emergence of the mass political party with the growth of electoral democracy has created further specialization within the political processes.

Modern educational systems and the mass media of communications share with the older institution of the Church the important function of articulating and disseminating those values and ideas which support a particular social order. Within the economic system, the growth of powerful trade unions counters the power of "private" ownership of productive instruments with the power of collective refusal to work them. The labour leader is a person with whom the older entrepreneur rarely had to contend, and more often against whom he had extensive legal protection.

If the modern corporate elite do constitute a master class in the Marxian sense they must have successfully "mastered" these specialized institutional orders. It is possible that they have, but the question is an empirical one to be settled after careful study of authority and control within each of these institutional orders. There are ways in which a degree of control can be achieved. The economic elite can form coalitions with the elites of other institutions, such as the close association of corporate and political leaders in modern industrial societies. To enter coalitions is not the same as to master. As is often alleged the economic elite may control political parties, although in an epoch of mass electorates it is unlikely that their control would be complete because the elites of other institutions can also bring pressure on political leaders; for example, politicians will often not cross picket lines during a strike. The argument then is that leaders of the corporate world have to share power with the leaders of these other institutions. Power becomes diffused because of the specialized function of these other institutions. ...

Elites and the Structure of Power

Power means the recognized right to make effective decisions on behalf of a group of people. The group may be a boys' gang, a coffee club, a nation, or a far-flung empire. Here we are concerned with developing a theory of power at the level of the modern nation state. Most discussions of power deal with the power of the state, that is, political power, because it includes the particularly dramatic element of physical force. In stable societies it is only political power-holders who have the right to use such force. The loyalty of the police and the army to political power-holders is the acid test of power in the political system. In some societies, in contemporary France or Latin America, for example, this test is made frequently. In others, it is occasionally made when civil disturbances require the restoration of order or the enforcement of legislation, as at Little Rock in the United States, or when governments intervene to break strikes, as at Louisville in Quebec.

Power, however, is not something which belongs to political officeholders alone. Rather it is found in all the social institutions which over time have been created by a society as means of getting certain essential tasks accomplished. These institutions can be regarded as sub-systems of the total social system. We often speak of the political system and the economic system as separate but related parts of the total society. We also attribute to them a certain degree of autonomous functioning. This breaking up of the society into functioning parts has been a long historical process. It is a process of differentiation, an extension of the social division of labour.

In modern societies it is possible to identify, beyond the economic and the political, several sub-systems, each having a relatively autonomous life. Important among these are the military, the governmental bureaucracy, and those institutions, such as the mass media, educational institutions, and the Church, which create and propagate the ideas which hold the society together. All of these sub-systems perform essential social functions. All of them must be directed and co-ordinated. It is this need for direction and co-ordination which gives rise to power. The power which resides in all these other sub-systems circumscribes the power of the political system. Power in other words is distributed through these various institutional orders. ...

The Canadian Political System

Canada's political system has not been neglected by social scientists. Historians, political scientists, and constitutional lawyers have provided a comprehensive picture of the development and formal operation of the major political institutions of the society. If there are any underlying themes in all this work they are the emergence of an independent statehood for Canada, and the search for a "viable federalism" in which the relative importance of the federal and provincial governments changes in the process of their adapting to the paramount problems of the day. The material on Canadian political institutions is largely descriptive. With a few exceptions there is an absence of a political theory by which the descriptive materials take on some meaning. Although there are political theories general to all societies it seems necessary, as well, for particular societies to have theories about themselves.

The Political System

Canada has no resounding charter myth proclaiming a utopia against which, periodically, progress can be measured. At the roost, national goals and dominant values seem to be expressed in geographical terms such as "from sea to sea," rather than in social terms such as "all men are created equal," or "liberty, fraternity, and equality." In the United States there is a utopian image which slowly over time bends intractable social patterns in the direction of equality, but a Canadian counterpart of this image is difficult to find.

The question which we are seeking to explore here is what does a political system do, what is its function in the total society? Clearly the function of the economic system is to produce a society's wealth. But the function of a political system cannot be so clearly stated. Although there is unlikely to be agreement among social scientists, the view taken here is that the political system is the one through which the society as a group can achieve its major goals and values, if it has any.

Undoubtedly major goals and values can be stated only in very general terms such as progress, a high standard of living, equality. Often these major values can be traced to some charter instrument such as a bill of rights or a constitution which has acquired, over time, a charismatic aura. These values will be reaffirmed periodically through social movements, such as Jeffersonian liberalism in the United States. They will also appear as recurring themes in a society's literature. Because values and goals will be cast in general terms they can be appropriated by both conservative elements supporting the *status quo* and utopian liberal elements seeking social change. Freedom can be seen as "wearing a crown" and also as being achieved by the breaking of imperial ties. However, unless there are values general to the society, it is difficult for the society to make judgments about its progress, although reference can be made to standards and values of other societies.

In a discussion of the political system of the United States, Talcott Parsons has suggested that the value system centres on what he calls "instrumental activism." The values against which actions are judged are cast in terms of economic adaptation or mastery of the physical conditions of life. There are general goals also of progress and improvement in which economic production is the main instrument of advance. It is the task of the political system and the leadership roles within it to mobilize the society's resources to these broad ends. In a differentiated pluralistic society there will not be general agreement on the means to be employed to reach these general values. There will, however, be some agreement on the ground rules. There are constitutional ground rules, but at the same time there is a body of political conventions which political parties observe, one of the most important being that the political party in power permits its rivals to exist. The two-party system is a functionally appropriate way of mediating the "conservative" and "progressive" social forces.

In his discussion of right and left in American politics Parsons argues that the focus of the American right is the organization of the free enterprise economy. The "right" becomes politically conservative because positive political action is seen as a threat to this free enterprise economy. The "left" on the other hand focuses on positive political action and is favourable to reform, to control of the economy, to the promotion of welfare, and to intervention in foreign affairs. These right and left foci distinguish in general terms the Republican and Democratic parties. Both parties seek to mobilize support. They alternate in office so that there is a swinging back and forth between the two dominant trends, but some dynamic development is achieved, because although the pressure for change comes from the left, and change is bitterly opposed by the right, the right, when it gets into office, does not destroy the advances made by the left. Although not all will agree that the Republican and Democratic parties are so distinguishable, it would be difficult to refute their respective foci to the right and left, the conservative and the progressive. The important point here is that in political systems and through political parties there is a polarization of the progressive and conservative forces, even though in the United States there is still a general acceptance of the view that the major goals of the society are achieved through the economic system rather than the political.

This brief outline of Parsons' analysis of the political dynamic in the United States is not intended to suggest that a similar political process takes place in Canada. All too often Canadian social scientists draw analogies from American experience. Rather, Parsons' account is a model of a political dynamic which results from a polarization of the right and the left. A similar model could be built from British experience. Marx, of course, also presented a model except that, for him, the polarization was so complete that mediation within the same normative order was impossible.

National Unity: Canada's Political Obsession

It would probably be safe to say that Canada has never had a political system with this dynamic quality. Its two major political parties do not focus to the right and the left. In the sense that both are closely linked with corporate enterprise the dominant focus has been to the right. One of the reasons why this condition has prevailed is that Canada lacks clearly articulated major goals and values stemming from some charter instrument which emphasizes progress and equality. If there is a major goal of Canadian society it can best be described as an integrative goal. The maintenance of national unity has overridden any other goal's there might have been, and has prevented a polarizing, within the political system, of conservative and progressive forces. It has never occurred to any Canadian commentators that national unity might in fact be achieved by such a polarization. Rather a dissociative federalism is raised to the level of a quasi-religious political dogma, and polarization to right and left in Canadian politics is regarded as disruptive. Consequently the main focus of Canadian politics has been to the right and the maintenance of the *status quo*. The reason that the Liberal party in Canada was in office so many years until 1957 was not because it was a progressive party, but because it served Canada's major goal of national unity.

The major themes in Canadian political thought emphasize those characteristics, mainly regional and provincial loyalties, which divide the Canadian population. Consequently integration and national unity must be a constantly reiterated goal to counter such divisive sentiments. The dialogue is between unity and discord rather than progressive and conservative forces. The question which arises is whether the discord-unity dialogue has any real meaning in the lives of Canadians, or whether it has become, in the middle of the twentieth century, a political technique of conservatism. Canada must be one of the few major industrial societies in which the right and left polarization has become deflected into disputes over regionalism and national unity.

Canada's major political and intellectual obsession, national unity, has had its effect on the careers of men who take on political roles. It has put a premium on the type of man whom we shall label the administrative politician and has discounted the professional political career in which creative politicians can assume leadership roles. Creative politics at the national level has not been known in Canada since before World War I when the westward thrust to Canada's empire was still a major national goal. Since the empire of the west was secured national goals of development have not been known.

Creative politics is politics which has the capacity to change the social structure in the direction of some major social goals or values. By mobilizing human resources for new purposes, it has the initiative in the struggle against the physical environment and against dysfunctional historical arrangements. Creative politics requires a highly developed political leadership to challenge entrenched power within other institutional orders. It succeeds in getting large segments of the population identified with the goals of the political system and in recruiting their energies and skills to political ends.

Elites, Classes, and Power in Canada

Leo V. Panitch (1995)

EDITORS' INTRODUCTION

Leo Panitch is the Canada Research Chair in Comparative Political Economy and Distinguished Research Professor at York University, Toronto, and the co-editor of the Socialist Register. *He is a prominent scholar in the leftist political economy tradition. Much of his scholarly work, based on Marxist political analysis, examines global capitalism and global finance and the role the United States plays in creating and managing a capitalist world order.*

The essay excerpted here examines class power structures in Canada and the role those power structures play in creating class (and by implication racial, ethnic, and sexual) inequalities. Panitch argues that political scientists should move beyond an analysis of elites and the governing institutions they control, and instead focus on a class-based analysis of the material social relations that determine the composition of society, and the distribution of power within it.

"*In Toronto there are no classes … just the Masseys and the masses.*" This little ditty, perhaps reflecting a centralist bias characteristic of Canadian politics itself, captures graphically the way political scientists have often approached the study of power in Canadian society. Inequalities of political and economic power are rarely denied and indeed are frequently a direct object of study. In general, however, political scientists have operated with a somewhat impoverished—and misleading—set of concepts in trying to understand these inequalities. As in the case of "the Masseys and the masses," they have tended to categorize society in terms of a gradation of rich, middle, and poor, and to examine politics in terms of elites with power and masses without. In employing such imprecise and over-simplified generalizations, social scientists have obscured and mystified the real links between social, economic, and political power in Canada.

Who, then, are these "elites" and "masses"? Occasionally, and most usually in the context of voting behaviour studies, the "masses" are divided into statistical classes grouped together on the basis of income, occupational status, or the "common-sense" self-perception of individuals themselves in class terms. Insofar as actual socioeconomic collectivities of people are dealt with, this has usually been done in terms of the concept of "interest groups"—formal organizations of farmers, workers, business-people, and the like. Those who lead such organizations are usually designated as "elites" and differentiated from the "non-decision-making" mass

Source: *Canadian Politics in the 1990s*, 4th edition, edited by Michael S. Whittington and Glen Williams. Scarborough, ON: Nelson, 1995. Some notes omitted. Reprinted by permission of the author.

of their members. In this view, *power* is seen in terms of *relations among elites*. It is extended to the study of relationships between elites and masses only through the highly structured contexts of elections, opinion polls, and interest group "demands."

The problem with this approach is not that it sees politics as isolated from socioeconomic structure. On the contrary, the behaviour of elites is very much seen as conditioned by the socioeconomic "background" of the individuals who compose them, and by the highly structured demands coming through voting or interest groups from society. As in the celebrated political system approach, which serves as a conceptual framework for Canada's most widely used introductory political science text, the determinant of politics is seen as "demands" coming from the "environment" of politics.

It is often alleged that what is wrong here is that the political system is a "black box" that reveals little of the inner workings of government, where the most salient elites make their decisions. There is something in this argument, but what is even more striking is the "black hole"—the environment. We are told that scarcity prevails here and that demands are generated by conflicts over resources, but a systematic examination of the way in which our economy is structured to cope with material scarcity, of the social relations that result between people, and thus of the concrete material clash of social forces that goes on is seldom undertaken. References to individual competition or intergroup competition, as with rich and poor, elite and mass, may give us clues, but because of their "gross-ness" as categories, because of their abstraction from concrete social relationships between people in a capitalist society such as Canada, they do not contribute enough to our understanding of what is acknowledged to be the determinant element of politics—the socioeconomic system in which politics is embedded.

To properly understand the relationship between society and politics involves taking an analysis of society seriously, which itself entails going beyond categories such as elite, mass, and group. It involves getting down to the material social relationships between people, their common experiences in terms of these relationships, and the actual collectivities they form and the struggles they enter into handling these experiences. This is what a *class analysis*, as opposed to an *elite analysis*, of society and politics is designed to do. In Canada—and even in Toronto—there *are* classes, and it is their history of contradictory relations to one another, and the balance of power that results at given periods and instances, that establishes the foundation of politics, including setting the extent and limit of the power of the Masseys, or that of any other "elite."

Elite Analysis in Canada

There is fairly widespread agreement among political scientists that what is meant by the term "democracy" as applied to a contemporary political system is "that institutional arrangement for arriving at political decisions in which individuals acquire the power to decide by means of a competitive struggle for the people's vote." The people themselves do not decide, and therefore power does not immediately reside with the people, but rather "the people have the opportunity of accepting or refusing the men [*sic*] who are to rule them." This is an "elitist" conception of democracy that does not require or expect high citizen participation in public affairs beyond the act of choosing between competing teams of leaders. A degree of *elite-pluralism* is guaranteed in this system, at least with a view to elections and formal parliamentary opposition, by a two-party or multiparty system. Moreover, in the case of a federal system like Canada's, the elite-teams compete for votes in various jurisdictions, and this further tends to multiply the extent of elite-pluralism. Finally, insofar as freedom of association prevails, it is recognized that the decision-making elites may be subject to a process of interest-group competition for influence upon them.

This system of elite-pluralism, however much it may be demarcated from broader, more mass-participatory conceptions of democracy, is not to be sneezed at as a minimal description of "actually existing" liberal democracies. It captures, albeit in too formal and nonhistorical a fashion, some of the basic differences between a polity such as ours and an authoritarian regime. Yet serious students of power in Canadian society have understandably not been willing to rest content with minimal descriptions of this sort. They have wanted to know *who* these competing teams of leaders are in socioeconomic terms and the extent to which they reflect in their competition and decision-making a narrow or broad range of approaches to public issues and concerns. They have wanted to know the relationship between the democratically elected political elites and those decision-makers in institutional spheres, such as the private corporations that dominate our economy, that are not democratically elected. To speak of elite-pluralism properly, they have recognized, entails examining the degree of *autonomy* political elites have from, at least, the elites that exercise power (in this sense of decision-making) in the economic sphere. ...

Turning to the tendency for elite analysis to treat social, political, and economic power in relation to equality of opportunity, it should be apparent that problems of domination and subordination are not reducible simply to patterns of recruitment. Even a perfect meritocracy implies a social division of labour, with people in authority and people subject to their authority. Authority positions, positions of control, set structural limits to what individuals can do in occupying decision-making roles within these institutions. If the president of INCO were to change places with a hard-rock miner, the structural position of the *place* occupied by each individual would strongly condition her or his behaviour. Elite analysis, in general, gives too much credence to the autonomous ability of "elites" to make unconstrained decisions. ...

It may be said that the main shortcoming of elite analysis is that it tends to ascribe *too much power*, indeed exclusive power, to those at the top. Restricting the concept of power, by definition, to authority in institutions obscures the fact that *power is a fluid social process* that, if stopped dead and anatomized in institutional terms, constantly evades analysis. The very private property market economy that corporate elite members seem to dominate by virtue of their institutional authority and cohesiveness is at the same time a limit on their authority and cohesiveness. Their positions are dependent on maintaining a rate of profit relatively high in relation to other corporations. Even if corporation executives don't lose their positions by the corporation going bankrupt, capital will flow form the less profitable corporations to the more profitable, and thus those in the less profitable will lose a good deal of their power. It is less institutional control than control over capital, a much more fluid thing, that is the foundation of the power of the corporate elite.

Similarly, by looking for power only among the elites one is forced to treat the masses as inert political clay, without self-activity (except perhaps in the highly structured context of elections). Yet the ways in which collectivities outside the "confraternity of power" engage in struggles to further their interests both limit and influence the decisions of institutional officeholders. Indeed, in the very definition of democracy that introduced this section it may be noted that the political elites' power finds its source in "the people's vote." This already implies that the power in question cannot be atomized only by examining the elites but must instead be seen in terms of a relationship between masses and elites. This would mean paying attention to the social collectivities that make up the "masses," inquiring whether these have modes of activity, of exercising power, outside of the electoral process—as indeed they do. If would also mean examining whether and where the relations between the collectivities intersect and overlap within and between the spheres of economy, state, and culture that the elite theorists look at only in terms of those at the top.

It is one of the ironies of elite theory that it often takes its intellectual root in the argument that Marxist class analysis assumes an all-powerful ruling class that does not fit 20th-century reality. Yet elite theory ends up seeing power much more monolithically than class analysis ever does, for class analysis entails seeing power as a *relational* concept, involving the necessity of tension, conflict, and struggle between social classes. ...

Class Analysis

The concept of class which finds the significant determinant of social and political behaviour in the ability or inability of labour—one's own and others'—demonstrated its value in nineteenth-century historical and sociological analysis, but has been rather scorned of late years. No doubt it is inadequate in its original form to explain the position of the new middle class of technicians, supervisors, managers, and salaried officials, whose importance in contemporary society is very great; yet their class positions can best be assessed by the same criteria: how much freedom they retain over the disposal of their own labour, and how much control they exercise over the disposal of others' labour. Nor is this concept of class as readily amenable as are newer concepts to those techniques of measurement and tabulation which, as credentials, have become so important to modern sociology. Yet it may be thought to remain the most penetrating basis of classification for the understanding of political behaviour. Common relationship to the disposal of labour still tends to give the members of each class, so defined, an outlook and set of assumptions distinct from those of the other classes.

This does not necessarily mean that the members of a class, so defined, are sufficiently conscious of a class interest to act mainly in terms of it in making political choices. Nor need it mean that their outlook and assumptions are a conscious reflection of class position or needs as an outside observer or historian might see them.

These words by C.B. Macpherson, from *Democracy in Alberta*, are as relevant today as when they were written 30 years ago. The central notion here is that it is people's *relationship* to property, to the ownership and control of the means of production, that is the main guide to the social composition of society and to the power relations that pertain therein. Macpherson has noted in another context that a "somewhat looser conception of class, defined at its simplest in terms of rich, middle or poor, has been prominent in political theory as far back as one likes to go." It is this looser definition of class that is employed in elite analysis in Canada. Insofar as the object of attention is the elite and its characteristics, the 80–90 percent of the population that is excluded from the upper or middle class (defined by elite family backgrounds, private-school or university education, fathers with professional occupations, or an income above a certain level) remains an undifferentiated "mass." ...

A class analysis always begins with *social relationships* that people enter into, or are born into, in producing their material means of livelihood. For production to take place in any society—and without it no society can exist—three elements are necessary: producers—the people doing the work themselves; objects of labour—the natural materials to work on (land, mineral, fish, etc.); and means of labour—instruments to work with (hoes, nets, tractors, boats, machines, computers, etc.). These elements may be owned by the producers themselves (collectively as in many primitive tribal societies, or individually as in the case of the family farm or the craftsperson's workshop) or by someone else who is a nonproducer. In a slave society, all the elements—including the producers— are predominantly owned by slaveholders. Under feudalism, the most important object of labour—the land—is predominantly owned by landlords. In a capitalist society, the means of labour—the machines, factories, offices, etc.—are predominantly owned by capitalists, individually or as groups of capitalists (as in the modern corporation).

Thus, the relationships between owners and nonowners, producers and nonproducers, vary in different modes of production. Under slavery, the direct producers are in a position of servitude to the nonproducers and can be bought and sold or born into servitude. Under feudalism, the peasants are not themselves owned and possess their own tools, but are legally tied to the land and required to pass over a portion of their produce to the landlord. Under capitalism, the producer is free, in the sense of having a proprietary right over his or her own labour, but is disposed of proprietary holdings of the objects and means of labour. In order to obtain the wherewithal to exist, therefore, the producer must sell his or her labour for a wage or salary to those who own the means of production and who control this labour directly—or indirectly through managers—in the production process. On this basis we can locate the predominant social classes of each society.

Classes are large groups of people, differing from each other by the places they occupy in a historically determined system of social production, by their relation (in most cases fixed and formulated in law) to the means of production, by their role in the social organization of labour, and consequently by the dimensions of the share of social wealth of which they dispose and the mode of acquiring it. Classes are groups of people one of which can appropriate the labour of another owing to the different places they occupy in a definitive system of social economy.[12]

It will be seen immediately that classes thus approached are not ordered in a higher and lower fashion, as rungs on a ladder, but rather in terms of people's *relationship* to one another. While it is a multidimensional relationship in that people are dependent on one another (the elements must be brought together in order for production to take place), it is unequal dependence in that one class appropriates the labour of another. Because the mutual dependence is therefore one of dominance of one class and subjection of another by the appropriation of labour, the social relationship is a *contradictory* one, entailing the potential of antagonism, of conflict, between the classes. This is not to say that the permanent condition of society is one of strikes, demonstrations, revolts, and revolutions. These are but the more explosive outcomes of the contradictory relations in question. But in the sense of an irreconcilable *basis* of conflict, over how much and under what specific conditions labour will be appropriated from the direct producers, the system is a conflictual one. This has historically been expressed in struggles over control of the labour process, over the length of the working day, and over remuneration, over new machines that displace labour and/or require labour to work more intensively.

But if these kinds of struggles have been more common than struggles to "change the system" itself, this reflects the balance of power between the classes. Class analysis is precisely about assessing that balance of power. This does not mean that those who sell their labour to others—the working class in capitalist society—have power only at the moment of social revolution. For it will be seen that what is operating in the relations between classes is never all power on one side and the lack of it on the other. Because the classes are constituted in terms of their mutual, contradictory dependence on one another, both sides always have power. The balance of power may be unequal, and may structurally favour those who own and control the means of production, but depending on given economic, cultural, and political conditions, the balance may change. This may alter the terms and conditions of the appropriation of labour, and it may give rise to struggles over changing the historically structured relations between classes themselves. But all this is the object of inquiry within a class analysis.

It should be stressed that in talking about classes in this way, we are talking about actual historical groups, real collectivities of people, who therefore cannot ever be examined in terms of economic categories alone. Classes, as societies, are constituted on a material basis in terms of producing the material means of livelihood, but they exist simultaneously in terms of culture, ideology, politics, consciousness. Insofar as we speak of classes in terms of statistical economic categories (so many owners, so many workers, etc.), we miss the point that we are dealing with real men and women. This is usually seen to be important—and it is—in terms of assessing the degree to which class relations as defined above are expressed in cultural, political, and ideological differentiations and conflicts. But it is important as well in terms of understanding the basis of social cohesion and stability of a society in the face of the inherently contradictory relations between classes, since the maintenance and reproduction of the relations of production is itself dependent not only on economic relations but on the degree of cultural, political, and ideological homogeneity that keeps these contradictory relations in check. This too, then, is part of the balance of power, which means that to undertake a class analysis of society we do not just map out economic relations, but rather examine the totality of cultural, ideological, and political, as well as the economic, relations between classes as the relevant "variables" in the overall balance of power. ...

Political Science and Social Change

The study of politics is not just the study of parliaments or bureaucracies or even a broader study of the most powerful decision-makers in all spheres of society. It must be a study as well of the social forces "from below." Some will say that is the proper field of sociology, especially insofar as the activities of those below, even if they influence the decision-makers, do not have enough power "to change the system." But this is an impoverished view of political science. Indeed, as Antonio Gramsci wrote half a century ago,

> If political science means science of the State, and the State is the entire complex of practical and theoretical activities with which the ruling class not only justifies and maintains its dominance, but manages to win the active consent of those over whom it rules, then it is obvious that all essential questions of sociology are nothing other than questions of political science.

There is another important dimension to political science, of course, which precisely has to do with "changing the system"; which is not just about analyzing what the state and ruling class do, criticizing it on this basis, or even coming forward on the basis of this analysis with "public policy" proposals for enabling the state to manage the system better. Rather, this other dimension of political science is about developing analyses of the processes and strategies involved in changing the system from one based on class competition, exploitation, and conflict to a different system based on the elimination of classes and the development of as fully a democratic, egalitarian, and cooperative society as possible. Here we begin to raise larger questions about what "science" is really all about. And Gramsci is again a valuable guide:

> Is not science itself "political activity" and political thought, in as much as it transforms men, and makes them different from what they were before? ... If science is the "discovery" of formerly unknown reality, is this reality not conceived of in a certain sense as transcendent? And is it not thought that there still exists something "unknown" and hence transcendent? And does not the concept of science as "creation" then mean that it too is "politics"? Everything depends on seeing whether the creation involved is "arbitrary," or whether it is rational—i.e., useful to men in that it enlarges their concept of life, and raises to a higher level (develops) life itself.

We can see, in this sense, the importance of a political science that is trying to know more than how to uncover how the power elites rule the world, but that also has an understanding that the majorities subjected to that rule also have power capacities, and is trying to discover how those capacities might be enhanced—not just to criticize the elites or ruling classes, not just to influence their decisions through struggles "from below," but to "transcend" the present system of power relations entirely. This is less a matter of constructing Utopian visions of a "good society" than of discovering the means whereby the subordinate classes have increased their power historically, and of trying to discover further and better means. Political science has a role to play in demonstrating that most people are not just passive recipients of someone else's power, that they currently exercise some power even if just in relation to the greater power of the dominant classes. It could have a larger and more creative role to play by discovering the limits to the ways in which subordinate classes have organized so far, and by trying to think through and offer advice on how to organize for a fundamental challenge to the powers that be. This will, above all, be a matter of discovering the kind of political organizations that enhance the intellectual capacities of working people themselves, so that they can become leaders and educators in their own communities and develop their capacities to run society and state in a fully democratic manner. To be a political scientist, in this conception, is to be someone who knows how to do more than criticize the power elite. It is to be someone who is orientated to discovering how to help those who have the potential power to change the system to realize that they have that potential—and then actually to act upon that potential. Philosophers, a great social scientist once said, have always tried to understand the world, but the point of this understanding, he appropriately insisted, was to change it.

Note

12. V.I. Lenin, "A Great Beginning" (1919), *Selected Works*, vol. 3 (Moscow: 1971), p. 231.

74 Income Inequality in Canada: What Can Be Done

Armine Yalnizyan (2013)

EDITORS' INTRODUCTION

In September 2011 the grassroots protest movement Occupy Wall Street and its corollaries around the world brought attention to the issue of income inequality and the uneven distribution of wealth, a state of affairs that had become even more apparent after the global economic crisis that began in 2008. The movement's slogan, "We are the 99 percent," refers to the staggering income disparity between the wealthiest 1 percent of Americans and the rest of the population. A number of similar #Occupy protests occurred in major Canadian cities. Though income inequality in Canada is not the ideological rallying cry it often is in the United States, Armine Yalnizyan, senior economist for the Canadian Centre for Policy Alternatives, demonstrates in this 2013 report to the House of Commons Standing Committee on Finance that income disparity is indeed real, growing, and detrimental, but that it can also be alleviated through adequate policy responses at the federal level.

Presentation to the House of Commons Standing Committee on Finance, April 30, 2013

Thank you for the opportunity to address your Committee on the issue of income inequality, and what can be done in Canada to offset its growth.

Income inequality used to widen in the wake of recessions, and shrink in times of solid job growth. But over the past generation, income inequality has risen in periods of robust economic growth too, in Canada and around the world.

Income inequality has become another inconvenient truth of our era, as challenging to our economy, our health, and our future as climate change. And, as with climate change, it attracts its share of deniers. But Canada would be wise to consider not only the message, but the messengers on the global scene who have issued strong warnings on what inaction could mean for both equity and efficiency.

The International Monetary Fund has shown that higher income inequality is associated with greater market volatility and less economic growth over the longer term.

Source: Transcript of presentation to the House of Commons Standing Committee on Finance, Ottawa, April 30, 2013. Reprinted by the Canadian Centre for Policy Alternatives. Notes omitted.

Analysis from the World Bank links the relationships between globalization, growing income inequality and democracy, and raises the provocative question whether inequality, unchecked, undermines democratic capitalism.

Internationally referenced Canadian academic Miles Corak has documented that the greater the income inequality of adults in a nation, the less the economic mobility of their children.

These are not trends only happening elsewhere, to other people. They are also occurring in Canada.

The Conference Board of Canada has warned that growing income inequality, left unchecked, will lead to lost potential, increased costs, squandered opportunity and potential social unrest.

Data from the Organization for Economic Cooperation and Development (OECD) shows that whereas Canada bucked the international trend towards rising income inequality between the mid 1980s and mid 1990s, since then Canada has been the country that slipped most rapidly down the international rankings, from 14th most equal to 22nd, from above-average to below-average equality. During this period, 15 of 34 OECD nations reduced inequality.

University of Toronto's Centre for Urban and Community Studies has launched pathbreaking research on Canada's major cities, visualizing how income polarization has led to spatial polarization, through the evolution towards more rich and poor neighbourhoods and fewer middle class ones.

The promise of equality of opportunity rings hollow for children whose opportunity is increasingly hardwired into their environments, through the quality of their schools, recreational outlets, and access to jobs. Create cities where you can predict poverty by postal code, and you are asking for trouble.

Between 1981 and 2010, the economy more than doubled in inflation-adjusted terms, but poverty has grown for working age adults and seniors. For children under 18, poverty is approaching rates of the mid 1970s, but is higher than it was in 1989 when all Parliamentarians unanimously voted to eliminate child poverty by the year 2000. What may seem a utopian rhetorical flourish has been close to accomplished in other developed nations such as Denmark, Sweden, Norway, Finland.

The economic pie has more than doubled yet the share of Canadians with inflation-adjusted earnings between $30,000 and $60,000—what could be termed the "middle class"—continues to decline. It needs to be noted that this class is above the middle. That is because, by 2010, over 50% of Canadians earned less than $30,000, a slightly larger share of the working population than in the mid 1970s in inflation-adjusted terms.

More of the gains from growth are ending up in the pockets of higher-income individuals and households than in the past. Based on individual tax data, the top 1% in Canada accounted for 32% of all income growth in the decade 1997–2007. Think that is normal? It is four times the gain during a period of similar growth in the 1960s, and almost double the gains accruing to the top 1% during the Roaring Twenties. We are in uncharted territory economically.

Over the course of 35 years, half of Canada's working aged population would be living on much less income than their predecessors were it not for government actions. As it is, the poorest 40% of working-age Canadians are living on less after-tax income, in inflation-adjusted terms, than their counterparts in the mid 1970s.

Figure 1   Percent of People With Incomes Below the Low Income Measure (After Tax), By Age, Canada, 1976–2010

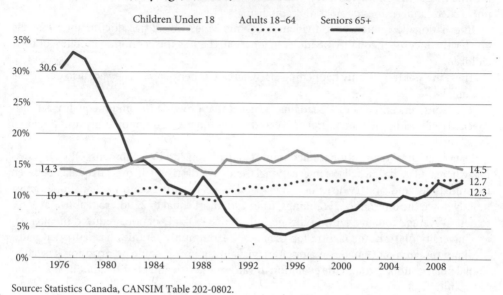

Source: Statistics Canada, CANSIM Table 202-0802.

Figure 2   Percent of Canadians Earning In Low, Middle, and High Income Classes (in Constant $2010), Canada, 1976–2010

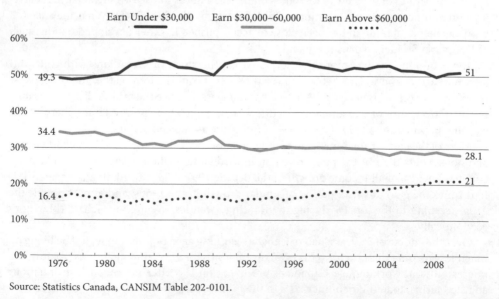

Source: Statistics Canada, CANSIM Table 202-0101.

Figure 3   Share of Income Gains Captured By Top 1%, Canada, 1920–2007

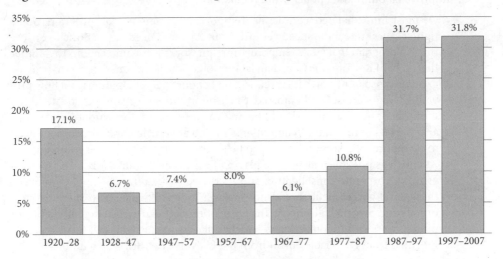

Source: Yalnizyan, Rise of Canada's Richest 1%. www.policyalternatives.ca.

Globalization and technological change are often cited as reasons for the widespread growth in income inequality. But the trends are not inevitable, as evidenced by variations across and within nations.

The federal government of Canada has a key role to play in offsetting growing income inequality, and has a broad suite of options for action:

1. Direct income measures: Enhance the Working Income Tax Benefit, refundable tax credits, Child Tax Benefit, Guaranteed Income Supplement or Old Age Security. Or introduce more sweeping reforms such as a Guaranteed Income. Improving EI would also increase incomes for jobless individuals, as well as help our macro-economy become more recession-proof.

2. Indirect support: The governments of eight provincial and territorial jurisdictions have committed to poverty reduction strategies. The federal government should support these initiatives, which would be distinctive in each region, and showcase best practices. The Alternative Federal Budget has outlined such a plan.

3. Tax measures: If new taxes are ruled out, it is critical that the existing tax regime is not further compromised. Enforcing rules on the books will require enhancements, rather than staff cuts, at the Canada Revenue Agency; and follow-through on prosecutions of tax evasions. Avoid expanding tax shelters through the Tax Free Savings Account and do not introduce income splitting for families with young children. Both measures widen, rather than reduce, disparities, as identified by the Library of Parliament in 2007, and the Department of Finance in February 2013.

4. Improve supports and services: Target additional revenues raised or not foregone from proposals in 3) to invest in the things that can greatly alleviate the pressure on middle- and low-income households: childcare, transit, housing, post-secondary education.

5. Improve labour market policies and regulations:

- Of most immediate concern is the Temporary Foreign Worker program. Some tighter rules were announced yesterday but far more needs to be done to ensure this is a program that views temporary foreign workers as complements to—rather than substitutes for—the Canadian labour force. The government needs to provide greater transparency on who is requesting Labour Market Opinions and how prevailing wages are set and enforced. Such information needs to be updated on a monthly basis. A website should be dedicated to such information. Exemptions and waivers to minimum requirements for job advertising and recruitment need to be reduced. Existing rules need to be enforced, and shown to be enforced.
- As much as possible, balance the playing field in the labour market: In an era of growing corporate consolidation and increased bargaining power of employers, the federal government should not make it more difficult for workers to form unions and bargain collectively. The correlation between greater equality, a bigger middle class and unionization is widely documented, as you will hear later this morning from Dr. Nicole Fortin from the University of British Columbia.

Any of these steps can reduce income inequality and improve opportunity. At the very least, public policy should not exacerbate market forces that have tended to increase income inequality in Canada.

The Pattern of Prairie Politics

75

Nelson Wiseman (1981)

EDITORS' INTRODUCTION

Nelson Wiseman teaches political science at the University of Toronto and is an expert on Canadian politics and Canadian political culture. He deploys the tools of history and other qualitative methods to observe regional variation in Canada's political culture. His 2007 volume In Search of Canadian Political Culture *provides a comprehensive distillation of five regional political cultures in Canada (Atlantic Canada, Quebec, Ontario, the midwestern provinces of Manitoba and Saskatchewan, and the far western provinces of Alberta and British Columbia).*

The article excerpted here, first published in Queen's Quarterly, *provides a succinct statement of his thesis regarding the importance of studying regional political cultures in order to understand both federal and provincial elections and party politics, and is both a critique of and builds upon Gad Horowitz's famous essay, "Conservatism, Liberalism, and Socialism in Canada: An Interpretation."*

Canadian historians and social scientists have usually thought of the prairies as a more or less homogeneous unit whose politics have been essentially a response, a reaction, to externally imposed conditions: the tariff, the withholding of authority over natural resources by the federal government, discriminatory transportation policies, etc. This approach tells us substantially about east–west Canadian relations. By itself, however, it tells us little about diversity of political traditions *on* the prairies. What is needed is an interpretive analysis which comes to terms with intra-regional differences. Why, until quite recently, has Manitoba politics been so dominated by Liberal and Conservative regimes? Why has Saskatchewan been so receptive to the CCF-NDP? Why did Alberta spawn such a durable and unorthodox farmers' government (the UFA) and then, overnight, become the bastion of an equally unorthodox Social Credit regime?

Answers to these questions do not lie (although some clues do) in an analysis of the east–west relationship. Nor do the answers lie in analyses which focus strictly on party systems or economic conditions. An economic analysis may be used to explain why, in the landmark federal election of 1911, Saskatchewan and Alberta endorsed the Liberals and freer trade, but it will not explain why Manitoba endorsed the Conservatives and protection. An analysis of party systems may be used to explain why, at the provincial level, Saskatchewan

Source: Excerpted from "The Pattern of Prairie Politics," *Queen's Quarterly*, vol. 88, no. 2 (Summer 1981). Reprinted by permission.

and Alberta rejected the two older parties in favor of third parties. It will not explain, however, why those two third parties are at opposite poles of the Canadian political spectrum. Identifying and accounting for the differences among the three prairie provinces, therefore, is essential. But this too is insufficient because striking diversities are to be located not only among but also *within* the provinces. By the 1890s, for example, Manitoba had been remade in the image of western Ontario. Yet in 1919, Winnipeg exhibited a level of class consciousness and class conflict that was decidedly more reminiscent of the European than the North American scheme of things. In Saskatchewan, until 1945, the federal Liberal party was consistently stronger than in any other English Canadian province. But it was this same province that returned North America's first social democratic government, a CCF government whose ideology was rooted in the British Labour party. Inconsistent political patterns seem no less profound in Alberta where governing parties that are defeated at the polls have faded almost immediately.

The analysis employed here utilizes the concepts of ideology and ethnicity. Elements of Canadian toryism, liberalism and socialism have been present in varying proportions in each province. Political representatives of these ideological tendencies on the prairies include men as diverse as Rodmond Roblin, John Diefenbaker, Charles Dunning, J.W. Dafoe, J.S. Woodsworth, Tommy Douglas, Henry Wise Wood, and William Aberhart, none of whom were born on the prairies. Because the prairie provinces and their societies were moulded in the late nineteenth and early twentieth centuries this is not surprising. Ideas and ideologies first appeared on the prairies as importations.

It is very unlikely that a Rodmond Roblin or a Tommy Douglas, preaching what they did, could have become premiers of Alberta. William Aberhart would not likely have succeeded in Manitoba or Saskatchewan. Politicians are reflectors of their society, their environment, their times. They may be examined in terms which transcend quirks of personality. Their ideas and actions may be seen as reflections of the popular and ideological-cultural basis of their support.

The key to prairie politics is in the unravelling of the dynamic relationship between ideological-cultural heritage and party. In Manitoba, the imported nineteenth-century Ontario liberal party tradition (with "a tory touch") maintained political hegemony until 1969. In Saskatchewan, the dominant tone of politics has reflected a struggle between Ontario liberal and British socialist influences. In Alberta, American populist-liberal ideas gained widespread currency beginning in the very first decade of that province's existence. In all three provinces minorities of non-Anglo-American origins have, in their voting, helped make and break governments. These minorities, however, have not determined the ideological coloration of any major party.

Prairie political culture is best seen as the product of the interaction of four distinct waves of pioneering settlers. The first wave was a Canadian one. More precisely, it was largely rural Ontarian. This wave was a westward extension of English Canada's dominant charter group. Ontarians were a charter group in each prairie province but their impact was greatest in Manitoba. It seemed both fitting and telling, that one of Manitoba's premiers (Hugh John Macdonald) was the son of Canada's first prime minister. Tory-touched Canadian liberalism was the ideological core of nineteenth-century Ontario and its prairie offshoot.

A second distinct wave in prairie settlement was a new, modern, British group. Coming near the turn of this century, it was largely urban and working class. Transformed and battered by nineteenth-century industrialism, Britain's working class had begun to turn to socialism. Despite the cultural and ideological differences between the Ontario and new-British waves, their social status in the west was roughly equal, both groups being British subjects and Anglo-Saxon pioneers in British North America. The new-British wave had its greatest impact in the cities, most powerfully in the largest prairie city, Winnipeg. In Saskatchewan relatively large numbers of new British (and European-born) immigrants settled in rural areas and they produced Canada's most successful provincial social democratic party. It seemed both fitting and telling that Saskatchewan's premier in this labor-socialist tradition (Tommy Douglas) was British-born and grew up and was politically socialized in Winnipeg's new British labor-socialist environment.

The third wave in prairie settlement was American. More specifically it was midwest, great plains American. Like the Ontario wave, but unlike the new-British wave, it came out of an agrarian setting with deeply rooted agrarian values and settled, in overwhelming numbers, in rural areas. Because of their values and racial origin American Anglo-Saxons became the only non-Canadian, non-British charter group on the prairies. The dominant ideological strain carried by the American wave was similar but not identical to that carried by the Ontarians. It was, to be sure, liberal, but its liberalism was devoid of toryism. It was a radical "populist" liberalism that stressed the individual rather than the community or the state as a tory or socialist would. This wave's greatest impact was in rural Alberta, the continent's last agricultural frontier. Populist liberalism expressed itself in an unconventional farmers' movement/government known as the United Farmers of Alberta (UFA) and in the long tenure of Social Credit. It seemed both fitting and telling, that this wave's leading representative figure was a veteran Missouri populist (Henry Wise Wood).

The fourth and last wave of prairie settlement consisted of continental Europeans. Because of their numerous national origins, their roots and traditions were the most diverse of the four waves. They were, however, neither a charter group nor did they have a significant ideological impact (the eastern European and Finnish influences in the Communist Party being a minor exception). The non-Anglo-Saxons were "alien" and suspect in the eyes of the other three groups. At times their very presence was attacked and challenged; at best they were tolerated. The ideological and political role of the continental wave became largely one of deference. The continental wave had its greatest urban impact in Winnipeg and its greatest rural impact in Saskatchewan. These areas were also those in which the new-British wave had its greatest impact. The combined voting strength of these two waves was to lead to CCF-NDP victories in Manitoba and Saskatchewan in later years. The Old World ideological attributes of the continentals were dismissed as illegitimate on the prairies. Because of this continentals deferred to the parties based on the other three groups; but the continentals represented the largest swing factor in voting of the four waves. They helped elect and defeat parties anchored by the other waves; they neither anchored nor led a major party.

The foregoing description of the four distinct waves of prairie settlers is not intended to imply that all Ontarians were tory-touched liberals, that all new Britons were labor-socialists, that all Americans were populist-liberals, and that all continentals deferred ideologically and politically. Furthermore, it should be understood that not all Ontarians voted for the Liberals and Conservatives, not all new Britons voted CCF, and not all Americans voted UFA-Social Credit. The contention here, simply, is that without the new-British impact the CCF would never have attained the stature it did (indeed, it might not have been created at all); similarly, without the American impact the UFA-Social Credit phenomenon in Alberta would not have been anything like what it was; and without the Ontarians, prairie Liberal and Conservative parties would not have gained early hegemony. ...

American populist influences were greater in Saskatchewan than in Manitoba but they were secondary and not nearly as significant as in Alberta. In Alberta the American-style populist farmers association (the UFA) determined the complexion of successive provincial governments for years. Alberta populism, like American populism, attracted some socialists, but it rejected socialist ideology. CCF socialism, embraced in Saskatchewan, was rejected by Alberta farmers on the peculiarly American grounds that it represented a repudiation of their "rugged individualism."

Manitoba was the province most true to the values of rural Ontario. In the language rights debates it was more Orange than Ontario. Manitoba imported its early American-inspired farm organization—the Grange and the Patrons of Industry—only after they had become established in Ontario. Manitoba's Tory farmers rejected any suggestion of possible secession from Confederation and American annexation in the 1880s. ...

Although Manitoba Liberal and Conservative governments relied on rural support from continental-born immigrants, few Europeans, of either British or continental origins, were to be found in the higher echelons of either of these parties. Nor were many to be found in the United Farmers of Manitoba (UFM). "Canadian Ukrainians do not have any influence," declared one Ukrainian paper in 1932, the year of the CCF's birth. "We are poor and need political help. Ukrainian farmers and workers depend for their livelihood on the more powerful. This forces us to support a politically influential party. Affiliation with small radical parties brings us Ukrainians only discredit, and ruin." Such deference, however, did little for continental immigrants in the city. In the 1930s none of Winnipeg's banks, trust companies, or insurance firms would knowingly hire a Jew or anyone with a Ukrainian or Polish name. Nor would Anglo-Saxon premiers pick them for their cabinets.

Labor-socialist politics in Manitoba were as much determined by newly arrived Britons and Europeans as agrarian politics were determined by Ontarians. Winnipeg became the home of Canada's first independent Labour party (ILP), and by 1899, twenty-seven separate unions appeared at the May Day parade. A year later, the editor of Winnipeg's labor newspaper *The Voice* was elected to the House of Commons.

Within a decade the labor-socialist sectarianism of Europe was reproduced in Winnipeg. Two groups working outside of the dominant ILP influence were the Social Democratic party and the Socialist Party of Canada. By 1920–21 the two permanent parties that emerged were the British-led laborist ILP and the continental-based Communist party. Every imprisoned 1919 strike leader, except one, came from Britain to Winnipeg between 1896 and 1912. So too did most of the ILP leadership. The Communists, on the other hand, drew their inspiration from the Russian Revolution and scientific socialism. A small and insignificant British minority, including One Big Unionist and strike leader, R.B. Russell, stayed out of both camps. In Manitoba, as in Britain, laborism won over Marxism and syndicalism. By 1923, when the Ontario ILP was falling apart, the Manitoba ILP could boast that it held more than two dozen municipal and school board seats, the mayoralty of Winnipeg and representation in both federal and provincial parliaments. This modern, turn of the century British laborist tradition had its greatest Canadian urban impact in Winnipeg and Vancouver and, thus, the strength of the CCF-NDP in these cities. ...

Manitoba was ripe for an NDP victory in 1969 in a way that Ontario was not. In Ontario the impact of Anglo-Saxon voters, most of them long established in Canada, was more powerful than in Manitoba. This is another way of pointing out that Ontario is ideologically older than Manitoba in its liberalism and its conservatism, particularly in the rural areas, but in the cities too. There was a significant new British laborist impact in Ontario (e.g. Toronto mayor Jimmie Simpson in the 1930s) but, because of Ontario's relative oldness, it was not as profound as it was further west.

Manitoba had enough of Ontario in it to have sustained the only provincial Conservative party west of Ontario that has never collapsed. But it also had enough of modern Britain and continental Europe to provide CCFer J.S. Woodsworth and provincial Communist leader Bill Kardash with parliamentary seats between the 1920s and 1950s. Manitoba also had enough of the prairies in it to produce national and provincial Progressive parties in the 1920s. Their Ontario-born liberal leadership, however, led both of them back to the Liberal party.

As in Manitoba, provincial politics in Saskatchewan initially meant transplanting Ontarian politics. The provincial Liberal government operated at the pleasure of the Saskatchewan Grain Growers Association, the dominant political and economic organization in the province. Both the Liberals and the SGGA were led by the same figures and most of them had Ontario roots. The Progressive debacle in Ottawa, however, and the inability of the SGGA to break with the Liberals fuelled the formation of a rival agrarian organization: the Farmers Union of Canada. It was founded and first led by L. B. McNamee, a former British railway worker and trade unionist. This difference between the SGGA's Ontarian leadership and the Farmers Union British leadership broadly represented the difference between Ontario liberal and British socialist influences. The division became a central feature of Saskatchewan politics. ...

In Saskatchewan, however, unlike Manitoba and Alberta, there was a significant new-British *rural* presence. Although Saskatchewan attracted fewer Britons than either Manitoba or Alberta, it had almost as many British-born farm operators as the other two provinces combined. This British influence, coming later than the Ontario influx, took a longer time to assert itself. The farmer–labor connection in the Farmers Union was unique among prairie farm organizations of any significant size. Much of its support came from farmers in continental-based areas, areas that switched from the Liberals to the CCF between 1934 and 1944. The SGGA, like the neighboring UFM and UFA, had largely ignored the non-Anglo-Saxon farmers and had almost no following in areas settled by Europeans. All three organizations were rooted in the oldest and most established areas. ...

A contributing factor to the rise of socialism in Saskatchewan was that the cooperative movement was stronger there than in any other province. Moreover, Saskatchewan's co-operators were more socialist than their provincial neighbors. The cooperative movement became an integral part of the CCF's constituency in Saskatchewan and the movement's growth in the province was aided by a provincial government branch headed by a British immigrant experienced in the British cooperative movement. This "British" link reappears often in Saskatchewan history. ...

The CCF succeeded because it was British-led and ideologically British-based. The CCF's Britishness, its cultural acceptability, made it difficult to attack as alien. Its cultural legitimacy made it politically acceptable. It could therefore become an alternative to the Liberals for Saskatchewan's continental-origin citizens. Even more than in Manitoba, continental-origin citizens represented a large potential swing factor in voting. This helps explain why the

CCF-NDP's success in Saskatchewan came twenty-five years before it did in Manitoba and why it was more profound in terms of votes and seats. The large rural British presence, combined with a large rural continental presence relative to Manitoba and Alberta, made it easier for continental-origin citizens in Saskatchewan to attach themselves to the CCF. This was exhibited in 1943 when another barrier to CCF aspirations was lowered: the Catholic Church declared its support for the cooperative movement, expressed concern respecting social welfare, and told its members they were free to vote for any party that was not communist. The CCF victory in 1944, therefore, was no surprise. ...

In the late 1950s Saskatchewan produced another political phenomenon, John Diefenbaker, who made it possible for the Conservatives to become a national party for the first time since 1935. In the 1940s, Manitoba preferred the Liberals, Saskatchewan the CCF, and Alberta Social Credit. Diefenbaker, unlike other national leaders, was neither an Anglo-Saxon nor was he identified with Central Canadian financiers. This made it possible for European-origin farmers to flock, for the first time, to the Conservative banner. Ethnic interaction and the passing of earlier prejudices no longer crippled the Conservatives in Saskatchewan's European-origin areas. At the same time, Diefenbaker's toryism and commitment to agricultural interests made him equally acceptable to rural, Anglo-Saxon, prairie farmers. They recognized him as an established, Ontario-born Canadian not as a European, naturalized one. Diefenbaker's populist image, another side of this phenomenon, helped him in Alberta where agrarian populism, as in the United States, eased its way into agribusiness. The prairies could therefore embrace the federal Conservative party after the 1950s because it was a qualitatively different party under Diefenbaker than it had been under Arthur Meighen, R.B. Bennett, John Bracken, and George Drew. ...

The politics of rural Alberta was as much influenced by the values of the American great plains as the politics of rural Manitoba by the standards of rural Ontario. In Alberta the various cultural waves, from Ontario, Britain, continental Europe, and the United States, came closest to arriving simultaneously. Early Ontario settlers in rural Alberta, as in Saskatchewan, encountered another ideological strain. It was not, however, a socialist challenge as it had been in Saskatchewan. It was, rather, a more militant, more radical, less tory form of petit-bourgeois liberalism than was the Canadian norm. It was not so much a challenge as a reinforcement, a radicalization, of the natural liberalism of transplanted Ontarians. There seemed little need, as there had been in Saskatchewan, for two rival agrarian organizations or for an ideologically distinct opposition party. The older parties simply re-oriented themselves. The Liberals and Conservatives became competitors vying for support from the American-influenced UFA. An MP remarked in the House of Commons that Alberta, "from the border northward to Edmonton, might be regarded as a typical American state." ...

American analogies are logical in Alberta. There is something to the argument that Aberhart comes closest among Canada's premiers to looking and sounding like a radical, populist, American governor. Many of his supporters referred to him as Alberta's Abraham Lincoln. But no one could compare prairie CCF leaders such as Douglas, Coldwell, Woodsworth, Queen, or even Irvine to American populists. One could identify them with a Norman Thomas but, to be more accurate, one would have to look to a Briton like Ramsay MacDonald, Labour's first prime minister.

An examination of Alberta's voting patterns reveals that they may be related directly to the patterns of settlement and to the ideological-cultural heritages of the settlers. Initial

Ontario settlers in the south, particularly those who came before 1896 and settled along the CPR line, voted for the party of the railroad, the federal Conservatives. The early twentieth-century American influx altered this. The American impact was most pronounced in southern and eastern Alberta, an area representing the key to political power in the province just as the southwest represented that key in Manitoba. The southern, American-settled parts of Alberta which were most favorable to prohibition in 1915 became the most favorable to the UFA from 1921 to 1935 and to Social Credit from 1935 to the early 1970s. Those areas in northern Alberta that tended toward the UFA were those whose population most closely resembled the American-anchored south. ...

The new British labor-socialist element in Alberta was largely isolated in the urban centres. Consequently, the CCF floundered. The British-anchored provincial CCF never managed to win more than two seats in Alberta. Significantly, both CCF MLAs in the 1950s were from the north and were second generation Ukrainians, as were large numbers of their constituents. These northeastern areas were among the very few where, in the 1920s, continental-born farmers outnumbered American-born ones. The CCF success here confirmed the shift, in a much less dramatic fashion than in Saskatchewan, from the Liberals to the CCF among non-Anglo-Saxons of continental, particularly eastern European, origin. In Saskatchewan, large numbers of rural continentals had swung their votes to support the party of large numbers of rural Britons, the CCF. In Alberta, however, there were both fewer continentals and fewer rural Britons. Thus, the CCF was a relatively minor force in Alberta's rural areas.

Manifestations of the American influence in Alberta abound. One example of a republican liberal tendency was the Alberta government's refusal to appear in 1938 before the Royal Commission on Dominion–Provincial Relations, addressing its comments instead to "the Sovereign People of Canada." Parliamentary government was described as a form of state dictatorship. Another example was the complaint of a Nebraska-born MLA who called the caucus form of government undemocratic and criticized the speech from the throne for making more of the 1937 coronation festivities than of Social Credit. Could such a sentiment respecting the coronation have been expressed at Queen's Park or in any other English Canadian provincial legislature?

In the 1970s prairie politics continued to be tied to prairie history. The hegemony of Ontario-anchored politics in Manitoba had succumbed temporarily to an alliance of an urbanized multi-ethnic working class and poorer non-Anglo-Saxon farmers led by the NDP. This alliance was unlike Saskatchewan's because it had little rural Anglo-Saxon support. In Saskatchewan, the CCF "formula" of 1944 has repeated itself with some consistency. Urbanization and ethnic assimilation in both provinces have generally aided the CCF-NDP, although this pattern may yet reverse itself as intermarriage and acceptance of ethnic leaders in the older parties increases. In Alberta, Social Credit gave way to the Conservatives; both are right-wing liberal parties which have, for half a century, offered policies that are either American in origin or in benefit. In part, Social Credit led to the Conservatives in the evolutionary, not radical, way that the UFA led to Social Credit. Although the conditions of the 1980s are different from those of the 1930s, Alberta Social Credit may yet disappear, just as the UFA did. The Conservatives have captured the ideological and popular base of Social Credit support just as Social Credit captured the ideological and popular base of UFA support.

76 The Shame of (Ignoring) the Cities

Caroline Andrew (2001)

EDITORS' INTRODUCTION

Caroline Andrew is the director of the Centre on Governance in the School of Political Studies at the University of Ottawa. In this article, she notes how Canadian cities have long been considered nothing more than creatures of provincial governments—that is, their existence and governing structures are dictated by provincial legislatures. And yet, Canada is an increasingly urban society, with over two-thirds of its population living in metropolitan areas. Canadian cities have become important sites of social and political contestation over racial and ethnic segregation, the integration of immigrants, the wealth gap, socio-economic disparities between urban centres and suburbs, and conflicting agendas for the redistribution of tax revenue. Professor Andrew argues that it is for these reasons that the concerns and responsibilities of Canada's big cities should be higher on the national agenda, and deserve greater recognition in the Canadian political system.

Why Cities Must Have a Larger Role

Cities and their governments need to have greater recognition because hugely important political issues are being played out in the cities and these issues are not being sufficiently considered, debated and/or managed in our present political system. The challenges of polarization and exclusion and of social diversity are, I would argue, urban questions. Not only can they not be understood without reference to the fact that they occur in urban settings, but also this understanding has to be part of their solution. ...

The evidence for increasing polarization in the large Canadian cities is widespread. To cite one author, Larry Bourne concludes, "Within cities ... there is considerable evidence that levels of income polarization and poverty have indeed increased." The 1990s saw the growth of the homeless population, particularly in the large cities, and the increase in other particularly vulnerable groups—single mothers and their children, the frail, the elderly, and refugees. These developments are not incidentally urban. The large cities have seen the development of the greatest wealth, but also, because social services exist at least to some extent, the

Source: Excerpted from the *Journal of Canadian Studies*, vol. 35, no. 4 (Winter 2001), 100–110. References omitted. Reprinted by permission.

poorest and most marginalized move to the central areas of the large cities to access these services. The inner cities increasingly become the places for the very rich and the very poor, and this juxtaposition accentuates processes of marginalization and exclusion. A number of trends come together to produce this "yawning income and social gap": segmentation of the job market, gentrification, deinstitutionalization without resources, major cuts in social housing activity, etc.

Another huge challenge for Canadian society to manage in the twenty-first century is that of social diversity. And this is clearly urban, in fact, metropolitan. Toronto, Vancouver, Montreal, and to a lesser degree, Ottawa-Hull are absorbing the vast majority of new immigrants. Immigration, of course, is not new—with the exception of the Aboriginal population, we are a country of immigrants. But today the immigration is massively non-white and from the economic South. This raises different questions and somewhat different challenges in relation to social integration. Again, this is not just incidentally urban; it relates to patterns of economic development, organization of the job markets, the existence of community supports and services. If we do not want to see an overlay of racial and socio-economic marginalization, we must think of a complete strategy of action, including policies for primary and secondary schools, ways of ensuring that social institutions are open to diversity, employment strategies, housing strategies, and so on. But how can these be formulated and implemented if the relevant unit for implementation has no power and/or no existence and/or no legitimacy?

The large cities in Canada will increasingly experience polarization and social diversity. We will either deal successfully with these challenges or face the consequences. The urgency of thinking about this comes also from the fact that these challenges are not being thought about or dealt with elsewhere. The trends towards decentralization are visible all across the world and Canada is no exception. Both Ottawa and the provinces have been moving responsibilities down to lower levels of government. Many of the areas central to action on polarization and on managing social diversity have been or are being decentralized, usually without financial resources.

Moves to decentralize need to be seen in the same context as moves towards privatization. In fact, the motivation often comes from a government wanting to get rid of some of its expenditures and therefore some of its obligations. A number of solutions are possible: reduce services, privatize them or decentralize them. Often, the politically most palatable solution is decentralization because the government cutting the service does not have to deal with the political costs of reductions in services. Fundamental to these processes is the initial government willingness to abandon some policy area. I would argue that this has been true for issues of social diversity and polarization, that these have not been seriously considered by senior levels of government. The preoccupation of senior levels of government over the past 15–20 years with trying to cut costs has meant that worrying about social policy was not a priority; it was either decentralized, abandoned, or privatized. …

Up to this point, I have argued that cities need to be better recognized and better governed because they are the political arenas for some of the most important public policy issues that Canadian society must deal with. If we are to have even minimal levels of social solidarity and social support, we have to be concerned as a society about the trends to polarization that are developing, particularly in the urban centres, just as we have to be concerned about the capacity of Canada to create an inclusive society on the base of the growing social diversity. We have to be able to act on these social problems, which are intimately linked to the development of large cities. ...

How Cities Can Gain Greater Recognition

In theory, a number of policy paths can be followed, combining variations around two central directions. The local level, that is, the cities themselves, can be given greater political power, or the senior levels of government can give higher priority to urban questions. ...

Federal Involvement

Concern for managing social diversity has become more visible on the federal agenda, and this leads to reflections about urban centres. A number of federal programmes are now pushing in the same direction. The initiative on homelessness, for example, is explicitly putting 80 per cent of its funding into the 10 urban centres with the highest numbers of homeless people. The programme, Supporting Communities Partnership Initiative, involves the federal government in trying to evolve policies for defining "community" and "community involvement." In the case of the three Ontario communities included in the programme (Toronto, Hamilton, Ottawa), the municipal governments act as the community entity, but elsewhere a combination of community structures plus Human Resources Development Canada (HRDC) involvement implements the programme.

Other federal programmes, such as those relating to crime prevention, also end up posing questions about the relation of federal activity to urban communities. If federal actors are clear that community action is the solution, federal policy-makers are then concerned with how this can be encouraged and how the federal government can ensure effective action from the community.

There is now some federal government concern that ignorance of urban issues means that federal programmes will be ineffective and that federal policy objectives will not be met. Because of federal lack of understanding of how large urban centres operate and how the roles of large urban centres play into global economic, social and cultural development, federal policy capacity is being hampered in areas central to the development of the twenty-first century knowledge-based society and economy that federal policy-makers hope to achieve.

The problem is that this federal concern is right—they do not understand urban issues, they do not understand how local communities operate and, therefore, they are not able to support community action effectively. And this raises questions about strengthening federal interest and intervention in urban affairs. Would a federal Ministry of Urban Affairs be effective, given the current low level of federal understanding of urban dynamics? On the other hand, perhaps adding some policy direction that is not obsessed with the federal–provincial relationship might be a positive addition to thinking about federal policy-making in areas that impact on urban centres.

Provincial Capacity and Interest

As for the provinces, should we be counting on them to increase their interest in urban questions and to increase their capacity for urban policy-making? ...

Answers differ across provinces; certainly some of the provincial governments have little policy capacity for urban questions. In some provinces, there is only one large city and policy relating to this city is dealt with on an *ad hoc* basis. In these provinces improved policy capacity in general would be a good thing and certainly would lead to greater capacity in urban policy. But in other cases, general policy capacity certainly exists but policy interest is lacking in questions of urban development. In Quebec, it has often been a push to get the government to be concerned about urban policy. ...

The combination of those provincial governments whose general policy capacity is weak with those whose political direction is not pro-urban certainly suggests that we cannot depend entirely on provincial government policy to recognize the importance of cities and to translate this into effective policy. At the same time, increasing provincial policy capacity in regard to urban issues and increasing provincial sensitivity to urban issues are clearly vital. Provincial policy capacity is inevitably one of the requirements for better recognizing the urban dimensions of the major policy challenges facing Canadian society. But, while this capacity is necessary, it is not sufficient. And it will not come about through the initiative of the provincial governments—if it is to come, it will come through pressure from the urban areas.

City-Building: Strengthening the Local Level

This brings us back to the other broad policy direction—strengthening the local level so that cities themselves have more clout in Canadian politics. Let us start by acknowledging clearly that this has not been the direction of the last century—Canadian municipalities lost power and autonomy over the course of the twentieth century. The evolution of Canadian federalism with the growth of the provincial governments is the central story of the twentieth century and this has meant that municipalities have increasingly become in reality what they are in theory, the "creatures of the provinces." ...

Several possibilities for strengthening city governments come to mind; they could be given greater responsibilities, more resources, different structures and/or greater recognition. Decentralization policies have certainly given greater responsibilities to cities in certain areas. Ontario has been the recent leader in this, with decentralization in such areas of social policy as housing, public health and public transit. This has been more the decentralization of financial responsibility, however, and the result has been for local governments to think more of cost-cutting than of increased services. Given existing local politics, an increase in the financial responsibilities for activities tends not to lead to greater city policy capacity.

There have been few instances of provincial governments increasing resources to cities. In the case of the federal government there are a few recent examples, particularly in the area of homelessness, but the administrative complexity of these initiatives has not given cities the sense that the senior governments are really trying to increase their capacity.

A third possibility is for the local level to be restructured or given a different territory or set of political institutions. This certainly has been taking place—Toronto, Halifax, Ottawa and now Montreal, Quebec City, Hull-Gatineau, etc. Huge debates have taken place and in certain cases, considerable opposition has arisen. Provincial governments have imposed the new structures, arguing not so much for better capacity to act but for less expensive city government. It is too early to be able to see clearly the impact of the municipal amalgamations on the policy capacity of local governments, but the fiscal context of the amalgamations has limited debate on increasing policy capacity.

Finally, cities could get increased recognition within the Canadian political system. Some people have argued for constitutional recognition but the likelihood of this seems almost non-existent. The federal–provincial dynamic is too strong at the present time; the inclusion of municipalities would be seen by the provinces as a federal tactic to weaken the provincial position. …

Conclusion

Urban governance must be recognized as important because this is the way cities work and the way city governments work. Even more, this is how the policy capacity of local governance regimes can be increased so as to meet the challenges of a world-city world. If we are to be able to act on questions of polarization and social diversity, our urban governance regimes have to give a greater role to women, to ethnocultural communities, to gays and lesbians, to the disabled and, generally, to the voices of the marginalized and the excluded. We have to develop local governance networks that will allow local government to act more effectively. City governments will not become more effective actors through provincial or federal recognition or power-sharing arrangements; rather, they can become more effective through *their* creation of more inclusive urban governance regimes. This is not to say that provincial and federal actions are unimportant, but such actions are not the central question. Through the democratic processes of politics, urban dwellers must recognize that their local governments should act on certain issues and in certain ways, and they must organize and mobilize to put pressure on these governments. These forms of organization and activity will operate through networks and partnerships if they are to be successful and will therefore require a governance framework. We should not ignore the cities, but this will happen only after they demonstrate to us and to the other levels of government that we cannot ignore them.

Atlantic Canada in the Twenty-First Century: Prospects for Regional Integration

77

Robert Finbow (2004)

EDITORS' INTRODUCTION

In discussions of the historical and contemporary regional cleavages that have defined Canadian politics and society, Atlantic Canada is rarely mentioned. While some argue that it is an overgeneralization to group together the four provinces commonly subsumed under the label "Atlantic Canada," these provinces—Nova Scotia, Prince Edward Island, Newfoundland and Labrador, and New Brunswick—often face similar political and economic challenges. In this excerpt, Robert Finbow, a professor and chair of the Political Science Department at Dalhousie University with a cross-appointment in Canadian Studies, examines the institutional, cultural, political, and economic forces that distinguish the four provinces of Atlantic Canada.

Canada's Atlantic provinces are often treated as an afterthought in academic texts. Robert Young refers to the dearth of inquiry about the Maritime provinces—Nova Scotia, New Brunswick and PEI—as analysis is replaced by stereotypes of patronage, with "petty princelings" fighting for the "spoils of office." Traditional attitudes of "distaste, fascination and disdain," which extend also to Newfoundland, give the region's critics a "soothing sense of bemused condescension." For many scholars, it is often easiest to lump these provinces together, despite the risk of over-generalization. This chapter will criticize these superficial analyses by looking at the institutional, economic, cultural and historical forces that distinguish these four provinces. It will assess the feasibility for greater integration or even outright union in the region, which is often advocated by outside observers as a simple panacea for regional dependence and underdevelopment. It will consider current common challenges that may force them to seek greater integration, cooperation or political union in the future. Finally, it will note the institutional constraints that will limit the prospects for integration and union, however desirable.

Observers are divided on the merits of referring to Atlantic Canada as a "region." There are similarities among these provinces, notably proximity to the sea and the maritime orientation to economic activity. They also share a population with fewer recent immigrants, mostly

Source: Excerpted from *Regionalism in a Global Society: Persistence and Change in Atlantic Canada and New England*, edited by Stephen G. Tomblin and Charles S. Colgan. Peterborough, ON: Broadview Press, 2004. Notes omitted. Reprinted by permission.

old-stock British and Acadian, with First Nations and African-Canadian minorities. In addition all four provinces share marginal resources, limited economic prospects, and regional disparities, marked by high unemployment and reliance on federal transfers for provincial and individual incomes. But diversities are also evident between them which are reinforced by the institutions of federalism and their inducements to province building, "parochialism," and "competitive statecraft." Murray Beck referred to a single Atlantic political culture as a "chimera," as citizens express provincial, not regional loyalties. ...

Some observers suggest that, despite the persistence of nineteenth-century provincialism, a weaker transcendent regionalism has developed in Canadian federalism, which created similar grievances, political marginalization, and dependence on federal programmes. As Jim Bickerton phrases it, "Atlantic Canadian regionalism in a very real sense can be considered a *creation* of the federal government or at the very least a socio-political phenomenon that exists, and has always existed, in symbiosis with the federal government." Initially, Atlantic Canada produced the federal regime's fiercest critics, including the first separatists in Nova Scotia in the late 1880s. Decreased economic and political influence in the federation induced transitory movements for regional cooperation, such as the Maritime rights agitation of the 1920s or the Maritime union discussion in the 1960s.

Subsequently, the region supported use of the federal spending power for cost-sharing in post-secondary education and health care, for equalization grants to provinces facing fiscal shortfalls, and for unemployment insurance to individuals with benefit duration tied to local unemployment rates. Ottawa poured millions into regional development to address disparities in incomes and unemployment by attempting, largely unsuccessfully, to create industrial "growth poles." Despite initial intentions, federal governments diluted these policies, caving in to political pressures from more populous regions. Bickerton notes that: "Regional development, which had originally been conceived and designed as a targeted, tightly controlled, rationally planned diversion of industrial growth from the over-heated and inflation-prone industrialized core to the chronically underdeveloped periphery, had become instead a pork-barrel accessible to federal and provincial politicians in every region." This dependence on federal programmes, alongside resentment of declining political and economic power, induced a dual conception of confederation, balancing central authority in redistribution with provincial control of economic destiny.

As the Atlantic provinces enter the new millennium, they retain historical characteristics in their cultures, economies and societies. These distinctions make their treatment as a single region questionable, and hamper any move toward union or coordination of policy and institutions. These differences are accentuated by the institutions of federalism, especially electoral fetishism and institutional structuring associated with province building, which augment provincial distinctions. However, Atlantic Canadians also confront economic and political forces that may force them to consider cooperation or even union, notwithstanding their differences. Fiscal crisis has caused the federal regime to reduce its contributions via transfers to provinces and individuals, leaving token programs for political purposes, while orienting major national policies towards more populous provinces. The small regional caucus in Parliament has limited influence on policy, though occasionally regional ministers do secure high profile expenditures, often with limited long-term benefits. Globalization and technology require more efficient use of public monies, and cause some to question the viability of four small, competitive provinces. In this chapter I will briefly survey political life in each province, and I will assess how difficult it will be to bridge the gaps between them in search of integration or cooperation in the common interest.

Newfoundland and Labrador

Newfoundland's dominion status and late entry into Confederation, and the isolation and lifestyle of its dispersed outport communities, separate it from the Maritimes. This province is overwhelmingly British and Irish in social origin, and dependent on fishing, forestry, and mining. The indigenous Beothuk were entirely wiped out by conflict with settlers and European disease; Innu peoples remain in isolated, impoverished towns in Labrador. French influence is felt in the traditional fishing concession known as the French Shore on the west coast, but this is a small element of the contemporary population. ...

Newfoundland was led into Confederation by the charismatic Joey Smallwood after a referendum in 1948, in which only 52 per cent preferred union with Canada. Smallwood convinced this slim majority that Newfoundland would benefit from Canada's social programs and from integration into the national economy. The province experienced an increase in living standards, as many took advantage of new economic opportunities and federal employment and income support. Smallwood spoke expansively of the "miracles ... as the benign air of Confederation breathed over us ... [as] our poor, downtrodden, backward Newfoundland ... was launched at last upon her astonishing career as a Canadian province."

But while the post-confederation period improved conditions, the province never achieved the expected economic miracle. ...

Dissatisfaction with Confederation lingered as some harked nostalgically to Dominion status, and blamed Ottawa for poor conditions. Federal and provincial development efforts both failed and forced reliance on overproduction in fisheries, with disastrous consequences for fish stocks. Sean Cadigan argues that the failed development policies merely continued a pre-confederation pattern that inadequate social welfare measures could not rectify:

> Together, Newfoundland and Canada established a ruinous cycle. They relied in the short term on social programs to deal with the dislocation caused by the failure of modernization programs, while in the long term turning even more to modernization, especially overexpansion in the fishing industry, to minimize the need for social programs. Overexpansion led to fisheries collapse and dependence on even more social programs, such as the fisheries moratoria program ... TAGS.

A "neo-nationalist" movement emerged in response to the economic "trump" of oil, with the discovery of the Hibernia oil field in the early 1970s. This cultural revival was compared with peripheral nationalism in Western Europe. Under the leadership of Brian Peckford, Newfoundland challenged Ottawa on constitutional reform and fiscal federalism. Peckford sought control of the offshore to allow the province to set the pace of development and maximize local benefits and linkage development from offshore oil and gas. Newfoundland joined Quebec and Alberta in opposing Pierre Trudeau's centralist vision. But the province lost key legal decisions on offshore jurisdiction. Liberal Premier Clyde Wells emerged as a defender of Trudeau's centralism against the decentralist proposals of Brian Mulroney's Meech Lake Accord. His successor, Brian Tobin, who served in the federal cabinet, defended Ottawa's role in setting national standards for social policy. ...

Tobin looked to Ireland for a model to reinvigorate the provincial economy via new technologies, manufacturing, entrepreneurship and tourism. His success in diversifying the economy remains uncertain, but statistics indicate that the provincial workforce is now shifting to the service sector, with merely 15 per cent left in primary industries. The collapse of the cod stocks, which was the mainstay for hundreds of isolated outports, was a profound economic and cultural blow, and contributed to alienation from Ottawa, which was accused of mismanaging this resource. The people of Canada's poorest province were forced into even greater dependence on federal social assistance, as plans were devised to retire fishermen and retrain the young. ...

Nova Scotia

Nova Scotia was a reluctant entrant into Confederation, and produced the country's first open secessionists with Joseph Howe's opposition to union in 1867 and the Repeal movement led by W.S. Fielding in 1886–87. Confederation corresponded with (and perhaps contributed to) economic eclipse as the province, once home to the world's fourth largest merchant navy, experienced decline. National policies, notably tariffs and railway construction, were blamed for Nova Scotia's predicament, generating tensions with Ottawa, as provincial politicians sought "better terms." After the Diefenbaker victory in 1957 and the start of equalization payments, regional development programmes and health care cost-sharing, federal–provincial relations improved. ...

Nova Scotia was a divided society at the time of Confederation, with those favouring union looking to integration around railway towns and industries, and those opposing confederation seeking self-determination as a global trading and shipping centre. Deep socio-economic divisions persist, with continued effects on governance. The province's agrarian, fishing, mining, forestry and urban communities are distinct worlds, making it curiously difficult to govern. Historically, ethnic fragmentation among Gaelic Scots Catholics in Cape Breton, Pictou Scottish Protestants, Loyalists and Englishmen, German speakers in Lunenburg, francophone Acadians, African-Canadian settlers, and indigenous Mi'kmaqs created political diversity. As Miller has noted, these regions "might unite for specific political action" particularly "to assault the political, economic or religious privilege of Halifax but there was no fusion." Religion dominated political discourse, with Catholic–Protestant divisions in education and services. This has receded, but the effects can still be seen in the plethora of small colleges serving different constituencies. ...

Recently, the two major parties have alternated in power. These centrist clones focus on issues of public management and leaders' personalities, not distinct policies. Governments are forced to compromise provincial interests with particular concerns of diverse constituencies in order to govern. This contributes to a patronage culture, with questionable public management and numerous scandals over the use of public funds. Patronage is an important political motivator in this have-not society, as supporters of each party routinely secure government contracts and employment. ...

More recently, the province has fragmented into three competing political zones: Cape Breton, where the Liberals and NDP compete for seats; Metro Halifax with a three-way competition where the NDP made inroads; and the rural mainland, where the Tories remain strongest. This creates a competitive three party system. The province's regionalized party system may produce an enduring period of three-way competition and minority government, depending on the NDP's durability and potential expansion. [*Editor's note: In the June 2009 election, the Nova Scotia NDP won a majority, marking the first time the NDP has formed a provincial government in the history of Atlantic Canada.*]

Nova Scotia remains among the worst provinces in the area of public management. The province has failed to balance the budget, and has one of the highest per capita debt loads in Canada. The Conservative government of John Hamm has borrowed rhetoric from Mike Harris's common sense revolution, declaring in its 1999 Throne Speech that "self-reliance and personal responsibility are the keys to building strong families, strong communities and a better province." It is unclear if Hamm's downsizing efforts will be sufficient to restore fiscal balance. But the current conflict between urban and rural municipalities over fiscal equalization indicates that old divisions are still evident.

New Brunswick

New Brunswick takes pride in its status as the only officially bilingual province. The francophone Acadians, returnees from the expulsion from Nova Scotia in 1755, settled mainly in the north and northeast of the province, adjacent to Quebec. The anglophone community originated with Loyalists in the Saint John River valley, with later arrivals of Yorkshiremen and Irish Catholics. New Brunswick is closer to continental markets than its Maritime cousins. The potato industry spawned the McCain's frozen food empire; the Irvings built on car dealerships and gasoline to become a provincial giant spanning numerous sectors (including a near media monopoly). Forestry is the largest primary industry, and the mining industry is diverse, led by zinc, lead and silver. Politics has centered on ethnic and geographic divisions, with the Liberals supported mainly in the rural, poor, Acadian north and the Conservatives in the largely English, more urban, prosperous south. This split has affected most elections, with important swing ridings of mixed ethnicity in the centre of the province near Moncton making the difference between Conservative and Liberal victories. Periods of long Conservative rule alternated with Liberal regimes, though early governments included coalitions of both parties, which were themselves loose associations of county parties, reflecting traditions of localism and patronage. …

After sweeping all 58 seats in 1987, the Liberal government of Frank McKenna adjusted to fiscal constraint and the telecommunications revolution. McKenna was remarkable as perhaps the only leader in the region to impose severe restraint measures and still retain popular support (winning three majority governments before retiring in 1997). To balance the books, he closed hospital beds, laid off nurses, froze civil-service wages, consolidated government departments and cut up to 3700 jobs from the public service. Somehow McKenna managed to inspire confidence from New Brunswickers about their province's potential. He attracted many new businesses to the province, like courier services and telemarketing, with up to 7000 jobs in call centers and big name investors like Purolator Courier, United Parcel Service, Federal Express Canada, and CP Express and Transport. He was accused by other provinces of using unfair, costly subsidies and tax breaks to lure these firms from away. …

Despite his achievements in fiscal discipline, welfare reform, and economic and entrepreneurial cultures, unemployment, debt and dependence on federal transfers still limit prospects. McKenna's job creation programme, using tax concessions and grants to lure firms from away produced short-term benefits but left an uncertain legacy for permanent and balanced economic development.

Some policies initiated in the McKenna years, such as an ill-fated scheme for an American company to build private prisons and construction of a toll road linking some of the province's largest cities, created problems for his successor, Camille Theriault. Discontent also emerged over school closures, elimination of elected school boards, hospital wait lists, workfare, and other austerity measures. Theriault soon lost to the youthful Conservative leader Bernard Lord.

Lord, 33 when elected in 1999, ran on promises of tax cuts, health spending and elimination of the highway tolls. He hoped to be the latest in a pattern of young, energetic leaders—from Robichaud to Hatfield to McKenna—to win multiple elections for both parties, which contributes to the province's reputation for vigour and innovation in governance. Despite protests from farmers and labour, Lord carried forward with his election promises of restraint and tax reductions, and limited new spending to address pressing needs in education and health care. It remains to be seen if Lord can sustain the tradition of multi-term premierships by young, bold, reformist premiers. ...

The demise of the Confederation of Regions party (a libertarian party of popular protest) does not spell the end of ethnic politics in the province; while the majority continue to support bilingualism, former COR supporters returned to the Conservative ranks to campaign against Theriault and may have contributed to Lord's surprise win. Some suggested that the COR's collapse could allow the Canadian Alliance to make inroads at the federal level in the province, but they did not win a seat here in the 2000 election. Despite occasional reactionaries, New Brunswick has bridged its linguistic differences, though violent confrontations with Mi'qmaks over lobster and forest resources have flared recently.

Prince Edward Island

Prince Edward Island, the "garden in the gulf," is an insular community, where the birthdays of children are noted on the provincial website. Its government operates like a municipality, with local concerns predominant. The province relies on farming (especially potatoes) and fisheries (notably shellfish) and its bourgeoning tourism industry (featuring its remarkable beaches and gentle countryside). Its politics initially revolved around the issues of absentee landlords, who won much of the island in a 1756 lottery; the reversal of this situation after Confederation instilled a fierce loyalty to the land on the Island.

Insularity is another enduring theme, as this small colony resisted confederation at first. Contact with the mainland was by ferry for over a century after Confederation. Politicians often promised a fixed link to the rest of the Maritimes, but some citizens resisted this possible disruption of island life. The construction of the Confederation Bridge, an engineering marvel, in the 1990s brought new prospects of economic integration, but rekindled fears. In a community where everyone knows your name, and where a murder a decade is the norm, the intrusion of the North American mainstream is resisted, even though young people often migrate elsewhere to find it. The fixed link project was opposed by environmentalists and community activists fearful of the loss of the Island way of life, but 59 per cent supported it in a 1988 plebiscite. ...

Confederation, entered reluctantly in 1873 because of railway debts and the end of reciprocity with the US, is still perceived as a mixed blessing. Some considered it a conspiracy of the British colonial office and Ottawa, imposed against the will of the majority. This province carries little weight in federal politics, though it is over-represented in population terms, with its four seats in the House of Commons protected by the Senate floor rule. Like its Maritime neighbours, it relies heavily on federal transfers, though the levels of federal support have dropped from 60 to 40 per cent of the provincial budget. ...

Political participation is the highest in the land, with over 85 per cent voter turnout in provincial elections. Politics is intensely contested, and the province is given to political extremes, with frequent landslides multiplied by the small chamber, where the opposition is often minimal (one member only after the 1999 election). While some families vote according to inherited loyalties or on patronage lines, the voters are well informed and a few votes can decide an election. In 1996, a mere 2,108 votes produced a majority for Pat Binns' Conservatives. ...

Though often accused of traditionalism, PEI was the first province to elect minority and female premiers (Joe Ghiz and Catherine Callbeck, respectively). Ghiz, of Lebanese origin, withstood racial slurs in the legislature to win the confidence of the population. He gained credibility on the national scene with his reasoned, moderate interventions in the Meech Lake debate. For a brief period in the 1990s, women simultaneously served as premier, lieutenant-governor, opposition leader, and Speaker of the House, an unprecedented circumstance in any province. ...

Outsiders often question PEI's viability and the expense to the nation of preserving a separate province for such a small population. However, there is a fierce commitment to autonomy here, reflected in the concern about the cultural impact of the fixed link to the mainland completed in the 1990s. Although often depicted as a virtual "ward" of Ottawa because of its small size and fiscal dependence, the Island has shown some independence. For instance, it is the only Atlantic province not to harmonize its sales taxes with Ottawa's GST.

Prospects for Atlantic Cooperation

Many observers suggest that these four historical units are no longer effective as self-governing provinces. The existence of 4 governments for 2.25 million people, versus one province for 12 million in Ontario, is considered wasteful. Critics speak of "overgovernment" and urge Atlantic or Maritime union as a potential solution to dependence and underdevelopment. Cooperation, including closer integration of policies and services, may be a necessary response to fiscal crisis and decentralization of authority. While Quebec sovereignty has faded as an immediate threat, it remains a possibility, which would isolate Atlantic Canada physically. Asymmetry, decentralization, fewer transfers, and more provincial powers are also possible. The fiscal and ideological climate in other regions has reduced support for interprovincial transfers, which could threaten the ability of these small provinces to provide essential services to their people.

Interprovincial cooperation has achieved some results, but many important elements of industrial development have not been included. And these arrangements can be undermined or abandoned by these provinces, in response to internal electoral pressures. Essential regional cooperation can only progress so far without political integration because of provincial sovereignty, which encourages both governments and societies to orient on provincial, not regional, lines. Union advocates believe that these provinces need to go beyond creating a single economic space, to creating shared facilities, services, and programmes if the citizens of this region are to retain services of national quality.

Political union could promote consolidation of government resources, and give the region a more coherent position in national forums. It could reduce expensive legislative and bureaucratic duplication and permit economies of scale in programmes. It could reduce spending on administration, while directing more revenues to services like health and education. It might allow cooperation in tourism, resource management and economic integration. And it could promote region-wide development and end competition for limited investment through costly tax concessions, loans or grants. Finally, a larger unit might simply be more credible as a voice for regional interests in the federation, even facilitating changes like Senate reform. Acadians outside New Brunswick might favour union to secure some of the benefits of their brethren in that province.

However, political union would be difficult if not impossible to implement. There is no constitutional means to force provinces together, given their veto power over changes to their jurisdiction and borders. In addition, there would be losses for the region, including the constitutional veto under the 7-of-10 provinces rule, and an end to the protection of the Senate floor rule for smallest provinces prompting a decline in the number of MPs from the region. Furthermore, these provinces could face the loss of distinctive identities, which are especially important to residents. For instance, PEI might reject submersion in a larger, less personal unit, in which its distinctive entity would disappear. New Brunswick's Acadians would become more of a minority in a united province. Newfoundland also feels little sense of identity with the Maritimes. There could be more tangible costs, like the loss of government employment, which would affect the health of the regional economy in the short run. There would also be the loss of experimentation with better approaches by different regimes. Public opinion on union remained divided in 1990s polls, with 35 per cent supportive of union, 38 per cent opposed and 26 per cent undecided.

These figures could indicate the need for slower integration to bring population onside and to demonstrate the benefits of closer cooperation in the preservation of services and standard of living. This could include the use of constitutionalized agreements between provinces, to enshrine cooperative arrangements and to allow for the merging of key institutions and bureaucracies. It could also permit the creation of a single economic space, tax and expenditure coordination, enshrined procurement rules and durable agreements to reduce interprovincial competition via costly investment incentives and tax breaks. The provinces could create innovative pools of investment capital using merged public sector pension funds. They could create self-sufficient interprovincial agencies with their own sources of revenue independent of individual provincial regimes (for example, a regional transportation agency funded by fuel taxes).

Eventually, the region might create joint bureaucracies in key areas such as health, post-secondary education, or create a common federal court for the region. An agency like the Council of Atlantic Premiers could direct the process and assign the major institutions to different provincial capitals to share employment benefits equitably. Ottawa could contribute to this process by promoting greater certainty in cost-sharing arrangements and by making some transfers to regional agencies. This level of cooperation could become an end in itself or a possible first step towards political union.

It may be in the region's interest to coordinate policies trans-provincially while retaining separate provinces, with four votes in constitutional and federal–provincial forums. However, any scheme of integration or cooperation would have to be implemented carefully to maximize savings and minimize costs. Some economists warn the benefits of economic integration without full union would be minimal. There would also be concerns about how to keep interprovincial institutions democratically accountable without a joint assembly. Careful steps will be needed to ensure that these institutions do not become a super-government that fails to reduce the cost or size of bureaucracy. It would be difficult to balance community input into policy from all four provinces, and debates over the degree of influence (or even location of new agencies) could be anticipated. It may be hard to promote cooperation in government services if independent provincial bureaucracies persist, with their own interests at stake. And politicians will always be tempted to pull back from cooperation for their own electoral purposes.

Current experience with cooperation is mixed. Maritime initiatives in higher education, and municipal training and development, lottery corporation, and veterinary and police education have existed for years. Newfoundland joined in Atlantic agreements on procurement and internal trade in the 1990s. Integration of some economic regulations, taxation, and insurance legislation has progressed more recently. A Council of Atlantic Premiers was formalized in 1989 to promote Atlantic concerns. Despite this progress, the continued existence of four sovereign provinces has created continual problems of competition which the region can ill afford. There has been infighting such as Nova Scotia's threatened withdrawal from the Atlantic Lottery Corporation and the police academy, PEI and Newfoundland's conflict over shrimp quotas, and Nova Scotia and Newfoundland's arbitration case on offshore boundaries. Intense economic need makes these provinces competitors, not cooperators; substantial institutional integration may be required to overcome this parochialism and encourage durable, mutually beneficial cooperation.

But long-time advocates of union see it as a costly and distant prospect, which is unlikely to materialize. This is not surprising in light of the distinct historical trajectories and very different cultural, economic, and social conditions affecting contemporary politics in the four Atlantic provinces. While outside observers tend to lump them together into a residual category, as parochial political and economic backwaters, this brief survey reveals profound variations in these political systems. These different traditions and contemporary practices constitute a significant barrier to intra-provincial cooperation, let alone political union. It is not easy for people accustomed to provincial loyalties and cultural identifications, and especially provincial-level organization in civil and pressure groups, to reorient on a regional basis. If anything, global homogenization encourages peoples to hold ever more strongly to particularities, even while integrating with distant nations. Therefore, it may not be easy for Atlantic Canadians to dispense with provincial symbols and cultures or to accept a new homogenized bureaucratic regionalism, however efficacious for expenditure and services.

Indeed, it is difficult to imagine how union or cooperation will occur within the Canadian federation as it is currently constituted. Observers of Canadian politics have long argued that the institutions of federalism interact with social forces to create durable provincialisms, which are resistant to any trans-provincial regionalism. Institutions set the boundaries for political conduct and provide incentives and constraints for political actors, limiting and shaping their behaviours. In the current constitutional context, political leaders in Atlantic Canada have little incentive to cooperate across borders, even to improve the cost-effective delivery of services and programmes. As long as they are accountable only to their own electors, Atlantic governments will often undertake policies that place them in destructive competition.

Whatever will to cooperate may exist, it will require a restructuring of federal institutions to provide sufficient rewards for cooperation. Such restructuring may not occur at all unless a crisis of sufficient magnitude (for example, Quebec sovereignty or radical decentralization of powers) forces these provinces to collaborate. Whether the costs of such a crises can be mitigated by intra-provincial cooperation short of union is uncertain. Meanwhile, analysts can do no more than to urge creation of trans-provincial institutions and funding arrangements to limit the damage of decentralization, duplication and under-funding of essential public services.

This brief survey of provincial politics in Atlantic Canada indicates that portrayals of the homogeneity of this region are misguided. The distinctive political histories and trajectories of these provinces, coupled with very diverse and distinct socio-cultural bases, indicate why it has been so difficult to create a sustained movement for unification. Newfoundland's neo-nationalism and cultural revival are clearly oriented along provincial lines, with provincialist tendencies at times approaching Quebec's in intensity. Nova Scotia is a regional leader in commerce, education and economics, yet it is plagued by internal diversities and fragmentation which make its own governance problematic, and which undermine its ability to cooperate with its neighbours. New Brunswick's unique accommodation of bilingual communities and vigorous public policy innovation could suffer in a homogenized Atlantic entity. Prince Edward Island retains a distinct, insular identity that will be challenged via increased contacts with mainland North America, let alone by submersion in a unified region.

Yet necessity is the mother of invention: challenges of globalization, Quebec sovereignty, decentralization, hemispheric integration, and technological innovation could still require greater integration and cooperation among these four small, vulnerable provinces. The challenge will be to get leaders here to look beyond electoral interests and parochial sentiments and accept durable cooperative arrangements in the interest of retaining world-class public services. This may be the fundamental challenge confronting the region, as it seeks to improve its competitive position in the integrated global economy of this new century.

Suggested Reading

Beck, J. Murray. "An Atlantic Region Political Culture: A Chimera" in D.J. Bercuson and Phillip Buckner, eds. *Eastern and Western Perspectives*. Toronto: University of Toronto Press, 1981.

Bickerton, James and Alain-G. Gagnon. "Regions and Regionalism in Canada" in James Bickerton and Alain-G. Gagnon, eds. *Canadian Politics* (5th edition). Toronto: University of Toronto Press, 2009.

Forbes, E.R. *Challenging the Regional Stereotype: Essays on the 20th Century Maritimes*. Fredericton: Acadiensis Press, 1989.

Smallwood, Joseph R. *I Chose Canada*, Vol. II. Scarborough: Signet, 1975.

Tomblin, Stephen. *Ottawa and the Outer Provinces*. Toronto: Lorimer, 1995.

Stephen Harper and the Rise of Western Conservatism

William Johnson (2009)

EDITORS' INTRODUCTION

Stephen Harper became Canada's 22nd prime minister in 2006. After a merger with the Canadian Alliance and Progressive Conservative parties, the newly formed Conservative Party of Canada won minority governments in 2006 and 2008. In 2011, after a non-confidence vote that deemed the Cabinet to be in contempt of Parliament, leading to an election, Harper's Conservatives were voted back into power with the first majority government since the Liberal victory in the 2000 federal election.

Harper has been sharply criticized by those who believe he has used his office to undermine Canada's democratic processes and the role of Parliament. But he has also remained in power through numerous controversies and crises, including the global financial crisis of 2008, and as the results of the 2011 election show, Harper has apparently achieved his goal of making Canada more conservative, and conservatism more popular among various constituencies. Indeed, one might consider this selection in light of André Blais' explanations for the success of the Liberal Party (Reading 28), which, prior to Harper, had often been referred to as "the natural governing party."

In this excerpt of an article published after Harper's victory in the 2008 election, William Johnson charts the rise of Harper, and Western Canada itself, as examples of demographic, economic, and political shifts in power that have occurred in recent decades. Although born in Toronto, Harper moved to Alberta as a young man, and it was there, seeing the economic damage wrought by Trudeau's National Energy Program in the early 1980s, that he underwent a political conversion. Ultimately, he would lead a reconstituted Conservative party, with roots planted firmly in the West, to a decade in power and electoral success comparable to any other string of victories in Canadian political history.

When Stephen Harper stepped up to the podium at the Conservative party's convention in Winnipeg in November 2008, the grassroots members were expecting a triumphant pep talk. He delivered. This was the party's second convention. At the first, in Montreal in 2005, he had arrived as the Opposition leader, with little chance of defeating the Liberals. Now he was back before them as the prime minister of Canada. They basked in his aura.

The Conservatives had returned to power [in October 2008] with an increased plurality. True, a setback in Quebec had kept the government to a minority. But outside that province,

Source: Excerpted from "The Outsider" by William Johnson. *The Walrus*, March 2009. Reprinted by permission.

where they had won 133 seats to their opponents' 100, they were now the undisputed majority party. The Liberals, their constant adversaries since 1867, had been crushed, humiliated, deserted by long-time supporters, and were now stuck with a lame-duck leader in Stéphane Dion. Despite the economic storm gathering over the country, for the Tories the future looked bright.

Harper's speech, more than a cry of victory, suggested the Exodus story, set in Canada. The Conservatives had wandered in the wilderness. Now they had fought their way back to the promised land. "The Conservative party is Canada's party," he announced. This proud claim became his leitmotif, the counterpoint to the travails his people had known.

"As we gather together here as a party, let us pause for a moment, and truly reflect and appreciate how far we have come, in so short a time," he told his supporters. "Five years ago, the Conservative movement in this country was divided, defeated, and demoralized. The government of the day ridiculed us. The pundits discounted us. And the public said, 'Don't bother talking to us until you've got your act together.'"

Two former warring parties, the Canadian Alliance and the Progressive Conservatives, had united under a new vision, which had led them through the desert. Harper enumerated its tenets: "Lower taxes and prudent spending focused on the priorities of Canadians. A commitment to free enterprise, free markets, and free trade. *La croyance en un gouvernement plus responsable, plus transparent.* A justice system that puts the welfare of law-abiding citizens before the interests of criminals. Strong support for rebuilding this country's too-long-neglected Canadian Forces. An unwavering commitment to asserting our sovereignty over the Arctic. A belief in a foreign policy that is both strong and independent. And a passionate belief in the unity of this country!" These were the principles that Harper had long fought for; now they were embraced by a mainstream party. His party and Canada were moving closer together, and closer to him.

Not so long ago, the Conservatives had been considered ideological aliens, outside the pale of Canadian values. But things had changed. "We made important inroads with women voters and with new Canadians," Harper reminded them. "From Comox to Iqaluit to Summerside, we painted large swaths of this great country Tory blue. Because, friends, the Conservative party is once again Canada's party!"

His exuberance, although understandable, was overstated. True, only the Conservatives were strong in almost every corner of the country. But their share of the vote was only 37.6 percent. Their 143 members in the Commons improved on the 124 of 2006, but Canadians had also returned 165 MPs from other parties: 77 Liberals, 49 members of the Bloc Québécois, 37 New Democrats, and two independents. The Conservatives remained weak in the largest metropolitan centres: Toronto, Montreal, and Vancouver. The country was still a rainbow, not Tory blue.

But Harper was already looking to the future. He had come to elected politics reluctantly, only because he believed that something was terribly wrong with the country, and that its elites were blind to the danger. Derided at first, he had seen Canada gradually move closer to the vision he'd formed in the wilderness. The Conservatives were still poised for a breakthrough, if Harper could stay the course, continue to learn from his mistakes, and adapt. A steady hand on the economy, a new strategy in Quebec, and next time the majority would be theirs. If they weren't yet Canada's party, they would be soon …

• • •

[While working on his master's degree in the mid-1980s,] Harper and his friend John Weissenberger were impressed with Peter Brimelow's *The Patriot Game*, in which the former business editor of *Maclean's* cast the obsession with placating Quebec as the futile governing principle of Liberal politics in Canada. Since Harper's birth on April 30, 1959, just a year before the outbreak of Quebec's Quiet Revolution, the province's alienation from Canadian federalism had indeed been the dominant concern of Canada's national politics. "What does Quebec want?" was the country's central existential question, and no answer had ever proved adequate.

Harper's sense of identification with the West escalated in the fall of 1986, when Brian Mulroney announced that a new fleet of 138 CF-18 fighter planes would be serviced by Montreal's Canadair rather than Winnipeg's Bristol Aerospace. The awarding of the $1.2-billion contract, which contradicted the recommendation of the government's own experts, sparked indignation across the prairies. Mulroney's minister of energy, Pat Carney, later wrote in her memoir, *Trade Secrets*, that the decision "changed Canadian history by hardening western alienation, breathing life into the Reform movement and bringing on the slow death of the Progressive Conservative Party."

Harper and Weissenberger were at the time planning a "Blue Tory network" within the PC party that would move the party to the right, but the CF-18 fiasco made them despair of the possibility of internal reform. Then, at an informal economics department meeting, they met Preston Manning.

In May of 1987, Harper found himself in Vancouver for the Western Assembly on Canada's Economic and Political Future, held under a banner proclaiming The West Wants In. He had prepared a paper with Weissenberger that sat on a table at the back of the room. Entitled "A Taxpayers Reform Agenda," it expressed a commitment to "strong conservative principles." It urged, for example, that activist government must be countered by bringing to bear the views of the taxpayers, and advocated "the implementation of the new economics—of smaller government, regional diversification, non-discriminatory or discretionary spending, privatization, fair trade, and less expensive and less bureaucratic income transfers." It also opposed the constitutional amendments accepted three weeks earlier by the first ministers meeting at Meech Lake. It contained no trace of social or religious conservatism.

The assembly voted to found a new party, and Harper attended the founding convention in Winnipeg as a featured speaker. "This paper is about justice and injustice, about fairness and unfairness, and about compassion and selfishness, in the economic treatment of western Canada under Confederation," he began. Using facts and figures, he laid out how Alberta and the West had been plundered. He was given a standing ovation, prompting the *Alberta Report* to comment, "The speech was acknowledged by delegates, party officials, and media as a highlight of the convention." Manning soon named Harper the Reform Party's chief policy officer; they alone were authorized to speak in the name of the party.

The media was immediately patronizing toward Reform. Delegates woke up on November 1 to a story in the *Toronto Star* by Val Sears that treated them like spooks:

WINNIPEG—A broomstick load of revolutionary ghosts rode Winnipeg's Halloween sky last night, summoned by the West's newest political bloc, the Reform Party of Canada.

The memory of the new party's treatment by the country's political establishment would stay with Harper. Still, it confirmed the beginning of a new phase of his life. He was developing a vision, a mission, and now had a vehicle for implementing them.

From that time on, Harper would be in the public sphere. He decided to run in the 1988 federal election as a Reform candidate in Calgary West, against his old mentor, Jim Hawkes. Quebec was one of his greatest concerns at the outset. In his nomination speech to the constituency association, he explained that he had turned against the policy of official languages. Mulroney had put Lucien Bouchard, the ardent separatist and promoter of Quebec as a French-only jurisdiction, in charge of the file. "Many are like me," Harper said, "individuals who once supported official bilingualism but now realize that federal language policy is collapsing under the weight of its own hypocrisy." A few years later, he would famously write, "As a religion, bilingualism is the god that failed. It has led to no fairness, produced no unity, and cost Canadian taxpayers untold millions."

Harper and his party both went down to defeat. He soon started strategizing for the next election, laying out a vision for Reform that placed him somewhat at odds with the organization he had only recently helped create. On March 10, 1989, he sent Manning a confidential 21-page memo that brazenly challenged his leader's most cherished assumptions.

Manning was a populist, Harper a conservative. Manning envisaged his party surging to power as part of a movement that animated a whole people, on the model of Social Credit's ascent to power in Alberta in 1935. He wanted Reform to draw support indifferently from Tories, Liberals, and New Democrats. In a "leader's foreword" to the 1988 election platform, he had written, "We reject political debate defined in the narrow terminology of the Left, Right, and Centre." He looked for support not in the big cities, but in the hinterland. So committed was he to this vision that he insisted on a sunset clause in Reform's constitution: if the party had not achieved power by the year 2000, it would be dissolved, barring a contrary vote from two-thirds of its members.

As a conservative, Harper wanted a long-term, patiently constructed, permanent party that would build coalitions of economic and social conservatives to form a government. Unlike Manning, he believed Canada needed the kind of ideological polarization and political realignment exemplified by Margaret Thatcher in the UK and Ronald Reagan in the US. This would mean a conflict between the ever-burgeoning public sector and the overtaxed urban middle class of the private sector. "It was a battle," he wrote in his memo, "not only for tax dollars, but about social values and social organization, especially over the size and role of government."

Around this central axis of political conflict, Harper saw secondary alignments based on interests and values. Whole sectors of society, even regions, benefited from state subsidies. The "political class" tended to be liberal on such issues as crime, unconventional lifestyles, and family values, while the working and rural classes tended to be "outrightly hostile to the liberal intellectualism of the Welfare State class." He proposed that the Reform Party become a political movement that would defend the private sector and moderate social conservatism. Only when economic and social conservatives worked together could a right-wing party take power in Canada.

That same month, Reform gained its first seat in Parliament, winning a by-election in the central Alberta riding of Beaver River. Manning prevailed on a reluctant Harper to suspend his studies for a year in order to assist the new member, schoolteacher Deborah Grey. Once again back in Ottawa, he witnessed the death throes of the Meech Lake Accord and the attendant surge of separatism in Quebec. Later, he devised Reform's strategy for opposing the 1992 referendum on the Charlottetown constitutional accord. As with Meech, the establishment denounced and derided Reform's opposition, but most Canadians supported the party's stance.

When the 1993 federal election was called, Harper again ran in Calgary West, again expecting to lose. But the country turned mid-campaign against the new government of Kim Campbell, who had inherited Brian Mulroney's legacy of distrust—a country polarized, region against region. The Mulroney government had also run eight deficits in a row and more than doubled the national debt.

Harper had warned for years that the nation was at risk of hitting a wall, and now led the team that crafted Reform's chief policy plank for the election, called Zero in Three. Its central proposal was to eliminate the $36-billion deficit within three years by cutting $18 billion in federal spending. Jean Chrétien's Liberals accused the Reformers of a slash-and-burn policy that would drive the country to ruin, and promised instead to merely diminish the deficit rather than eliminate it.

The election reduced Campbell's party to two seats. The Liberals took power, and fifty-two newly minted Reform MPs, including Harper, took their seats across the aisle. Soon, the Liberals became aware that the country was in danger of a fiscal crisis. As Paul Martin recounts in his memoir, *Hell or High Water*, international investors, spooked by the Mexican peso crisis, "began looking around for other vulnerable countries with unresolved fiscal problems, and we were near the top of the list." Martin's 1995 budget brought the deficit down to zero in three years, and subsequently produced budget surpluses. He made deeper spending cuts than Zero in Three had proposed, without spinning the country into turmoil. This would be the Chrétien-Martin government's proudest achievement—but it was Reform that had first foreseen the crisis and proposed the solution. And it was the party's support in the Commons that made eliminating the deficit politically feasible. Martin's greatest success in fact implemented Stephen Harper's earlier vision. This was the country's first big step toward what Harper stood for from the start. …

[Shortly after the failed 1995 Quebec referendum,] Harper introduced private member's bill C-341, the Quebec Contingency Act (Referendum Conditions), which laid down stringent conditions for Quebec to secede. Years later, in 1998, the Supreme Court of Canada delivered its response to the reference on secession, spelling out a doctrine that vindicated Harper's vision. When the Chrétien government finally passed the Clarity Act, in 2000, it fell short of Harper's bill, failing to lay out what the government would do if Quebec passed a unilateral declaration of independence—the most likely path of secession.

Characteristically, Harper didn't complete his first mandate as a member of Parliament. In January 1997, he dropped out to take a position as vice-president (later president) of the National Citizens Coalition, where he could agitate for policies concordant with the organization's slogan: "More freedom through less government." His decision stemmed mainly from differences between his and Manning's visions. He had gone public with his views in the spring of 1995, in a *Globe and Mail* article with the headline, "Where Does the Reform Party Go from Here? To be credible as the logical alternative to the Liberals, says a Reform MP, the party can't just fight elections on the popular protests of the day." When his plea to Reform's rank and file failed, Harper quit.

He returned to electoral politics only when his conservative vision was threatened by the leadership of Stockwell Day. Manning morphed the Reform Party into the Canadian Alliance in 2000, attracting a fringe of Progressive Conservatives. But in 2001, thirteen Alliance MPs left the caucus to sit with Joe Clark's Progressive Conservative MPs. Day called a leadership convention to settle the strife, but most of the candidates favoured uniting the Alliance with the PCs. This would have meant a shift to the left, as long as Joe Clark, a Red Tory, was their leader.

So Harper ran for the Alliance leadership, and on March 20, 2002, took over a party that was battered, broke, and discredited. In the *Toronto Star*, Richard Gwyn dismissed him as "yesterday's man." Edward Greenspon, now editor-in-chief of the *Globe and Mail*, described him as an ideologically displaced person in Canada: "Stephen Harper: A Neo-con in a Land of Liberals." The *Vancouver Sun* wrote, "He presents himself as unbending, unwilling to make the compromises to appeal to the middle-of-the-road voters and traditional support-ers of the Progressive Conservatives."

Perhaps so, but in just two years Harper restored the Alliance's unity and finances and merged the party with the Progressive Conservatives. He won the leadership of the new entity, then was thrust almost immediately into the 2004 election, which was called by Paul Martin before the new party could get organized. Lacking the time to hold a policy conven-tion, the Conservatives couldn't craft a ratified program, and Martin was therefore able to define the party as he chose.

He portrayed their leader as scary. Harper had a hidden agenda. He was an American-style conservative who would destroy medicare and demolish the social safety net that protected the poor, the unemployed, and the disabled. He would strike down women's right to abortion and probably bring back the death penalty. This complex of messages was compressed into one slogan: "Harper is another George Bush." It didn't help that other Conservative candi-dates affronted progressive public opinion during the campaign—one, for instance, equated homosexuality with pedophilia.

In reality, Harper was not a social conservative, and had differed on social issues even with the Reform Party. During Reform's annual assembly in October 1994, the party had tabled the following motion: "Resolved, that the Reform Party support limiting the defin-ition of a legal marriage as the union of a woman and a man, and that this definition be used in the provision of spousal benefits for any program funded or administered by the federal government." Manning supported the resolution, and the convention voted 87 percent in favour. But Harper protested: "Those are not partisan issues; those are moral issues. People have to be able to belong to political parties regardless of their views on those issues. It's perfectly legitimate to have moral objections as well as moral approval of homosexuality, but I don't think political parties should do that." His judgment was far-sighted. Had he prevailed, Reform and its successors would have been spared much future strife and public distrust.

Despite the obstacles, the Conservatives reduced the Liberals to a minority. At the party's first convention, in 2005 in Montreal, Harper urged it to adopt a moderate program. A resolution condemning abortion was subsequently defeated, and Harper promised never to introduce a bill on the issue. After the convention, he insisted on strict adherence to the official program—nothing more, nothing less.

During the 2006 election campaign, he imposed an unprecedented control on his candi-dates: if they spoke publicly, they had to stick to the program. Harper knew he was mistrusted, and that the Liberals would again paint him as scary, so he focused his campaign not on himself, but on a daily unveiling of goodies that targeted broad clusters of voters. The Martin Liberals had expected him to announce a platform of spending cuts. Instead, he matched their cornucopia of spending promises with policies that were as much populist as conservative. He countered the Liberals' pledge to cut income taxes by offering to reduce the GST by two points, for example, and countered their program of subsidized public daycare with a subsidy of $100 a month for every child under the age of six. The policies were designed to appeal to as many Canadians as possible, and they succeeded.

And so it was that on January 23, 2006, Stephen Harper became prime minister. ...

As prime minister, he devoted more time and blandishments to seducing Quebecers—the key to the Conservatives' prospects for a majority—than to any other objective. He knew he was distrusted for his past criticisms of the Official Languages Act, and for his opposition to the Meech Lake and Charlottetown accords and the premiers' 1997 Calgary Declaration. But during the campaign for the 2006 election, he attenuated his objections to some nationalist articles of faith, and then, after he was in office, celebrated French as Canada's founding language. After promising a "federalism of openness," he gave Quebec a voice in the Canadian delegation at UNESCO, turned over billions to settle the "fiscal imbalance," recognized Quebec as a nation within a united Canada, and routinely began his speeches in French. This would provide his greatest achievement: in the Quebec provincial elections of 2007 and 2008, secession was almost ignored as an issue.

At the outset of the 2008 campaign, polls showed Harper to be Canadians' preferred choice as leader. So this time the Conservatives' campaign was more personal, focusing on Harper as the best manager for the country during threatening economic times. He was shown in ads as a kindly, solicitous dad in a navy blue sweater vest. No longer the outsider, he was positioned as a father, a family man like any other. The strategy largely succeeded outside Quebec. In that province, the Conservative campaign was dominated by the announcement of $45 million in cuts to certain arts programs, which provoked Quebec's intellectual and artistic communities to mount a spectacular campaign that presented the Conservatives as being at war with Quebec's culture and very identity.

Following the October 14, 2008 election, which returned the strengthened Conservative minority, Harper invited the other party leaders to work with him, and promised to be flexible. As he told his followers in Winnipeg, "We will have to be both tough and pragmatic, not unrealistic or ideological, in dealing with the complex economic challenges that confront us." The G-20 nations, meeting in Washington the next day, called for massive government spending to reverse the accelerating worldwide economic decline. Harper concurred, and even acknowledged that the Canadian government would likely have to incur budget deficits—a move he had disavowed during the campaign.

But then, on November 19, the celebrated strategist made a monumental blunder: he presented the country with a Throne Speech that sounded like a summons to austerity. "Hard decisions will be needed to keep federal spending under control and focused on results," the Governor General read. "Departments will have the funding they need to deliver essential programs and services, and no more." Taken on its own, this position was defensible enough. In the United States, Barack Obama was warning that to spend massively in some areas, the government would have to cut back in others, in order to avoid structural deficits. But Harper decided to split his economic program into two parts, announcing the bad news of spending cuts on November 27, in Finance Minister Jim Flaherty's fiscal statement, while remaining silent for the moment on measures to stimulate the economy and bail out failing industries. ...

Harper ultimately withdrew the proposals to eliminate political subsidies and public servants' right to strike, and announced that bailouts and stimuli were coming—but it was too late. The three opposition leaders had taken Flaherty's fiscal statement as a declaration of war, forming a coalition that sought to topple the Conservatives immediately and replace them with a Stéphane Dion–led Liberal-NDP government, supported by the Bloc Québécois. The coalition would be able to muster 163 votes in the House, compared with the Conservatives' 143.

Harper fought back, first postponing the confidence vote he'd planned for December 1, then denouncing the coalition in terms akin to treason: "The highest principle of Canadian democracy is that if one wants to be prime minister one gets one's mandate from the Canadian people and not from Quebec separatists. The deal that the leader of the Liberal party has made with the separatists is a betrayal of the voters of this country, a betrayal of the best interests of our economy, and a betrayal of the best interests of our country, and we will fight it with every means that we have."

Polls showed that the coalition was widely viewed as illegitimate. None of the three opposition leaders had campaigned on a coalition; on the contrary, all had explicitly rejected the possibility. It appeared that the election results would be overturned by politicians seeking partisan advantage, in response to a prime minister who appeared to many to be doing the same. In an extraordinary televised address to the nation on December 3, a combative Harper vowed, "Tonight I pledge to you that Canada's government will use every legal means at our disposal to protect our democracy, to protect our economy, and to protect Canada." Duceppe, in reply, began, "The Bloc Québécois is a party devoted exclusively to the service of the Québécois." He could have added "and to the objective of Quebec's separation."

The following day, Harper met Governor General Michaëlle Jean, who consented to his request to prorogue Parliament until January 26, 2009. The vote of confidence was in abeyance.

No one came out of this tragicomic episode looking innocent, but as in past battles Harper showed a more sound appreciation of the public interest than did his opponents. An Ipsos Reid poll published December 5 showed that 61 percent of Canadians supported the elimination of the $1.95 subsidy (granted annually to political parties for each vote received in the previous election)—the issue that had sparked the opposition parties' furor in the first place. The threat to national unity had emerged not from Harper's provocation, but from the coalition, which would have imposed on Canada an incoherent, unstable, and illegitimate government, with Gilles Duceppe as the kingmaker. When polls made it obvious that Dion had grievously misjudged the situation, he resigned and was replaced as leader by Michael Ignatieff, whose support for the coalition had never been more than lip service. The crisis was over, at least for a time.

Still, the country had become needlessly mired in partisan politics on Harper's watch. His dogged pursuit of his vision, however sage that vision might have been, had left the country dug in on all sides at a moment that demanded consensus. If, as he claimed, the Conservatives were Canada's party, they had still further to travel in proving it. And Harper himself, who usually learned from his errors, would have to take lessons in the politics of consensus.